T0230290

Lecture Notes in Computer Science   5460

Commenced Publication in 1973
Founding and Former Series Editors:
Gerhard Goos, Juris Hartmanis, and Jan van Leeuwen

Ozalp Babaoglu   Márk Jelasity
Alberto Montresor   Christof Fetzer
Stefano Leonardi   Aad van Moorsel
Maarten van Steen (Eds.)

Self-star Properties in Complex Information Systems

Conceptual and Practical Foundations

 Springer

Volume Editors

Ozalp Babaoglu
Márk Jelasity
Alberto Montresor
Università di Bologna
Departimento di Scienze dell'Informazione
40126 Bologna, Italy
E-mail: {babaoglu,jelasity,montresor}@cs.unibo.it

Christof Fetzer
Technische Universität Dresden
Fakultät Informatik
01062 Dresden, Germany
E-mail: christof.fetzer@inf.tu-dresden.de

Stefano Leonardi
Università di Roma "La Sapienza"
Dipartimento di Informatica e Sistemistica
00198 Rome, Italy
E-mail: leon@dis.uniroma1.it

Aad van Moorsel
University of Newcastle upon Tyne
School of Computing
Newcastle upon Tyne, NE1 7RU, UK
E-mail: aad.vanmoorsel@newcastle.ac.uk

Maarten van Steen
Vrije Universiteit Amsterdam
Department of Computer Science
1081 HV, Amsterdam, The Netherlands
E-mail: steen@cs.vu.nl

Library of Congress Control Number: 2005925758

CR Subject Classification (1998): C.2.4, C.2, D.2, F.1, F.2, I.2.11, H.4

ISSN	0302-9743
ISBN-10	3-540-26009-9 Springer Berlin Heidelberg New York
ISBN-13	978-3-540-26009-7 Springer Berlin Heidelberg New York

Springer is a part of Springer Science+Business Media

springeronline.com

Typesetting: Camera-ready by author, data conversion by Scientific Publishing Services, Chennai, India
Printed on acid-free paper   SPIN: 11428589   06/3142   5 4 3 2 1 0

Preface

Information systems can be complex due to numerous factors including scale, decentralization, heterogeneity, mobility, dynamism, bugs and failures. Deploying, operating and maintaining such systems can be not only very difficult, but also very costly. A flurry of recent activity has been directed at this problem, and future information systems are envisioned as self-configuring, self-organizing, self-managing and self-repairing. Collectively, we call these properties self-⋆ properties.

This book is a "spin-off" of a by-invitation-only Bertinoro workshop on self-⋆ properties in complex systems which was held in summer 2004 in Bertinoro, Italy. The Self-star workshop brought together researchers and practitioners from different disciplines and with different backgrounds to discuss complex information systems. The theme of the workshop was to identify the conceptual and practical foundations for modeling, analyzing and achieving self-⋆ properties in distributed and networked systems. Partly based on these discussions, we solicited papers from the workshop participants and a set of invitees for this book.

We sought original contributions in which authors explicitly take a position concerning requirements, usefulness, potential and limitations of technologies for self-⋆ properties of complex systems. This position needed to be founded on research results that were put clearly in context with respect to the position statement. We strongly encouraged visionary statements, thought-provoking ideas, and exploratory results that will help the reader form her or his own opinions on the importance of self-⋆ properties in current and future complex information systems.

We structured the book according to our goal of having such visionary statements. The first part of this book contains a set of separate 1-page summaries of the positions taken by the various authors. This gives the reader a chance to get a quick overview of the various positions. The second part of the book contains the full papers that explain in more detail the positions taken by the different authors.

Without further ado, we wish you a pleasant and stimulating read.

Bologna, Dresden, Rome,   Ozalp Babaoglu

Newcastle upon Tyne, Amsterdam   Márk Jelasity

February 2005   Alberto Montresor

                                                               Christof Fetzer

                                                       Stefano Leonardi

                                                      Aad van Moorsel

                                                    Maarten van Steen

Organization

Organizing Committee

Ozalp Babaoglu	University of Bologna, Italy
Márk Jelasity	University of Bologna, Italy
Alberto Montresor	University of Bologna, Italy
Christof Fetzer	Technical University of Dresden, Germany
Stefano Leonardi	University of Rome "La Sapienza," Italy
Aad van Moorsel	University of Newcastle upon Tyne, UK
Maarten van Steen	Free University of Amsterdam, The Netherlands

Referees

Vinay Aggarwal	Márk Jelasity	Aad van Moorsel
Ozalp Babaoglu	Zbigniew Jerzak	Maarten van Steen
Luca Becchetti	Stefano Leonardi	Andrea Vitaletti
Christof Fetzer	Alberto Montresor	Berthold Vöcking

Special Thanks

We would like to thank the sponsors of Self-star 2004 for making the Workshop possible:

FET Open Project BISON
FET Integrated Project DELIS
FET Open Project COSIN
BICI: Bertinoro International Center for Informatics
UNESCO Office Venice, Regional Bureau for Science in Europe (ROSTE)

We are grateful to Dr. Dum of the European Commission for his enthusiasm and support of research in "Complex Systems" through the projects BISON, COSIN and DELIS. We would also like to thank the University Residential Centre of Bertinoro for hosting the Workshop.

Table of Contents

Self-awareness vs. Self-organization

Supporting Self-★

Peer-to-Peer Algorithms

The Self-star Vision

Achieving various self-⋆ properties has been a grand challenge of computer science and engineering since the building of the first computer. The latest reincarnation of this challenge is due to the fact that large, complex and dynamic information systems have suddenly become a key part of the infrastructure of modern societies. Accordingly, it has become very important to be able to build, manage, and exploit these systems in the most efficient way possible. In other words, these systems have to become self-⋆.

We are now in the process of finding out how to deal with this challenge. It is a complex problem because information systems are deployed over a very wide range of environments from wireless sensor networks to powerful supercomputing clusters, from home networks to the entire Internet. It is very likely that to meet this challenge, we need to draw ideas from many disciplines that have been dealing with the design or explanation of large and/or complex systems, such as the space shuttle, an operating system, the Internet, human intelligence, an ecosystem, evolution, living organisms, etc. The goal of this book is to explore the widest possible range of ideas and approaches that can potentially be relevant in understanding how to build self-⋆ information systems. We invited experts from different disciplines and asked them the same questions:

> Why and where do you think self-⋆ properties are important? How can your field of research contribute to these goals? What are the most promising directions to explore in the future?

This chapter contains a selection of the most visionary answers we received. To make navigation easier, we organized the contributions into the following, rather fuzzy, categories:

Self-organization. A typical approach in this group emphasizes the importance of *emergence* and *self-organization* of fully distributed and independent components. Biological and social (agent-based.) inspiration belongs here. For some fields, like in wireless ad hoc networks, this approach is a must, in other fields it is an interesting alternative. This approach is often also *radical* in that it proposes to build systems from scratch as opposed to enhance existing systems.

Self-awareness. This approach seeks to achieve self-⋆ properties via a *meta-model* of the system: self-⋆ is an add-on. An external component controls the system via a control loop, or a decision mechanism based on the (perhaps precomputed) model of the system and its environment. This approach is often incremental, and therefore more practical, in that it allows the extension of existing systems with little or no modification.

Self-organization Versus Self-awareness. A small but interesting set of approaches explicitly investigate the relation (synergies, differences) between the first two approaches and therefore cannot be classified in either of those.

O. Babaoglu et al. (Eds.): SELF-STAR 2004, LNCS 3460, pp. 1–20, 2005.

Supporting Self-⋆. We included here contributions that aim at developing methodologies, environments, tools, abstractions, systems support; in short, things that make it easier (or possible) to develop self-⋆ systems. These approaches are often highly ambitious, because their scope is quite generic.

We hope that you will find browsing the visions below as much fun as we have.

Self-organization

Natural Technology
Peter Bentley

Every salamander is a superhero. It is seemingly invulnerable to harm. Cutting off a leg won't stop it. It will grow a new one back, complete with bones, muscles and blood vessels. Cutting off its tail also has no real effect. A few weeks later it will have grown a new one. Try blinding it, and it will regrow the damaged parts of its eye. No stake through the heart or silver bullet will stop our superhero salamander. Damage its heart and it'll regrow that too.

The salamander is doing more than simple healing here. It is able to regenerate parts of itself. Even when major structures (such as a whole leg) are lost, it can regrow them from nothing. It's positively miraculous.

Salamanders can do these things and we can't because their cells have evolved to be a little bit different to ours. They're not the only ones. Plants are also clever in similar ways. You can amputate all of the limbs of a tree and in a couple of years it will grow a new set. Cut a leg (or "ray" as it is called) from a starfish and it will grow a new one — and the ray you've cut off will grow a new body. Snails can even regrow their entire head if they loose it.

Imagine trying to design a piece of technology that could do the same thing. A car that healed itself after a crash. A house that regrew its roof after damage from a storm. A computer that repaired itself after its circuits had been fried. Such ideas are so beyond our current abilities that they seem ludicrous. We can't design such technologies. We don't know how. Not only that, we can't even design technology that is several orders of magnitude simpler and have it work.

There's something going wrong with contemporary design. Complexity is overwhelming us. For certain types of design, it has already overwhelmed us — software is now too complex to work reliably. Economies are too complex to manage reliably. Societies are too complex to govern reliably.

But we are surrounded by complexity that is orders of magnitude more complex than all these examples. Life is designed by evolution at molecular scales and grows to macro scales. Every cell in our bodies contains a molecular computer made from genes and proteins, which instructs the cell what to do. We have hundreds of billions of cells in us. We are the most complex entities in the known universe — and yet we work.

I believe that complexity should not cause our designs to fail. We must look at successful complex designs in nature and learn from them. We should attempt to discover not only how they work, but how they are formed. Nature does not perform conscious design, but her designs are better than anything a human is capable of designing. I aim to discover how this happens by working with biologists and modelling the processes of evolution and development. I aim to harness these processes by enabling new forms of technology that can evolve and develop.

I strongly believe that one day we will achieve some of the capabilities of living organisms in our technology. We will have self-adaptive, self-designing, self-building, self-repairing, ... self-★ devices. This "natural technology" is not just a pip-dream of ambitious scientists. It is necessary for us to progress in our technology. It will be the only way we can construct complex devices that work reliably in the future.

Evolutionary Computing
A.E. Eiben

The main point advocated here is that evolutionary computing is one of the key technologies that can help meeting some of the grand self-★ challenges. The arguments backing up this point roughly fall into three categories.

The first argument considers evolutionary computing as a technology that can be used to solve optimisation problems. EC is widely applicable, it requires almost no assumptions about the problem to be solved, an evolutionary solver can be usually developed with limited efforts and it produces good quality solutions at acceptable computational costs for a wide range of problems. The EC community describes the "niche" of EC (i.e., the class of problems where it offers competitive performance) by attributes including: many parameters with highly complex non-linear interactions, many local optima, the presence of noise, dynamically changing circumstances (constraints and/or optimisation objectives), the lack of an analytical problem model, etc. Mind you, it is not suggested that EC is always applicable; for instance, automatic translation would be very "EC-hard".

The second line of argumentation observes that self-★ properties are mainly required in complex, distributed information systems. In such systems the macro-level behaviour is often a result of complex interactions of numerous of micro-level entities (for instance, system components, parameters, configurations, etc). Therefore, population-based adaptive systems (PAS), such as evolutionary algorithms (EA) or adaptive multi-agent systems, can naturally match the essence of the information systems in question. EAs are inherently distributed and if only one can identify the individual units, define their utility, and specify how to create and test new variants on-the-fly, the system is "evolutionarised". The example about optimising web services discussed in the paper illustrates this. The use of a PAS, in particular an EA, offers specific advantages for self-★ applications. By the presence of a population there is an inherent ability to adapt to changes, which is a key feature in, for instance, self-healing, self-optimisation, self-reconfiguration, etc.

The third argument is based on the fact that EAs are capable to perform real-time self-optimisation by adjusting (some of) their parameters on-the-fly. Solutions to realise this in evolutionary computing, for instance self-adaptation of EA parameters, could be transportable to the context of autonomic computing. Even though an existing EC trick does not work directly, evolutionary weaponry can very well serve as a source of inspiration.

The second point in my paper concerns the relevance of autonomic computing to evolutionary computing. An evolving system can be seen as a special case of an autonomic system and it can be expected that some solutions invented within autonomic computing can be transferred to EC helping to realise parameter-free evolutionary algorithms.

What Is Self-★?
Wolfram Krause and Martin Greiner

Complex self-★ systems are widespread in nature. Maybe the most fascinating example is given by ourselves and automatically leads to the question "What is life?" Here, self-★ reveals itself on various scales: the biochemical feed-back control system within the microscopic cell and, built on top of that, e. g., the immune system and the brain. We should not hesitate to mention also the next rougher scale, which is represented for example by social networks and our inter- actions as part of the ecosystem. Herewith it becomes clear that nature defines self-★ as the self-organizing control of highly complex, interacting and networked systems.

Recently physics has started a new branch, which will be key to a generic un- derstanding of self-organization in nature and beyond: the Statistical Physics of complex networks. It discusses the structure and formation of complex networked systems, their dynamics and their function. The new insight which along these lines has already been given for example to gene and metabolic networks consti- tutes for sure a remarkable highlight and complements the current endeavor to understand the proteomic function of the deciphered, but hieroglyphic (human) genome. Applicationwise, this new physics branch not only focuses on complex networks in nature, but also on social, technical and information systems.

Some of the complex technical systems are beginning to ask similar ques- tions about self-organization and function as the networked nature. Examples are production and logistic networks, traffic networks and communication net- works. Their parallelism results from a common interplay between a material flow, consisting of either goods, vehicles or data packets, and an information flow. As these technical networks are up-scaling in size, efficiency requires that the control of the flow interplay should no longer rely on a central approach alone. Elements of decentralized control are becoming increasingly important, which first gather and process local information and then use this for a local feedback control action. In the limit of a purely decentralized control such net- worked systems become self-organizing.

Our research focuses on information systems in general and wireless commu- nication networks in particular. Coordination and synchronization of different tasks shall be performed in a distributive manner. In this context, self-⋆ refers to self-configuration, self-management, self-repair, self-adaption and related topics. But these systems are still far from perfect. A deep understanding of the processes in biological systems might be the basis for new technological methods that allow improved system characteristics. Regarding sensor networks, a distributed, parallel processing of collected data can speed up the data acquisition and reduce the traffic load of the network. One might even think about nodes that can act autonomously and start certain actions, based on data acquired at their own sensors or communicated by neighbors.

However, self-⋆ has also other meanings. The principles of self-⋆ are playing an important role in a large variety of other research topics. In solid state physics, self-organization is discussed in the context of the "magic" growth of very specific surface structures, even down to the placement of single atoms. The magical creation of clusters and other macro-molecules are other examples for self-⋆ processes. Delicate tasks, like the assembly of carbon atoms to a fullerene or nanotube, cannot be performed directly. But given certain environmental conditions, self-organization enters the stage and the process *just happens automatically.*

Cooperative Agents
Jim Dowling, Raymond Cunningham, Anthony Harrington,
Eoin Curran and Vinny Cahill

Our vision of self-managing distributed systems is based on building decentralised systems using coooperative agents that can adaptively coordinate their local behaviour to solve system self-management problems. In such a model, each agent gathers information on its own and takes independent decisions on how to behave or adapt itself, but in order to establish and maintain self-managing system properties, agents must also coordinate their local behaviour models through interaction with their neighbours or a shared environment.

The design of decentralised algorithms to build self-managing systems presents a number of challenges. One approach is to use decentralised algorithms that enable consensus between groups of agents on optimal, local behaviour models that produce the desired, system self-management behaviour. The main challenge in designing such algorithms is the establishment of common behaviour models in agents, given the inherent uncertainty and dynamism in the environment, and the impossibility of using centralised techniques. Designers must also not resort to pseudo-centralised techniques, such as using an agent's local view of the system to infer properties of the system as a whole, as such assumptions in dynamic environments may break down quickly. In designing decentralised systems, we have found as much inspiration in the fields of statistics and optimisation as in natural, self-organising systems. Decentralised algorithms will be important in designing self-managing systems areas such as mobile ad-hoc networks, wireless sensor networks, peer-to-peer systems and very large distributed systems.

Specific challenges in designing these decentralised algorithms for self-managing systems include:

- the representation of an agent's local view of the world
- techniques that improve the accuracy of the agent's local view using changes in the agent's environment and changes in neighbouring agents' local views
- enabling the establishment of consensus on optimal local behaviour models that can produce self-managing system behaviour

To conclude, decentralised self-managing computing systems should establish and maintain self-management properties in dynamic and uncertain environments with minimal external intervention. Finally, we define a self-managing decentralised system as follows: "A self-managing decentralised system has externally observable self-management properties, that are established and maintained solely by the coordination and adaptation of its agents that execute using only a partial, estimated view of the system, and without knowledge of any system-wide self-management property".

The Emergent Thinker
Sergio Camorlinga and Ken Barker

Systems research is a large research area within computer science. Systems research works on operating systems, distributed systems, networks, systems management, and many other aspects of computer systems. Algorithms and models have been developed that provide feasible solutions to many of the problems encountered in computer systems within constrained environments. However, the increased complexity of computer systems that are brittle limits the applicability of some solutions. The augmented complexity is due to many factors such as the large number of components, component interdependencies and heterogeneity, systems' ubiquity (i.e. pervasiveness), and nonstop appearance of new technologies; among other factors. This complexity is calling for better solutions that are scalable and reliable assuming continuous growth in the number of components and component technology, while maintaining the quality of service in the pervasive use of computing components. Terms like self-organization, self-configuration, self-monitoring, self-control and many others "self's" (i.e. self-$\star$ properties) are being defined as system properties that are needed to cope with the new challenges.

An essential question is how to achieve the self-$\star$ properties necessary to provide services in large computing environments? For this we are proposing the *Emergent Thinker* paradigm. The Emergent Thinker provides a shift in the way we achieve computation by means of *Complex Adaptive Systems* emergent computations (a.k.a. swarm intelligence). The Emergent Thinker paradigm is proposed as an alternative approach for new and current design and implementation challenges in systems research. The solutions that emerge from the simple activities of a swarm's members and the metaphor variety for complex adaptive systems models in our lives (e.g. biological systems, economic systems, ecologies, brain, social systems, immune systems, etc.) present a fruitful area to explore for mechanisms and processes with emergent computations that provide self-⋆ properties.

The *Biologically Inspired Distributed File System* (BPD) implements the Emergent Thinker paradigm and corroborates our hypothesis by means of emergent computations achieved by simulating squirrels biological behaviors. The BPD provides file system services in a complex information system environment that is dynamic, self-organized, *ad-hoc*, and decentralized. The BPD is an initial step for the Thinker. Many pieces remain to be investigated and implemented. The Thinker establishes a computing framework and we use it to prove and instantiate the paradigm with the BPD implementation described later in our paper.

The Emergent Thinker paradigm offers an alternative computational model for complex information systems design; and nature presents the mechanisms required for the emergent thinker computations. Mechanisms and processes remain unknown and waiting for us to uncover. The know-how achieved by applying the Emergent Thinker could lead us to build up new computing algorithms and models (some generic, some specific) by uncovering biological, economic, social and others real systems mechanisms. Thus, a new way to provide computing will emerge and change our thinking in systems research for large computer systems.

Evolutionary Games
Spyros Kontogiannis and Paul Spirakis

Evolutionary Game Theory is a field of science that examines strategic (and perhaps antagonistic) interactions among members of a large population of agents. The individuals base their decision on simple rules. The dynamics of such interactions, under certain conditions, tend to converge to the adaptation of certain strategies that are "more stable" than others. Interestingly, these strategies are also robust against invasion. In the general case, evolutionary dynamics may also lead to chaotic behaviour.

We consider the notions of Evolutionary Game Theory as a solid framework that allows a concrete examination of self–organization procedures in a large number of selfish individuals. This theory originated from a fruitful interaction of Biology, Economics, Game Theory and (rather recently) Computer Science. Our work examines a yet quite unexplored but crucial aspect of Evolutionary Game Theory, namely the combinatorial, algorithmic and computational complexity issues involved.

Indeed, the effort of deriving concrete conclusions in any non-trivial model of antagonistic evolutionary behaviour, poses interesting computational questions and complex decision problems. The further, pragmatic growth of the field seems to depend on how efficiently these questions can be answered, or even approximated. This view seems to invite an interaction of the field with the field of Algorithmics and Computer Science. We highlight such issues here and provide initial evidence of the usefulness of algorithmic way of thought in the strategic evolution domain.

Self-awareness

Self-⋆: A New Paradigm
Robert Laddaga and Paul Robertson

Software development technology is critically in need of new paradigms supporting increased robustness. Robustness is of great concern now because our systems are becoming more complex, and because they are increasingly sensing and controlling our physical environment and processes. One such paradigm is self-⋆, a collection of properties such as self reconfigurable, self adaptive, self aware, and self checking. We believe that all self-⋆ systems share the following traits:

- Deferral of design decisions to runtime (a form of late binding)
- Metaprogramming
- Explicit attention to state of the world
- Attention to program state

Software design consists in large part in analyzing the cases the software will be presented with, and ensuring that requirements are met for those cases. A design decision in the context of any possible program state, any possible input, and any possible condition of the environment is inherently more complex than deciding what to do given a specific input in the context of a specific state of the program and the environment. Self-⋆ systems attempt to use various forms of metaprogramming to enable them to defer decisions to runtime, when attention to the state of the world and the state of the program can be used to reduce the complexity that would otherwise be overwhelming.

Self Adaptive Software (our new self-⋆ paradigm) monitors its own operation and attempts to correct deviations from required behavior. In the self adaptive architectures we are developing, it accomplishes this by diagnosing the sources of deviant behavior, whether internal program problems, or contextual changes in an embedded program's environment. The software then responds by reconfiguring itself, to use alternate procedures that either correct the malfunction, or perform better in the current context. The diagnosis and reconfiguration are in part accomplished by storing models of the goals, structure, design and requirements of a program such that they are available to the program at run time. Since most of our self adaptive systems are also embedded systems, models of the physical plant which the software controls or effects are also stored and referenced at run time.

Self Adaptive Software provides some advantages over some other self-⋆ approaches, that utilize a more reactive programming technique, and which are inherently less self aware. these advantages include:

- Explicit management of contexts is used to increase robustenss and reduce effective complexity
- Existing functions can be "wrapped" and used in self adaptive architectures
- Use of the descriptions and models in the software motivates their production, and they are also valuable for development and maintenance

– It is easier to control (rather than depend on) emergent behavior
– It is easier to make self aware systems explain their behavior

Important open research issues for Self Adaptive Software are the following:

– Providing assurance of software behavior – convergence on correct solutions, stability, limits on emergent behavior
– Providing tools to assist in development of self evaluation code
– Providing tools to assist in development of descriptions and models of software and controlled systems
– Incorporating learning into Self Adaptive systems.

Online Performance Models
Daniel A. Menascé, Mohamed N. Bennani and Honglei Ruan

Modern computing environments are becoming increasingly complex in nature and exhibit highly varying and unpredictable workloads. Such systems have a multitude of parameters whose settings may significantly affect performance. Under these circumstances, it is virtually impossible for human beings to continuously tune a system's configurable parameters. Therefore, these systems must be self-managing and self-organizing.

We present an approach that consists of a *controller* that continuously determines the configuration that optimizes a given goal function, which is typically a function of the system performance metrics. The size of the state space of possible configurations grows in a combinatorial way with the number of controlled parameters. Therefore, the controller uses combinatorial search techniques to find a configuration for which the value of the goal function is as close as possible to its desired level.

The goal function for a system's current configuration is evaluated as a function of performance metric measurements. However, as the search technique explores the configuration state space, the goal values for potential new configurations have to be computed through the use of models that can predict the value of performance metrics for these configurations. We use analytic performance models—typically queuing network models—of the controlled system to obtain the values of these performance metrics for each configuration.

This *online* use of predictive performance models is a departure from their common use in capacity planning, where performance models are used to analyze and compare scenarios over relatively long (in the order of months) periods of time. In the case of self-configuring and self-managing systems, configurations may have to change very frequently (at a few-minute intervals).

Our technique has been implemented and evaluated in many different settings. In the paper presented in this book we show the effectiveness of the controller on a real Web server. We also show that the controller becomes more effective when the frequency of its invocation is a function of the relative error between the desired performance level and the current performance. The controller effectiveness improves even more if it uses workload intensity forecasting techniques. The techniques discussed here are shown to be robust to high variability of the interarrival time and service time distributions. Finally, we showed how online performance models can be used to design QoS-aware service oriented architectures.

Proactive Failure Prediction
Felix Salfner, Günther Hoffmann and Miroslaw Malek

Massively distributed, heterogeneous hardware-software systems day by day reach higher and higher complexity levels and their behavior is in parts, especially with respect to certain properties such as dependability and security, unpredictable. A naive belief, that non laboratory systems are deterministic, manually manageable or fault free, is a myth. A number of reasons lead to this increased complexity: rapidly increasing size of individual software components, growing heterogeneity of components, decentralization, emerging new technologies such as ad-hoc reconfiguration and accelerated software development through code reuse techniques. Additionally, fault tolerance techniques and performance boosters can introduce stochastic dynamics, which further complicates matters. This has been leading to a change in the way software systems are perceived and to changing concerns from fault centric — *whether* a system will work to *how well* it will work. There is reason to believe that future systems will grow in complexity making them even more failure prone and unpredictable.

In order to sustain an acceptable level of dependability, radically new methods have to be incorporated in addition to a mix of formal methods, attempts to prove correctness or at least consistency and testing. No amount of proving or testing will at present certify the system's correctness. Therefore, we need to learn to coexist with unpredictable systems and learn to react and adapt in case of unpredictable changes.

Self-⋆ properties have been proposed as a potential solution to this problem. We propose an aggressive, preventive maintenance by developing automatic stochastic software failure prediction methods which provide for downtime minimization, graceful degradation or outright failure avoidance. In our work we focus on self-managing properties, or in other words *anticipating software systems*. We advocate a proactive approach which capitalizes on probabilistic failure prediction by selecting appropriate methods for avoiding the failure (e.g., load decrease, process retry, failover) or for minimizing the recovery time in case of a crash.

Since failures are stochastic events, it is our belief that the system's behavior can be captured by its probabilistic representation. Machine learning techniques are a class of algorithms that are able to handle the complexity of software systems. They are also capable of finding non-obvious relationships in data and identifying suspicious patterns and deviations from normal behavior. We present two approaches which are Universal Basis Functions (UBF) and Similar Events Prediction (SEP). In our study we model and predict failures of a telecommunication system.

Making Self-adaptation an Engineering Reality
Shang-Wen Cheng, David Garlan and Bradley Schmerl

We posit our vision of a software engineering reality where engineers can develop self-adaptive software-intensive systems cost-effectively. Imagine a world where a software engineer could take an existing software system, specify for a set of properties of interest (1) an objective, (2) conditions for change, and (3) strategies for their adaptation and, within a few man-weeks, make that system self-adaptive where it was not before. An engineer might take an existing client-server system and make it self-adaptive with respect to a specific performance concern such as high latency. He might specify an objective to maintain response latency below some threshold, a condition to change the system if the latency rises above the threshold, and a few strategies to adapt the system to fix the high-latency situation.

Systems increasingly require mechanisms to monitor and adapt themselves to failures or surrounding changes, that is, to *self-adapt*. Currently such capabilities are realized in somewhat limited forms through programming language features such as exceptions and in algorithms such as fault-tolerant protocols. These mechanisms are often highly specific to the application and tightly bound to the code, making them costly to build and difficult to maintain once added. Rather than rely on internal mechanisms, we apply a closed-loop control paradigm using external mechanisms to monitor, model, and control a running system. We further use architectural models to get global system perspective and system constraints, and architectural styles to give us leverage on analysis and guidance for self-adaptation.

To achieve self-adaptation as we envisioned, in addition to mechanisms for monitoring, techniques for diagnosis and problem correction, and capabilities for run-time reconfiguration, we need to make it possible for engineers to use these in cost-effective and principled ways. In particular, we would like to be sure that engineers can augment existing systems to be self-adaptive without having to rewrite them from scratch, that self-adaptation policies and strategies can be used across similar systems, that multiple sources of adaptation expertise can be synergistically combined, and that all of this can be done in ways that support maintainability, evolution, and analysis.

We show how our Rainbow approach, supported by three case studies, fulfills the important properties of *generality, cost-effectiveness*, and *composability*. Specifically, we focus on the separation between the general parts of Rainbow that can be applied across different styles of systems and different concerns, and the tailorable parts that need to be written to apply Rainbow to specific systems and concerns.

Control-Theoretic Concepts
Nagarajan Kandasamy, Sherif Abdelwahed, Gregory C. Sharp and John P. Hayes

Our ongoing research effort focuses on the theory and practice of designing self-managing distributed computing systems. To operate such systems effectively, multiple performance-related parameters must be continuously tuned to dynamic operating conditions, and the current state-of-the-art involves substantial human effort. To cope with the complexity expected of future computing systems, it is highly desirable for such systems to manage themselves, given high-level quality-of-service (QoS) objectives from administrators.

Our position is that control-theoretic concepts are applicable to selected and important resource management problems in computing systems, including self-optimization where the system aims to improve its performance and efficiency continuously. Control theory provides a systematic approach to resource management in general settings; if the underlying system is correctly modeled and its operating environment accurately estimated, the actions required to maintain a set QoS level and/or optimize a given utility (cost) function can be derived. It also provides well-established mathematical techniques to analyze system performance and correctness.

We are currently developing online control techniques that allow multiple QoS objectives and operating constraints to be explicitly represented as an optimization problem and efficiently solved at each time step. This approach can manage systems exhibiting both simple and complex nonlinear dynamics. Our research also studies how to build self-healing capabilities within the control framework where the system reconfigures itself in response to hardware (software) resource failures. Stability and feasibility analysis of these control algorithms is another important part of this work. We have, so far, applied this approach to problems such as power management in microprocessors and real-time data processing under a dynamic workloads with promising results. We plan to extend the approach to tackle other important resource management problems in distributed systems such as energy-efficient load balancing in server clusters and dynamic resource provisioning between multiple applications in data centers, among others.

If successful, this research will result in systematic and theoretically sound techniques to design and operate large-scale self-managing computer systems.

Restart
Katinka Wolter

Modern information systems are becoming increasingly complex, powerful and at the same time very widely used. They are being used not only by experts, but in first place by people who quickly want to buy a train ticket, people who want to look up something on the Internet, or people who must write a text. Most users want to have their service delivered by the computer system, but they do not want to know why and when and how the system works.

Obviously, every system will not always work. Computer systems need maintenance, repair and management. Very often, nowadays, some of these can be done remotely, facilitating this task enormously for customers and management service providers.

If the deployment of modern computer systems will continue to spread as it did in the past, management has to become a very simple and easy task. Otherwise there will soon be not enough people available to support all existing computer systems. To what extent a system has 'self' properties will become a very important characteristic. And 'self' capabilities of systems include as an essential part easy solutions for complex problems.

Our field of research, the 'black-box' restart of jobs is an extremely easy solution for an extremely hard problem. The addressed problem is the reduction of long job execution times. We do not try to understand why jobs take extremely long or fail, we only want to know for a given job, whether it is of the 'extremely long' type. This reduces the problem complexity enormously and makes it amenable to a simple solution such as restart. Such simple and pragmatic solutions are the only way to handle complex information systems in the future.

We take in our work a pragmatic view and propose an algorithm that is designed for one metric, but works for arbitrary completion time problems. It provides on-line a recommendation for when a job should be aborted and restarted, so that system performance is maximised. This will in many cases solve the problem of 'pending jobs' and we see it as a first step on the way to automatic, or semi-automatic system management.

Restart cannot replace all system management, but it can solve some management problems, so that in those situations not even someone is needed to analyse the system and its problem. Some of the management issues are transferred from people to the system itself.

Mathematical Foundations
Tomasz Nowicki, Mark S. Squillante and Chai Wah Wu

Many original concepts and ideas for self-⋆ properties of complex information systems have come from the natural sciences where there are various examples of self-managing systems. An an example, the autonomic function of the human central nervous system is one often cited inspiration. Hence, in the same way that mathematics plays important roles in the natural sciences, mathematical methods must provide the foundations for self-⋆ systems. In particular, mathematical methods must be exploited in a manner that is as central as it is in, e.g., physics, to best achieve the diverse goals of providing self-⋆ properties. This is required in at least 3 fundamental areas: The models and methods to analyze and understand self-⋆ systems; The laws and properties that characterize and predict the complex dynamics of any aspect of a self-⋆ system; The algorithms and policies to control, manage and optimize any aspect of a self-⋆ system and its complex dynamics to achieve any objective of interest.

This fundamental and pervasive role for mathematical methods in self-⋆ systems is important for a variety of reasons. Many different issues and problems associated with self-⋆ systems essentially reduce, either in part or as a whole, to a much smaller number of fundamental mathematical problems. The corresponding solutions are required across a wide range of temporal and spatial scales in order to meet a common overall goal. These and other complexities of current and future self-⋆ systems pose new challenges whose solutions must be based on sophisticated mathematical methods. We simply cannot afford approaches based on forcing elementary solutions that do not fit or are inappropriate, as the consequences of doing so will be disastrous; e.g., consider the chaotic behavior exhibited in various markets which share some of the characteristics of self-⋆ systems. Furthermore, new mathematical results and methods must be developed as needed, and these mathematical results/methods must also be tailored to the data available and time scale(s) of the problem at hand. These solutions are often best obtained through a combination of different mathematical methods working together in a unified manner. They must also balance the quality of solution with its costs.

In support of this position, our study investigates the mathematical foundations of two fundamental aspects of management in self-⋆ systems: the optimization of the entire range of autonomic system objectives, and the dynamic control of achieving these optimal solutions. We first establish several important results regarding decentralized optimization, including showing that there is no loss of quality in the (static) solution obtained under a decentralized approach versus a centralized approach. We then turn to study the dynamics of this system in which optimization decisions are made continually over time and at multiple time scales. Our analysis illustrates some of the potential problems and complicated behavior of such continual decentralized optimization when the system environment changes over time, which can include phase transitions, chaos and instability. One of the fundamental problems then is to determine this complex interaction between dynamics and optimization as we consider in our study.

Self-awareness Versus Self-organization

The Conflict Between Self-⋆ Capabilities and Predictability
Rogério de Lemos

This paper takes the position that autonomy (the basis for enabling self-⋆ capabilities) and predictability are conflicting aspects when building systems. Starting from the premise that there is a dichotomy on how systems are described, either process or data, this paper argues that uncertainties associated with these forms of system description dictate the ability that a system has in adapting to changes. The difference between process and data representations can be interpreted from the perspective of accuracy and precision. While process descriptions might be precise but not accurate, data descriptions might be accurate but not precise. In process descriptions, the assumptions that allow a process to be realizable introduce uncertainties. However, when these assumptions are discharged more accurate models can be obtained, thus eliminating uncertainties from the system. On the other hand, data descriptions are an abstraction of the actual behaviour of the system, and in some cases for the data to be meaningful it has to undergo through some generalizations. These two issues inevitably lead to the introduction of uncertainties on how systems are described, and it is from these uncertainties that emergent behaviours materialize.

The above argument is supported by two examples on how process and data descriptions of systems can handle predictability and autonomy. In the first example, we present an architectural solution based on exceptional handling to tolerate faults. The solution relies on a process description for building adaptable, but deterministic systems. Uncertainties are eliminated from the system behaviour, however the solution is not scalable since exceptional handling based solutions are invariably application dependent, i.e., there is no single mechanism that is able to deal with a general class of faults. For example, it would be feasible to apply such architectural solution to handle intrusions because of the uncertainties associated with these. In the second example, we present an artificial immune system solution (AIS) for the detection of anomalies. The solution relies on a data description for generating error detectors that are able to identify new unexpected circumstances. The rationale associated with this approach is that if systems are to be autonomous when reacting to changes, in this case undesirable, then it is essential that the system should be able to recognise new erroneous states, and adapt its set of detectors accordingly. In this particular context, it has been observed that the generalisation of potential detectors has lead to a decrease on the detection coverage, and an increase in the number of false positives, i.e., false alarms.

The idea of developing systems that rely on both process and data representations, which explores the complementary benefits of these, is not new. Such hybrid systems have mostly been confined to stand alone closed systems, however the challenge ahead is whether the same idea can be applied to more complex systems that are open and collaborative in their nature, and which are expected to show self-⋆ capabilities and be predictive at the same time.

Self-aware Software
Peter Andras and Bruce G Charlton

Research on self-aware software systems is an active part of computer science almost since its inception. This research led to many interesting theories and applications, but no truly self-aware software system has been developed so far. It appears that a critical barrier that could not be overcome is that software systems are unable to generate appropriately adaptive responses in previously unknown situations.

One possible way towards the development of self-aware software is to imitate natural self-aware systems. The theory of abstract communication systems, built on works of Niklas Luhmann about abstract social systems, provides a very effective framework for the analysis of such systems. Analysing natural self-aware systems, like cells or organisations, reveals features that are critically related to their self-awareness abilities. Such features are: (1) they possess both short- and long-term memories, (2) they have an information subsystem, which processes and creates new memories; (3) they have a set of long-term memory communications representing a self-model that is referenced by identity check communications of the information subsystem; (4) their self-model is adaptive and is changing in response to faulty communications, errors and failures experienced by the system.

We see computer software as a communication system of many components executed on computer hardware. The software in this context is the set of interactions between communication units (e.g., objects). In our view software systems should have comparable features to natural self-aware systems in order to become truly self-aware. Software systems need to expand their memory communications, by creating memories of most interactions between software communication units. The extensive sets of memories will provide the foundations for the development of the information subsystem of the software (see aspect oriented programming). Self-monitoring should be based on memory communications and on identity-check communications of the system. The software system itself should emerge to large extent from identity-check communications. Self-aware software systems should aim to reproduce and expand themselves as communication systems. They should perform their functionality by adapting to their environment and reproducing and expanding within this environment. The software should adapt its self-model, the code of itself, in response to faulty interactions, errors and failures experienced by the system. Building such systems will need a novel 'from within' approach to software development.

Supporting Self-⋆

Design Methodology
Indranil Gupta, Steven Ko, Nathanael Thompson, Mahvesh Nagda, Chris Devaraj, Ramsés Morales and Jay A. Patel

Today, designing new protocols for self-⋆ distributed systems such as peer-to-peer systems, autonomic Grid applications, etc., is an extremely challenging task. The only resources available to a researcher designing new protocols are her basic distributed systems knowledge, prior research literature, and the designer's experiences. This "seat of pants" approach to protocol design has resulted in long research project timelines, long lag times to production, and complex final system designs when pieces are assembled.

We believe these shortcomings can be addressed for future systems by populating and enriching a new resource for the protocol designer – Protocol Design Methodologies. Loosely, a protocol design methodology is *an organized, documented set of building blocks, rules and/or guidelines for design of a class of distributed protocols. It is possibly amenable to automated code generation.*

Given a distributed computing problem then, a collection of methodologies can be brought to bear, for either innovating novel protocols, or for composing existing protocols. This results in a more *systematic* approach to protocol design. It augments the creative activity of protocol innovation, rather than stifle it. Methodology research has already matured in other fields such as hardware synthesis, operating systems, and software engineering, etc.

Methodologies for distributed systems can be either *innovative*, i.e., create novel unknown protocols, or *composable*, i.e., combine existing protocols, thus enriching their properties. Methodologies can also be have retroactive or progressive, i.e., they can help in understanding design principles of existing protocols, or create new protocols (or both).

For instance, many protocols derived from natural phenomena suffer from hand-wavy descriptions and analyses. This is due to the lack of systematization. We have created a new innovative and progressive methodology that translates systems of differential equations (that can be used to represent a natural phenomenon) into equivalent distributed protocols. The use of a methodology guarantees that the protocol can be specified formally, and its self-stabilization and fault-tolerance properties can be proved.

Many of the creative distributed protocol ideas, designed by the community over the years, are either never read or never used in a real system. Retroactive and composable methodologies can help systematize the understanding of large classes of protocols, increasing not only chances of their use but also the possibility that they will be composed with other popular protocols.

Autonomic Grid Applications
M. Parashar, Z. Li, H. Liu, V. Matossian and C. Schmidt

Pervasive information and computational Grid environments are inherently large, complex, heterogeneous and dynamic, globally aggregating large numbers of independent computing and communication resources, data stores and sensor networks. Furthermore, emerging Grid applications are similarly complex and highly dynamic in their behaviors and interactions. Together, these characteristics result in application development, configuration and management complexities that break paradigms based on passive components and static compositions and interactions, and impose new requirements on programming systems for Grid applications. Grid programming systems must be able to specify applications that can detect and dynamically respond during execution to changes in both, the state of execution environment and the state and requirements of the application. This requirement suggests that: (1) Grid applications should be composed from discrete, self-managing components, which incorporate separate specifications for all of functional, non-functional and interaction-coordination behaviors. (2) The specifications of computational (functional) behaviors, interaction and coordination behaviors and non-functional behaviors (e.g. performance, fault detection and recovery, etc.) should be separated so that their combinations are composable. (3) The interface definitions of these components should be separated from their implementations to enable heterogeneous components to interact and to enable dynamic selection of components.

Addressing these challenges requires redefining the programming framework to address the separations outlined above. Specifically, it requires (1) static application requirements and system and application behaviors to be relaxed, (2) the behaviors of elements to be sensitive to the dynamic state of the system and the changing requirements of the application and be able to adapt to these changes at runtime, (3) required common knowledge be expressed semantically rather than in terms of names, addresses and identifiers, and (4) the core enabling middleware services be driven by such a semantic knowledge.

In this paper we first investigate the challenges and requirements of programming Grid applications, and present self-managing applications as a means for addressing these requirements. We then introduce Project AutoMate, which investigates autonomic solutions, based on strategies used by biological systems, to realize Grid applications that are capable of managing (i.e., configuring, adapting, optimizing, protecting, healing) themselves.

System-Level Support
Simon Patarin and Mesaac Makpangou

Recently, autonomic computing has received much consideration and many efforts have been put in the various aspects of this emergent domain. However, several years after the identification of this research area (the term "autonomic computing" was first coined in 2001, while "trouble-free systems" had been already mentioned in 1999), autonomic applications have still not modified our day-to-day relationships with a computer.

Although some progresses have made their way into grid computing and enterprise-class software, the standard end-user is left behind. What should expect end-users from a forest fire application, an oil-reservoir application or a self-healing cluster (all examples taken from the most recent literature)? What about an autonomic Web server, an autonomic proxy-cache, an autonomic mail server or an autonomic peer-to-peer file-sharing application instead? This fact is rather paradoxical as the former applications seem much more complex to apprehend rather than the latter ones. Perhaps, this could be risen as an explanation: complex, unpredictable, applications are required to exercise autonomic systems appropriately. But, we do not believe it to be true. Internet is more than enough complex and unpredictable so that any distributed application is a good candidate to demonstrate autonomic capabilities.

According to us, it is a good system-level support for autonomic applications that is currently missing. One that would present the right abstractions to the developers, which would allow them to prototype autonomic applications rapidly. One that would be flexible enough to cope with the diversity and the heterogeneity of current platforms. One that would be efficient in terms of performance, because you simply cannot pretend maintaining any sort of quality of service if the service you propose is of poor quality right from the beginning. And one that would keep simple applications easy to implement. It is our belief that such a basis would allow researchers with different motivations and experiences to put their ideas in practice, free from the painful details of low-level system implementation. As the first simple autonomic elements become available, it will be easier and easier to build more complex system or to plug one's strategy into an existing element: a bottom-up development strategy does seem appropriate in building autonomic applications.

After having defined how autonomic systems should work and outlined possible approaches, time has come to see them actually working and to make them available to the largest possible audience. We are coming very close to systems that "just work", all we need now is the right system support to federate current efforts and reify them.

Spatial Computing
Marco Mamei and Franco Zambonelli

A number of approaches to support self-⋆ properties in computing are being proposed since the past few years. In general, we fully agree on the opinion that future computing systems will have to exploit self-⋆ properties in nearly all of their facets: self-configuration, self-tuning, self-healing etc. Whether you call it proactive computing or autonomic computing or — better and more compre-hensive — "self-ware", it is becoming rather clear that the intrinsic complexity and decentralization of today and future computing scenarios requires humans to be out of the loop. Any approach that requires software and complex network systems to be "manually" managed by human will soon become practically and economically unfeasible. In this context, most of current scientific and technolog-ical researches on "self-⋆" computing propose special-purpose and specially-tune solutions to specific kinds of problems. Most of these works are indeed interesting and are providing useful insights on the general problems.

However, we think that to effectively leverage self-⋆ approaches from a sci-entific curiosity to both a sound science and a practical engineering discipline we must also definitely look for general purpose approaches and solutions. Such general purpose approaches should provide a uniform set of abstractions and tools for deploying a variety of self-⋆ properties in a variety of heterogeneous computing scenarios that are emerging. These include: (i) micro-networks, i.e., networks of low-end computing devices typically distributed over a geograph-ically small area (e.g., sensor networks and spray computers); (ii) ubiquitous networks, i.e., networks of medium-end devices, distributed over a geographi-cally bounded area, and typically interacting via short/medium range wireless connections (pervasive computing systems, smart environments and cooperative robot teams); (iii) global networks, characterized by high-end computing systems interacting at a world-wide scale (the physical Internet, the Web, P2P networks and multiagent systems).

Starting form such a motivation, our current research work is aimed at iden-tifying the role that can be possibly played by spatial abstractions and by their adoption as building blocks for a novel general-purpose "spatial computing" approach for distributed system development and management. A spatial com-puting approach — by providing application components with an explicit rep-resentation of their operational environment in terms of a space encoding some application-specific features, and by having application level activities expressed in terms of sensing the properties of space and navigating in it — can effectively deal with network dynamics in large scale systems, can facilitate the integration of variety of self-⋆ properties in distributed systems, and also suit those systems whose activities are intrinsically situated in an environment. More important: (i) a spatial computing approach, by providing application components with an ab-stract — high-level perspective of the operational environment, appears suitable for a wide range of heterogeneous scenarios; (ii) most of current approaches to self-ware in distributed systems can be easily mapped into phenomena of spatial self-organization, thus making to model in spatial computing terms a variety of very diverse self-⋆ approaches. Our paper included in this book elaborate around spatial computing, its relations with self-⋆ approaches, and sketches some of our current research work in the area of "spatial computing middleware".

QoS-Enabled Peer-to-Peer Systems
Vana Kalogeraki, Fang Chen, Thomas Repantis and Demetris Zeinalipour-Yazti

Current efforts on P2P systems have focused on organizing the nodes in the network, improving resource usage, minimizing network latencies and reducing the volume of unnecessary traffic incurred in the P2P overlays. These have shown that P2P systems have been used successfully in the context of large scale file systems, resource sharing, multicast and information retrieval. Thus far, most of the work has concentrated in the sharing of "small" objects including MP3 music files, images, and audio.

Our position is that we can support distributed applications with Quality of Service (QoS) demands on Peer-to-Peer (P2P) systems. It is our belief that by exploring the self-⋆ properties such as self-organization, self-configuration and self-monitoring of the nodes of the P2P infrastructure and the necessary provisions, we will simplify the management and be able to support distributed applications that have QoS demands.

We believe that the decades of research in middleware technologies will help to achieve these goals. Examples include OMG's Common Object Request Broker Architecture (CORBA), Microsoft's Distributed Component Object Model (DCOM), Sun's Java Remote Method Invocation (RMI) and the Simple Object Access Protocol (SOAP). These represent mature, extensive and portable infrastructures that simplify the management of the applications and enable them to interoperate independently of their computing platforms and networking protocols. This work should be fully considered when developing distributed applications in P2P systems.

However, there are significant challenges that must be addressed. These applications demand multiple end-to-end QoS guarantees, such as predictable latency and jitter, reliability, and scalability. Large-scale environments have unpredictable latencies and changing resource availability, thus require systems that are easy to manage and able to adapt to dynamic changes in the utilization or availability of the resources.

To achieve our goals, we need to explore mechanisms for managing local resources, prioritizing application requests and propagating resource and timing measurements system-wide, and adaptive self-organization algorithms that improve application latencies and balance the load across multiple peers to meet the application end-to-end soft real-time and QoS requirements. These will help us to achieve high levels of performance and scalability and truly create self-managing QoS-enabled P2P systems.

Evolving Fractal Gene Regulatory Networks for Graceful Degradation of Software

Peter J. Bentley

Department of Computer Science, University College London,
Malet Place London, WC1E 6BT, UK
P.Bentley@cs.ucl.ac.uk
http://www.cs.ucl.ac.uk/staff/p.bentley/

Abstract. Fractal proteins are an evolvable method of mapping genotype to phenotype through a developmental process, where genes are expressed into proteins comprised of subsets of the Mandelbrot Set. The resulting network of gene and protein interactions can be designed by evolution to produce specific patterns that in turn can be used to solve problems. In this paper, adaptive developmental programs, capable of developing different solutions in response to different signals from an environment, are investigated. The evolvability of solutions and the capability of these solutions to survive damage is assessed. Evolution is used to create a fractal gene regulatory network (GRN) that calculates the squareroot of the input (its environment). This is compared with a GP-evolved squareroot function and a human-designed squareroot function. The programs are damaged by corrupting their compiled executable code, and the ability for each of them to survive such damage is assessed. Experiments demonstrate that only the evolutionary developmental code shows graceful degradation after damage. This provides evidence that software based on gene, protein and cellular computation is far more robust than traditional methods. Like a multicellular organism, with its genes evolved and developed, it shows graceful degradation. Should it be damaged, it is designed to continue to work.

1 Introduction

Human designs are carefully-crafted, consciously-created fusions of experience and skill. Our designs usually work reliably and well under the conditions they were designed for. Unfortunately, they rarely work well under unforeseen conditions. A ship will sink in the wrong kinds of seas, a car will crash on the wrong kinds of roads. A program will fail in the wrong kind of software environment. And sadly for computer-users worldwide, the mess of different software on an average computer causes such complex environments that programs fail with tired regularity.

Natural systems are also carefully crafted, but there is no conscious mind or skill needed to produce her designs. Generations of past experience drives evolution to create robust, damage-tolerant solutions. Organisms don't fail if they sustain minor damage. A broken finger hardly slows us. The equivalent damage to a human-designed program would produce terminal failure.

The work described here continues an ongoing investigation into the use of developmental systems with evolutionary computation. Here, fractals are employed as a

O. Babaoglu et al. (Eds.): SELF-STAR 2004, LNCS 3460, pp. 21–35, 2005.

computer representation of proteins. Earlier work has shown that fractal proteins are highly evolvable by a genetic algorithm (Bentley 2004, 2003c), that specific patterns of activation in a fractal gene regulatory network (GRN) can be evolved (Bentley, 2004, 2003b), that they can perform computational tasks such as function regression and robot control (Bentley 2003a), and that evolved fractal GRNs naturally show fault-tolerance (Bentley 2003c). This work now focuses on the evolution of developmental programs that display graceful degradation when damaged.

2   Background

Questions of reliability and graceful degradation occur frequently in fields focusing on embedded systems. To date, most solutions seem to depend on architectures that partition software into separate components, organised in such a way that the failure of non-critical components will not induce the failure of the whole system (Shelton & Koopman, 2001).

In Evolutionary Computation, scientists have been focussing on the ability of evolution, and more commonly developmental methods, to enable self-repairing behaviour and graceful degradation of solutions. The work of Andy Tyrrell and his group create fault-tolerant hardware inspired by ideas of embryology and immune systems (Jackson and Tyrrell, 2002). More recently, Julian Miller has described experiments evolving developmental programs to create "French Flag" patterns (Miller and Banzhaf, 2003). He shows that development is able to regenerate these patterns should some of their cells be removed. Current work by Mahdavi and Bentley (2003) demonstrates how adaptive evolutionary control can enable a "Smart Snake" to redevelop new movement strategies even after the loss of a crucial muscle (Nitinol wire).

In his research on fault-tolerant systems, Thompson (1997) describes how "graceful degradation for free" can be achieved in theory and in practice for robot controllers, "from the nature of the evolutionary process." Thompson suggests that mutation-insensitive individuals will, in the long term, survive better, thus producing a pressure towards fault-tolerant solutions. More recently, the same results were demonstrated with fractal developmental processes (Bentley 2003c), where there are no direct mappings: pleiotropy and polygeny are prevalent, and genes are reused over many developmental iterations. It was shown that through the Baldwin Effect, solutions "naturally" became more efficient and fault-tolerant (Bentley 2003c). In more detail, the work demonstrated that if evolution was permitted to run for a further 1000 generations after a perfect solution had evolved, the fractal GRNs continued to evolve: the number of genes and proteins that made up the solution was reduced (so there is less to be damaged), and duplicate genes were added, which provide redundancy and protection against damage.

This paper extends this work, showing that damage directly to the executable code (and not just a gene in the system) can be survived by evolved developmental programs.

3   Fractal Proteins

Development is the set of processes that lead from egg to embryo to adult. Instead of using a gene for a parameter value as we do in standard EC (i.e., a gene for long legs), natural development uses genes to define proteins. If expressed, every gene generates a specific protein. This protein might activate or suppress other genes, might be used for signalling amongst other cells, or might modify the function of the cell it lies within. The result is an emergent, asynchronous, parallel "computer program" made from dynamically forming gene regulatory networks (GRNs) that control all cell growth, position and behaviour in a developing creature (Wolpert et al, 2001).

Table 1. Types of objects in the model

fractal proteins	defined as subsets of the Mandelbrot set.
Environment	contains one or more fractal proteins (expressed from the environment gene(s)), and one or more *cells*.
Cell	contains a *genome* and *cytoplasm*, and has some *behaviours*.
Cytoplasm	contains one or more fractal proteins.
Genome	comprising *structural genes* and *regulatory genes*. In this work, the structural genes are divided into different types: *cell receptor genes, environment genes* and *behavioural genes.*
regulatory gene	comprising operator (or promoter) region and coding (or output) region.
cell receptor gene	a structural gene with a coding region which acts like a mask, permitting variable portions of the environmental proteins to enter the corresponding cell cytoplasm.
environment gene	a structural gene which determines which proteins (maternal factors) will be present in the environment of the cell(s).
behavioural gene	structural gene comprising operator and cellular behaviour region.

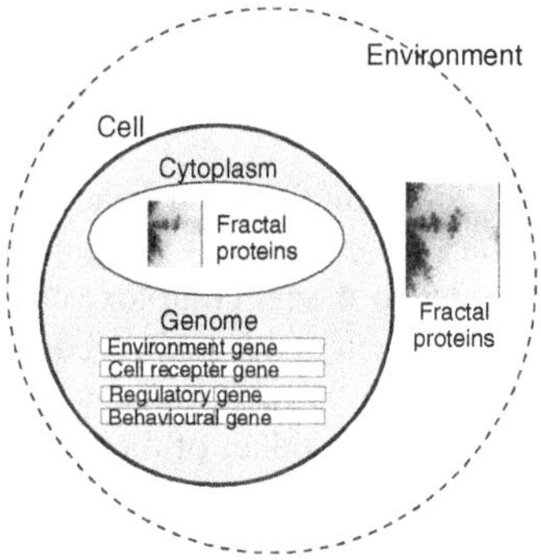

FRACTAL DEVELOPMENT

For every developmental time step:

    For every cell in the embryo:

        Express all environment genes and calculate shape of merged environment fractal proteins

        Express cell receptor genes as receptor fractal proteins and use each one to mask the merged environment proteins into the cell cytoplasm.

        If the merged contents of the cytoplasm match a promoter of a regulatory gene, express the coding region of the gene, adding the resultant fractal protein to the cytoplasm.

        If the merged contents of the cytoplasm match a promoter of a behavioural gene, use coding region of the gene to specify a cellular function.

        Update the concentration levels of all proteins in the cytoplasm. If the concentration level of a protein falls to zero, that protein does not exist.

Fig. 1. Representation using fractal proteins

Fig. 2. The fractal development algorithm

In this work, a biologically plausible model of gene regulatory networks is constructed through the use of genes that are expressed into *fractal proteins* – subsets of the Mandelbrot set that can interact and react according to their own fractal chemistry. Further motivations and discussions on fractal proteins are provided in (Bentley, 2004 & 2003a,b,c). Table 1 describes the object types in the representation; Figure 1 illustrates the representation. Figure 2 provides an overview of the algorithm used to develop a phenotype from a genotype. Note how most of the dynamics rely on the interaction of fractal proteins. Evolution is used to design genes that are expressed into fractal proteins with specific shapes, which result in developmental processes with specific dynamics.

3.1 Defining a Fractal Protein

In more detail, a fractal protein is a finite square subset of the Mandelbrot set (Mandelbrot 1982), defined by three codons (x,y,z) that form the coding region of a gene in the genome of a cell. Each (x, y, z) triplet is expressed as a protein by calculating the square fractal subset with centre coordinates (x,y) and sides of length z, see fig. 3 for an example. In addition to shape, each fractal protein represents a certain *concentration* of protein (from 0 meaning "does not exist" to 200 meaning "saturated"), determined by protein production and diffusion rates.

Fig. 3. Example of a fractal protein defined by $(x=0.132541887, y=0.698126164, z=0.468306528)$

3.2 Fractal Chemistry

The model incorporates the notions of cell cytoplasm – a "container" which holds the proteins belonging to the corresponding cell) and (cellular) environment – the global "container" which holds proteins visible to all cells. In order to model complex protein-protein and protein-gene interactions, multiple fractal proteins are allowed to interact according to their fractal shapes. The interaction occurs by merging separate protein shapes to form new, complex compounds. The result is a product of their own "fractal chemistry" which naturally emerges through the fractal interactions.

Fractal proteins are merged (for each point sampled) by iterating through the fractal equation of all proteins in "parallel", and stopping as soon as the length of any is unbounded (i.e. greater than 2). Intuitively, this results in black regions being treated as though they are transparent, and paler regions "winning" over darker regions. See fig 4 for an example.

3.3 Calculating Concentration Levels

The total concentration of two or more merged fractal proteins is the mean of the different concentrations seen in their merged product. For example, fig. 4 shows how fractal proteins are merged to form a new fractal shape. Figure 5 illustrates the

Fig. 4. Two fractal proteins (left and middle) and the resulting merged fractal protein combination (right)

Fig. 5. The different concentrations of the two fractal proteins (left and middle) and the concentration levels in their merged product (right)

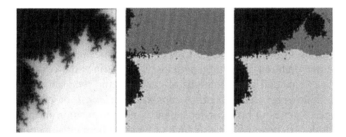

Fig. 6. The shape of the desired protein as defined by a promoter (left), the shape and concentration levels of merged proteins in the cytoplasm (middle) and the concentration levels seen on that promoter (right), where total concentration is taken as mean. Note that although a merged protein may decrease affinity (similarity) to the promoter, should the second protein have a higher concentration level to the first, it will boost overall concentration seen by the promoter, i.e., act like a catalyst to speed up (or slow down, if lower) the "reaction"

resultant areas of different concentration in the product. When being compared to the $(xp,\ yp,\ zp)$ promoter region of a gene (the "conditional" part of the gene to be matched, see later section on genes), the concentration seen on that promoter is described by all those regions that "fall under" the promoter, see fig. 5. In other words, the merged product is masked by the promoter fractal, and the total concentration on the promoter is the mean of the resulting concentrations, see Fig. 6.

3.4 Updating Protein Concentration Levels

Every developmental time step, the new concentration of each protein is calculated (synchronously). This is formed by summing two separate terms: the previous concentration level after diffusion (*diffusedconc*) and the new concentration output by a gene (*geneoutputconc*). These two terms model the reduction in concentration of proteins over time, and the production of new proteins over time, respectively, where:

diffusedconc = *prevconcentration* $\times$ (1 − 1/ PROTEINDEC + 0.2)
      (PROTEINDEC is a constant normally set to 5)
and:

geneoutputconc = *totalconc* $\times$ tanh((*totalconc* − *ct*) / CWIDTH) / CINC

where: *totalconc* is the mean concentration seen at the promoter,
        ct is the concentration threshold from the gene promoter
            CWIDTH is a constant (normally set to 30)
            CINC is a constant (normally set to 2)

3.5 Genes

The environment gene, cell receptor gene, regulatory genes, and behavioural genes all contain 7 real-coded values:

xp	yp	zp	Affinity threshold	Concentration threshold	x	y	z	type

where (*xp, yp, zp, Affinity threshold, Concentration threshold*) defines the promoter (operator or precondition) for the gene and (*x,y,z*) defines the coding region of the gene. The *type* value defines which type of gene is being represented, and can be one or all of the following: *environment, receptor, behavioural,* or *regulatory*. This enables the type of genes to be set independently of their position in the genome, enabling variable-length genomes. It also enables genes to be multi-functional, i.e. a gene might be expressed both as an environmental protein and a behaviour.

When *Affinity threshold* is a positive value, one or more proteins must match the promoter shape defined by (*xp,yp,zp*) with a difference equal to or lower than *Affinity threshold* for the gene to be activated. When *Affinity threshold* is a negative value, one or more proteins must match the promoter shape defined by (*xp,yp,zp*) with a difference equal to or lower than |*Affinity threshold*| for the gene to be repressed (not activated).

To calculate whether a gene should be activated, all fractal proteins in the cell cytoplasm are merged (including the masked environmental proteins, see later) and the combined fractal mixture is compared to the promoter region of the gene.

The similarity between two fractal proteins (or a fractal protein and a merged fractal protein combination) is calculated by sampling a series of points in each and summing the difference between all the resulting values. (Black regions of fractals are ignored.) Given the similarity matching score between cell cytoplasm fractals and gene promoter, the activation probability of a gene is given by:

$activationprob = (1 + \tanh((matchnum - Affinity\ threshold - Ct) / Cs)) / 2$

where: *matchnum* is the matching score,
                         Affinity threshold is the matching threshold from the gene promoter
                         Ct is a threshold constant (normally set to 50)
                         Cs is a sharpness constant (normally set to 50)

Regulatory Gene

Should a regulatory gene be activated by other protein(s) in the cytoplasm (which have concentrations above 0) matching its promoter region, its corresponding coding region (x,y,z) is expressed (by calculating the subset of the Mandelbrot set) and new concentration level calculated. To do this, the concentration of the resulting protein is modified by incrementing with *geneoutputconc*, the result of a function of the concentration threshold (*ct*) and the mean total concentration seen at the gene promoter (*totalconc*), as given in section 3.5. In this way, higher concentrations of protein on the promoter will cause an increased rate of output protein concentration growth, while lower concentrations (below the *ct* threshold) will increase the diffusion rate of the output protein (its concentration will decrease at a higher rate).

The cell cytoplasm, which holds all current proteins, is updated at the end of the developmental cycle.

Cell Receptor Gene

At present, the promoter region of the cell receptor gene is ignored, and this gene is always activated. As usual, the corresponding coding region (x,y,z) is expressed by calculating the subset of the Mandelbrot set. However, the resultant fractal protein is treated as a mask for the environmental proteins, where all black regions of the mask are treated as opaque, and all other regions treated as transparent. For an example, see fig. 7. If there is more than one receptor gene, only the first in the genome is used.

Fig. 7. Cell receptor protein (left), environment protein (middle), resulting masked protein to be combined with cytoplasm (right)

Environment Gene

Like the cell receptor gene, this gene is always activated. It produces environmental factors for all cells: fractal proteins of concentration 200. If there is more than one environmental gene, the expressed environmental proteins are merged before being masked by the receptor protein. If one or more values are being input to the system, the concentration of the environmental fractal proteins are set to those values, i.e. an input to the system disturbs the environment during development.

Behavioural Gene

A behavioural gene is activated when other protein(s) in the cytoplasm match its promoter region (using the *affinity threshold*). For this application, a gradual activation between not activated and activated was required, using the x value of the coding region (x,y,z) triplet as a *fate* value to define a function, calculated as follows:

If the gene is being activated with a negative *Affinity threshold*,
output = output - (totalconcentration - concentrationthreshold) * fate
If the gene is being activated with a positive *Affinity threshold*,
output = output + (totalconcentration - concentrationthreshold) * fate

Note how the total concentration of proteins seen on the promoter is offset against the *Concentration Threshold* gene and scaled by the *fate* gene (x value of the coding region), allowing evolution to adjust the range of values seen on the output, and used to specify behaviours. (If there is more than one behavioural gene, the change to *output* is averaged over all behavioural genes, each developmental step.)

3.6 Fractal Sampling

All fractal calculations (masking, merging, comparisons) are performed at the same time, by sampling the fractals at a resolution of 15x15 points. Note that the comparison is normally performed between the single fractal defined by (xp,yp,zp) of a gene and the merged combination of all other proteins currently in the cytoplasm. The fractal being compared is treated a little like the cell receptor mask – only those regions that are not black are actually compared with the contents of the cytoplasm.

3.7 Development

As was illustrated in figure 2, an individual begins life as a single cell in a given environment. To develop the individual from this zygote into the final phenotype, fractal proteins are iteratively calculated and matched against all genes of the genome. Should any genes be activated, the result of their activation (be it a new protein, receptor or cellular behaviour) is generated at the end of the current cycle. Development continues for d cycles, where d is dependent on the problem. Note that if one of the cellular behaviours includes the creation of new cells, then development will iterate through all genes of the genome in all cells.

3.8 Evolution

The genetic algorithm used in this work has been used extensively elsewhere for other applications (including GADES (Bentley 1999)). A dual population structure is employed, where child solutions are maintained and evaluated, and then inserted into a larger adult population, replacing the least fit. The fittest n are randomly picked as parents from the adult population. The degree of negative selection pressure can be controlled by modifying the relative sizes of the two populations. Likewise the degree of positive selection pressure is set by varying n. When child and adult population sizes are equal, the algorithm resembles a canonical or generational GA. When the child population size is reduced, the algorithm resembles a steady-state GA. Typically the child population size is set to 80% of the adult size and $n = 40\%$. (For further details of this GA, refer to (Bentley 1999).)

Unless specified, alleles are initialised randomly, with (xp,yp,zp) and (x,y,z) values between -1.0 and 1.0 and *thresh* between -10000 and 10000. The ranges and precision of the alleles are limited only by the storage capacity of *double* and *long* 'C' data types – no range constraints were set in the code.

Genetic Operators
Genes are real-coded, but genomes may comprise variable numbers of genes. Given two parent genomes, the crossover operator examines each gene of parent1 in turn, finding the most similar gene of the same type in parent 2. Similarity is measured by calculating the differences between values of operator and coding regions of genes. One of the two genes is then randomly allocated to the child. If the genome of parent2 is shorter, the child inherits the remaining genes from parent 1. If the genomes are the same length, this crossover acts as uniform crossover.

Mutation is also interesting, particularly since these genes actually code for proteins in this system. There are four main types of mutation used here:

1. Creep mutation, where (xp,yp,zp) and (x,y,z) values are incremented or decremented by a random number between 0 and 0.5, *Affinity Threshold* is incremented or decremented by a random number between 0 and 16384 and *Concentration Threshold* is incremented or decremented by a random number between 0 and 200.
2. Duplication mutation, where a (xp,yp,zp) or (x,y,z) region of one gene randomly replaces a (xp,yp,zp) or (x,y,z) of another gene. (This permits evolution to create matching promoter regions and coding regions quickly.)
3. Gene mutation, where a random gene in the genome is either removed or a duplicate added.
4. Sign flip mutation, where the sign of *Affinity Threshold* is reversed.

Crossover is always applied; all mutations occur with probability 0.01 per gene.

4 Squareroot Function Regression

Previous work has demonstrated how evolution can generate specific fractal proteins that interact with each other in order to produce desired patterns of activation (Bentley 2004) or to produce a specific set of commands for a robot, to guide it past obstacles (Bentley 2003a). Here, the task is to produce the square root of a number. The input to the system is provided by setting the concentration of the first environment fractal protein (all others have a default value of 200). The output is produced by the behavioural gene(s) as described previously. Each genotype was developed ten times in succession with random input (concentration) values between 0 and 199. The fitness was the sum of the differences between the values obtained and true squareroot of the input.

To evolve the controllers, the fractal development system was initialised with a single cell, 2 environment genes, 2 receptor gene, 2 behavioural genes and 6 regulatory genes. (With variable length genomes, evolution was free to modify these gene numbers). The operator and coding regions of the genes were randomly initialised with the alleles that defined 10 previously evolved protein fractals (Bentley, 2004). 8 developmental steps were employed (ten times, each with a different environmental protein concentration, corresponding to the ten random inputs), and the evolutionary algorithm used a population size of 100, running for 1000 generations.

To provide some assessment of how effective fractal proteins are in improving performance or evolvability, the same system was also run with all fractal proteins disabled. In this non-fractal version, the triplet of three real values were used directly (the affinity value now defined how small the sum of differences between the cis-region of the gene and the protein should be before the gene is activated). There were no protein-protein interactions; no fractal shapes were calculated, merged or compared. All other parameters were kept the same.

5   Squareroot Function Regression Results

Figure 8 shows the final fitness scores achieved by the fractal developmental system and the system using no fractal proteins, for thirty runs. Fitnesses below 40,000 achieved an acceptable accuracy. It should be clear that the system using fractal proteins achieved acceptable fitnesses in 20 out of 30 runs. The system without fractal proteins only achieved acceptable fitnesses in 7 out of 30 runs. In addition, solution quality often suffers without fractal proteins – no solutions achieved the same accuracy as those produced with fractal proteins.

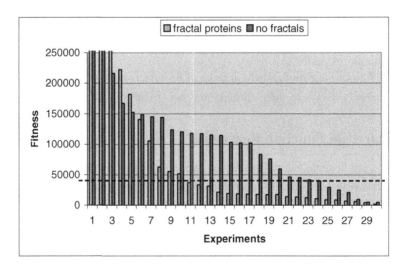

Fig. 8. Fitness of developmental squareroot program using fractal proteins and the developmental squareroot program without fractal proteins. Results are shown sorted into descending order of fitness for clarity and ease of comparison. The dotted line denotes a fitness of 40,000 – any solutions with fitnesses at or below this line are considered sufficiently accurate at calculating the squareroot of the input

The reason for the difference in performance seems to be *evolvability*. Without fractal proteins, solutions become trapped in local optima – GRNs that produce a linear output are common, instead of the required non-linear squareroot curve. Without the ability for new proteins and genes created by evolution to affect existing proteins and genes (through complex protein-protein and protein-gene interactions), there is no way for evolution to overcome the trap. With fractal proteins, evolution is free to add new genes which produce proteins that modify existing solutions subtly and in nonlinear ways. Evolvability is caused by the ability of this representation to enable gradual modifications to any solutions - not just by changing existing genes but also by adding new ones that act in combination with existing ones where necessary. This is evident during evolution as poor solutions gain large numbers of genes, and good solutions prune the genes down to more robust sizes. Without fractal proteins, each gene has a much more binary role - it is either critical to the GRN or has no effect at all - meaning evolution cannot make small changes quite as easily (despite still being able to duplicate genes).

Previous work (Bentley 2003c) has shown other aspects of evolvability: even after evolution has found a perfect solution, it continues to evolve, changing genes, proteins and entire GRNs constantly. This representation enables never-ceasing evolution, which also results in the solutions becoming compact and robust against damage.

6 Damage Tolerant Developmental Programs

Having shown that fractal proteins do convey a significant advantage for evolutionary development, a further experiment was performed in order to assess how fractal developmental programs show graceful degradation, when damaged. Using the results from the previous experiment, the fittest solution was picked (see figure 9a), the evolved fractal proteins were written into the code as a short list of real-valued constants (the x, y, z values described earlier), the genetic algorithm removed, and the resulting fractal developmental squareroot program compiled into a stand-alone executable. (The compiler was GCC 3.3, using xcode on a Mac Powerbook G4, Mac OS 10.3.2.)

6.1 Comparison Methods

Two other programs were used as comparisons in the experiments. The first was a fast squareroot function, written for speed of execution, provided by Hsieh[1]. This is written in C and was simply compiled to produce a stand-alone executable. The second was evolved by Landon's simple GP (Langdon 1998)[2]. This standard genetic programming engine used a function set comprising "+", "-", "*" and "/", population size of 100, max program size of 100 nodes, number of generations = 1000, probability of crossover 0.7, and mutation 0.01. Each individual was evaluated by presenting 10 random inputs and calculating the sum of the difference between the outputs and the true squareroot of the inputs. After twenty runs, only five solutions close to the

---

[1] http://www.azillionmonkeys.com/qed/sqroot.html#fast
[2] http://www.cs.ucl.ac.uk/staff/w.langdon/ftp/gp-code/simple/simple-gp.c

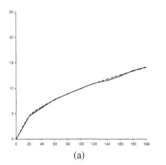 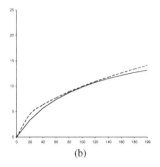

(a)   (b)

Fig. 9. (a) Output of the evolved developmental squareroot function. (b) Output of the GP-evolved squareroot function. (True squareroot shown by dotted line.)

```
((GPdiv(x+x+x+GPdiv(((x)-((x)*(x)))-((x)*(x)),(x)*(x))+x+((x+x+x+x)*(x))-(x),((x+x+
x+x+x+x+x+x+x+x+x+x+x+x+x+x+x+x+x+x+x+x)*(x))-(GPdiv((x)*(x),GPdiv(x+x+x+x+x,(x)-
((x)*(x)))))))))*(x));
```

Fig. 10. GP-evolved squareroot. "GPdiv" divides, trapping divide-by-zero errors

function of squareroot had evolved. Figure 9b shows the output of the best GP square-root function. Fig. 10 shows its code. The evolved code was then isolated and compiled to produce a stand-alone GP-evolved squareroot executable.

7 Damage Tolerance Experiments and Results

Although it was observed that the evolved fractal developmental squareroot function was more accurate and this accuracy was achieved more consistently than the GP version, this was not the objective of the work. (Note that all three compiled square-root programs are set to calculate the squareroot of 11 values from 0 to 199 in steps of 20, so accuracy is measured in terms of these sample points only.) Here we are more concerned with the ability of the evolved solutions to survive damage to their compiled executables. In order to assess this, a "corruption" program was written, which reads a specified file in a series of 2048 byte chunks, flipping a single, randomly chosen bit in each chunk, before saving in a new file. This was performed 50 times for all three squareroot programs, resulting in 150 corrupted executables. These were then executed and the results noted.

The initial results were perhaps predictable. Both the fast squareroot program and the GP-evolved program were approximately 16 kilobytes in size, smaller than the 28 kilobytes of the developmental squareroot program. This meant they were corrupted less, resulting in more reliable performance. Indeed, the fast squareroot program ran perfectly 15/50 times, and ran providing incorrect solutions twice. The GP-evolved program ran perfectly 10/50 times, and provided incorrect solutions twice. The developmental program ran perfectly twice, provided approximately correct solutions 3 times, and incorrect solutions twice.

With all three programs being different lengths and containing different code, it was clear that the comparison was flawed. The developmental program contained many more calls to memory-handling routines and library functions, resulting in more code (which was corrupted more), and thus code more likely to fail. To overcome this, the three squareroot programs were combined into a single program. By changing a simple compiler directive, the program could be compiled in three different ways:

1. Output result of method 1 only if methods 2 and 3 executed correctly.
2. Output result of method 2 only if methods 1 and 3 executed correctly.
3. Output result of method 3 only if methods 1 and 2 executed correctly.

where method 1 was the fast squareroot function, method 2 was the GP-evolved function, and method 3 was the fractal developmental squareroot function. This way, all three programs contained the same code with the same susceptibility to damage, except that the code that generated the output was different in each program.

The three executables were corrupted 200 times using the method described previously. The corrupted programs were then executed and the results noted, see table 2.

Table 2. Results of running 200 corrupted executables for three squareroot programs. Graceful degradation is defined as solutions producing 10 non-zero values within 50 percent of the correct values

	Square root	GP square root	Ev. Dev. square root
Fail	197	198	177
Incorrect run	1	0	13
Graceful degradation	0	0	8
Perfect	2	2	2

8 Analysis

The results are fascinating. Despite all three programs suffering from the same proportion and type of errors (see fig. 11), there is marked difference in performance between the developmental squareroot program and the fast squareroot and GP-evolved programs. The latter both only manage to execute correctly 2 out of 200 corrupted executables. They display zero graceful degradation – they simply fail to execute (or in a single case, execute with incorrect results).

The developmental squareroot program manages to run 23 times out of 200. 13 of those produce incorrect results (usually all zeros). Only 2 produce perfect results (as good as the uncorrupted program). But in 8 cases, the developmental squareroot produces *approximately correct* solutions, fig 12. The damage to the executable has perhaps corrupted the genes or fractal proteins, and the developmental program recovers. As was described in section 2, evolution has not only evolved a good solution, it has created a solution that copes with damage. It seems that this protection even extends to damage done to the executable code, as well as simple mutation-driven damage to genes.

Note that the GP-evolved code does not display this property. It is conceivable that should the GP solution contain bloat (unused code), then it might survive damage more readily. However, this would not be the same phenomenon observed in the developmental system, which has no bloat (Bentley 2003c). In the developmental system, damage to the code *that is actually being used*, can be survivable (Bentley, 2003c). It seems probable that only highly evolvable developmental systems enable this kind of "natural" graceful degradation to emerge.

It should also be noted that all three squareroot programs were calculating the squareroot results according to their inputs. The developmental program did not, in any sense, have the answer "wired in" as constants – indeed it performed more calculation using the input to produce the results than the other two programs. The ability to survive damage arises because of the way the calculation was performed – the dynamic (gene) networks in the code are able to survive despite having "holes punched in them" by the corruption program.

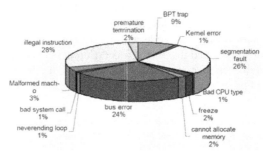

Fig. 11. Percentage & type of errors obtained in all runs of the corrupted programs

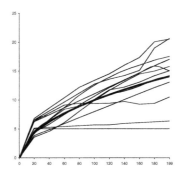

Fig. 12. Outputs produced by different runs of the damaged developmental squareroot function, true squareroot shown in bold. Note that most produce results that are approximately correct (within 2 of the true value), displaying remarkably graceful degradation

9 Conclusions

Development is the process used by evolution to construct complex, adaptive and robust forms. Computer algorithms based on development can share some of these properties. Here, experiments have shown that fractal proteins increase the evolvability of developmental programs by allowing new protein-protein and protein-gene interactions to incrementally modify solutions over several generations. Experiments have also shown that, unlike traditional software, evolved fractal developmental programs show graceful degradation after damage to their executable code. While surviving only around 14 bits (0.05%) of damage 10% of the time is not a great achievement compared to the robustness of natural systems, given the conventional (brittle) nature of the programming language, compiler and hardware, it is still considered impressive. It seems likely that should computer science remove its brittleness and embrace evolutionary and developmental systems more fully, abilities such as graceful degradation will improve further.

Acknowledgments

This material is based upon work supported by the European Office of Aerospace Research and Development (EOARD), Airforce Office of Scientific Research, Airforce Research Laboratory, under Contract No. F61775-02-WE014. Any opinions, findings and conclusions or recommendations expressed in this material are those of the author and do not necessarily reflect the views of EOARD. MOBIUS is an project.

References

[1] Bentley, P. J. Fractal Proteins. 2004. In Genetic Programming and Evolvable Machines Journal.

[2] Bentley, P. J. Evolving Fractal Gene Regulatory Networks for Robot Control. 2003a. In Proceedings of ECAL 2003.

[3] Bentley, P. J. Evolving Fractal Proteins. 2003b. In Proc. of ICES '03, the 5th International Conference on Evolvable Systems: From Biology to Hardware.

[4] Bentley, P. J. Evolving Beyond Perfection: An Investigation of the Effects of Long-Term Evolution on Fractal Gene Regulatory Networks. 2003c. In Proc of *Information Processing in Cells and Tissues* (IPCAT 2003).

[5] Bentley, P. J. From Coffee Tables to Hospitals: Generic Evolutionary Design. 1999. Chapter 18 in Bentley, P. J. (Ed) Evolutionary Design by Computers. Morgan Kaufmann Pub. San Francisco, pp. 405-423.

[6] A.H. Jackson, A.M. Tyrrell Implementing Asynchronous Embryonic Circuits using AARDVArc. 2002. In *Proceedings of 2002 NASA/DoD Conference on Evolvable Hardware* (EH-2002), IEEE Computing Society, Alexandria, Virginia, pp. 231-240.

[7] S. Kumar and P. J. Bentley. Computational Embryology: Past, Present and Future. 2003. Invited chapter in Ghosh and Tsutsui (Eds) Theory and Application of Evolutionary Computation: Recent Trends. Springer Verlag (UK).

[8] Langdon, W. (1998) *Genetic Programming + Data Structures = Automatic Programming!* Kluwer Pub.

[9] Mahdavi S. and Bentley P. J. Adaptive Evolutionary Motion of Smart Robots. 2003. In Proc. of EvoROB2003, 2nd European Workshop on Evolutionary Robotics.

[10] Mandelbrot, B. *The Fractal Geometry of Nature.* 1982. W.H. Freeman & Company.

[11] Miller, J. and Banzhaf, W. Evolving the Program for a Cell: From French Flags to Boolean Circuits. 2003. Invited chapter in Kumar, S. and Bentley, P. J. (Eds) *On Growth, Form and Computers.* Academic Press, 2003.

[12] Shelton, C. & Koopman, P. Developing a Software Architecture for Graceful Degradation in an Elevator Control System. *Workshop on Reliability in Embedded Systems.*

[13] Thompson, A. Evolving Inherently Fault-Tolerant Systems. 1997. In Proc. Instn. Mech. Engrs 1997.

[14] Lewis Wolpert, Rosa Beddington, Thomas Jessell, Peter Lawrence, Elliot Meyerowitz, Jim Smith. *Principles of Development, 2nd Ed.* 2001. Oxford University Press.

Evolutionary Computing and Autonomic Computing: Shared Problems, Shared Solutions?

A.E. Eiben

Vrije Universiteit Amsterdam

Abstract. The purpose of this paper is to present evolutionary computing (EC) and to identify a number of issues where EC and autonomic computing, a.k.a. self-*, are mutually relevant for each other. We show that Evolutionary Algorithms (EA) form a metaheuristic that can be used to tackle the problem of self-optimisation in autonomic systems and suggest that an evolutionary approach can also help solving other challenges in autonomic computing. Meanwhile, an evolving system can be seen as a special case of an autonomic system. From this perspective, the quest for parameterless EAs can be positioned in a broader context and it can be expected that some solutions invented within autonomic computing can be transferred to EC.

1 Introduction

This position paper is aiming at linking evolutionary computing and autonomic computing. Autonomic computing is assumed to be known, therefore it is not reviewed here. Evolutionary computing is discussed emphasizing those facets that are most relevant to make the main points about the mutual relevance of the two areas.

We argue that the evolutionary mechanism is inherently capable of optimising a collection of entities. This capability comes forth from the interplay of three basic actions: reproduction, variation, and selection. Whenever the entities in question reproduce they create a surplus, variation during reproduction amounts to innovation of novel entities[1], and finally selection takes care of promoting the right variants by discarding the poor ones. This process has led to the Homo Sapiens on Earth and to numerous superior solutions of engineering and design problems in evolutionary computing [6]. Technically, an evolutionary process can be perceived as a generate-and-test search algorithm regulated by a number of parameters and it has two very interesting properties from a self-* perspective. First, evolution is able to evolve itself, that is, to tune its own parameters on-the-fly. Second, it is able to adapt itself to changing circumstances, that is, to track optimal solutions after the objective function is changed.

We also argue that evolutionary computing is one of the key technologies that can help meeting some of the grand challenges of autonomic computing.

---

[1] That is, in our case reproduction is not simply cloning.

O. Babaoglu et al. (Eds.): SELF-STAR 2004, LNCS 3460, pp. 36–48, 2005.

EC is widely applicable, it requires almost no assumptions about the problem to be solved, an evolutionary solver can be usually developed with limited efforts and it produces good quality solutions at acceptable computational costs under a wide range of circumstances. To illustrate our point we describe an evolutionary approach to self-optimisation in a distributed system. Our example is a problem concerning web services offered to a large number of users via a (possibly large) number of servers. The quality of service is the key measure to be optimised and re-optimised if the circumstances change, for instance, if the behaviour of the users changes over time. The key to our approach is to have each user session regulated by a number of parameters and allow variations in these parameters. Adding selection based on the quality of service belonging to given parameter values introduces survival of the fittest and makes the system evolutionary.

The paper is organised as follows. In Section 2 a general introduction to EC is given. Section 3 provides more details on a specific type of EAs, evolution strategies, and illustrates how self-adaptation works in EC. Thereafter, in Section 4, an example application is described and an evolutionary approach is presented to realise self-optimisation in the system. Besides specifying a concrete EA to solve this problem, we also consider general properties of an evolutionary approach in such a context. The paper is concluded by Section 5, where we discuss how and why developments in these two fields can be expected to help solving great challenges in the other field.

2   Evolutionary Computing in a Nutshell

Evolutionary Computing encompasses a variety of so-called evolutionary algorithms [2, 5, 6] that all share a common underlying idea: given a population of individuals, the environmental pressure causes natural selection (survival of the fittest), which causes a rise in the fitness of the population over time. The main principle behind evolution, be it natural or computer simulated, can be summarised as follows. If a collection of objects satisfies that

- they are able to reproduce,
- their offspring inherits their features,
- these features can undergo small random, undirected variations,
- these features effect their reproduction probabilities,

then the features of these objects will change over time in such a way that they will fit their environment better and better.

In a formal setting, the environment is represented by a given quality function to be maximised.[2] The population is created by randomly generating a set of candidate solutions, i.e., elements of the function's domain, and the quality function is used as an abstract fitness measure – the higher the better. Based on

---

[2] Handling minimisation problems only requires a trivial mathematical transformation.

this fitness, some of the better candidate solutions are chosen to seed the next generation by applying recombination and/or mutation to them. Recombination is an operator applied to two or more selected candidates (the so-called parents) and results one or more new candidates (the children). Mutation is applied to one candidate and results in one new candidate. Executing recombination and mutation leads to a set of new candidates (the offspring) that compete – based on their fitness (and possibly age)– with the old ones for a place in the next generation. This process can be iterated until a candidate with sufficient quality (a solution) is found or a previously set computational limit is reached.

In this process there are two fundamental forces that form the basis of evolutionary systems:

- Variation operators (recombination and mutation) create the necessary diversity and thereby facilitate novelty.
- Selection acts as a force pushing quality. As opposed to variation, selection reduces diversity.

Based on the biological analogy one often distinguishes phenotypes and genotypes of candidate solutions. The phenotype of a candidate is its "outside", the way it looks and/or acts. The genotype denotes the code, the "digital DNA", that encodes or represents this phenotype. It is an important to note that variation and selection act in different spaces.

- Variation operators act on genotypes. Mutation and recombination never take place on phenotypical level, for instance, changing a leg into a wing. Rather, variation effects on the level of genes that determine the phenotype.
- Selection acts on phenotypes. A gene is never evaluated directly, it has to be expressed as a physical feature or behaviour and it is this feature or behaviour that gets evaluated by the environment and influences the survival and reproduction capabilities.

The combined application of variation and selection generally leads to improving fitness values in consecutive populations. It is easy (although somewhat misleading) to see such a process as if the evolution is optimising, or at least "approximising", by approaching optimal values closer and closer over its course. Alternatively, evolution it is often seen as a process of adaptation. From this perspective, the fitness is not seen as an objective function to be optimised, but as an expression of environmental requirements. Matching these requirements more closely implies an increased viability, reflected in a higher number of offspring. The evolutionary process makes the population increasingly better at being adapted to the environment.

It is important to note that many components of such an evolutionary process are stochastic. During selection fitter individuals have a higher chance to be selected than less fit ones, but typically even the weak individuals have a chance to become a parent or to survive. For recombination of individuals the choice of which pieces will be recombined is random. Similarly for mutation, the pieces that will be mutated within a candidate solution, and the new pieces replacing them, are chosen randomly. The general scheme of an evolutionary algorithm can is given in Fig. 1 in a pseudocode fashion.

```
BEGIN
  INITIALISE population with random candidate solutions;
  EVALUATE each candidate;
  REPEAT UNTIL ( TERMINATION CONDITION is satisfied ) DO
    1 SELECT parents;
    2 RECOMBINE pairs of parents;
    3 MUTATE the resulting offspring;
    4 EVALUATE new candidates;
    5 SELECT individuals for the next generation;
  OD
END
```

Fig. 1. The general scheme of an evolutionary algorithm in pseudocode

It is easy to see that EAs fall in the category of generate-and-test algorithms. The evaluation (fitness) function represents a heuristic estimation of solution quality, and the search process is driven by the variation and the selection operators. Evolutionary algorithms possess a number of features that can help to position them within in the family of generate-and-test methods:

- EAs are population based, i.e., they process a whole collection of candidate solutions simultaneously.
- EAs mostly use recombination to mix information of more candidate solutions into a new one.
- EAs are stochastic.

Example: The Travelling Salesman Problem
In the Travelling Salesman Problem (TSP) the task is to find a tour (Hamiltonian circle) through n given locations with minimal length. An evolutionary approach considers tours as phenotypes that are evaluated by their length, the shorter a tour the higher its fitness. An appropriate genotype can be for instance a permutation of n location IDs with the obvious genotype-phenotype mapping. The essence of designing an EA for the TSP is to specify appropriate variation and selection operators (followed by defining the initialisation procedure, termination condition, etc). To keep things really simple one could decide to use mutation as the only variation operator and chose to mutate a permutation by swapping the values on two randomly chosen positions. As for selection –remember, it is independent from what genotypes we use – one can use fitness proportional random drawing. Whenever a good individual needs to be selected from a population of m, any candidate c_i is selected by a probability $p_i = fitness(c_i)/\sum_{i=1}^{m} fitness(c_i)$.

As mentioned before there are different EA variants. The most important types, or "dialects", are (in alphabetical order) evolution strategies, evolutionary programming, genetic algorithms, and genetic programming [2, 5, 6]. These dialects differ only in technical details. For instance, the representation of a candidate solution is often used to characterise different streams. Typically, the candidates are represented by (i.e., the data structure encoding a solution has the form of) strings over a finite alphabet in genetic algorithms (GA), real-valued vectors in evolution strategies (ES), finite state machines in classical evolutionary programming (EP), and trees in genetic programming (GP). These differences have a mainly historical origin. Technically, a given representation might be preferable over others if it matches the given problem better; that is, it makes the encoding of candidate solutions easier or more natural. It is important to note that the recombination and mutation operators working on candidates must match the given representation. Thus, for instance, in GP the recombination operator works on trees, while in GAs it operates on strings. As opposed to variation operators, selection takes only the fitness information into account; hence it works independently from the actual representation.

Technically, an EA has numerous parameters. The precise list of parameters and the way they are set are depending on the type of EA at hand. However, in all cases one has to arrange the population, selection, and variation. The following list illustrates some common parameters.

- Population size: the number of candidate solutions (typically kept constant during a run). A small population allows faster progress but increases the risk of getting stuck in a local optimum because it can only maintain fewer alternatives, hence less diversity.
- Selection pressure: the extent of bias preferring the good candidates over weak ones. High selection pressure causes faster progress but increases the risk of getting stuck in a local optimum by being too greedy. Zero selection pressure degrades evolutionary search into random walk.
- Mutation magnitude[3]: the parameter regulating the influence of mutation, e.g., how often, how big, etc. Using more/larger mutation speeds up the search but can prevent fine tuning on the optimum.

In the early days of EC it has been claimed that EAs have robust parameters, i.e., that EAs are to a large extent insensitive to the exact parameter values. Later on this claim has been revised and the contemporary view acknowledges that using the right parameter values can make a big difference in algorithm performance. The effects of setting the parameters of EAs has been the subject of extensive research by the EA community and recently there is much attention paid to self-calibrating EAs. The ultimate goal is to have a parameter-free algorithm that can calibrate itself to any given problem while solving that problem. For an extensive treatment of this issue [4] and [6–Chapter 8] are recommended,

---

[3] *Mutation magnitude* is not an established technical term in EC. It is used here as an umbrella term covering the commonly used ones, like mutation rate, mutation step size, etc.

[1] provides an experimental comparison between EAs using different levels of self-calibration.

3   Evolution Strategies and Self-adaptation

In this section we outline evolution strategies. Hereby we present a member of the evolutionary algorithm family in details and illustrate a very useful feature in evolutionary computing: self-adaptation. In evolutionary computing self-adaptivity means that some parameters of the EA are varied during a run in a specific manner: the parameters are included in the chromosomes and co-evolve with the solutions. This feature is inherent for evolution strategies, i.e., from the earliest versions ESs are self-adaptive, and during the last couple of years other EAs are adopting self-adaptivity.

Evolution strategies are typically used for continuous parameter optimization problems, i.e., functions of the type $f : \mathrm{IR}^n \to \mathrm{IR}$, using real-valued vectors as candidate solutions. Parent selection is done by drawing λ individuals with a uniform distribution from the population of μ, where $\lambda > \mu$ (very often μ/λ is about $1/7$). After creating λ offspring and calculating their fitness the best μ of them is chosen *deterministically* either from the offspring only, called (μ, λ) selection, or from the union of parents and offspring, called $(\mu + \lambda)$ selection. Recombination in ES is rather straightforward, two parent vectors $\bar{u}$ and $\bar{v}$ create one child $\bar{w}$, where

$$w_i = \begin{cases} (u_i + v_i)/2 & \text{in case of intermediary recombination} \\ u_i \text{ or } v_i \text{ chosen randomly in case of discrete recombination} \end{cases} \tag{1}$$

The mutation operator is based on a Gaussian distribution requiring two parameters: the mean, which is always set at zero, and the standard deviation σ, which is interpreted as the mutation step size. Mutations then are realised by replacing components of the vector $\bar{x}$ by

$$x_i' = x_i + \sigma \cdot N(0, 1), \tag{2}$$

where $N(0,1)$ denotes a random number drawn from a Gaussian distribution with zero mean and standard deviation 1. By using a Gaussian distribution here, small mutations are more likely then large ones. The particular feature of mutation in ES is that the step-sizes are also included in the chromosomes. In the simplest case one σ that acts on each x_i, in the most general case a different one for each position $i \in \{1, \ldots, n\}$. A typical candidate is then $\langle x_1, \ldots, x_n, \sigma_1, \ldots, \sigma_n \rangle$ and mutations are realised by replacing individual $\langle x_1, \ldots, x_n, \sigma_1, \ldots, \sigma_n \rangle$ by $\langle x_1', \ldots, x_n', \sigma_1', \ldots, \sigma_n' \rangle$, where

$$\sigma' = \sigma \cdot e^{\tau \cdot N(0,1)} \tag{3}$$

$$x_i' = x_i + \sigma' \cdot N_i(0, 1) \tag{4}$$

and τ is a parameter of the method.

By this mechanism the mutation step sizes are not set by the user, they (the $\bar{\sigma}$ part) are co-evolving with the solutions (the $\bar{x}$ part). To this feature it is essential to modify the σ's first and mutate the x's with the new σ values. The rationale behind it is that an individual $\langle \bar{x}, \bar{\sigma} \rangle$ is evaluated twice. Primarily, it is evaluated directly for its viability during survivor selection based on $f(\bar{x})$. Secondarily, it is evaluated for its ability to create good offspring. This happens indirectly: a given $\bar{\sigma}$ evaluates favourably if the offspring generated by using it turns viable (in the first sense). Thus, an individual $\langle \bar{x}, \bar{\sigma} \rangle$ represents a good $\bar{x}$ that survived selection and a good $\bar{\sigma}$ that proved successful in generating this good $\bar{x}$.

Observe that using self-adaptive mutation step sizes has two advantages: 1) the user does not have to bother about it, the EA does it itself, 2) parameter values are changing during the run. In general, modifying algorithm parameters during a run is motivated by the fact that the search process has different phases and a fixed parameter value might not be appropriate for each phase. For instance, in the beginning of the search exploration takes place, where the population is wide spread, locating promising areas in the search space. In this phase large leaps are appropriate. Later on the search becomes more focused, exploiting information gained by exploration. During this phase the population is concentrated around peaks on the fitness landscape and small variations are desirable.

There are various techniques in evolutionary computing to adjust algorithm parameters (also called strategy parameters) on-the-fly [6–Chapter 8]. Self-adaptivity is one such technique, where the parameters are changed by the algorithm itself with only minimal influence from the user. In case of self-adaptation of parameters the algorithm is performing two tasks simultaneously: It is solving a given problem and it is calibrating (and repeatedly re-calibrating) itself for solving that problem. While in theory this implies a computational overhead that could lead to reduced performance, the practice of ES –and many other EAs adopting self-adaptive features– show the opposite effect.

A convincing evidence for the power of self-adaptation is provided in the context of changing fitness landscapes. In this case the objective function is changing and the evolutionary process is aiming at a moving target. When the objective function changes, the present population needs to be re-evaluated, and quite naturally the given individuals may have a low fitness, since they have been adapted to the old objective function. Often the mutation step sizes will prove ill-adapted: they are too low for the new exploration phase required. The experiment presented in [8] illustrates how self-adaptation is able to reset the step sizes after each change in the objective function without any user intervention. Fig. 2 shows that the location of the optimum is changed after every 200 generations (*x-axes*) with a clear effect on the average best objective function values (*y-axis, left*) in the given population. Self-adaptation is adjusting the step sizes (*y-axes, right*) with a small delay to larger values appropriate for exploring the new fitness landscape, thereafter the values of σ start decreasing again once the population is closing in on the new optimum.

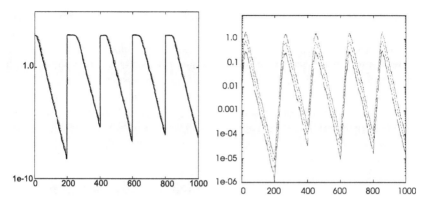

Fig. 2. Moving optimum ES experiment on the 30 dimensional sphere function. See text for explanation

Over the last decades much experience has been gained over self-adaptation in ES. The accumulated knowledge has identified necessary conditions for self-adaptation:

- $\mu > 1$ so that different strategies are present
- Generation of an offspring surplus: $\lambda > \mu$
- A not too strong selective pressure (heuristic: $\lambda/\mu = 7$, e.g., (15,100))
- (μ, λ)-selection (to guarantee extinction of misadapted individuals)
- Recombination also on strategy parameters (especially intermediate recombination)

4   The Web Service Example

In this section we show how an evolutionary approach can be used to build autonomic computing systems, or at least how EC can be utilized to solve some of the key problems raised within autonomic computing, in particular that of real-time self-optimisation. To this end, we introduce an example problem that serves to illuminate the matter. Note, that the point is not to solve the example problem, but to show how the generic "evolutionary trick" can be applied to solve challenges in autonomic computing.

4.1   The Web Service Example: The Optimisation Problem

Let us assume some web service to a large number of visitors. Without loss of generality we can also assume that the service is provided by a number of service units, e.g., M web-servers offering the same service through the same URL such that the visitors do not even notice whether their session is conducted by unit A or unit B. The main task here is to maximise the service level g. We can assume that the service level g is defined as some combination of the time spent with obtaining the service (shorter session, higher service level) and the degree to which a request could be satisfied (higher degree, higher service level). Furthermore, we

postulate that each session conducted with a visitor of the given web site is regulated by a parameterized procedure, using a parameter vector $\bar{p}$. This parameter
vector can consist of values encoding, for instance, colour, arrangement, etc.
of the web pages used, the (type of) messages presented to the visitor, applied
pricing strategy, the sub-page hierarchy, subroutines used in a session, ordering
of databases consulted in a session, etc. Formally, the values within $\bar{p}$ can be
Booleans, integers, reals, or even a mixture of them and we have a parameter
optimization problem, since we want to use those $\bar{p}$ vectors that maximise g, that
is, we want to conduct sessions that maximise service level. In the following we
will illustrate how this can be done in self-* style using an evolutionary approach.

4.2   The Web Service Example: Individuals, Population, Fitness

The basis of this evolutionary approach is to consider a given $\bar{p}$ as an individual
whose fitness is $g(\bar{p})$ and to set up a system where a population of individuals
undergoes variation and selection.

To introduce a population we must allow that different values of $\bar{p}$ are used
simultaneously, i.e., visitor 1 can be serviced by using a procedure belonging to
$\bar{p}_1$, while the interaction with visitor 2 can take place by using $\bar{p}_2$. After finishing
a session the quality of the parameter $\bar{p}$ used in the session can be determined by
calculating the corresponding service level $g(\bar{p})$. It can be argued that calculating $g(\bar{p})$ should be based on more than one sessions with $\bar{p}$. Technically, this is a
simple extension having no influence for the present discussion. Having specified
parameter vector $\bar{p}$ and the utility function g we have the most fundamental requirement for an evolutionary process: an evaluation function or fitness function
applicable to a population of individuals. Then, at all times we can maintain a
set of N parameter values (and call N the population size). Invocation of parameter values, that is assigning some $\bar{p}$ from the given population to a new session,
must be also regulated in some way, but these details are not important for the
present discussion either. What is important is the distinction between the pool
of service units (consisting of M elements) and the pool of N $\bar{p}$ values, being the
population to be evolved. The key to real-time self-optimisation of the system
consisting of the service units is to evolve this population of parameter values.
Technically this requires variation and selection operators.

4.3   The Web Service Example: Variation

Variation can be handled in a rather straightforward way: using common mutation operators from EC we can specify small random perturbations to a given
value $\bar{p}$, yielding $\bar{p}'$. Alternatively, if there are no appropriate off-the-shelf mutation operators, one can design application specific mutation – this is mostly not
too difficult. For a well-defined procedure we also have to define when to apply
variation. A simple heuristic for this is to create a child $\bar{p}'$ to $\bar{p}$ as soon as $\bar{p}$ gets
evaluated, i.e., $g(\bar{p})$ is calculated. Of course, there is no need to restrict ourselves
to mutation only, and also recombination can be used to create new individuals. Here again common recombination operators from EC can be applied to
two parent vectors $\bar{p}_1$ and $\bar{p}_2$, or designed for the specific needs. (This might be

more difficult than inventing mutation operators.) Depending on the operator the result can be one or two new vectors. For specifying when recombination is applied we can use a heuristic similar to that concerning mutation.

4.4   The Web Service Example: Selection

Selection is a bit more complicated than variation in our case. To begin with parent selection, we can keep it very simple and unbiased, that is, not related to the fitness of the individuals (utility of the parameter vectors). This can be achieved by the heuristic mentioned above and mutate every individual after it gets evaluated, regardless to its fitness. As for recombination we can apply this heuristic too but we also need to specify how to select a second parent $\bar{p}_2$, for a given $\bar{p}_1$. Here we can use a random choice based on the uniform distribution, giving every other individual in the population an equal chance.

Concerning survivor selection we will consider two options: local competition and global competition. The basic idea behind local competition is that each newborn child competes with its parent(s) directly. In this case each new $\bar{p}'$ must be used in a session as soon as possible after its "birth" to calculate its utility, that is, its fitness value. This might imply a requirement for the invocation procedure, but we do not discuss this aspect here. What is important for meaningful selection is that a parent $\bar{p}$ is kept in the population (and probably used again) until its offspring $\bar{p}'$ gets evaluated. When $g(\bar{p})$ and $g(\bar{p}')$ are both known then we select either of them based on g and delete the other one. This selection can be deterministic (keep the winner) or probabilistic giving the winner a higher chance to survive. Note that some form of additional population management might be required here if we allow that a waiting parent (a given $\bar{p}$ whose offspring $\bar{p}'$ is not evaluated yet) can be invoked and used in a session. This extra bookkeeping is needed to ensure that no individual is being deleted too early, yet minimising the period during which parents and offspring under evaluation co-exist.[4]

Global competition is based on the idea to let parents and children co-exist for a while and consequently to let populations grow. During such a predefined period of growth, called epoch, no individual is deleted. The length of an epoch can be specified as a given number of fitness evaluations (parameter vector invocations), successful sessions, wall-clock time, etc. Children born in this period are added to the population without restriction and are being used to seed sessions, thereby getting evaluated. At the end of an epoch, the population size can be reset to its initial value N by selecting N individuals for survival based on their fitness. Here again, the selection can be deterministic (keeping the best N) or probabilistic giving better individuals a higher chance to survive.

4.5   The Web Service Example: System Review

Our web service application has a number of properties worth further consideration. From the perspective of the whole system, it is an example of self-

---

[4] Notice that such a co-existence would mean that the population size is not constant.

optimisation. Starting with a set of randomly generated or manually engineered session handling strategies (that is, a population of vectors $\bar{p}$), the system is continuously improving the service level (optimising $g(\bar{p})$). In principle, the system is also able to cope with changing circumstances, for instance changes in the types of visitors requiring new strategies to provide high quality service. Population-based search methods, like EAs, are in general capable of tracking moving optima, although for applications where coping with time varying objectives is essential specific extensions might be required to boost this property, cf. [3] and [6–Chapter 13.4].

From an evolutionary computing perspective we can observe that the EA as described above has no selection pressure (i.e., positive bias towards fitter candidates) during parent selection, only during survivor selection. This is, in principle, no problem. To prevent degradation to random walk, an EA must have selection pressure *somewhere*, either in parent or in survivor selection, but not necessarily in both. Many common EAs have fitness-related bias only in one selection procedure, e.g., generational GAs have no survivor selection (all children survive), while evolution strategies "lack" parent selection. It would not be difficult, however, to add bias when selecting parents in our system. We could simply require that invocation of a vector $\bar{p}$ from the population for a new session be based on fitness information (the utility function g).

As opposed to regular EAs, where population updates are neatly arranged consecutively, here we have a completely asynchronous process, where at a given time some individuals might undergo evaluation (by being used in a user session), some others might be mutated (because their session has just been finished), and yet others might be being deleted. For this reason, the evolutionary process in our example shows more resemblance with natural evolution than most EAs do. Technically, we could say that our EA is performing distributed optimisation in the sense that different candidate solutions are processed independently (in different sessions), possibly on different machines (web servers). A good solution found in some "corner" of the system, however, can quickly proliferate – in an evolutionary system highly fit individuals will always dominate weaker ones and spread over time.

Another aspect where our system is more "natural" than many other EAs is the behaviour based evaluation. In most EA applications the problem at hand can be modelled in such a way that the fitness function is a straightforward input-output mapping, a formula. Think, for instance, of the TSP example in Section 2 of this paper, where we only need a simple sum of distances of the edges represented by a permutation to calculate its fitness. In the web service example application a candidate solution has to *do* something, rather than just *be* something. A trivial consequence of this is that fitness evaluations can take a long time, in our case a whole session with a visitor of the web site. In general, this implies that relatively few candidates can be evaluated in a given amount of time. In other words, evolution will be relatively slow. Large populations and/or many generations are usually advantageous for getting good results, but in our case these might not be feasible. This might cause progress at a slow rate and necessitate special (application dependent) tricks to obtain satisfactory performance.

Last, but not least, let us note that there is no self-adaptation, or any other mechanism, in this EA to change its own parameters on-the-fly. The EA is applied for real-time (self-)optimisation of the system providing the web services without optimising itself. This shows that self-adaptation on EA level is not a requirement for self-optimisation on system level.

5 Links Between Evolutionary and Autonomic Computing

From the self-* perspective we can summarise the most important properties of evolutionary algorithms as follows:

1. EAs form a (meta)heuristic that can be used to solve optimisation problems. By the presence of a population of candidate solutions EAs are inherently suited to cope with time varying optimisation objectives.
2. EAs need to be optimised themselves, in particular, their parameter settings have to be determined appropriately for maximum performance. Because evolutionary search consists of different stages, optimal parameter values depend on time.
3. EAs are capable to perform real-time self-optimisation. To this end, self-adaptation is a particularly successful technique that is able to determine appropriate algorithm parameters following the progress of the search process, thus handling time dependency of optimal parameters given a stationary problem. Furthermore, it can also deal with changing objectives, resetting and re-optimising parameters automatically, without any user intervention.
4. EAs are inherently distributed and parallelisable because different members of the population can be naturally allocated to different processors.

It is rather clear from this list that evolutionary computing in general, and existing techniques within evolutionary computing in particular, can be used to meet some canonical challenges in autonomic computing, for instance, self-optimisation. Additionally, the evolutionary paradigm can serve as a source of inspiration, or let us say as a generic approach, to achieve other self-* properties, like self-configuration or self-healing. There exists related work also advocating population based approaches, such as multi-agent systems and ant-colony optimisation [9, 7].

To see the relevance of autonomic computing to evolutionary computing let us recall the problem of parameter control in EC. During the last decade it become increasingly clear within the field that the numerous EA parameters have a complex relationship with each other, or more precisely, a combined, non-linear influence on algorithm performance. Since non-linear problems with many interacting parameters belong to the niche of EC, it is a natural idea to use an evolutionary system to optimise itself on-the-fly, cf. [4] and [6–Chapter 8]. Self-optimisation or self-configuration has thus became one of the great challenges of evolutionary computing. Existing techniques, like self-adaptation of mutation step-sizes, can solve this problem partially, but a completely parameterless EA requires much more, for instance regulating selection pressure, population size, mutation and recombination parameters *simultaneously*. From this perspective, an evolving system can be seen as a special case of an autonomic system and it can be expected that some solutions invented within autonomic computing can be transferred to EC, meaning indeed that the two fields would share solutions to common problems.

Acknowledgement

I am grateful for M. Jelasity for the discussions about a suitable application example.

References

1. T. Bäck, A.E. Eiben, and N.A.L. van der Vaart. An empirical study on GAs "without parameters". In M. Schoenauer, K. Deb, G. Rudolph, X. Yao, E. Lutton, J.J. Merelo, and H.-P. Schwefel, editors, *Proceedings of the 6th Conference on Parallel Problem Solving from Nature*, number 1917 in Lecture Notes in Computer Science, pages 315–324. Springer, Berlin, Heidelberg, New York, 2000.
2. T. Bäck, D.B. Fogel, and Z. Michalewicz, editors. *Evolutionary Computation 1: Basic Algorithms and Operators*. Institute of Physics Publishing, Bristol, 2000.
3. J. Branke and H. Schmeck. Designing evolutionary algorithms for dynamic optimization problems. In A. Ghosh and S. Tsutsui, editors, *Advances in Evolutionary Computating: Theory and Applications*, pages 239–262. Springer, Berlin, Heidelberg, New York, 2003.
4. A.E. Eiben, R. Hinterding, and Z. Michalewicz. Parameter control in evolutionary algorithms. *IEEE Transactions on Evolutionary Computation*, 3(2):124–141, 1999.
5. A.E. Eiben and M. Schoenauer. Evolutionary computing. *Information Processing Letters*, 82:1–6, 2002.
6. A.E. Eiben and J.E. Smith. *Introduction to Evolutionary Computing*. Springer, Berlin, Heidelberg, New York, 2003.
7. Luca Maria Gambardella. Engineering complex systems: Ant colony optimization to model and to solve complex dynamic problems. In *SELF-STAR: International Workshop on Self-* Properties in Complex Information Systems*. Bolgna, Italy, June, 2004.
8. F. Hoffmeister and T. Bäck. Genetic self-learning. In F.J. Varela and P. Bourgine, editors, *Toward a Practice of Autonomous Systems: Proceedings of the 1st European Conference on Artificial Life*, pages 227–235. MIT Press, Cambridge, MA, 1992.
9. Gerald Tesauro, David M. Chess, William E. Walsh, Rajarshi Das, Alla Segal, Ian Whalley, Jeffrey O. Kephart, and Steve R. White. A multi-agent systems approach to autonomic computing. Technical Report RC23357 (W0410-015), IBM research Division, October 2004.

Self-⋆ Topology Control in Wireless Multihop Ad Hoc Communication Networks

Wolfram Krause[1,2], Rudolf Sollacher[1], and Martin Greiner[1]

[1] Corporate Technology, Information & Communications, Siemens AG,
D-81730 München, Germany
{rudolf.sollacher, martin.greiner}@siemens.com
[2] Frankfurt Institute for Advanced Studies,
and Frankfurt International Graduate School for Science,
Johann Wolfgang Goethe-Universität,
Postfach 11 19 32, D-60054 Frankfurt am Main, Germany
krause@th.physik.uni-frankfurt.de

Abstract. Wireless multihop ad hoc communication networks represent an infrastructure-less generalization of todays cellular networks. Since a central control authority is missing, the complex network has to self-⋆ itself for various operating tasks. Key to a self-⋆ realization is the design of simple, yet robust distributive control rules, which allow the overall network to perform well. Two examples from topology control are given. The first one addresses the connectivity issue, where a self-⋆ rule is presented and shown to lead to strong network connectivity almost surely. A generic system analysis is used in the second example to first develop a phenomenological description of the network's end-to-end throughput capacity and then to sketch further steps towards a self-⋆ rule for obtaining a large throughput performance.

1 Introduction

What means self-⋆? A general answer remains obscure. It depends on the context within which the question is posed. For example, in material physics self-⋆ stands for selforganization of surface growth. In bio-chemistry it would be selforganized growth of macromolecules. Self-configuration, self-management and self-repair are aspects of self-⋆ in computer science. In this paper we pick an example from electrical engineering and present selected issues on its self-⋆.

The challenging technical system of our choice are wireless multihop ad hoc networks [1, 2, 3]. They represent a very complex and infrastructure-less communication network, which has no central controller. Each device, which according to the network jargon we will denote as node, does not only act as a communication source and sink, but also forwards communication for others. This requires a lot of coordination amongst all nodes. Fig. 1 helps to explain the key mechanisms and the associated problems. Each node has to build up wireless communication links to its neighbors. With regulation of its transmission power, it is able to

O. Babaoglu et al. (Eds.): SELF-STAR 2004, LNCS 3460, pp. 49–62, 2005.

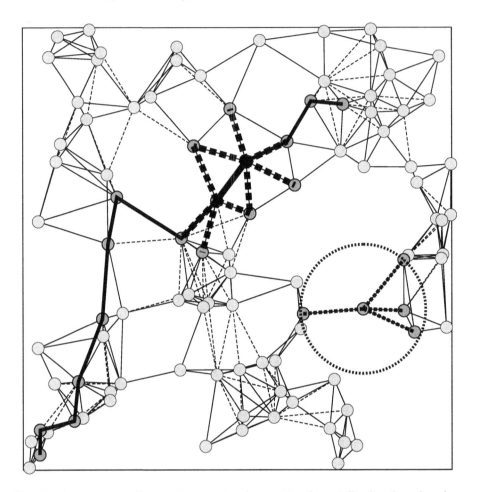

Fig. 1. A wireless multihop ad hoc network consists of spatially distributed nodes, which are connected by wireless links. One-hop neighbors of a node all lie inside its transmission range (shown as dotted circle). An end-to-end communication hops from one node to the next along an end-to-end route (shown as thick line). To avoid interference all neighbors (shown attached to thick dashed links) of an ongoing one-hop transmission (shown as a very thick link) are blocked by medium access control

modify its transmission range and its neighborhood. Here the node faces frustration for the first time. On the one hand it wants to save energy and to keep its transmission power as low as possible, but on the other it might have to choose a larger neighborhood and help the network to gain strong connectivity, so that each node will be able to communicate to any other via multihop routes. This brings us to another protocol layer, from link control to routing control. End-to-end routes have to be explored and maintained. During their execution the communication hops from one node to the next. This is where another protocol layer, called medium access control, sets in. It blocks all neighbors attached to an ongoing one-hop transmission in order to avoid interference. This represents another frustration, now across layers. Whereas routing efficiency prefers short end-to-end routes with the consequence of large one-hop neighborhoods, medium access control prefers to block small neighborhoods with the consequence of long end-to-end routes. A delicate balance between these two layers is necessary for the overall network to gain a large end-to-end throughput performance, which measures the amount of communication traffic the network is able to handle without overloading.

Link, medium access and routing control represent the most basic layers within the protocol stack of wireless multihop ad hoc networks. For the overall network to perform well those have to be intra- as well as interlayer efficient. It is here, where self-⋆ has to appear. For demonstration we focus on topology control throughout this paper, but note that this is only a subclass of control actions. Since a global control master is missing, the topology control actions have to be distributive and initiated locally by single-node actions. By in- or decreasing its transmission power a node modifies its local topology, eventually forces its new and old neighbors to respond, accumulates and evaluates their feedback, upon which it decides whether to accept or reject the explorative move. As a result of the sum of many such local control actions, the network then runs into certain topology patterns. Of course we are interested only in such network structures which lead to a good network performance. It is our primary goal to engineer the local topology control rules in such a way, that their collective iterative action leads to a good global topology defined by a good global network performance. This may be taken to the records as an engineering definition of self-⋆. In some sense the situation is similar to what we have learned from cellular automata, where the self-organizing emergence of specific macroscopic spatio-temporal patterns is already encoded in the CA update rules [4].

During the last years, the first sensor networks using multihop ad hoc network technology were deployed. Transmission power control algorithms are used to minimize the power consumption of the nodes, but topology optimization for throughput enhancement has not yet been considered in these implementations.

The organization of the paper is as follows. In sect. 2 a local self-⋆ connectivity control is presented for static wireless multihop ad hoc networks. Sect. 3 presents important preparatory steps for a self-⋆ throughput-optimized topology control for such networks. It focuses on a generic system analysis, provides an understanding as to what limits the end-to-end throughput performance, and presents a search for performance-optimized network topologies. A brief outlook is given in sect. 4 and includes some suggestions for self-⋆ large-throughput control rules.

2   Self-⋆ Connectivity

We begin with the case that each node i of the network has exactly the same transmission power $P_i = P$ [5,6]. Then according to a simple isotropic propagation-receiver model, a node will have wireless links to those nodes which are located within its transmission radius $R = (P/\beta)^{1/\alpha}$. α is a spatial fading exponent and β represents the signal-to-noise ratio. Excluding finite-size effects, a node will then on average have $\langle k \rangle_\infty = \rho \pi R^2$ neighbors. The total number of nodes N distributed over some area L^2 determine the node density $\rho = N/L^2$. The question now is, how large does P, or equivalently R or $\langle k \rangle_\infty$, have to be so that the overall network becomes strongly connected? Strong connectivity requires that each node can reach any other node via at least one multihop route. This question falls into the regime of continuum percolation [7]. For an ensemble of spatial point patterns, where points have been randomly and homogeneously thrown into a square area, Fig. 2 illustrates the logarithmic N-dependence of $\langle k \rangle_\infty$, for which 99 % of the thrown realizations are strongly connected. To be on the safe side, the value $\langle k \rangle_\infty = 24$ guarantees strong connectivity almost surely for network sizes up to several thousands. Fig. 3 (left) exemplifies the structure of such a network. However, there are major problems with rules like $\langle k \rangle_\infty = 24$. If the nodes would not be randomly distributed in a homogeneous manner, but in a more clustered way, then the average neighborhood has to be significantly larger than 24 [7]; consult again Fig. 2. In such cases, nodes of small- and even medium-sized networks would have direct links to almost every other node, thus putting the multihop idea at stake. An even more striking problem with $\langle k \rangle_\infty = const$ is its distributive implementation. Only with additional internal and external information input on quantities like ρ, α, β, a node is able to adjust its transmission power to a respective value $P = const$. Clearly, there is a strong need for a different kind of connectivity control, one with a self-$\star$ property.

The minimum-node-degree rule [7] is designed to resolve the shortcomings of the $P = const$ rule. Each node finds its transmission power in a self-$\star$ way, only communicating with its neighbors. Starting from the smallest possible transmission power, ECHO REQUESTS are send, containing the current list of neighbors and the currently used transmission power. If another node receives such an ECHO REQUEST, and does not already belong to the neighbor list, it replies. The transmission power is increased until a given minimum number k_{min} of neighbors is reached. To ensure that all nodes have at least k_{min} neighbors, eventually a node with already enough neighbors is forced to further increase its own transmission power: once an ECHO REQUEST from another node, which suffers a lack of neighbors, but is currently outside the transmission range, is received, the own power is increased to build up a bidirectional communication link to the requesting node. Note, that as a result of all nodes having at least k_{min} bidirectional neighbors the transmission power values differ from node to node. This heterogeneity leads to the occasional emergence of one-directed links, which do not qualify as communication links used for routing. More explicit details of this connectivity rule are given in Ref. [7].

Fig. 2 also illustrates the required k_{min} values to guarantee strong connectivity with a 99 % confidence level for networks based on random homogeneous point patterns. Even for network sizes of several thousands the minimum-node degree remains below $k_{min} = 8$. It turns out that this value also holds for net-

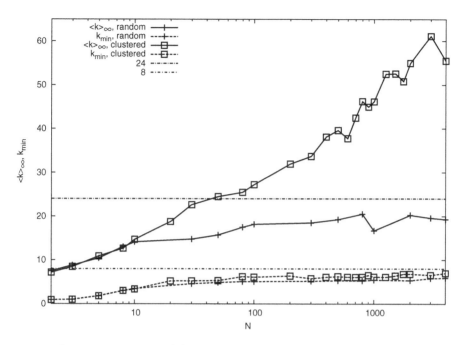

Fig. 2. Average node degree $\langle k \rangle_\infty$ (solid curve with crosses) and minimum-node degree k_{min} (dashed curve with crosses) required to guarantee strong connectivity with a 99 % confidence level for wireless multihop ad hoc networks with N randomly and homogeneously distributed nodes. For comparison the two respective curves with squared symbols are for a clustered distribution of nodes, for which the parameters have been chosen as in Ref. [7]. The lines $\langle k \rangle_\infty = 24$ and $k_{min} = 8$ are shown for guidance

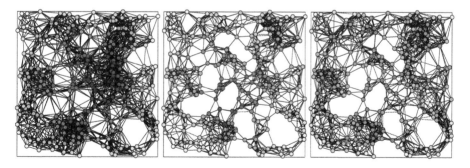

Fig. 3. Various structures for wireless multihop ad hoc networks: (left) const-P rule with $\langle k \rangle_\infty = 24$, (center) minimum-node-degree rule with $k_{min} = 8$, (right) e2e-throughput optimized according to (6). The same random homogeneous spatial point pattern with $N = 300$ nodes has been used for all three cases

works based on random clustered point patterns; see again Fig. 2 and Ref. [7].
This demonstrates the robustness and adaptivity of this simple connectivity
rule. A visualization of a resulting network structure is given in Fig. 3 (center).
Compared to a respective $P = const$ structure, the average node degree $\langle k \rangle$
and, consequently, also the average transmission power is significantly smaller.
This proves that the minimum-node-degree does not only self-$\star$ into a strongly
connected network structure, but that it is also energy efficient.

3   Towards Self-$\star$ End-to-End Throughput

Maybe the most important performance measure of wireless multihop ad hoc networks is given by the end-to-end throughput capacity. It represents the amount
of data traffic the network is able to handle without overloading. For sure, the
end-to-end throughput depends on the underlying network structure. Hence, it
is a self-$\star$ goal to construct a topology control that beyond strong connectivity
also ensures a large throughput capacity. This goal is ambitious and requires a
careful preparation. In this section we will focus on a preparatory system analysis
and a subsequent search for throughput-optimized network structures.

3.1   Back-on-the-Envelope Estimate of End-to-End Throughput

A crude estimate of the end-to-end throughput is given by

$$T_{e2e} = \frac{1}{D}\frac{N}{\text{MAC}} \ . \tag{1}$$

On average an active one-hop transmission involves MAC nodes. It is not only
the one-hop sending and receiving node, but also all neighbors attached to them
by outgoing links. Before the one-hop communication takes place, the outgoing
neighbors are being blocked by medium access control to avoid interference. The
ratio N/MAC then counts the maximum number of one-hop transmissions which
can take place at the same time. The diameter D of the network is defined as
the mean of all shortest end-to-end routes. Hence, expression (1) measures the
maximum number of end-to-end communications which can be completed per
time.

   It is interesting to look at how the expression (1) scales with the network
size N. Whereas the quantity MAC is of the order one to two times the N-
independent average node degree $\langle k \rangle$, the diameter $D \sim \sqrt{N}$ scales with the
reciprocal embedding dimension of planar geometrical networks. This leads to
the capacity estimate $T_{e2e} \sim \sqrt{N}$, which increases with the network size. Within
the employed rough picture, this has to be compared with a one-channel central-
hub network, where all intra-cellular end-to-end communications go directly from
the sender to the base station and then to the receiver. This makes $D = 2$ and
MAC $= N$, resulting in $T_{e2e} = 0.5$. Hence, for networks larger than a certain size,
the multihop ad hoc mode of wireless networks will produce a larger end-to-end
throughput than the cellular mode.

Due to its simplicity, the expression (1) is too crude and overestimates the end-to-end throughput capacity. It assumes the one-hop traffic to be homogeneously distributed over the network. This is of course not the case. Due to the multihop nature of the end-to-end routes, spatially central nodes have to forward more communication traffic for others than nodes lying at the periphery. The central nodes will become congested first and will be most critical to the network's overall performance. The questions are, how much does this most-critical-node effect lower the end-to-end throughput and how does this affect its scalability. First answers to these questions will be provided by a generic packet traffic simulation.

3.2   Generic Packet Traffic Simulation

For the investigation of the throughput scaling behavior, the simulation must be able to calculate results for network sizes up to 2000 nodes within a resonable amount of time. Therefore, we employ a generic packet traffic simulation with the implementation of a generic packet creation and a forwarding algorithm based on a generic MAC protocol.

The simulation implements random end-to-end packet traffic. Time is divided into discrete steps. During each time step a node can either create a new packet with probability μ, forward or receive a packet, become blocked due to medium access control, or remain idle. During packet creation, a respective receiving node is selected at random, to which the packet will be forwarded one hop after the other along the respective shortest-path route during successive time steps. Nodes with non-empty packet queues are competing for one-hop transmissions. They are sequentially checked in random order and, if successful, they as well as their intended one-hop receiver MAC-block the attached outgoing neighbors, which are then not allowed to send or receive other packets during the remainder of this time step. Once a packet arrives at its final destination, it is immediately removed from the network. More details of this generic packet traffic simulation can be found in Ref. [8].

During simulations the single-node in- and out-packet flux rates μ_i^{in} and μ_i^{out} are monitored. For sub-critical packet creation rates μ the inequality $\mu_i^{\mathrm{in}} < \mu_i^{\mathrm{out}}$ holds for all nodes. Once this inequality turns into an equality for the first time for one node, the critical network load is reached. This defines the critical packet creation rate μ_{crit} and the end-to-end throughput capacity $T_{e2e} = \mu_{\mathrm{crit}} N$. The latter represents the maximum rate of end-to-end communications without network-wide overloading.

Fig. 4 illustrates the end-to-end throughput obtained from the generic packet traffic simulation for network structures generated with the $k_{\mathrm{min}} = 8$ connectivity rule. An average over a large enough number of random homogeneous point patterns has been taken. For very small network sizes the end-to-end throughput starts with $T_{e2e} = 1$, then drops down to about $T_{e2e} = 0.7$ for a little larger N, only then to bounce back and cross $T_{e2e} = 1$ around $N \approx 100$. Beyond this network size the end-to-end throughput increases further and scales as $T_{e2e} \sim (N - N_0)^\gamma$. The exponent turns out to be $\gamma = 0.22$, which is lower than $\gamma =$

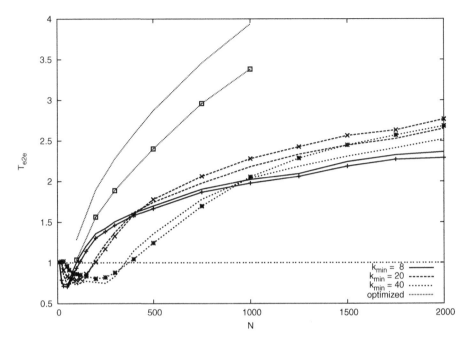

Fig. 4. Network-size dependent end-to-end throughput for various network structures based on random homogeneous point patterns: minimum-node-degree $k_{min} = 8$ (solid), 20 (dashed), 40 (large dots), and throughput-optimized (small dots) according to (6). Curves with symbols are results from a generic packet traffic simulation. Respective curves without symbols represent the estimate (6)

0.5 from the simple-minded expression (1). Again, the main reason for this is the heterogeneous distribution of the one-hop traffic. Note however, that for all network sizes the end-to-end throughput stays above the $T_{e2e} = 0.5$ central-hub limit. Note also, that a fully connected network, where each node has one-hop links to any other node, produces the N-independent value $T_{e2e} = 1$.

Different sparse network structures will lead to different heterogeneities of the one-hop traffic and, most likely, to a different end-to-end throughput behavior. This suspicion is confirmed with Fig. 4, where $T_{e2e}(N)$ is also shown for minimum-node-degree network structures based on values other than $k_{min} = 8$. The resulting small-N behaviors are similar, and so does the scaling behavior $T_{e2e} \sim (N - N_0)^\gamma$ for sufficiently large network sizes. However, the scaling exponent changes with k_{min}. For example, for $k_{min} = 20$ and 40 we find $\gamma = 0.24$ and 0.29. Given this clear proof that the end-to-end throughput depends on the underlying network structure, it is now most natural to pose the next question in line: what is the network structure that optimizes the end-to-end throughput? The answer is far from simple and requires several steps with more system analysis. The first step needs to find a translation of the simulational findings into an analytic function, which in a second step serves as objective function for optimization.

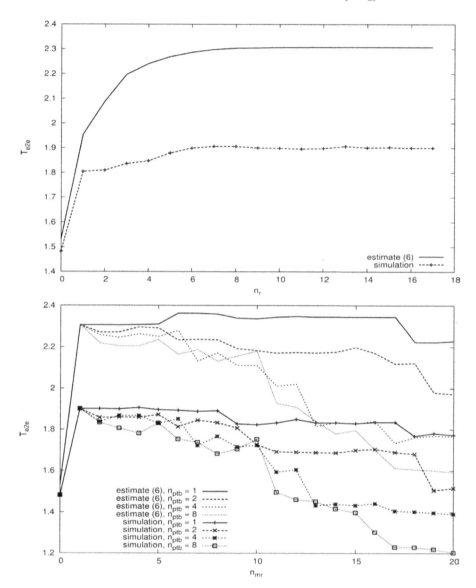

Fig. 5. (a) The evolution of the end-to-end throughput in dependence of the optimization rounds n_r until the first local maximum of expression (6) is reached. The initial $N = 300$ network realization has been constructed with the self-⋆ ($k_{\min} = 8$) connectivity rule, applied to a random homogeneous point pattern. The upper curve is for (6), whereas the lower curve represents its counterpart from the packet traffic simulations. (b) The subsequent evolution of the end-to-end throughput, according to expression (6) (upper curves) as well as packet traffic simulations (lower curves), in dependence on the number of meta-rounds n_{mr}. Each meta-round is kicked off with a random perturbation of $n_{\mathrm{ptb}} = 1, 2, 4, 8$ randomly selected nodes from a local-maximum network configuration

3.3   Most Critical Node Effect

Within the single-node description the in-packet flux rate can be described with

$$\mu_i^{\text{in}} = \mu N \frac{B_i}{N(N-1)} \ . \tag{2}$$

On average μN new packets are inserted into the network per time step, of which the fraction $B_i/N(N-1)$ will be routed via node i during successive time steps. The betweenness centrality

$$B_i = \sum_{\substack{m \neq n=1 \\ (n \neq i)}}^{N} \frac{b_{mn}(i)}{b_{mn}} \tag{3}$$

counts the number of shortest paths going through i out of all $N(N-1)$ end-to-end combinations. b_{mn} represents the number of shortest paths from m to n, of which $b_{mn}(i)$ pass by i. Compared to μ_i^{in}, the modeling of the out-packet flux rate

$$\mu_i^{\text{out}} = \frac{1}{\tau_i^{\text{send}}} \tag{4}$$

is more delicate. Due to the competition between neighbors to gain medium access for one-hop transmissions, node i can not send a packet right away, but has to wait a characteristic time τ_i^{send}. A convenient empirical ansatz for this sending time is given by

$$\tau_i^{\text{send}} = 1 + \frac{1}{B_i} \sum_{j \in \mathcal{N}_i^{in}} B_j = \frac{B_i^{cum}}{B_i} \ . \tag{5}$$

It compares the betweenness centrality B_i to its cumulative counterpart B_i^{cum}, the latter being a respective sum over the ingoing neighbors. Equating relations (2) and (4) yields an expression for the critical packet creation rate μ_{crit} and for the end-to-end throughput,

$$T_{e2e} = \mu_{\text{crit}} N \approx \frac{N(N-1)}{\sup_i B_i^{cum}} \ . \tag{6}$$

At least, this expression is consistent with the finding $T_{e2e} = 1$ for fully connected networks, where each node has the same $B_i = N - 1$, resulting in $B_i^{cum} = N(N-1)$. As another quick consistency calculation reveals, it also produces $T_{e2e} = 0.5$ of a central-hub network. However, the fate of (6) is decided with the minimum-node-degree networks. In Fig. 4 it is compared with the throughput curves obtained earlier from the generic packet traffic simulations. For various $k_{\min}$ values the overall agreement is remarkable. Except for minor deviations the simulationally found scaling exponents $\gamma = \gamma(k_{\min})$ are reproduced.

3.4   Throughput Optimization of the Network Topology

Due to the good reproduction of the simulational findings, the analytic expression (6) qualifies as objective function for the search of optimized network structures, producing a maximum end-to-end throughput. This search is quite challenging. First of all, the expression for the end-to-end throughput depends on the network structure in a complicated non-linear and non-local manner, which does not allow for a local decomposition [9, 10]. Moreover, the space of all testable network structure configurations is very large. It is of the order $(N - 1)^N$: each of the N nodes has its own transmission power ladder with $N - 1$ rungs; being on rung k means that the picked node is able to reach its k closest neighbors. Of course not all of these configurations are meaningful for wireless multihop ad hoc networks. It is important to confine the search operations only to the meaningful ones.

As initial configuration the network structure obtained with the minimum-node-degree ($k_{min} = 8$) connectivity rule is chosen. This sets a minimum node degree $k_i^{min} \geq k_{min}$ for each node i. During subsequent optimization operations, the respective transmission power values of all nodes are not decreased below their initial value, thus ensuring strong connectivity for all times. Search operations are performed in rounds. Per round, each node is randomly picked once. A picked node explores in two directions. In the first move it increases its transmission power by one rung and, if the newly reached node does not already have a large enough transmission power, forces the latter to climb up its ladder until its rung suffices to successfully build a new mutual bidirectional communication link. In the other move the picked node steps down its transmission power ladder by one rung, implying that the lost neighbor might also move down its ladder until it reaches the rung just before another communication link is broken. Both moves modify the local network structure, require a global update of the end-to-end routes and the betweenness centralities for all nodes, and lead to two modified estimates of the end-to-end throughput (6), which are then compared to the old estimate before the two explorative moves. The network structure yielding the largest estimate is accepted. This update procedure, which has its motivation from the ECHO REQUESTS of the self-⋆ connectivity rule presented in sect. 2, guarantees meaningful wireless multihop ad hoc network structures and keeps the occurrence of interfering one-directed links to a minimum.

A local maximum of (6) is reached, if during a complete search round no improvement of the throughput estimate is found. Fig. 5a shows a typical evolution of the end-to-end throughput in dependence of the number of search rounds until the first local maximum is reached, which only takes a modest number of rounds. The increase of the throughput performance is already remarkable. Once a local maximum is reached, the respective network realization is perturbed by forcing a small, randomly chosen fraction of the nodes to step up or down by one rung on their transmission power ladder, including respective new or lost neighbor actions as explained before. We denote the period until the next local maximum is found as a meta-round. Fig. 5b illustrates the evolution of the end-to-end throughput in terms of meta-rounds. The striking feature is that if more than one node is perturbed out of its local-maximum state, the throughput perfor-

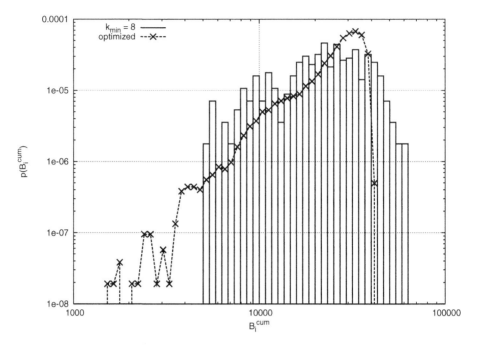

Fig. 6. Distribution of B_i^{cum} for an ensemble of minimum-node-degree networks with $k_{min} = 8$ as well as for an ensemble of throughput-(6)-optimized networks. The network size is $N = 300$

mance decreases with the number of meta-rounds. If only one node is perturbed, the throughput performance remains more or less the same as found for the first local-maximum network realization, but there is no further improvement.

It is important to check all of these results with packet traffic simulations. As demonstrated in Fig. 5a+b, a strong correlation between the simulation results and the throughput estimate (6) is found. This is a non-trivial and important statement. This analysis shows that the first local maximum yields the highest throughput and all further maxima show a lower performance. Therefore, the optimization can be terminated after reaching the first local maximum. Nevertheless, the fraction of the explored search space is small. Other maxima might exist, but we do not know any algorithm to find them within the constraint of reasonable cpu time.

Fig. 3(right) shows such a first-local-maximum network structure. It is still similar to the initial network structure, which is illustrated in Fig. 3(middle). It appears that only a few more communication links have been added. However, those have been introduced in such a careful way that end-to-end routes are modified to decrease the largest B_i^{cum} values. For the initial as well as the optimized network topologies the B_i^{cum} distribution is shown in Fig. 6. The optimization process strongly decreases large B_i^{cum} values, thus leading to an increase of the throughput performance.

For various network sizes, ranging from $N = 100$ to 1000, ensembles consisting of 100 throughput-optimized network realizations have been generated. Besides the optimized estimate (6) the end-to-end throughput has also been calculated from packet traffic simulations. Results are shown as small-dotted curves in Fig. 4. The optimized network topologies have an end-to-end throughput significantly larger than for the other networks. This shows again that the expression (6) qualifies as a useful objective function for optimization, although the discrepancy between estimated and simulated throughput has increased to some extend. The end-to-end throughput of the optimized topologies again reveals the scaling behavior $T_{e2e} \sim (N - N_0)^\gamma$. For the estimate (6) we find $\gamma = 0.43$ and from the packet traffic simulations we get $\gamma = 0.46$. These values are very close to the mean-field estimate $\gamma = 0.5$ following from (1). It demonstrates that within the optimized network topologies the heterogeneities of the one-hop traffic have been considerably reduced. With other words, the network structure has been modified in such a way that the new end-to-end routes distribute the overall network traffic more evenly and reduce the peak traffic loads of the bottleneck nodes.

So far, a self-⋆ topology control to construct wireless multihop ad hoc network structures with a large end-to-end throughput performance has not been put forward. The presented preparatory steps, including the generic system analysis and a subsequent search for optimized network structures, serve as a proof of principles. They motivate and justify future self-⋆ efforts. Clearly, a careful characterization of the structural properties of the obtained throughput-optimized network topologies is needed next. In particular, a precise understanding of the small, but decisive topology differences between the networks, obtained from the first local maximum of the performance optimization, and their initial, minimum-node-degree counterparts are key to the development of successful self-⋆ proposals.

4   Conclusions and Outlook

Another, admittedly very intriguing approach to self-⋆ topology control could be network game theory. In Ref. [11] a coupling of playing games with neighboring nodes and network structure evolution has been introduced. Consequently, the goal of network game theory would be: give a game to the nodes, let them play, and by doing so they will automatically end up in a self-⋆ construction of a game-dependent network structure. Of course, for the moment this is only an idea and a lot of tough conceptual work is still necessary to prove it right (or wrong).

Although we have focused on topology control so far, there is plenty of self-⋆ open range beyond it. For example, in Ref. [12] a reinforced load dependent routing metric has been proposed, which adapts to packet traffic congestion, is able to increase the end-to-end throughput and to decrease the end-to-end time delay in wireless multihop ad hoc communication networks. Other important self-⋆ issues, which should be addressed not only in wireless multihop ad hop networks, but also in extensions like sensor-actutator networks, are efficient medium-access-control assignments, network robustness, network security and more network function. Some preliminary, biology-inspired investigations in these directions have already been presented [13].

Acknowledgments

W. K. gratefully acknowledges support by the Frankfurt Center for Scientific Computing and the Ernst von Siemens-Scholarship.

References

1. Proceedings of the 3rd ACM Int. Symp. on Mobile Ad Hoc Networking and Computing (MobiHoc 2002), ACM, Lausanne, Switzerland, 2002.
2. Proceedings of the 4th ACM Int. Symp. on Mobile Ad Hoc Networking and Computing (MobiHoc 2003), ACM, Annapolis, MD, USA, 2003.
3. Proceedings of the 5th ACM Int. Symp. on Mobile Ad Hoc Networking and Computing (MobiHoc 2004), ACM, Roppongi, Japan, 2004.
4. A. Deutsch, S. Dormann, Cellular Automaton Modeling of Biological Pattern Formation, Birkhäuser, Boston, 2004.
5. P. Gupta, P. R. Kumar, The capacity of wireless networks, IEEE Trans. Info. Theory IT–46 (2) (2000) 388–404.
6. C. Bettstetter, On the minimum node degree and connectivity of a wireless multihop network, in: MobiHoc 2002 [1], pp. 80–91.
7. I. Glauche, W. Krause, R. Sollacher, M. Greiner, Continuum percolation of wireless ad hoc communication networks, Physica A 325 (2003) 577–600.
8. W. Krause, I. Glauche, R. Sollacher, M. Greiner, Impact of network structure on the performance of wireless multihop ad hoc communication, Physica A 338 (2004) 633–658.
9. R. Montemanni, L. M. Gambardella, Exact algorithms for the minimum power symmetric connectivity problem in wireless networks, Computers and Operations Research.
10. R. Montemanni, L. M. Gambardella, A. Das, Mathematical models and exact algorithms for the min-power symmetric connectivity problem: an overview, in: J. Wu (Ed.), Handbook on Theoretical and Algorithmic Aspects of Sensor, Ad Hoc Wireless, and Peer-to-Peer Networks, CRC Press, to appear.
11. H. Ebel, S. Bornholdt, Evolutionary games and the emergence of complex networks, cond-mat/0211666.
12. I. Glauche, W. Krause, R. Sollacher, M. Greiner, Distributive routing & congestion control in wireless multihop ad hoc communication networks, Physica A 341 (2004) 677–701.
13. J.-Y. Le Boudec, S. Sarafijanović, An artificial immune system approach to misbehavior detection in mobile ad-hoc networks, in: A. J. Ijspeert, D. Mange, M. Murata, S. Nishio (Eds.), Bio-ADIT 2004, Lausanne, Switzerland, 2004, pp. 96–111.

Emergent Consensus in Decentralised Systems Using Collaborative Reinforcement Learning

Jim Dowling, Raymond Cunningham, Anthony Harrington,
Eoin Curran, and Vinny Cahill

Distributed Systems Group, Trinity College, Dublin, Ireland

Abstract. This paper describes the application of a decentralised coordination algorithm, called Collaborative Reinforcement Learning (CRL), to two different distributed system problems. CRL enables the establishment of consensus between independent agents to support the optimisation of system-wide properties in distributed systems where there is no support for global state. Consensus between interacting agents on local environmental or system properties is established through localised advertisement of policy information by agents and the use of advertisements by agents to update their local, partial view of the system.

As CRL assumes homogeneity in advertisement evaluation by agents, advertisements that improve the system optimisation problem tend to be propagated quickly through the system, enabling the system to collectively adapt its behaviour to a changing environment. In this paper, we describe the application of CRL to two different distributed system problems, a routing protocol for ad-hoc networks called SAMPLE and a next generation urban traffic control system called UTC-CRL. We evaluate CRL experimentally in SAMPLE by comparing its system routing performance in the presence of changing environmental conditions, such as congestion and link unreliability, with existing ad-hoc routing protocols. Through SAMPLE's ability to establish consensus between routing agents on stable routes, even in the presence of changing levels of congestion in a network, it demonstrates improved performance and self-management properties. In applying CRL to the UTC scenario, we hope to validate experimentally the appropriateness of CRL to another system optimisation problem.

1   Introduction

In the future, many distributed systems will consist of interacting, autonomous components that organise, regulate and optimise themselves without human intervention. However, with increasing system size and complexity our ability to build self-managed distributed systems using existing programming languages, top-down design techniques and management infrastructures is reaching its limits [1], as solutions they produce require too much global knowledge.

Self-managing distributed computer systems, on a scale comparable with biological autonomic systems, require a decentralised, bottom-up approach to their

O. Babaoglu et al. (Eds.): SELF-STAR 2004, LNCS 3460, pp. 63–80, 2005.

construction. Self-managing decentralised systems can be modelled as collections of self-managing agents using decentralised coordination to enable a weak form of consensus to emerge between a group of agents partial views of the system [2, 3]. Consensus between the agents' partial views of the system can be used as a basis for system optimisation, coordinating the execution of self-management actions and the collective adaptation of agents to a changing and uncertain environment. The benefits of such an approach include improved scalability, the possibility of establishing self-management properties, self-optimisiation, the lack of centralised points of failure or attack, as well as possible system evolution by evolving the coordination models of the agents.

The construction of self-managing distributed systems using decentralised coordination models presents a number of challenges. These include designing a suitable representation for an agent's local view of the system, the provision of self-management actions for agents that allow them to adapt to changes in their local environment, and the design of feedback models that update the agent's local view of the world.

This paper discusses collaborative reinforcement learning (CRL), as a technique for building decentralised coordination models that addresses these challenges. CRL extends reinforcement learning (RL) with positive and negative feedback models to update an agent's policy, i.e., its local model of how to interact with the system, and enable a certain degree of consensus to emerge between agent policies. We introduce two application areas for CRL, a routing protocol for Mobile Ad Hoc Networks (MANETs) called SAMPLE and an Urban Traffic Control (UTC) system called UTC-CRL. Both of these systems are designed to leverage consensus between agent policies to implement self-managing system properties as system optimisation behaviours. The goal of CRL is to enable agents to produce collective behaviour that establishes and maintains the desired system-wide self-management properties. However, in open, dynamic distributed systems, the environment is non-stationary and CRL enables agents to continually update their consensus on more optimal policies in order to be able to maintain the system-wide self-management properties in a changing environment. In the evaluation of SAMPLE we show how the protocol enables routing agents to continually maintain consensus on any stable routes in the network to improve system routing performance.

This paper is structured as follows. Section 2 introduces decentralised coordination and is followed in section 3 by a description of the CRL model. Section 4 presents SAMPLE as both a CRL system and an on-demand routing protocol for ad hoc networks. We compare simulation results for SAMPLE with two widely used on-demand MANET routing protocols in different scenarios and explain the differing abilities of the protocols to adapt and optimise to a view of the MANET environment. Section 5 introduces our approach to applying CRL to the problem of Urban Traffic Control. The final section provides some conclusions to the work presented in this paper.

2   Self-managing Systems Using Decentralised Coordination

Coordination is the process of building programs by gluing together active pieces [4], where active pieces can be processes, autonomous objects, agents or applications. Coordination is the logic that binds independent activities together into a collective activity. Both centralised and decentralised coordination models have been developed to describe the "glue" that connects computational activities. A multi-agent system built using a centralised coordination model is one where the behaviour of the agents in the system is controlled either by an active manager agent or by a predetermined design or plan followed by the agents in the system [5]. A system built using a decentralised coordination model is a self-organising multi-agent system [5], whose system-wide structure or behaviour is established and maintained solely by the interactions of its agents that execute using only a partial view of the system.

Coordination models are necessary for the construction of self-managing distributed systems as they organise the self-management and self-adaptive behaviour of agents towards system goals. A lack of coordination among agents in a distributed system can lead to interference between the different agents' self-management behaviour, conflicts over shared resources, suboptimal system performance and hysteresis effects [6]. For example, a distributed system that is composed of self-managing agents, where agents optimise their behaviour towards agent goals is not necessarily optimised at the system-level, as there is the possibility that conflicting greedy decisions taken by agents may result in sub-optimal resource utilisation or performance at the system-level. In order to optimally adapt a system to a changing environment the agents must respond to changes in a coordinated manner, but in decentralised environments, the coordination mechanism cannot be based on centralised or consensus-based techniques.

Increasingly, researchers are investigating decentralised coordination approaches to establish and maintain system properties [7, 8, 9, 10]. Decentralised control is based on defining local coordination or control models for components that only have partial views of the system, support only localised interaction and have no global knowledge. Agents typically store locally a partial, estimated model of the system and interaction protocols defined between neighbouring agents enables them to collectively improve the accuracy of their local, estimated models [11, 12]. This can often result in convergence between the estimated models of neighbouring agents on a common view of the system or environment [13]. Agents that have converged models can coordinate their behaviour using their local models to perform collective adaptive behaviour that can establish and maintain system-wide properties. These system properties emerge from the local interaction between neighbouring agents and with no explicit representation of system properties on the level of the individual agent [7, 8].

Decentralised coordination techniques have been developed that are based on cooperation [10, 11] and competition [14] between agents. Both approaches are typically evaluated by how they optimise some system property, such as a self-managing property of the system. There is also the possibility that the system may attempt to optimise more than one system property. Multiple objective functions can be used to describe optimisation problems where there is more than one competing objective function.

Some problems associated with decentralised models include the uncertain outcome of control actions on agents, as their effect may not be observable until some unknowable time in the future. Also, optimal decentralised control is known to be computationally intractable [9], although systems can be developed where system properties are near-optimal [15, 16, 13, 12], which is often adequate for certain classes of applications.

3   Collaborative Reinforcement Learning

CRL is a decentralised approach to establishing and maintaining system-wide properties in distributed systems. CRL is an extension to Reinforcement Learning (RL) [17] for decentralised multi-agent systems. CRL does not make use of system-wide knowledge and individual agents only know about and interact with their neighbouring agents.

CRL can be used to implement decentralised coordination models based on cooperation and information sharing between agents using coordination actions and various feedback models, respectively. The feedback models include a negative feedback model that decays an agent's local view of its neighbourhood and a collaborative feedback model that allows agents to exchange the effectiveness of actions they have learned with one another. In a system of homogeneous agents that have common system optimisation goals and where agents concurrently search for more optimal actions in different states using Reinforcement Learning (RL), collaborative feedback enables agents to share more optimal policies [17], increasing the probability of neighbouring agents taking the same or related actions. This process can produce positive feedback in action selection probability for a group of agents. Positive feedback is a mechanism that reinforces changes in system structure or behaviour in the same direction as the initial change and can cause the emergence of system behaviour or structure [3, 18]. In CRL, the positive feedback process continues until negative feedback, produced either by constraints in the system or our decay model, causes agent behaviour to adapt so that agents in the system converge on stable policies. In effect, agents can establish consensus with their neighbours on more optimal self-management actions to take given a particular system state.

Given a certain degree of consensus between agents on their policies, the goal of system optimisation is to have the agents' policies converge on values that produce collective behaviour that meets the system optimisation criteria [19]. However, in open dynamic distributed systems, the system's environment is non-stationary and we require agents than can collectively adapt their behaviour to the changing environment to continue to meet the system optimisation criteria. We believe that the adaptability of system behaviour to changes in its environment is as important an evaluation criterion for complex adaptive distributed systems as the more traditional criterion for static environments of convergence and stabilisation on optimal system behaviour.

3.1   Reinforcement Learning

In RL, an agent associates actions with system states in a trial-and-error manner and the outcome of an action is observed as a reinforcement that, in turn, causes an update to the agent's *action-value policy* using a reinforcement learning strategy [17]. The goal of reinforcement learning is to maximise the total *reward* (reinforcements) an agent receives over a time horizon by selecting optimal *actions*. Agents may take actions that give a poor payoff in the short-term in the anticipation of higher payoff in the longer term. In general, actions may be any decisions that an agent wants to learn how to make, while states can be anything that may be useful in making those decisions.

RL problems are usually modelled as Markov decision processes (MDPs) [17, 20]. A MDP consists of a set of states, $\mathcal{S} = \{s_1, s_2, \ldots, s_N\}$, a set of actions, $\mathcal{A} = \{a_1, a_2, \ldots, a_M\}$, a reinforcement function $R : \mathcal{S} \times \mathcal{A} \to \mathbb{R}$ and a state transition distribution function: $P : \mathcal{S} \times \mathcal{A} \to \Pi(\mathcal{S})$, where $\Pi(\mathcal{S})$ is the set of probability distributions over the set $\mathcal{S}$.

3.2   Coordination in CRL

CRL system optimisation problems are decomposed into a set of discrete optimisation problems (DOPs) [7] that are solved by collaborating RL agents. The solution to each DOP is initiated at some starting agent in the network and terminated at some (potentially remote) agent in the network. Each agent uses its own policy to decide probabilistically on which action to take to attempt to solve a DOP. In CRL the set of available actions that an agent can execute include *DOP actions*, $\mathcal{A}_{p_i}$, that try to solve the DOP locally, *delegation actions*, $\mathcal{A}_{d_i}$, that delegate the solution of the DOP to a neighbour and a *discovery action* that any agent can execute in any state to attempt to find new neighbours.

The goal of CRL is to coordinate the solution to the set of DOPs among a group of agents using delegation and discovery actions. This is achieved by ensuring that an agent is more likely to delegate a DOP to a neighbour when it either cannot solve the problem locally or when the *estimated cost* of solving it locally is higher than the estimated cost of a neighbour solving it.

3.3   Partial Views of System

In dynamic distributed systems, agents typically have a changing number of neighbouring agents that can be used to help solve a given DOP. To model an agent's dynamic set of neighbours, CRL allows agents to execute discovery actions and then establish *causally-connected states* with any newly discovered neighbour. Causally-connected states represent the contractual agreement between neighbouring agents to support the delegation of DOPs from one to the other. Causally-connected states map an *internal state* on one agent to an *external state* on at least one neighbouring agent. An internal state on one agent

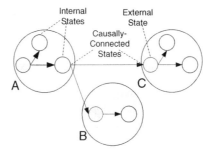

Fig. 1. Causally-Connected States between the MDPs in Agents A, B, C

can be causally-connected to external states on many different neighbouring agents, see Figure 1. An agent's set of causally connected neighbours represents its *partial-view* of the system.

3.4   Feedback Models

There are various feedback models in CRL, including a collaborative feedback model that allows agents to exchange the effectiveness of actions they have learned with one another and a negative feedback model that decays an agent's local view of its neighbourhood.

Collaborative Feedback as Advertisement. In CRL, neighbours are informed of changes to $V_j(s)$ of a causally-connected external state, s, at agent n_j using an *advertisement* . Each agent maintains a local view of its neighbours by storing V values for causally-connected states to neighbours in a local cache, $Cache_i$. The cache consists of a table of Q-values, for all delegation actions, a_d, at agent n_i, and the last advertised $V_j(s)$ for successful transition to the causally connected state. A $Cache_i$ entry is a pair $(Q_i(s, a_j), r_j)$, where r_j is the cached $V_j(s)$ value. When the agent n_i receives a $V_j(s)$ advertisement from neighbouring agent n_j for a causally-connected state s, it updates r_j in $(Q_i(s, a_j), r_j)$. Examples of implementation strategies for V advertisement in distributed systems include periodic broadcast/multicast, conditional broadcast/multicast, piggybacking advertisement in transmission/acknowledgement packets and event-based notification.

Decay as Negative Feedback. In certain decentralised systems an agent's set of neighbours changes dynamically and to overcome problems related to unreachable neighbours, an agent's cached V_j values become stale using a *decay* model [7]. In CRL, we decay cached V_j information in the absence of new advertisements of V_j values by a neighbour as well as after every recalculation of Q_i values. The absence of V_j advertisements is one aspect of negative feedback and allows the removal of stale cache entries. The rate of decay is configurable, with higher rates more appropriate for more dynamic network topologies.

3.5   Distributed Model-Based Reinforcement Learning

CRL enables system optimisation in multi-agent RL systems, and states in the multi-agent system may be distributed over different agents in the network. As a result, state transitions can be either to a local state on the current agent or to a remote state on a neighbouring agent. In distributed systems, when estimating the cost of the state transition to a remote state on a neighbouring agent we also have to take into consideration the network *connection cost* to the neighbouring agent. For this reason, we use a *distributed model-based reinforcement learning algorithm* that includes both the estimated optimal value function for the next state at agent n_i, $V_j(s')$, and the connection cost, $D_i(s'|s,a) \in \mathbb{R}$ where $a \in \mathcal{A}_{d_i}$, to the next state when computing the estimated optimal state-action policy as $Q_i(s,a)$ at agent n_i (see equation (1)).

In the learning algorithm of CRL, our reward model consists of two parts. Firstly, a *MDP termination cost*, $R(s,a) \in \mathbb{R}$, provides agents with evaluative feedback on either the performance of a local solution to the DOP or the performance of a neighbour solving the delegated DOP. Secondly, a connection cost model, $D_i(s'|s,a)$, provides the estimated network cost of the attempted delegation of the DOP from a local agent to a neighbouring agent. The connection cost for a transition to a state on a neighbouring agent should reflect the underlying network cost of delegating the DOP to a neighbouring agent, while the connection cost for a transition to a local state after a delegation action should reflect the cost of the failed delegation of the DOP. The connection cost model requires that the environment supplies agents with information about the cost of distributed systems connections as rewards.

The update rule used in the learning algorithm or CRL is:

$$Q_i(s,a) = R(s,a) + \sum_{s' \in S_i} P_i(s'|s,a).$$

$$(D_i(s'|s,a) + Decay\,(V_j(s'))) \tag{1}$$

where $a \in \mathcal{A}_{d_i}$. If $a \notin \mathcal{A}_{d_i}$, this defaults to the standard model-based reinforcement learning algorithm [20] with no connection costs or decay function. $R(s,a)$ is the MDP termination cost, $P(s'|s,a)$ is the state transition model that computes the probability of the action a resulting in a state transition to state s', $D_i(s'|s,a)$ is the estimated connection cost and $V_j(s')$ is $r_j \in Cache_i$ if $a \in \mathcal{A}_d$, and $V_i(s')$ otherwise.

3.6   Emergent Consensus

We advocate an experimental approach to the validation of the emergence of consensus in CRL systems. Due to the lack of a global view of the system, individual agents cannot validate the existence of system properties and their existence cannot be validated analytically. We can only validate their existence through external observation of the system, e.g., through experimentation. The process through which agents can achieve consensus in CRL systems is decentralised coordination using coordination actions and feedback. They enable consensus to emerge between groups of agents on more optimal actions to execute actions given shared system states. The convergence of agent policies in CRL is a feedback process in which a change in the optimal policy of any RL agent, or a change in the system's environment as well as the passing of time causes an update to the optimal policy of one or more RL agents. In CRL, changes in an agent's environment can provide feedback into the agent's state transition model and connection cost model, while changes in an agent's optimal policy provides collaborative feedback to the cached V values of its neighbouring agents using advertisement. Time also provides negative feedback to an agent's cached V values and allows converged policies to be 'forgotten', enabling policies to converge again on different behaviours.

As a result of the different feedback models in CRL, agents can utilise more information about the state of the system and their neighbouring agents to enable groups of agents to converge on similar policies. In particular, collaborative feedback enables agents to share policy information with their neighbours and achieve consensus on more optimal actions to execute in given system states. This consensus between neighbouring agents on the actions to execute, assuming the agents perceive the system to be in a similar state, can be the basis for collective behaviours such as system self-management behaviour.

4   SAMPLE and CRL

The CRL model was used to build a MANET routing protocol called SAMPLE [12]. SAMPLE is a probabilistic on-demand ad hoc routing protocol that contains system-wide self-managing properties, such as the adaptation of network traffic patterns around areas of congestion and wireless interference and the exploitation of stable routes in the environment.

Ad hoc routing is a challenging problem as it exhibits properties such as the lack of global network state at any particular node in the network and frequently changing network topology due to node mobility. This ensures that system properties of the protocol only emerge from local routing decisions based on local information and that routing agent's behaviour has to frequently adapt to a changing environment.

Two major assumptions of the two most popular MANET routing protocols, Ad-Hoc On-Demand Distance Vector routing (AODV) [21] and Dynamic Source Routing (DSR) [22], is that the network has a random topology and that all radio links function perfectly. Both protocols make these static assumption about the MANET environment in order to avoid route maintenance problems typically encountered by proactive routing protocols in MANETs. AODV and DSR use on-demand routing where routes to destinations are only discovered when needed using flooding [21, 22] and these routes are discarded when a number of transmission failures over a network link occur, even though that transmission failure may be due to a temporary phenomena such as congestion or wireless interference.

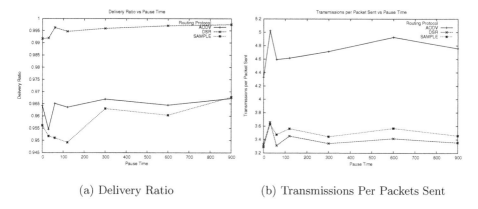

(a) Delivery Ratio   (b) Transmissions Per Packets Sent

Fig. 2. Perfect Network Links in a Random Topology. Performance with Varying Load. 64 byte packets

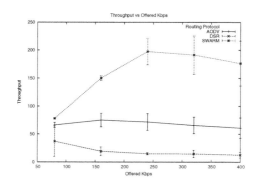

Fig. 3. At a varying load, 512 byte packets, SAMPLE delivers a data throughput of up to 200Kbps. This throughput approaches the theoretical limit of the throughput achievable in a multi-hop 802.11 mobile ad hoc network scenario

In our evaluation of SAMPLE, in sections 4.1 and 4.4, we show how CRL enables routing agents in SAMPLE to establish consensus on the location of stable routes in a network with different quality network links and use this consensus to optimise system routing performance. In SAMPLE we attempt to optimise multiple, often conflicting system routing performance criteria, including maximising overall network throughput, maximising the ratio of delivered packets to undelivered packets and minimising the number of transmissions required per packet sent.

4.1   SAMPLE Experiments

We have implemented the SAMPLE routing protocol in the NS-2 network simulator [23]. We compare the performance of the SAMPLE routing protocol to that

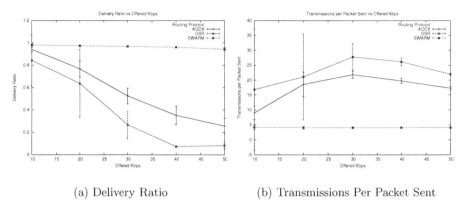

(a) Delivery Ratio   (b) Transmissions Per Packet Sent

Fig. 4. Stable Route Topology. Performance with Varying Load. 64 byte packets

of AODV and DSR, in two different scenarios. The first scenario is a random network scenario that is designed to test how SAMPLE compares with AODV and DSR when the MANET environment reflects their static design assumptions. The second scenario is a metropolitan area MANET, where a subset of the links in the network are stable, that is designed to test the ability of the protocols to adapt their routing behaviour to achieve consensus on the location of the stable routes in the network. We also introduce congestion into both scenarios to investigate the effectiveness of the protocols in adapting their routing behaviour to a changing MANET environment. Our goal here is to compare the performance of the SAMPLE routing protocol in different, changing environments with on-demand protocols that make static assumptions about the MANET environment using the system optimisation criteria identified in Section 4.

The SAMPLE routing protocol combines routing information with data packets, and as a result the metric of *number of routing packets* is not a valid one for comparison with AODV and DSR. For this reason, we use the number of transmissions (unicast or broadcast) that each protocol makes per application packet sent during the simulation run as a metric to compare the protocols. This metric represents the cost to the network of routing each data packet.

4.2   Perfect Network Links in a Random Topology

The comparative performance of the protocols in a scenario that mimics the random topology used in [24] is first evaluated. A simulation arena of 1500m x 300m is used, with the transmission power of the radio interfaces set to 250m. The random way-point mobility model is used, with a maximum speed of 20 m/s and varying pause times. Constant bit rate traffic of 64 byte packets, 4 packets per second, with 10 flows between random pairs of nodes is used.

We compare the SAMPLE routing protocol to AODV and DSR in an idealised experiment with no packet loss added to the simulation. Figure 2 shows the packet delivery ratio and transmissions-per-packet metrics as they vary with the level of mobility in the network. In this scenario, both AODV and DSR have near-optimal packet delivery ratios, while SAMPLE has between 1% and 4% worse packet delivery ratios, and all protocols have a near-minimal cost (in terms of network transmissions). As there is no packet loss and all links are of perfect quality, AODV's favouring of routes with the shortest hop-count shows the best performance.

4.3   Achieving Consensus on Stable Links in a Metropolitan Area MANET

We have also evaluated the performance of SAMPLE against that of AODV and DSR in a network scenario based on a metropolitan ad hoc network. In this scenario, there are a subset of nodes in the network that are not mobile. The network scenario is motivated by the recent appearance of ad hoc networks designed to supply Internet access to mobile nodes.

In this scenario, we anticipate that certain nodes in the network will be immobile for extended periods of time, resulting in stable links between them, and that the traffic patterns in the network will be concentrated on the subset of nodes that have Internet connectivity. In the experiments presented here we use 3 server nodes. Each client sends constant-bit-rate traffic to one of the servers at a rate of 4 packets per second. The number of client nodes in the network is varied in order to create congestion in the network. There are 33 fixed nodes in these simulations, and 50 mobile nodes. The fixed nodes in the simulation provide stable links in the network which the routing protocols could exploit. SAMPLE's configurable parameters have been tuned to provide improved performance for this scenario, see [12] for more details.

Figure 4 shows the variation in performance of the three routing protocols as the number of clients in the network is increased. The packet size sent by clients was kept fixed at 64 bytes, sent 3 times a second.

As the number of clients in the network is increased, the offered throughput to the routing protocols is increased. This in turn increases the level of packet loss and the amount of contention that the Media Access Control (MAC) protocol must deal with. This increased congestion increases the number of failed MAC unicasts in the network. Figure 4 shows that increased packet loss results in lower throughput and packet delivery ratios in AODV and DSR, but that SAMPLE is able to maintain high throughput and packet delivery ratios with high levels of packet loss.

In [25] it was demonstrated that for multi-hop 802.11 networks, the achievable throughput is significantly less than the transmission rate of the radio interfaces. The maximum achievable data throughput in an 802.11 ad hoc network is approximately 0.25Mbps (which [25] achieved using 1500 byte packets). Figure 3 shows that SAMPLE manages to approach this limit in this scenario. This shows experimentally that using CRL, SAMPLE can meet the system optimisation criteria of maximising network throughput in the metropolitan area MANET scenario.

4.4   Emergent Consensus and System Optimisation in SAMPLE

In the metropolitan area MANET environment, there are a subset of the links in the network that are stable. Collaborative feedback adapts routing agent behaviour to favour paths with stable links, producing the emergent stable routes in the network. AODV and DSR do not allow nodes to differentiate between multiple available links in this manner, due to their static assumptions about network links. In SAMPLE positive feedback in link selection by routing agents means that the routing behaviour of agents converges on the stable network links in the environment. SAMPLE maintains a near-optimal delivery ratio and using a minimal number of transmissions even at high offered throughput for 802.11 MANETs. An important lesson from SAMPLE is the need for experimentation, as the emergence of more optimal routing properties is sensitive to tunable parameters in CRL and to the update rule of the learning algorithm used in SAMPLE.

5   Urban Traffic Control and CRL

We believe that Urban Traffic Control is an appropriate application domain for the CRL technique. The UTC and MANET application domains exhibit some similar characteristics. Road traffic-signal controllers can be modelled as autonomous agents. Routing network traffic along a link is analogous to running a green signal-control phase for this street and the system goal is to maximise overall road network throughput by altering signal timings to minimise congestion and vehicle delay.

The suburban road network provides the links between agent controllers. The vehicle density or flow-rate provides a measure of the attractiveness or general fitness of this link. If the quality of service or throughput of the link degrades suddenly due to traffic incidents, sudden increase in traffic volumes or traffic signal operation then the link will become congested and it will be sub-optimal to route vehicles along this link.

The signal-control agent obtains information about its local environment from its sensor infrastructure. The overall UTC system objective may be to optimise vehicle throughput the network however this policy must be implemented by autonomous agents that only possess timely and verifiable information about their local environment. The key challenge of trying to implement a global optimisation strategy based on partial knowledge of a dynamic system is therefore common to both the UTC and MANET application domains.

5.1   Optimisation in Urban Traffic Control

Advances in sensor infrastructure resulting in online vehicle and traffic flow detection have enabled the advent of adaptive traffic control systems capable of online generation and implementation of signal timing parameters[26]. Adaptive control systems such as SCOOT[37] and SCAT [38] are widely deployed throughout the world.

However the adaptive traffic control systems that are currently deployed are hampered by the lack of an explicit coordination model for junction or agent collaboration and are typically reliant on prespecified models of the environment that require domain expertise to construct. These models are typically used as an aid to sensor data interpretation and strategy evaluation and may often be too generic to adequately reflect highly dynamic local conditions[28].

These systems have a limited rate of adaptivity and are designed to respond to gradual rather than rapid changes in traffic conditions. They employ centralised data processing and control algorithms that do not reflect the localised nature of traffic disturbances and flow fluctuations. Yagar and Dion[36] state that: "smooth traffic and uncomplicated networks provide good opportunities for progression, in which case a centralised quasi real-time model, such as SCOOT is appropriate as a model of central control. However, when faced with significant demand fluctuation or interference..., a distributed real-time model is required".

Current research on next generation UTC systems is focusing on applying novel control strategies and AI techniques to the domain. Hoar et. al [27], have investigated the application of swarm intelligence to cooperative vehicle control and isolated signal setting optimisation. Their approach is based on the stigmergic model of environment mediated communication to enable inter-vehicle and vehicle-signal controller cooperation. The fitness function evaluated seeks to minimise the average waiting time of all vehicles in the network. Initial tests indicate promising results and increased adaptivity to high rates of change in traffic flow.

Abdulhai et. al [28], have applied reinforcement learning techniques to UTC control. Using an unsupervised learning technique they have demonstrated that an AI approach can at least match the performance of expert-knowledge based pre-timed signal plans without the requirement of a network model or traffic engineering expertise. The system attempts to minimise the total delay incurred by vehicles in all queues on a junction approach. The evaluation results relate to the operation of a single intersection controller and does not substantially address distributed signal coordination between agent junctions.

The authors cited above have applied novel techniques to the UTC domain however they are essentially adopting centralised approaches to the problem. Their evaluation scenarios are not representative of a real-sized UTC network. Such approaches are not scalable and Lo and Chow[39] highlight the difficulty faced by attempting to optimise a real-sized UTC problem in a centralised fashion. They apply a genetic algorithm based control strategy with possible solution sets encoded as binary strings. For a network with 3 agent junctions operating with a constrained number of control variables the sample solution space expands to 2^{70}. The addition of agent junctions capable of a normal set of control actions causes the solution space to grow exponentially and results in an intractably large solution space.

We believe that adopting a decentralised approach to UTC optimisation is the only feasible method of tackling the problem on a large scale. We believe this decentralisation is best attained by modelling individual junctions as agents and

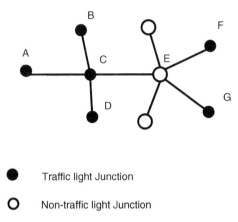

Fig. 5. Sample Layout of a set of Junctions

allowing consensus to emerge between cooperating agents on a suitable system control strategy.

5.2   UTC-CRL

The similarities between the UTC and MANET environments coupled with difficulties exposed by current UTC strategies has prompted the application of the CRL model to the UTC domain. A large scale UTC system may be modelled in a decentralised manner using CRL. Using the UTC-CRL approach, traffic lights would act as agents, choosing a particular action to take, such as changing from one phase to another and receiving a reward from the environment, for taking this action. UTC-CRL allows traffic light agents to share their local view of the congestion at their junction with neighbouring agents to enable convergence towards a shared view of the congestion in the surrounding area.

Using CRL to tackle this problem has a number of advantages. Firstly, CRL gives an explicit framework to model the collaboration and coordination between agents. Secondly, as CRL is a distributed learning technique, traffic light agents collaborate to allow consensus to be established on the optimal phases to choose at a junction in an UTC environment that is uncertain and dynamic. This in turn allows the flows of traffic in an area to be optimised by the collaborating traffic light agents. Positive feedback is used to reinforce the selection of such optimal phases. Negative feedback discourages traffic light agents to act in a greedy fashion as this adversely impacts on congestion levels at neighbouring traffic light agents.

For example in figure 5, a traffic light agent at junction C uses information from its neighbouring traffic light agents, $\{A, B, D, F, G\}$ to optimise the flow of traffic in the area surrounding junction C. Similarly, junction C communicates with its neighbours to allow them to optimise the flow of traffic in their individual area. The traffic light agent would then communicate its view of the environment to the traffic light agents that are both upstream and downstream of it.

Indirect feedback is given by vehicles crossing the junction from one or more approaches to one or more exits. Secondly, traffic light agents advertise their view of their local environment to neighbouring agents. Instead of advertising the cost to a particular destination as in SAMPLE, a traffic light agent in UTC-CRL advertises its view of the level of congestion associated with a particular approach from an upstream junction or associated with a particular exit towards a downstream junction.

For example in figure 5, junction C would advertise to junction A its view of the congestion on the approach from junction A. Similarly, junction A would advertise to junction C its view of the congestion on the exit from junction A towards junction C. By incorporating each of these views into their calculations, junctions A and C can establish convergent views of the congestion level which can then in turn inform their collective decisions of which action is most appropriate.

The type of system optimisation achievable in UTC-CRL depends on the actions, states and rewards used. The actions available to a particular junction correspond to a subset of the possible phases at that junction. The set of possible states relate to the type of system optimisation desired. For example, one optimisation criteria may be to minimise average number of vehicles waiting at a junction. Given such a criteria, the states of the traffic light agent at that junction correspond to a tuple of values that represent the number of vehicles waiting on each approach to that junction. Another possible optimisation criteria would be to maximise the average velocity of vehicles in the system. This would require the average velocity of vehicles on each approach to be wirelessly communicated to the traffic light agent at the junction.

The reward model depends on the particular optimisation strategy being pursued. When trying to minimise the number of vehicles waiting at a junction, the reward received by an agent on executing an action should be related to the number of vehicles that traverse the junction as a result of the particular action being selected. Alternatively, when trying to maximise the average velocity, the reward received by executing an action should be related to the change in the velocities of the vehicles on the various approaches to the junction.

Finally, as CRL is a completely decentralised approach with agents having a similar number of states and actions, this should allow UTC-CRL to scale to a large number of traffic light junctions.

5.3   Evaluation Strategy

As highlighted in section 4.1, SAMPLE takes an experimental approach to validate the emergence of consensus between mobile hosts in a MANET. In a similar approach, UTC-CRL is taking an experimental approach to validate the appropriateness of CRL in a large scale UTC setting. In particular, an objective of the UTC-CRL experimental approach is to verify that consensus can emerge between collaborating traffic light agents and this emergence of consensus allows optimisation of traffic flows in this large scale setting. The envisioned setting for this work corresponds to the Dublin city area which consists of 248 traffic light junctions, over 750 non-traffic light junctions and over 3000 links joining these junctions. Given this layout of junctions, models of traffic flows between different areas of the city are currently under development that correspond to currently available census data for the greater Dublin area [31]. We have constructed a model of the road network for Dublin city centre and a traffic model containing realistic vehicle volumes. We are currently evaluating MDPs to validate the appropriateness of CRL in this domain.

6   Conclusions

Decentralised computing systems should establish and maintain consensus on environmental or system properties with minimal external intervention in order to provide system-wide self-managing behaviour. The challenges of how to achieve consensus between agents' local, partial views of the system in order to establish such properties can be met using decentralised coordination techniques. CRL is one such coordination technique that enables consensus on optimal policies to emerge between interacting agents in a decentralised system. In this paper we described CRL as a decentralised coordination technique and discussed its application to a MANET routing protocol called SAMPLE and Urban Traffic Control problems. From our evaluation of SAMPLE as a CRL system, we show that CRL through feedback, advertisement and decay enables consensus to emerge on stable routes in a MANET and how this can be used to improve the system routing performance in MANETs with stable nodes.

References

1. Montresor, A., Meling, H., Babaoglu, O.: Towards self-organizing, self-repairing and resilient distributed systems. Future Directions in Distributed Computing. vol LNCS 2584 (2003).
2. Visscher, P.: How self-organization evolves. Nature. vol.421 799–800 (2003).
3. Camazine, S., Deneubourg, J., Franks, N., Sneyd, J., Theraulaz, G., Bonabeau, E.: Self-Organization in Biological Systems. Princeton University Press (2003).
4. Gelernter, D., Carriero, N.: Coordination languages and their significance. Commun. ACM vol.35 no.2 97–107 (1992).
5. Goldin, D. and Keil, K.: Toward domain-independent formalization of indirect interaction. 2nd Int'l workshop on Theory and Practice of Open Computational Systems (TAPOCS) (2004).
6. Efstratiou, C., Friday, A., Davies, N., Cheverst, K.: Utilising the event calculus for policy driven adaptation in mobile systems. Proceedings of the 3rd International Workshop on Policies for Distributed Systems and Networks (2002) IEEE Computer Society 13–24 June (2002).
7. Dorigo, M. Di Caro, G.: The ant colony optimization meta-heuristic. New Ideas in Optimization (1999).
8. Andrzejak, A., Graupner, S., Kotov, V., Trinks, H.: Adaptive control overlay for service management. Workshop on the Design of Self-Managing Systems. International Conference on Dependable Systems and Networks (2003).

9. De Wolf, T. and Holvoet, T.: Towards autonomic computing: agent-based modelling, dynamical systems analysis, and decentralised control. Proceedings of IEEE International Conference on Industrial Informatics 470–479 (2003).
10. Boutilier, C., Das, R., Kephart, J., Tesauro, G., Walsh, W.: Cooperative negotiation in autonomic systems using incremental utility elicitation. Uncertainty in Artificial Intelligence (2003).
11. Khare, R., Taylor, R.N.: Extending the representational state transfer (rest) architectural style for decentralized systems. Proceedings of the International Conference on Software Engineering (ICSE) (2004).
12. Curran, E., Dowling, J.: Sample: An on-demand probabilistic routing protocol for ad-hoc networks. Technical Report Department of Computer Science Trinity College Dublin (2004).
13. Jelasity, M., Montresor A., Babaoglu, O.: A modular paradigm for building self-organizing peer-to-peer applications. Proceedings of ESOP03 International Workshop on Engineering Self-Organising Applications (2003).
14. Panagiotis, T., Demosthenis, T., Mackie-Mason, J.-K.: A market-based approach to optimal resource allocation in integrated-services connection-oriented networks. Operations Research vol.50 4 July-August 2002.
15. Littman, M., Boyan, J.: A distributed reinforcement learning scheme for network routing. Technical Report CS-93-165 (1993).
16. Di Caro, G., Dorigo, M.: AntNet: Distributed Stigmergetic Control for Communications Networks. Journal of Artificial Intelligence Research vol 9 317–365 (1998).
17. Sutton, R., Barto, A.: Reinforcement Learning. MIT Press (1998).
18. Bonabeau, E., Dorigo, M., Theraulaz, G.: Swarm Intelligence: from natural to artificial systems. New York Oxford University Press (1999).
19. Crites, R., Barto, A.: Elevator group control using multiple reinforcement learning agents. Machine Learning volume 33 2-3 235–262 (1998).
20. Kaelbling, L., Littman, M., Moore, A. Reinforcement learning: A survey. Journal of Artificial Intelligence Research vol 4 237–285 (1996).
21. Perkins, C.: Ad Hoc On Demand Distance Vector (AODV) Routing. IETF Internet Draft November (1997).
22. Johnson, D., Maltz, D., Broch, J.: DSR: The dynamic source routing protocol for multihop wireless ad hoc networks. Ad Hoc Networking 139–172 Addison-Wesley (2001).
23. NS-2 network simulator. Information Sciences Institute (2003).
24. Broch, J., Maltz, D., Johnson, D., Hu, J., Jetcheva, J.: A Performance Comparison of Multi-Hop Wireless Ad Hoc Network Routing Protocols. Mobile Computing and Networking 85–97 (1998).
25. Li, J., Blake, C., De Couto, D., Lee, H., Morris, R.: Capacity of ad hoc wireless networks. Proceedings of the 7th International Conference on Mobile Computing and Networking 61–69 (2001).
26. Klein, L.: Sensor Technologies and Data Requirements for ITS. Artech House (2001).
27. Hoar, R., Penner, J., Jacob, C.: Evolutionary Swarm Traffic: If Ant Roads had Traffic Lights. Proceedings of the IEEE Conference on Evolutionary Computation Honolulu Hawaii 1910–1916 (2002).
28. Abdulhai, B., Pringle, R., Karakoulas, G.: Reinforcement Learning for True Adaptive Traffic Signal Control. Transportation Engineering vol.129 May (2003).
29. Findler, N.: Harmonization for Omnidirectional Progression in Urban Traffic Control. Computer-Aided Civil and Infrastructure Engineering vol 14 Honolulu Hawaii 369–377 (1999).

30. Pendrith, M.: Distributed Reinforcement Learning for a Traffic Engineering Application. Proceedings of the Fourth Internation Conference on Autonomous Agents Barcelona Spain (2000).
31. Dublin Transportation Office: DTO Strategy Update - Full Report - Platform For Change. Available on: http://www.dto.ie/strategy.htm (2001).
32. Guestrin, C., Lagoudakis, M., Parr, R.: Coordinated reinforcement learning. Proceedings of The Nineteenth International Conference on Machine Learning 227–234 (2002).
33. Schneider, J., Wong, W., Moore, A. and Riedmiller, M.: Distributed value functions. Proceedings of the Sixteenth International Conference on Machine Learning 371–378 Morgan Kaufmann Publishers 1999.
34. Stone, P.: TPOT-RL applied to network routing. Proceedings of the Seventeenth International Conference on Machine Learning (2000).
35. Mariano, C, Morales, E.: A new distributed reinforcement learning algorithm for multiple objective optimization problems. Advances in Artificial Intelligence, International Joint Conference 7th Ibero-American Conference on AI 15th Brazilian Symposium on AI (2000).
36. Yagar, S. Dion, F.: Distributed Approach to Real-Time Control of Complex Signalized Networks. Transportation Research Record Vol.1 1–8 (1996).
37. Hunt, P. Robertson, R. Winton, R. Bretherton, R.: SCOOT- A Traffic Responsive Method of Coordinating Signals. Road Research Laboratory, TRRL Report 1014 (1981).
38. Sims, A.: The Sydney Coordinated Adaptive Traffic System. Proceedings of the ASCE Engineering Foundations Conference on Research Priorities in Computer Control of Urban Traffic Systems (1979).
39. Lo, H., Chow, A.: Control Strategies for Oversaturated Traffic. Transportation Engineering vol.130 July (2004).

The Biologically Inspired Distributed File System: An Emergent Thinker Instantiation

Sergio Camorlinga[1] and Ken Barker[2]

[1] Computer Science Department, University of Manitoba, Winnipeg MB, R3T 2N2 Canada
sergio_camorlinga@sbrc.ca
[2] Computer Science Department, University of Calgary, Calgary AB, T2N 1N4 Canada
barker@cpsc.ucalgary.ca

Abstract. This paper introduces the *Emergent Thinker* paradigm, an area-wide logical computing entity, named after a philosopher that continuously analyses information and has emergent computed solutions for new and/or existing requests. The Complex Adaptive System (CAS) emergent computation model and the CAS propagation model are proposed as mechanisms to achieve the Emergent Thinker. The Thinker is proposed as an alternative approach for new and existent design and implementation challenges in systems research. The Biologically Inspired Peer-to-Peer Distributed File System (BPD) is an instantiation of the Emergent Thinker paradigm and corroborates our hypothesis that CAS based computation is an alternative paradigm to provide scalable computation for large distributed systems.

1 Introduction

Systems research has produced solutions to many of its design and implementation challenges. These solutions are usually based on algorithms and models that have predetermined, predefined centralized and distributed techniques. However, these models and algorithms are limited when subject to computing environments that are dynamic, self-organized, *ad-hoc* (e.g. in terms of connectivity, operatively, *etc.*) and decentralized like those found in peer-to-peer systems, pervasive computing environments, some grid systems (e.g. grids with no common domain across the Internet), autonomic systems, *etc.* Some workarounds are often implemented to alleviate these system's limitations. However, it is clear that different approaches are required for these environments.

Complex adaptive systems (CAS) are defined as systems characterized by having a large number of members with simple functions and limited communication among them. The emergence of swarm intelligence [1] from simple members activities boasts autonomy and self-sufficiency, which allows them to adapt quickly to changing environmental conditions. The emergent global outcome may be applied to solve particular distributed system problems. Emergent outcomes (i.e. self-* properties) providing solutions to specific problems have been documented in

O. Babaoglu et al. (Eds.): SELF-STAR 2004, LNCS 3460, pp. 81–96, 2005.

different research work published previously. Several examples are available in the literature [2-11].[1]

This paper introduces a new computing paradigm, the *Emergent Thinker* [12], and an instantiation of the paradigm, the *Biologically Inspired Peer-to-Peer Distributed File System* (BPD). The Emergent Thinker uses CAS domains to provide emergent computation for large, highly dynamic distributed systems. The BPD implements the Emergent Thinker and experimentally corroborates our hypothesis that CAS based computation is an alternative valid paradigm to provide scalable computation for large distributed systems.

Section 2 describes the Emergent Thinker paradigm and the two models the paradigm is based on: the CAS Emergent Computation model and the CAS Propagation model. Section 3 explains how the paradigm is applied to design and implement the BPD. It then continues with a description of the BPD CAS algorithms utilized and provides a generic description of the architecture. Section 4 presents some representative results of the BPD implementation. Section 5 discusses and overviews future work in the Emergent Thinker paradigm to conclude and give final thoughts in Section 6.

2   The Emergent Thinker Paradigm

2.1   The CAS *Emergent Computation* Model

A common feature of previous CAS related work is the existence of simple agents[2] with local functions[3] and a simple communication mechanism[4] that is either direct or indirect. For this, we propose a basic computing model that generalizes previous work. We call it the *CAS Emergent Computation* model. See Figure 1.

In the CAS Emergent Computation model, agents follow simple rules to affect their states and/or environment to generate an emergent pattern formation[5] that produces a system wide result (Figure 1). The system wide result is interpreted as an emergent computation (i.e. self-* property) that solves a particular distributed system problem (e.g. aggregation, resource allocation, classification, assignment, path selection, decision, *etc.*). A model hypothesis is that all computation to be provided can be obtained by emergent computations of simple activities.

It is important to stress the difference between an *emergent* computation and a *regular* computation. A regular computation is a CPU computation like arithmetic and logical operations. An emergent computation is at a higher abstraction level. The emergent computation outcome is a self-* property that resolves a particular distributed computing problem. Emergent computations can make use of regular

---

[1] Some authors do not call their mechanisms CAS-based. However in essence they are, if we assume that these mechanisms have similar characteristics.

[2] The terms 'agent', 'individual', and 'member' mean the same across the paper.

[3] The terms 'function', 'property', 'action', and 'activity' mean the same across the paper.

[4] The communication mechanism exists within the domain environment.

[5] 'Emergent pattern formation' means pattern formations in agents, domain environment, or both.

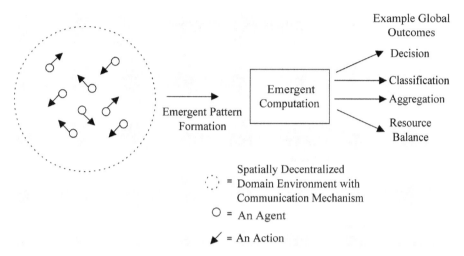

Fig. 1. CAS Emergent Computation Model

computations to achieve its outcomes, and could also use other emergent computations (e.g. hierarchical emergent computations) as part of their computations.

A basic question[6] is identifying the relationship that exists between the emergent computation and the local agents' properties or actions. By focusing on the cause-effect relationships, which are dynamic and non-linear, it could lead us to identify necessary and sufficient conditions to obtain emergent computations (i.e. self-* properties). Further, it helps us to understand how a specific property produces an emergent outcome. All these will allow us to control and manage the agent's properties to obtain desired global outcomes. This leads to a key question: How can we identify these relationships? We propose the *CAS Propagation* model to answer this question.

2.2 The CAS *Propagation* Model

The CAS Propagation model is based on the simple idea of amplification by propagation. The way the different agents connect and exchange information (directly and/or indirectly) will have a direct consequence in the action's impact on the other agents and in the system as a whole. In the past, different approaches have been used to interconnect CAS agents (e.g. fully connected, small world pattern, random, small set of neighbors, local paths, etc). These connectivity approaches generate different global outcomes from the same local properties. We could attribute this to the way the local properties were propagated and exchanged across the domain and are consequently amplified for different global, emergent self-* properties. The main point that the CAS Propagation model makes concerns the spread and its affects on the amplification of the agents' actions to eventually give an emergent result, called a global self-* property (Figure 2).

---

[6] Other questions include issues like message exchanges, speed, property sets, feedbacks, edge of chaos, limit theory, *etc.*

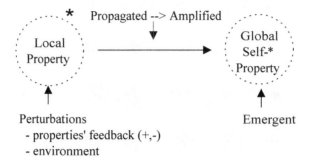

Fig. 2. CAS Propagation Model

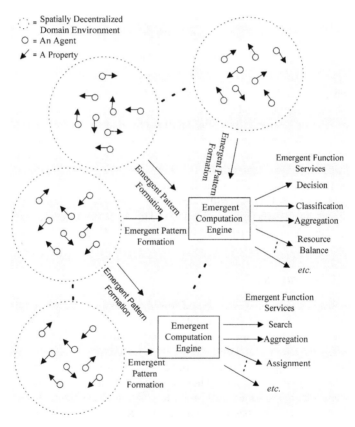

Fig. 3. The Emergent Thinker

Furthermore, the way the actions are propagated and exchanged will have an impact in the perturbations (i.e. properties' feedback, environment feedback), which subsequently affect the local agents' properties, which then adapt their agents' behaviors accordingly. If these perturbations are too high, it can force the system into chaos. The CAS Propagation model is a fertile area of experimental research that can lead to an understanding of the fundamentals linkages between local properties and emergent, global self-* properties that eventually can lead us to develop the theory and mathematical formulations that represent them.

Based on our clear understanding of the CAS Emergent Computation (Figure 1) and the CAS Propagation (Figure 2) models, these models are extended to develop what we call the *Emergent Thinker* paradigm. The Emergent Thinker paradigm provides computing services by means of CAS Emergent Computation model instantiations. The Emergent Thinker is named after a philosopher that continuously analyses information and has emergent computed solutions for new and/or living requests. Living requests mean those computations that the Emergent Thinker continuously works on.

2.3 The Emergent Thinker Paradigm

The Emergent Thinker is defined as an area-wide logical computing entity (Figure 3) based solely on CAS models and algorithms to provide function services. Function services are the mechanisms used by an application program to request services from the Emergent Thinker. The Emergent Thinker uses the CAS Emergent Computation model (Figure 1) as its building block. It has CAS domain environments that are implemented in decentralized contexts (e.g. P2P environment, pervasive environments, multi-processors computers, grids, *etc.*) providing emergent function services. The emergent function services are equivalent to system calls provided by a regular operating system, but with a completely different functionality and purpose (i.e. at a higher abstraction level). The emergent computation engines are located wherever the emergent service is required (i.e. pervasive engines). This is possible because the services or functions (i.e. self-* properties) are continuously emerging from the system itself. These engines are access points to observable and/or interpreted global properties. The CAS Propagation model is then used to experimentally test the properties and the emergent computations utilized by the Emergent Thinker.

3 The Biologically Inspired Peer-to-Peer Distributed File System

The *Biologically Inspired Peer-to-Peer Distributed File System* (BPD) is an instantiation of the Emergent Thinker paradigm. The BPD merges CAS models with Peer-to-Peer (P2P) computing to implement a Distributed File System (DFS). The BPD design and implementation presents a novel alternative to existing deterministic, centralized or distributed techniques proposed in the majority of current P2P and DFS research. BPD implementation has shown promising results by modeling natural behaviors in its foundation services to solve distributed systems' design challenges. This section reviews the BPD and how the Emergent Thinker paradigm is applied. Another will detail the BPD architecture design and implementation.

The BPD assumes an environment that has computing devices with *ad hoc* behavior (i.e. joining and leaving the network) and no central server or controller. The BPD is intended to scale from a few peers to thousands of peers allocated across a distributed system within an organization. The BPD targets an environment where users can seamlessly and dynamically share their storage resources to provide a peer-to-peer distributed file system.

Figure 4 shows a high level view of the BPD. A P2P system with hundreds or thousands of computing devices forms a complex environment where peers (Figure 4 circles) continuously connect and disconnect. Each peer has agents that execute basic actions (in Figure 4 these are depicted with arrows) independent from each other, with minimum or no communication among them. The emergent computations achieved by the agents' actions provide computing services required by the DFS. The DFS is spread out across the P2P environment. A user or application[7] accesses File System (FS) services for its file management needs through calls to the DFS emergent computation engine. A DFS emergent computation engine resides in each peer that provides access to the environment. When an application requires a FS service, the engine inserts the request into the complex environment and the response emerges from it and it is delivered to the application that initially made the request. For each BPD DFS service provided, there is an independent spatially decentralized domain of agents' actions that execute on the same physical P2P system.

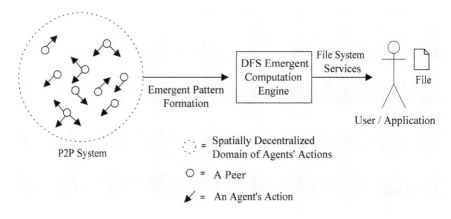

Fig. 4. BPD High Level View

Before the CAS Propagation model can be experimentally used within the Emergent Thinker paradigm, essential DFS building block functions must be identified. These DFS building block functions must be suitable to be provided by emergent computation and eventually constitute major components of the FS services to the applications. A top-down approach is used to analyze application FS services and identify the common building block functions. For example, Bach [13] describes the Unix operating system FS services provided to applications. The analysis gives us the following primary DFS building block functions:

1.   Allocation services to implement storing data blocks and/or complete files across the P2P.

---

[7] The terms 'user', and 'application' mean the same across the paper.

2. Retrieval services to implement reading data blocks and/or complete files from the P2P system.
3. Replication services to implement a data replication scheme to increase storage reliability and availability.
4. Discovery services to implement a P2P system wide data search.

After the analysis, the four primary DFS functions are the prime candidates to be implemented by emergent computations. However, further study shows that replication services (in its different variants) can be implemented with allocation services. Also, directory and file tables, which are resident at the local peer, can control retrieval services of known data, while discovery services can control retrieval services of unknown data. Thus, retrieval services can be implemented with local data management techniques (known data) and with discovery services (unknown data). These leave us with two essential DFS building block functions: Allocation and discovery[8] function services.

Allocation and discovery services are essential distributed services and consequently we hypothesize that they can be implemented by emergent computations. We define *emergent function services* as those basic DFS services that emerge out of CAS emergent computations.

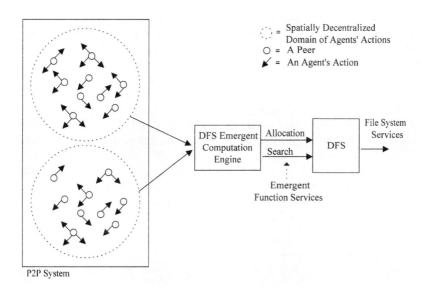

Fig. 5. BPD Instantiation of the Emergent Thinker Paradigm

Figure 5 shows the BPD instantiation of the Emergent Thinker paradigm. The current BPD implementation uses one CAS (i.e. spatially decentralized domain of agents' actions) for each emergent function service identified (i.e. allocation and discovery services). However, these CAS domains run on the same physical P2P

---

[8] The terms 'discovery' and 'search' are used interchangeably throughout the paper.

complex environment so, each CAS domain is logically independent but physically run on one physical P2P complex environment.

3.1   The BPD Emergent Computing Algorithms Overview

Research has been carried on to use the CAS Emergent Computation and the CAS Propagation models to experiment and implement the BPD emergent computations based on natural or biological behaviors. The CAS algorithms utilized are based on squirrel natural behaviors and provide a novel metaphor for this kind of CAS. Camorlinga, Barker *et al.* [6][14] provide details on the BPD CAS algorithms utilized for allocation and search emergent services. The algorithms are based on CAS squirrel hoarding mechanisms. The squirrel behaviors modeled and applied to the DFS emergent function services are briefly described next.

3.1.1   CAS Algorithms for DFS Allocation Services

Many ecological and environmental protection groups have studied the hundreds of squirrel species found worldwide [15][16].[9] Squirrels eat various nuts, acorns, and other small foodstuffs[10] by caching acorns in small hoards over a large geographic area. When food becomes scarce they return to the caches. Their failure to recover a great percentage of the horded acorns facilitates the growth of new trees. Squirrels, in conjunction with Jays [15], are responsible for the vast oak extensions through North America after the glacial age 10,000 years ago. From a computational perspective, squirrels are allocating resources (land space) to storage demands (acorns) in such a way that resources are balanced. The global or corporate consequence emergent from the behavior of these individuals is a populated forest of oak trees across a wide geographic area.

For allocation services (e.g. storing data), the most interesting squirrel behavior is hoarding, rather than foraging, as hoarding leads to a global outcome of which the individual squirrels cannot possibly be aware. The hoarding approach also reflects a more natural reflection of the allocation activity. We are interested in the way squirrels spread out acorns, nuts and other small food pieces in an area to obtain a resource allocation balance. We exploit these techniques to design and implement resource allocation services suitable for distributed systems [6].

The squirrel hoarding behaviors can be summarized as:

- Random gathering and burying of small acorn amounts in an area geographically close to its nest,
- Investigation of various random locations ("sniffing" several places) before deciding where to put the acorn,
- Possibly deciding not to hoard its food if there are other squirrels around, and
- Possibly working in small teams with others with whom they are familiar, while avoiding places inhabited by unknown squirrels.

---

[9] A web search on 'squirrel resources' provides reference to squirrel information sources describing additional behaviors.

[10] We speak of these foodstuffs collectively using the exemplar "acorns" as we are interested in the consequence of the hording activities.

The "squirrels" CAS based system consists of a P2P environment. Each peer has one or more caches where squirrels hoard acorns. Squirrels live in these peers in small groups. When they have acorns, they go through the peers, "sniffing" to find a cache suitable for the acorn following one of the behaviours described above. Each peer is a producer and consumer of caches (storage resources). Figure 6 illustrates such an environment.

Each acorn is a data block that must be stored within the DFS. Each cache is a group of data blocks available that can be allocated. The goal is efficient allocation of storage resources by balancing resource allocation across peers' caches. Each cache has the same characteristics across peers. What it is different is the number of caches available per peer. Consequently, if we balance caches then a well-balanced P2P DFS system is achieved according to peer capabilities (number of caches available in the peer). How well balance the system is will be measured by the variance of acorns allocated per cache. The lower the variance (i.e. close to zero), the better allocation balance obtained.

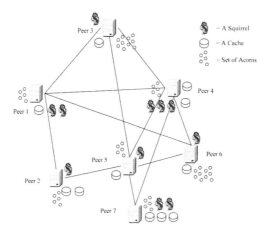

Fig. 6. CAS Allocation Based on Squirrel Behaviors

3.1.2 CAS Algorithms for DFS Discovery Services

We also apply a slight variation of the squirrel behaviors to discovery services (e.g. data search). The basic idea is that squirrels with simple hoarding activities disseminate acorns that contain identifiers. These acorn identifiers are used to dig out data acorns stored in the peer storage caches where they were allocated [14] and help us to determine their locations.

Initially each peer has its own squirrels (up to a maximum) according to its capabilities (Figure 7.a). Each peer shares resources (e.g. files in sharable folders). Squirrels from different peers are independent of each other. The squirrels are unaware that their hoarding activities are used to search data. The search emerges as a global outcome of the activities of the independent members (i.e. squirrels) that work with simple activities but generate a system wide result. When a new member joins the P2P environment, there is no administrative activity to do besides joining the P2P environment. When a new search arrives at a peer (Figure 7.b), the peer's squirrel puts the acorn id in a sack together with other acorn ids already existing that have been put there by other squirrels (if any) and hoards them in nearby peers.

If a sack with acorn ids is placed in a peer, the acorn ids are searched within this peer. Any acorn id that is found is notified of the original search peer, otherwise either the acorn id remains in the sack or the acorn identifier expires, terminating the data acorn search. New searches from this peer are added to this sack (if any) and together continue to be disseminated by the local squirrel to other peers (Figure 7.c).

The whole P2P environment is a living organism that has members joining and leaving continuously with no administrative burden. Once a member joins, its sharable resources are available and actively participate in the emergent search scheme according to its capabilities (i.e. by the number of sharable resources and by the number of peer's squirrels available). Each squirrel works locally so that if the peer disappears, the emergent search algorithm self-adapts to its new context without interruption. Neither loss of administrative statistics nor waste of resources occurs. Furthermore, by packing several acorn ids in sacks, the squirrels reduce the number of messages they carry by a factor of 'n', where 'n' is the average number of acorn ids per sack. The more activity the P2P environment has, the greater the message reduction factor.

In both DFS CAS-based services, experimental research with the CAS propagation model help us to identify agent actions (i.e. properties) suitable for the BPD. Essential properties in the squirrel behaviors are identified to provide DFS emergent computations (i.e. search and allocation services). The BPD implementation uses these properties and behaviors to become a biologically inspired DFS with emergent computations.

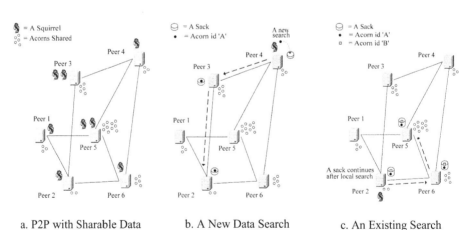

a. P2P with Sharable Data   b. A New Data Search   c. An Existing Search

Fig. 7. CAS Search Based on Squirrel Behaviors

3.2 BPD Design Overview

After we investigate the CAS based algorithms for the identified DFS emergent computations (Section 3), the next question is how to integrate them within a P2P

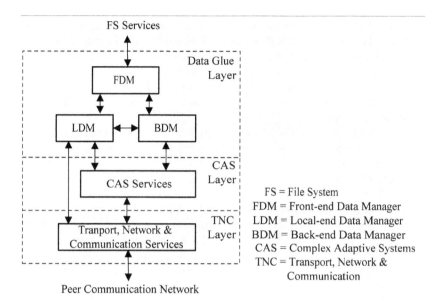

Fig. 8. BPD Architecture Stack

DFS design? For this, a BPD architecture stack (Figure 8) is designed that merges FS services with CAS algorithms in a layered structure. The BPD architecture stack runs in every peer and provide mechanisms for CAS member communication with the use of the P2P network. It is divided in three layers that together provide file system services to applications running on the peer. Camorlinga and Barker [17] provide an extended description of the BPD architecture.

Briefly the layers are:

- Data glue layer that processes file system calls and provides metadata services to keep control of files and directories. It consists of Front-end Data Manager, Local-end Data Manager, and Back-end Data Manager. These managers are responsible for the metadata services and the FS interface. The data glue layer also has the Application Programming Interface (API), the Common Line Interface, and the Graphical User Interface to client applications.

- CAS layer that provides DFS emergent computation engine responsible for the complex adaptive systems models and algorithms to provide data allocation[11], retrieval, replication and search emergent function services. The CAS layer algorithms [6][14] model and apply the behaviors and properties that are briefly described in Section 3.1.1 and 3.1.2.

- Transport, Network, and Communication (TNC) layer that interconnects peers across the distributed system with networking and communication services. It interfaces to the physical peer communication network.

---

[11] Allocation and search emergent services implement the retrieval and replication emergent services as discussed in Section 3.

The BPD also introduces the concept of a *bag* to represent a container where related data is kept. A *bag* is defined as a complete directory hierarchy of related files. The implicit locality of the CAS models used by the BPD localizes files that are under the same *bag*. In this way data locality is implemented by the use of *bags*. *Bag items* (i.e. *items*) are used to manage *bags*. An *item* is defined as a file, a folder within a bag or the bag itself. All FS application-programming interface (API) is defined around the *bag item* concept.

A *bags' holder* (i.e. *holder*) is a virtual place where multiple bags can dynamically exist. There is one *holder* per client computer. A *holder* grows as more bags are loaded, and shrinks as bags are unloaded. Bags are loaded automatically by changing to a different bag not already loaded (i.e. equivalent to a directory change in Unix).

Each BPD peer is independent of the others. A peer collaborates with other peers as shown in Figure 9. The TNC layer provides a communication path between them. The peers with their software entities (i.e. agents[12]) within the CAS layer work together when executing CAS models. A global DFS outcome emerges that balance resources, search data, maintains locality and scales according to the peer network characteristics. Figure 9 also shows how the BPD architecture layers are implemented in each peer.

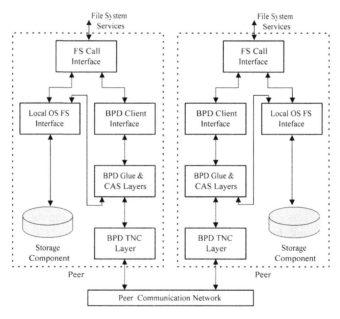

Fig. 9. The BPD Peer Network

It is important to stress that the software entities live in each peer at the CAS layer. The software entities execute natural behaviors analogies, briefly described in Section 3.1, which produce DFS emergent computations required within the P2P complex environment.

---

[12] Also known as squirrels in our CAS analogy.

4   Results

A BPD software prototype has been built and utilizes the CAS algorithms developed earlier [6][14] for its emergent function services. Our initial goal was to prove BPD concepts and instantiation of the Emergent Thinker paradigm. We develop the BPD architecture software in Java so it runs in each BPD peer (Figure 9).

The data glue layer implements the bag item concept introduced in section 3.2. The glue layer provides services to store, retrieve, manage, and search bag items (i.e. files) across the P2P complex environment. These glue layer services constitute the DFS API interface to client applications. The CAS layer implements both CAS algorithms for DFS allocation and discovery services. The CAS algorithms follow the biological behaviors described in Section 3.1. The TNC layer communication is TCP/IP socket-based among the peers. A more robust peer communication network could be implemented easily (e.g. JXTA-based P2P communication platform [18]) but this is sufficient for our purposes.

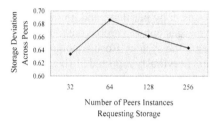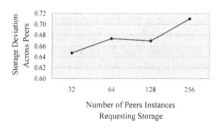

| a. P2P System with 500 Peers | b. P2P System with 700 Peers |

Fig. 10. Storage Allocation

Figure 10 shows representative results in two P2P systems with 500 and 700 peers respectively. The CAS allocation obtains a balance of storage resources under a variety of P2P characteristics (e.g. P2P size, number of peers storing data, P2P system-wide storage capacity utilization, and peer storage capacity among others). The storage allocation deviation is usually less than one, which means that each peer participates according to its storage capabilities and a system wide resource balance is achieved. Figure 10 results are similar to those obtained in CAS algorithm simulations carried on in P2P systems with more than 25000 peers [6]. BPD implements the CAS algorithms with the squirrel behavior properties that emerge with a self-adaptable system-wide resource allocation balance.

Representative discovery service results are shown in Figure 11. For the first group of results (Figure 11.a), we vary the number of peers in the environment and keep fixed the number of concurrent peers searching data. We obtain the average number of messages with its standard deviation that the BPD takes to discover the search items. A message is an acorn sack transfer from one peer to another (section 3.1.2). The number of peers searching is set to 10 in each P2P size. Each peer searches for 2 items. In terms of sharable storage, there are 100 peers with 10 sharable items per peer. All stored and search data are randomly generated in each experiment. The peers that participate in the experiments are randomly selected as well.

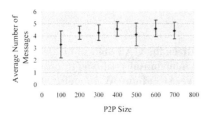
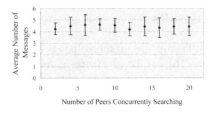

a. DFS Search Scalability

b. DFS Concurrent Search

Fig. 11. Data Discovery

For the second group of results (Figure 11.b), we fix the number of peers to 400 peers and vary the number of concurrent peers searching data. We also obtain the average number of messages with its standard deviation. In this experiment group, there are 128 peers with 10 sharable items per peer. Peers and data are randomly selected and generated in each experiment too. It is important to stress that in both groups there is no data replication; there is only one copy per item; and no indexes or auxiliary item location tables exist. The search emerges out as a global outcome of the CAS members that disseminates acorn sacks across the system. Results compare with emergent search simulations of thousands of peers previously reported [14].

5 Extended Work

The Emergent Thinker paradigm offers a large experimental area to expand current system research. BPD touches only a small piece where the paradigm can be applied. An operating system has many service areas where the paradigm can be instantiated. For example program execution, security, error detection and response, system accounting, *etc.* to mention a few. These areas could use a methodology similar to the one employed in BPD to achieve emergent computations that provide building functional blocks for their services. Eventually we can have a complete computing device based on CAS emergent computations. The more we experiment with CAS models, the more it will help us to understand its mechanisms and applicability in system research. Eventually this could facilitate development of a formal generic mathematical description of the Emergent Thinker paradigm.

In our BPD design analysis (Section 3), we conclude that the emergent computations on allocation and discovery services are essential. Retrieval and replication services are considered a higher level and easily implemented with the use of allocation and discovery services together with local directory tables. However, another design could try to implement these additional services and others with emergent computations to expand current work so it includes more emergent processing.

We believe it is appropriate to apply the Emergent Thinker paradigm to application domains where emergent computations are used to resolve specific, domain-oriented problems. Some examples of area domains include artificial intelligence, cognitive sciences, computational economics, optimization, biology, psychology, neurosciences, and engineering.

Current BPD work assumes logically isolated CAS domains. The CAS domains are logically isolated from the perspective that they compute independent from each other, however they might be running on the same physical hardware. Future agendas can analyze and obtain the fundamental bases when the CAS domains are interrelated at different levels and forms (e.g. hierarchical, intersected, dependant, *etc.*).

6   Conclusion

Systems research is an area where complex adaptive systems can provide innovative schemes and models. These schemes and models can provide emergent solutions (i.e. self-* properties) to a variety of design and implementation challenges in large distributed systems; some already exist but others have not been conceived before.

We have proposed a generic CAS emergent computing model. This model is later extended to become the Emergent Thinker paradigm that provides a different approach to distributed systems computing with the use of self-* properties. The CAS propagation model is proposed as an experimental means to understand and layout the fundamentals of the CAS emergent computing model.

The Biologically Inspired Peer-to-Peer Distributed File System (BPD) implements the Emergent Thinker paradigm. BPD provides file system services in a complex information system environment that is dynamic, self-organized, *ad-hoc* and decentralized. Some of the characteristics that make BPD distinctive include an architecture design and implementation that merges CAS models with P2P computing; CAS models for distributed services (storage, retrieval, search, and replication); and the use of commodity peers for storage and retrieval in a complex dynamic environment.

The Emergent Thinker paradigm offers an alternative computational model for complex information system environments with the use of Complex Adaptive Systems models and the self-* properties that emerge out it.

Acknowledgements

We want to thank Peter Graham, John Anderson and Jeff Diamond from University of Manitoba, Canada for their participation in useful discussions about emergent computations. We are grateful to the St. Boniface Research Center and the Medical Informatics Group by sponsoring this research work.

References

1. Bonabeau, E., Theraulaz, G. Swarm Smarts. Scientific American. Vol. 282, No. 3. (2000) 54-61
2. Dorigo, M., Maniezzo V., Colorni, A. The Ant System: Optimization by a Colony of Cooperating Agents. IEEE Transactions on Systems, Man and Cybernetics. Vol. 26, No. 1. (1996) 29-41
3. Babaoglu, O., Meling, H., Montresor, A. Anthill: A Framework for the Development of Agent Based Peer-To-Peer Systems. University of Bologna Technical Report UBLCS-2001-09. (2002)

4. Montresor, A. Anthill: A Framework for the Design and Analysis of Peer-To-Peer Systems. 4th European Research Seminar on Advances in Distributed Systems, Bertinoro, Italy. (2001)

5. Montresor, A., Meling, H., Babaoglu, O. Messor: Load-Balancing through a Swarm of Autonomous Agents. Proceedings of the 1st International Workshop on Agents and Peer-To-Peer Computing. Bologna, Italy, (2002) 125-137

6. Camorlinga, S., Barker, K., Anderson, J. Multiagent Systems for Resource Allocation in Peer-to-Peer Systems. Proceedings of the Winter International Symposium on Information and Communication Technologies. Cancun, Mexico. (2004) 173-178

7. Bonabeau, E., Meyer, C. Swarm Intelligence, a New Way to Think About Business. Harvard Business Review, (2001) 106-114

8. Solnon, C. Ants Can Solve Constraint Satisfaction Problems. IEEE Trans. on Evolutionary Computation. Vol. 6, No. 4. (2002) 347-357

9. Bourjot, C., Chevrier, V., Thomas, V. A New Swarm Mechanism Based on Social Spiders Colonies: From Web Weaving to Region Detection. Web Intelligence and Agent Systems: An International Journal. Vol. 1, No. 1. (2003) 47-64

10. Jelasity, M., Kowalczyk, van Steen, M. An Approach to Massively Distributed Aggregate Computing on Peer-to-Peer Networks. Proceedings 12th Euromicro Conference on Parallel, Distributed and Network based Processing. La Coruña, Spain. (2004)

11. White, T. Swarm Intelligence and Problem Solving in Telecommunications. Canadian AI Magazine. No 41. (1997) 14-16

12. Camorlinga, S., Barker, K. The Emergent Thinker. International Workshop on Self-* Properties in Complex Information Systems. Bertinoro, Italy. (2004) 69-71

13. Bach, M.J. The Design of the Unix Operating System. Prentice Hall. Englewood Cliffs, New Jersey USA (1986)

14. Camorlinga, S., Barker, K. Emergent Search in Large Distributed Systems. 8th International Conference on Parallel Problem Solving from Nature, Workshop on Games and Emergent Behaviors in Distributed Computing Environments. Birmingham, UK (2004)

15. Shulman, A., Nelson, E. Foraging Behavior of Squirrels as a Function of Season Progression From Early Fall Towards Winter. University of the South Ecology. See docs at www.sewanee.edu/biology/journal/2001/squirrels/squirrelbehavior.html.

16. Bureau of Natural Resources, Wildlife Division. Wildlife in Connecticut: Gray Squirrel. The Connecticut Department of Environmental Protection. See docs at dep.state.ct.us/burnatr/wildlife/factshts/gsqrl.htm

17. Camorlinga, S., Barker, K. The Design and Implementation of a Biologically Inspired Peer-to-Peer Distributed File System. University of Calgary Technical Report 2004-737-02. Department of Computer Science. Calgary AB Canada (2004)

18. The JXTA project. See docs at http://www.jxta.org

Evolutionary Games: An Algorithmic View[*]

Spyros Kontogiannis[1,2] and Paul Spirakis[1]

[1] Computer Technology Institute,
Riga Feraiou 61, 26221 Patras, Greece
{kontog, spirakis}@cti.gr
[2] Department of Computer Science,
University of Ioannina, 45110 Ioannina, Greece

Abstract. Evolutionary Game Theory is the study of strategic interactions among large populations of agents who base their decisions on simple, myopic rules. A major goal of the theory is to determine broad classes of decision procedures which both provide plausible descriptions of selfish behaviour and include appealing forms of aggregate behaviour. For example, properties such as the correlation between strategies' growth rates and payoffs, the connection between stationary states and the well-known game theoretic notion of Nash equilibria, as well as global guarantees of convergence to equilibrium, are widely studied in the literature.

Our paper can be seen as a quick introduction to Evolutionary Game Theory, together with a new research result and a discussion of many algorithmic and complexity open problems in the area. In particular, we discuss some algorithmic and complexity aspects of the theory, which we prefer to view more as *Game Theoretic Aspects of Evolution* rather than as *Evolutionary Game Theory*, since the term "evolution" actually refers to strategic adaptation of individuals' behaviour through a dynamic process and not the traditional evolution of populations. We consider this dynamic process as a *self-organization procedure* which, under certain conditions, leads to some kind of stability and assures robustness against invasion. In particular, we concentrate on the notion of the Evolutionary Stable Strategies (ESS). We demonstrate their qualitative difference from Nash Equilibria by showing that symmetric 2-person games with *random* payoffs have on average exponentially less ESS than Nash Equilibria. We conclude this article with some interesting areas of future research concerning the synergy of Evolutionary Game Theory and Algorithms.

1 Introduction

Game Theory is the study of *interactive* decision making, in the sense that those involved in the decisions are affected not only by their own choices, but also by the decisions of others.

---

[*] This work was partially supported by the EU within the Future and Emerging Technologies Programme under contract IST-2001-331116 (FLAGS) and within the 6th Framework Programme under contract 001907 (DELIS).

O. Babaoglu et al. (Eds.): SELF-STAR 2004, LNCS 3460, pp. 97–111, 2005.

This study is guided by two principles:

(1) The choices of players are affected by well-defined (and not changing) *preferences* over outcomes of decisions.
(2) Players act *strategically*, ie, they take into account the interaction between their choices and the ways other players act.

The dominant notion of conventional game theory is the belief that players are *rational* and this rationality is common knowledge. This common knowledge of rationality gives hope to equilibrium play. That is, players use their equilibrium strategies because of what would happen if they had not.

The point of departure for **Evolutionary Game Theory** is the view that the players are not always rational. In evolutionary games, "good" strategies *emerge* from a trial-and-error learning process, in which players discover that some strategies perform better than others. The players may do very little reasoning during this process. Instead, they simply take actions by rules of thumb, social norms, analogies for similar situations, or by other (possibly more complex) *methods* for converting stimuli into actions.

Thus, in evolutionary games we may say that the players are "programmed" to adopt some strategies. Typically, the evolution process deals with a huge population of players. As time proceeds, many small games are played (eg, among pairs of players that "happen" to meet). One then expects that strategies with high payoffs will spread within the population (by learning, copying successful strategies, or even by infection).

Indeed, evolutionary games in large populations of players create a *dynamic process*, where the frequencies of the strategies played (by population members) *change in time* because of the learning or selection forces guiding the players' strategic choices. Clearly, the rate of changes depends on the current strategy mix in the population. Such dynamics can be described by stochastic or deterministic models. The subject of evolutionary game theory is *exactly* the study of these dynamics. A very good presentation of evolutionary game dynamics can be found in [5]. For a more thorough study the reader is referred to [1].

Numerous paradigms for modeling individual choice in a large population have been proposed in the literature. For example, if each agent chooses its own strategy so as to optimize its own payoff ("one against all others" scenario) given the current population state (ie, other agents' strategies), then the aggregate behaviour is described by the **best-response dynamics** [8]. If each time an arbitrary user changes its strategy for any other strategy of a strictly better (but not necessarily the best) payoff, then the aggregate behaviour is described by the **better-response dynamics** or **Nash dynamics** [11]. In case that pairs of players are chosen at random (repeatedly) and then they engage in a bimatrix game ("one against one" scenario) whose payoff matrix determines according to some rule the gains of the strategies adopted by these two players, then we refer to **imitation dynamics**, the most popular version of which is the **replicator dynamics**[12].

If we allow sufficient time to pass, then the global "state" of the whole population "system" will respond to the forces of selection/learning by either *self-*

organizing and approaching a seemingly stationary state, or by leading to complicated behaviour, such as chaos. In fact, chaos is a very realistic possibility, appearing even in seemingly very simple systems. One of the goals of Evolutionary Game Theory is to *characterize* those cases where such chaotic behaviour does not occur.

In the "lucky" cases where the behaviour of the system is self-organizing and approaches some stationary configuration, we start to wonder how does this configuration "looks like". One major question here is whether the stationary configuration is "structurally stable". One can easily understand non-stable stationary states as follows: Simply check whether an arbitrarily small perturbation in the specification of the system can completely alter the properties of the stationary state.

Not surprisingly, evolutionary game processes that converge to stable states have usually the property that those states are also self-confirming equilibria (eg, Nash equilibria). This is one of the most robust results in Evolutionary Game Theory, the "folk theorem" that stability implies Nash equilibrium. In fact, one of the main approaches in the study of evolutionary games is the concept of **Evolutionary Stable Strategies** (ESS), which are nothing more than Nash Equilibria together with an additional stability property. This additional property is interpreted as ensuring that if an ESS is established in a population, and if a small proportion of the population adopts some *mutant* behaviour, then the process of selection (or learning) will eliminate the latter. Once an ESS is established in a population, it should therefore be able to withstand the pressures of mutation and selection.

It should be obvious by the above discussion that Evolutionary Game Theory is a very suitable framework for the study of self-organization. The framework draws on the rich tradition of Game Theory. It is mathematically precise and rigorous; it is general enough to be applied in many example areas such as Biology and species evolution, infection and spread of viruses in living populations or in the Internet, self-stabilization codes in distributed computing, etc. We would like to especially stress the suitability of such a theory for the study of self-stabilizing distributed protocols (eg, Dijkstra). To us it seems that ESS is the right concept.

However, Evolutionary Game Theory will become much more useful if we can *efficiently handle* its mathematical models. For example, suppose that we adopt a dynamic model for the strategic evolution of a population. How efficiently (if ever) can we answer the model's long-run behaviour? Can we predict that an evolutionary game process will stabilize, say, to an ESS? Even more, given the simple games that the population members play (ie, their payoffs) and given the description of the adaptation and learning forces, can we claim that such an evolutionary game process will indeed have any ESS? Can we compute how this ESS will look like, in the case of an affirmative answer?

Till now, the prime concern of evolutionary game mathematicians has been to understand the dynamics of evolutionary games (usually via tools of the rich field of nonlinear differential equations). We propose here a complementary concern: namely, the precise characterization of the *computational complexity* of the question of convergence in such games. This concern is tightly coupled with the quest for *efficient* techniques by which one can predict the long-term behaviour of evolutionary systems, or compute the precise structure and properties of the equilibria involved. Such an *algorithmic* examination may in addition allow for the understanding of how the *environment* of the population (its graph of allowable motions of players, its constraints on how players meet, etc) affects the evolution. It may also allow for *efficient comparison* of the the evolution trajectories of two phenomenally different evolving populations, in the spirit of isomorphisms or similar notions.

The proposed blend of the algorithmic thought with Evolutionary Game Theory, in fact, intends even to highlight *design rules* for self-organizing systems and to complement the older experimental, simulations-based approach, with efficient computational ways that calculate the impact of such design rules. A good example here is the rigorous computation of the *speed of convergence* for such self-organizing evolutionary systems.

For such a problem, several paradigms of the algorithmic thought may become handy. Such a paradigm is that of the *rapid mixing* of discrete stochastic combinatorial processes and its implications on the efficient approximate enumeration of the cardinality of the stationary state space.

The purpose of this paper is exactly to propose this algorithmic view of evolutionary game theory; we do so, by discussing some concrete open problems; and by offering some new research results on the ESS structure of the vast majority of evolutionary games.

2   Key Notions of Evolutionary Game Theory

2.1   Non-cooperative Games and Equilibria

We restrict our view to the class of *finite games in strategic form*. More precisely, let $I = \{1, 2, \ldots n\}$ be a set of **players**, where n is a positive integer. For each player $i \in I$, let S_i be her (finite) set of allowable actions, called the **pure strategies set**. The choice of a specific action $s_i \in S_i$ of a player $i \in I$, is called a **pure strategy** for this player. A vector $\mathbf{s} = (s_1, \ldots, s_n) \in \times_{i \in I} S_i$, where $s_i \in S_i$ is the pure strategy adopted by player $i \in I$, is called a **pure strategies profile** or a **configuration** of the players. The space of all the pure strategies profiles in the game is thus the cartesian product $S = \times_{i \in I} S_i$ of the players' pure strategies sets (usually called the **configuration space**).

For any configuration $\mathbf{s} \in S$ and any player $i \in I$, let $\pi_i(\mathbf{s})$ be a real number indicating the payoff to player i upon the adoption of this configuration by all the players of the game. In Economics, the payoffs are, eg, firms' profits, while in Biology they may represent *individual fitness*. In computer networks, where the players are users (eg, exchanging files), the payoff may be the opposite of a user's delay, when her data travel from a source to a destination in the network.

The finite collection of the real numbers $\{\pi_i(\mathbf{s}) : \mathbf{s} \in S\}$ defines player i's pure strategies payoff function. Let $\pi(\mathbf{s}) = (\pi_i(\mathbf{s}))_{i \in I}$ be the vector function of all the players' payoffs. Thus, a game in strategic form is simply described by a triplet $\Gamma = (I, S, \pi)$ where I is the set of players, S is the configuration space of the players, and π is the vector function of all the players' payoffs.

A **mixed strategy** for player $i \in I$ is a *probability distribution* (as opposed to a deterministic choice that is indicated by a pure strategy) over the set S_i of her allowable actions. We may represent any mixed strategy as a vector $\mathbf{x_i} = (x_i(s_{i,1}), x_i(s_{i,2}), \ldots, x_i(s_{i,m_i}))$, where $m_i = |S_i|$, $\forall j \in [m_i]^1$, $s_{i,j} \in S_i$ is the jth allowable action for player i, and $x_i(s_{i,j})$ is the probability that action $s_{i,j}$ is adopted by player i. In order to simplify notation, we shall represent this vector as $\mathbf{x_i} = (x_{i,1}, x_{i,2}, \ldots, x_{i,m_i})$. Of course, $\forall i \in I$, $\sum_{j \in [m_i]} x_{i,j} = 1$ and $\forall j \in [m_i]$, $x_{i,j} \in [0,1]$. Since for each player i all probabilities are non-negative and sum up to one, the **mixed strategies set** of player i is the set $\Delta_i \equiv \left\{ \mathbf{x_i} \in \mathbb{R}^{m_i}_{\geq 0} : \sum_{j \in [m_i]} = 1 \right\}$. Pure strategies are then just special, "extreme" mixed strategies in which the probability of a specific action is equal to one and all other probabilities equal zero.

A **mixed strategies profile** is a vector $\mathbf{x} = (\mathbf{x_1}, \ldots, \mathbf{x_n})$ whose components are themselves mixed strategies of the players, ie, $\forall i \in I$, $\mathbf{x_i} \in \Delta_i$. We denote by $\Delta = \times_{i \in I} \Delta_i \subset \mathbb{R}^m$ the cartesian product of mixed strategies sets of all the players, which is called the **mixed strategies space** of the game ($m = m_1 + \cdots + m_n$).

When the players adopt a mixed strategies profile $\mathbf{x} \in \Delta$, we can compute what is the *average* payoff, u_i, that player i gets (for $\mathbf{x}$) in the usual way: $u_i(\mathbf{x}) \equiv \sum_{\mathbf{s} \in S} P(\mathbf{x}, \mathbf{s}) \cdot \pi_i(\mathbf{s})$ where, $P(\mathbf{x}, \mathbf{s}) \equiv \prod_{i \in I} x_i(s_i)$ is the occurrence probability of configuration $\mathbf{s} \in S$ wrt the mixed profile $\mathbf{x} \in \Delta$. This (extended) function $u_i : \Delta \mapsto \mathbb{R}$ is called the **(mixed) payoff function** for player i.

Let us indicate by $(\mathbf{x_i}, \mathbf{y_{-i}})$ a mixed strategies profile where player i adopts the mixed strategy $\mathbf{x_i} \in \Delta_i$, where all other players adopt the mixed strategies that are determined by the mixed strategies profile $\mathbf{y} \in \Delta$. This notation is particularly convenient when a single player i considers a unilateral "deviation" $\mathbf{x_i} \in \Delta_i$ from a given profile $\mathbf{y} \in \Delta$. One of the cornerstones of Game Theory is the notion of Nash Equilibrium (NE in short) [10]:

Definition 1. *A* **best response** *of player i to a mixed strategies profile $\mathbf{y} \in \Delta$ is any element of the set $B_i(\mathbf{y}) \equiv \arg\max_{\mathbf{x_i} \in \Delta_i} \{u_i(\mathbf{x_i}, \mathbf{y_{-i}})\}$ (usually called the* **best response correspondence** *of player i to the profile $\mathbf{y}$). A* **Nash Equilibrium** *(NE) is any mixed strategies profile $\mathbf{y} \in \Delta$ having the property that, $\forall i \in I$, $\mathbf{y_i}$ is a best response of player i to $\mathbf{y}$. That is, $\forall i \in I$, $\mathbf{y_i} \in B_i(\mathbf{y})$.*

The nice thing about NE is that they always exist in finite strategic games:

Theorem 1 ([10]). *Every finite strategic game $\Gamma = (I, S, \pi)$ has at least one Nash Equilibrium.*

---

[1] For any integer $k \in \mathbb{N}$, $[k] \equiv \{1, 2, \ldots, k\}$.

2.2   Symmetric 2-Player Games

The subclass of symmetric 2-player games provides the basic setting for much of the Evolutionary Game Theory. Indeed, many of the important insights can be gained already in this (special) case.

Definition 2. *A finite strategic game* $\Gamma = (I, S, \pi)$ *is a* **2-player game** *when* $I = \{1, 2\}$. *It is called a* **symmetric** *2-player game if in addition,* $S_1 = S_2$ *and* $\forall (s_1, s_2) \in S, \pi_1(s_1, s_2) = \pi_2(s_2, s_1)$.

Note that in the case of a symmetric 2-player strategic game, the payoff functions of Γ can be represented by two $|S_1| \times |S_2|$ real matrices Π_1, Π_2 such that $\Pi_1[s_i, s_j] = \pi_1(s_i, s_j)$, $\forall (s_1, s_2) \in S$ and $\Pi_2 = \Pi_1^T$ (the transpose matrix of Π_1).

For any mixed strategies profile $\mathbf{x} = (\mathbf{x_1}, \mathbf{x_2}) \in \Delta$, the expected payoff of player 1 for this profile is $u_1(\mathbf{x}) = \mathbf{x_1}^T \Pi_1 \mathbf{x_2}$ while the payoff of player 2 is $u_2(\mathbf{x}) = \mathbf{x_2}^T \Pi_2 \mathbf{x_1}$.

In a symmetric 2-player game $\Pi = \Pi_1 = \Pi_2^T$ and thus we can fully describe the game by common action set S and the payoff matrix Π of the row player.

Two useful notions, especially in the case of 2-player games, are the **support** and the **extended support**:

Definition 3. *In a 2-player strategic game* $\Gamma = (\{1, 2\}, S, \pi)$, *the support of a mixed strategy* $\mathbf{x_1} \in \Delta_1$ ($\mathbf{x_2} \in \Delta_2$) *is the set of allowable actions of player 1 (player 2) that have* non-zero *probability in* $\mathbf{x_1}$ ($\mathbf{x_2}$). *More formally,* $\forall i \in \{1, 2\}, supp(\mathbf{x_i}) \equiv \{j \in S_i : x_i(j) > 0\}$. *The* **extended support** *of a mixed strategy* $\mathbf{x_2} \in \Delta_2$ *of player 2 is the set of* pure best responses *of player 1 to* $\mathbf{x_2}$. *That is,* $extsupp(\mathbf{x_2}) \equiv \{j \in S_1 : u_1(j, \mathbf{x_2}) \in \max_{\mathbf{x_1} \in \Delta_1} \{u_1(\mathbf{x_1}, \mathbf{x_2})\}\}$. *Similarly, the* **extended support** *of a mixed strategy* $\mathbf{x_1} \in \Delta_1$ *of player 1, is the set of* pure best responses *of player 2 to* $\mathbf{x_1}$. *That is,* $extsupp(\mathbf{x_1}) \equiv \{j \in S_2 : u_2(\mathbf{x_1}, j) \in \max_{\mathbf{x_2} \in \Delta_2} \{u_2(\mathbf{x_1}, \mathbf{x_2})\}\}$.

The following lemma is a direct consequence of the definition of a Nash Equilibrium:

Lemma 1. *If* $(\mathbf{x_1}, \mathbf{x_2}) \in \Delta$ *is a NE of a 2-player strategic game, then* $supp(\mathbf{x_1}) \subseteq extsupp(\mathbf{x_2})$ *and* $supp(\mathbf{x_2}) \subseteq extsupp(\mathbf{x_1})$.

Proof. The support of a strategy that is adopted by a player is exactly the set of actions which the player takes with positive probability. At a NE $(\mathbf{x_1}, \mathbf{x_2}) \in \Delta$, each player assigns positive probability only to (not necessarily all the) pure strategies which are best responses to the other player's strategy. On the other hand, the extended support of, say, $\mathbf{x_2}$ is exactly the set of all the actions (ie, pure strategies) of player 1 that are best responses to $\mathbf{x_2}$, and vice versa. That is, $supp(\mathbf{x_1}) \subseteq extsupp(\mathbf{x_2})$ and $supp(\mathbf{x_2}) \subseteq extsupp(\mathbf{x_1})$.

When we wish to argue about the vast majority of symmetric 2-player games, one way is to assume that the real numbers in the set $\{\Pi[i, j] : (i, j) \in S\}$ are independently drawn from a probability distribution F. For example, F can be the uniform distribution in an interval $[a, b] \in \mathbb{R}$. Then, a typical symmetric 2-player game Γ is just an instance of the implied random experiment that is described in the following definition.

Definition 4. *A symmetric 2-player game $\Gamma = (S, \Pi)$ is an instance of a (symmetric 2-player) random game wrt the probability distribution F, if and only if $\forall i, j \in S$, the real number $\Pi[i, j]$ is an independently and identically distributed random variable drawn from F.*

Definition 5. *A strategy pair $(\mathbf{x_1}, \mathbf{x_2}) \in \Delta^2$ for a symmetric 2-player game $\Gamma = (S, \Pi)$ is a symmetric Nash Equilibrium, if and only if (1) $(\mathbf{x_1}, \mathbf{x_2})$ is a NE for Γ, and (2) $\mathbf{x_1} = \mathbf{x_2}$.*

Not all NE of a symmetric 2-player game need be symmetric. However it is known that there is at least one such equilibrium:

Theorem 2 ([10]). *Every symmetric 2-player game has at least one symmetric Nash Equilibrium.*

2.3   Evolutionary Stable Strategies

We will now restrict our attention to symmetric 2-player strategic games. So, fix a symmetric 2-player strategic game $\Gamma = (S, \Pi)$, for which the mixed strategies space is Δ^2. Suppose that all the individuals of a large population are programmed to play the same (either pure or mixed) *incumbent* strategy $\mathbf{x} \in \Delta$, whenever they are involved in the game Γ. Suppose also that a small group of *invaders* appears in the population. Let $\varepsilon \in (0, 1)$ be the share of invaders in the postentry population. Assume that all the invaders are programmed to play the (pure or mixed) strategy $\mathbf{y} \in \Delta$ whenever they are involved in Γ.

Pairs of individuals in this *dimorphic* postentry population are now repeatedly drawn at random to play always the same symmetric 2-player game Γ. If an individual plays, the probability that her opponent will play strategy $\mathbf{x}$ is $1 - \varepsilon$ and that of playing strategy $\mathbf{y}$ is ε. This is equivalent with a match with an individual who plays the *mixed* strategy $\mathbf{z} = (1 - \varepsilon)\mathbf{x} + \varepsilon\mathbf{y}$. The postentry payoff to the incumbent strategy $\mathbf{x}$ is then $u(\mathbf{x}, \mathbf{z})$ and that of the invaders' is just $u(\mathbf{y}, \mathbf{z})$ ($u = u_1 = u_2$). Intuitively, evolutionary forces will select *against* the invader if $u(\mathbf{x}, \mathbf{z}) > u(\mathbf{y}, \mathbf{z})$.

Definition 6. *A strategy $\mathbf{x}$ is **evolutionary stable** (ESS in short) if for any strategy $\mathbf{y} \neq \mathbf{x}$ there exists a barrier $\bar{\varepsilon} = \bar{\varepsilon}(\mathbf{y}) \in (0, 1)$ such that $\forall 0 < \varepsilon \leqslant \bar{\varepsilon}$, $u(\mathbf{x}, \mathbf{z}) > u(\mathbf{y}, \mathbf{z})$ where $\mathbf{z} = (1 - \varepsilon)\mathbf{x} + \varepsilon\mathbf{y}$.*

One can easily prove the following characterization of ESS, which sometimes appears as an alternative definition:

Proposition 1. *Let $\mathbf{x} \in \Delta$ be a (mixed in general) strategy profile that is adopted by the whole population. The following sentences are equivalent:*

(i) $\mathbf{x}$ is an evolutionary stable strategy.
(ii) $\mathbf{x}$ satisfies the following properties, $\forall \mathbf{y} \in \Delta \setminus \{\mathbf{x}\}$:
    [P1] $u(\mathbf{y}, \mathbf{x}) \leqslant u(\mathbf{x}, \mathbf{x})$
    [P2] *If $u(\mathbf{y}, \mathbf{x}) = u(\mathbf{x}, \mathbf{x})$ then $u(\mathbf{y}, \mathbf{y}) < u(\mathbf{x}, \mathbf{y})$*

Observe that the last proposition implies that an ESS $\mathbf{x} \in \Delta$ has to be a Nash Equilibrium of the underlying symmetric 2-player strategic game Γ (due to [**P1**]) and has to be strictly better than any invading strategy $\mathbf{y} \in \Delta \setminus \{\mathbf{x}\}$, against $\mathbf{y}$ itself, in case that $\mathbf{y}$ is a best-response strategy against $\mathbf{x}$ in Γ (due to [**P2**]).

Definition 7. *A mixed strategy* $\mathbf{x} \in \Delta$ *is* **completely mixed** *iff and only if* $supp(\mathbf{x}) = S$ *(that is, it assigns to all the allowable actions non-zero probability).*

It is not hard to prove the following lemma:

Lemma 2 (Haigh 1975, [4]). *If a completely mixed strategy* $\mathbf{x} \in \Delta$ *is an ESS, then it is the* unique *ESS of the evolutionary game.*

An Example. A classical example in Evolutionary Game Theory is the Hawk-Dove game, in which there are two possible pure strategies for the players in the population: fighting (ie, being a hawk) or withdrawing (ie, being a dove). Let's denote these two strategies by H and D respectively. Strategy H obtains a payoff $V > 0$ and strategy D gets a zero payoff, when H is played against strategy D (ie, hawk eats dove). However, when both players are determined to fight (ie, they both adopt strategy H), then each of them gets a payoff $\frac{V-C}{2}$, where $C > 0$ is the cost for losing the fight (ie, due to injury). Finally, when both players are willing to retreat (ie, they both adopt strategy D), then each player gets a payoff of $\frac{V}{2}$. The above described 2-player strategic game is symmetric and has the following payoff matrix:

$$\Pi = \begin{bmatrix} \frac{V-C}{2} & V \\ 0 & \frac{V}{2} \end{bmatrix}$$

We assume that the cost of losing a fight exceeds the profit of a victory, ie, $C > V$. For example, for $C = 6$ and $V = 4$ the payoff matrix is

$$\Pi = \begin{bmatrix} -1 & 4 \\ 0 & 2 \end{bmatrix}$$

and the (unique) symmetric NE for the symmetric 2-player game $\Gamma = (\{H, D\}, \Pi)$ is the completely mixed strategy $\mathbf{x} = (\frac{2}{3}, \frac{1}{3})$. One can easily prove that $\mathbf{x}$ is also an ESS. So, by the previous lemma we deduce that it is the *unique* ESS of the Hawk-Dove evolutionary game.

2.4   Population Dynamics

A simple way to think about the evolution of a population whose members play a 2-player game whenever they meet, is to consider the "state" of the population at time t to be a vector $\mathbf{x}(t) = (\mathbf{x_1}(t), \mathbf{x_2}(t), \ldots, \mathbf{x_m}(t))$, where $S = \{1, 2, \ldots, m\}$ is a set of actions, individuals are only allowed to adopt *pure strategies* in S, and $\mathbf{x_i}(t)$ is the population share playing strategy $i \in S$ at time (ie, round) t.

Let's assume that when two individuals meet, they play the symmetric 2-player game $\Gamma = (S, \Pi)$, where $\Pi = \Pi_1 = \Pi_2^T$. We can interpret for example the payoff value $\Pi_1[i,j]$ as the number of offsprings of the individual that played strategy i, against an individual who played strategy j. (Similarly, $\Pi_2[i,j] = \Pi[j,i]$ is the number of offsprings of the individual playing strategy j, against an individual playing strategy i). How are the generated offsprings programmed? There are various ways to define this. For example, they may play the *same strategy as their parents*. Then, we have a particular kind of dynamics (usually called the **replicator dynamics**). Of course, for the model to be complete, one has to say how often they are selected from the population.

In general, such a way of thought usually results in defining $\mathbf{x}(t)$ via either a *stochastic* process, or via a system of differential equations describing its rate of change (that is, $\dot{\mathbf{x}}(t) = f(\mathbf{x}(t),t)$, where f is usually a non-linear deterministic function). Then the model becomes a sample of a vast variety of dynamical system models and one can study its evolution by finding how $\mathbf{x}(t)$ changes in time. It is not hard to modify these models in order to capture effects like noise, random choice of the strategy $\mathbf{y}$ to play, or some particular rule of "learning" which are the good strategies, based on the payoffs that the individuals get (and perhaps, some desirable payoff values that act as thresholds for changes in strategy). For more details, we recommend that the interested readers have a look at [5, 13].

3   The Expected Number of ESS in Random Games

Let $\mathcal{P}_k \equiv \{(v_1,\ldots,v_k) \in \mathbb{R}^k_{\geqslant 0} : \sum_{i \in [k]} v_i = 1\}$. In this section we study the number of ESS in a generic evolutionary game with an action set $S = [n]$ and a payoff matrix which is an $n \times n$ matrix U whose entries are **iid** random variables drawn from a probability distribution F. For any non-negative vector $\mathbf{x} \in \mathcal{P}_k$ for some $k \in \mathbb{N}$, let $Y_{\mathbf{x}} \equiv \mathcal{P}_k \setminus \{\mathbf{x}\}$. The following statement, proved by Haigh, is a necessary and sufficient condition of a mixed strategy $\mathbf{s} \in \mathcal{P}_n$ being an ESS, given that $(\mathbf{s},\mathbf{s})$ is a symmetric NE of the symmetric game $\Gamma = (S,U)$.

Lemma 3 (Haigh 1975, [4]). *Let $(\mathbf{s},\mathbf{s}) \in \mathcal{P}_n \times \mathcal{P}_n$ be a symmetric NE for the symmetric game $\Gamma = (S,U)$ and let $M = extsupp(\mathbf{s})$. Let also $\mathbf{x}$ be the projection of $\mathbf{s}$ on M, and C the submatrix of U consisting of the rows and columns indicated by M. Then $\mathbf{s}$ is an ESS if and only if $\forall \mathbf{y} \in Y_{\mathbf{x}}$, $(\mathbf{y} - \mathbf{x})^T C(\mathbf{y} - \mathbf{x}) < 0$.*

We observe that the following lemma also holds, whose proof is straightforward (comes from the definition of ESS):

Lemma 4. *Let $\mathbf{s} \in \mathcal{P}_n$ be an ESS of $\Gamma = (S,U)$. Then $(\mathbf{s},\mathbf{s})$ is a symmetric NE for Γ.*

Combining lemmas 3 and 4 we observe that it is enough to examine only symmetric NE of $\Gamma = (S,U)$ in order to find out whether this game possesses an ESS. The following lemma will be useful in our investigation:

Lemma 5. *Let X_1, X_2 be two independent random variables of the same mean $\mu = \mathbb{E}\{X_1\} = \mathbb{E}\{X_2\}$, whose densities are symmetric around μ (we call them* **symmetric random variables**). *Then* $\mathbb{P}\{X_1 \geqslant X_2\} \leqslant \frac{1}{2}$.

Proof. Since X_1 and X_2 are symmetric around μ, we have that $\mathbb{P}\{X_i < \mu\} \leqslant \frac{1}{2}$, $i \in \{1, 2\}$ and also $\mathbb{P}\{X_i > \mu\} \leqslant \frac{1}{2}$, $i \in \{1, 2\}$. Now,

$$\mathbb{P}\{X_2 > X_1\} \geqslant \mathbb{P}\{X_2 > X_1 | X_1 < \mu\} \cdot \mathbb{P}\{X_1 < \mu\} \geqslant 1 \cdot \frac{1}{2} \Rightarrow$$

$$\Rightarrow \mathbb{P}\{X_1 \geqslant X_2\} = 1 - \mathbb{P}\{X_2 > X_1\} \leqslant 1 - \frac{1}{2} = \frac{1}{2}$$

We now show our main theorem:

Theorem 3. *Let $\Gamma = (S, U)$ be an instance of a random symmetric 2-player game in which the payoff entries are* **iid** *random variables drawn from the uniform distribution F that assigns values from the range $[0, A]$, for some constant A. Then $\mathbb{E}\{\#ESS\} = o(\mathbb{E}\{\#SymmetricNE\})$.*

Proof. Consider an arbitrary symmetric NE $\mathbf{s} \in \mathcal{P}_n$, and assume wlog that $extsupp(\mathbf{s}) = [m]$ for some $1 \leqslant m \leqslant n$ (by reordering the action set S). Assume also that $s_1 \geqslant s_2 \geqslant \cdots \geqslant s_r > 0 = s_{r+1} = \cdots = s_m$ for some $1 \leqslant r \leqslant m$ (ie, its support is $supp(\mathbf{s}) = [r]$). Let $\mathbf{x} = \mathbf{s}|_{[m]} \equiv (s_1, \ldots, s_m) \in \mathcal{P}_m$ be the projection of $\mathbf{s}$ to its extended support. Let also $C = U|_{[m],[m]}$ be the submatrix of U consisting of its first m rows and columns. By lemmas 3 and 4 we know that a necessary condition for $\mathbf{s}$ being an ESS is that C is negative definite, ie, $\forall \mathbf{y} \in Y_{\mathbf{x}}$, $(\mathbf{y} - \mathbf{x})^T C (\mathbf{y} - \mathbf{x}) < 0$. We shall prove that this is highly unlikely to hold for any mixed strategy $\mathbf{s}$ with support of size $r \gg 1$. Set $\varepsilon = s_r > 0$. Consider the following collection of vectors from $Y_{\mathbf{x}}$: $\forall 1 \leqslant k \leqslant \min\{r, m-1\}$,

$$\mathbf{y}^{\mathbf{k}} = \left(x_1, \ldots, x_{k-1}, x_k - \varepsilon, x_{k+1} + \frac{\varepsilon}{m-k}, \ldots, x_m + \frac{\varepsilon}{m-k}, x_{m+1}, \ldots, x_n\right)$$

and

$$\mathbf{z}^{\mathbf{k}} = \mathbf{y}^{\mathbf{k}} - \mathbf{x} = \left(0, \ldots, 0, -\varepsilon, \frac{\varepsilon}{m-k}, \ldots, \frac{\varepsilon}{m-k}, 0, \ldots, 0\right)$$

Then we have: $\forall 1 \leqslant k \leqslant \min\{r, m-1\}$,

$$(\mathbf{z}^{\mathbf{k}})^T C \mathbf{z} = \varepsilon^2 \cdot C_{k,k} - \frac{\varepsilon^2}{m-k} \sum_{j=k+1}^{m} [C_{k,j} + C_{j,k}] + \frac{\varepsilon^2}{(m-k)^2} \sum_{k+1 \leqslant i,j \leqslant m} C_{i,j} \quad (1)$$

By lemma 3 we know that a necessary condition for the mixed strategy $\mathbf{s}$ (for which we already assumed that it is such that $(\mathbf{s}, \mathbf{s})$ is a symmetric NE for (S, U)) to be an ESS is that $\forall 1 \leqslant k \leqslant \min\{r, m-1\}$,

$$(\mathbf{y}^{\mathbf{k}} - \mathbf{x})^T C (\mathbf{y}^{\mathbf{k}} - \mathbf{x}) = (\mathbf{z}^{\mathbf{k}})^T C \mathbf{z} < 0 \quad \overset{/\ast\ \varepsilon > 0\ \ast/}{\Longrightarrow}$$

$$\frac{1}{m-k} \sum_{j=k+1}^{m} [C_{k,j} + C_{j,k}] > C_{k,k} + \frac{1}{(m-k)^2} \sum_{k+1 \leqslant i,j \leqslant m} C_{i,j}$$

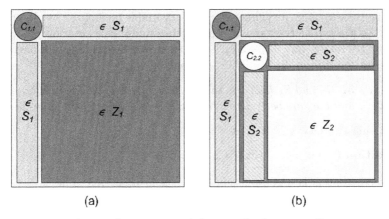

Fig. 1. The partition of the payoff sub-matrix C

Consider now the collection of events $E = \left\{ \mathcal{E}_k \equiv \mathbb{I}_{\{S_k > C_{k,k} + Z_k\}} \right\}_{1 \leqslant k \leqslant \min\{r, m-1\}}$ where $S_k \equiv \frac{1}{m-k} \sum_{j=k+1}^{m} [C_{k,j} + C_{j,k}]$ and $Z_k \equiv \frac{1}{(m-k)^2} \sum_{k+1 \leqslant i,j \leqslant m} C_{i,j}$. Now observe that

(a) Z_k does not include in this sum any of $C_{k,j}, C_{j,k}, C_{k,k}$. Thus, Z_k is independent of S_k and $C_{k,k}$.

(b) S_k is not affected at all by the values of $C_{k,k}$. Therefore, S_k is also independent of $C_{k,k}$.

Let $R_k \equiv C_{k,k} + Z_k$. By our previous remarks, we get the following corollary:

Corollary 1. R_k *is a random variable independent of* S_k.

By linearity of expectation and assuming that any random variable that is distributed according to F has an expectation μ, we have that $\mathbb{E}\{R_k\} = \mathbb{E}\{C_{k,k}\} + \frac{1}{(m-k)^2} \sum_{k+1 \leqslant i,j \leqslant m} \mathbb{E}\{C_{i,j}\} = \mu + \frac{(m-k)^2 \cdot \mu}{(m-k)^2} = 2\mu$. Similarly, $\mathbb{E}\{S_k\} = \frac{1}{m-k} \sum_{k+1 \leqslant j \leqslant m} [\mathbb{E}\{C_{k,j}\} + \mathbb{E}\{C_{k,j}\}] = \frac{(m-k) \cdot 2\mu}{m-k} = 2\mu$. That is, we deduce that

Corollary 2. $\mathbb{E}\{R_k\} = \mathbb{E}\{S_k\}$.

Notice also that the following lemma holds, whose proof is straightforward:

Proposition 2. *Let* $X_1, \ldots, X_t$ *be* **iid** *uniform random variables drawn from* $[0, A]$. *Then* $X = \sum_{j=1}^{t} X_i$ *is a symmetric random variable around its expectation* $\mathbb{E}\{X\} = \frac{tA}{2}$, *in the interval* $[0, tA]$.

Since $\{C_{k,j}, C_{j,k}\}_{k+1 \leqslant j \leqslant m}$ is a collection of $2(m-k)$ **iid** uniform random variables on $[0, A]$, then $(m-k)S_k$ is symmetric random variable around its expectation $2(m-k)\mu$ in the interval $[0, 2(m-k)A]$, or equivalently, S_k is a symmetric random variable around its expectation 2μ in the interval $[0, 2A]$. Similarly, $\{C_{i,j}\}_{k+1 \leqslant i,j \leqslant m}$ is a collection of $(m-k)^2$ **iid** uniform random variables on $[0, A]$

and thus, $(m-k)^2 Z_k$ is a symmetric random variable on $[0, (m-k)^2 A]$, or equivalently, Z_k is a symmetric random variable (around its expectation $\mathbb{E}\{Z_k\} = \mu$) on $[0, A]$. Therefore, $R_k = Z_k + C_{k,k}$ is also a symmetric random variable (around its expectation 2μ) on $[0, 2A]$. Thus, we conclude that

Corollary 3. R_k and S_k have the same expectation 2μ, they are independent of each other, and they are both symmetric random variables in the interval $[0, 2A]$.

By applying lemma 5 we get that

Proposition 3. $\forall k \geqslant 1$, $\mathbb{P}\{\mathcal{E}_k\} = \mathbb{P}\{S_k > R_k\} \leqslant \frac{1}{2}$.

Observe that E is a conjunction of *independent* events. This is because $\mathcal{E}_1$ actually describes a structure of the entries in C, by comparing twice the average value of those entries involved in S_1 against the value of $C_{1,1}$ plus the average value of the entries in Z_1. Nevertheless, $\mathcal{E}_1$ says nothing about the *internal* structure of the coordinates involved in Z_1. It only considers their average value. On the other hand, $\mathcal{E}_2$ (conditioned on the total value of the entries in Z_1) actually partially describes the *internal* structure of the coordinates in Z_1 by comparing twice the average value of the coordinates in S_2 with the value of $C_{2,2}$ plus the average value of the coordinates in Z_2 and does not care about the values of $C_{1,1}$ or the coordinates in S_1. Yet, this event says nothing about the *internal* structure of the coordinates in Z_3, except for its total value, a.s.o. To have an idea about the nested grouping of the coordinates of C, the reader is referred to figure 1. More formally, $\mathbb{P}\{E\} = \mathbb{P}\{\mathcal{E}_1\}\,\mathbb{P}\{\mathcal{E}_2 \mid \mathcal{E}_1\}\cdots\mathbb{P}\left\{\mathcal{E}_{r*} \mid \bigcap_{j=1}^{r^*-1}\mathcal{E}_j\right\}$ where $r^* = \min\{r, m-1\}$. But, due to our structural argument, $\mathbb{P}\left\{\mathcal{E}_i \mid \bigcap_{j=1}^{i-1}\mathcal{E}_j\right\} = \mathbb{P}\{\mathcal{E}_i\}$ for any $i \in [r^*]$, since $\mathcal{E}_i$ compares the values inside a sum, while $\bigcap_{j=1}^{i-1}\mathcal{E}_j$ compares the total value of that sum as a whole with the total value of variables out of this sum. Hence, by proposition 3 we conclude that

$$\mathbb{P}\{E\} = \prod_{j=1}^{r^*}\mathbb{P}\{\mathcal{E}_j\} \leqslant \left(\frac{1}{2}\right)^{r^*} \tag{2}$$

It is worth mentioning that for the random 2-player games considered in [9] (where each entry of the payoff matrices is uniformly distributed in the unit sphere) almost all the NE have supports whose sizes are approximately $0.315915n$. The scaling of the unit interval $[0,1]$ to $[0,A]$ for any $A > 0$ does not affect this result, since a NE is determined by linear constraints wrt the support (each support is defined as a system of *linear* inequalities for a 2-player game, cf. [6]) and we can scale by A each inequality, so long as $A > 0$.

Let now $q = \#NE$ be the number of NE in our game, that is of course a random variable. For each NE $\mathbf{x}$ of the game, let $I(\mathbf{x}) = \mathbb{I}_{\{\mathbf{x}\text{ is ESS}\}}$ be the corresponding indicator variable of $\mathbf{x}$ being also an ESS. Since an ESS implies our event E, we have that

$$\mathbb{E}\{I(\mathbf{x})\} = \mathbb{P}\{I(\mathbf{x}) = 1\} = \mathbb{P}\{\mathbf{x}\text{ is an ESS}\} \leqslant \mathbb{P}\{E\} \Rightarrow \mathbb{E}\{I(\mathbf{x})\} \leqslant \left(\tfrac{1}{2}\right)^{r^*}$$

$$\Rightarrow \qquad \mathbb{E}\{\#ESS\} = \mathbb{E}\left\{\sum_{\mathbf{x}=NE} I(\mathbf{x})\right\} \leqslant \left(\tfrac{1}{2}\right)^{r^*} \cdot \mathbb{E}\{\#NE\}$$

by Wald's inequality for a random sum of random variables. So, we have established that, since $0.315915n \leqslant r \leqslant m$, $\mathbb{E}\{\#ESS\} = \mathcal{O}\left(\frac{\mathbb{E}\{\#NE\}}{2^{0.315915n}}\right)$ which proves our main theorem.

Remark 1. If we also adopt the numerical analysis of [9] on the expected number of NE in such a game, according to which the expected number of NE is $\exp(0.281644n + \mathcal{O}(\log n))$, then we will come to the conclusion that $\mathbb{E}\{\#ESS\} = \frac{\exp(0.281644n + \mathcal{O}(\log n))}{2^{0.315915n}} = \exp(0.281644n + \mathcal{O}(\log n) - 0.2189755n) = \exp(0.0626675n + \mathcal{O}(\log n))$ as $n \to \infty$. This is still exponential, but also exponentially smaller than the expected number of NE.

4   Open Algorithmic and Complexity Problems in Evolutionary Game Theory

4.1   ESS Existence and Construction

Simple symmetric 2-player games with no ESS are known to exist. For example, if an evolutionary game uses the matrix (see Samuelson 1997, [7] p. 46)

$$\Pi = \begin{bmatrix} (1,1) & (2,-2) & (-2,2) \\ (-2,2) & (1,1) & (2,-2) \\ (2,-2) & (-2,2) & (1,1) \end{bmatrix}$$

has no ESS.

Given the matrix of a symmetric 2-player game, with $|S| = s$:

(a) Can we decide whether an ESS exists or not?
(b) If there is an ESS, can we compute it (or even approximate it) in polynomial time?

In [2] it has been shown that the decision problem above is both $\mathcal{NP}$–complete and co-$\mathcal{NP}$–complete. However, this does not exclude the possibility of efficient algorithms for both problems when s is moderately small, or at least efficient approximation algorithms.

In addition, assume that we are given a symmetric 2-player game Γ with a NE strategy $\mathbf{x}$ as input. How efficiently can we check whether $\mathbf{x}$ is an ESS? That is, how hard is the additional stability condition [**P2**] in terms of computational complexity?

4.2   Imposing Structural Properties of a Game into the Evolutionary Dynamics

Our last question deals with some new ways of interaction in the evolutionary dynamics of a game, that will also depict the special structure of the corresponding traditional game. For example, when a virus spreads in a network, the architecture of the network itself and the starting points of the virus in it should affect somehow the success of the virus. The proposed game theoretic models of evolution proposed so far in the literature, mainly focus on the case where the individuals in a population collide with each other in a random fashion. Ie, the underlying "interaction" infrastructure is represented by a clique. What if this is not the case, and we have instead some special graph representing the interactions? We need new evolutionary models to capture such cases, that will somehow encode the structure of this graph in the dynamics, via elementary properties (eg, the connectivity or the expansion of the graph).

To make an example here, let's assume an initial population of hawks and doves with the following rules:

- When a hawk meets a dove, it kills it.
- When two hawks meet, they kill each other.
- When two doves meet, they both survive.

The matrix of the game is thus

$$\Pi = \begin{bmatrix} (0,0) & (1,0) \\ (0,1) & (1,1) \end{bmatrix}$$

If the hawks are all (say) in a connected graph and the doves are isolated, then if we assume random moves of individuals along the edges of the graph, then all the doves will survive for ever and at most one hawk will survive in the network. However, if the doves coexist with the hawks in the same connected graph (eg, a clique) then the probability of eventual survival of doves is almost zero. We can thus state the following problem:

> Given the matrix A of the game as above, a graph G and an initial placement of the hawks and doves on its vertices, and given that each animal follows a random walk on G, compute the survival probability of each species.

The complexity of this problem is wide open.

4.3   Evolutionary Games as Algorithms

Perhaps the most classical problem in Computational Game Theory is the following:

> **NE-CONSTRUCT** Given the payoff matrix $A \in \mathbb{R}^{n \times n}$ of a 2-player strategic game, find a Nash Equilibrium.

Only exponential-time algorithms are known for this problem today. If A is symmetric, consider instead an evolution process where the possible strategies are allt eh strategies of A initially. Since "stability implies Nash" (see property[**P2**]), by the folklore theorem of Evolutionary Game Theory, we could impose some stable dynamics on the population that plays A and find (via solving the dynamical system) its stable states. This would give a NE for A. Thus, we reduce the problem **NE-CONSTRUCT** to the problem of (efficiently) finding an (asymptotically) stable state of an evolutionary process. While this approach is not yet explored in full generality, some progress has been made for simple congestion games [3]).

4.4   Other Issues

Many other issues can inspire algorithmic and complexity questions. Examples are equilibrium selection, trajectory prediction, isomorphism of two evolutionary processes, etc. We advocate here that a new subfield is wide open.

References

1. Cressman R. *Evolutionary dynamics and extensive form games.* MIT Press, 2003.
2. Etessami K., Lochbihler A. The computational complexity of evolutionary stable strategies. Technical Report 55, Electronic Colloquium on Computational Complexity (ECCC), 2004. ISSN 1433-8092.
3. Fischer S., Vöcking B. On the evolution of selfish routing. In *Proc. of the 12th European Symposium on Algorithms (ESA '04)*, pages 323–334. Springer, 2004.
4. Haigh J. Game theory and evolution. *Advances in Applied Probability*, 7:8–11, 1975.
5. Hofbauer J., Sigmund K. Evolutionary game dynamics. *Bulletin of the American Mathematical Society*, 40(4):479–519, 2003.
6. Koutsoupias E., Papadimitriou C. Worst-case equilibria. In *Proc. of the 16thAnnual Symposium on Theoretical Aspects of Computer Science (STACS '99)*, pages 404–413. Springer-Verlag, 1999.
7. Samuelson Larry. *Evolutionary Games and Equilibrium Selection (Economic Learning and Social Evolution).* The MIT Press, 1997.
8. Matsui A., Gilboa I. Social stability and equilibrium. *Econometrica*, 59:859–867, 1991.
9. McLennan A., Berg J. The asymptotic expected number of nash equilibria of two player normal form games. Working document, Department of Economics, Univ. of Minnesota, 2004.
10. Nash J. F. Noncooperative games. *Annals of Mathematics*, 54:289–295, 1951.
11. Rosenthal R.W. A class of games possessing pure-strategy nash equilibria. *International Journal of Game Theory*, 2:65–67, 1973.
12. Taylor P. D., Jonker L. Evolutionary stable strategies and game dynamics. *Mathematical Biosciences*, 40:145–156, 1978.
13. Weibull, Jörgen W. *Evolutionary Game Theory.* The MIT Press, 1995.

Model Based Diagnosis and Contexts in Self Adaptive Software

Paul Robertson and Robert Laddaga

Computer Science and Artificial Intelligence Laboratory,
Massachusetts Institute of Technology,
Cambridge, Massachusetts, USA
rladdaga@ai.mit.edu

Abstract. Self Adaptive Software monitors its own operation and attempts to correct deviations from required behavior. In the self adaptive architectures we are developing, it accomplishes this by diagnosing the sources of deviant behavior, whether internal program problems, or contextual changes in an embedded program's environment. The software then responds by reconfiguring itself, to use alternate procedures that either correct the malfunction, or perform better in the current context. We present the GRAVA architecture as an example, and show how it utilizes diagnosis of the external context to limit complexity and enhance robustness in several vision applications.

1 Introduction

Software development technology is critically in need of new paradigms supporting increased robustness. Robustness is of great concern now because our systems are becoming more complex, and because they are increasingly sensing and controlling our physical environment and processes. One such paradigm is self-*, a collection of properties such as self reconfigurable, self adaptive, self aware, and self checking. We believe that all self-* systems share the following traits:

- Deferral of design decisions to runtime (a form of late binding)
- Metaprogramming
- Explicit attention to state of the world
- Attention to program state

A design decision in the context of any possible program state, any possible input, and any possible condition of the environment is inherently more complex than deciding what to do given a specific input in the context of a specific state of the program and the environment. Self-* systems attempt to use various forms of metaprogramming to enable them to defer decisions to runtime, when attention to the state of the world and the state of the program can be used to reduce the complexity that would otherwise be overwhelming.

O. Babaoglu et al. (Eds.): SELF-STAR 2004, LNCS 3460, pp. 112–127, 2005.

Our own version of the self-* paradigm, Self Adaptive Software, uses diagnosis of the environmental context to control complexity and increase robustness. In order to present this idea, we first describe Self Adaptive Software, then describe model based diagnosis. We then present the GRAVA vision architecture in general, and the concept of context in a vision application. Next, we present principal component decomposition, the technique we use to generate contexts from a corpus of examples. Finally, we present our conclusions.

2   Self Adaptive Software

Software design consists in large part in analyzing the cases the software will be presented with, and ensuring that requirements are met for those cases. It is always difficult to get good coverage of cases, and impossible to assure that coverage is complete. If program behaviors are determined in advance, the exact runtime inputs and conditions are not used in deciding what the software will do. The state of the art in software development is to adapt to new conditions via off-line maintenance, and the required human intervention delays change. In contrast, the premise of self adaptive software is that the need for change should be detected, and the required change effected, while the program is running (at run-time).

The goal of self adaptive software is the creation of technology to enable programs to understand, monitor and modify themselves. Self adaptive software understands: what it does; how it does it; how to evaluate its own performance; and thus how to respond to changing conditions. We believe that self adaptive software will identify, promote and evaluate new models of code design and runtime support. These new models will allow software to modify its own behavior in order to adapt, at runtime, when exact conditions and inputs are known, to discovered changes in requirements, inputs, and internal and external conditions.

A definition of self adaptive software was provided in a DARPA Broad Agency Announcement on Self-adaptive Software [11]:

> Self-adaptive software evaluates its own behavior and changes behavior when the evaluation indicates that it is not accomplishing what the software is intended to do, or when better functionality or performance is possible.

> This implies that the software has multiple ways of accomplishing its purpose, and has enough knowledge of its construction to make effective changes at runtime. Such software should include functionality for evaluating its behavior and performance, as well as the ability to replan and reconfigure its operations in order to improve its operation. Self adaptive software should also include a set of components for each major function, along with descriptions of the components, so that components of systems can be selected and scheduled at runtime, in response to the evaluators. It also requires the ability to impedance match input/output of sequenced components, and the ability to generate some of this code from specifications. In addition, DARPA seek this new basis of adapta-

tion to be applied at runtime, as opposed to development/design time, or as a maintenance activity.

Self adaptive software constantly evaluates its own performance, and when that performance is below criteria, changes its behavior. To accomplish this, the runtime code includes the following things not currently included in shipped software:

1. descriptions of software intentions (i.e. goals and designs)
2. descriptions of program structure;
3. descriptions of the environment that the program is running in, both computational and (for embedded software) physical;
4. a collection of alternative implementations and algorithms (sometimes called a reuse asset base).

We will return to further discussion of the first three items above, in a later section: Model Based Diagnosis. Three metaphors have been useful to early researchers on self adaptive software: coding an application as a dynamic planning system, or coding an application as a control system, or coding a self aware system, [12]. The first two are operational metaphors, and the third deals with the reflective nature of the program.

In programming as planning, the application doesn't simply execute specific algorithms, but instead plans its actions. That plan is available for inspection, evaluation, and modification. Replanning occurs at runtime in response to a negative evaluation of the effectiveness of the plan, or its execution. The plan treats computational resources such as hardware, communication capacity, and code objects (components) as resources that the plan can schedule and configure. See [2], [9], [16], and [20].

In program as control system, the runtime software behaves like a factory, with inputs and outputs, and a monitoring and control unit that manages the factory. Evaluation, measurement and control systems are layered on top of the application, and manage reconfiguration of the system. Explicit models of the operation, purpose and structure of the application regulate the system's behavior. This approach is more complex than most control systems, because the effects of small changes are highly variable, and because complex filtering and diagnosis of results is required, before they can serve as feedback or feed-forward mechanisms. Despite the difficulties of applying control theory to such highly non-linear systems, there are valuable insights to be drawn from control theory, and also hybrid control theory, including for example the concept of stability. See [9], [10], and [14].

The key factor in a self aware program is having a self-modeling approach. Evaluation, revision and reconfiguration are driven by models of the operation of the software that are themselves contained in the running software. Essentially, the applications are built to contain knowledge of their operation, and they use that knowledge to evaluate performance, to reconfigure and to adapt to changing circumstances (see [12], [20], and [15]). The representation and meta-operation issues make this approach to software engineering also intriguing as an approach to creation of artificial intelligence.

3   Model Based Diagnosis

We said before that self adaptive software will include descriptions of:

1. software intentions (i.e. goals and designs)
2. program structure;
3. the environment that the program is running in, both computational and (for embedded software) physical;

Each of these descriptions will generally be in the form of a model. That is, the descriptions must involve a significant functional abstraction, so as to support operations on the descriptions that can in turn affect the functional behaviors of the things described. So for example, we must be able to recompute the subgoals of a goal in the light of new contextual information. Also, we want to use the models of program structure to diagnose problems and support reconfiguration of the program. Finally, models of the physical environment can be used to:

1. diagnose program failures and performance problems,
2. provide contextual basis for subgoaling and reconfiguring,
3. provide a basis for choosing new strategies for the computation.

We also said earlier that the chief engineering issue for self adaptive software was evaluation of program performance. It is of course possible to do evaluation without actually diagnosing a problem, even when one is determined to respond to the evaluation. For example, given a poor evaluation (which may itself provide no diagnostic information) we might simply respond by randomly picking a different algorithm or implementation. Although this fits a broad definition of self adaptive software, our goals are much higher.

Instead, the kind of evaluation we envision is one that includes and partially depends on a diagnosis of at least the proximate cause, and where possible the root cause, of the failure or performance problem. In this sense, the entire self adaptive apparatus in the program can be thought of as a model based diagnosis system, in support of the program's main goals. The program, its goals, and the environment that it runs in are all modeled in the running system, and diagnostic reasoning is employed to evaluate program performance. Thus model based diagnosis realizes the self aware metaphor for self adaptive software.

In the next sections, we introduce a computer vision system that uses diagnosed changes in the current context, in order to adapt to those changes.

4   Complexity and Context in Vision

Image understanding programs have tended to be very brittle and perform poorly in situations where the environment cannot be carefully constrained. Natural vision systems in humans and other animals are remarkably robust. We believe that recognition of (and adaptation to) changes in the environment is what allows natural vision to be so much more robust than computer vision. A premise of the self-adaptive approach is that it should be possible, at runtime, to synthesize context specific systems, to determine the need to change context and to self-adapt the program so that the program's context matches the state of the environment and operates robustly because each of its components is operating well within their optimal range.

The idea of self-adaptation is to adapt the program to a particular "context". In order to achieve this adaptation we build structural descriptions that facilitate dividing the model space into contexts and provide a mechanism for determining when a context is a good fit to the environment, and diagnosing when we have a poor context fit. AI has long understood the importance of contexts. In 1975 Minsky introduced the notion of *frames* [13] which was essentially an approach to contexts. Frames have been used extensively in AI research, especially for natural language. Riseman's Schemas [6] was a similar idea specifically for Computer Vision.

The first application of the GRAVA architecture [19, 18] was to the interpretation of satellite aerial images. In GRAVA (for Grounded Reflective Adaptive Vision Architecture), satellite images were segmented into regions of homogeneous content and the regions were parsed, much as words are in a sentence to form a structural understanding of the image. Different image types are comprised of different kinds of regions, different colors and textures, and different parse rules. Rather than making one huge grammar that includes all textures and region types, it is better to have grammars, and optical models tailored to the context because tailored contexts provide greater accuracy and constraint. In that program the contexts as well as the grammars and region content models were learned from a corpus of images annotated by a human photo interpreter.

The use of corpora in building trainable intelligent systems has been a growing trend in A.I. in recent years especially in natural language [5, 4], speech understanding [8], and computer vision [17]. These problems are far too difficult to tackle in their full generality, and require techniques for managing that complexity. One common and beneficial use of corpora is in managing complexity by learning contexts. Contexts introduce constraints that bound the choices to be made (or learned) about attributes and their values.

Contexts occur for a variety of reasons, at different levels of processing, and in different parts of the corpus. Given a set of images it is generally not possible to divide the images into separate piles with each pile representing a different context. Contexts for different aspects of the problem can be composed in a variety of ways. The explosion of possible combinations of contexts is one reason why the self-adaptive approach is attractive. That is, rather than generating all possible combinations of contexts in advance—and then having a "big switch" to choose which to use—it is better to generate the particular combination of contexts on demand.

4.1   An Overview of the GRAVA Architecture

The purpose of the reflective architecture is to allow the image interpretation program to be aware of its own computational state and to make changes to it as necessary in order to achieve its goal. The steps below provide a schematic introduction to the GRAVA architecture.

1. The desired *behavior* is specified in the form of statistical models with the help of a corpus.
2. The behavior, which covers several different imaging scenarios, is broken down into contexts. Contexts exist for different levels of the interpretation problem. Each context defines an expectation for the computational stage that it covers. Contexts are like frames and schemas; but because the contexts are gathered from the data automatically it is not necessary to define them by hand.
3. Given a context a program to interpret the image can be generated from that context. This is done by *compiling* the context into a program by selecting the appropriate agents.
4. The program that results from compiling a context can easily know the following things:
   (a) What part of the specification gave rise to its components.
   (b) Which agents were involved in the creation of its components.
   (c) Which models were applied by those agents in creating its components.
   (d) How well suited the current program is to dealing with the current input.
5. The division of knowledge into agents that perform basic image interpretation tasks and agents that construct programs from specifications is represented by different reflective levels.

4.2   Context in Aerial Image Interpretation

To better understand the idea of contexts, consider the case of optical model contexts and language model contexts.

Figure 1 shows four multi-spectral color SPOT images from the color corpus that demonstrate different contexts. Images (1) and (2) are similar in content (mostly farmland and small towns) but the colors and textures of the regions are very different. In fact, the images are taken under different imaging conditions. In the case of these two images, the major difference is with the optical models, since, grammatically, the two are rather similar. In images (3) and (4) the nature of the terrain is very different. Image (3) shows part of a major city whereas image (4) shows a rural setting with only small villages. The grammar that is suitable for parsing images 3 and 4 is quite different. Attempting to interpret any of these images with the wrong collection of optical or grammatical models may be expected to produce a poor result especially since knowledge weak segmentation algorithms often give poor results. In this case, the reason for the differences between image (1) and image (2) were changes in the SPOT technology used to image them.

(1)   (2)

(3)   (4)

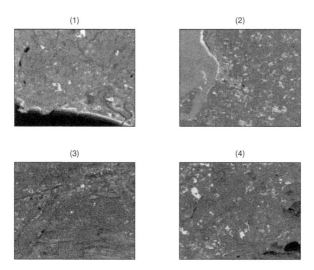

Fig. 1. Image Contexts

4.3   Context and Face Recognition

We next consider an example from the application of computer vision to face recognition. Most face recognition systems work by measuring a small number of facial features given a canonical pose and matching them against a database of known faces. Frequently however, in practical applications, few frames show a full frontal face. By building a face recognizer that can seamlessly switch between different contexts such as pose and lighting we can construct a recognizer that is robust to normal changes in the natural environment. This permits a much wider application of face recognition technology. (See [22] for a more complete description of the face recognition system).

Our application involves recognizing people as they move about an intelligent space [3] in an unconstrained way. An intelligent(or smart) space is a room or collection of rooms and corridors that have an abundance of sensors so that computer monitoring can track and understand activities in the space and provide intelligent support for the activities of the participants. Although the use of a space may in general be very complex, most spaces have a number of frequently repeated uses. By modeling the relationship between contexts the system can predict activities that occur in sequences within a space. For example the sequence of "assembling", "meeting", and "adjourning" can be learned as a hidden markov model (HMM) [23, 1].

To better understand contexts for face recognition consider the face "pose" contexts:

Figure 2 shows four pose contexts: "profile", "oblique", "off-center", and "frontal". The profile view, for example, is supported by agents that measure points along the profile of the face, the corner of the eye, and the lips. The oblique view, on the other hand, is supported with measurements of the ear and

Fig. 2. Four Pose Contexts

measurements of the position of the ear, eye, and nose. The triangle formed by the eye, ear, and nose help to determine the angle of the face to the camera which allows measurements to be normalized before recognition. The different contexts control, among other things, what models can be used for matching, what features can be detected and what transformations must be made to normalize the measurements prior to matching. This example shows contexts for pose but there are also contexts for lighting, race, gender, and age.

The recognizer supports a collection of face candidate finders, face models, feature finders, and normalization algorithms implemented as agents. Face candidate finder agents look for face like shapes in the image and generate evidence that supports the selection of a set of contexts based on the shape and shading of the face candidate. Agents appropriate to the context are selected to make a special purpose face recognizer. If the recognizer doesn't succeed in finding appropriate features where they are expected to be the system self-adapts by using available evidence to select a more appropriate context, constructing a new recognizer, and trying again.

5   Principal Component Decomposition

The architecture discussed above can adapt to a changing environment, given a decomposition of the problem space into contexts. We now describe how we derive our set of context models from a corpus, automatically.

A corpus provides multiple positive examples of a structure (such as faces) that we wish to model. The structures in question have one or more dimensions, for example orientation, and the corpus provides examples of the structure that enable us to model the location within the appropriate multidimensional space. One way of doing this is to model the structures as a probability distribution function (PDF). The natures of the structures may be very different but the essential nature of a corpus is the same: positive examples of structures in a multi-dimensional space.

Principal component decomposition is the interpretation of a set of data points into the component collections by analyzing the principal components of the interpretation space. After the space has been divided into separate clusters conventional PCA is applied to produce the models.

The algorithm builds upon two earlier works. The first is a classification program developed by Wallace [24], and the second is the practice of using principal component analysis [7] to reduce the dimensionality of high dimensional problems to model separate populations. Our algorithm applies principal component analysis recursively in order to separate the collection into successively smaller clusters. At each point the criterion for separating a population is that it reduces the global description length of the original population. A more complete description can be found in [21].

5.1   A Statistical Model for Clusters

Given an n-dimensional space S_n containing m points. we can interpret the points in this space as being unrelated points, all members of a single cluster, or grouped into a number of clusters.

A premise of the GRAVA architecture is that knowledge of the world in the form of models can be used to produce better descriptions of an image. A good description of the world in the GRAVA architecture is one that has a minimum description length. A model allows a shorter description length if the model reduces the amount of uncertainty about the values of features in the image.

The entropy of the collection data points in the corpus is given by:

$$H = - \sum_{d \in S_n} P(d) log_2 P(d) \tag{1}$$

The lower bound MDL of a description that represents all of the points in the S_n is given by:

$$DL = - \sum_{d \in S_n} log_2 P(d) \tag{2}$$

In order to compute this theoretical description length, it is necessary to know the PDF for points in S_n. A corpus doesn't specify every possible point in the space. A corpus provides a collection of *representative* points in the space. The job of interpreting the corpus involves modeling the PDF. There are many choices for modeling a PDF. One model that is simple, predictive, and which often pertains to naturally occurring distributions is the Gaussian.

The description of a Gaussian model consists of a mean and variance of the distribution $< \mu, \sigma^2 >$. For a set of points the Gaussian model can be fitted simply by computing the mean μ and the variance σ^2. Given this characterization, for any point d we can compute the probability $P(d)$ as follows:

$$\begin{aligned} P(d) = erf\left(\frac{(pos(d) - \mu_n + \epsilon/2)}{\sigma_n} \right) \\ -erf\left(\frac{(pos(d) - \mu_n - \epsilon/2)}{\sigma_n} \right) \end{aligned} \tag{3}$$

where $pos(d)$ is the position of the point d, ϵ is the position resolution, μ_n is the n-dimensional mean, σ_n^2 is the n-dimensional variance, and erf() is the error function.

The choice of whether to consider the points in the corpus as (1) unrelated individual points, (2) all members of the same model, or (3) divided into groups each of which is modeled, is to select the choice that yields the minimum description length.

The interpretation task can therefore be characterized as dividing the data points in S_n into n proper subsets $C_{i,n}$ such that:

$$S_n = \bigcup_{i=1}^{n} C_i \tag{4}$$

The MDL is

$$arg \min_{C_{1,n}} \sum_{i=1}^{n} \left\{ \left(\sum_{d \in C_i} -log_2 P(d|C_i) - log_2 P(d \in C_i) \right) \right.$$
$$\left. + ddl(C_i) \right\} \tag{5}$$

where $ddl(C_i)$ is the description length of the distribution used to model C_i. The description of a point is divided into two parts. The first part identifies its position in the space $(-log_2 P(d|C_i))$ and the second part identifies to which collection it belongs $(-log_2 P(d \in C_i))$.

The statistical models chosen for C_i determine the size of the point descriptions. In order to specify the position of a point we choose a resolution ϵ to be used uniformly since otherwise a point can have an arbitrary precision and its representation would be arbitrarily large.

If the representation of a collection includes its mean position μ, the positions of the points in the collection can be described as distances δ from the mean. So any point d can be described as an n-dimensional mean and an n-dimensional displacement:

$$\mu + \delta - \frac{\epsilon}{2} \leq d \leq \mu + \delta + \frac{\epsilon}{2} \tag{6}$$

To Communicate the collections, all that is required is the mean position represented to an accuracy of ϵ. The points are represented as a description of which collection they belong to and the offset from the mean: $< C_i, \delta >$.

As the data points in a corpus are divided up into smaller collections the description length of the individual points is reduced if the distribution that characterizes the collection is more predictive about the position of its component points than the distribution for the entire corpus was. Any suitable statistical distribution can be chosen for a collection.

5.2   Algorithm for Decomposition

Having defined the criteria for an optimal division of the data points into separate models we are left with the task of defining an effective procedure for achieving such a division. To accomplish this we developed an efficient algorithm that approximates a solution to Equation 4.

Our algorithm, which we call "principal component decomposition" (PDC), attempts to divide the data by searching for dividing hyper planes along the eigenvectors of the data. The idea behind the algorithm is that the principal eigenvectors represent the dimensions with the greatest spread. The spread can be caused by a single phenomenon with a large variance, or it can be caused by more than one phenomenon distributed throughout the space. To distinguish these two cases we compute the entropy of the data points as a whole and then we compute the sum of the entropies of the two collections formed by dividing the data points into two collections with a hyper plane perpendicular to the eigenvector[1]. We do this for all possible cut points along the eigenvector. If all sums of divided collections yield a higher description length than the original combined collection the collection is not divided, otherwise the collection is divided at the place that yields the minimum description length. This point can be seen as the minimum point in the entropy curve.

This procedure is repeated for each eigenvector of the collection starting from the eigenvector that corresponds to the largest eigenvalue until either a division occurs or until all eigenvectors have been tried. Once a collection has been split the algorithm is applied to each of the newly divided collections. Eventually there are no collections of points that split. The algorithm consists of two parts CHOP and MERGE.

CHOP looks for places to divide a collection of data points into two collections by finding a dividing hyperplane. CHOP thus produces two collections that have the property that if collection C_0 is divided into C_1 and C_2, $C_0 = \cup\{C_1 C_2\}$, and $DL(C_0) > DL(C_1) + DL(C_2)$. MERGE finds two collections of data points (say C_1 and C_2) that have the property that $DL(\cup\{C_1 C_2\}) < DL(C_1) + DL(C_2)$. If the collection of data points is non-convex CHOP can cause some points to become separated from the collection that they naturally belong to. MERGE re-associates points severed in this way with their natural collection. The advantage of this approach is that it is possible to construct non-convex collections of data points.

First we describe the algorithm for $CHOP(S)$ that chops the collection into separate collections.

$CHOP(S)$:

1. S is a set of n-dimensional data points. Let $\bar{m}$ be the mean and C be the co-variance matrix.
2. Let $v_1 \ldots v_n$ and $\lambda_1 \ldots \lambda_n$ be the eigenvectors and corresponding eigen values, respectively, sorted into decreasing order of eigenvalue.
3. For each eigenvector v_i starting with v_1 (the one with the largest eigenvalue—the principal eigenvector), search for the best place to cut the data points into two collections as follows:

   (a) Establish the cutting hyper plane. The cutting hyper plane is the plane that is perpendicular to the eigenvector v_i. We arbitrarily choose the hyper plane that passes through the mean $\bar{m}$.

---

[1] A 2-dimensional hyper plane is a line.

$$n = \bar{m}^T v_i$$
$$\bar{r} v_i = n$$
(7)

where $\bar{r}$ is a point specified as a row matrix.

This is the perpendicular form of the equation of a hyper plane. This representation is convenient because it permits fast calculation of the distance of a point from the hyper plane. For any point d the distance from the plane in equation 7 is given by $n - dv_i$.

(b) Sort the points in S in order of distance from the cutting hyper plane. Since the hyper plane cuts through the mean, approximately half of the points will be on one side of the hyper plane, with the rest on the other side. Approximately half of the points, therefore, will have a negative distance from the plane. The distance is not the absolute distance from the plane, it is how far to move along the normal to the hyperplane to reach the plane in the direction of v_i.

(c) Let A be the sorted list of data points.

(d) Let B be an empty list.

(e) Let the $cutPoint = 0$ and $position = 0$

(f) Let $minDL = DL(A)$ the description length of the entire set of data points.

(g) Now we simulate sliding the cutting plane along the eigenvector from one end of the set of data points to the other, by taking points one at a time from A, putting them into B, and computing the description length of the two collections as follows:

For each point d_j in A do:

    i. Remove d_j from A.

    ii. Add d_j to B.

    iii. Increment the position ($position = position + 1$).

    iv. Compute the new description length as $newDL = DL(A) + DL(B)$.

    v. If $newDL < minDL$ set $minDL = newDL$ and $cutPoint = position$.

(h) If $cutPoint > 0$ divide the data points S into two collections S_1, and S_2 at the position indicated by $cutPoint$. Then recursively apply $CHOP$ to both of the sub-collections to see if further chopping can be performed. Finally return the complete list of chopped collections:

$return\ append(CHOP(S_1), CHOP(S_2))$

4. At this point, all of the eigenvectors of S have been searched for chop points, and none have been found. The data points cannot be represented with a smaller description length by chopping along an eigenvector so return the list of collections as the single collection S:

$return\ list(S)$

The nature of the way the collections are divided up results in some groups of data points being divided unnecessarily.

The PCD algorithm described above has a number of interesting characteristics:

1. PCD produces a structural description of the data points that is an approximation to a global MDL description of the points.
2. Each remaining collection of points can be represented efficiently by the statistical model chosen for it since if the collection could not be represented well it would have been divided.
3. Each collection is a good candidate for PCA modeling because of (2). If the data points were for faces of dogs or humans, as discussed earlier, we may end up with a good PCA model for human faces and a good PCA model for dog faces rather than one general model for faces.
4. The algorithm can be implemented efficiently and can produce good decompositions very quickly. The number of "chop" and "merge" operations that are performed in producing a decomposition is very small compared to the number of points.
5. The algorithm can produce non-convex collections.

The final point (5) is an interesting feature of the algorithm that is not obvious from the example given above. Non-convex collections cannot be disentangled by using the "chop" operation alone but inclusion of the "merge" operation allows two convex collections to be joined so as to produce a non-convex merged collection.

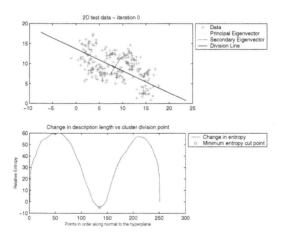

Fig. 3. Intertwined Non-Convex Shapes

To demonstrate this capability we generated a set of data points by picking points randomly along two interlocking 'C' shapes in a ying yang configuration. Even though the data is quite dense and intertwined the algorithm manages to "chop" it apart and then "merge" the severed parts back together. Figure 3 shows the first iteration on the data.

The second and third iterations chop the data down further and later iterations merge the severed portions back into their rightful places as shown in Figure 4.

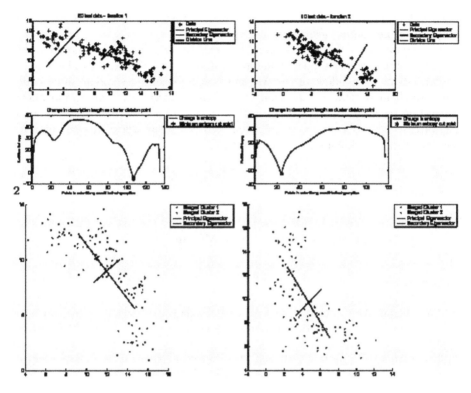

Fig. 4. Curved example data

6   Conclusion

The GRAVA system effectively uses model based diagnosis of context models to adapt to changing environments. This adaptation has been demonstrated in aerial image interpretation as well as in face recognition applications.

So, in addition to knowledge of content (faces or aerial images), that the GRAVA agents use to interpret images, GRAVA brings to bear two other kinds of knowledge. One of these is knowledge of the contexts that can be presented by the environment (contextual awareness), and the other is self-awareness, or meta-knowledge about the state of the program and the agents. What is unique about the recognizer outlined above is that it has multiple ways of interpreting images. For example, in face recognition, it divides up a complex space of lighting, age, race, sex, and pose into contexts that can be composed in a huge number of ways and self-adapts the recognizer at runtime.

In addition, we have developed a novel algorithm for the decomposition of complex models into collections of simpler models. This forms a backbone mechanism for automatically interpreting corpora, and automatically building both contexts and code for diagnosing context changes.

Since contexts are not random but are structurally related, transitions between contexts can be modeled as hidden Markov models (HMM). We are currently extending the architecture described in the paper to use HMM reasoning to optimize the context switching mechanism.

The adaptations that the system can exhibit are limited by the contexts that are well represented in the hand annotated corpus. We expect to be able to extend the system to allow for the system to capture examples and automatically annotate them by tracking previously recognized instances. This would allow the system to learn to adapt to situations that were not in the original human annotated corpus. We have not yet attempted this form of learning but plan to perform such experiments in the near future.

Acknowledgements

Effort sponsored in part by MIT Project Oxygen, and the Project Oxygen partners: Acer, Delta, Hewlett-Packard, Nokia, NTT and Philips.

References

1. L.E. Baum. An inequality and associated maximization technique in statistical estimation for probabilistic functions of a markov process. *Inequalities*, 3:1–8, 1972.
2. I. Ben-Shaul, H. Gazit, O. Holder, and B. Lavva. Dynamic self adaptation in distributed systems. In P. Robertson, R. Laddaga, and H. Shrobe, editors, *Self-Adaptive Software*, pages 134–142. Springer-Verlag, 2000.
3. R. A. Brooks. The intelligent room project. In *Proceedings of the Second International Cognitive Technology Conference (CT'97), Aizu, Japan*, 1997.
4. E. Charniak. *Statistical Language Learning*. MIT Press, 1993.
5. E. Charniak. Statistical techniques for natural language parsing. pages 33–43, 1997.
6. B. Draper, R. Collins, J. Brolio, A. Hansen, and E. Riseman. The schema system. Technical Report COINS TR88-76, Computer and Information Science, Univ. Massachusetts at Amherst, 1988.
7. J.E. Jackson. *A user's guide to Principal Components*. John Wiley and Sons, New York, 1991.
8. F. Jelinek, J.D. Lafferty, and R.L. Mercer. Basic methods of probabilistic context-free grammars. In Pietro Laface and Renato De Mori, editors, *Speech recognition and understanding. Recent advances, trends, and applications, volume F75*. NATO ASI Series. Berlin: Springer Verlag, 1992.
9. G. Karsai and J. Sztipanovits. A model-based approach to self-adaptive software. *IEEE Intelligent Systems*, 14(3):46–53, May/June 1999.
10. M.M. Kokar, K. Baclawski, and Y.A. Eracar. Control theory-based foundations of self-controlling software. *IEEE Intelligent Systems*, 14(3):37–45, May/June 1999.
11. R. Laddaga. Self-adaptive software sol baa 98-12. 1998.
12. R. Laddaga. Creating robust software through self-adaptation. *IEEE Intelligent Systems*, 14(3):26–29, 1999.
13. M. Minsky. A framework for representing knowledge. In P. H. Winston, editor, *The Psychology of Computer Vision*. McGraw-Hill, New York, 1975.

14. D.J. Musliner, R.P. Goldman, M.J. Pelican, and K.D. Krebsbach. Self-adaptive software for hard real-time environments. *IEEE Intelligent Systems*, 14(4):23–29, July/August 1999.

15. G. Nordstrom, J. Sztipanovits, G. Karsai, and A. Ledeczi. "metamodeling rapid design and evolution of domainspecific modeling environments". In *Proceedings of the IEEE Conference and Workshop on Engineering of Computer Based Systems*, 1999.

16. Peyman Oreizy, Michael M. Gorlick, Richard N. Taylor, Dennis Heimbigner, Gregory Johnson, Nenad Medvidovic, Alex Quilici, David S. Rosenblum, and Alexander L. Wolf. An architecture-based approach to self-adaptive software. *IEEE Intelligent Systems*, 14(3):54–62, 1999.

17. P. Robertson. A corpus based approach to the interpretation of aerial images. In *Proceedings IEE IPA99*. IEE, 1999. Manchester.

18. P. Robertson. An architecture for self-adaptation and its application to aerial image understanding. In P. Robertson, R. Laddaga, and H. Shrobe, editors, *Self-Adaptive Software*, pages 199–223. Springer-Verlag, 2000.

19. P. Robertson. *A Self-Adaptive Architecture for Image Understanding*. PhD thesis, University of Oxford, 2001.

20. P. Robertson and J.M. Brady. Adaptive image analysis for aerial surveillance. *IEEE Intelligent Systems*, 14(3):30–36, May/June 1999.

21. P. Robertson and R. Laddaga. Principle component decomposition for automatic context induction. In *Proceedings Artificial and Computational Intelligence 2002, Tokyo, Japan*, 2002.

22. P. Robertson and R. Laddaga. A self-adaptive architecture and its application to robust face identification. In *Pacific Rim Conference on Artificial Intelligence 2002*. Springer-Verlag, 2002.

23. A.J. Viterbi. Error bounds for convolution codes and an asymptotically optimal decoding algorithm. *IEEE Transactions on Information Theory*, 13:260–269, 1967.

24. C.S. Wallace. Classification by minimum-message-length inference. In G. Goos and J. Hartmanis, editors, *Advances in Computing and Information–ICCI'90*, pages 72–81. Springer-Verlag, 1990.

On the Use of Online Analytic Performance Models in Self-managing and Self-organizing Computer Systems

Daniel A. Menascé, Mohamed N. Bennani, and Honglei Ruan

George Mason University, Department of Computer Science, MS 4A5,
Fairfax, VA 22030, USA
{menasce, mbennani}@cs.gmu.edu
hruan@gmu.edu

Abstract. Current computing environments are becoming increasingly complex in nature and exhibit unpredictable workloads. These environments create challenges to the design of systems that can adapt to changes in the workload while maintaining desired QoS levels. This paper focuses on the use of online analytic performance models in the design of self-managing and self-organizing computer systems. A general approach for building such systems is presented along with the algorithms used by a Quality of Service (QoS) controller. The robustness of the approach with respect to the variability of the workload and service time distributions is evaluated. The use of an adaptive controller that uses workload forecasting is discussed. Finally, the paper shows how online performance models can be used to design QoS-aware service oriented architectures.

1 Introduction

The next generation of large distributed systems will consist of millions of interconnected heterogeneous devices and of a very large number of sources that generate data in widely different formats. These devices have significantly different characteristics in terms of processing power, bandwidth, reliability, battery life, and connectivity (wired or wireless). Many different types of applications with different and competing Quality of Service (QoS) requirements may share a common computing, communication, and data storage infrastructure. Applications running in these environments will i) be component-based for increased reusability, ii) service-oriented, iii) need to operate in unattended mode and possibly in hostile environments such as battlefields or natural disaster relief situations, iv) be composed of a large number of "replaceable" components discoverable at run-time, and v) have to run on a multitude of unknown and heterogeneous hardware and network platforms.

Under these circumstances, systems must be adaptable and self-configurable in order to continuously meet QoS requirements at the application and component level in the presence of changes in workload intensity. Adaptability and self-configuration is also necessary to cope with attacks and failures in order to

O. Babaoglu et al. (Eds.): SELF-STAR 2004, LNCS 3460, pp. 128–142, 2005.

meet availability and security requirements. Therefore, because of the dynamic aspects of complex distributed computer systems, they must be self-configurable, self-optimizing, self-healing, and self-protecting.

Some important challenges must be addressed:

- The structure of applications changes dynamically as new services are added or removed.
- The workload is hard to characterize due to its unpredictable nature, dynamically changing services, and application adaptation.
- It is difficult to build static performance models because the system is in constant evolution.
- There is a multitude of QoS metrics at various levels. Some examples include response time, jitter, throughput, availability, survivability, recovery time after attack/failure, call drop rate, access failure rate, packet delays, packet drop rates.
- There are tradeoffs between QoS metrics (e.g., response time vs. availability [15], response time vs. security [18]).
- Transient analysis of QoS compliance, and not just steady-state analysis, of system behavior is necessary in critical times such as terrorism attacks or catastrophic failures.
- Global QoS goals have to be mapped to locally enforced and monitored QoS goals [14].
- There is a need for protocols and mechanisms for efficient QoS goal negotiation, monitoring, and enforcement. Given the heterogeneous nature of these systems, QoS goals and contracts have to be specified in platform-neutral terms.
- Resource management mechanisms including resource reservation, resource allocation, and admission control in non-dedicated resources, as in Grid computing [13], are generally complex.

There has been a growing interest in self-managing systems and self-configuring systems as illustrated by the papers in a recent workshop [5] and in [1, 2, 6, 7, 8, 9, 10, 11, 17, 20, 22, 25]. In this paper, we describe our approach which consists of using analytic performance models in the design of self-configurable and self-managing computer systems. This approach is exemplified in various of our papers [4, 16, 17, 19, 20]. We provide here an all encompassing framework, describe the challenges, and summarize result obtained. Section two discusses our general approach to controlling computer systems. Section three presents an example of the results obtained by applying these ideas to control a Web server. The next section shows how analytic performance models are robust when the workload and service time distributions exhibit high variability. Section five describes the design of an adaptive controller that uses workload forecasting and presents an example of results for such a controller. Section six shows how online performance models can be used to build QoS-aware service oriented architectures that perform QoS negotiation and admission control. Finally, Section seven presents some concluding remarks.

2   General Approach

We use Fig. 1 to illustrate our general approach to designing self-organizing and self-managing computer systems. We consider that a system is subject to a workload, which may consist of any mix of online transactions and batch jobs. There is a multitude of parameters and settings that may affect the performance of such systems. Examples of these parameters include, among others, TCP, web server, application level, database server, operating system, and load balancer parameters. An analysis of the effects of various configurable parameters in E-commerce systems can be found in [23].

The set of parameters is divided into uncontrolled parameters and controlled parameters. Uncontrolled parameters (1) are those that are not changed dy-

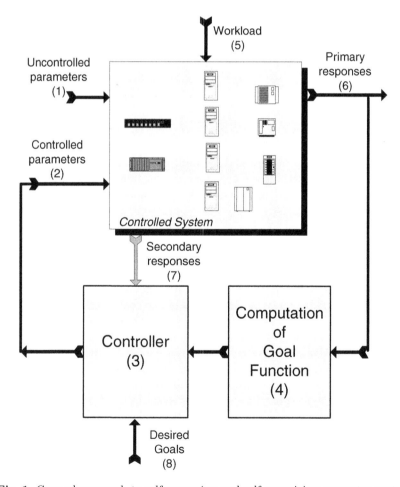

Fig. 1. General approach to self-managing and self-organizing computer systems

namically by the controller. Typically, these parameters are the ones that have relatively little impact on performance or that require a system restart or reboot in order for their effect to take place. Controlled parameters (2) are those whose settings are changed dynamically by the *controller* (3) by executing a controller algorithm. The goal of this algorithm is to find settings of the controlled parameters that optimize a given *goal function* (4), which can be expressed in the form of a utility function [24] or any other function of the values of the primary responses. Examples will be given in the remaining sections of the paper. The result of the current goal is passed to the controller, which may request goal evaluations for different possible settings of the controller parameters.

A set of responses are generated as a result of the workload (5) and of the settings for all parameters—controlled and uncontrolled. The responses are typically divided into primary responses (6) and secondary responses (7). The former are those whose values must be kept within desired ranges as specified by Service Level Agreements (SLAs) or QoS goals (8). Examples of primary responses may include response time, throughput, and probability of rejection. Secondary responses are those for which no QoS goals are set but that may be used by the controller algorithm. An example is the utilization of the various devices of the controlled system.

2.1   The Controller Algorithm

The size of the state space of possible configurations grows in a combinatorial way with the number of controlled parameters. Therefore, an exhaustive search of that space is not feasible. The controller uses combinatorial search techniques [21] such as hill-climbing and beam-search to find a close-to-optimal configuration for which the value of the goal function is as close as possible to its desired level.

Figure 2 displays an example of a portion of a state space. Each point represents a configuration of the controlled parameters and the numerical value associated with each point represents the value of the goal function. Suppose that the current configuration is point A, which has value 10, and that through a hill-climbing search, a new configuration, point B with value 35, is found.

An important question is how is the goal value computed for each configuration point? The goal value for the current configuration is obtained from measurements obtained from the system. However, as the search technique explores the state space, the goal values have to be computed through the use of models that can predict the value of response variables for configurations different from the current one. Our approach consists in using analytic performance models of the system to obtain the values of the primary responses.

This *online* use of predictive performance models is a departure from their common use in capacity planning [12]. In those cases, performance models are used to analyze and compare scenarios over relatively long (in the order of months) periods of time. In the case of self-configuring and self-managing systems, configurations may have to change very frequently (at a few-minute intervals).

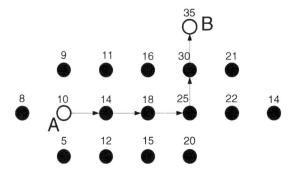

Fig. 2. Example of state space search

2.2   Controller Types

Controllers can be classified according to the control frequency and workload forecasting method used.

– Control frequency. The interval between two successive executions of the controller algorithm is called the *control interval (CI)*. Controllers can be classified according to the length of the controller interval as follows:
  - Fixed CI: the length of the control interval is constant.
  - Adaptive CI: If the CI is too small and the workload intensity is relatively stable, the controller algorithm will be executed too often with little or no effect. If the CI is too large and the workload intensity varies very rapidly, the controller will not run frequently enough to be effective. Thus, a CI that adjusts itself to the workload intensity can be more effective than a fixed CI.
– Workload forecasting. The online performance models used by the controller algorithm use two types of parameters: workload intensity (e.g., arrival rates of requests) and service demands of the requests on the various resources of the computer system [12]. The service demands can be obtained by monitoring the utilization of the various system resources (e.g., CPU, disks, and network segments). Controllers can be classified according to their use of the workload intensity as follows:
  - No forecasting: the workload intensity used to run the performance models in a given CI is the same as the workload intensity seen in the previous CI.
  - Workload forecasting: the workload intensity used to run the performance models in a given CI is a forecast of the workload intensity based on workload intensity values for a certain number of previous intervals. Workload forecasting techniques such as exponential smoothing,

weighted moving averages, and polynomial regression [12] can be used. It was shown [4] that the use of workload forecasting can improve the QoS of a controlled system, especially when the workload intensity approaches its saturation value.

3   An Example: A Controlled Web Server

In this section we show the results of applying the techniques described above to the QoS control of an actual Web server. The HTTP server is Apache 1.3.12, which was modified to allow for a dynamic change of the number of active threads (m) and the maximum number of requests in the system (n). These parameters, m and n, are the controlled parameters. The workload used to drive the server is generated by SURGE, a workload generator for Web servers [3], using two client machines sending requests to a third machine that runs the Web server. SURGE generates references matching empirical measurements regarding file size distributions, relative file popularity, embedded file references, and temporal locality of references. This workload generator was selected because it was demonstrated [3] that, unlike other Web server benchmarks, it exercises servers in a manner that is consistent with actual empirical distributions observed in Web traffic. A fourth machine runs the QoS controller. All four machines are Intel-based and run either Windows 2000 Professional or Windows XP Professional. All machines are connected through a 100-Mbps LAN switch.

The primary responses are the response time of an HTTP request (R), the throughput of the HTTP server (X_0), and the probability that a request is rejected (P_{rej}). The goal function is a QoS value defined as $QoS = w_R \times \Delta QoS_R + w_X \times \Delta QoS_X + w_P \times \Delta QoS_P$, where ΔQoS_R, ΔQoS_X, and ΔQoS_P are relative deviations of the average response time, average throughput, and probability of rejection, with respect to their SLAs, and w_R, w_X, and w_P are the relative weights of these deviations with respect to the QoS value [4, 17]. These deviations are defined in such a way that their value is in the range $[-1, 1]$. When the response metric meets its goal the deviation is zero. The deviation is negative when the response metric does not meet its goal and positive when the goal is exceeded. Therefore, the value of QoS is also in the range $[-1, 1]$ and the larger its value the better. The weights w_R, w_X, and w_P have to be chosen in a way that reflects the relative importance of the three performance metrics—response time, throughput, and probability of rejection—to the management of the Web site. The SLAs and respective weights for the experiment described here are: $R \leq 0.3$ seconds, $w_R = 0.5$, $X_0 \geq 50$ requests/sec, $w_X = 0.2$, $P_{\text{rej}} \leq 0.05$, and $w_P = 0.3$.

Figure 3 shows the variation of the QoS during the experiment. The x-axis is a time axis labeled in units of control intervals. The workload intensity started at 5 requests/sec and climbed to 19 requests/sec at CI = 19. Then, the workload intensity was reduced to 14 requests/sec. The experiment in question lasted 30 CIs and each CI is equal to two minutes. Results are shown for two types of combinatorial search techniques: hill climbing and beam search (see top two

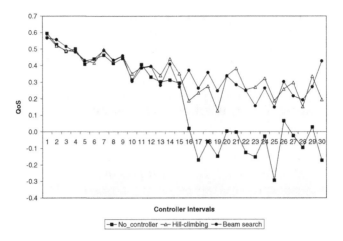

Fig. 3. A controlled Web server

curves). As it can be seen, the QoS for the uncontrolled Web server (bottom curve) becomes negative when the load reaches its peak value, indicating that at least one of the three metrics is not meeting its SLA. On the other hand, the QoS for the controlled Web server always remains in positive territory for both hill-climbing and beam search. We noticed in the various experiments we carried out that beam search tends to provide slightly better results than hill-climbing. This is probably due to the fact that the latter combinatorial search technique may at times be trapped at local optima. However, the difference between the two techniques was never significant.

4   The Robustness of Online Models

Many real workloads exhibit some sort of high variability in their intensity and/or service demands at the different resources. Therefore, it is important to investigate the behavior of the proposed technique for self-managing computer systems in such environments. To this end, we conducted a set of experiments to study the impact of the variability in the request inter-arrival time and service times distributions using a simulated multi-threaded server with one CPU and one disk. The server has m threads and at most n requests can be in the server, waiting for a thread or being executed by a thread. The goal function is the one used in Section 3. The SLAs and respective weights for the experiment described here are: $R \leq 1.2$ seconds, $w_R = 0.25$, $X_0 \geq 5$ requests/sec, $w_X = 0.3$, $P_{\text{rej}} \leq 0.05$, and $w_P = 0.45$.

The variability of the distributions of the inter-arrival time and service times distributions is represented by their respective coefficients of variation (COV) (i.e., the standard deviation divided by the mean): C_a and C_s. Figure 4 shows the value of the QoS during an experiment in which $C_a = C_s = 2.0$. The x-axis is labeled in CIs and each CI is equal to two minutes. The workload intensity

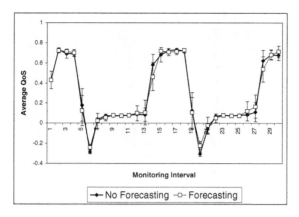

Fig. 4. QoS controller performance for $C_a = 2$ and $C_s = 2$

varies in the same manner as in Section 3. The top two curves correspond to hill climbing and beam search and the bottom curve corresponds to the situation in which the controller is disabled. It can be clearly seen that even at the peak intensity value (CI = 20), the QoS decreases only slightly (from 0.8 to 0.55) when the controller is used. On the other hand, the QoS decreases from 0.8 to less than 0.1 when the controller is disabled. Other results for different values of C_a and C_s are presented in our previous work [4]. These results show the robustness of analytic models when used for QoS control. Even though these models assume exponential service and interarrival times (i.e., $C_s = 1.0$ and $C_a = 1.0$), they do a good job at predicting the trends of QoS metrics when these assumptions are violated. The reason is that it is more important to correctly compare, QoS-wise, two points in the search space than knowing their absolute QoS values.

5   Adaptive Controller Intervals

Figure 5 shows an algorithm that can be used to dynamically vary the length of the control interval. This algorithm sets the length of the CI as a multiple, K, of the smallest possible control interval $\text{CI}_{\min}$. When the currently measured value of the QoS, QoS_{curr}, is less than or equal to a minimum value $\text{QoS}_{\min}$ for the QoS, the controller interval is set to its minimum value $\text{CI}_{\min}$. Otherwise, the controller interval is set to a multiple of $\text{CI}_{\min}$ according to the relative error ϵ between the QoS value, QoS_{prev}, measured last time the controller was activated and the currently measured value of the QoS, QoS_{curr}.

Figure 6 shows the variation of the QoS when the control interval varies according to the algorithm of Fig. 5 when $C_a = C_s = 1.0$. In these curves, workload forecasting is always used. The workload used in that experiment has two peaks: one at time 6 and another at time 20. It can be clearly seen from the figure that the use of a dynamically adjusted controller interval yields better QoS values. For example, at peak loads (see monitoring intervals 6 and 20), the QoS for the dynamically adjusted system is always positive. These curves also

If $\text{QoS}_{\text{curr}} < \text{QoS}_{\text{min}}$

then $CI \leftarrow \text{CI}_{\text{min}}$

else begin

$$\epsilon = \left| \frac{\text{QoS}_{\text{curr}} - \text{QoS}_{\text{prev}}}{\text{QoS}_{\text{prev}}} \right|$$

If $0 \leq \epsilon \leq 0.05$ then $K = 12$

If $0.05 < \epsilon \leq 0.1$ then $K = 6$

If $0.1 < \epsilon \leq 0.2$ then $K = 5$

If $0.2 < \epsilon \leq 0.3$ then $K = 4$

If $0.3 < \epsilon \leq 0.4$ then $K = 3$

If $0.4 < \epsilon \leq 0.5$ then $K = 2$

If $\epsilon > 0.5$ then $K = 1$

$CI \leftarrow K \times \text{CI}_{\text{min}}$

end

Fig. 5. Algorithm for adjusting control interval length

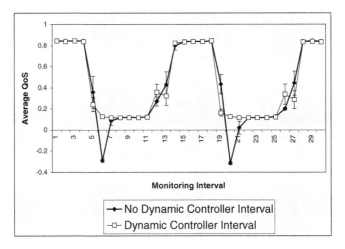

Fig. 6. Dynamic controller interval impact on QoS (forecasting always used)

show that the QoS values obtained when adaptive control intervals are used are generally higher than those achieved when the controller runs at fixed intervals.

One could ask the question whether these improvements come mainly from the dynamic adjustment of the control interval and not because of workload forecasting. To this end, we conducted another set of experiments in which we compare the average QoS values obtained for the cases when dynamic controller intervals were used alone against the cases when they were used jointly with workload forecasting. The results are reported in Fig. 7 for $C_a = C_s = 1.0$. The curves in this figure clearly show that there is a statistically significant performance gain when forecasting is enabled in conjunction with dynamic controller

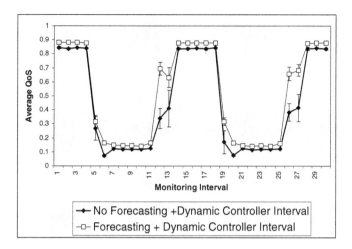

Fig. 7. Impact of workload forecasting on QoS (dynamic controller intervals always used)

interval. There is an accompanying increase in the QoS gain as a result of using dynamic controller intervals combined with workload forecasting.

6   QoS-Aware Service Oriented Architectures

In [16] we presented a framework for the design of QoS-aware software components. This section presents another application of online performance models in the design of QoS-aware Service Oriented Architectures (SOAs). Figure 8 presents an architecture that consists of QoS-aware service providers (SPs), clients that make requests to the SPs, and a QoS Broker (QB). SPs register with the QB. During the registration process, the QB engages in a protocol

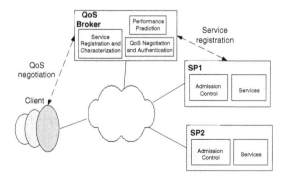

Fig. 8. A Service Oriented Architecture with a QoS broker

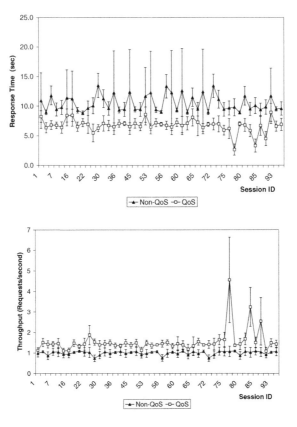

Fig. 9. Response time (top) and throughput (bottom) for the non-QoS and QoS negotiated cases for $f = 35\%$

aimed at characterizing the services provided by an SP in terms of their service demands. A client that needs a service contacts the QB to discover the service, authenticate itself, and negotiate QoS requirements in terms of response time and required throughput for its session with the SP. The QB keeps track of all accepted QoS requests and uses an online performance model to negotiate new requests. Based on the results of the performance evaluation, a request may be accepted, rejected, or a counteroffer may be sent to the client. Once a session is accepted, the SP is informed and the client makes requests directly to the SP, which is responsible for admission control.

We implemented the approach in Java and performed several experiments to validate the approach. A comparison between the QoS-based case and the non-QoS case (i.e., the case in which no QoS negotiation takes place) is shown in Fig. 9. The experiments generate a random workload which is submitted to the two SPs without using the QoS broker. The workload is replayed against the same SPs but this time using the QoS negotiation protocol. During this second phase, a reduction on the response time observed in the non-QoS case is requested. Let f be the reduction factor in the response time.

Figure 9 compares response times and throughputs between the QoS-brokered and the non-QoS brokered cases for all sessions executed by SP 1 for a reduction factor of $f = 35\%$. The top graph of that figure shows the average request response time for the two cases and the bottom one shows the throughput in requests/sec. The x-axis is labeled by session ID, each of which is unique in the experiments. The value at each point is an average over 500 values collected during the experiments. The curves also display the 95% confidence intervals for the average values. As it can be seen from the figure, there is a significant performance gain, i.e., decreased response time and increased throughput for the service provider. As shown in Table 1, with an $f = 35\%$ response time reduction requirement at QoS negotiation time, the actual response time reduction is 35.2%, which perfectly matches the QoS requirement.

Table 1. Summary of results for $f = 0.0$, $f = 0.20$, and $f = 0.35$

		$f = 0\%$	$f = 20\%$	$f = 35\%$
	% RT Reduction	4.1	16.7	35.2
	% XPUT Increase	9.0	24.0	54.7
SP 1	% Reject	17.0	22.7	36.9
	% Counter Offer	6.9	9.3	9.9
	% Acceptance	76.1	68.0	53.2
	% RT Reduction	4.9	21.2	35.0
	% XPUT Increase	12.1	24.0	54.7
SP 2	% Reject	15.2	29.3	39.8
	% Counter Offer	10.8	9.7	10.4
	% Acceptance	74.0	61.0	49.8

We also conducted similar experiments for $f = 0\%$ and $f = 20\%$. The summary results for the two SPs are shown in Table 1. In this table, %RT Reduction stands for the percentage reduction of the average response time and %XPUT Increase stands for the percent increase in throughput relative to the non-QoS case. Table 1 also shows, for each SP, the percent of sessions that are rejected, the percent of session requests that received a counter offer, and the percent of sessions that were accepted by the QoS broker. As it can be seen, with the QoS broker, the SPs always achieve better performance than without it. Moreover, the actual response time reductions achieved matched pretty closely the QoS goals for different values of f. These results demonstrate the applicability and effectiveness of online analytic performance models for building QoS-aware Service Oriented Architectures.

7   Concluding Remarks

This paper presented a general approach that can be used to build self-managing/organizing computer systems. We showed how online analytic performance models can be used in an efficient and effective manner for that purpose. We discussed and presented results for different design alternatives for the controller component of these autonomic systems. These design alternatives include the selection of a combinatorial search technique, the frequency at which the controller algorithm is invoked, and the importance of a workload forecasting feature. We provided promising results obtained from a real web server subject to a workload generated by the SURGE benchmark. The robustness of these techniques with respect to the variability of interarrival times and service times and the effectiveness of using an adaptive controller were evaluated on a simulated multithreaded server. We also showed how online performance models can be used to design QoS-aware service oriented architectures. We are currently expanding our work along several lines. First, we are looking into the use of online analytic performance models that are subject to heterogeneous classes of requests. We are also investigating how the techniques presented here can be used to determine optimal resource allocation for autonomic data centers. In this case, control has to be carried out in a distributed manner. Local controllers have to coordinate with global controllers to maximize a global utility function.

Acknowledgements

This work was partially supported by grant NMA501-03-1-2022 from the National Geospatial-Intelligence Agency (NGA) and by grant ACI 0203872 from the National Science Foundation.

References

1. Anderson, E., Hobbs, M., Keeton, K., Spence, S., Uysal, M., Veitch, A.: Hippodrome: running circles around system administration. Conference on File and Storage Technologies (FAST'02), Monterey, CA, Jan. (2002)
2. Babaoglu, O., Jelasity, M., Montresor, A.: Grassroots Approach to Self-Management in Large-Scale Distributed Systems. In Proceedings of the EU-NSF Strategic Research Workshop on Unconventional Programming Paradigms, Mont Saint-Michel, France, 15-17 September (2004)
3. Barford, P., Crovella, M.: Generating Representative Web Workloads for Network and Server Performance Evaluation. Proc. 1998 ACM Sigmetrics, Madison, Wisconsin, June 22-26, (1998)
4. Bennani, M., Menascé, D.A.: Assessing the Robustness of Self-managing Computer Systems under Variable Workloads. *Proc. IEEE International Conf. Autonomic Computing (ICAC'04)*, New York, NY, May 17–18, (2004)
5. Chase, J., Goldszmidt, M., Kephart, J.: eds., Proc. First ACM Workshop on Algorithms and Architectures for Self-Managing Systems. San Diego, CA, June 11, (2003)

6. Chase, J., Anderson, D., Thakar, P., Vahdat, A., Doyle, R.: Managing Energy and Server Resources in Hosting Centers. 18th Symp. Operating Systems Principles, Oct. (2001)
7. Diao, Y., Gandhi, N., Hellerstein, J. L., Parekh, S., Tilbury, D. M.: Using MIMO Feedback Control to Enforce Policies for Interrelated Metrics With Application to the Apache Web Server. Proc. IEEE/IFIP Network Operations and Management Symp., Florence, Italy, April 15-19, (2002)
8. Doyle, R., Chase, J., Asad, O., Jin, W., Vahdat, A.: Model-Based Resource Provisioning in a Web Service Utility. Fourth USENIX Symposium on Internet Technologies and Systems, March (2003)
9. Garlan, D., Cheng, S., Schmerl, B.: Increasing System Dependability through Architecture-based Self-repair. Architecting Dependable Systems, R. de Lemos, C. Gacek, A. Romanovsky (eds.), Springer-Verlag, (2003)
10. Jelasity, M., Montresor, A., Babaoglu, O.: A Modular Paradigm for Building Self-Organizing Peer-to-Peer Applications. In Post-Proceedings of ESOP03: International Workshop on Engineering Self-Organising Applications, Lecture Notes in Computer Science, vol. 2977, Springer-Verlag, Berlin (2004)
11. Kermarrec, A.: Self-clustering in Peer-to-Peer overlays. In International Workshop on Self-* Properties in Complex Information Systems, Bertinoro, Italy, February (2004) 89–92
12. Menascé, D. A., Almeida, V.A.F., Dowdy, L.W.: *Performance by Design: Computer Capacity Planning by Example*, Prentice Hall, Upper Saddle River, NJ, (2004)
13. Menascé, D.A., Casalicchio, E.: A Framework for Resource Allocation in Grid Computing, Proc. 12th Annual Meeting of the IEEE/ACM International Symposium on Modeling, Analysis, and Simulation of Computer and Telecommunication Systems (MASCOTS), Volendam, The Netherlands, October 5–7, (2004)
14. Menascé, D.A.: Mapping Service Level Agreements in Distributed Applications. IEEE Internet Computing (2004) September/October , Vol. 8, No. 5, 100–102
15. Menascé, D.A.: Performance and Availability of Internet Data Centers. IEEE Internet Computing (2004) May/June, Vol. 8, No. 3, 94–96
16. Menascé, D.A., Ruan, H., Gomaa, H.: A Framework for QoS-Aware Software Components. *Proc. ACM 2004 Workshop on Software and Performance*, San Francisco, CA, January 14–16, (2004)
17. Menascé, D.A., Bennani, M.: On the Use of Performance Models to Design Self-Managing Computer Systems. Proc. 2003 Computer Measurement Group Conf., Dallas, TX, Dec. 7-12, (2003)
18. Menascé, D.A.: Security Performance. IEEE Internet Computing (2003) May/June, Vol. 7, No. 3, 84–87
19. Menascé, D.A.: Automatic QoS Control. IEEE Internet Computing (2003) January/February, Vol. 7, No. 1, 92-95
20. Menascé, D. A., Dodge, R., Barbará, D.: Preserving QoS of E-commerce Sites through Self-Tuning: A Performance Model Approach. Proc. 2001 ACM Conf. E-commerce, Tampa, FL, Oct. 14-17, (2001)
21. Rayward-Smith, V. J., Osman, I. H., Reeves, C.R., eds, Modern Heuristic Search Methods, John Wiley & Sons, Dec. (1996)
22. Schintke, F., Schutt, T., Reinefeld, A.: A Framework for Self-Optimizing Grids Using P2P Components. Intl. Workshop on Autonomic Computing Systems, Sep. (2003)

23. Sopitkamol, M.: Ranking configuration parameters in multi-tiered e-commerce sites. ACM Sigmetrics Performance Evaluation Review, Special Issue in E-commerce and Services, Dec. 2004
24. Walsh, W.E., Tesauro, G., Kephart, J.O., Das, R.: Utility Functions in Autonomic Computing. *Proc. IEEE International Conf. Autonomic Computing (ICAC'04)*, New York, NY, May 17–18, (2004)
25. Wickremisinghe, R., Vitter, J., Chase, J.: Distributed Computing with Load-Managed Active Storage. IEEE Int. Symp. High Performance Distr. Computing, July (2002)

Prediction-Based Software Availability Enhancement

Felix Salfner, Günther Hoffmann, and Miroslaw Malek

Institut für Informatik, Humboldt-Universität zu Berlin
{salfner, gunho, malek}@informatik.hu-berlin.de

Abstract. We propose a new paradigm for software availability enhancement. We offer a two-step strategy: Failure prediction followed by maintenance actions with the objective of avoiding impending failures or minimizing the effort of their repair. For the first step we present two failure prediction methods: universal basis functions (UBF) and similar events prediction (SEP), which are based on probabilistic analysis. The potential of the presented methods is evaluated by a case-study where failures of a commercial telecommunication platform have been predicted. The second step includes existing maintenance methods fitting the proposed approach and a new recovery strategy called "adaptive recovery blocks". Since system availability enhancement is the overall goal, equations to calculate availability of such a system are given as well.

1 Introduction

Software failures have been identified as the single largest source of unplanned downtime and system failures (Sullivan et al. [1]). As software is becoming increasingly complex it also becomes more difficult to manage and is more prone to bugs. Research on software availability issues has largely focused on reducing the number of errors during software development, e.g., aspect oriented programming or service oriented computing, and on post mortem system repair, aiming at setting the system back into a fault free state. The disadvantage of the first approach is that it is extremely difficult if not impossible to build fault-free software. The drawback of the latter is its reactive approach which makes the system wait for a failure to happen and then reset it to a fault free state.

In this article we propose a two-step failure prevention and recovery approach. In the first step the probability of upcoming failures is assessed continuously during runtime. When a high failure probability has been predicted, in step two either preventive actions against the potentially upcoming failure are initiated, or reactive mechanisms are tuned such that time to recovery is shortened. To achieve this, we believe that the key is to apply machine learning techniques: to observe the system and to learn from the dynamics of its components in order to infer rules about component interactions and to correlate the learned rules with failures. These rules may be learned from previously recorded data: Once we have data describing the evolution of the system we may build and verify models which would allow us to predict the probability of the system being in a "healthy" or "failure prone" state.

Predicting system failures has been addressed by several authors. For example, a number of works are on reliability estimation, which inherently yields predictions for

O. Babaoglu et al. (Eds.): SELF-STAR 2004, LNCS 3460, pp. 143–157, 2005.

the probability of the next failure's occurrence. These models operate on a very high level of abstraction and are generated in an analytical manner. An analytical model for transaction processing systems has been presented by Garg et al. in [2]. Due to aging, the service rate of the system in question decreases over time and the software itself experiences hangs and crashes which result in unavailability. The authors present two preventive maintenance policies which increase the probability that an arriving transaction is carried out within a pre-specified response time. However, their analytical approach, quickly reaches its limits with increasing complexity of systems in practical use. A continuous time Markov chain model for a long running server-client type telecommunication system is described by Huang et al. in [3]. They express downtime and the cost induced by downtime in terms of the models parameters. In [4] the assumption of exponentially distributed time independent transition rates (sojourn time) made in [3] are relaxed and a semi-Markov model is built. This way the authors find a closed form expression for the optimal rejuvenation time.

In contrast to analytically generated models, a number of models that are built from previously recorded data have been proposed. Literature on applying linear modeling techniques to software systems has been dominated by approaches based on a single or a limited number of variables. Most models are either based on observations of workload, time, memory or file tables. In [5] Garg et al. propose a time based model for detection of software aging. Vaidyanathan and Trivedi [6] propose a workload based model for prediction of resource exhaustion in operating systems such as Unix. Li et al. [7] collect data from a web server which they expose to an artificial workload. The authors build time series ARMA (autoregressive moving average) models to detect aging and estimate resource exhaustion times. The idea of applying statistical learning theory to extract models from observed behavior of the system has been described more recently by Fox et. al [8]. Little attention has been given to detect potential nonlinear dependencies between various system resources and impending failures. In this paper we propose Universal Basis Functions that show the potential to make headway in this area.

Models operating on event-driven data include, for example, the Dispersion Frame Technique presented by Lin et al. [9]. Most of these models are based solely on the time of failure occurrence and do not incorporate additional information such as patterns of error messages or information that is contained in the messages itself. Similar Events Prediction, which is the second approach to failure prediction proposed in this paper, exploits this additional data.

The paper is structured as follows: A detailed problem statement is given in Section 2. In Section 3 two failure prediction methods are presented while maintenance and repair procedures are discussed in Section 4. In order to assess the impact on system availability equations to calculate availability from five quality measures are described in Section 5. In Section 6 a proof-of-concept case-study is presented in which the proposed failure prediction techniques have been applied to a commercial telecommunication platform.

2   Problem Statement and Research Challenges

Large industrial software systems can consist of millions of lines of code, with hundreds of programmers working on the system. The system can operate in a distributed way and there are many techniques in which fault tolerance and performance are boosted, sometimes in obscure and undocumented ways. The system may consist of many interacting parts, which may not be well specified. The widespread application of commercial-of-the-shelf-components (COTS) further adds to complexity. When we mention "large" systems we consider the fact that there is typically no single instance with full knowledge of the system's details.

Currently employed post mortem repair schemes are limited in their scope because by definition they always need time to identify a failure and they need resources to reconstruct a failure free system state. Consider, for example, a real-time system in which if we double system resources and have one system act as a standby, the time needed to identify a failure, switch over to the standby system, initiate the standby system and get the the the desired result may well exceed deadline guarantees.

There is always a trade-off between availability and the resources needed to achieve it. We believe that in order to gain a significant improvement in system availability under resource constraints by the order of a magnitude or so, we need a radically different approach. If we could predict the appearance of a failure in advance and early enough to initiate preventive measures, we might be able to alleviate the impending failure, or at least we might be able to prepare recovery for the upcoming failure in order to reduce resource consumption and time to repair.

However, "there is no free lunch" also holds for software systems. In order to get a prediction mechanism to work, we need to identify an adequate mechanism, to build a model of the system and then make correct predictions about impending failures during runtime. This procedure requires human as well as computation resources.

2.1 Problem Statement

Our objective is a development of failure prediction methods with high accuracy and a determination of automatically invoked actions that are effective, efficient and appropriate to the situation for industry scale software systems.

We believe machine learning techniques such as kernel or Markov based mechanisms are two of the most qualified approaches for failure prediction. Given that there is no way to obtain full knowledge of the system, the only practical way to learn about it is to "touch and observe" the system by collecting data about its status. This could include time series about system variables logged in regular time intervals (e.g., memory consumption or CPU load) as well as event-driven logfile data written by the application or the operating system.

The learning task in our scenario can be defined as follows: Given a set of labeled observations we compute a probabilistic classifier by a learning algorithm that predicts the target class label, which is either "*failure*" or "*no failure*". As classifier mechanism, we employ universal basis functions (UBF) and similar events prediction (SEP). Both methods are described in Section 3. The classifier needs to evaluate future events: If we make a prediction at time t we would like to know the future system status at time $t+\Delta t$. We call Δt the *lead time* (see Figure 1). Δt is necessary for a prediction to be of any use. It critically depends on the problem domain, e.g., how long does it take to restart a component, to initiate a fail over sequence or any other action. The *prediction period* t_p describes the length of the time interval for which the prediction holds. It can be adapted more flexibly: The larger t_p becomes the easier it is to predict failures, but the less meaningful the prediction will be. The *embedding dimension* δt specifies how far the observations used for prediction extend into the past.

Definitions of *accurate* failure prediction as well as *effective* and *appropriate* actions are given in Section 5.

$t - \delta t$ t $t + \Delta t$ $t+\Delta t+t_p$ time

Fig. 1. Definition of embedding dimension (δt), lead time (Δt) and prediction period (t_p)

2.2 Research Challenges

In addition to finding a solution to the objective given in the previous section, there are other challenges that have to be taken care of. We are interested in a practical way to increase availability without stressing the system in other parts. Another challenge is to cope with changing system dynamics, some of it introduced by changing system configurations, while at the same time keeping performance implications minimal. Additionally, data collection may introduce unwanted load to the system and the sheer volume of data collected is a serious challenge for any modeling algorithm.

Regarding the second step of our approach, open issues include investigation of actions with respect to their suitability to be combined with failure prediction. Methods that choose the most effective action depending on failure prediction, system state as well as other factors have to be developed. Furthermore, the combination of several failure prediction techniques and maintenance actions seems to be a challenging task.

3 Predicting Failures

The first of our proposed two-step approach is to predict failures. While failures have to be predicted online – while the system is running – the models used for prediction are generated off-line by training from previously recorded data. We propose two models: universal basis functions and similar events prediction and describe the process how to derive them.

3.1 Failure Definition

The initial step on the way to failure prediction is to exactly define failures. This is not a trivial task in a commercial environment. A typical definition is: "A system failure occurs when the delivered service deviates from fulfilling the system's function". It is important to mention that "system's function" means behavior from the user's perspective. In addition to this definition, probabilistic, real-time and quality-of-service aspects may also need to be taken into account. For example, in the case study described in Section 6 a failure is defined as "call failure rate exceeding a predefined level". Please note that a failure does not necessarily imply a collapse of the entire system.

From the modeling perspective failures must meet certain requirements, too. First, each failure must occur often enough to ensure that the modeling techniques have enough cases to learn what indicates upcoming failures. It is difficult if not impossible to identify the exact number of failures needed to build a failure prediction model. This is an area of ongoing research and currently we strongly depend on the modeler's intuition developed in the process of system observation. Further constraints are given by the fact that it is sometimes not practical to gather data on failures of certain types in a large software system.

3.2   Data for Failure Prediction

In our approach, the models for failure prediction are generated by analyzing previously recorded data in order to extract "symptoms" that indicate an upcoming failure. Therefore, both failure data and recordings of system variables from which a symptom can be extracted are needed for model generation – posing conceptual as well as technical challenges.

Technically, the data should be gathered non-intrusively with minimal implications on performance. Most software systems are not designed to yield insight information about their status at any given point in time. Log files have been found to be a feasible data source for historical system behavior. Issues concerning structure and design of logfiles have been discussed separately by Salfner et al. [10].

3.3   Variable Selection

An important concern is the selection of system variables that are significant to achieve good failure prediction. Performance of statistical machine learning models is closely related to the degrees of freedom in the model, which is strongly influenced by the number of variables being included in the model. Selecting too few as well as selecting too many variables can lead to poor forecasting performance. See for example Geman et al. [11]. In a real-world learning problem, the number of variables being monitored may be in the order of several hundreds, which is comparable to gene sequence analysis. There is no a-priori way of determining exactly the importance of each variable. The set of all observed variables may include noisy, irrelevant or redundant observations distorting the information set gathered. Thus it can be difficult to determine the most relevant variables with respect to our modeling task beforehand.

This problem is subject to ongoing research efforts and is known under a variety of names such as *variable selection*, *dimension reduction* or *feature detection*. It consists of finding the smallest subset of input variables which are sufficient to perform our modeling task. This type of problem is one of the most prevalent topics in the machine learning and pattern recognition community and has been addressed by a number of authors such as Weigend et al. [12]. Limiting the number of input variables to the ones contributing most to model quality not only decreases the number of free parameters in our model, the selected variables also can be used to assist an analytical approach in finding the root cause of a failure.

3.4 Two Models for Failure Prediction

We briefly describe two models we developed for failure prediction. Both models are inspired by machine learning techniques since we believe that this class of techniques is capable to handle the challenges imposed by today's complex software systems. See Hoffmann [13] for a more detailed description of these models.

Universal Basis Functions. We employ a novel data-based modeling approach we call Universal Basis Functions (UBF) that was introduced by Hoffmann [14]. UBF is a kernel based function approximation technique where the probability of a failure at some prespecified time in the future is estimated. UBF models are a member of the class of nonlinear non-parametric data-based modeling techniques. They operate with linear mixtures of bounded and unbounded activation functions such as Gaussian, sigmoid and multi quadratics [14][15]. Nonlinear regression techniques strongly depend on architecture, learning algorithms, initialization heuristics and regularization techniques and UBF addresses some of these issues. The kernel functions in a UBF can be adapted to build transfer functions that fit the task of failure prediction making them robust to noisy data and data with mixtures of bounded and unbounded decision regions. UBF produce parsimonious models which tend to generalize more efficiently than comparable approaches such as Radial Basis Functions. To perform online failure prediction we aim at finding the correlation between availability and observable input variables.

Failure Prediction by Similar Events. As UBF is tailored to equidistant time series, Similar Events Prediction (SEP) analyzes patterns in event-driven datasets [16]. Event patterns are represented by a discrete Markov chain (see Figure 2-a).

During model generation the states are automatically constructed by a hierarchical clustering technique applied together with additional algorithms to calculate relative frequencies of paths.

To achieve failure prediction for the running system that had been modeled, absorption probability distributions are computed to estimate the probability of a failure at time t in the future. The result is a discrete probability function as depicted by Figure 2-b.

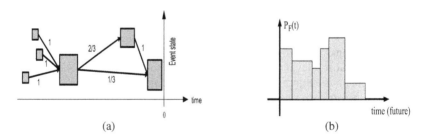

(a)   (b)

Fig. 2. Failure prediction with Similar Events Prediction (SEP). (a) Event patterns are represented as a Markov chain. Each state corresponds to a set of similar events. (b) Failure prediction is calculation of failure probability at time t in the future

4   Actions Fitting Failure Prediction

Obviously, failure prediction alone does not affect availability of a system. Therefore, after having predicted an upcoming failure an *action* has to be taken in order to proactively prevent the failure or to optimize its repair. In addition to a discussion of repair actions and preventive maintenance, a new recovery scheme called *adaptive recovery blocks* is introduced.

4.1 Repair Actions

Repairing the system after failure is the classical way of failure handling. These methods *react* to failures that have already occurred and are triggered by classical fault/failure detection mechanisms such as, e.g., coding checks, replication checks, timing checks or plausibility checks.

Roll-backward recovery reestablishes a previous, fault-free system state and tries to redo computations from that state (either by the same replica to account for temporary faults or by another hardware and/or software unit). Typical examples are recovery from a checkpoint or recovery blocks. Redo units comprise, for example, spares or redundant software modules.

Roll-forward recovery skips or approximates faulty computations and continues with the next – possibly using another computation unit or module. It is mainly used in real-time environments where meeting deadlines is more important than 100% correct results.

Combining reactive recovery methods with failure prediction can reduce mean-time-to-repair (MTTR). Time-to-repair is characterized by two factors: the time consumed to prepare the unit that performs the redo operation and the amount of operations that have to be computed again. The latter is mainly determined by the time between the last checkpoint and the failure's occurrence. Failure prediction has the potential to reduce both: With knowledge of upcoming failures, preparation of redo units can be started even before the failure occurs and checkpoints may be established short before failure. For example, in case of spares as redo units, a warm spare could be elevated to become a hot one such that it is almost ready when the failure actually occurs.

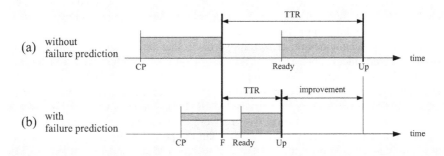

Fig. 3. Improved-Time-To-Repair (TTR) for prediction-driven repair schemes. (a) sketches classical recovery: Time from the last checkpoint (CP) to the occurrence of a failure (F) determines how much has to be recomputed (dark-gray interval). After a failure occurs, the substitution unit has to be initialized (light-gray interval). After repair, the unit is "ready" and starts to redo the lost computations. When it has finished, the system is "up" again. (b) shows two effects how failure prediction can reduce TTR: The checkpoint may be established closer to the failure, and the substituting unit can be initialized even before the failure occurs such that it is ready earlier after the failure

Figure 3 sketches both effects. Please note, that in the case of roll-forward recovery there are no redo operations, hence only a quick preparation of computation units improves MTTR.

4.2 Preventive Maintenance

In the context of the approach presented in this article, the goal of preventive maintenance is to perform actions in order to *prevent* an imminent failure, which has recently become an active field in research. We identified four categories of mechanisms: preventive restarts, state clean-up, preventive failover and system relief.

Preventive restarts reset parts of the system or the system as a whole when a failure is imminent but has not yet occurred. Software Rejuvenation – introduced in 1995 by Huang et al. [3] – is one of the first members of this group. It counteracts the aging process of software by preventively restarting specific components. Software aging describes misbehavior of software that does not cause the component to fail immediately such as, e.g., memory leaks and bugs that cannot be completely recovered from. Rejuvenation is based on the assumption, that restarting a component during normal operation is more efficient than restarting it after the component has failed.

State clean-up tries to prevent failures by cleaning up resources. Examples are garbage collection, clearance of queues, correction of corrupt data or elimination of useless processing.

Preventive failover techniques perform a preventive switch from a component that is likely to fail, to another more reliable component. For example, a preventive switch to a backup unit may be scheduled by failure prediction. Preventive failover can also include roll-forward techniques. An example for this is a real-time system where an imminent miss of deadlines (the failure that has been predicted) can be avoided in a roll-forward manner using faster but not 100% accurate methods. A third example is failure prediction driven load balancing aiming at relief of a component or a system (See Castelli et al. [17]).

System *mollification* (ease-up) tries to prevent failures by taking load of the system such that it has the chance to recover. For example, a web-server could reject connection requests depending on the risk of failure.

Some of the techniques described above can either be scheduled periodically or system state dependent. For periodic triggering several approaches exist to determine the optimal cycle duration: For example, Dohi et al. [4] use semi-Markov models, Pfening et al. [18] use a Markov decision process and Garg et al. [19] employ a Markov Regenerative Stochastic Petri Net (MRSPN). Trivedi et al. [20] show that state-dependent application of proactive recovery mechanisms has the potential to be more appropriate and hence more effective than the periodic alternative. The case of failure prediction-based invocation belongs to the class of state-dependent approaches. Several other techniques exist as well. For example, Vaidynathan et al. [6] use clustering of several operating system parameters to estimate system workload and to predict resource exhaustion by use of a semi-Markov process.

Preventive recovery mechanisms affect Mean-Time-To-Failure (MTTF) since these methods try only to prevent failures. However, if a failure happens nothing is done to improve repair. MTTF is affected in two ways: A portion of failures can be *prevented* (do not occur) but on the other side some *extra failures* may be induced. The incident of an extra failure could, for example, be caused by unnecessary recovery actions performed during peak load periods.

Adaptive Recovery Blocks. Failure prediction enables us to create a new recovery scheme: Adaptive recovery blocks. Recovery blocks as defined by Randell [21] save the state at the block's entry (checkpointing) and perform an acceptance test after computation to check the correctness of the result. Checkpointing produces heavy I/O traffic while acceptance tests put additional computational load on the system. *Adaptive* recovery blocks invest this overhead for reliability only if a failure is likely to occur whereas in case of low failure probability the overhead can be avoided. See Figure 4 for illustration.

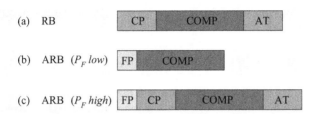

Fig. 4. Comparison of standard recovery blocks (RB) with adaptive recovery blocks (ARB). Case (a) shows standard recovery blocks: they first perform checkpointing (CP) then the computation (COMP) and an acceptance test (AT) at the end. Adaptive recovery blocks first perform failure prediction (FP). (b) If failure probability (P_F) is low, checkpointing and acceptance test can be avoided or limited. (c) shows the case for high failure probability. The proportion of failure prediction, checkpointing and acceptance test is application specific, but in many applications checkpointing and acceptance test will outweigh the failure prediction overhead

5   Calculating Availability Enhancement

One of the most widespread dependability measures is system availability. To show the potential of the presented approach, this section gives general equations to calculate the effect on system availability. A short computational example is given in the last part.

5.1   Measuring the Quality of Failure Prediction and Maintenance Actions

To evaluate the quality of a given failure prediction driven maintenance/repair strategy we propose five measures: Precision and recall assess the quality of failure prediction while the effects of maintenance/repair are gauged by three measures: repair time improvement, the probability of prohibiting failures as well as the probability of causing extra ones.

Failure prediction. Several measures exist to account for false positives and false negatives. We chose *precision* and *recall* that are commonly used in information retrieval [22]. Precision is defined as the portion how many of the generated alarms have been correct whereas recall is the portion of true failures that had been predicted:

$$precision = \frac{correct\,alarms}{number\,of\,alarms} \tag{1}$$

$$recall = \frac{correct\ alarms}{number\ of\ failures} \tag{2}$$

Both precision and recall can take values in the interval $[0,1]$.

Actions. Repair as well as preventive mechanisms that are driven by failure prediction affect mean-time-to-failure (MTTF) and mean-time-to-repair (MTTR). The effect on MTTR (see Figure 3) is measured by a *repair factor* r_f being the mean relative improvement in MTTR:

$$r_f = \frac{MTTR_{prep}}{MTTR}\ |a_c \tag{3}$$

where $MTTR_{prep}$ is Mean-time-to-Repair in the case that the repair action was prepared for the failure (hence the condition of correct alarm a_c). r_f can take values in $[0,\infty)$. Obviously, a repair factor less than 1 indicates improved MTTR whereas values greater than 1 imply a change for the worse. In the case of preventive actions r_f equals 1 since preventive actions do not affect MTTR.

The effect on MTTF is measured by two probabilities:

$$P_p = P(F_{prevented}\ |a_c) \tag{4}$$

$$P_e = P(\text{extra failure}) \tag{5}$$

$P(F_{prevented}\ |a_c)$ denotes the probability that a failure can be prevented by the maintenance procedure in the case that failure prediction identified the upcoming failure correctly and P_e denotes the probability that an alarm generates an extra (additional) failure caused by the failure prediction algorithm or the action itself.

5.2 Calculating Availability

As availability is defined in terms of *MTTF* and *MTTR*, we compute *MTTF'* and *MTTR'* for the system with prediction driven maintenance / repair. From that a formula for availability is derived.

MTTR', which is the effective mean-time-to-repair for a system with applied failure prediction-driven maintenance / repair, is a mixture of *MTTR* and *MTTR_{prep}* weighed by probabilities *recall* and $(1-recall)$, respectively. Therefore, it can be computed using Equation 3:

$$MTTR' = (1 + recall * (r_f - 1)) * MTTR \tag{6}$$

In order to compute *MTTF'*, we first assess the expected number of failures in an arbitrary time interval $[0,t]$ of the original system without prediction-driven maintenance / repair:

$$f = \frac{t}{MTTF + MTTR} \tag{7}$$

When applying failure prediction driven maintenance / repair, f is altered in two ways: The triggered action may prevent but may also add extra failures:

$$f' = f - f_{prevented} + f_{extra} \tag{8}$$

where the number of prevented / extra failures can be calculated by use of P_p and P_e as follows:

$$f_{prevented} = P_p * a_c \tag{9}$$

$$f_{extra} = P_e * a \tag{10}$$

The number of correct alarms (a_c) and the total number of alarms (a) can be calculated from the number of failures together with precision and recall.

Equation 7 is used to derive an equation for $MTTF'$:

$$MTTF' = \frac{t}{f'} - MTTR' \tag{11}$$

Insertion of Equations 6 and 8 delivers an equation for the mean-time-to-failure:

$$MTTF' = \frac{MTTF + MTTR}{1 - P_p * recall + P_e * \dfrac{recall}{precision}} - (1 + recall * (r_f - 1)) * MTTR \tag{12}$$

In order to compute system availability, Equations 6 and 12 have to be combined resulting in the following formula that express effects of our two-step approach – regardless whether it improves or worsens system availability:

$$\boxed{A' = A + k * \frac{MTTR}{MTTF + MTTR}} \tag{13}$$

where A, $MTTF$ and $MTTR$ characterize the original system and k is:

$$\boxed{k = 1 - (1 + recall * (r_f - 1)) * \left(1 - P_p * recall + P_e * \frac{recall}{precision}\right)} \tag{14}$$

In order to guarantee $0 \leq A' \leq 1$, k is bounded:

$$k \in \left[-\frac{MTTF}{MTTR}, 1 \right] \tag{15}$$

5.3 An Example

To get a grasp for the five measures and also to show the potential of the approach, we provide a short computational example. We chose the values for precision and recall according to the results achieved for one minute ahead failure predictions in a case study with a commercial telecommunication application (see next section): precision = 80%, recall = 92.3%. If we would be able to achieve a prevention probability $P_p = 90\%$, a probability of extra failure $P_e = 1\%$ and a repair time improvement factor $r_J = 0.5$, system availability would be improved by an order of magnitude. Please note, that the numbers are the same for all order of magnitude transitions, regardless of the availability of the original system.

6   Case Study

We applied the two machine learning techniques described in 3.4 to data of a commercial telecommunication platform. It is important to mention that the experiment only covers the failure prediction part of our proposed two-step strategy. The second part, which includes triggering appropriate maintenance / repair actions based on the failure prediction, is an ongoing research effort.

To describe the experiment more precisely, the objective was to predict that the system's failure rate exceeds 0.01% in successive five minute intervals, where a failure was defined as missing a pre-specified deadline.

6.1   Platform Characteristics

The main characteristics of the software platform we investigated is its component-based software architecture running on top of a fully-featured clustering environment consisting of two to eight nodes. The platform offers the ability to measure response times and hence to detect failures via an external stress generator. We measured data of a two node cluster non-intrusively using the Unix SAR (system activity reporter) tool and logfiles produced by the system.

6.2   Data

We have monitored 53 days of operation over a four month period providing us with approximately 30GB of data. Results presented in this section originate from a three days excerpt. We split data of the three days into equally proportioned segments (one day per segment) and used the first segment to build the models and the second to cross validate the models. The third segment was used as test data, which had been kept aside. We gathered the numeric values of 42 operating system variables once per minute and per node. This yielded 84 variables in a time series describing the evolution of internal states of the operating system, thus in a 24-hour period we collected $n = 120,960$ readings. Logfiles were concurrently collected and the same three days were selected for modeling and testing. System logfiles contain events of all architectural layers above the cluster management layer. The large variety of logged information includes 55 different, partially non-numeric variables in the log files. The amount of log data per time unit varies greatly: from two to 30,000 log records per hour.

6.3   Results

Using the test data, we calculated precision and recall (see Section 5 for details). We compared our models to a naive approach that predicts failures periodically with a period set to mean-time-between-failures calculated from the training and validation data set. Results are shown in Table 1.

Table 1. Precision and recall for Similar-Events-Prediction (SEP), Universal-Basis-Functions (UBF) and a naive approach using MTBF. In the case of UBF we report mean values. The reported results were generated on previously unseen test data

Model	Type of Data	Precision	Recall	Lead Time
SEP	log files	0.8000	0.9230	1 min.
UBF	SAR	0.4912	0.8295	5 min.
MTBF		0.2500	0.2000	MTTF

The SEP model was built based on a lead time of one minute, the UBF model with five minutes. Admittedly, this makes it somewhat difficult to compare the results. However, we expect a smaller lead time to increase the models quality as is demonstrated by the SEP model. UBF and SEP models clearly outperform the periodic model that assumes MTBF to remain constant, which is not the case.

7   Conclusions and Future Work

The speed at which complex and large software systems are built and deployed is a big obstacle to formally define and describe the exact behavior of these systems. We believe that in order to further significantly increase software availability under given resource constraints we need to support software systems during runtime. We proposed an approach where preventive maintenance to avoid failures as well as repair mechanisms are controlled efficiently and appropriately to the system state by failure prediction. This is in contrast to the currently predominant post-mortem approach that waits for failures to happen and reacts afterwards.

For failure prediction, we believe that machine learning techniques that are able to find relationships in data and to identify suspicious patterns and deviations from normal behavior, are one of the most promising class of techniques. Inspired by these techniques we developed two models: Universal Basis Functions (UBF) and Similar Events Prediction (SEP). Both methods are able to indicate whether or not a system works but moreover give a probabilistic evaluation on how well the system works. Additionally, these models can be powerful tools in understanding the behavior of complex software systems.

We investigated the effectiveness of both techniques to model and predict failures of a commercial telecommunication system. We compared UBF and SEP to an approach where failures are "predicted" periodically after Mean-Time-Between-Failure.

Our initial results are encouraging. For UBF we achieve a recall of 82% and a precision of 49% with 5 minutes lead time while SEP achieves 80% precision and 92% recall with 1 minute lead time. Both failure prediction methods compare most favorably to the MTBF prediction yielding a recall of 20% and a precision of 25%.

Preventive maintenance and repair techniques have been discussed and their effect on system availability has been investigated. Five quality measures have been identified covering all effects on availability: precision and recall evaluate the quality of failure prediction while the repair time improvement factor, probability of failure prevention and the probability of extra failures assess the outcome of the methods triggered by failure prediction. An equation concerning availability calculation of a system that employs such a two-step approach has been derived.

Our two-step approach is embedded in an ongoing research effort, where both failure prediction methods and preventive and recovery actions are being investigated. Future work will extend the experiments in terms of increasing the size of the data sets and assessing the stability of the models (e.g., with changing system configuration). As our experiments investigated only the first step of our two stage procedure, future efforts will have to focus on the problem of finding out which recovery scheme is best suited for which situation and will have to investigate their effectiveness. However, the ultimate question is: How far can we push the availability increase using our proposed approach - can we expect an improvement of an order of magnitude or more?

References

1. Sullivan, M. and Chillarege, R.: Software defects and their impact on system availability - a study of field failures in operating systems. 21st Int. Symp. on Fault-Tolerant Computing (FTCS-21) (1991) 2-9
2. Garg, S. and Puliafito, A. and Telek, M. and Trivedi, K.S.: Analysis of Preventive Maintenance in Transactions Based Software Systems. IEEE Trans. Comput. **47(1)** (1998) 96-107
3. Huang, Y. and Kintala, C. and Kolettis, N. and Fulton, N.: Software Rejuvenation: Analysis, Module and Applications. In: Proceedings of IEEE Intl. Symposium on Fault Tolerant Computing, FTCS 25. (1995)
4. Dohi, T. and Goseva-Popstojanova, K. and Trivedi, K. S.: Statistical Non-Parametric Algorihms to Estimate the Optimal Software Rejuvenation Schedule. In: Proceedings of the Pacific Rim International Symposium on Dependable Computing (PRDC). (2000)
5. Garg, S. and van Moorsel, A. and Vaidyanathan, K and Trivedi, K. S.: A Methodology for Detection and Estimation of Software Aging. In: Proceedings of the Int'l. Symp. on Software Reliability Engineering (ISSRE). (1998)
6. Vaidyanathan, K. and Trivedi, K. S.: A Measurement-Based Model for Estimation of Resource Exhaustion in Operational Software Systems. In: Proceedings of the International Symposium on Software Reliability Engineering (ISSRE). (1999)
7. Li, L. and Vaidyanathan, K. and Trivedi, K. S.: An Approach for Estimation of Software Aging in a Web Server. In: Proceedings of the Intl. Symposium on Empirical Software Engineering (ISESE). (2002)
8. Fox, A. and Kiciman, E. and Patterson, D. and Katz, R. and Jordan, M. and Stoica, I.: Statistical Monitoring + Predictable Recovery = Self-*. In: Proceedings of the Internation Workshop on Self-* Properties in Complex Information Systems (SELF-STAR). (2004)
9. Lin, T. and Siewiorek, Daniel P.: Error log analysis: statistical modeling and heuristic trend analysis. IEEE Transactions on Reliability **39(4)** (1990) 419-432

10. Salfner, F. and Tschirpke, S. and Malek, M.: Comprehensive Logfiles for Autonomic Systems. In: Proceedings of 9th IEEE Workshop on Fault-Tolerant Parallel, Distributed and Network-Centric Systems. (2004)

11. Geman S., Bienenstock E. and Doursat, R.: Neural Networks and the Bias/Variance Dilemma. Neural computation **4(1)** (1992) 1-58

12. Weigend A. S., Gershenfeld N. A., eds. : Time Series Prediction. First edition. Addison Wesley, (1994)

13. Hoffmann, G.A. and Salfner, F. and Malek, M.: Advanced Failure Prediction in Complex Software Systems. research report 172, Department of Computer Science, Humboldt University, Berlin, Germany, Available at www.informatik.hu-berlin.de/~salfner (2004)

14. Hoffmann, G.A.: Adaptive Transfer Functions in Radial Basis Function Networks (RBF). In: International Conference on Computational Science. (2004)

15. Schoelkopf B., Smola A.: Learning with Kernels. edition. MIT Press, (2002)

16. Malek, M. and Salfner, F. and Hoffmann, G.A.: Self-Rejuvenation - an Effective Way to High Availability. In: SELF-STAR: International Workshop on Self-* Properties in Complex Information Systems. (2004)

17. Castelli V. and Harper, R.E. and Heidelberger P. and Hunter, S.W. and Trivedi, K.S. and Vaidyanathan, K. and Zeggert, W.P.: Proactive management of software aging. IBM Journal of Research and Development **45(2)** (2001) 311-332

18. Pfening, A. and Garg, S. and Puliafito, A. and Telek, M. and Trivedi, K. S.: Optimal Software Rejuvenation for Tolerating Soft Failures. Performance Evaluation **27.28** (1996)

19. Garg, S. and Telek, M. and Puliafito, A. and Trivedi, K.S.: Analysis of Software Rejuvenation using Markov Regenerative Stochastic Petri Net. In: Proceedings of the International Symposium on Software Reliability Engineering (ISSRE 1995). (1995)

20. Trivedi, K. S. and Vaidyanathan, K. and Goseva-Popstojanova, K.: Modeling and Analysis of Software Aging and Rejuvenation. In: Proceedings of the IEEE Annual Simulation Symposium. (2000)

21. B. Randell: System structure for software fault tolerance. IEEE Transactions on Software Engineering **1(2)** (1975) 220-232

22. Ferber, Reginald: Information Retrieval: Suchmodelle und Data-Mining-Verfahren für Textsammlungen und das Web. edition. dpunkt.verlag, Heidelberg, Germany (2003)

Making Self-adaptation an Engineering Reality

Shang-Wen Cheng, David Garlan, and Bradley Schmerl

School of Computer Science,
Carnegie Mellon University,
5000 Forbes Ave, Pittsburgh, PA 15213
{zensoul, garlan, schmerl}+@cs.cmu.edu

Abstract. In this paper, we envision a world where a software engineer could take an existing software system, specify, for a set of properties of interest, an objective, conditions for change, and strategies for their adaptation and, within a few man weeks, make that system self-adaptive where it was not before. We describe how our approach generalizes to different classes of systems and holds promise for cost-effective, dynamic system self-adaptation to become an engineering reality.

1 Introduction

Imagine a world where a software engineer could take an existing software system, specify for a set of properties of interest, an objective, conditions for change, and strategies for their adaptation and, within a few man-weeks, make that system self-adaptive where it was not before. An engineer might take an existing client-server system and make it self-adaptive with respect to a specific performance concern such as high latency. He might specify an objective to maintain request-response latency below some threshold, a condition to change the system if the latency rises above the threshold, and a few strategies to adapt the system to fix the high-latency situation. Another engineer might make a coalition-of-services system self-adaptive to network performance fluctuations while keeping down cost of operating the infrastructure. Still another engineer might make a cluster of servers self-adaptive to certain security attacks.

Systems with mechanisms to monitor and adapt themselves to faults or surrounding changes are known variously as *self-adaptive*, *self-healing*, or *self-managing* systems. A decade in the past, systems that supported self-adaptation were rare, confined mostly to domains like telecommunications switches or deep space control software, where shutdown for upgrades was not an option and human intervention was not always possible.

Today, more and more systems have this requirement. Systems such as those in the e-commerce and mobile embedded system domains must operate continuously with only minimal human oversight. They must cope with variable resources (e.g., bandwidth and service availability), system errors (e.g., server components failing, or connections going down), and changing user priorities (e.g., high-fidelity video streams at one moment and low fidelity at another). Ubiquitous computing, in which

O. Babaoglu et al. (Eds.): SELF-STAR 2004, LNCS 3460, pp. 158–173, 2005.
© Springer-Verlag Berlin Heidelberg 2005

highly mobile users operate in heterogeneous environments under resource constraints, also motivates the need for self-adaptive systems. Finally, leading software companies like IBM [11] are pursuing ways to develop "self-managing and self-provisioning" infrastructure to help businesses streamline IT operations [10].

Over the past decade, engineers and researchers alike have responded to and met this self-adaptation need in somewhat limited forms through programming language features such as exceptions and in algorithms such as fault-tolerant protocols. But these mechanisms are often highly specific to the application and tightly bound to the code. As a result, self-adaptation in today's systems is costly to build, often taking many man-months to retrofit systems with the capabilities. Moreover, once added, the capabilities are difficult to modify and usually provide only localized treatment of system errors [14,27].

How might we achieve the kind of envisioned capabilities for self-adaptation? Clearly there are many lines of research that must contribute, including (a) new mechanisms for monitoring the behavior of systems in order to detect when problems occur; (b) new techniques for diagnosing and correcting problems once they are detected; and (c) new capabilities for run-time reconfiguration that will support on-line adaptation. However, even if these capabilities were somehow magically available, there would still remain the important problem of making it possible for engineers to use them in cost-effective and principled ways. In particular, we would like to be sure that engineers can augment existing systems to be self-adaptive without having to rewrite them from scratch, that self-adaptation policies and strategies can be used across similar systems, that multiple sources of adaptation expertise can be synergistically combined, and that all of this can be done in ways that support maintainability, evolution, and analysis.

In previous work, we have developed a framework incorporating some of the mechanisms mentioned above and demonstrated end-to-end self-adaptation support through two case studies [4,12,13]. We have also described the use of software architectural style to support analysis and guide decisions for system monitoring, diagnosis, and changes [3]. In this work, we show how our approach generalizes across different classes of systems, and re-examine in this context our existing case studies as well as a new case study on security concern.

2 Related Work

Our work builds on a rich set of existing technologies for dynamic system adaptation, and improves upon a number of prior approaches.

2.1 Technologies for Dynamic System Adaptation

Gross and colleagues at Columbia University have contributed substantial work on monitoring—probing and gauging—and effecting technologies [19,30]. The DASADA project has defined the probe and gauge infrastructures [1,15]. Event systems like SIENA [2] and MEET [18] provide the communication infrastructure necessary for monitoring. Workflow systems have been applied to support planning in self-adaptation, such as the Cougaar-based self-adaptation by BBN Technologies [6].

A similar body of research applies adaptation at the infrastructure or operating system level. In particular, adaptive components or multi-fidelity components provide useful capabilities in existing software systems and offer complementary approaches to self-adaptation [9,22]. In addition, a recent branch of middleware research attempts to support dynamically adaptive distributed systems by developing reflective, adaptive, and, in general, more "intelligent" middleware [20]. Adaptive middleware technology may prove synergistic with our approach.

Adaptive middleware monitors and controls software applications using interception or interposition techniques. Specifically, an adaptive middleware makes extensive use of interceptors to, for example, profile, trace, and even affect dynamic library usage [7,23]. Fault-tolerant CORBA provides transparent OMG-compliant fault tolerance through strong replica consistency, using techniques such as N-versioning, hot, warm, or cold swap, and redundant servers [24]. Some of the challenges include the ordering of operations, duplication of operations, recovery, and consistency in the face of multithreading.

A combination of existing dynamic adaptation technologies with a sound engineering approach holds promise to make self-adaptation an engineering reality.

2.2 Prior Self-adaptive Approaches

To date, several dynamic adaptation frameworks have been proposed and developed [8,16,31]. Of these, perhaps the most closely related systems are the architecture evolution framework of Taylor and colleagues from U.C. Irvine and the self-organizing systems of Kramer and colleagues from Imperial College, U.K.

Gorlick and colleagues have developed a framework, Weaves, that supports continuous observation and dynamic rearrangement of systems in the data-flow style to facilitate software construction and analysis, allowing parts of systems to be snipped and spliced without disruptions to data-flow [17]. Inspired by the dynamic observation and reconfiguration capability demonstrated in this work, our work broadens support to other styles.

In his dissertation on the "open architecture software" approach, Peyman Oreizy proposed the use of an application's architectural system model as a basis for decentralized software evolution for a greater degree of adaptability while supporting increased assured consistency over previous software evolution techniques [25]. His approach introduced an "architecture evolution manager" to validate changes to the architectural model and to carry out the changes on the application's implementation to reflect the model. Associated with his approach, the ArchStudio environment comprises a number of tools to support evolution of software via changes to the architectural model for C2-style applications. While Oreizy's thesis provided an approach for developers to evolve a system by changing its architectural model at *design time*, our work focuses on enabling monitoring and adaptation of a system consistent with its architectural model at *run time*.

As a natural extension, Oreizy and colleagues added a planning loop to his software evolution approach and introduced an architecture-based run-time software evolution framework [8,26]. As with all architecture-based adaptation, the UCI "architecture evolution framework" dynamically evolves systems using a monitoring and execution loop controlled by a planning loop. This framework, built over the course of several years, supports self-adaptation for systems built in the C2 hierarchical publish-subscribe style. Evolution of the architectural model uses architectural differencing and merging techniques similar to those used to version-control code. Although powerful and demonstrated on quite a number systems, this approach would be difficult and costly to apply on a target system that deviates from the publish-subscribe style or uses a completely different style. Our work overcomes this limitation by providing a general self-adaptation framework that can be tailored to specific classes of systems.

The work on self-organizing systems proposes an approach where self-managing units coordinate toward a common model, an architectural structure defined using the architectural formalism of Darwin [16]. Each self-organizing component is responsible for managing its own adaptation with respect to the overall system and requires the global architectural model to do so. While this approach provides some advantages of distributed control and eliminates a single point of failure, requiring each component to maintain a global model and keep the model consistent imposes significant performance overhead. Furthermore, the approach prescribes a fixed distributed algorithm for global configuration. Our approach aims to overcome that limitation by allowing tailorable global reorganization without imposing a high performance overhead.

3   Requirements for an Engineering Solution

To improve on the state of current practice and overcome the limitations of the current state-of-the-art, we need an engineering approach that helps software developers achieve external system adaptation in a principled and cost-effective way. In particular such an approach should have three important properties:

- *Generality*. The approach should be applicable to a wide variety of systems and properties. It should not be limited to a specific class of system such as client-server or a single system concern such as performance. For example, a developer should be able to apply the approach with relative ease to a pipe-filter, repository, or event-based system as well as client-server. The developer should also be able to tackle a combination of performance, security, reliability, as well as other prominent run-time system properties using this approach. In addition, the approach should be applicable to both new and existing software-based systems.
- *Cost-effectiveness*. The approach should allow developers to realize and implement self-adaptation capabilities on supported classes of systems at a relatively low-cost compared to development from scratch (perhaps order(s) of magnitude lower), and in a reasonably short amount of time (possibly on the order of a few man-weeks). The approach should not require substantial change to legacy systems. In addition, a self-adaptation solution previously applied to a system should be largely reusable in another system with similar self-adaptation needs.
- *Composability*. The approach should allow self-adaptation capabilities of different domains of concern, e.g., performance, cost, and security, to be specified independently by domain experts. Developers should then be able to

compose these capabilities to achieve self-adaptation for a combination of concerns. The property relies on an expert's ability to analyze the effectiveness of the capabilities he specified. Fortunately, separating the concerns facilitates such analysis. Another implication is that independently specified self-adaptation capabilities would be reusable for similar concerns in different systems.

3.1   Making Self-adaptation External

In practice, most systems deployed today do not satisfy these requirements. Systems that do self-adapt today have application-specific and ``hardwired'' self-adaptation capabilities that are difficult to generalize. Such built-in (*internal*) capabilities are often able to detect a problem close to its error source through low-level mechanisms such as exceptions and time-outs. Yet, at the same time, the code is limited to a localized view of the system, making it difficult to detect and correct overall system anomalies such as decreasing end-to-end system throughput. In addition, this internal approach disperses the adaptation logic throughout the system, making it costly and difficult to modify and maintain, hence *not* cost-effective. Embedded and dispersed logic also makes it challenging to reason about the outcome, making composability difficult to achieve. Finally, internal and dispersed logic makes reuse nearly impossible, so developing new self-adaptive systems requires significant duplication of effort and, thus, high cost.

To realize the goal of having general, analyzable, composable, and cost-effective adaptation requires that the adaptation be extracted from actual system code and treated as separate from the system. In fact, a number of recent research efforts use external mechanisms to monitor and adapt a running-system in a closed-loop control fashion [1,26,30]. The closed-loop control paradigm, as illustrated in Fig. 1, provides us leverage to "divide and conquer" the self-adaptation problem, separating the approach into three phases: monitoring, modeling, and control of the target system.

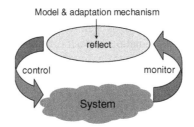

Fig. 1. Illustration of Closed-Loop Control

In principle, external adaptation mechanisms have a number of benefits over internal mechanisms. External control separates the concerns of system functionality from the concerns of "exceptional behaviors," enabling the engineer to systematically focus on and design solutions for dynamic adaptation. As a separate entity, the effectiveness of the adaptation logic is more analyzable and the mechanism more modifiable and extendible. These engineering traits allow the engineer to focus development, facilitate reuse, and reduce cost. In turn, the engineer can generalize techniques and solutions for adaptation to different and even multiple kinds of systems and system properties. Furthermore, the separation of mechanisms allows this technique to be applied to systems where the source code is not available. This relies on a key assumption that the target system provides, or can be wrapped to provide, hooks to get information out of the system and to make changes.

3.2 Scenarios for Self-adaptation

To clearly address the challenges of self-adaptation, one must understand the scenarios or conditions under which self-adaptation may need to occur. We recognize three major types of conditions for self-adaptation: system errors, changes in the environment of the target system including resource variability, and changes in user preferences. Understanding these different conditions for self-adaptation directly affects the development of capabilities for measuring, modeling, and controlling the target system to support self-adaptation.

A *system error* covers an undesirable condition that arises from the target system itself. For example, a server component may fail, or a set of network connections may go down. An *environment change* and, in particular *resource variability,* covers an undesirable condition that often arises outside the target system and causes problems for the target system. For instance, the wireless network on which an application depends may change beneath it, causing a sudden disruption of connection or change in available bandwidth. Or, the context in which a device is used, such as a room, may change, thus altering the set of resources available to that device. A *change in user priority or preference* constitutes a change in some requirements on the target system. For instance, the user may require high-fidelity video streams at one moment but be satisfied with low fidelity at another.

These three types of conditions share the common property of being a change that may not have been anticipated when assumptions about the intended use of the system were made during system development. These conditions at system run time thus provide opportunities for improvements to bring the system back within the boundaries of its requirements under the newly encountered conditions.

4   Role of Software Architecture

A key issue in applying an external control model is to determine the appropriate kind of models to use as a basis for control decisions. A recent branch of work suggests an architectural model of the software as a useful basis for making decisions about system adaptation [14,26].

4.1   Architectural Model

An *architectural model* represents the system architecture as a graph of interacting computational elements.[1] We adopt a standard view of software architecture that is

---

[1]   Although there are different views of architecture, we are primarily interested in the run-time component-connector view [5].

typically used today at design time to characterize a system to be built. Nodes in the graph, called components, represent the system's principal computational elements and data stores, including clients, servers, databases, and user interfaces. Arcs, called connectors, represent the path-ways for interaction between the components. Additionally, architectural elements may be annotated with various properties, such as expected throughputs, latencies, and protocols of interaction. Components themselves may represent complex systems, represented hierarchically as sub-architectures.

However, unlike traditional uses of software architecture as strictly a design-time artifact, our approach includes a system's architectural model in its run-time infrastructure. In particular, developers of self-adaptation capabilities use a system's software architectural model to monitor and reason about the system. Using a system's architecture as a control model for self-adaptation holds promise in several areas. As an abstract model, an architecture can provide a global perspective of the system and expose important system-level behaviors and properties. As a locus of high-level system design decisions, an architectural model can make a system's topological and behavioral constraints explicit, establishing an envelope of allowed changes and helping to ensure the validity of a change.

Using the architectural model as a basis to monitor and adapt a running system is known as *architecture-based self-adaptation*. A number of researchers have investigated this form of self-adaptation [17,21,26]. Their self-adaptive systems have been hand-crafted to provide strong support for particular classes of system (e.g., data-flow) and to target specific domains of concern (e.g., performance). Given a system in a supported system class, there will typically be an architecture description language and tool support to analyze and model the system, capture constraints on system behavior, detect constraint violations, and adapt the system.

4.2 Architectural Style

To capture system commonalities, we adapt the notion of an architectural style. Traditionally, the software engineering community has used architectural styles to help encode and express system-specific knowledge [29]. An architectural style characterizes a family of systems related by shared structural and semantic properties. The style is typically defined by four sets of entities:

- Component and connector types provide a vocabulary of elements, including components such as Database, Client, Server, and Filter; connectors such as SQL, HTTP, RPC, and Pipe; and component and connector interfaces.
- Constraints determine the permitted composition of the elements instantiated from the types. For example, constraints might prohibit cycles in a particular pipe-filter style, or define a compositional pattern such as the starfish arrangement of a blackboard system or a compiler's pipelined decomposition.
- Properties are attributes of the component and connector types, and provide analytic, behavioral, or semantic information. For example, load and service time properties might be characteristic of servers in a performance-specific client-server style, while transfer-rate might be a property in a pipe-filter style.
- Analyses can be performed on systems built in an appropriate architectural style. Examples include performance analysis using queuing theory in a client-server system, and schedulability analysis for a real-time-oriented style.

To support the needs of run-time system self-adaptation, we augment the notion of style with the notions of operators (to change an architecture) and adaptation strategies (to package changes for specific purpose). In previous work, we have extensively described the significant leverage that architectural style affords us [3]. That is, style provides opportunity for specific analysis of system behavior and properties. For self-adaptation, each style may uniquely guide the choice of metrics, help identify strategic points for system observation, and suggest possible adaptations.

5 The Rainbow Framework

In this section, we briefly introduce the Rainbow framework, which has already been reported in prior work [3,13]. In this paper, we focus on the separation between the general parts of Rainbow that can be applied to a wide variety of systems, and the tailorable parts that need to be written to apply Rainbow to specific systems and concerns.

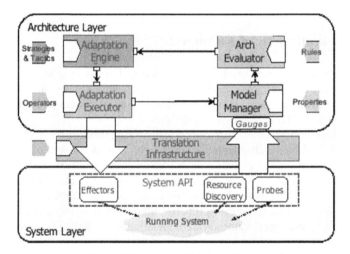

Fig. 2. The two-part Rainbow Framework

Rainbow uses the architectural model of the system to monitor the system and "reason" about appropriate actions. Monitoring mechanisms observe the running system. Observations are related to properties of the architectural model via *probes* and *gauges* [1,15]. The model is periodically evaluated to ensure that the system is operating within an envelope of acceptable range. If the evaluation determines that the system is not operating within the accepted range, the adaptation process is triggered, which determines the action to take. The adaptation is executed on the running system via system-level effectors.

The key idea for applying Rainbow in different situations is the separation of the framework into two parts (see Fig. 2). The first comprises a set of general, common infrastructures that are reusable across systems. The second consists of tailorable parts that can be specialized and customized for particular styles of system and various system properties of concern. The reusable infrastructures consist of the monitoring mechanisms, the model manager, the architectural evaluator, the adaptation engine, the executor, and various translators. The tailorable parts determine what properties of the system to monitor, what rules or constraints to evaluate, what adaptation actions to take when constraints are violated, and how to carry out those adaptations in terms of architectural as well as system-level operators.

This two-part self-adaptation approach has a number of advantages. By providing a substantial base of reusable infrastructure it greatly reduces the cost of development. By providing separate tailoring parts it allows engineers to tailor the framework to different systems with relatively small increments of effort. In particular, the tailorable model management and adaptation mechanisms give engineers the ability to customize adaptation to address different properties and domains of concern, and to add and evolve adaptation capabilities with ease. Furthermore, as described later, a modular adaptation language for tailoring the adaptation mechanism allows engineers to consider adaptation concerns separately and then put them to work together. In short, assessed abstractly, the Rainbow approach has the potential to satisfy the generality, cost-effectiveness, and composability requirements set forth initially.

6   Case Instantiations of Rainbow

To date, the Rainbow framework has been instantiated in two case study systems, and a third case study is in progress. Each case study has demonstrated the application of Rainbow to a different style of system, a different kind of system concern, as well as slightly different subsets of Rainbow capabilities.

The first case study provided an end-to-end investigation of the feasibility of the architecture style-based self-adaptation approach, and demonstrated effectiveness through an experiment on a dedicated testbed consisting of five routers and 11 machines communicating over 10-megabits-per-second lines [13]. The second case study demonstrated the potential generality of Rainbow applied to a different architectural style and an additional property of concern over the first case study, as well as revealed a moderate framework computational overhead [4]. Moreover, these two case studies helped to distill the reusable infrastructures of the framework [12]. The third case study in progress aims to show generality with a third data point on the kinds of system concern that Rainbow can address.

Here, we focus on how the two-part framework is instantiated for each of the case-studies to show how it can make self-adaptation an engineering reality.

6.1   Case 1: Client-Server Style with Performance Concern

In the first case study, we experimented with the application of Rainbow to a client-and-server style system, which consisted of a number of clients connected to one cluster of servers, with a specific performance concern of latency. The results show that for this application and the specific loads used in the experiment, self-adaptation significantly improved system performance. Fig. 3 shows sample results for system performance with and without adaptation. Fig. 3a shows that, without adaptation, once the latency experienced by each client rises above 2 seconds, it never again falls

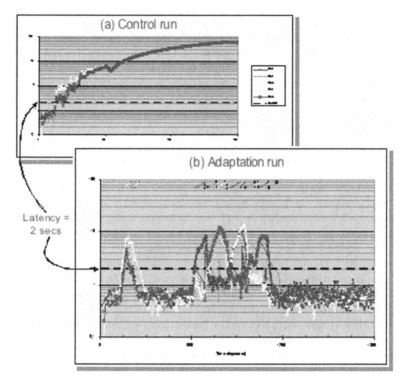

Fig. 3. System performance with and without self-adaptation. The dashed lines indicate the desired latency behavior

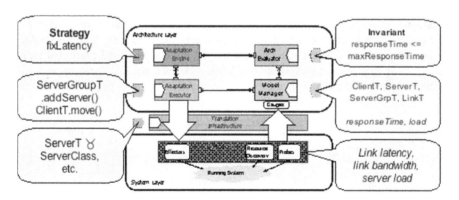

Fig. 4. Rainbow instantiation for client-server and performance

below this threshold. On the other hand, Fig. 3b shows that if Rainbow issues the adaptations, the client latencies return to optimal levels.

For this case study, as illustrated in Fig. 4, a vocabulary for the client-server style system elements is defined, along with performance-related properties. Specific performance properties—latency, bandwidth, load—are identified for monitoring. An invariant is defined over the system's architectural model to indicate the condition for adaptation. Thus, the architectural evaluator "sounds an alarm" when the response time of a client rises above some maximum threshold. A strategy has been defined to deal with this latency issue, and the strategy uses style-specific architectural operators such as *addServer*() and *move*(). A mapping helps to translate elements and actions in the architectural level to their counterparts in the system level. Note that, in general, mappings between architecture-layer and system-layer elements and actions may not be one-to-one, but will often be one-to-many.

6.2   Case 2: Service Coalition Style with Performance and Cost Concerns

In the second case study, we investigated the use of Rainbow on a service-coalition style, video-conferencing system with a simultaneous need to provide good-quality video service while keeping cost down to the customers using the service. Perhaps not surprisingly, this case study revealed that self-adaptation incurs some latency. In this system, the lapsed time for adaptation at the architecture, translation, and system layers were 230, 300, and 1,600 ms, respectively, for one scenario, and 330, 900, and 1,500 ms, respectively, for another. These results indicate that the software architecture-based approach best suits adaptations that operate on a system-wide scale and fix longer-term system behavior trends.

Because this system shared common performance properties with the first case study, we were able to reuse parts of the monitor and control infrastructures. In fact, from the first case study, the Rainbow prototype reused approximately 100 kilo-lines of code out of 102, plus an additional 73 kilo-lines of tool and utility code.

For this case study, as shown in Fig. 5, a vocabulary for the service coalition style system elements is defined, along with performance and cost-related properties. Specific properties—cost, load, bandwidth—are identified for monitoring. A few invariants are defined over the system's architectural model to indicate the conditions for adaptation. In particular, the architectural evaluator "sounds an alarm" either when the available bandwidth on certain connections drop below a minimum threshold, or the cost of serving the users rise above a maximum threshold. Adaptation strategies have been defined to deal with these two kinds of issues, and the strategies use style-specific architectural move() operators.

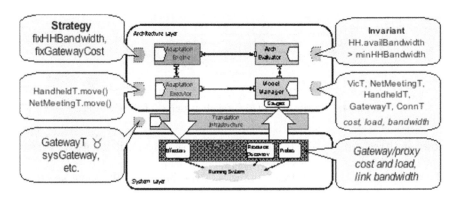

Fig. 5. Rainbow instantiation for service coalition and performance + cost

6.3   Case 3: Client-Server Style with Security Concern

The third case study is a straightforward client-server style system where a set of servers processes the requests of many clients, some of which can be malicious. The primary concern in this system is security, specifically, to appropriately detect and adapt against distributed denial of service attacks without greatly compromising such attributes as data integrity. Again, due to certain commonalities between this system and the previous two case studies, a significant subset of the framework, in addition to the common infrastructures, will be reusable.

In this case study, as illustrated in Fig. 6, a vocabulary for the specific kind of client-server style system elements is defined, along with security-related properties. Specific security properties—load, intrusion patterns—are identified for monitoring. An invariant is defined to trigger adaptation when the intrusion probability rises above a maximum threshold. Multiple adaptation strategies have been defined to deal with intrusion, including partitioning the network and securing data. The strategies use style-specific architectural operators supported by the various system elements.

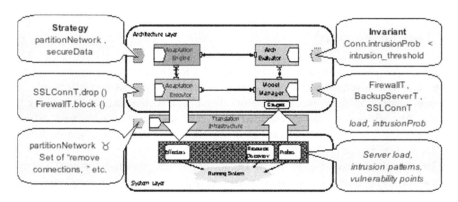

Fig. 6. Rainbow instantiation for client-server and security

6.4   Generalizing Across Cases

Table 1 summarizes the three case studies along two dimensions—architectural style and system concern. We believe that the Rainbow framework applies to a sufficient number of data points in these two dimensions to demonstrate generality.

Table 1. Summary of Rainbow case studies to date

Concern \ Style	Client-Server	Service-Coalition	...	Repository	...
Performance	X	X			
Cost		X			
Security	X				
....					
Reliability					
...					

These three case studies illustrate how we envision the application of Rainbow and give concrete examples to help characterize the tailorable parts. These case studies also bring into focus the aspects of the Rainbow framework that are (or need to be) reusable and generalized across systems. As a result, we have identified a number of key challenges to make the Rainbow approach possible.

In particular, we are presently investigating two research challenges that arise from the ability in Rainbow to tailor specific adaptation strategies for different styles of systems and different kinds of system concern, namely representing adaptation knowledge and coordinating adaptations. A general ability to represent adaptation knowledge allows engineers to "plug-in" different strategies, making adaptation external and modifiable. This marks an important step toward providing *cost-effective* self-adaptation. A general mechanism to resolve conflicts and coordinate adaptations allows system engineers to consider system properties of concern separately and *compose* adaptation strategies.

As these challenges are being resolved, the Rainbow framework holds promise to realize our vision and make self-adaptation an engineering reality.

7   Looking Forward

In this paper, we have expressed our vision of a software engineering reality where engineers can develop self-adaptive software-intensive systems cost-effectively. We have discussed the Rainbow approach and shown how it charts a path to realizing this vision. Specifically, we have described three case studies of systems with different concerns and qualitatively demonstrated how Rainbow generalizes across different styles of systems and different concerns.

In a larger context, the Rainbow framework holds potential for application in other forms of composition, particularly in relation to human task, autonomic computing, and software design. Recall that one of the conditions of self-adaptation is changes in user priority or preference. For Rainbow to be aware of such changes, it would provide appropriate interfaces to the user level. Specifically, a user would be able to influence the behavior of the framework via such variables as frequency and granularity of monitoring, choice of adaptations, and quality of actions taken.

Recently, there has been a push by IBM and others toward developing systems or elements of systems that are autonomic. That is, they are self-managing and exhibit self-configuring, self-healing, self-protecting, and self-optimizing properties [11]. Since Rainbow provides the mechanisms for self-adaptive systems, it is possible to apply Rainbow in the context of autonomic systems to construct a system of systems in which each constituent system exhibits self-adaptive capabilities.

Finally, certain insights from the Rainbow approach can influence how software engineers design future software. One of the main assumptions of the Rainbow approach is that we require the target system to provide hooks for measuring and changing the system. What if the software is designed to provide such hooks? Indeed, if the software engineering community standardizes interfaces for extracting information from and effecting changes on systems, engineers would be able to produce systems that plug-and-play with self-adaptation infrastructures like Rainbow.

Acknowledgements

This research was supported by DARPA under grants N66001-99-2-8918 and F30602-00-2-0616, by the US Army Research Office (ARO) under grant numbers DAAD19-02-1-0389 ("Perpetually Available and Secure Information Systems") to Carnegie Mellon University's CyLab and DAAD19-01-1-0485, and the NASA High Dependability Computing Program under cooperative agreement NCC-2-1298. The views and conclusions described here are those of the authors and should not be interpreted as representing the official policies, either expressed or implied, of DARPA, the ARO, NASA, the US government, or any other entity.

References

1. Robert Balzer. Probe run-time infrastructure. http://schafercorpballston.com/dasada/2001WinterPI/ProbeRun-TimeInfrastructureDesign.ppt, 2001.
2. Antonio Carzaniga, David S. Rosenblum, and Alexander L. Wolf. Design and evaluation of a wide-area event notification service. ACM Transactions on Computer Systems, 19(3):332–383, August 2001.
3. Shang-Wen Cheng, David Garlan, Bradley Schmerl, João Pedro Sousa, Bridget Spitznagel, and Peter Steenkiste. Using architectural style as a basis for self-repair. In Jan Bosch, Morven Gentleman, Christine Hofmeister, and Juha Kuusela, editors, Software Architecture: System Design, Development, and Maintenance (WICSA-3), pages 45–59, Massachusetts, USA, August 25–30, 2002. Kluwer Academic Publishers.
4. Shang-Wen Cheng, An-Cheng Huang, David Garlan, Bradley Schmerl, and Peter Steenkiste. An architecture for coordinating multiple self-management systems. In Proceedings of the 4th Working IEEE/IFIP Conference on Software Architecture (WICSA-4), Oslo, Norway, June 11–14, 2004.
5. Paul Clements, Felix Bachmann, Len Bass, David Garlan, James Ivers, Reed Little, Robert Nord, and Judith Stafford, editors. Documenting Software Architecture: Views and Beyond. The SEI Series in Software Engineering. Pearson Education, Inc., 2003.
6. Nathan Combs and Jeff Vagel. Adaptive mirroring of system of systems architectures. In Garlan et al. [14], pages 96–98.
7. Timothy W. Curry. Profiling and tracing dynamic library usage via interposition. In USENIX Summer, pages 267–278, 1994.
8. Eric M. Dashofy, Andre van der Hoek, and Richard N. Taylor. Towards architecture-based self-healing systems. In Garlan et al. [14], pages 21–26.
9. Jason Flinn, SoYoung Park, and Mahadev Satyanarayanan. Balancing performance, energy, and quality in pervasive computing. In Proceedings of the 22nd International Conference on Distributed Computing Systems (ICDCS'02), pages 217–226. IEEE Computer Society Press, July 02–05, 2002.

10. Colleen Frye. Self-healing systems. Application Development Trends, pages 29–34, September 2003.
11. A. G. Ganak and T. A. Corbi. The dawning of the autonomic computing era. IBM Systems Journal, 42(1):5–18, 2003.
12. David Garlan, Shang-Wen Cheng, An-Cheng Huang, Bradley Schmerl, and Peter Steenkiste. Rainbow: Architecture-based self-adaptation with reusable infrastructure. IEEE Computer, 37(10):46–54, October 2004.
13. David Garlan, Shang-Wen Cheng, and Bradley Schmerl. Increasing system dependability through architecture-based self-repair. In Rogério de Lemos, Cristina Gacek, and Alexander Romanovsky, editors, Architecting Dependable Systems, Lecture Notes in Computer Science, pages 61–89, New York, NY, USA, 2003. Springer-Verlag, Inc.
14. David Garlan, Jeff Kramer, and Alexander Wolf, editors. Proceedings of the First ACM SIGSOFT Workshop on Self-Healing Systems (WOSS'02), New York, NY, USA, November 18–19, 2002. ACM Press.
15. David Garlan, Bradley Schmerl, and Jichuan Chang. Using gauges for architecture-based monitoring and adaptation. In [28].
16. Ioannis Georgiadis, Jeff Magee, and Jeff Kramer. Self-organizing software architectures for distributed systems. In Garlan et al. [14], pages 33–38.
17. Michael M. Gorlick and Rami R. Razouk. Using Weaves for software construction and analysis. In 13th International Conference of Software Engineering, pages 23–34, Los Alamitos, CA, USA, May 1991. IEEE, IEEE Computer Society Press.
18. Phil Gross. MEET. http://www.psl.cs.columbia.edu/meet/index.html, 2002.
19. Philip N. Gross, Suhit Gupta, Gail E. Kaiser, Gaurav S. Kc, and Janak J. Parekh. An active events model for systems monitoring. In [28].
20. Fabio Kon, Fabio Costa, Gordon Blair, and Roy H. Campbell. The case for reflective middleware. In Communications of the ACM, 45(6), pages 33–38, June 2002.
21. Jeff Magee, Naranker Dulay, Susan Eisenbach, and Jeff Kramer. Specifying Distributed Software Architectures. InW. Schafer and P. Botella, editors, Proceedings of 5th European Software Engineering Conference (ESEC 95), pages 137–153, Sitges, Spain, September 26, 1995. Springer-Verlag, Berlin.
22. V. Markl, G. M. Lohman, and V. Raman. LEO: An autonomic query optimizer for DB2. IBM Systems Journal, 42(1):98–106, 2003.
23. Priya Narasimhan, Louise E. Moser, and P. M. Melliar-Smith. Using interceptors to enhance CORBA. IEEE Computer, pages 62–68, July 1999.
24. Priya Narasimhan, Louise E. Moser, and P. M. Melliar-Smith. Strongly consistent replication and recovery of fault-tolerant CORBA applications. Journal of Computer System Science and Engineering, Spring 2002.
25. Peyman Oreizy. Open Architecture Software: A Flexible Approach to Decentralized Software Evolution. PhD thesis, University of California, Irvine, 2000.
26. Peyman Oreizy, Michael M. Gorlick, Richard N. Taylor, Dennis Heimbigner, Gregory Johnson, Nenad Medvidovic, Alex Quilici, David S. Rosenblum, and Alexander L. Wolf. An architecture-based approach to self-adaptive software. IEEE Intelligent Systems, 14(3):54–62, May–June 1999.
27. Proceedings of the International Conference on Autonomic Computing, New York, NY, May 17-18, 2004.
28. Proceedings of the Working Conference on Complex and Dynamic Systems Architecture, Brisbane, Australia, December 12–14, 2001.

29. Mary Shaw and David Garlan. Software Architecture: Perspectives on an Emerging Discipline. Prentice-Hall, 1996.
30. Giuseppe Valetto and Gail Kaiser. A case study in software adaptation. In Garlan et al. [14], pages 73–78.
31. Alexander L. Wolf, Dennis Heimbigner, Antonio Carzaniga, Kenneth M. Anderson, and Nathan Ryan. Achieving survivability of complex and dynamic systems with the Willow framework. In [28].

An Online Control Framework for Designing Self-optimizing Computing Systems: Application to Power Management[*]

Nagarajan Kandasamy[1], Sherif Abdelwahed[2], Gregory C. Sharp[3], and John P. Hayes[4]

[1] Electrical and Computer Engineering Deptartment,
Drexel University, Philadelphia, PA 19104, USA
kandasamy@ece.drexel.edu
[2] Institute for Software Integrated Systems,
Vanderbilt University, Nashville, TN 37212, USA
sherif@isis.vanderbilt.edu
[3] Harvard Medical School,
Massachusetts General Hospital, Boston, MA 02114, USA
gcsharp@partners.org
[4] Electrical and Computer, Engineering Department,
University of Michigan, Ann Arbor, MI 48109, USA
jhayes@eecs.umich.edu

Abstract. Computer systems hosting critical e-commerce applications must typically satisfy stringent quality-of-service (QoS) requirements under dynamic operating conditions and workloads. Also, as such systems increase in size and complexity, maintaining the desired QoS by manually tuning the numerous performance-related parameters will become very difficult. This paper addresses the design of self-optimizing computer systems using a generic online control framework in which the control actions governing the operation of the system are obtained by optimizing its behavior, as forecast by a mathematical model, over a limited time horizon. As a specific application of this control technique, we show how to minimize the power consumed by a processor while satisfying the QoS requirements of a time-varying workload. We describe the processor model, formulate the power management problem, and derive the online control algorithm. The performance of the controller is evaluated using representative e-commerce workloads.

1 Introduction

Computer systems hosting applications crucial to commerce and banking, transportation, military command and control, among others, must typically satisfy

---

[*] A preliminary version of this paper appeared in the proceedings of the IEEE Conference on Autonomic Computing, Washington DC, USA, May 2004.

O. Babaoglu et al. (Eds.): SELF-STAR 2004, LNCS 3460, pp. 174–188, 2005.

stringent QoS requirements while operating in highly dynamic environments; for example, the workload to be processed may be time varying, and hardware and software components may fail during system operation. To operate such computer systems efficiently while achieving the desired QoS goals, multiple performance-related parameters must be continuously tuned to the dynamic operating conditions, and as these systems become more complex, it will become very difficult for human operators to manage their performance effectively.

To cope with the complexity expected of future computing systems, it is highly desirable for such systems to manage themselves, given high-level objectives by administrators. Such *self-managing systems* aim to achieve QoS objectives by adaptively tuning key operating parameters with minimal human intervention [16]. This paper focuses on one key aspect of such systems—*self-optimization*, where its performance and efficiency are continuously improved.

We address the design of self-optimizing computer systems within an online control framework. Control theory provides a systematic way to manage resources in a general setting; if the computer system is correctly modeled and its operating environment accurately estimated, the control actions required to maintain a certain QoS by optimizing a given cost function can be derived [20]. It also provides well-established mathematical techniques to analyze system performance and correctness, and recently, has been successfully applied to such problems as task scheduling [19] [11], QoS adaptation in web servers [2], load management in e-mail and file servers [14] [18], network flow control [21] [4], and power management [15] [27].

The above methods all use *feedback* or *reactive control* [22] to first observe the current system state and then take corrective action, if any, to achieve the specified QoS. Traditional feedback control has some inherent limitations. It usually assumes a linearized and discrete-time model for system dynamics, and a continuous input (output) domain. Many practical systems, however, have a finite set of possible control inputs, and exhibit *hybrid* behavior comprising both discrete-event and time-based dynamics [5].

We propose a *model-predictive control* approach where the actions governing system operation are obtained by optimizing its forecast behavior, described by a mathematical model, for the specified QoS criteria over a limited prediction horizon [20]. This scheme is more general and widely applicable than feedback control, allowing for multiple QoS objectives and system operating constraints to be explicitly represented as an optimization problem and solved for each control step. It can also control systems exhibiting event-driven and/or nonlinear dynamics, as well as those with delays and dead times. Finally, the approach can accommodate run-time modifications to the system model itself, caused by resource failures and time-varying parameter changes.

As a specific case study, we apply the above control technique to manage the power consumed by a processor subject to a time-varying workload comprising HTTP and e-commerce requests. Assuming a processor capable of dynamic voltage scaling [23], an online controller is developed to achieve a specified response time for these requests while minimizing the corresponding power consumption.

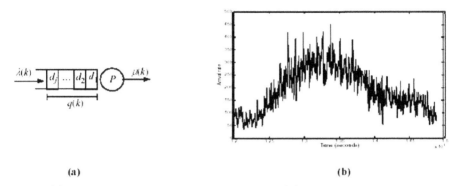

(a)   (b)

Fig. 1. (a) A queuing model of the processor and (b) HTTP requests made to an Internet service provider in the Washington DC area [7]

Note that power consumption relates quadratically to processor supply voltage which can be reduced at lower frequencies. Therefore, power savings can be quite significant. Furthermore, many processors such as the AMD-K-2 [3] and StrongARM [25] support dynamic voltage scaling by offering a limited number of frequency settings, eight and ten, respectively. We describe the processor model, formulate the power management problem, and develop the online controller to operate the processor efficiently within a limited and discrete frequency domain. Controller performance is evaluated using a representative e-commerce workload. Finally, we also discuss how online control can be applied to other resource management problems in computer systems.

The rest of this paper is organized as follows. Section 2 formulates the processor power management problem while Section 3 discusses basic predictive-control concepts and develops the online control algorithm. Section 4 evaluates controller performance and we conclude the paper with a discussion on future work as well as other applications of online control in Section 5.

2   Preliminaries

This section discusses system modeling assumptions, specifies the desired QoS objectives, and formulates the resource management problem.

2.1   System Model

Figure 1(a) shows the queuing model corresponding to a processor P where $\lambda(k)$ and $\mu(k)$ denote the arrival and processing rates, respectively, of incoming requests $\{d_j\}$, and $q(k)$ denotes the queue size at time step k. We do not assume an *a priori* arrival-rate distribution for $\{d_j\}$ but use real-world workload traces such as that shown in Fig.1(b). Also, requests are processed by P in a first-come first-serve fashion. We assume a processor capable of operating within a limited set of frequencies U. Therefore, if the time required to process d_j while operating at the maximum frequency $u_{\max}$ is c_j, then the corresponding processing time while operating at some frequency $u(k) \in U$ is $c_j/\alpha(k)$ where $\alpha(k) = u(k)/u_{\max}$ is the scaling factor. The average response time achieved by the processor during time step k is denoted by $w(k)$; this includes both the waiting time in the queue and the processing time on P. We use the model proposed in [28] to estimate the average power consumed by the processor while operating at $u(k)$ as $\psi(k) = \alpha^2(k)$. This simple model has been shown to provide reasonably accurate estimates for power consumption.

The above system model corresponds to a special class of hybrid systems having a finite control set—called *switching hybrid systems* [1]. The following discrete-time form of the state space equations describes their dynamics:

$$x(k + 1) = f(x(k), u(k), \Omega(k))$$

where $x(k) \in \mathbb{R}^n$ denotes the current system state, and $u(k) \in U \subset \mathbb{R}^m$ and $\Omega(k) \in \mathbb{R}^r$ the control and environment inputs, respectively, at time k. The system state is given by the achieved response time and the corresponding power consumption as $x(k) = (w(k), \psi(k))$. The function f (described in Section 3.2) models the system dynamics, and computes the next state for time step $k + 1$, given $x(k)$, the control input $u(k)$, and the environment inputs $\Omega(k) = (\lambda(k), c(k))$ where $\lambda(k)$ and $c(k)$ denote the request arrival rate and average processing time, respectively.

2.2   Performance Specification

At each time step, the controller aims to satisfy a designer-specified response time w^* for incoming requests while minimizing processor power consumption. We pose this resource management problem as one of *utility optimization* that maximizes (minimizes) a performance measure given as a function of both the system state and input variables. Typically, this function is a weighted norm, where the corresponding variables are lumped together with different weights reflecting their individual contributions to overall system utility. Operating requirements may also include hard and soft constraints on system variables. *Hard constraints* are generally expressed as a feasible domain for a composite set of system variables, possibly including the control inputs themselves. A *soft constraint* is similarly expressed, and represented by a cost function mapping each point in the composite space to a scalar value denoting the corresponding penalty. A soft constraint, therefore, is another way to specify system performance requirements where the controller aims to minimize the associated cost function.

We now pose the problem of interest. Let $J(k)$ be the cost function corresponding to some system state $x(k)$. Soft constraints may be added to $J(k)$ using *slack variables*, defined such that they are non-zero only if the corresponding constraints are violated. Their non-zero values may be heavily penalized in the cost function. Therefore, the controller has a strong incentive to keep them at zero if possible. We define an appropriate slack variable $\epsilon(k)$ such that:

$$\epsilon(k) = \begin{cases} 0 & : \quad w(k) \leq w^* \\ w(k) - w^* & : \quad \text{otherwise} \end{cases}$$

Therefore, the cost function $J(k)$ is now a weighted norm of the form:

$$J(k) = \|\epsilon(k)\|_Q + \|\psi(k)\|_R$$

where Q and R denote user-defined weights.

2.3   Problem Formulation

The control problem is to satisfy the QoS specification during the operating period of the system, i.e., for each time step k, and is formulated as follows:

$$\text{Minimize} \sum_k J(k)$$

$$\text{Subject to}\ \ x(k+1) = f(x(k), u(k), \Omega(k))$$

$$u(k) \in U$$

Note that the control inputs are constrained by the frequency settings available on the processor. Also, since the underlying control set is discrete and finite, traditional optimal control techniques cannot be applied directly to solve this problem, and in most cases, a closed expression for feedback control cannot be obtained. Moreover, in practice, the operating parameters including $\Omega(k)$ may vary continuously at run time.

3   Controller Design

This section introduces key predictive control concepts and develops the online control algorithm.

3.1   Predictive Control Concepts

We solve the optimization problem in Section 2.3 under dynamic operating conditions using a predictive control technique [20]. The basic ideas behind this approach are now briefly discussed. As noted in Section 1, the control actions governing system operation are obtained by optimizing its forecast behavior, described by the mathematical model f, for the specified QoS criteria over a limited prediction horizon of length N. Therefore, the original control problem is written as follows:

$$\text{Minimize} \sum_{i=k+1}^{k+N} J(k)$$

$$\text{Subject to}\ \ \hat{x}(i+1) = f(x(i), u(i), \hat{\Omega}(i))$$

$$u(i) \in U$$

where $\hat{x}(i)$ and $\hat{\Omega}(i)$ denote the estimated system state and environment inputs, respectively. Since U is finite, the above problem is clearly solvable, though, in

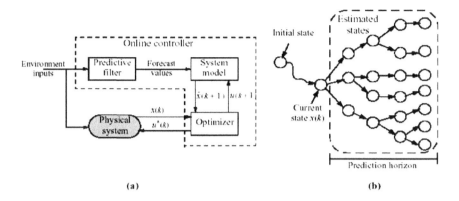

Fig. 2. (a) The overall controller architecture and (b) the look-ahead optimization process

general, it will not produce an optimal solution for the original control problem. In many practical situations, however, the main concern is *controller feasibility*, namely its ability to drive the system towards the desired operating region quickly and maintain it there even under dynamic operating conditions.

Figure 2(a) shows the overall structure of the online controller to solve the above optimization problem. Relevant parameters of the operating environment such as workload arrival patterns and processing times are estimated, and used by the system model to forecast future behavior over the look-ahead horizon. The controller optimizes the forecast behavior as per the specified QoS requirements by selecting the best control input to apply to the system.

- As shown in Figure 2(b), future system states, in terms $\hat{x}(k+i)$, for a prediction horizon of $i = 1, \ldots, N$ steps are estimated during each sampling time step k using the corresponding behavioral model. These predictions depend on known values (past inputs and outputs) up to the sampling instant k, and on the future control signals in terms of $u(k+i), i = 1, \ldots, N-1$ which are inputs to the system that must be calculated.
- A sequence of control signals resulting in the desired system behavior is obtained for each step of the prediction horizon by optimizing the cost function.
- The control signal $u^*(k)$ corresponding to the first control input in the above sequence is applied to the system during time k while the other inputs are rejected. During the next sampling instant, $x(k+1)$ is known, and the above steps are repeated. Finally, note that the observed state $x(k + 1)$ may be different from that estimated by the controller at time k.

3.2 Model Dynamics

To estimate system behavior over the prediction horizon, characteristics of the workload including the request arrival rate and processing times must also be estimated. Various prediction models have been previously proposed for performance estimation of computer systems. In [26], an autoregressive model to predict trends in network traffic is developed, while [29] combines a Kalman filter with an autoregressive model to detect changes in web server workloads. The authors of [13] present both short- and long-term prediction algorithms to estimate various performance variables in a computer system including abnormal events such as QoS violations and system failures.

Based on key characteristics of representative e-commerce workloads, we now develop an appropriate forecasting model to predict request arrival rates. Figure 1(b) shows HTTP requests made to a computer at ClarkNet, an Internet service provider in the Washington DC area over a day [7]. Request arrivals, plotted using a granularity of 30 seconds, clearly show a cyclical trend, as do many other published workloads [7] [6]. Therefore, we conclude that such workloads may be predicted using a trend model, used when the increase (decrease) in a series of values persists for an extended time. The following equations describe this forecasting model [12]:

$$\hat{\lambda}(k) = \alpha \cdot \lambda(k) + (1 - \alpha) \cdot (\hat{\lambda}(k-1) + \delta(k-1))$$
$$\delta(k) = \beta \cdot (\hat{\lambda}(k) - \hat{\lambda}(k-1)) + (1 - \beta) \cdot \delta(k-1)$$
$$\hat{\lambda}(k+1) = \hat{\lambda}(k) + \delta(k)$$

where $\lambda(k)$ and $\hat{\lambda}(k)$ denote the observed and estimated arrival rates for time k, respectively. The estimate $\hat{\lambda}(k)$ is obtained using a weighted moving average of recent past estimates and the current observation. The smoothing constant α determines the weight given to past observations and controls the rate of averaging. The trend $\delta(k)$ present in the arrival rate is detected using a smoothed average of first differences, i.e., the change in request arrivals from period k to $k+1$. The smoothing constant β controls the rate of averaging. This model is validated using a real-world workload in Section 4. The processing time estimate for time $k+1$ is given by an exponentially-weighted moving average model as $\hat{c}(k+1) = \gamma \cdot c(k) + (1 - \gamma) \cdot \hat{c}(k-1)$ where γ is the smoothing constant.

The following equations describe the dynamics of the processor model:

$$\hat{q}(k+1) = q(k) + \left(\hat{\lambda}(k+1) - \frac{\alpha(k+1)}{\hat{c}(k+1)}\right) \cdot t_{\mathsf{s}}$$
$$\hat{\omega}(k+1) = (1 + \hat{q}(k+1)) \cdot \hat{c}(k+1)$$
$$\hat{\psi}(k+1) = \alpha^2(k+1)$$

Given the observed queue length $q(k)$, the estimated length $\hat{q}(k+1)$ for time step $k+1$ is obtained using the workload predictions. The sampling period of the controller is denoted by t_s. The average response times of requests arriving during the interval $[k, k+1]$ is estimated as $\hat{\omega}(k+1)$ and the corresponding power consumption estimate is $\hat{\psi}(k+1)$.

3.3   Control Algorithm

To solve the look-ahead optimization problem presented in Section 3.1, the controller explores the prediction horizon starting from the current state $x(k)$. It constructs, in breadth-first fashion, a tree comprising all possible future states up to the specified horizon as follows. Given some $\hat{x}(i)$ within the prediction horizon, we first estimate the workload $\hat{\Omega}(i+1)$, and generate the next set of reachable system states by applying all possible control inputs from the set U. The cost function $J(k)$ corresponding to each generated state is then computed. Once the prediction horizon is fully explored, a sequence of reachable states with the minimum cumulative cost is obtained and the control input corresponding to the first state in this sequence is provided to the processor while the rest are discarded. The above control action is repeated for each sampling step.

In our experiments, the weights in the cost function $J(k)$ were set to $Q = 100$ and $R = 1$ to penalize the controller heavily if a chosen operating frequency fails to satisfy ω^*. However, if multiple frequencies satisfy ω^*, the lowest frequency is chosen to minimize energy consumption. Also, since the controller exhaustively evaluates all possible operating states within the prediction horizon to determine the best input to apply at time step k, the overhead due to this approach must be analyzed. If $|U|$ denotes the size of the control-input set, and N the prediction horizon depth, then the number of explored states is given by $\sum_{i=1}^{N} |U|^i$.

When both the prediction horizon and the number of control inputs are small, the computational overhead is negligible—as confirmed by experiments in Section 4. Since control actions are taken after exploring a limited number of states, we must also guarantee that the underlying physical system is online controllable. Our system is, since given a state $x(k)$, it is always possible to find a control input $u(k)$ that forces the system into a different state. This implies that the controller can make continuous progress towards achieving the desired QoS objective without a deadlock. We do not analyze the stability of the on-line controller here; a more detailed analysis is left as future work.

4   Performance Evaluation

The performance of the controller is now evaluated using a representative e-commerce workload. We first describe how the workload is generated and then discuss the obtained results.

The authors of [15] propose a feedback controller to balance both energy consumption and QoS requirements on a processor executing multimedia applications. Our approach cannot be directly compared to [15] since is assumes a processor capable of operating at arbitrary frequencies. By contrast, we assume a processor with a limited number of frequency settings—an AMD Athlon with possible operating frequencies of 532, 665, 798, 1197, and 1529 MHz [24].

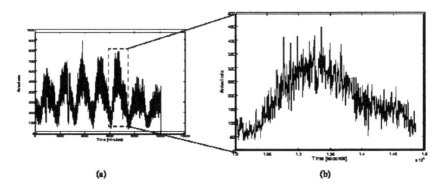

Fig. 3. (a) Workload arrival pattern generated using the HTTP logs of an internet service provider; (b) requests received by the computer during a day, plotted in 30-second intervals

4.1   Workload Generation

Our experiments simulated a busy server processing a synthetic yet realistic workload comprising HTTP requests. To generate the workload, we require a time-varying request arrival rate, execution times of the individual requests, and their distribution within the arrival stream. The workload arrival rate shown in Fig. 3(a) was obtained by combining real-world traces—HTTP requests made to a computer at Clarknet over a week [7]. (Unfortunately, the published log files do not have any execution-time information for these requests).

Using the rate information in Fig. 3(a), the distribution of individual requests within the arrival sequence was determined using two important characteristics of most web workloads: popularity and temporal locality. First, we generated a virtual store comprising 10,000 objects, and the time needed to process an object request was randomly chosen from a uniform distribution between $(25, 50)$ ms. Simulated requests to the store had the following characteristics:

- *Popularity*: It has been widely observed that some files are more popular than others, and that the popularity distribution commonly follows Zipf's law [7]. (A few files are extremely popular while many others are very rarely requested). Therefore, we partitioned the virtual store in two—a "popular" set with 1000 objects receiving 90% of all requests, and a "rare" set containing the remaining objects in the store receiving only 10% of requests.
- *Temporal locality*: This is the likelihood that once an object is requested, it will be requested again in the near future. In many web workloads, temporal locality follows a lognormal distribution [9].

4.2   Analysis of Results

We first calibrated the trend model used to forecast arrival rates (described in Section 3.2). The best fit to the arrival pattern in Fig. 3(a) was obtained for smoothing constants of $\alpha = 0.17$ and $\beta = 0.1$; the goodness-of-fit measure was

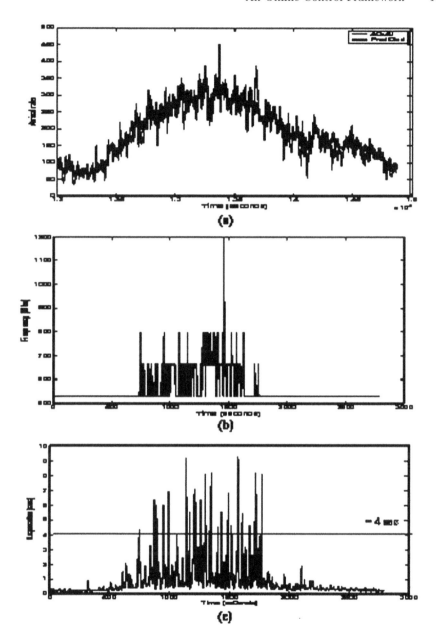

Fig. 4. (a) An overlay of the workload arrival rates from Fig.3(b) and the corresponding predictions made by the online controller; (b) the processor operating frequencies specified by the controller, and (c) the achieved response times

$\bar{R}^2 = 0.82$ and the predicted values had a mean absolute percentage error of 16% when compared to observed ones. Figure 4(a) shows the observed and predicted values overlaid on each other. Though the trend model predicts the arrival rate well in most cases, it fails to track sudden surges (or spikes) in request arrivals. We compared the performance of the trend model with another widely used forecasting technique; a Box-Jenkins ARIMA model [10] was generated using Freefore [8] to best fit the observed data in Fig. 3(a). The generated model had and an average error of 15% between predicted and observed values. Therefore, we conclude that the trend model provides an adequate fit to the data used in our experiments; the sudden spikes simply correspond to noise in the data values. Request processing times were estimated using $\gamma = 0.35$.

The performance of the controller was evaluated over a smaller portion of the overall workload, shown in Fig. 3(b), where the requests received by the computer during one day are plotted in 30-second observation intervals. We note that this interval is sufficient to smooth the variability in arrival rates and adequately track them using the prediction model. Therefore, the sampling period of the controller was set to $t_s = 30$—no smaller that the observation interval. Also, the overhead due to controller execution as well as the system dead time (the delay between changing the operating frequency and its completion) is negligible and therefore ignored in our experiments. The response time to be achieved by the controller was set to $\omega^* = 4$ sec.

Figures 4(a)-4(c) summarize the performance of the controller for a prediction horizon of two time steps. Figure 4(b) shows how the controller changes processor frequency to accommodate the time-varying workload in Fig. 4(a). The achieved response times are shown in Fig. 4(c). The controller does not achieve the desired QoS during some time periods since it cannot predict sudden (and short-term) spikes in the arrival rate. The frequent switching activity in Fig. 4(b) occurs since the cost function $J(k)$ does not include a corresponding switching penalty. Though control actions in general systems typically incur some penalty, in the specific case of power management, this penalty is negligible; for example, a frequency change in the AMD-K-2 processor incurs a time overhead of only 41 μs [24]. Therefore, our cost function ignored this switching penalty.

The overall controller performance is promising; in our experiments, it achieved the desired response time ω^* for about 91% of the received requests. We also evaluated the effect of different prediction horizons on controller performance in terms of the percentage of requests satisfying their QoS requirement. Increasing the horizon in this case does not improve performance; in fact, performance suffers slightly. It may be that for this specific workload, model forecasting errors accumulate with increasing horizon depth, degrading controller performance.

To summarize, our experiments imply that optimal solutions for such on-line control problems do not exist, particularly when the arrival rates are unpredictable and potentially unbounded. The system designer must, therefore, decide upon an acceptable controller configuration after sufficient experimentation. In this specific case, a short-term forecasting horizon of depth two appears appropriate. Also, controller performance may be enhanced by improving the processor model and the cost function—both are topics for future work. Finally, the controller overhead corresponding to prediction horizons of two, three, and four was found to be negligible, and hence not reported.

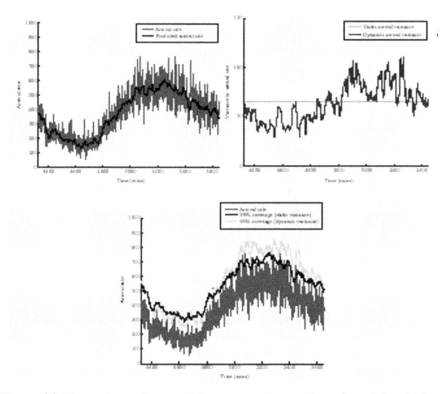

Fig. 5. (a) Observed arrival rate and the corresponding predictions made by a Kalman filter, (b) the variance between the observed and predicted values, and (c) conservative predictions accounting for noise in the observed arrival rate

5 Discussion

This paper has addressed the design of self-optimizing computer systems using a generic online control framework. As a specific application of this technique, we showed how to minimize the power consumed by a computer by designing a controller to satisfy the QoS requirements of a time-varying workload while operating the processor at the lowest possible frequency. Its performance was evaluated using representative e-commerce workloads with encouraging results. As future work, we plan to improve the performance of the predictive controller and extend the control scheme to manage distributed systems. The QoS violations seen in Fig. 4(c) suggest that the system model is somewhat sensitive to noise in the observed data. We can enhance model accuracy and robustness by including prediction errors while forecasting arrival and processing rates. Figure 5(a) shows a portion of the workload previously shown in Fig.3(a) and the corresponding predictions, obtained using a constant velocity Kalman filter that implements the trend model presented in Section 3.2. Note that for this workload, the variance between predicted and actual values changes over time. In fact,

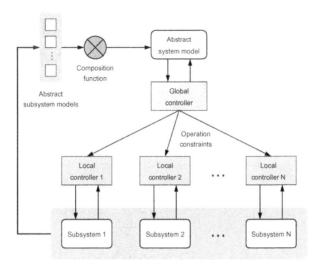

Fig. 6. The multi-level control structure

the variance increases for higher arrival rates. Figure5(b) compares a statically estimated variance (obtained while tuning the Kalman filter) against a dynamic estimation. These variance estimates can now be used to obtain conservative arrival-rate predictions by providing some "spare capacity" to the original predictions in Fig.5(a). Predictions covering 99% of the noise in the original workload are shown in Fig.5(c) using both static and dynamic variance estimation. When using dynamic estimation, a higher capacity is required during periods of high variance. Conversely, during periods of low variance, the error margin is tighter.

The proposed control approach is very general and is applicable to other resource management problems in computer systems. In [17], we developed an online controller to operate a distributed computer system in energy-efficient fashion while satisfying the QoS requirements of a dynamic workload; computers are switched on (off) as needed to accommodate the time-varying workload. Online predictive control is especially useful when control actions have substantial dead times (such as switching on a computer). We have evaluated this approach on real-world e-commerce workloads with encouraging results. We also believe a similar control approach can help design self-healing distributed systems. Certain computer failures may be predicted shortly before their occurrence by analyzing the corresponding performance variables [13]. The controller can then initiate the appropriate reconfiguration action such as switching on a backup computer in anticipation of such failures to prevent service disruptions.

Finally, in a distributed system with several components, each may have its own requirement specification defining a desired operating region. In addition, a global performance requirement for the overall system may also be specified. Therefore, the controller must effectively coordinate (complex) interactions between the various components to ensure overall system performance.

The nature of such systems suggests a *hierarchical control structure* where each component has a local controller. Interaction between these controllers is managed via a global controller that aims to satisfy the global specifications of the overall system. Fig. 6 shows the structure of a two-level control scheme where local-controller interactions are managed by a higher-level controller using an abstract system model containing information relevant to its objectives. The model includes, for instance, details of interactions between system components in terms of specific local variables contributing to a global objective. The abstract dynamics then represent how these variables would change in response to certain settings that the global controller enforces via commands to local ones.

We envision a hierarchical structure where the high-level controller takes a long-term perspective of system dynamics, while the local ones act to optimize their components on a shorter-term basis. High-level commands are directed towards satisfying global QoS objectives, and act as a set of operating constraints on each local controller. Each local controller then tries to optimize the performance of its underlying component using specific utility functions while satisfying any constraints imposed on it. Interaction between these controllers takes place as follows. Each local controller has a finite set of operating modes corresponding to specific parameter settings within its controlled component, e.g., a different operational requirement or input domain. The global controller then places (or restricts) each one in a mode aimed at satisfying the QoS objective. Local controllers optimize relevant parameters within that mode.

References

1. S. Abdelwahed, G. Karsai, and G. Biswas. Online safety control of a class of hybrid systems. In *41st IEEE Conference on Decision and Control*, pages 1988–1990, 2002.
2. T. F. Abdelzaher, K. G. Shin, and N. Bhatti. Performance guarantees for web server end-systems: A control theoretic approach. *IEEE Trans. Parallel & Distributed Syst.*, 13(1):80–96, January 2002.
3. Advanced Micro Devices Corp. *Mobile AMD-K6-2+ Processor Data Sheet*, June 2000.
4. E. Altman, T. Başar, and R. Srikant. Congestion control as a stochastic control problem with action delay. *Automatica*, 35:1937–1950, 1999.
5. P. Antsaklis. Special issue on hybrid systems: theory and applications a brief introduction to the theory and applications of hybrid systems. *Proceedings of the IEEE*, 88(7):879–887, July 2000.
6. M. Arlitt and T. Jin. Workload characterization of the 1998 world cup web site. Technical Report HPL-99-35R1, Hewlett-Packard Labs., September 1999.
7. M. F. Arlitt and C. L. Williamson. Web server workload characterization: The search for invariants. In *Proc. ACM SIGMETRICS Conf.*, pages 126–137, 1996.
8. Automatic forecasting systems, http://www.autobox.com. *Freefore.*
9. P. Barford and M. Crovella. Generating representative web workloads for network and server performance evaluation. In *Proc. ACM SIGMETRICS Conf.*, pages 151–160, 1998.
10. G. P. Box, G. M. Jenkins, and G. C. Reinsel. *Time Series Analysis: Forecasting and Control.* Prentice-Hall, Upper Saddle River, New Jersey, 3 edition, 1994.

11. A. Cervin, J. Eker, B. Bernhardsson, and K. Arzen. Feedback-feedforward scheduling of control tasks. *J. Real-Time Syst.*, 23(1–2), 2002.
12. S. A. DeLurgio. *Forecasting Principles and Applications*. McGraw-Hill International, Singapore, 1998.
13. R. Vilalta et al. Predictive algorithms in the management of computer systems. *IBM Systems Journal*, 41(3):461–474, March 2002.
14. S. Parekh et al. Using control theory to achieve service level objectives in performance management. *J. Real-Time Syst.*, 23(1-2):127–141, July/September 2002.
15. Z. Lu et al. Control-theoretic dynamic frequency and voltage scaling for multimedia workloads. In *Intl Conf. Compilers, Architectures, & Synthesis Embedded Syst. (CASES)*, pages 156–163, 2002.
16. A. G. Ganek and T. A. Corbi. The dawn of the autonomic computing era. *IBM Systems Journal*, 42(1):5–18, 2003.
17. N. Kandasamy and S. Abdelwahed. Designing self-managing distributed systems via on-line predictive control. Technical Report ISIS-03-404, Vanderbilt University, December 2003.
18. C. Lu, G. A. Alvarez, and J. Wilkes. Aqueduct: Online data migration with performance guarantees. In *Proc. USENIX Conf. File Storage Tech.*, pages 219–230, 2002.
19. C. Lu, J. Stankovic, G. Tao, and S. Son. Feedback control real-time scheduling: Framework, modeling and algorithms. *Journal of Real-Time Systems*, 23(1-2):85–126, July/September 2002.
20. J. M. Maciejowski. *Predictive Control with Constraints*. Prentice Hall, London, 2002.
21. S. Mascolo. Classical control theory for congestion avoidance in high-speed internet. In *Conf. Decision & Control*, pages 2709–2714, 1999.
22. K. Ogata. *Modern Control Engineering*. Prentice Hall, Englewood Cliffs, NJ, 1997.
23. T. Pering, T. Burd, and R. W. Brodersen. The simulation and evaluation of dynamic voltage scaling algorithms. In *Intl Symp. Low Power Electronics & Design (ISLPED)*, pages 76–81, 1998.
24. P. Pillai and K. G. Shin. Real-time dynamic voltage scaling for low-power embedded operating systems. In *Proc. Symp. Operating Syst. Principles*, pages 89–102, 2001.
25. J. Pouwelse, K. Langendoen, and H. Sips. Dynamic voltage scaling on a low-power microprocessor. In *Proc. Conf. Mobile Computing & Networking (MOBICOM)*, pages 251–259, 2001.
26. D. Shen and J. L. Hellerstein. Predictive models for proactive network management: Application to a production web server. In *Proc. Network Operations & Management Symp.*, pages 833–846, 2000.
27. T. Simunic and S. Boyd. Managing power consumption in networks on chips. In *Proc. Design, Automation, & Test Europe (DATE)*, pages 110–116, 2002.
28. A. Sinha and A. P. Chandrakasan. Energy efficient real-time scheduling. In *Proc. Intl Conf. Computer Aided Design (ICCAD)*, pages 458–463, 2001.
29. F. Zhang and J. L. Hellerstein. An approach to online predictive detection. In *Proc. Modeling, Analysis & Simulation Computer & Telecom. Syst.*, pages 549–556, 2000.

Self-management of Systems Through Automatic Restart

Katinka Wolter

Humboldt-Universität zu Berlin,
Institut für Informatik,
Unter den Linden 6, 10099 Berlin, Germany
wolter@informatik.hu-berlin.de

Abstract. Modern complex information systems require management mechanisms that operate to a large extent independently and autonomously. One such mechanism is the restart of components or transactions in case a failure in the system occurs. In this paper we introduce a pragmatic algorithm to determine close to optimal restart times on-line.

We present a method for choosing best restart times based on empirical data, if no theoretical distribution is known. The best restart time is determined based on the empirical hazard rate. We study the sample size required to come to a reasonably good estimate, the effect of the failure probability of a job and issues of parameter selection for the hazard rate estimation. The application considered in this paper is the connection setup time in HTTP GET necessary for the download of web pages.

1 Introduction

In various situations in computer systems a restart of system components, a re-issuing of a request, or a re-establishment of a network connection improves the performance or availability of the component under consideration significantly. Not always is it known why precisely restart of a process or job becomes necessary or beneficial. Most Internet users, however, are familiar with the fact that clicking the reload button often helps in speeding up the download of a page, although we understand only to a limited extent what is happening exactly in the Internet. Another example is software 'aging', for which rejuvenation - the restart of the software environment - helps in preventing application failures hence also improves the completion time. But little understanding exists about the causes of aging and we are not usually able to identify the source of the problem and remove it. In practical situations, therefore, we will not be able to come to the required understanding to remove the problems, instead we want to optimise the deployment of 'black-box' restart to improve system availability or performance.

The use of restart has first been proposed for optimising Internet agent activities in [2], and further experiments have been carried out in [6]. [3] presents mathematics to optimise the expected download time, and based on this, [5]

O. Babaoglu et al. (Eds.): SELF-STAR 2004, LNCS 3460, pp. 189–203, 2005.

introduces a proxy server based architecture for restart including a software module for the computation of the optimal timeout value. Our objective is to automate restart, building on the above work. We decide on-line whether restart will be beneficial and when to do it. In this paper we simulate an on-line procedure by using increasingly more data from measurements taken earlier [5], but the applied methods can easily be included in a software module like the proxy server in [5] to be executed in real-time.

The shape of the hazard rate of a probability distribution indicates whether restart is beneficial. For empirical data the correct theoretical distribution is unknown and the hazard rate therefore needs to be estimated based on observations. Estimating the hazard rate is not a straightforward task, since it needs numerical computation of the derivative of the cumulative hazard rate. In this paper we derive and implement a new and simple rule based on the hazard rate that allows us to find the optimal restart time to maximise the probability of making a deadline. This rule approximates the optimal restart time independent of the exact value of the deadline, and is asymptotically exact (when the deadline increases). Moreover, the rule is very simple, making it a likely candidate for run-time deployment. Not in all cases doe the optimal restart time exists. Restart is applicable to a system if (and only if) the rule finds an optimal restart time. So, our simple rule actually serves a two-fold purpose: it enables us to decide whether restart will be beneficial in the given situation, and if so, it provides us with the optimal restart time.

We apply the rule to data sets we collected for HTTP, thus mimicking the on-line execution of the algorithm. We explore how much data is required to arrive at reasonable estimates of the optimal restart time. We also study the effect of failed HTTP requests by artificially introducing failures in the data sets. Based on these explorations we provide engineering insights useful for run-time deployment of our algorithm.

Finally, an important technical detail when using the hazard rate is the value of the bandwidth in the required smoothing algorithm. Based on many experiments, we obtain a reasonably robust rule for setting the bandwidth based on the variance of observations. This greatly speeds up the execution of the algorithm, thus improving its on-line performance.

2   The Restart Model

To automate restart, we need to decide the metric of interest, and postulate a mathematical model. In our earlier work, we use restart to minimise the expected download time of a web page in an algorithm that does not make use of the hazard rate [5]. But restart can also be used to increase the probability of making a deadline and for a finite deadline and a finite number of restarts algorithms based on the theoretical distribution and lognormally distributed completion times have been presented in [4]. In our experiments we measured different variables involved in the download of a web page. In this paper we only use the connection setup time from data sets already studied in [5]. We again study the probability of making a deadline, but unlike the formulation in [4] here we use an approximation to estimate the optimal restart time. Using the approximation we can formulate a very simple rule based on the hazard rate, which in fact is independent of the deadline to be met.

Our mathematical model assumes statistical independence of consecutive preemptive tries. We found this very often to be a realistic assumption in HTTP downloads from one URL [5]. Let the random variable T denote the completion time of a job, with probability distribution $F(t), t \in [0, \infty)$. Assume τ is a restart time, and introduce the random variable T_τ to denote the completion time when an unbounded number of retries is allowed. That is, a retry takes place periodically, every τ time units, until completion of the job or until the deadline has passed, which ever comes first. We write $f_\tau(t)$ and $F_\tau(t)$ for the density and distribution of T_τ. A distribution can equally well be described by the hazard rate

$$h(t) = \frac{f(t)}{1 - F(t)}$$

and the cumulative hazard

$$H(t) = \int_{s=0}^{t} h(s)ds$$

which both are very important throughout our analysis. One useful relation between the cumulative hazard rate and a distribution function is given by

$$H(t) = -\log(1 - F(t)).$$

Restart at time τ is beneficial only if the probability $F_\tau(t)$ of making the deadline t under restart is greater than the probability of making the deadline without restart, i.e.

$$F_\tau(t) > F(t). \tag{1}$$

As we have shown in [4], one can intuitively reason about the completion time distribution with restarts as Bernoulli trials. At each interval between restarts there is a probability $F(\tau)$ the completion 'succeeds.' Hence, if the time t is a multiple of the restart time τ, we can relate the probability of missing the deadline without and with restart through:

$$1 - F_\tau(t) = (1 - F(\tau))^{\frac{t}{\tau}}. \tag{2}$$

Eqn. (2) is correct only for values of t and τ such that t is an integer multiple of τ. But if we ignore this fact, or simply accept (2) as an approximation, we can find the optimal restart time in a straightforward way. Surprisingly, it turns out that the approximation gives us a restart time independent of the deadline t, which is optimal in the limit $t \to \infty$. That is, it optimises the tail of the completion time distribution under restarts, and is therefore beneficial for many other metrics as well, such as higher moments of the completion time.

Theorem 1. *If the restart time τ^* is an extreme (in τ) of $(1 - F(\tau))^{\frac{t}{\tau}}$ for any deadline t then τ^* is a point where $\tau^*.h(\tau^*) = -\log(1 - F(\tau^*))$;*

Proof. We use that

$$\frac{d}{dx}(g(x))^x = (g(x))^x \left(\frac{x \frac{d}{dx} g(x)}{g(x)} + \log(g(x)) \right). \tag{3}$$

τ^* is an extreme when the derivative of $(1 - F(\tau))^{\frac{t}{\tau}}$ equates to 0:

$$\frac{d}{d\tau}(1 - F(\tau))^{\frac{t}{\tau}} = (1 - F(\tau))^{\frac{t}{\tau}} \left(\frac{f(\tau)\tau}{1 - F(\tau)} + \log(1 - F(\tau)) \right) = 0. \tag{4}$$

Irrespective of the value of t it immediately follows that

$$\frac{f(\tau)}{1 - F(\tau)} = \frac{-\log(1 - F(\tau))}{\tau}, \tag{5}$$

and thus the conclusion holds if and only if the premiss holds.   □

Eqn. (5) can be rewritten as

$$\tau \cdot h(\tau) = H(\tau) \tag{6}$$

where $H(\tau)$ can be interpreted as the surface under the hazard rate curve up to point τ. We can therefore reason that (5) expresses the fact that if (1) holds there exists a point on the hazard rate curve such that the rectangle defined by x- and y-value of this point equals the integral under the hazard rate curve up to this point. We will refer to 6 as the *rectangle equals surface rule*. This very appealing and simple rule is used in this paper for an empirical hazard rate to find an empirical optimal restart time that maximises the probability of completion, that is the probability of making an infinite deadline.

It should be noted that if the hazard rate is monotonously increasing, no value of τ exists, such that (6) holds. In that case restart will not help increasing the probability of completion. Only if the hazard rate decreases after some point a value of τ exists, such that (6) holds. Only then restart can be applied successfully.

3   Estimating the Hazard Rate

It follows from (6) that an estimate $\hat{h}(t)$ of the hazard rate curve is needed to determine the optimal restart time following the *rectangle equals surface* rule. We will in this section provide the main steps of how to estimate the hazard rate and implement the rule (6) in an algorithm. Some details are shifted to the appendix. We use the theory on survival analysis in [1].

The hazard rate $h(t)$ can not be estimated directly from a given data set. Instead, first the cumulative hazard rate $H(t)$ is estimated and then the hazard rate itself is computed as a numerical derivative.

Let us consider a sample of n individuals, that is n completions in our study. We sample the completion times and if we order them, we obtain a data set of

D distinct times $t_1 \leq t_2 \leq \ldots \leq t_D$ where at time t_i there are d_i events, that is d_i completions take time t_i. The random variable Y_i counts the number of jobs that need more or equal to t_i time units to complete. We can write Y_i as

$$Y_i = n - \sum_{j=1}^{i-1} d_j$$

All observations that have not complete at the end of the regarded time period, usually time t_D, are called *right censored*. There are $Y_n - d_n$ right censored observations. The experimental data we use falls in that category, since Internet transactions commonly use TCP, which aborts (censors) transactions if they do not succeed within a given time.

The hazard rate estimator $\hat{h}(t)$ is the derivative of the cumulative hazard rate estimator $\hat{H}(t)$, which is defined in Appendix A. It is estimated as the slope of the cumulative hazard rate. Better estimates are obtained when using a kernel function to smooth the numerical derivative of the cumulative hazard rate. The smoothing is done over a window of size $2b$. A bad estimate of the hazard rate will yield a bad estimate of the optimal restart time and the optimised metric is very sensitive to whether the restart time is chosen too short. Therefore a good estimate of the hazard rate is needed.

Let the magnitude of the jumps in $\hat{H}(t)$ and in the estimator of its variance $\hat{V}[\hat{H}(t)]$ at the jump instants t_i be $\Delta\hat{H}(t_i) = \hat{H}(t_i) - \hat{H}(t_{i-1})$ and $\Delta\hat{V}[\hat{H}(t_i)] = \hat{V}[\hat{H}(t_i)] - \hat{V}[\hat{H}(t_{i-1})]$. Note that $\Delta\hat{H}(t_i)$ is a crude estimator for $\hat{h}(t_i)$.

The kernel-smoothed hazard rate estimator is defined separately for the first and last points, for which $t - b < 0$ or $t + b > t_D$. For inner points with $b \leq t \leq t_D - b$ the kernel-smoothed estimator of $h(t)$ is given by

$$\hat{h}(t) = b^{-1} \sum_{i=1}^{D} K\left(\frac{t - t_i}{b}\right) \Delta\hat{H}(t_i). \tag{7}$$

The variance of $\hat{h}(t)$ is needed for the confidence interval and is estimated by

$$\sigma^2[\hat{h}(t)] = b^{-2} \sum_{i=1}^{D} K\left(\frac{t - t_i}{b}\right)^2 \Delta\hat{V}[\hat{H}(t_i)]. \tag{8}$$

The function $K(.)$ is the Epanechnikov kernel defined in Appendix B.

A $(1 - \alpha) \cdot 100\%$ point wise confidence interval around $\hat{h}(t)$ is constructed as

$$\left[\hat{h}(t)\exp\left[-\frac{z_{1-\alpha/2}\sigma(\hat{h}(t))}{\hat{h}(t)}\right], \hat{h}(t)\exp\left[\frac{z_{1-\alpha/2}\sigma(\hat{h}(t))}{\hat{h}(t)}\right]\right]. \tag{9}$$

where $z_{1-\alpha/2}$ is the $(1 - \alpha/2)$ quantile of the standard normal distribution.

The choice of the right bandwidth b is a delicate matter, but is important since the shape of the hazard rate curve greatly depends on the chosen bandwidth (see figure 2) and hence a badly chosen bandwidth will have a serious effect on the optimal restart time. One way to pick a good bandwidth is to use a cross-validation technique of determining the bandwidth that minimises some measure of how well the estimator performs. One such measure is the *mean integrated squared error* (MISE) of $\hat{h}$ over the range $\tau_{\min}$ to $\tau_{\max}$. The mean integrated squared error can be found in Appendix C. To find the value of b which minimises the MISE we find b which minimises the function

$$g(b) = \sum_{i=1}^{M-1} \left(\frac{t_{i+1} - t_i}{2} \right) (\hat{h}^2(t_i) + \hat{h}^2(t_{i+1})) -$$

$$2b^{-1} \sum_{i \neq j} K \left(\frac{t_i - t_j}{b} \right) \Delta \hat{H}(t_i) \Delta \hat{H}(t_j). \quad (10)$$

Then $g(b)$ is evaluated for different values of b. Each evaluation of $g(b)$ requires the computation of the estimator of the hazard rate. The optimal bandwidth can be determined only in a trial-and-error procedure. We found in our experiments that the optimal bandwidth is related with the size of the data set and the variance of the data. We use the standard deviation to determine a starting value and then do a simple step-wise increase of the bandwidth until $g(b)$ takes on its minimal value. In case the hazard rate is increasing in the first steps, we decrease b and start again, since then we are obviously beyond the minimum already. In our experiments and in the literature we always found a global minimum, never any local minima. Advanced hill-climbing algorithms can be applied to find the minimum more quickly and more accurately than we do here.

Once the best estimate of the hazard rate is found we need to determine the point i^* that satisfies the *rectangle equals surface* rule (6).

The following simple algorithm determines the optimal restart time τ^* by testing all observed points $t_i, i = 1, \ldots, n$ as potential candidates.

Algorithm 1 (Optimal restart time).

```
Input ĥ, Ĥ and t;
i = 1;  #(t = t₁,...,tₙ)
While((i < n) and (tᵢ · ĥ(tᵢ) > Ĥ(tᵢ)) ) {
    i + +;
}
return tᵢ;
```

This algorithm returns in the positive case the smallest observed value that is greater than the estimated optimal restart time τ^*.

In many cases, however, the studied data set does not contain observations large enough to be equal or greater than the optimal restart time. Then we extrapolate the estimated hazard rate to find the point where the rectangle equals the surface under the curve. Assuming we have a data set of n observations $t_i, i = 1, \ldots, n$, at first the slope of the estimated hazard rate at the end of the curve is determined as the difference quotient

$$\text{slope} = \frac{\hat{h}(t_n) - \hat{h}(t_{n-1})}{t_n - t_{n-1}}. \quad (11)$$

Then $t_\tau = t_n + \Delta t$ is determined such that for t_τ eqn. (5) holds.

$$(t_n + \Delta t) \cdot (\hat{h}(t_n) + \text{slope} \cdot \Delta t) = \hat{H}(t_n) \cdot \text{slope} \cdot \Delta t \cdot t_n$$

$$\Longleftrightarrow \quad \Delta t = \frac{\hat{H}(t_n) - t \cdot \hat{h}(t_n)}{\hat{h}(t_n) - 2 \text{ slope } t_n - \hat{H}(t_n) - \text{slope}}. \quad (12)$$

3.1   Complexity

The computational complexity depends in first place on the number of iterations needed to find the optimal bandwidth for the hazard rate estimator. In our experiments we used a heuristic based on the standard deviation of the data set that gave us the optimal bandwidth often in less than 5 iterations, but sometimes took up to 20 iterations.

The second important parameter is the number of observations considered. Each iteration on the bandwidth requires the computation of the estimated hazard rate, which in turn needs traversing all observations and uses for each point a window of size $2b$. Complexity of the hazard rate estimator is therefore at most $O(n^2)$. Improving on the heuristic for the bandwidth, so that in all cases only few iterations are needed is certainly worth while.

4   Experiments

We have implemented the algorithm to estimate the hazard rate and determine the optimal restart time as defined in theorem 1. The implementation is done in Mathematica and has been applied to the HTTP connection setup data studied in [5]. This data in fact consists of the time needed for TCP's three-way handshake to set up a connection between two hosts.

In our experiments we investigate various issues. One is the uncertainty introduced by small sample sizes. The available data sets consist of approximately one thousand observations for each URL, that is thousand connection setup times to the same Internet address. We use these data sets and take subsets of first one hundred then two hundred observations etc. as indicated in the caption of the figure and in the table. We do not use data of different URLs in one experiment since we found that very often different URLs have different distributions or at least distribution parameters. Furthermore, the application we have in mind is web transactions between two hosts.

The data we study is data set '28' consisting of the connection setup times to http://nuevamayoria.com, measured in seconds. This data set shows characteristics such as a lower bound on all observation and a pattern of variation which we found in many other data sets as well, even though usually not with the same parameters. The chosen data set is therefore to be seen as one typical representative of a large number of potential candidates. The considered connection setup times are shown in figure 1. The largest observation in this data set is 0.399678 seconds.

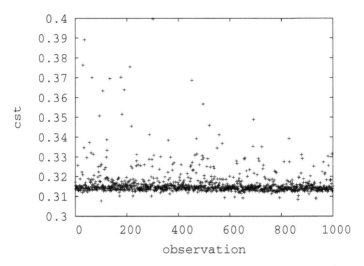

Fig. 1. Data set No. 28; connection setup times (in seconds)

For each of the mentioned subsamples the optimal smoothing factor, or bandwidth, is computed by evaluating (10) several times, finding the minimum in a simple search. Figure 2 shows estimates of the hazard rate for different values of the bandwidth. Parameter $b1$ is too large, whereas $b2$ is too small, $b3$ is the one that minimises the error and is therefore the optimal bandwidth. One can see that too large a bandwidth leads to an extremely smooth curve, whereas too small a bandwidth produces over-emphasised peaks. From the figure one might conclude that rather too large a bandwidth should be chosen than one that is too small, but more experiments are needed for a statement of this kind. Using the optimal bandwidth, the hazard rate and its 95% confidence interval are estimated according to (7) and (9). Finally, for each estimated hazard rate the optimal restart time τ^* is computed using algorithm 1. In some cases, the algorithm finds the optimal restart time, since the data set includes still an observation greater than the optimal restart time. If the data set has no observation large enough to be greater than the optimal restart time, we extrapolate according to (12). The optimal restart times are drawn as vertical bars in the plots in figures 3 and 4. Note that in figure 3 although it looks like all optimal restart times are extrapolated in fact none of them is. The extrapolated optimal restart times are indicated by an asterisk in table 1.

The hazard rate curve has no value at the point of the largest observation, since for the numerical derivation always two data points are needed. Furthermore, because of the limited amount of data in the tail, it is not surprising that the confidence interval at the last observations grows rapidly.

Table 1 shows some characteristics obtained in the program runs for data set 28. Each block of the table belongs to a subset of size n with corresponding standard deviation. The standard deviation changes as more observations come into consideration. For each subsample three different cases are studied. In the

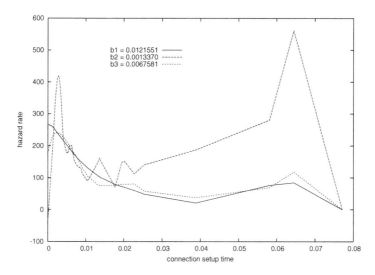

Fig. 2. Hazard rate for data set No. 28 and different values of the bandwidth b

first one only the n observations are used and the failure probability equals either zero, or the relative fraction of observations that are greater than 3.0. This threshold is the first retransmission timeout of TCP and hence observations greater 3.0 are (somewhat arbitrarily) censored and retried. We treat them as censored observations and all censored observations contribute to the failure probability. Data set '28' does not have any such censored observations, but many other data sets do. The second group consists of the n observations plus $2n$ censored ones and has therefore failure probability 2/3, or a little higher if there are additional censored observations present in the data set. Analogously, the third group has $n + 4n$ observations and a failure probability of $n/5n = 0.8$ (or more if there are censored observations in the data set).

If we look at the results for failure probability zero, also plotted in figure 3 for $n = 100, 200, 400, 600, 800$ we see that the small data sets lead to an overestimated optimal restart time (if we assume that the full 1000 observations give us a *correct* estimate), but the 'correct' value is overestimated by less than 5%.

We used such high, and perhaps unrealistic, failure probabilities in our study since a failure probability of e.g. 0.1 does not show in the results at all. Looking at the results for the different sample sizes in the group with high failure probability, we also find that with the small samples the optimal restart time gets overestimated.

We also investigate the impact of the failure probability within a group of fixed sample size. The failure probability is increased by subsequently adding more failed (and hence censored) observations and then estimates for the hazard rate and optimal restart time are computed. The failed attempts of course increase the sample size. We notice (as can be seen in table 1) that the bandwidth used for estimating the hazard rate decreases for increasing failure rate, while the

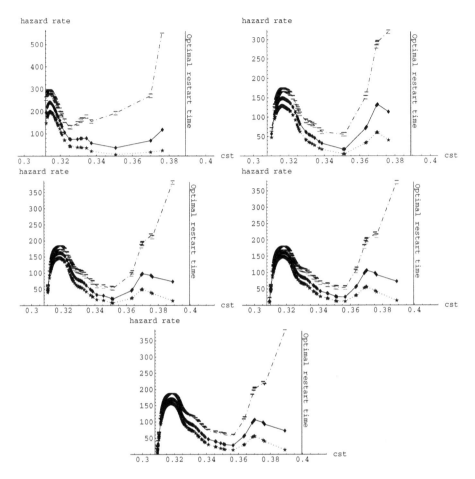

Fig. 3. Estimated hazard rates and confidence intervals for the estimates for increasing sample size (top row $n = 100$ and $n = 200$, middle row $n = 400$ and $n = 600$, bottom row $n = 800$) and failure probability 0.0

sample standard deviation is computed only from non-failed observations and hence does not change with changing failure probability. We found in [4] that for theoretical distributions the optimal restart time decreases with increasing failure probability. Typically our experiments agree with this property, which, however, is not true for some subsets of data set '28'.

An additional purpose of the experiments was to find out whether we can relate the optimal bandwidth to any characteristic of the data set. In the literature no strategy is pointed out that helps in finding the optimal bandwidth quickly. In our implementation we set the standard deviation as a starting value for the search. If we have no censored observations (failure probability zero) we always find the optimal bandwidth within less than five iterations. If the data set has many censored observations the optimal bandwidth roughly by factor 5

Table 1. Optimal restart time (τ^*) and optimal bandwidth (bw) for different subsample sizes of data set 28 and different failure probabilities

$n = 100$, StdDev $= 0.0121551$			$n = 200$, StdDev $= 0.0117341$		
failure prob.	bw	τ^*	failure prob.	bw	τ^*
0.0	0.006758	0.389027	0.0	0.011557	0.389027
0.666667	0.001779	0.597251*	0.666667	0.001398	0.674306*
0.8	0.001779	0.554513*	0.8	0.001271	0.638993*
$n = 300$, StdDev $= 0.0106746$			$n = 400$, StdDev $= 0.010383$		
failure prob.	bw	τ^*	failure prob.	bw	τ^*
0.0	0.011742	0.389027	0.0	0.010226	0.399678
0.666667	0.001272	0.333271	0.666667	0.001124	0.333271
0.8	0.001156	0.333271	0.8	0.001124	0.333271
$n = 500$, StdDev $= 0.00997916$			$n = 600$, StdDev $= 0.00941125$		
failure prob.	bw	τ^*	failure prob.	bw	τ^*
0.0	0.010977	0.399678	0.0	0.010352	0.399678
0.666667	0.001081	0.333271	0.666667	0.001138	0.333271
0.8	0.001081	0.333271	0.8	0.001019	0.333271
$n = 700$, StdDev $= 0.00895504$			$n = 800$, StdDev $= 0.00851243$		
failure prob.	bw	τ^*	failure prob.	bw	τ^*
0.0	0.009850	0.309209	0.0	0.0103	0.399678
0.66667	0.000970	0.333271	0.66667	0.000922	0.332014
0.8	0.000970	0.333271	0.8	0.000922	0.332014
$n = 900$, StdDev $= 0.00816283$			$n = 1000$, StdDev $= 0.00784583$		
failure prob.	bw	τ^*	failure prob.	bw	τ^*
0.0	0.009877	0.308456	0.0	0.009493	0.308456
0.6667	0.000884	0.332014	0.6667	0.000949	0.333271
0.8	0.000884	0.332014	0.8	0.000850	0.332014

and we need more iterations to find that value, since our heuristic has a starting value far too large in that case.

Figure 4 compares two hazard rates using another data set for data with identical sample size, the first has zero failure rate and the second has failure rate 0.8. It can be seen that the high number of added censored observations leads to a much more narrow hazard rate, with lower optimal restart time. Note that this figure is based on a different data set than the ones above.

In summary, we have provided an algorithm that gives us an optimal restart time to maximise the probability of meeting a deadline only if restart will indeed help maximising that metric. So if the algorithm returns an optimal restart time we can be sure that restart will help. We found a heuristic based on the variance of the data that helps in finding quickly the bandwidth parameter needed for the hazard rate estimator. We found that small data sets usually lead to an overestimated optimal restart time. But we saw earlier (in [4]) that an overestimated restart time does much less harm to the metric of interest than an underestimated one and we therefore willingly accept overestimates.

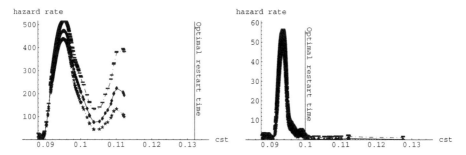

Fig. 4. Estimated hazard rates and confidence intervals for sample size $n = 1000$, failure probability 0.0 (left) and 0.8 (right)

5   Discussion and Conclusions

Self-management of modern, complex systems can include among others the automatic restart of jobs, or transactions if they are performing badly. As the considered metric we chose in this paper the probability of completion before an arbitrary deadline under unlimited number of allowed restarts. We derived a *surface equals rectangle* rule for the optimal restart time that is based on the hazard rate. We implemented an algorithm to estimate the hazard rate from a given data set and to determine the optimal restart time. The *surface equals rectangle* rule provides an answer to the question of whether restart makes sense in a given scenario. If an optimal restart time is found at all we can be sure that the shape of the hazard rate is such that restart makes sense and (1) holds. A very simple heuristic was used to quickly find the best bandwidth for the hazard rate estimation. The benefit of our algorithm is that it gives reasonably good estimates on small data sets and can hence be used for fast estimates in on-line automatic restart.

The run-time of the algorithm depends on the considered number of observations and on the number of iterations needed to find a good bandwidth for the hazard rate estimation. We found that for our smaller data sets with up to 400 observations less than 5 iterations are needed and the algorithm is very fast. We did not evaluate CPU time and the Mathematica implementation is not run-time optimised, but a suggestion for an optimal restart time in the above setting can be provided within a few seconds. If, however, the data set grows large, has e.g. more than 800 observations, each iteration on the bandwidth takes in the order of some one or two minutes. The polynomial complexity becomes relevant and the method is no longer applicable in an on-line algorithm.

A good heuristic for choosing the optimal bandwidth is a key part in the whole process. The better the first guess, the less iterations are needed and the faster we obtain the optimal restart time. We cannot compare our heuristic to others since in the literature nothing but pure 'trial and error' is proposed. But we can say, that for small data sets and failure probability zero the optimal restart time is obtained very fast since the heuristic provides a good first estimate of the bandwidth.

In our experience the smallest data sets were usually sufficient for a reasonably good estimate of the optimal restart time. The optimal restart time will always be placed at the end of the bulk of the observations and some few hundred observations are enough to get a notion of 'bulk' and 'end of the bulk'. If we consider that some web pages consist of up to 200 objects a data set of 100 samples is not hard to obtain or unrealistic. In Internet transactions some hundred samples are very quickly accumulated. Furthermore, small samples seem to overestimate the optimal restart time, which does the maximised metric much less harm than underestimation.

In practical applications the required number of observations is no limitation to the applicability of our method and having not too much data has a positive effect on the run-time while it does not deteriorate the obtained result. The proposed method is well-suited as an on-line restart module.

One may argue that if everybody applies restart networks become more congested and response times will drop further. And in fact restart changes the TCP timeout - for selected applications. In our measurements we found that less than 0.5% of all connection setup attempts fail. Our method tries to detect failures faster than the TCP timeout and to restart failed attempts, since for slow connections restart typically does not lead to improved response time, whereas for failed connections in many cases it does. Failed attempts, however, are so rare that restarting those does not impose significant extra load on a network, while potentially speeding those up enormously.

References

1. J. P. Klein and M. L. Moeschberger. *Survival Analysis, Techniques for Censored and Truncated Data.* Springer, 1997.
2. S. M. Maurer and B. A. Huberman, "Restart strategies and Internet congestion," in *Journal of Economic Dynamics and Control,* vol. 25, pp. 641–654, 2001.
3. A. van Moorsel and K. Wolter, "Analysis and Algorithms for Restart," in *Proc. 1st International Conference on the Quantitative Evaluation of Systems (QEST),* pp. 195-204, Twente, Netherlands, Sept. 2004.
4. A. van Moorsel and K. Wolter, "Making Deadlines through Restart," in *Proc. 12th GI/ITG Conference on Measuring, Modelling and Evaluation of Computer and Communication Systems (MMB 04),* pp. 155–160, Dresden, Germany, Sept. 2004.
5. P. Reinecke, A. van Moorsel and K. Wolter, "A Measurement Study of the Interplay between Application Level Restart and Transport Protocol," in *Proc. International Service Availability Symposium,* Munich, Germany, May 2004.
6. M. Schroeder and L. Buro, "Does the Restart Method Work? Preliminary Results on Efficiency Improvements for Interactions of Web-Agents," in T. Wagner and O. Rana, editors, *Proceedings of the Workshop on Infrastructure for Agents, MAS, and Scalable MAS at the Conference Autonomous Agents 2001,* Springer Verlag, Montreal, Canada, 2001.

Appendix

A   Cumulative Hazard Rate

The cumulative hazard rate is estimated using the Nelson-Aalen estimator, which has especially good small sample performance. The Nelson-Aalen estimator is

$$\hat{H}(t) = \begin{cases} 0 & \text{if } t \leq t_1 \\ \sum_{t_i \leq t} \frac{d_i}{Y_i} & \text{if } t_1 \leq t. \end{cases} \tag{13}$$

The estimated variance of the Nelson-Aalen estimator is

$$\sigma_H^2(t) = \sum_{t_i \leq t} \frac{d_i}{Y_i^2}. \tag{14}$$

B   Epanechnikov Kernel

For the kernel $K(.)$ the Epanechnikov kernel is used

$$K(x) = 0.75(1 - x^2) \qquad \text{for } -1 \leq x \leq 1 \tag{15}$$

as it is shown in [1] to be often more accurate than other kernel functions. When $t - b < 0$ or $t + b > t_D$ the symmetric kernel must be transformed into an asymmetric one, which is at the lower bound with $q = t/b$

$$K_q(x) = K(x)(\alpha + \beta x), \qquad \text{for } -1 \leq x \leq q, \tag{16}$$

where

$$\alpha = \frac{64(2 - 4q + 6q^2 - 3q^3)}{(1 + q)^4(19 - 18q + 3q^2)} \tag{17}$$

$$\beta = \frac{240(1 - q)^2}{(1 + q)^4(19 - 18q + 3q^2)} \tag{18}$$

For time-points in the right-hand tail $q = (t_D - 1)/b$ the kernel function is $K_q(-x)$.

C   Bandwidth Estimation

The *mean integrated squared error* (MISE) of the estimated hazard rate $\hat{h}$ over the range $\tau_{\min}$ to $\tau_{\max}$ is defined by

$$\begin{aligned} MISE(b) &= E\left(\int_{\tau_{\min}}^{\tau_{\max}} [\hat{h}(u) - h(u)]^2 \, du\right) \\ &= E\left(\int_{\tau_{\min}}^{\tau_{\max}} \hat{h}^2(u) \, du\right) - 2E\left(\int_{\tau_{\min}}^{\tau_{\max}} \hat{h}(u)h(u) \, du\right) \\ &\quad + E\left(\int_{\tau_{\min}}^{\tau_{\max}} h^2(u) \, du\right). \end{aligned} \tag{19}$$

This function depends on the bandwidth b used in the Epanechnikov kernel. The last term does not contain b and can be ignored when finding the best value of b. The first term is estimated by $\int_{\tau_{min}}^{\tau_{max}} \hat{h}^2(u)\,du$. We evaluate $\hat{h}(u)$ at a not necessarily equi-distant grid of points $\tau_{min} = u_1 < u_2 < \ldots < u_M = \tau_{max}$ and apply the trapezoid rule. The second term we approximate by a cross-validation estimate suggested by Ramlau-Hansen where we sum over the event times between τ_{min} and τ_{max}.

Fundamentals of Dynamic Decentralized Optimization in Autonomic Computing Systems

Tomasz Nowicki, Mark S. Squillante, and Chai Wah Wu

Mathematical Sciences Department,
IBM Thomas J. Watson Research Center,
Yorktown Heights, NY 10598, USA

Abstract. We consider the fundamentals of a mathematical framework for decentralized optimization and dynamic optimal control in autonomic computing systems that provide self-∗ properties. In particular, we first study conditions under which decentralized optimization can provide the same quality of solution as centralized optimization. After establishing such equivalence results under mild technical conditions, we exploit our mathematical framework to investigate the dynamic control properties of decentralized optimization including the communication between hierarchical levels. We then study the dynamic case when the parameters and input to the system changes, and how the additional dynamics can cause behavior which deviates from the static case, including complicated behavior such as phase transitions, chaos and instability.

1 Introduction

An autonomic computing system is a complex information system comprised of many interconnected components that operate at different time scales in a largely independent fashion and that manage themselves to satisfy high-level system management requirements and specifications [1]. This includes providing the self-∗ properties of self-configuring, self-organizing, self-protecting, and self-repairing. Fundamental problems involved in achieving these goals of self-management concern the general mathematical framework that provides the underlying foundation and supports the design, architecture and algorithms employed throughout the autonomic computing system. Two fundamental aspects of this mathematical framework are of interest in this paper: the optimization of the entire range of autonomic system objectives, and the dynamic control of achieving these optimal solutions.

The increasing complexity of current and future information systems suggests a decentralized approach for the optimization model of autonomic computing systems, which is a natural and appropriate way to design and implement large-scale information systems that provide self-∗ properties. On the other hand, a centralized approach with complete knowledge over all constituent system components has the potential to provide significant improvements over a decentralized approach (ignoring associated overheads, delays, etc.), in the same way that

O. Babaoglu et al. (Eds.): SELF-STAR 2004, LNCS 3460, pp. 204–218, 2005.

solutions to global optimization problems (if attainable) are often superior to the corresponding locally optimal solutions. This fundamental problem involving the tradeoff between centralized and decentralized approaches arises in a wide range of applications, and its solution is especially important to achieve the goals of self-management in autonomic computing systems.

Autonomic computing systems that provide self-* properties are dynamic environments in which optimal self-management decisions must be made continually over time and at multiple time scales. Dynamic optimal control is needed to achieve these optimal solutions over time. When the input parameters to the system change with time, or when the system environment changes over time for any other reason, the additional dynamical behavior of the resulting continual optimization problem can be quite complex and a fundamental problem is to determine this interaction between dynamics and optimization. The complicated behavior caused by these additional dynamics can include phase transitions, chaos and instability.

Our study focuses on both of these fundamental problems as an important step toward providing a mathematical foundation for decentralized optimization and dynamic optimal control in autonomic computing systems with self-* properties. We first establish conditions under which a decentralized optimization approach is as good as a centralized approach. In particular, we show that there is no loss of quality in the optimal self-management of complex information systems when a decentralized approach is used. Our study also considers implementation schemes where additional information is passed between system components at different levels of this hierarchical decentralized optimization model in order to significantly increase the efficiency with which the optimization algorithms compute the optimal solution. We then turn to the dynamic case and illustrate some possible difficulties and added complexities of optimization under uncertainties in the ever changing data that is communicated among parts of the system over time. This uncertainty can be caused by inaccuracies in the measurement, but can be also due to delay in the measurement and/or communication links of the system. In both cases, a representative application of our general mathematical framework is presented and used to illustrate some of the fundamental properties of decentralized optimization and dynamic optimal control in autonomic computing systems.

2   Mathematical Framework for Optimization

2.1   System Model

We consider a hierarchical and decentralized model for optimal self-management in which a complex information system is partitioned into multiple application environments (AEs) each of which has an application manager (AM) that controls and optimizes the resource management and operations within the application environment. The collection of application managers are in turn controlled and optimized by a central manager (CM) that allocates the system resources among the application environments; refer to Figure 1. The system hierarchy

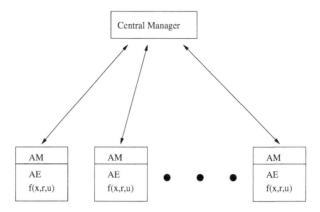

Fig. 1. System model

can contain many levels, i.e., each application environment can itself recursively include a manager controlling and optimizing subenvironments within the application environment. It is the goal of the central manager to optimize the overall objective function for the entire information system.

This overall objective function can be based on any combination of self-∗ properties (e.g., self-configuring, self-organizing, self-protecting, self-repairing) and measures (e.g., availability, costs, overheads, penalties, performance, reliability, revenues, risk, robustness, utility [2]) and depends upon the resources, workloads and other parameters of the information system. In particular, it is important to note that our use of the overall objective function in this study is not limited to the more typical measures based on performance, but rather can be based on any quantitative measure of interest to support any combination of self-∗ properties. This can include objectives based on measures of the robustness of the desired solution, as well as objectives based on minimal deviations from "good" states or maximum deviations from "bad" states. Furthermore, our use of the overall objective function is not limited to any specific self-∗ property such as those that have been traditionally considered as optimization problems. Instead, the scope of our study is intended to cover any aspect of any self-∗ property, or combination of self-∗ properties, that can be solved, either in part or as a whole, using a quantitative objective function. Optimization should play an important role in these aspects of the design and implementation of autonomic computing systems.

2.2   Optimal Total Cost

To formally express the problem in the standard form of optimization problems, we consider without any loss of generality minimizing a *cost* function (since maximizing f is equivalent to minimizing $-f$). A cost function $f_i(x_i, r_i, u_i)$ is associated with each application environment i, where x_i is the set of variables that can be changed in application environment i, r_i is the set of resources allocated to application environment i, and u_i is the set of external variables that affect application environment i. Examples of r_i include the set of servers assigned to application environment i, or the amount of disk space or processing time made available to application environment i. Examples of u_i include the current workload of application environment i or conditions imposed by external events such as failures. The set of variables x_i must also satisfy the set of constraints C_i, i.e., $x_i \in C_i$ is the feasible region of operation for application environment i. In general, C_i will depend on r_i and u_i. Examples of C_i include conditions imposed by application environment i, such as an upper limit on the percentage of requests having end-to-end response times that exceed some threshold when the resources of application environment i are organized in a multi-tier architecture.

The total cost function for the entire system is given by

$$h(f_1(x_1, r_1, u_1), \ldots, f_n(x_n, r_n, u_n)),$$

where h aggregates the cost of each application environment i into a single total cost. Examples of h of interest in this paper include summation (SUM), weighted summation with nonnegative weights, the maximum function (MAX), and the minimum function (MIN).

The total set of resources in the system is finite, and the set of resources assigned to the application environments is required to satisfy a constraint: $(r_1, \ldots, r_n) \in R$. Examples of this constraint include bounds on the amount of disk space or number of servers, or in the case when the servers are organized in multiple tiers, bounds on the end-to-end response or processing time. By allowing elements of R to represent a strict subset of the resources, the central manager can reserve a set of available resources for direct allocation to any application environment i rather than being moved from application environment j to application environment i.

Then the goal of the autonomic computing system is to globally minimize the total cost function h subject to constraints. That is,

$$h_c = \min_{x_i, r_i} h(f_1(x_1, r_1, u_1), \ldots, f_n(x_n, r_n, u_n)) \tag{1}$$

such that $(r_1, \ldots, r_n) \in R$, $x_i \in C_i(r_i, u_i)$. The value h_c is the optimal cost of the information system (which in general depends on the set of external variables $u_1, \ldots, u_n$) under a *centralized* approach as it is the globally minimal cost among all feasible resource allocations r_i and all feasible sets of variables x_i. The cost h_c can be computed by an optimization algorithm which has knowledge about the operations of all application environments i including the cost functions f_i.

Now we seek to find conditions under which h_c can be obtained using a hierarchical, decentralized approach.

2.3   Decentralized Optimization

For each application environment i, the corresponding application manager i minimizes the cost function for application environment i by solving the optimization problem:

$$g_i(r_i, u_i) = \min_{x_i} f_i(x_i, r_i, u_i) \tag{2}$$

such that $x_i \in C_i(r_i, u_i)$, where r_i are the set of resources allocated by the central manager to application environment i. In turn, the central manager determines the resource allocation by solving the optimization problem:

$$h_d = \min_{r_i} h(g_1(r_1, u_1), \dots, g_n(r_n, u_n)) \tag{3}$$

such that $(r_1, \dots, r_n) \in R$.

Notice the decentralized nature of this approach. Each application environment i optimizes the cost within its environment and passes this optimal cost to the central manager. In particular, there is no need for the central manager to know the exact form of the cost function f_i. As we will show in Section 2.4, additional information can be sent from each application environment i to the central manager to aid in the optimization of the total cost.

For vectors in $\mathbb{R}^n$, let $\geq$ be the partial order generated by the positive orthant, i.e., $x \geq y$ if $x_i \geq y_i$ for all i.

Definition 1. *A function* $g : \mathbb{R}^n \to \mathbb{R}^m$ *is called* order-preserving *with respect to* $\geq$ *(OPGT) if* $g(x) \geq g(y)$ *whenever* $x \geq y$.

We will refer to such a function as OPGT. Examples of OPGT functions are SUM, MAX and MIN.

Suppose the external variables u_i are constant (in a stationary stochastic sense) so that we can ignore them for the moment. Section 3 will consider the case when this assumption is removed. We then have the following equality result between centralized and decentralized optimization.

Theorem 1. *If the aggregation function* h *is OPGT, then* $h_c = h_d$, *i.e., the decentralized optimal solution is as good as the centralized optimal solution.*

Proof. Clearly $h_d \geq h_c$. Let x_i^* and r_i^* be the optimal set of variables and resource allocations such that

$$h(f_1(x_1^*, r_1^*, u_1), \dots, f_n(x_n^*, r_n^*, u_n)) = h_c$$

while satisfying the constraints $(r_1^*, \dots, r_n^*) \in R$, $x_i^* \in C_i(r_i^*, u_i)$. Then by definition

$$g_i(r_i^*, u_i) \leq f_i(x_i^*, r_i^*, u_i),$$

and from the OPGT property of h we have:

$$h_d \leq h(g_1(r_1^*, u_1), \dots, g_n(r_n^*, u_n))$$
$$\leq h(f_1(x_1^*, r_1^*, u_1), \dots, f_n(x_n^*, r_n^*, u_n)) = h_c.$$

$\square$

2.4   Hierarchical Implementation

In general, continuous optimization algorithms to solve Equation (3) perform much more efficiently and effectively if, in addition to the ability to evaluate the objective function

$$\widetilde{h}(r_1,\ldots,r_n) = h(g_1(r_1,u_1),\ldots,g_n(r_n,u_n)),$$

the gradient $\nabla\widetilde{h}$ of the objective function is also available.

Note that

$$\nabla\widetilde{h} = \sum_i \nabla_i h \cdot \frac{\partial g_i}{\partial r}$$

with $\frac{\partial g_i}{\partial r_j} = 0$ for $i \neq j$. Assuming the constraints $x_i \in C_i(r_i,u_i)$ are written as $c_i(x_i,u_i) = r_i$ or as $c_i(x_i,u_i) \leq r_i$, then $-\frac{\partial g_i}{\partial r_i}$ are the Lagrange multipliers in solving Equation (2); e.g., refer to [3]. Thus by having each application manager i send to the central manager both $g(r_i,u_i)$ and the corresponding Lagrange multipliers, the gradient $\nabla\widetilde{h}$ can be efficiently computed by the central manager. In this case, the following hierarchical implementation scheme between the central manager and the application environments can be employed.

1. The central manager sends r_i to each application manager i.
2. Depending on the architecture of the system, the central manager might also send the set of external variables u_i to each application manager i. In other cases, the external variables u_i are readily available to each application manager i.
3. Each application manager i computes $g_i(r_i,u_i)$ and sends it to the central manager along with the corresponding Lagrange multipliers.
4. The central manager uses this information to compute $\widetilde{h}$ and $\nabla\widetilde{h}$ and find the next resource allocation $(r_1,\ldots,r_n)$.
5. This is iterated until a suitable resource allocation is found or the algorithm converges.

Note that this iterative scheme need not require communication between the central manager and every application manager at each step, as application manager i can provide its objective and the gradient of this objective both as functions of r_i, for all (or a subset of) feasible r_i. In any case, the computation of $g_i(r_i,u_i)$ for each application environment i does not have to be performed very accurately (e.g., run too many iterations to compute $g_i(r_i,u_i)$) at the beginning of the iterative scheme.

For environments where derivatives are not available or cannot be computed efficiently, the above hierarchical implementation scheme can be used together with derivative-free trust-region methods [4] to realize similar benefits. In particular, when derivative-free trust-region methods are used to compute g_i, the trust region radius and (internal) trust region model used in computing g_i can be sent to the central manager in place of the Lagrange multipliers. This information can be sent to the central manager in a compact form and used in an efficient manner that is analogous to the hierarchical implementation scheme provided above.

2.5   Application of Decentralized Optimization

Let us now consider a representative application of our mathematical framework for decentralized optimization in which a set of M heterogeneous computing servers, $S_1, \ldots, S_M$, and a set of routers are used by a common service provider to host a set of N client application environments, $E_1, \ldots, E_N$. The router assigned to application environment i immediately routes all incoming requests to one of the servers allocated to and under the control of application manager i. A service-level agreement (SLA) is created for each application environment to define the corresponding quality-of-service (QoS) requirements and the revenues (respectively, penalties) for satisfying (respectively, failing to satisfy) these requirements. To elucidate the exposition, we consider SLAs with a single QoS class within each application environment.

Optimal self-management in such an autonomic computing system includes the allocation of servers among the set of application environments, the routing of requests within each application environment, and the scheduling of requests at each server within an application environment, all in order to minimize the global objective function based on the collection of SLAs. Specifically, each application manager i solves the optimization problem in Equation (2) and the central manager solves the optimization problem in Equation (3), where r_i are the set of servers and the router allocated by the central manager to application environment i, $(r_1, \ldots, r_N) \in R$, u_i are the set of workload characteristics for application environment i, and $x_i \in C_i(r_i, u_i)$ are the set of router and per-server scheduling variables that can be changed in application environment i. With our focus here on single-class QoS requirements, there is no need to set or adjust any scheduling variables at each server, and thus x_i consists solely of a vector of the proportional weights for routing requests among the set of servers allocated to application environment i. The set R is the set of all possible N-way partitions of the set of servers $\{S_1, \ldots, S_M\}$, together with a router for each application environment.

The details of the cost functions in Equations (2) and (3), as well as the corresponding constraints $C_i(r_i, u_i)$, depend upon the specific client environments being served. We shall thus focus on a typical scenario in which the QoS requirements are based on the response times of client requests. In particular,

$$f_i(x_i, r_i, u_i) \ = \ f_i(\mathbb{E}T_i(x_i, r_i, u_i)),$$

where $\mathbb{E}T_i(x_i, r_i, u_i)$ denotes the expectation of the stochastic response time process for application environment i given the allocation of resources r_i and under the routing and scheduling variables x_i and the workload u_i. We also shall consider a linear aggregate cost function that is given by

$$h(g_1(r_1, u_1), \ldots, g_N(r_N, u_N)) \ = \ \sum_{i=1}^{N} \widehat{H}_i \, g_i(r_i, u_i)$$

where $\widehat{H}_i$ is the holding cost per unit time associated with application environment i, although MAX and MIN could be used instead of SUM in a similar fashion.

The workloads u_i can be accurately modeled as stationary stochastic processes [5]. When the functions $f_i(\cdot)$ are linear, the optimization problem in Equation (2) for each application manager i, under the assumptions of this section, has been considered in [6] within the context of closed-form approximations based on heavy-traffic stochastic-process limits to accurately model the per-server response time processes in each application environment i under general conditions in an online fashion. Further assuming independence within and among the stochastic processes, we obtain from the results in [6] that Equation (2) is given by

$$g_i(r_i, u_i) = \min_{x_i} \sum_{S_j \in r_i} H_j \left(\frac{1}{\mu_{i,j}} + \frac{x_{i,j}\alpha_i + \beta_i}{\mu_{i,j} - \lambda_i x_{i,j}} \right) x_{i,j}, \qquad (4)$$

such that $\sum_{S_j \in r_i} x_{i,j} = 1$, $x_{i,j} \geq 0$, $\lambda x_{i,j} < \mu_{i,j}$, where $\alpha_i = (\mathcal{C}_{A_i}^2 - 1)/2$, $\beta_i = (\mathcal{C}_{B_i}^2 + 1)/2$, H_j is the holding cost per customer per unit time at server S_j, λ_i^{-1} and $\mathcal{C}_{A_i}^2$ are the mean and squared coefficient of variation of the overall interarrival time process for application environment i, $\mu_{i,j}^{-1}$ and $\mathcal{C}_{B_i}^2$ are the mean and squared coefficient of variation of the service time process for application environment i on server $S_j \in r_i$, and $x_{i,j}$ is the proportional weight for routing requests of application environment i to server $S_j \in r_i$. The corresponding central manager optimization problem consists of solving for the set of servers $(r_1^*, \ldots, r_N^*) \in R$ in Equation (3) with respect to (4), which can be expressed as

$$h_d = \min_{(r_1, \ldots, r_N)} \sum_{i=1}^{N} \widehat{H}_i \min_{x_i} \sum_{S_j \in r_i} H_j \left(\frac{1}{\mu_{i,j}} + \frac{x_{i,j}\alpha_i + \beta_i}{\mu_{i,j} - \lambda_i x_{i,j}} \right) x_{i,j}, \qquad (5)$$

such that $(r_1, \ldots, r_N) \in R$, $\sum_{S_j \in r_i} x_{i,j} = 1$, $x_{i,j} \geq 0$, $\lambda x_{i,j} < \mu_{i,j}$. The solutions of both of these optimization problems can be computed very efficiently using the hierarchical implementation scheme of Section 2.4 together with known methods in convex programming; e.g., refer to [3]. Similarly, the corresponding centralized optimization problem can be solved via (1) and the above equations, subject to the same set of constraints.

We have implemented these optimal solutions with which we have conducted many numerical experiments. Using this approach, we find that even though the total amount of computation is larger for the decentralized approach, the optimization is distributed and the work performed by the central manager is in general less than having the central manager perform centralized global optimization.

3   Mathematical Framework for Dynamic Control

3.1   System Model

The previous section considered decentralized optimization in a static system environment where the external (workload) variables u_i are constant (in a stationary stochastic sense). On the other hand, autonomic computing systems that provide self-* properties are clearly dynamic environments in which optimal self-management decisions need to be made continually over time and at multiple time scales. The optimal self-management of such complex information systems therefore must also involve dynamic optimal control for achieving the optimal solutions that are computed at points in time.

More precisely, the external (workload) variables u_i vary over time. These external (workload) variables u_i, however, can be accurately modeled as stochastic processes that vary over time [5]. To achieve the global objectives of autonomic computing systems with self-* properties under such nonstationary behavior, the decentralized optimization decisions are made periodically at time epochs t_ℓ, $\ell = 0, 1, 2, \ldots$. That is, $\{t_0, t_1, t_2, \ldots\}$ represents the sequence of points in time when the decentralized optimization process makes its optimal decisions, where $0 \equiv t_0 < t_1 < t_2 < \ldots$.

The time scales at which these optimal decisions are made depend upon several factors, including the delays, overheads and constraints involved in making changes to decision variables, the QoS requirements of each application environment i, and the properties of the underlying (nonstationary) stochastic processes. Then the optimization problems in (2) and (3) are solved at each optimization decision epoch t_ℓ based on measurements collected during previous optimization intervals $\tau_k \equiv [t_k, t_{k+1})$, $k = 0, \ldots, \ell - 1$, in order to determine the optimal variables x_i^* and r_i^* that should be deployed during the next optimization interval τ_ℓ, while satisfying the constraints limiting the changes to the decision variables. We shall assume the intervals τ_ℓ, $\ell \geq 0$, are sufficiently long that each application environment reaches steady state within every interval, and thus the functions in (2) and (3) are bounded, provided that the constraints for each application environment are satisfied.

The data from the interval $\tau_{\ell-1}$ can be used together with data from previous intervals to parameterize stochastic models related to the optimization decision process for τ_ℓ, to forecast these models to characterize the corresponding system behavior for the interval τ_ℓ, to use these forecasted stochastic models to analyze the decision process during this interval, and finally to make the appropriate self-management decisions for the interval τ_ℓ of the optimization decision process which can include interactions with other decision processes.

3.2   Dynamic Control Properties

The control, decision making and optimization mechanisms cannot always be continuous (due to granularity) and may include some time-delay dependencies. One of the reasons is that any change requires time and resources. For example, switching a resource from one application environment to another even if done in the same physical domain requires some clean-up and quarantine time (due to, e.g., privacy restrictions in SLAs). The time delays can also be caused by different time scales of the workloads as well as the operations of several applications within an environment. It is well known that even very simple (e.g., linear) models which are only piecewise continuous or contain a feedback element may exhibit chaotic (in the sense of difficult to predict and qualitatively very sensitive to initial or control conditions) behavior [7]. This chaotic behavior may appear in some regimes of parameters, however the sets of vulnerable parameters may also be very complex – excluding an envelope (e.g., closure or convex hull) of them might exclude an overly large portion of the parameter space.

As an elementary example of how adding time delay can produce locally unstable behavior (and hence can produce chaos on the larger scale), consider a linear dynamical system

$$y_{n+1} = (s - d)y_n + D \tag{6}$$

with constant parameters, where the new state depends only on the closest previous one. This system is stable whenever for $\xi = s - d$ we have $|\xi| \leq 1$ and asymptotically stable when $|\xi| < 1$, where ξ denotes the eigenvalue of the dynamical system. However, if the balance of $s - d$ is spread over time, we get a system

$$y_{n+1} = sy_n - dy_{n-1} + D. \tag{7}$$

Now the stability condition is that both solutions of $\xi^2 - s\xi + d$, the characteristic polynomial of the new system, satisfy $|\xi| \leq 1$. In the bifurcation cases, when one of the eigenvalues is ± 1, then the other is $\pm d$, and clearly we may have $|d| > 1$ even when $|s - d| < 1$. We skip the detailed analysis of the complex (conjugate) eigenvalues; e.g., refer to [7].

When the dynamical system near a fix point is as described above and it is globally bounded (by some non-linear dependencies) in such a way that the trajectories return to this fix point, then the instability of the fix point produces very chaotic behavior due to the irregular number of iterates involved in returns to this fix point.

In special cases chaos can be controllable, for example many stochastically stable systems exhibit individual chaotic trajectories, but with very well behaved distributions or moments. The transitions from a deterministic regime, where all trajectories are predictable at all times, to a stochastic regime, where most of the trajectories are predictable over long intervals of time, may go through all kinds of uncontrollable evolutions.

It is therefore essential for any given control system to determine the types of possible asymptotic behavior, the stability of such behavior under small perturbations of the system (a robustness issue), and to conceive of mechanisms exposing the type of behavior the system is currently in.

3.3   Application of Dynamic Optimal Control

Let us now investigate a representative application of our mathematical framework for dynamic optimal control by extending the (static) decentralized optimization application of Section 2.5 to include the dynamic control for achieving these optimal solutions. In particular, we consider each application environment i during any optimization interval τ_ℓ in which the corresponding workload processes u_i are stationary. Every application manager i determines the optimal routing and scheduling variables $x_i^* \in C_i$ by solving the optimization problem in Equation (4), and the central manager determines the optimal allocation of servers $(r_1^*, \ldots, r_N^*) \in R$ by solving the optimization problem in Equation (5). Then the router variables for each application environment i are obtained by minimizing the weighted sum of expected response times within application environment i, and the central manager allocates servers among the set of application environment i in order to minimize the overall weighted sum of the corresponding expected response times.

When $\lambda_i x_{i,j} \geq \mu_{i,j}$, the response time process for application environment i on server $S_j \in r_i$ blows up. In particular, under this condition, the value of $\mathbb{E}T_{i,j}$ within an interval τ_ℓ increases with the length of τ_ℓ such that $\mathbb{E}T_{i,j} \to \infty$ as $\tau_\ell \to \infty$. While this condition violates key constraints in the decentralized optimization problem, time delays can cause this situation to occur as we will demonstrate below. Hence, the smaller the length of τ_ℓ, the smaller the explosion in the value of $\mathbb{E}T_{i,j}$ during the interval τ_ℓ. On the other hand, the smaller the length of τ_ℓ, the larger the delay in the dynamical system (due to fairly constant overheads and communication delays) which can lead to the instability problems illustrated below. Furthermore, the likelihood that a backlog of customers from interval τ_ℓ is not served within this interval and thus spills over into intervals $\tau_{\ell+k}$, for $k \geq 1$, also depends upon the length of τ_ℓ.

There is an analogy between this model and the dynamical systems from Section 3.2. The rate of growth in the backlog of customers corresponds in Equations (6) and (7) to the growth rate s, while the server allocation is related to the decay rate d. In Equation (6) the growth rate and the decay rate cancel each other immediately within the same time interval and we deal with the net effect which, by assumption, is such that the backlog remains bounded. In the presence of time delay as in Equation (7), the decay rate (or the server allocation) corresponds to a different time interval than the growth rate (or the backlog rate), which in some cases produces instabilities. We see these effects in Figures 4 and 5, where the time delay produces high spikes in the total response time.

In fact, there is a singularity at the point $\lambda_i x_{i,j} = \mu_{i,j}$ resulting in a phase transition between the regions where $\lambda_i x_{i,j} < \mu_{i,j}$ and $\lambda_i x_{i,j} > \mu_{i,j}$, and numerical issues can cause problems in the computation of the optimal solutions. The optimization algorithms used to compute these optimal solutions need to carefully address these issues.

Dynamic optimal control is clearly needed to achieve the optimal solutions of Equations (4) and (5) continually over time and at multiple time scales. This, however, is a very difficult problem within the context of the representative application of our mathematical framework, as illustrated by some of the important issues raised above. Moreover, when the system environment changes over time (e.g., a change in the workload), the additional dynamical behavior of the resulting continual optimization problem can be very complex in terms of both the mathematical analysis of the system and the insights gained from this analysis. In order to gain a better understanding of the fundamental interactions between dynamics and optimization in autonomic computing systems, we consider a simplification of (4) and (5) that reduces to the sum of the corresponding expected

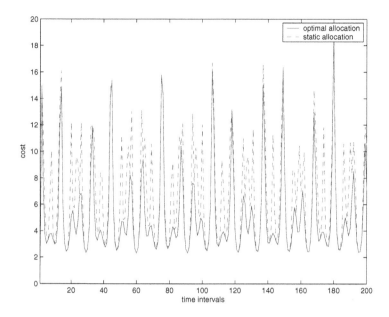

Fig. 2. Total response time for optimal allocation and for a constant static allocation

response times. We further assume for clarity of presentation that the servers are homogeneous and that the decision variables represent the fraction of a large set of servers allocated between the $N = 2$ application environments.

This version of the problem is simple enough to understand and gain important insights while still being a meaningful representation of dynamic optimal control in autonomic computing systems. In particular, we expect that the key trends obtained from our analysis of this simplified version of the problem will continue to hold even for the more general problem. A deeper mathematical analysis of the general problem and related issues is outside of the scope of this paper and is the subject of ongoing research.

Using this simplified version of the problem, the resulting continual optimization problem in canonical form is reduced to:

$$\min_{K_1,K_2} (\mathbb{E}T_1 + \mathbb{E}T_2) = \min_{K_1,K_2} \left(\frac{K_1}{K_1 - \lambda_1} + \frac{K_2}{K_2 - \lambda_2} \right)$$

subject to the constraints $K_1 + K_2 = 1$, $K_i > \lambda_i \geq 0$, where K_1 and K_2 represent the portion of the servers assigned to each application environment with workload traffic intensities λ_1 and λ_2. An explicit optimal solution for K_1 and K_2 is then obtained in a straightforward manner by the Lagrangian method.

The dynamics of the two time-varying traffic intensities are modeled as sinusoidal functions of time. In order to illustrate the various behaviors due to different server allocations, we consider several methods of adjusting the server allocation and compare them to a static allocation scheme which assigns a constant server allocation across all time intervals. This static allocation is chosen to

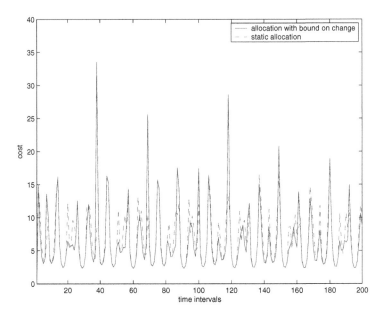

Fig. 3. Total response time for static allocation and allocation which limits the change between succesive time intervals

be the optimal allocation for the average traffic intensity, assuming its behavior is known.

In Figure 2 we show the total response time $\mathbb{E}T_1 + \mathbb{E}T_2$ for the static allocation scheme and the optimal allocation scheme. The optimal allocation scheme assigns the optimal allocation at each time interval given the traffic intensities at that interval. As expected, the static allocation is always no better than the optimal allocation.

Now we impose a bound on the change in the allocation allowed between successive time intervals. This is one way to represent the constraint that a large change in server allocation is undesirable. Figure 3 shows that this limits the ability of the server allocation to "chase" the optimal allocation and can result in allocation between intervals which is suboptimal and even can be worse than static allocation.

Next we consider the effect of allocation based on previous traffic intensity information due to delays. In Figure 4 we show the total response time if the optimal allocation is computed based on the traffic intensity of the previous time interval. As can be expected from using incorrect traffic intensities to allocate servers, we see that in some time intervals the constraint $K_i > \lambda_i$ is violated, resulting in very large response times. In such cases, one might prefer to use forecasted traffic intensities based on the data from the previous time interval(s) to allocate servers rather than using the (incorrect) traffic intensities obtained directly from the data of the previous time interval.

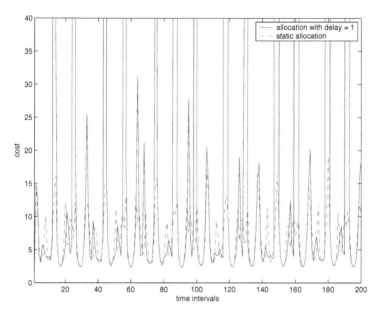

Fig. 4. Total response time for static allocation and optimal allocation based on traffic intensity of previous time interval

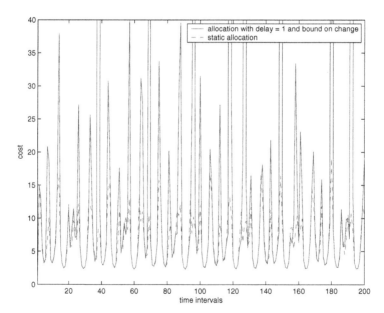

Fig. 5. Total response time for static allocation and allocation based on traffic intensity of previous time interval while limiting the change in allocation between time intervals

On the other hand, combining the two restrictive effects above does not necessarily make things worse. In particular, for the system under consideration, the combination of bounded change on allocation and delayed traffic intensities results in allocation that is better than delayed traffic intensities alone. In Figure 5 we see that the number of violations is less than Figure 4 if we impose a limit on the change in allocation between time intervals as in Figure 3.

4   Conclusions

We have considered the fundamentals of a mathematical framework for decentralized optimization and dynamic optimal control in autonomic computing systems with self-∗ properties. This framework provides a mathematical foundation for these important aspects of self-management in complex information systems and supports the design, architecture and algorithms employed throughout such self-∗ system. Using this framework, we first established conditions under which decentralized optimization can provide the same quality of solution as centralized optimization, both in a static environment and under mild technical assumptions. Our study also considered implementation schemes that significantly increase the efficiency with which the hierarchical decentralized optimization algorithms compute the optimal solution. We then further exploited our mathematical framework to investigate the dynamic control of continual decentralized optimization over time. In particular, our study illustrated how the additional dynamics can cause complicated behavior that deviates considerably from the static case, yielding potential problems and added complexities for continual optimization in environments which change over time. This complicated behavior can include phase transitions, chaos and instability.

References

1. Kephart, J.O., Chess, D.M.: The vision of autonomic computing. Computer **36** (2003) 41–52
2. Walsh, W.E., Tesauro, G., Kephart, J.O., Das, R.: Utility functions in autonomic systems. Technical report, IBM Research Division (2004)
3. Bertsekas, D.P.: Nonlinear Programming. 2nd edn. Athena Scientific (1999)
4. Conn, A.R., Gould, N.I., Toint, P.L.: Trust-Region Methods. SIAM (2000)
5. Gamarnik, D., Lu, Y., Squillante, M.S.: Fundamentals of stochastic modeling and analysis for self-∗ properties in autonomic computing systems. Technical report, IBM Research Division (2004)
6. Guo, X., Lu, Y., Squillante, M.S.: Optimal stochastic routing in distributed parallel queues. Technical report, IBM Research Division (2003) Revised, April 2004.
7. Katok, A., Hasselblatt, B.: Introduction to the Modern Theory of Dynamical Systems. Cambridge University Press (1995)

The Conflict Between Self-* Capabilities and Predictability

Rogério de Lemos

Computing Laboratory,
University of Kent, UK
r.delemos@kent.ac.uk

Abstract. Although it would be desirable for any system to have self-* capabilities when faced with changes that might occur either in the system or its environment, there is a certain classes of systems in which the incorporation of such capabilities would be difficult to justify. These systems are mainly those that uncertainties in their behaviours are not desirable. In this paper, we discuss how the expected degree of autonomy of a system is related to the way in which a system is described, either process or data. The discussion is presented in the context of predictability. The type of system being considered are mission-critical system that are likely to restrict the degree of uncertainty associated with their behaviour, or the infrastructure that enables this behaviour.

1 Introduction

As computer based systems become more complex, design solutions that promote their operational autonomy have become the holy grail of system architects and designers. Autonomy, in this context, would enable the system to react to either internal or external changes without any outside interference. However, system autonomy should not be restricted to the actual services delivered by the system, but it should also be associated with the infrastructure that enables the system to deliver its services. In other words, autonomy is not necessarily something that should be observed only at the system interface, it could be a system capability that enables it to deliver its specified service with a certain degree of quality.

Self-* capabilities are the means by which a system attains its autonomy, and these capabilities have an impact upon the system's fundamental properties, which are functionality, usability, performance, cost, and dependability. In this paper, properties and capabilities are considered to be two different concepts, the former is a system attribute that can be directly measured and quantified, while the latter are the means that enable one or more of the system properties. Although some aspects of self-* capabilities might allow the system to provide different kinds of services, the view taken in this paper is that system capabilities are essentially enablers for improving the system non-functional properties. In addition to self-* capabilities, the system might have other capabilities whose purpose is also to enhance the quality of services provided by the system, and reduce the cost for providing them.

O. Babaoglu et al. (Eds.): SELF-STAR 2004, LNCS 3460, pp. 219–228, 2005.

This paper explores the relationship between self-* capabilities and predictability, which is a fundamental aspect in the design, operation and evaluation of a certain class of systems. The objective of this exercise is to identify, from the perspective of predictability, what type of systems should the self-* capabilities be associated with, and what techniques could be used to attain such capabilities. This would allow establishing the theoretical and practical limits that can be associated with the different approaches that are employed in the development of systems.

The rest of the paper is organised as follows. In the next section, the dichotomy between data and process descriptions of systems is described. Section 3 presents how self-* capabilities can be incorporated into systems that are essentially represented as data and process. In the final section some concluding remarks are presented.

2   Dichotomy in the Descriptions of Systems

Simon has distinguished two fundamentally different ways in which systems can be described [15]: state and process. Since well-established notion of state is used in a different way in dynamics and control, MacFarlane has suggested instead the usage of the terms of *process* and *data* for making the distinction initially suggested by Simon [13].

Data description of systems characterises the system as acted upon, by providing the criteria for identifying objects, often by modelling the objects themselves [15]. In this type of description a circle could be described as a locus of all points equidistant from a give point, such as the representation of a circle as a bit map. Other examples include pictures, blueprints, most diagrams, and the chemical structure of formulas [15]. *Process description* of systems characterises the system as sensed, by providing the means for producing or generating objects having the desired characteristics [15]. In this type of description, the construction of a circle could be described as the rotation of a compass with one arm fixed until the other arm has returned to its starting point. Alternatively, a circle could be represented as an equation. Other examples include recipes, differential equations, and equations for chemical reactions [15]. A major difference between these two forms of description is the amount of information required for modelling a system. The process description of a system usually involves less information than its counterpart. Moreover, it might be the case that due to its very nature, the data description of systems becomes unbounded, which is not the case in the process description of systems.

Architects and designers of complex distributed systems are currently facing the prospect that existing techniques would not scale for the envisaged future systems, such as, decentralised peer-to-peer, self-organised ad hoc networks, and pervasive computing. Existing approaches make use of traditional engineering principles in which system properties are specified and evaluated in a step-wise manner, mainly top-down. These are essentially based on process descriptions that are amenable to rigorous or mathematical analysis. For that, it is needed to identify key system variables that allow monitoring its state and controlling its behaviour, such as, inputs, outputs, and internal and environmental variables. On the other hand, architects and designers are seeking alternative decentralised control techniques that can be used when building complex distributed systems. These approaches are based on large population of entities that independently gather information and decide how to behave. The functionality of these entities is very simple, and their communication is very limited. With these characteristics, the intent is to obtain desirable macroscopic behaviours from microscopic behaviours and interactions. These approaches are based on data descriptions, and it is claimed that the emergent macroscopic behaviours would be able to provide solutions to specific problems.

The difference between process and data representations can be interpreted from the perspective of accuracy and precision. While process descriptions might be precise but not accurate, data descriptions might be accurate but not precise. In process descriptions, the assumptions that allow a process to be realizable introduce uncertainties. However, when these assumptions are discharged more accurate models are obtained, thus eliminating uncertainties from the system. On the other hand, data descriptions are an abstraction of the actual behaviour of the system, and in some cases for the data to be meaningful it has to undergo through some generalisations. These two issues inevitably lead to the introduction of uncertainties on how systems are represented, and it is from these uncertainties that emergent behaviours materialize.

This dichotomy between process and data descriptions of systems is clearly recognised in the context of decentralised solutions for complex systems, while the distributed systems community take the consensus view, the computational intelligence community takes either the emergence or learning view. Consensus approaches are based on protocols that reach agreement under particular failure loads. Emergence is based on a collection of simple autonomous and self-sufficient entities that are able to adapt to changing environments. Different from emergent behaviours, but based on the same principles, learning refers to the automatic mining of information from available data for the purpose of creating knowledge. In the following, this dichotomy between process and data descriptions will be used as a basis for investigating the provision of self-* capabilities in different classes of systems. Depending on the system, expectations on the degree of autonomy of a system might be curtailed depending on the assumptions made and the properties of that system.

3   Self-* and Predictability

The complexity of systems and the way they are integrated will require new approaches for their development, operation and maintenance. As already mentioned, conventional deterministic approaches based on process descriptions may not be sufficient for enabling the provision of a wide range of services that are expected from these systems. Several new approaches have recently emerged from different areas, such as, biologically inspired computing being applied to a general class of problems, control systems being applied to software engineering, and social and economic models being applied to agent technology, just to mention a few. In this paper, we restrict ourselves to the first two areas. Issues related to agent technology and dependability were recently discussed on two panels [5][10].

The provision of self-* capabilities by software engineering solutions essentially relies on the representation of systems as processes, in which solutions are normally based on the feedback control loop principle. Meta-parameters of system behaviour and structure, and its environment, are monitored for eventual changes so that the system can be adjusted for delivering required services in a stable way. The degree of self-* capabilities that can be achieved by employing these solutions is limited because of the need for having predictive behaviours, otherwise reaction to changes would not be deterministic. Predictability is achieved by removing operational uncertainties from the system otherwise these could disrupt the normal operation of the system. In other words, it is fundamental that during the development of these systems the complete state specification is identified, or else the occurrence of unexpected states can lead to system failures. Considering such restrictions, can a process oriented system be able to show self-* capabilities? They might be able, but the degree of autonomy is restricted, and it might be the case that these capabilities need to be established during design time.

On the other hand, the provision of self-* capabilities by biologically inspired solutions essentially relies on the representation of systems as data. Such solutions exploit clever mechanisms from nature by defining algorithms and implementations that are appropriate for the problem at hand. The inspiration is usually based on the logical characteristics of biological systems rather than physical. The reason for this is that logical aspects tend to be more generic, and more appropriate to analyse data in a virtual data space. Since biological inspired solutions are based on a sample of the whole data associated with a system, complete system models are difficult to obtain, which explains why uncertainties are an inherent aspect of these models. Incorporating learning capabilities into a system might eliminate this deficiency, however these are likely to introduce another degree of uncertainty. Emergent behaviours might be useful in dealing with unexpected circumstances, but the system reaction to these might become unpredictable.

In the following, we focus on two approaches for exemplifying how process and data descriptions of systems can handle predictability and autonomy.

4 Example of Process and Data Descriptions

In the first example, we present an architectural solution based on exceptional handling to tolerate faults. The solution relies on a process description for building adaptable, but deterministic systems. Uncertainties are eliminated from the system behaviour, however the solution is not scalable since exceptional handling based solutions are invariably application dependent, i.e., there is no single mechanism that is able to deal with a general class of faults. For example, it would be feasible to apply such architectural solution to handle intrusions because of the uncertainties associated with these [18]. In the second example, we present an artificial immune system solution (AIS) for the detection of anomalies. The solution relies on a data description for generating error detectors that are able to identify new unexpected circumstances. The rationale associated with this approach is that if systems are to be autonomous when reacting to changes, in this case undesirable, then it is essential that the system should be able to recognise new erroneous states, and adapt its set of detectors accordingly. In this particular context, it has been observed that the generalisation of potential detectors has lead to a decrease on the detection coverage, and an increase in the number of false positives [2].

4.1 Architectural Approaches

Architectural representations of systems have shown to be effective in assisting the understanding of broader system concerns by abstracting away from details of the system. To leverage the dependability properties of systems, solutions are needed at the architectural level that are able to guide the structuring of undependable components into a fault tolerant architecture. Fault tolerance, one of the means to dependability, is related to the self-repair and self-healing capabilities [7].

Architectural flexibility for supporting run-time change can be achieved by using specialised co-operative connectors to change the pattern of collaboration between components: components are rigid entities, and how they interact provide the basis for adaptability [4][6]. Each collaboration is identified in terms of pre- and post-conditions, and invariants. Depending on the required change, a different collaboration is selected that makes the system to change its behaviour. All the collaborations are defined during design time together with their respective trigger conditions. Uncertainty between the alternative collaborations does not exist because choice has to be deterministic, and uncertainties associated with a particular collaboration is restricted because behavioural invariants have to be maintained.

In a different work, in order to deal with undesirable, though expected circumstances, an idealised architectural component was defined with structure and behaviour equivalent to that of the idealised fault-tolerant component concept [11]. This approach was later extended to deal with commercial off-the-shelf (COTS) software components [12]. The basic mechanism to deal with the expected circumstances employed in these approaches was exception handling. The system architect must know from the outset what exceptions might occur, the causes associated with these exceptions, and how to match these exceptions with their respective handlers. The predictability in these systems is obtained by clearly identifying what is expected, and avoiding the system to become brittle towards the unexpected. How a system reacts towards expected circumstances should be know beforehand and should be incorporated in the design of the system.

Alternative techniques could be employed if undesirable circumstances, i.e. faults, could be grouped in terms of classes. Instead of the need for identifying specific handlers for each type of undesirable circumstance, as mentioned above, general solutions based on replication, diversity, and consensus could be devised. However, although these systems would be robust towards certain classes of faults, they are not considered sufficiently robust towards general classes of faults. In all these approaches, there is almost no degree of autonomy for the sake of obtaining predictable behaviour, which was an essential requirement of the applications involved.

4.2 Artificial Immune Systems

Nature has been good in solving problems, hence biological inspired approaches are enthused by nature but do not copy it blindly. There are several areas associated with computational intelligence, such as evolutionary algorithms and artificial neural networks, and one of its recent additions is the area of artificial immune systems (AIS). Artificial immune system is an example of nature-inspired problem solving system, which is based on the current understanding of the mammal immune system, without copying exactly its biological steps.

The immune system is a defence mechanism against body invaders (viruses, bacteria, and fungi). Since the study of the immune system is still progressing, is no surprise that there are three main theories for describing it: clonal selection, immune network, and danger. It consists of four layers of defence: physical barriers, chemical barriers, innate immunity, and adaptive immunity [3]. In terms of computational intelligence metaphors, the most relevant layer of defence is the adaptive immunity, whose role is to defend the body against specific foreign organisms, and to learn and remember about past invaders. From the perspective of clonal selection, adaptive immunity is responsible for training the immature lymphocyte cells for distinguishing between self molecules and foreign antigens, since immune response is undertaken by mature lymphocyte cells. During the immune response, mature lymphocyte cells multiply for effective defence, and differentiate for perfect recognition. After immune response, efficient mature lymphocyte cells are stored for subsequent encounters. The motivation for immune system to be found interesting as a metaphor is because its general characteristics: pattern recognition (anomaly detection, noise tolerance), diversity, learning, memory, redundancy, robustness, feature extraction, distributed, multi-layered, and adaptive.

Artificial immune systems (AIS) are adaptive systems inspired by theoretical immunology and observed immune functions, principles and models, which are applied to complex problems [3]. For the engineering of AIS algorithms, a high-level framework has been proposed that contains three basic elements [3]. The first layer is related to the *representation* of the basic entities of the system, which can be the antigens and antibodies. This representation can either be numerical (discrete or continuous) or symbolic. The second layer is the *affinity measures* that quantify the interactions between the antigens and antibodies. For the case of discrete representations the Hamming distance can be employed, while Euclidean distance can be used for continuous representations. The last layer captures the *immune algorithms* that actually define the system dynamics. There are several AIS techniques, just to mention a few, negative selection algorithms, immune network models, bone marrow models, clonal selection algorithms, and danger theory [3]. In this paper, for the purpose of anomaly detection, the negative selections algorithm has been selected, for several reasons: it was one of the first algorithms to be proposed [8], and since its understanding is quite intuitive, it became popular, sometimes for the wrong reasons [9]. Self/non-self discrimination metaphor behind the negative selection of T-cells in the thymus provided inspiration for the negative selection algorithm: in the *censoring phase* T-cells that match self are eliminated, and in the *monitoring phase* mature T-cells will in general match only non-self. The negative selection algorithm has been used to generate detectors that are able to identify undesirable changes to normal patterns or behaviour (self) of a system.

A number of works have attempted to build artificial immune systems for fault tolerance, virus detection, and computer security. Avizienis was one of the first ones to identify key characteristics of the immune system that were relevant for fault tolerance [1]: autonomy, distributed lymphatic vessels among the body, exclusive communication links, redundancy, and diversity. The immune system metaphor is actually quite relevant to fault tolerance principles: the self molecules of the immune system correspond to normal states/behaviours, the non-self molecules (antigenic patterns) correspond to abnormal states/behaviours, and the T-cells correspond to error detectors. Based on this metaphor, the creation of immunised fault tolerant embedded systems has been proposed [16][17][19], which explores negative selection, an immune inspired algorithm, for the generation of error detectors [2]. More recently, this work has been extended to incorporate the capability of generating adaptable error detectors during run-time, thus providing the means for the system to adapt itself to previously unexpected and undesirable circumstances. The incorporation of this capability has come to a price: the accuracy in detecting erroneous states has decreased when compared with that of an equivalent well craft engineered system; other studies have drawn the same conclusions [14].

Concerning the application of the negative selection algorithm to anomaly detection there are several problems in the classification of self/non-self [9]. First is related to the fact that the whole process is inefficient and time consuming because it relies on the generation of random detectors: this is a random search, which it does not use any information from the self. The second problem is that during the training phase, only negative examples (in this case self) are used. And finally, the whole approach is not adaptive, once the detectors are identified these will not change during run-time. Other more pragmatic inconveniences include, the discrete representation of the entities of system, which creates problems in the definition of affinity because small mutations in the representations might lead to a great impact on the meaning of the data. It also includes the trade off between specialisation and generalisation of detectors, which might have an impact on the run-time efficiency of the system: specialisation tends to maximise the coverage, while generalisation tends to minimise the size of the detector set. Based on the above limitations, alternative approaches have to be investigated in which detectors are able to adapt to changes in the environment. Recent investigations have adopted the immune network theory as a metaphor for two reasons. First, its self-assertion view in which there is no knowledge of self, instead it is developed over time. Second is the support for adaptability that is obtained through metadynamics, which is the recruitment of new individuals to the network structure.

The application of data oriented to minimise the size of the detector set approaches to error detection, that could be either the consequence of faults or intrusions, clearly illustrates the limitations associated with these approaches. Since faults and intrusions are considered rare events, the question to be asked is how the system is able to learn from rare events. If some correlation could be established between rare events, then the process of identifying new undesirable events could be based on the extrapolation of what is already known. However, this assumption cannot be generalised, since it is difficult to establish the correlation between undesirable events. An alternative approach could be that of learning new undesirable events from what is already known about the non-erroneous behaviours of the system. This is a daunting challenge if we consider that the state space of normal behaviours might be much larger if compared with that of abnormal behaviour. Either the normal behavioural state can be encoded in such way that facilitates the search process, or such an approach becomes prohibitive in terms of efficiency and storage.

Another limitation in applying data descriptions to anomaly detection is how to improve coverage of the detectors and reduce at the same time the false positives. The main problem, as already mentioned, is that data is an abstraction of the actual behaviour of the system. This inevitably introduces uncertainties that have to be solved by finding a good balance between specialisation and generalisation.

Another problem that is inherent in data oriented approaches is the data itself. In addition for the need to the data to be representative of the actual system, there is also the need to have a deep understanding what the data represents. If either of these issues are not observed the predictability of the system is affected.

4.3 Predictability in Data Descriptions

It has been claimed that data oriented approaches might be appropriate for new emerging applications, but in what capacity is not yet clear. One issue however is clear: if predictability has to be an essential capability in the development and operation of a system, then a data oriented approach might not be an appropriate solution. This is particularly significant in those classes of systems in which performance and dependability constraints are critical, such as mission-critical systems. However, data oriented approaches could nevertheless be employed in such systems if sufficient protections are incorporated into their designs. Again such conservative solution would restrict one of the major benefits of data oriented approaches, which is that of emergent behaviours. An alternative approach, yet not fully explored, would be to build massively redundant systems, in which the failure of some the components would not affect the expected outcome of the whole system. However, for such solution to be successful, diverse data oriented approaches should be composed in order to increase their combined effectiveness, or coverage. However, a major weakness in such configuration would be the quality of the training data. If the data is not good, it does not matter how many approaches are employed if all of them suffer the same deficiencies.

Still considering the idea of exploring data oriented approaches in the context of systems containing trillions of components, issues like the identification of the source of change is important for establishing the appropriate mechanisms to deal with the change. For example, changes that occur internally to a component and that eventually affect the behaviour of that component, how these should be handled in the wider system? If the rest of the system was able to accommodate the unknown behaviours, what should be the threshold to which the system should react either for eliminating a whole group of abnormal components, or incorporating these components as normal? The reverse also raises very interesting questions. If the environment of a system changes, how these changes are reflected upon the components of that system: either the components are eliminated from the system, or the components have to be modified for coping with the changes. All these decisions affect the predictability of the overall system behaviour if clear strategies are not implemented. However, as already mentioned, it might be the case that the combined usage of diverse strategies might be the only way of bringing out the best of the system, which eventually might lead to unpredictabilities.

Most of work on the data descriptions has dealt with emergent behaviours or functional properties. Still to be investigated are the non-functional properties of these systems, such as, performance, usability and dependability. Concerning in particular dependability, although it is easy to build a system out of dependable (sub)systems, though this does not always guarantee the resulting system is dependable, what about building dependable systems from a collection of individual undependable entities? Although it is not at all clear how dependability can become an emergent property, it might be the case that in a large population of entities sufficient redundancies can be obtained for maintaining the reliability of the system as a whole. Of course that, solutions intrinsically depend on the application being considered and the levels of risk associated with it.

5   Conclusions

Although in this paper, the issues concerning self-* capabilities of systems were presented in terms of the dichotomy on how systems can be described, i.e. *process* versus *data*, we have not overlook the possibility of systems relying on both representations for achieving different degrees of autonomy depending on the services to be delivered. The idea of developing systems that rely on both process and data representations, which explores the complementary benefits of these, is not new. Such hybrid systems have mostly been confined to stand alone closed systems, however the challenge ahead is whether the same idea can be applied to more complex systems that are open and collaborative in their nature, and which are expected to show self-* capabilities and be predictive at the same time.

References

[1]   A. Avizienis. "Towards Systematic Design of Fault-tolerance Systems". *Computer 30(4)*. 1997. pp. 51-58.
[2]   M. Ayara, J. Timmis, R. de Lemos, L. N. de Castro, R. Duncan. "Negative Selection: How to Generate Detectors". *Proc. of the 1st International Conference on Artificial Immune Systems*. Canterbury, UK. September 2002. pp. 89-98.
[3]   L. N. de Castro, J. Timmis. Artificial Immune Systems: A New Computational Intelligence Approach. Springer-Verlag. 2002.
[4]   R. de Lemos. "A Co-operative Object-Oriented Architecture for Adaptive Systems". *Proc. of the 7th IEEE International Conference and Workshop on the Engineering of Computer-Based Systems (ECBS'00)*. Edinburgh, Scotland. April 2000. pp. 120-128.
[5]   R. de Lemos. "Novel Approaches in Dependable Computing". *Proc. of the 4th European Dependable Computing Conference (EDCC-4)*. Lecture Notes in Computer Science 2485. Eds. P. Thevenod-Fosse, A. Bondavalli. Springer-Verlag. Toulouse, France. October 2002. pp. 79-80.
[6]   R. de Lemos, J. L. Fiadeiro. "An Architectural Support for Self-adaptive Software for Treating Faults". *Proc. of the 1st ACM SIGSOFT Workshop on Self-Healing Systems (WOSS'02)*. Eds. A. Wolf, D. Garlan, J. Kramer. Charleston, SC, USA. November 2002. pp. 39-42.
[7]   R. de Lemos, C. Gacek, A. Romanovsky (Eds.). *Proc. of the ICSE 2003 Workshop on Software Architectures for Dependable Systems*. Portland, OR. April 2003. http://www.cs.ukc.ac.uk/events/conf/2003/wads/ (October 2003).

[8]   S. Forrest, et al. "Self-Nonself Discrimination in a Computer". *Symposium on Research in Security and Privacy*. 1994: p. 202-212.

[9]   A. A. Freitas, J. Timmis. "Revisiting the Foundations of Artificial Immune Systems: A Problem-Oriented Perspective". *Artificial Immune Systems: Proc. 2nd Int. Conf. (ICARIS-2003)*. Lecture Notes in Computer Science 2787. Springer-Verlag. 2003. pp. 229-241.

[10] A. Garcia, J. Sardinha, C. Lucena, J. Castro, J. Leite, R. Milidiú, A. Romanovsky, M. Griss, R. de Lemos, A. Perini. "Software Engineering for Large-Scale Multi-Agent Systems – SELMAS 2003: Workshop Report". *ACM Software Engineering Notes 28(5)*. November 2003.

[11] P. A. de C. Guerra, C. Rubira, R. de Lemos. A Fault-Tolerant Software Architecture for Component-Based Systems. *Architecting Dependable Systems*. Lecture Notes in Computer Science 2677. Springer. Berlin, Germany. 2003. pp. 129-149.

[12] P. A. de C. Guerra, C. Rubira, A. Romanovsky, R. de Lemos. "Integrating COTS Software Components into Dependable Software Architectures". *Proc. of the 6th IEEE Int. Symposium on Object-Oriented Real-Time Distributed Computing (ISORC'03)*. Hokaido, Japan. May 2003.

[13] A. G. J. MacFarlane. "Information, Knowledge and Control". *Essays on Control: Perspective in the Theory and its Applications*. Eds. H. L. Trentelman, J. C. Willians. Birkhäuser. 1993.

[14] R. A. Maxiom, K. M. C. Tan. "Anomaly Detection in Embedded Systems". *IEEE Transactions on Computers 51(2)*. February 2002. pp. 108-120.

[15] H. A. Simon. *The Sciences of the Artificial*. Second Edition. MIT Press. Cambridge, MA, USA. 1981.

[16] J. Timmis, R. de Lemos, M. Ayara, R. Duncan. "Towards Immune Inspired Fault Tolerance in Embedded Systems". *Proc. of 9th International Conference on Neural Information Processing*. IEEE Computer Society. November 2002. pp. 1459-1463.

[17] A. M. Tyrell. "Computer Know Thy Self!: A Biological Way to Look at Fault-Tolerance." *Second Euromicro/IEE Workshop on Dependable Computing Systems*. 1999. pp. 129- 135.

[18] P. Veríssimo. "Uncertainty and Predictability: Can they be reconciled?" *Fudico: Future Directions in Distributed Computing*. Lecture Notes in Computer Science 2584. Springer. Berlin, Germany. May 2003.

[19] S. Xanthakis, et al. "Immune System and Fault Tolerant Computing". *Lecture Notes in Computer Science*. Ed. J.M. Alliot. Springer-Verlag. 1995. pp. 181-197.

Self-aware Software – Will It Become a Reality?

Peter Andras[1] and Bruce G Charlton[2]

[1] University of Newcastle Upon Tyne,
School of Computing Science,
Newcastle upon Tyne, NE1 7RU, UK
peter.andras@ncl.ac.uk
[2] University of Newcastle Upon Tyne,
School of Biology(Psychology),
Newcastle upon Tyne, NE1 7RU, UK
bruce.charlton@ncl.ac.uk

Abstract. The possibility of building self-aware software fascinated computer scientist since the beginning of computer science. Research in AI, and in particular on software agents, agent system, computational reflection and reflective software delivered interesting results which moved towards the development of software systems with features of self-awareness. However, these approaches have not so far generated any clear success in terms of real and useful self-aware software. Here we introduce the theory of abstract communication systems, which describes the world in terms of systems and their environment. Systems comprise dense, inter-referencing clusters of communications. We analyse natural self-aware systems highlighting the critical features which make them able to be self-aware. We analyse software systems in terms of abstract communication systems theory and compare their critical features with these natural self-aware systems. We describe the necessary features of hypothetical self-aware software, discuss the existing barriers that stand in the way of realization of such systems and how these might be overcome.

1 Introduction

The concept of self-aware software appeared very early after the building of first large programmable computers and provided the foundation for science fiction novels and films (e.g., 2001: A Space Odyssey). In scientific terms these ideas led to the emergence of the domain of artificial intelligence as part of computer science [11], [17]. An early failed attempt to build software with self-awareness used perceptron neural networks, which were believed to lead to the emergence of some kind of consciousness (e.g., [57]). Other attempts based on symbolic reasoning also led to failures in terms of producing truly self-aware software systems [13], [49].

The idea of building an adaptive self-aware software system that is able to sense itself and maintain itself producing appropriate adaptive behaviours (dependent on the environmental stimuli and on the state of the system) appears

O. Babaoglu et al. (Eds.): SELF-STAR 2004, LNCS 3460, pp. 229–259, 2005.

perpetually fascinating for many computer scientists (e.g., [23], [28], [37], [42], [54], [63], [64]). A direction that grew out from classical artificial intelligence research is focusing on intelligent agents and multi-agent systems (e.g., [2], [31]). The aim of this research is to build software agents that can behave intelligently in a limited sense (e.g., within a strictly defined knowledge domain, like collecting, selecting, categorizing and packaging for delivery of financial news items) and which can support the professional activity of their owner. One step further the aim is to build systems of such agents, which are able to perform meaningful negotiations over exchanging services, representing the interests of their owners [2].

Another important direction is the research on computational reflection [36], [42], [51] and on reflective software systems [14], [18], [21], [52]. Reflective software systems aim to be able to evaluate themselves and generate adaptive responses to external stimuli, such that the response is appropriate for the state of the software system. Reflective software research also feeds into the research on intelligent agents, by providing core software for some of these agents [62]. A more application oriented related area is the research on self-monitoring and self-healing software [6]. The aim of this research is to build software systems that are able to evaluate their own state, detect faults and errors and automatically correct them returning the system to a 'healthy' state. Recent works on aspect-oriented software development [19], [33], [54] are very promising in terms of building self-monitoring applications, which is an important step towards self-aware software systems.

The above mentioned works on building software systems that show some level of self-awareness in an adaptive and responsive manner led to limited success. It appears that the most critical barrier that these systems cannot overcome yet is that of generating adaptive novel responses to previously unseen situations. In other words these systems are able to do what they were programmed for and to make the decisions that their programmers considered when they programmed them, but they cannot surpass these pre-programmed behaviours by generating new ones, which were not hard-coded by their programmers. In our view a major reason behind this lack of progress is that all these systems are designed to perform an externally implied function in some kind of efficient manner. This approach implies that there is no 'self' in a real sense of the software system from the point of the view of its design, and that the resources of the system are usually optimized sufficiently to prevent the emergence of suboptimal behaviours (these are usually considered erroneous ones), which otherwise is the usual way of emergence of new behaviours in the case of natural self-aware systems (e.g., bacteria, plants, animals, social organizations) [3], [16], [41], [48].

We note that there are positive signs towards software development environments, which may allow the emergence of the 'self' of software systems. Languages like Java and Smalltalk which implement reflection allow some level of structural self-inspection and self-modification (i.e., structural reification) [22], [28], [51], [61]. Component-based (e.g., JavaBeans, web services) [30]and aspect-oriented programming [19], [33], [54] may represent a way away from strict functional optimality, which in our view prevents the emergence of self-aware software.

The abstract communication systems approach offers a new way to look at software systems, and in particular offers an insider view of these systems. The theory of abstract communication systems [4], [15], [16], [41] was developed originally in the context of social systems by Luhmann (1996), having its roots in works on autopoetic systems [45] and in works on decision making in organizations [10], [58], [44].

In the interpretation followed here, the abstract communication systems approach views systems as dense collections of inter-referencing communications generated by communication units, which themselves are not part of the system. Such communication systems can be used to describe biological and social systems providing revelatory insights into the nature of these systems. We propose here to use this approach to analyse software systems and highlight the requirements for the building of self-aware software systems.

First, we provide a brief overview of the theory of abstract communication systems, explaining key concepts and providing examples that highlight key features of the explained concepts. Next, we discuss two natural self-aware systems, living cell and social organizations, emphasizing their critical components that provide the foundation for their self-awareness. This is followed by the analysis of software systems using concepts of abstract communication systems theory, focusing on components of software systems that are required for self-awareness in our view. Finally, the paper is closed by a discussion about how realizable we see the generation of self-aware software systems considering the requirements for this discussed previously.

2   Abstract Communication Systems

In this section we introduce fundamental concepts of abstract communication systems theory following the work of Luhmann (1996) and our earlier works [4], [15], [16], [5]. Each introduced concept is explained in theoretical terms supported by practical examples highlighting the relevant features of the concept.

Communications and Communication Systems. Communications are sequences of symbols communicated between communication units. Abstract communication systems are made of such communications between communication units. The communication units are not part of the system, since they are not themselves communications but instead transmit and receive communications. Communications reference other communications, in the sense that the sequence of symbols contained in a communication is dependent on the contents of other earlier or simultaneous communications and thereby refer to them. A dense cluster of inter-referencing communications surrounded by rare set of communications constitutes a communication system. In quantifiable terms it may be said that a system is a 'significantly' dense concentration of inter-referenced communications which persists over a 'significant' timescale - in which the cut-off levels of significance define the probability that there is indeed a system.

For example the system of computer science contains all communications which reference earlier scientific communications from the domain of computer science and which follow the rules of these scientific communications (e.g., allowing the possibility of falsification, using logical reasoning, discussing admissible topics using admissible arguments etc.). A large part of these computer science communications are scientific papers, which explicitly reference other scientific papers, and use the conclusions of earlier papers as premises of the logical reasoning presented in the paper. According to systems theory, the human computer scientists are not part of the system of computer science, only their scientific communications about computer science topics are part of this system.

A communication system is defined by the regularities that specify how referenced communications determine the content of a referencing communication. All communications that follow the set of rules defining the system are part of the system. Other communications that do not follow the rules of the system are part of the system's environment. Therefore from the systems perspective the world is constituted by the system under consideration and its environment - and there are as many such 'worlds' as there are systems, such that the same communication will have different meanings in different systems or be included in one system but not another. The set of regularities of referencing constitutes an abstract grammar, which defines an abstract language, characteristic of the system. For example the sciences of economics and medicine have different specialist languages, and scientific communications belong to one of these sciences according to whether they follow the rules of the specific language.

Systems Are Self-reproducing. Communication systems reproduce themselves by recruiting new communications, which follow the referencing rules of the system. How successful the recruitment of new communications is, depends on earlier communications generated by the system and on the match between the system and its environment. We can view the system as a self-describing system made of communications, which at the same time describes its environment in a complementary sense. (In other words, the system's only knowledge of its environment is within the system itself - the system models the environment, and that model is the sum of its knowledge of the environment.) Better - ie. more complex and adaptive - descriptions of the systems environment potentially lead to higher success in recruiting new communications and more rapid reproduction and expansion of the system.

For example we may consider the case of artificial intelligence of the 1950s-1960s. During this period AI research used relatively simple assumptions about natural intelligent systems (e.g., relatively simple artificial neural networks were supposed to simulate biological neural networks) and made high promises. AI research expanded fast in this period. In a relatively short term the promises made were proved to be unachievable (e.g., the works of Minsky and Papert on perceptrons). This led to a massive reduction of funding for AI research and the shrinking of the volume of science communications in the area of AI. After the 1980s revival of AI research science communications in this domain developed better descriptions of the environment, which led to fewer and smaller failures and supported the recent expansion in the domain of novel AI (e.g., data mining, intelligent control). Better descriptions of the system environment in case of recent AI fuel the expansion of the system of this science, while the not so good environment descriptions of classical AI led to the shrinking of AI during the 1970s.

The system communications are about the system itself. Taking another approach, the system communications reference other system communications in order to prove that they are part of the system (i.e., that they are correct according to the rules of the system). If the communications lead to continuation the process of proving that they are correct continues. If the system is able to exist, i.e., to generate/recruit new communications according to the rules of the system, this implies that the proving process of the correctness of earlier communications continues. In general it is not possible to prove the correctness of system communications; it is possible to prove only the incorrectness of them, when there is not further continuation of communications rooted from the original communication. We call this the Popper Principle, i.e., that only the falsity of system communication can be proven by stopping the generation of communications rooted from the communication in question.

More Adaptive Systems Out-Compete Less Adaptive Ones. Systems that reproduce and expand faster than other systems may drive to extinction the slower reproducing and expanding systems. The limits of system expansion are determined by the probabilistic nature of referencing rules. A communication may reference several earlier communications indirectly through other referenced communications constituting referencing sequences of communications. The indeterminacies of referencing rules determine how long can be such referencing sequences of communications before the later communications become a random continuation. Longer referencing sequences of communications (i.e., more detailed descriptions) allow better descriptions of the systems and its environment. The optimal size of the system (i.e., the number of simultaneous communications being part of the system) is also determined by the indeterminacies of referencing rules. Systems that overgrow their optimal size may split into similar systems.

For example we may consider the introduction of electronic storage and management of information in companies. Before this, information was mainly stored on paper. Paper storage of accounting data for example increases the likelihood of making errors in calculations compared to electronic handling of the same data, and also makes it difficult to handle very large amounts of data. Electronic storage and data management decreases the likelihood of calculation errors and allows efficient organisation and handling of huge amounts of data. In both cases the data describes the environment of the company, but in the case of electronic data it is possible to reliably perform much more complicated operations with the data (i.e., longer sequences of such operations) than in the case of paper based data. This implies according to systems theory that the environment descriptions of companies using electronic data are better than the environment descriptions of companies using paper based data. Indeed, companies adopting electronic data easily out- compete companies using paper based data.

Systems Increase Complexity by Developing Subsystems. Communication systems may develop subsystems that are systems within the system, i.e., they constitute a denser inter-referencing cluster within the dense communication cluster of the system. Communications that are part of subsystems follow system rules with additional constraints that are characteristic of the subsystem. More constrained referencing rules decrease indeterminacies and allow the system to generate better complementary descriptions of the environment and expand itself faster than systems without subsystems. Systems may also change by simplification of the set of their communication symbols (i.e., reduction of the number of such symbols). This may lead to reduction of indeterminacies in the referencing rules. Consequently systems with simpler sets of communication symbols may expand faster than systems with larger sets of communication symbols.

For example we may consider early computer software systems that aimed to deal with a wide range of problems and had a monolithic architecture. Extending such software systems was difficult, and led very fast into the generation of inconsistent data and conflicts between components of the system. More recent software systems are modular, having specialized parts dealing with specific classes of problems. Expanding these software systems is much easier, and the likelihood of running into major integration problems is relatively low. Recent advances in the area of software development led to the building of template libraries and design patterns, which simplify the building of software systems, providing standardised building blocks for them. Due to the availability of such standard components large software systems can be developed and upgraded faster than before, and current software systems grow much larger than any previous software system.

Systems with Memory. Another way of extending reliable descriptions of the environment (i.e., non-random sequences of referencing communications) is by retaining records of earlier communications, i.e., by having memories of earlier communications that can be referenced by later communications. In a sense we can view such memories as the creation of new communication units (or recruitment of communication units) that produce for a certain period a certain communication that can be referenced in place of some other communication (i.e., the one which is represented by the memory). Having memories reduces the indeterminacies in referencing by allowing direct referencing of much earlier communications, instead of referencing them through a chain of references.

An alternative way of considering memory systems is that they are communication systems that 1. model the communications of the main system and 2. communicate using longer lasting communications than the main system. This means that the communications in the memory system provide a longer-lasting record of events in the main system.

However, in strict systems theory terms, this is not quite accurate - since the 'memory function' of a system only refers to its function as perceived by another system. Furthermore, the 'memory function' only refers to the memory systems communications with its environment, yet by definition a complex system has a much denser communication referenced to itself than its communications with its environment.

The implication is that a memory system is first and foremost a densely self-referencing complex system with the implicit function of self-reproduction and growth in complexity by means of modelling its environment. Therefore, memory systems arise in the context of an environment, differentiate and expand due to their self-reproductive qualities; from this it follows that the internal evaluation processes of memory systems are not primarily concerned with providing an accurate data base for other systems.

What makes such a system able to function as a memory for another system is firstly that the memory system has longer lasting communications than the system using it as memory, and secondly that the memory system's model of its environment is under selection by the system which is using it as memory. This implies that the memory systems model of another system using it as memory is not a representation of the other system, but is a model which has been selected by that other system.

This illustrates that memory systems communications are (like all systems) mainly internal, and the vast majority of the communications of history have nothing directly to do any environmental system. But the environmental systems usage of some of the communications of memory systems will amplify some parts of the memory system and suppress others, reinforcing some random changes in the evaluation criteria of memory systems and suppressing others such that the memory system will evolve, will grow in complexity in particular ways, and to an external observer can be seen to perform its 'memory function' more efficiently.

Consequently, systems with memory can expand faster than systems without memory. In the context of human communications such memories of communications are written or otherwise recorded verbal communications and human artefacts that can be seen as memories of human behavioural, verbal and written communications that led to the creation of the artefact.

As an example we may consider the effect of printing on science. Before printing was invented science developed slowly, as it was based on difficult and time consuming reproduction of scientific texts by handwriting. After the invention of printing the system of science was able to expand much faster than before, having more available memory communications (written texts) because each individual written scientific communication is longer-lasting than verbal communications-especially when these written communications are incorporated into a specifically archival system which generates new forms of complex communication based around these long lasting communications (i.e., science librarianship).

Identity-Checking Subsystems. Systems with memory may develop an information subsystem (the memory is information about the past of the system) consisting of communications between communication units generating memory communications.

Information system communications reference memory communications and can be seen as representations of information processing operations - so that an information system may be defined as communications about memory communications. Hence, the discipline of history may be considered a type of information system, since history consists of communications about communications concerning the past.

Memories of information systems communications are referenced in future information system communications and provide the blueprint for processing of memories. Information system communication memories last longer than memories of other communications, and constitute long-term memories of the system, while memories of other communications are the short-term memories of the system. The information subsystem emerges if information processing communications constitute a dense cluster of inter-referencing communications determined by a set of characteristic referencing rules. Having an information subsystem allows combination of memories and by this the generation of descriptions of the environment which are better than such descriptions in systems with memory but without information subsystem.

But the information system is not primarily concerned with functioning as a memory system - its memory function is an interpretation reached by an external observer analysing the relationship between two systems, and concluding that one system is functioning as memory for another. For example, the system of the discipline of history (as exemplified by the written communications of professional historians) is - from the perspective of historians, its own justification- its implicit aim being to do ever more history. But from the perspective of the political system, the function of the discipline of history is (approximately) to be a repository of information about the past of the society which can be used for political purposes (ie. for getting and retaining political power). In modern democratic societies political and other social systems (such as the legal system, science, education and the mass media) combine to exert a selection pressure on the discipline of history such that the evaluation criteria of history become 'scientific' - in other words history is meant to be true and internally consistent, as a basis for understanding the past and planning the future for many social systems. But in traditional or 'totalitarian' societies, the political/ military/ religious ruling system exerts a monolithic selection pressure o the discipline of history, which evolves to have a quite different (and non-scientific) function of justifying the perpetuation in power of the ruling system.

We may consider as another example the solving of a software development problem by having a series of ad-hoc meetings. The participants of the meetings may remember ideas discussed at previous meeting and occasionally may reference them, but it will be very difficult to arrive to a reasonably good solution without systematic analysis of earlier ideas and developing elaborations of these ideas. Finding the desired solution will happen much faster if the meetings are minuted, analysis and synthesis tasks are assigned to participants, and communications about memories of earlier communications are generated in form of reports that are referenced during the next and later meetings. In this way the group of developers will progress relatively fast towards an acceptable solution and the system of the software developer company will expand faster.

The information subsystem of a system provides the references for identity checking communications of the system. The blueprints of information processing held in long-term memories of the system are referenced by identity check communications and allow checking the validity of communications within the context of the system. Having an information subsystem that provides references for identity check communications decreases the likelihood of generating wrong communications that cannot be referenced according to the rules of the system. Reducing the likelihood of wrong communications helps the expansion of the system by providing guarantees that the system communications are correct and can be referenced by further system communications. The identity checking communications turn the information processing blueprints into a self-model of the system. The self-model of the system is a simplified representation of the system and of its environment in a complementary sense, containing the information processing rules of the system.

For example we may consider a small start-up company having the founders and a couple of other people as employee. The company runs mostly in an informal manner, although standard record keeping is already in place and the company has its statutes regulating the structure of the company (which is almost invisible during the everyday work), decision rights of shareholders, etc. As the company grows and gets larger contracts and hires more employees it turns into an established company, with specialised departments (e.g., sales, HR, development), sets of rules that describe how information is processed within the company, and an elaborate visible multilevel structure (e.g., offices indicating status within the company). The company builds an extensive self-model and an elaborate identity checking system based on its information system communications. Identity check communications guarantee that within company processes and services delivered outside of the company meet the expected quality standards and together with the self-model of the company provide the foundation for the building of the company identity. The company would not be able to meet its growing commitments without this transformation. Having in place the information subsystem, the identity checking communications and the self-model allows the company to grow fast and conquer its market.

Faulty Communications. Faulty communications may occur in systems. Faulty communications are defined as those which do not fit the lexicon of the system's language or, which have zero likelihood to be produced in a certain context according to the rules of the system's grammar.

For example in case of human speech the pronunciation of meaningless words (a sequence of phonemes not associated with any word of the lexicon of the language of the speaker), such words are faulty communications. To differentiate between faulty communications of the system and communications, which are outside of the system (although produced by communication units, which produce communications that are part of the system), we need to consider the referencing set of the communication. If the referencing set contains exclusively or dominantly system communications, and the communication in question is produced instead of a regular system communication that should follow by application of some system rules, the communication in question is a faulty communication.

For example, if the meaningless word occurs during meaningful speech, we have a faulty communication, while if a human produces a meaningless 'word' by the understanding of another human, this may not be the case of faulty communication (e.g., if somebody speaks Chinese words in an English environment, without the intention of linking these communications to other English communications).

In some cases faulty communications do not lead to any continuation communication within the system (e.g., communications outside of the lexicon of the system). In other cases system communications may reference faulty communications. Such cases may lead to further problems within the system and may cause the system to fail. However this is not necessarily the case - for example evolution by natural selection proceeds by genetic mutations which are faulty communications. Most genetic mutations are fatal to survival, or deleterious and damage the organism, however a minority of mutations are 'mis-interpreted' by the system as being meaningful, and by chance these mutations improve the adaptiveness of the organism enabling it to reproduce relatively more effectively than the organisms without the mutation - hence the system constituted by organisms of the same species can grow in complexity.

Communication Errors. Errors of communication systems are defined as cases when communications happen according to the rules of the system, but the system of communications cannot lead to continuation because of environmental constraints. In other words, communication units that are expected to produce the continuation communication are unable to do this, due to their participation in other environmental communications - for instance when an organism with no visual system is dessicated by sunlight since it cannot detect or respond to the light. The death of the organism is not due to a fault in the system communications, but to the error constituted by limitations of the organisms system of communications.

Errors therefore mean that the system's description of the environment is not correct in the specific circumstance being experienced. Of course, all system descriptions of the environment are necessarily incorrect in an absolute sense because the environment is more complex than the system. However there is no error so long as the environment description is 'good enough' to enable the system communications to continue. An error is said to occur when the incorrectness of environmental description leads to an actual failure in continuation of communications.

Continuations of faulty communications may lead to errors in the above sense. If there is no continuation of the faulty communication, the error occurs there, as there in no continuation of the system communications. If there are continuations of the faulty communication, these continuations aim to decide whether the faulty communication is part of the system or not. Such communications may reach the 'not part of the system' decision according to the rules of the system, with the consequence of ending the sequence of communications by a terminating communication, implying no continuation within the system. If the halting of continuation communications happens when there are communications supposed to be the continuation of the most recent communications, the system reaches an error in the above defined sense.

Errors may occur even when there is no faulty communication at the root. Occurrence of such system errors are signs of the mismatch between the system's description of the environment and the actual environment. Mismatch errors imply that some of the rules defining the system are pragmatically wrong (i.e., they do not fit the environment as it is being experienced). The system's action on finding errors is the generation of communications that check the validity of communications that led to the communication triggering the error. These checks aim to find the root of the error, and terminate the continuations of communications branching out from the root of the error.

For example, in natural sciences hypotheses and theories are built and incorporated into ongoing scientific work. But when the experimental results 'falsify' the theories by not confirming their predictions, this prevents continuations of communications until the science is revised to remedy this. The root of the wrong theory is invalidated, together with scientific communications branching from this root, and these are eliminated from that science so that communications can continue. This may be described as 'purging' the system after an error- to excise the error and its continuations.

Purging the system after an error may have very severe implications for the system. The invalidation of the branches emerging from the root of the error will probably shrink the system considerably in the short term. If large scale shrinking of the system happens the system encounters a failure. System failure may even lead to the dissolution of the system. For example, the experimental findings invalidating the roots of alchemy theories led to the elimination of the alchemy from the system of sciences. In case of the Enron company (an US electricity distribution giant until 2000), the finding that the roots of the accounting of the company were false led to the rapid collapse of the company. The attempts to purge the errors from the Russian economic system caused a collapse in economic output which has lasted 15 years, so far.

Self-awareness in Systems. Abstract communication systems are self-aware systems if they have an information subsystem which generates an adaptive self-model of the system providing reference for identity check communications. In other words, self awareness implies the evolution of an information sub-system in the first place, and evolution of particular properties of this information sub-system. It is important to recognize that, like all systems, the internal communications of the information subsystem is differentially much greater than the external communications, and this differential increases as the complexity of the information subsystem increases. This implies that the function of self-awareness (like all memory functions) represents only a minority of the communications of the system which enables self-awareness.

Consequently, self-aware systems generate adaptive actions and form adaptive perceptions representing the adaptive changes in their self-model. The adaptive changes in the self-model happen in response to faults, errors and failures experienced by the system. Purging the system of communications leading to errors imply imposing new structures and possibly new information processing rules. Simplification of communications, emergence of subsystems and interactions with other systems may also imply changes in the information processing rules. Changes in the rules of information processing are reflected in changes of long-term memories and corresponding changes in the self-model of the system.

For example a company may experience difficulties in selling their products in their market. These difficulties are errors within the system, as expected continuation communications (i.e., selling of products) do not follow previous communications (i.e., those which lead to the production and packaging for selling of the products). In response the company may revise its own regulations and other communications to identify the roots of the problem. If it is found that the company's technology is unable to produce sufficiently competitive products in some market of the company the company may change its technology or may turn its resources and technologies to produce different products. This change happens by modifying the regulations of the company and by adapting the self-model of the company. After the adaptive change of the self-model of the company identity check communications will change and the company will generate new adaptively changed actions and experience adaptively changed perceptions. In some cases the company may survive for very long time, while moving from one market to another, adaptively changing its self-model and identity in order to fit better to its environment (e.g., the BARCO company produces visualisation and optical monitoring equipment today, while originally it was founded as the Belgian - American Radio Company, which produced radios and later TVs).

3   Memory and Information Subsystems

We discuss in this section two natural systems, which feature self-awareness. The first system that we discuss is the cell which is a biological self-aware system producing adaptive responses to external stimuli in function of the state of the system. The second system that we discuss is the system of a human organization (e.g., a company or government department), which is again a self-aware system (i.e., a type of 'management'), which senses itself and produces adaptive and possibly innovative responses depending on external stimuli and the state of the system.

The critical features of the discussed systems for the presence of self-awareness are that they possess both short- and long-term memories and an information subsystem, which processes and creates new memories, and that they have an adaptive self-model that is referenced by their identity check communications. ('Adaptive' means that the self-model has evolved under selection pressure from the system for which it serves the self-awareness function.). The memories are produced by communication units, which reproduce earlier communications that happened within the system. The information subsystem is a part of the communication system which generates new communications about memory communications (i.e., by referencing memory communications) and leads to the generation of long-term memory communications representing processes of combinations and derivations of existing memory communications.

3.1   Cells: Proteins, RNA and DNA

Living cells can be analysed in phenomenological terms by listing their components and the properties and behaviours of these components. This traditional approach is followed by most biology books, describing cells as a complex machinery made of cell membrane, cytoplasm, ribosomes, mitochondria, chloroplasts, Golgi organelle, cilia, flagella, centrosome, lysosomes, endoplasmic reticulum, nucleus and possibly various other cellular organelles [48]. For each of these components their structure and behaviour can be described, listing proteins, lipids and other molecules that compose them, and describing changes of them in response to various stimuli (e.g., pump molecules residing in the cellular membrane may introduce or expulse some ions or smaller molecules into/from the intracellular fluid).

An alternative way of looking at cells is to consider them as abstract communication systems, in which proteins and other molecules are the communication units and their interactions are the communications. In this sense the cell is identified as the set of interactions between proteins and other molecules (e.g., ATP, RNA) (Andras and Andras in press). All cellular components can be seen as well organized spatio-temporal patterns of interactions between such molecules, the proteins playing a central role in most of these interactions. Molecular interactions reference earlier interactions in the sense that the participating molecules are results of earlier interactions between molecules (e.g., proteins form intermediary complexes, which lead to new molecules, including proteins and possibly now conformations of the participating proteins, the resulting proteins participate in new molecular interactions, referencing earlier interactions which led to their formation or transformation). Such inter-referencing interactions form a dense cluster within the cell, surrounded by relatively rare interactions with molecules, which are outside of the cell. The density boundary of the cell system is materialized as the cell membrane.

Memories of interactions between proteins are contained in RNA molecules. The appropriate decoding of RNA molecules into proteins at the ribosomes guarantees that the appropriate types of proteins are available within the cell and that the appropriate molecular interactions happen within the cell delivering the expected functionality of cellular organelles into which the produced proteins are incorporated. The RNA molecules may change during evolution. Frequent or important interactions between proteins leading to stable protein complexes may become encoded by a single RNA, coding directly for protein complex emerging from the interactions of proteins. The RNA molecules produce the primary memory subsystem of the cell, allowing the reproduction of earlier communications (i.e., molecular interactions) by allowing the reproduction of proteins. The RNA memory system is a short-term memory system, the RNA molecules being able to exist for a relatively limited time period (e.g., half-life of mRNA molecules is around 6 hours [55]).

The short-term memory molecules of the cell participate in many interactions between such memory molecules (i.e., RNAs). Well known and newly discovered RNA molecules, like mRNA, rRNA, tRNA, siRNA [1], [47], microRNA [39]and others interact with each other regulating the translation of memories encoded in mRNA molecules into proteins. The result of these regulatory interactions is the appropriate production of types and quantities of proteins within the cell. The interactions between RNA molecules rearrange some of them (e.g., splicing of immature mRNA) and produce RNAs corresponding to the right sequence of proteins that need to be produced or RNAs which can communicate with others in further regulatory interactions. The system of communications between RNA molecules constitutes an information subsystem of the cell.

The interactions between RNA molecules are reproduced using memories of such communications. These memories are the DNA molecules organized into the genome of the cell. The DNA molecules produce RNA molecules by interacting with proteins and RNA molecules. The produced RNA molecules participate in RNA interactions and ultimately lead to the generation of various regulatory and protein encoding RNA molecules and finally to proteins within the cell. The DNA molecules constitute a secondary memory subsystem of cell consisting of long-term memories (the DNA molecules usually survive with minor changes during the whole lifetime of the cell). In bacteria and archaea the DNA contains mostly segments which encode RNA molecules which lead to protein generation. In higher organisms the DNA contains a large amount of non-protein coding segments, which are believed to participate in regulatory interactions between DNA segments [40]. These regulatory interactions lead to the production of appropriate RNA molecules in appropriate quantities. The regulatory interactions between DNA segments constitute a communication system, which can be seen as the secondary information system of the cell (i.e., the information subsystem regulating RNA interactions).

Following the abstract communication systems theory interpretation we identified two levels of memory subsystems within the cell constituted by RNA and DNA molecules, providing memories of protein interactions (short-term memories) and RNA interactions (long-term memories), respectively. These memories generate and information subsystem made of interactions between RNA molecules and segments of DNA molecules, which regulate the expression of memories under their control including the creation of new memories (e.g., spliced RNA molecules, simultaneous production of various combinations of RNA molecules). The long-term memories contain a blueprint description of the cell, constituting the self-model of the cell.

The cell performs self-monitoring through the interactions between proteins, RNA molecules and segments of the DNA [46]. These communications trigger further communications which reference them. Some of the protein interaction communications lead to interactions with RNA molecules. The results of such interactions can be seen as short term memories (i.e., possibly modified RNA molecules). These short term memories participate in RNA interaction communications contributing to the selection of appropriate RNA molecules for translation into proteins. RNA interactions may generate RNA molecules or proteins that interact with DNA molecules (e.g., siRNA molecules), driving the DNA expression into RNA accordingly to the cell's needs. Other RNA molecules may even create new DNA molecules (e.g., RNA retroviruses), creating new memories of RNA interactions. The self-monitoring ultimately refers to the self-model (i.e., the DNA blueprint) in order to check the identity of intracellular communications (i.e., whether they are correct or not, or expected or less expected).

The actions of the cell system are sequences or spatio-temporal patterns of protein interactions (e.g., secretion of molecules into the extra-cellular space, movement of the cell). These actions aim to validate the correctness of earlier cell communications and implicitly to reproduce and expand the cell. The actions are generated using the memories and the information processing subsystems of the cell, which regulate the generation of the right proteins in the right amounts and right places, such that the appropriate cell actions can be generated.

The cell perceptions are the differences between the expected distribution of protein interactions and the actual distribution of these interactions. The first is specified through the blueprint of the cell, the second emerges from self-monitoring identity check communications. For example the presence or absence of antibiotics in case of bacteria may lead to very different patterns and distributions of protein interactions (i.e., in the presence of ribosome-blocking antibiotics many wrong proteins are produced, generating many protein interactions, which do not fit into the system of protein interactions of the cell). The different pattern and distribution of protein interactions leads to changed patterns of RNA-protein expression and possibly to change patterns of DNA-RNA expressions (e.g., previously inactive DNA segments are expressed in neurons after long-term potentiation [12]).

Faults, errors and failures occur in cells. Faults are interactions between proteins that do not follow the language of the cell (i.e., the set of regular interactions). For example such interactions may lead to protein malformations like prions, which are proteins having a wrong conformation, preventing them from their regular interactions. Faults may lead nowhere, and in many cases the cell can simply ignore them, eliminating the possibly hazardous results of faulty interactions (e.g., toxins produced by such wrong interactions). Errors occur, when interactions happen according to the rules, but they cannot be continued by further appropriate interactions. For example, in the case of bacteria in the presence of antibiotics many appropriate protein interactions cannot be followed by such interactions because of the lack of appropriate proteins. When errors happen at the large scale, and large part of the cell system halt the cells may experience failure, which may lead to the disintegration of the cell (e.g., bacteria in presence of antibiotics).

Self-monitoring makes possible for the cells to perceive themselves and implicitly their environment and to select appropriate actions in order to increase their chance of self reproduction and expansion. In case of faults, errors and failures these are perceived in terms of deviations form the expected interactions and the cell invokes new parts of its memory subsystem using its information subsystem to generate responses to avoid catastrophic effects (i.e., the disintegration or large scale shrinking of the system) of these problems. Adaptive responses are generated by the cell reflecting the environment of the cell and its own state. Some of these adaptive responses lead to new memories and fuel the evolution of the system. For example, bacteria may develop antibiotic resistance in the presence of antibiotics, and may loose antibiotic resistance after residing in antibiotic-free environment.

Our analysis shows that cell systems constitute self-aware systems. They are able to monitor themselves and produce adaptive responses reflecting the state of their environment and of themselves. They are also able to build upon these adaptive responses and innovate themselves evolving into new forms adapted to their environment in such ways that increases their chance to reproduce and expand.

3.2   Organizations and Bureaucracies

Human communications (verbal, written, gesture based, etc.) constitute a communication system, which is the human society. Human society has many subsystems, like subsystems defined by natural languages (e.g., English, Chinese, etc. societies), and subsystems defined by their specific logic, with associated functionality in the context of their society (e.g., political system, legal system, economic system, etc.) [16], [16], [41], [53]. Organizations constitute subsystems within many parts of the human society, e.g., political parties within the political system, companies within the economic system, and universities in the higher education system.

Organizations can be viewed as communication systems made of communications between humans, these humans acting as communication units for the organization [4], [10], [15], [44]. The organization is defined by its own language, which restricts the distributions over possible continuation communications, conditioned by previous communications. The language of the organization is usually described in terms of statutes, regulations, contracts, rules (rules differ from regulations in the sense that rules have a limited range of applicability and restrict the relationship between a few factors, while regulations are large consistent sets of rules with a wide range of applicability and constraining the relationships of many factors), and rituals (interpreted in a wide sense, including all kinds of expected behavioural patterns). The language of the organization imposes structures (i.e., restrictions on communications) within the organization (e.g., organizational hierarchies).

Organizations produce memories that contribute to the success of reproduction and expansion of the organization. Such memories are products and services, which represent in a compressed form the human communications that lead to their production, written paper and electronic records of organizational communications, and repeatedly told stories of organizational events. The memories of the organization are organized into a memory subsystem by communications about these memories in form of generating organizational rituals, traditions, rules and regulations. The latter constitute the foundation of the identity checking information subsystem of the organization. Products, services and records of organizational communications constitute short-term memories of the organization, they being referenced for relatively short time period. Memories about processing of short-term memories, like rituals or regulations are long-term memories of the organization, they persist for long time periods and are referenced during this time when memory communications are processed. The long-term memories of the organization describe a self-model of the organization (e.g., the constitution of a party describes the organizational units of the party, the rights and responsibilities of these units and of their members, the decisional procedures, etc.).

Large organizations have well developed information subsystems, which use and generate memories and check the identity of organizational communications by referencing traditions, rules and regulations. The information subsystem of such organizations takes the form of organizational bureaucracy. Thus, the bureaucratic subsystem of the organization deals primarily with production of records, assessment of records, and production of new identity checking communications in forms of particularized orders based on existing regulations, formulation of new rules, contracts and regulations. The organizational bureaucracy in particular generates the long-term memories of the organization.

Organizations self-monitor themselves by checking the identity of organizational communications and by generating records of organizational communications for later identity checks. Organizational bureaucracies perform to large extent the self-monitoring of the organization by generation and assessment of records of organizational communications. Self-monitoring drives the appropriate application of rules by referencing long-term memories of the organization (the organization's blueprint) contained in regulations defining the what is allowed and what is not in the context of organizational communications.

The actions of an organization are organizational communications that modify the communications in the environment of the organization (e.g., selling products, conquering a part of a market, changing a part of the political discourse etc.). Communications constituting organizational actions follow the rules of the organization (e.g., rules describing the delivery of a service). The perceptions of the organization are the differences between the expected distribution of organizational communications and their actual distribution. These perceptions are assessed using memories of earlier communications usually by the organizational bureaucracy. Actions generate perceptions and perceptions generate actions all aiming to increase the reproduction and expansion ability of the organization. If the rules of the organization (i.e., the identity of the organization) match its environment the perceptions and actions will allow the organizations to recruit more organizational communications, which usually materializes in the expansion of the organization in the sense of having more humans communicating within the organization, more products and services sold and gaining new parts of markets.

Organizations also experience faults, errors and failures. Faults are those organizational communications which do not follow the rules of the organization. These many times are eliminated without providing reference for many further organizational communications. Errors occur when organizational communications follow the rules, but they cannot be continues due to environmental constraints. For example, an inappropriate marketing campaign does not lead to increase in sales. A major functional role of the organizational bureaucracy is to discover faults and errors and limit their effects on the organization. By applying identity checks (i.e., assessing memories of communications - records to find out whether they comply with the rules) and forming expectations about future communications according to the rules an effective organizational bureaucracy can spot faulty communications and recognize errors. In case of errors the bureaucracy aims to find the roots of it by analyzing records of organizational memories, i.e., those communications that led to the generation of the error, and generates new identity checks, i.e., new communications about rules that are intended to be used to prevent the occurrence of similar errors. Failures happen when errors halt the continuation of communications within a large part of the organizations. Failures may lead to the disintegration of the organization, and usually lead to major restructuring of it, changing rules and regulations, and reorganizing the organizational bureaucracy.

Organizations adapt to their environment in response to faults, errors and failures by changing their rules, regulations, structure, and possibly even their identity (e.g., companies may move completely from one market to another). These changes in organizations often take the form of adding and modifying the regulations of the organization, and many times this leads to standardisation / simplification of organizational communications. Such changes trigger the reorganization of the organization, provision of new products and services, the change of its bureaucracy and possibly of its identity. The changes may be beneficial or not for the organization. In a competitive environment, where many organizations compete for communications generated by the same communication units (i.e., humans) maladaptive change leads to the shrinking and possibly to the dissolution of the organization. In less competitive environment (e.g., state monopolies or very large corporations) maladaptive changes are likely to lead to overgrowing bureaucracy as new regulations are put in place to prevent earlier errors and failures triggering the growth of the organizational bureaucracy in charge of generating and imposing regulations and checking adherence to regulations.

Organizations are self-aware systems, which monitor themselves using their memories and information subsystem (i.e., the organizational bureaucracy), sense their environment and act upon their environment, and adapt to their environment. Organizational adaptations are generated by the organizational bureaucracy in form of new or revised rules and regulations aimed to prevent faulty communications, errors and the occurrence of failures, guaranteeing increased ability of the organization to reproduce and expand.

4   Self-aware Software

Computer software drives the computer hardware and it is present in increasingly many machines and appliances, including cars, fridges, and mobile phones. Computer software is made of computer programs written in some programming language (e.g., Java, C++) and executed on some computer hardware, which is able to understand the programs and translate them into behaviours of the machine. In the early times (1950s - 1960s) computer programs were independent of each other, were executed sequentially, and mainly dealt with processing and transforming some data records and possibly producing some additional data records. More recently computer software is composed of many concurrently active components which communicate with each other.

The usual way is to view computer software in functional terms, associating with them a set of functions that they can perform and which might be useful for their user (e.g., word processing, graphics generation, web browsing, etc.). An alternative way to consider computer software is to view them as part of the human society interpreted as an abstract communication system. In this context computer programs can be seen as recorded memory of human communication (i.e., the communication of the programmers with computers, which transformed their typed communications into stored records containing the program). This memory can be recalled by using a computer (or some computing hardware in general), and the recalled communication will be used to process new society communications (human or indirectly related to human communications) and generate possibly new communications and records of earlier communications. The software is part of the information subsystem of the society allowing the processing of memories (i.e., electronic records of earlier communications) and to generate new society communications (e.g., a printed page, a spoken sentence, or stored data). Unsurprisingly, computer software is used to a very large extent in the context of information subsystems (i.e., bureaucracies) of various social subsystems, like companies, government agencies, and other kinds of organizations. (We note that computers themselves are products of human communications and can be seen as memories of these communications that led to the design and assembly of them.)

In alignment with the above presented view, computer software can be seen as a communication system of many processes or components executed on computer hardware. In the context of object-oriented software, we may consider each object (i.e., an instantiation of a class, which is specified in the code of the software) as a communication unit, and view the software itself as the set of interactions between these communication units. In current large scale software systems such objects appear and disappear frequently, communicating with many other objects, some of these being created by other programs. Some objects may create copies of themselves or other objects on distant hardware, and may reproduce and expand the communication system of which they are part of (e.g., spyware).

Here we aim to investigate the ways by which computer software may become self-aware. First let us review the features of self-aware communication systems that we highlighted in the previous section of the paper. Systems with self-awareness all have short- and long-term memories and identity check communications that reference these memories. Memories provide the foundation for self-monitoring, which is performed by the information subsystem of the system using identity check communications and generation of new long-term memory communications by processing existing memory communications. The system of long-term memories defines a self-model of the system, which is ultimately referenced by identity check communications. Self-aware systems perceive their environments in terms of differences between expected and actual system behaviour, perform actions by which they modify their environment, and aim by their perceptions and actions to reproduce and expand the system. In principle these systems may expand infinitely, although in practice they may reach some limits of their expansion. Self-aware systems adapt to their environment by changing themselves in response to experienced faulty communications, errors and system failures. System adaptations change the information subsystem of the system, by imposing new or modified identity checks, or smaller or larger scale reorganizations of the information subsystem, changing the rules defining the identity of the system. The rest of the section will analyse each of the listed features of self-aware systems in the context of software systems.

In the case of software systems we can identify short and long term memories in forms of data and software code. The data is allowed to change frequently in most cases. Stored data represents to some extent the memories of communications between objects (although not all communications are represented by stored data). The software code constitutes long term memories (the blueprint or self-model of the system), which allow the recreation of objects many times, and store the rules of communications that lead to creation of these objects in computer memories. The software code is usually not changing. More recently new software systems emerged, which allow to some extent the change of their code by incorporating new pieces of code into the system's long term memory, e.g., security patches installed by human user or possibly installed automatically. These changes in the long term memory of the system represent adaptations based on processing memories of recent communications within the system, which led to faults, errors and failures. We need to note that all these changes to the software code reference human communications, which created the software patches. Recent software environments like Smalltalk, Java and .NET implement computational reflection [21], [42], which allows in principle changes to the program code, but the range of practically allowed changes is very limited (e.g., asking for names and types of exposed variables and methods in newly added components [24]). Elementary structural changes, like using new methods available in newly added components are allowed in the context of component-based programming [34]. Software systems usually do not create memories of communications between objects (except in cases of faults or errors that can be interpreted by exception handling components of these objects) and in consequence are unable to develop an information subsystem that would process memories and possibly generate new memories, including changes to the long term memory of the system. However, we note that recent advances in the area of aspect-oriented programming [19], [33] allow the software system to track communications between objects. This can be seen as a critical first step towards the creation of memories of communications between objects (see logging of object communications in the context of aspect-oriented programming). In order to make software systems able to develop self-awareness it is very important to expand their memory subsystem to provide the foundation for an information subsystem within the software system.

Self-monitoring is performed by the information subsystem of self-aware systems. In case of software systems we can find some basic level of self-monitoring in form of correctness monitoring using methods of exception handling, type checking and execution pattern matching (in context of aspect-oriented programming). These can be seen analogous to basic identity check communications in self-aware systems. These communications usually check the correctness of data; they do not check the correctness of communications between objects or processes in any more general sense (this is usually done during the compiling of the software by checking that the long term memory of the software system conforms the rules of the programming language in which it is written). Recent advances in aspect-oriented programming [19], [33] and design patterns [28]indicate significant progress in terms of self-monitoring, by allowing tracking of object communications (aspect-oriented programming) and using blueprints of relatively simple communication patterns to enforce appropriate communications (design patterns; we note also the similar role of 'interface'-s in the context of Java). Self-aware software systems need much larger scale self-monitoring comparable to self-monitoring of natural self-aware systems. Self-monitoring should be based on memories of communications that happen between objects and processes, should check the identity of these communications referencing identity check communications of the software system (in particular the self-model of the system, the software code), and generating new memory and identity checking communications (including new parts of the software code).

In case of natural self-aware systems the identity check communications generate a large part of communications within the system, and we may see the system emerging from such identity check communications. Due to the Popper principle the system's correctness cannot be proven, and identity checking (or correctness proving) communications may continue infinitely, guaranteeing the reproduction and expansion of the system. Existing software systems have basic mechanisms to check the correctness of data (e.g., type checks, exception handling methods), but most of them do not check the correctness (or identity) of communications between communication units (i.e., objects) during runtime and consequently do not lead to the expansion of the software system interpreted as a communication system. We note that run-time type checking is present in Smalltalk and also to some extent in Java, and the identity check of communications may become a practical possibility following current trends in aspect-oriented programming [19], [33] and use and development of design patterns [56]. In case of software systems reproduction and expansion can be seen to some extent in form of re-use (template libraries [29], design patterns [26], component-based programming [30]) and in form of installation and running of many copies of them. Some of them, like software viruses, are able to replicate themselves by creating new copies of their own code, which is run on the same or on different computer hardware. Importantly, software systems usually do not adapt autonomously to their environment (software patches distributed automatically over the Internet can be seen as a basic form of adaptive change triggered by human communications generating the patch) or their adaptation is very limited (recognizing methods and types of variables of a new component). Perhaps the most autonomous adaptive behaviour can be seen in the context of implementation of continuation in programs developed using functional languages, which allows capturing of continuations of executions and the adaptive recombination of such captured continuations [20], [7]. To overcome the present limitations of software systems, and to develop self-aware software systems a major change is needed in the design and analysis of software systems. While current systems are designed and analysed in terms of their functionality imposed on them in the context of their environment, self-aware software systems should be designed and analysed using a 'from within' view, which permits the development of the system such that its own identity check communications lead to the emergence of the system. Self-aware software systems should aim to reproduce and expand themselves as communication systems and they should perform their intended and externally imposed functionality by adapting to their environment and reproducing and expanding within this environment. Steps that may lead to such systems include works on cellular automata [25], multithread parallel systems [59], software viruses [35], the concept of continuation [20], [7], development of persistent systems [8], self-monitoring and self-healing systems [6], component based programming [30]and aspect-oriented programming [19], [33], [54].

Actions of software systems are sequences of communications with effect on the environment of the system. These effects can be triggered actions of human users (e.g., pressing a button or clicking the mouse on a certain place of the screen) or communications originating from other software systems (e.g., arrival of data through the Internet connection). The actions of the software system follow the rules established by the self-model of the system (i.e., procedures described in the software code), but the referencing of the self-model happens mostly during the compilation of the code into objects (notable exceptions are programs written in scripting languages, e.g., the use of the function 'eval' to include new code from an additional file). In contrast, natural self-aware systems reference their self-model communications frequently during the identity check communications. They also generate short-term memories of their action communications, which are checked for their identity by referencing other memory communications, self-model communications, and by generating new memory communications. Perceptions of software systems are the detections of changes in their environment. Typically such perceptions are implemented in the form of 'if-then-else' rules or multiple variants of this (e.g., 'switch', 'case-of'), or in form of exception handling (i.e., equivalent of a final or possibly branching 'else'). The expectation about possible communications is usually characterized by a flat prior distribution, i.e., there is no prior information represented in the encoding of the perception interpretation code. The difference between the flat prior expectation and the experienced distribution (i.e., one of the possibilities appears with certainty, while others have zero experienced probability) triggers communications within the software systems. Similarly to the case of actions, perception communications reference the self-model of the software system only at time of compilation of the objects. Natural self-aware systems have expectations based on prior experience. These expectations are usually characterized by non-flat distributions over the space of possibilities. Prior experience changes the expectations adaptively, so that the system can generate the most appropriate communications in response to its perceptions. Self-aware systems also reference their self-model and memory communications frequently when the generate perception triggered communications. To turn software systems into self-aware systems they need to have frequent references to their short- and long-term memories, adaptive expectations encoding non-flat prior distributions of possibilities, and more flexibility of the behaviour of the software system that might be achieved by on-line adaptation of the self-model (i.e., the software code) and frequent recompilation (or partial recompilation) of objects.

Works on dependable systems and software reliability [9], [38] created an elaborated theory of faults, errors and failures in the context of software systems. The most common mechanisms to deal with faults are the data validation combined with roll-back and the exception handling methods. The roll-back is triggered by invalid data and restores the previous correct state of the system. In case of databases the roll-back restores previous data that satisfied the validity checks before, in case of more complex software systems recovery blocks executed in parallel may be used to restore a valid state of the system [38]. Exception handling methods include the handling of invalid data, type mismatch, and invalid access rights, providing essentially an 'if-then-else' type solution of dealing with unexpected communications grouped in one or a few categories. Related recent work addresses the concept of 're-start', i.e., when does a program or communication need to be re-initiated [65]. 'Re-start' can handle in principle a general class of errors, when the expected continuation communications do not happen. Natural self-aware systems check the identity (validity) of communications permanently by referencing their short- and long-term memory communications and creating new identity check communications. Identity check communications eliminate most of the faulty communications, errors are limited by structures that may change adaptively, and failures trigger major adaptive changes in the self-model of the system. This suggests that self-aware software systems need to expand their response repertoire to deal with faults, errors and failures, by employing frequent identity check communications to validate data and communications between objects, including communications referencing long-term memory communications (i.e., the software code), use of adaptive structures, re-start methods and parallel multi-thread execution to limit errors and to create slack resources (i.e., enough many communications so the system can continue its own reproduction even if many communications lead to faults and errors), and by adapting its own self-model in response to errors and failures by changing and adding to the software code.

Adaptation is a key feature of natural self-aware systems. Adaptation includes the generation of appropriate actions and forming of appropriate perceptions in order to increase the reproduction and expansion ability of the system, and also the modification of the self-model of the system in response to errors and failures experienced by the system. Software systems are able to form appropriate perceptions and generate appropriate actions to some extent, but they are unable to adapt their self-model by themselves during their existence in response to errors and failures experienced by them. Software systems are most adaptive in terms of stored data that is changing frequently and to lesser extent in terms of changing access interfaces of objects (e.g., using methods of a newly added component). Adding new security patches and updates is a relatively new way of adaptation of software systems, which changes the self-model of the software system in response to errors and failures. At the same time we have to note that all these adaptations are triggered by communications with humans (even in the case of automated updates the new modules are written by human software developers). Just-in-time compilation, run-time type checking, and garbage collection are the beginnings of more adaptive behaviour, which allow adaptive changes with respect to the actively referenced part of the self-model and introduce more frequent references to the self-model. The concept of 're-start' [65] represent a new pathway that may lead to novel ways of adaptation in software systems in response to errors (i.e., lack of continuation of communications as expected). Analysing natural self-aware systems suggests that a much wider range of adaptive responses is needed in software-systems to achieve self-awareness. Memories of runtime interactions between objects/processes need to be created. These should generate new communications by referencing identity check communications and other memory communications in order to check the identity (validity) of these interactions, eliminating faulty communications when they appear. Identity check communications should reference frequently the self-model of the system and should lead to changes in the self-model of the software system (i.e., the software code) in response to errors and failures. These changes of the self-model should manifest in new structural constraints imposed on communications between objects, possibly in simplification / standardisation of object communications, in specialisation of communications between objects, leading to the emergence of specialist subsystems of the software system, and possibly in the generation or recruitment of new types of objects into the software system.

In general, comparison of software systems with natural self-aware systems suggests that current software systems need many changes to become similar to self-aware systems and possibly to become self-aware software systems. A fundamental difference from current practice that seems to be needed is that self-aware software systems need to be designed using a 'from within' perspective, aiming to build a system that reproduces and expands itself and becomes associated with externally perceived functions by adaptation to its environment. The self-reproduction and expansion of the system should happen by generating short-term memories of object communications and endless number of identity checking communications that reference short- and long-term memory communications. The self-aware software system should be able to adapt to its environment by choosing appropriate actions and perceptions, and also by adapting its own self-model contained in its long-term memories the software code. The adaptation of the self-model is critical for self-awareness, and should include changes to the code, generation of new structures, and incorporation of new classes and generation of new objects.

5   Will Self-aware Software Become a Reality?

In this section we discuss to what extent we expect that self-aware software that satisfies our descriptions outlined in the previous section will become an existing reality. We discuss aspects that we consider critical in terms of resources and approaches.

In our view self-aware software systems will aim in principle to grow without any limit. In practice the environmental constraints may limit this growth very much as they do this in the case of existing natural self-aware systems (e.g., bacteria, animals, organizations). In most cases of natural systems the growth limits of the system imposed by scarcity of resources needed for communication units and communications do not limit the growth of the system in practical sense, and the habitable environment of the system is apparently infinite from the system's point of view. We believe that in order to generate self-aware software we need to achieve the state in which the habitable environment of the software system becomes apparently infinite. The habitable environment of software systems is provided by available hardware and software components (i.e., objects, processes run on the large amount of hardware). At the moment this habitable environment is relatively small, which does not offer apparently limitless resources for the expansion of software systems. Simple replicating software, like viruses spread on the Internet, are able to populate very rapidly the existing available software/hardware environment, exhausting their resources for growth, and collapsing as a system. In order to have the environmental conditions for self-aware software we need many magnitudes increase of available software and hardware resources, so that the environment provided by them allows practically limitless growth for self-aware software systems.

As we noted earlier it is very critical that self-aware software is developed using a 'from within' approach. A similar approach can be seen in the case of the Smalltalk [27] programming language, in which everything is an object, including the development environment, and programs are built by combining existing objects and building new objects [22], [61]. The main difference of the proposed approach from most current software development approaches is that it does not subordinate the development of the software system to the function imposed on the system from outside. The proposed 'from within' approach will allow to associate functions to the software system as it reproduces and expands under environmental constraints. This does not mean that software components (e.g., objects) or the software system is not developed to fulfil some specific role; it rather means that components, communications, and the self-model of these is selected and composed such that the system emerges to fulfil its designated role. We do not know at the moment what would be the detailed features of the software development 'from within', but we think that current trends in component-based programming and aspect-oriented programming are pointing towards the 'from within' approach to software development.

Self-aware software in our view will be the sum of communications between objects that follow the rules described in the self-model of the software system (i.e., the software code). We believe that such systems will be based on re-use of many existing components (runtime objects, coded classes), and will recruit communications involving such existing components. Similar to human organizations or cells the focus of the system will be only partly to produce its communication units (humans and proteins, respectively), but to a larger extent will be to use the existing ones, involving them in communications according to the rules of the system. This means that self-aware software systems will become a possibility when an apparently infinite number (obviously objectively this will be still a finite number) of available software components will exist in an apparently infinite supporting environment provided by computer hardware. The self-aware software system may still produce many objects according to its own self-model so it can build up itself, but it will be necessary for the software system to be able to incorporate in itself communications with existing objects. Existing objects of which code is not part of the software system may provide new segments for the adaptive self-model of the software system, making it better able to reproduce and expand in its environment. Today we already can see beginnings of a hardware/software environment which might become able to support the development of self-aware software according to our vision. The increasing re-use of software components, the availability of template libraries [29], design patterns [26], [56], and in some cases of their source code (i.e., open source versions of them or the bytecode of Java objects), the development of standardised communication interfaces and communication protocols between objects, hint that it might not be in the too distant future that building software by combining existing objects and source code will be possible. An early step towards self-aware software might be the building of software systems by specifying the design of communication patterns between existing components, without adding any new component or explicitly rewriting the behaviour of existing components (see design patterns).

As we pointed out in the previous section natural self-aware systems extensively use memory communications, and they create memories of many communications. Having these memory communications provides the foundation for their self-monitoring by their information subsystem and for the adaptation of their self-model. The critical missing component of software systems in this respect is the lack of creating memories of communications between objects/processes, however recent advances in aspect-oriented programming address this issue at least at a basic level by allowing the logging of object communications [19]. Consequently, the analysis of natural self-aware systems suggests that in order to develop self-aware software systems we need to have memories of communications between objects and these memory communications need to be referenced frequently by communications constituting the software system. Although it is not completely clear for us how the creation of object communication memories should be implemented, we believe that such memory communications can be realized in the form of creating new objects which generate repeatedly a representation of the memorized communication (or combining simple existing objects by creating re-occurring communications between them or by extension logging communications implemented in the context of aspect-oriented programming). These memories should work as short-term memories, implying that they can be discarded after a relatively short time, making their sustaining components (i.e., objects which produce the memory communications) available to store new memory communications or to participate in other communications. The development of these short-term memories will bring us closer to the method of 'from within' for software system development.

Natural self-aware systems grow to a large extent due to identity check communications. In other words, due to the Popper principle, the asymmetry of true and false decisions about the identity/validity of communications, systems that are able to exist check their identity for infinity (at least in principle), systems that cease to exist conclude at some moment that their identity does not exist by ceasing the continuation of their communications. In our opinion self-aware software systems should expand largely due to identity checking communications, which check the identity/validity of communications between objects, generating new communications between objects, including memory communications, and guaranteeing the reproduction and expansion of the system according to its own rules. We believe that the 'from within' method of development of self-aware software will include methodology that allows the expansion of the software system by the generation of identity check communications. As we already noted, the function of the self-aware software system will be achieved by adaptation to its environmental constraints, which limit its growth and trigger the generation of additional identity check communications by contributing to the generation of some actual communications that differ to some extent from the expected communications (at least in their distribution). We note that our view of growing the software system by identity check communications is similar to the method of development of programs by elaborating the proof of initial statements representing the problem and assumptions [32], [43], [60]. The main difference between our approach and program development by proof is that in our view the proving process should continue infinitely in case of self-aware software systems, while in the context of program development by proof the proving process ends by proving the correctness of the program. While program development by proof operates in a world supposed to be static and completely known (i.e., represented by the assumptions and the problem statement, of which validity is assumed to be provided), in our view self-aware software develops in a world that is infinitely complex and variable, the software system being able to capture (i.e., describe in a complementary sense) at any time a limited part of this world. In the context of our assumption, if the proving process halts that means the end of the software system, and the infinite continuation of the proving process means the reproduction and possibly expansion of the software system.

Adaptation of the self-model of natural self-aware systems is their core critical feature. Existing software systems are limited in adapting their self-model as we discussed in the previous section. If the previously discussed issues will be solved according to our expectations, the adaptation of the software code in response to faults, errors and failures will become possible. The use of existing objects and the access to their source code (their self-model) will allow the inclusion of new parts into the self-model of the software system. Self-monitoring, memories of runtime interactions, and frequent references to the self-model of the system, and accessibility of new self-model components will make possible to search for roots of errors, to find appropriate simplifications and standardisations, and to find appropriate changes to the self-model of the system, which will increase its reproduction and expansion ability.

Finally, an interesting question is whether the self-aware software will show anything similar to human consciousness, including feelings and emotions. In our view there is a wide variety of natural self-aware systems, which include bacteria, plants, simple and complex animals, social animals like humans, human organizations, and possibly other natural self-aware systems. These systems perform their self-awareness in many different ways, but all maintain the critical features of self awareness (including the adaptive change of their own self-model). One of these systems, the humans, show consciousness, while others may show similar features to some extent (e.g., animals), but others do not show any behaviour that would resemble human consciousness (at least in terms of communications/interactions with humans). This indicates that self-aware software systems may not show any behaviour that would resemble human consciousness, and in principle there is no reason why we should expect any such behaviour. Our view is that self-aware software systems (if they become reality) will show the critical features of self-awareness, but they will not behave like conscious humans.

References

1. Agrawal, N, et al. (2003). RNA Interference: Biology, Mechanism, and Applications. Microbiology and Molecular Biology Reviews, 67: 657-685.
2. Alonso, E, Kudenko, D and Kazakov, D (eds.) (2003) Adaptive Agents and Multi-Agent Systems. Springer-Verlag, Berlin,
3. Andras, P and Andras, CD (in press). Protein interaction world - an alternative hypothesis about the origins of life. To appear in Medical Hypotheses.
4. Andras, P and Charlton, BG (2004). Management from the Perspective of Systems Theory. In Proceedings of Practising Philosophy of Management - 2004.

5. Andras, P and Charlton, BG (2002). Democratic Deficit and Communication Inflation in the Health Care System. Journal of Evaluation in Clinical Practice, 8: 291-298.

6. Appavoo et al. (2003). Enabling autonomic behavior in systems software with hot swapping. IBM Systems Journal, 42: 60-76.

7. Ariola, ZM, Herbelin, H, and Sabry, A (2004). A type-theoretic foundation of continuations and prompts. ACM SIGPLAN Notices, 39: 40-53.

8. Atkinson, MP and Morrison, R (1995). Orthogonally persistent object systems. VLDB Journal, 4: 319-401.

9. Aviziensis, A, Laprie, JC, and Randell, B (2001). Fundamental concepts of dependability. Newcastle University Report no. CS-TR-739.

10. Barnard, CI (1938). The Functions of the Executive. Harvard University Press, Cambridge, MA.

11. Barr, A and Feigenbaum, EA (1989). The Handbook of Artificial Intelligence. Volume II, 2nd printing, Addison-Wesley, Reading, MA.

12. Behnisch T, Matsushita S, and Knopfel T (2004). Imaging of gene expression during long-term potentiation. Neuroreport, 15: 2039-2043.

13. Born, R (Ed.) (1989). Artificial Intelligence: The Case Against. Routledge, London, UK.

14. Cazzola, W, Stroud, RJ, and Tisato, F (2000). Reflection and Software Engineering. Springer-Verlag, Heidelberg.

15. Charlton, BG and Andras, P (2004). The Nature and Function of Management - a perspective from systems theory. Philosophy of Management, 3: 3-16.

16. Charlton, BG and Andras, P (2003). The Modernization Imperative, Imprint Academic, Exeter, UK.

17. Cohen, PR and Feigenbaum, EA (1989). The Handbook of Artificial Intelligence. Volume III, 2nd printing, Addison-Wesley, Reading, MA.

18. DiStefano, A, Fragetta, M, and Tramontana, E (2003). Computational reflection for embedded Java systems. LNCS 2889, Springer Verlag, Heidelberg, pp.437-450.

19. Douence, D, Fradet, P, and Sudholt, M (2004). Composition, reuse, and interaction analysis of stateful aspects. In: Proceedings of AOSD 2004, ACM, pp.141-150.

20. Duba, B, Harper, R, and MacQueen, D (1991). Typing first-class continuations in ML. In: Proceedings of the 18th ACM SIGPLAN-SIGACT Symposium on Principles of Programming Languages, ACM, pp.163-173.

21. Ferber, J (1989). Computational reflection in class based object-oriented languages. ACM SIGPLAN Notices, 24: 317-326.

22. Foote, B and Johnson, RE (1989). Reflective facilities in Smalltalk-80. ACM SIGPLAN Notices, 24: 327-335.

23. Frank, MR and Szekely, P (1997). Adaptive forms: an interaction paradigm for entering structured data. In: Proceedings of the 3rd International Conference on Intelligent User Interfaces, ACM, pp.153-160.

24. Furicht, R, Prahofer, H, Hofinger, T, and Altmann, J (2002). Components: A component-based application framework for manufacturing execution systems in C# and .NET. In: Proceedings of TOOLS Pacific 2002, ACM, pp.169-178.

25. Gacs, P (2001). Reliable cellular automata with self-organization. Journal of Statistical Physics, 103: 45-267.

26. Gamma, E, Helm, R, Johnson, R, and Vlissides, E (1995). Design Patterns: Elements of Reusable Object-Oriented Software. Addison-Wesley, Reading, MA.

27. Goldberg, A and Robson, D (1983). Smalltalk - 80. The Language and its Implementation. Addison-Wesley, Reading, MA.

28. Grothoff, C (2003). Walkabout revisited: The runabout. In: LNCS 2743, pp. 103-125.

29. Jarzabek, S (1995). From reuse library experiences to application generation architectures. ACM SIGSOFT Software Engineering Notes, 20: 114-122.

30. Jarzabek, S and Knauber, P (1999). Synergy between component-based and generative approaches. ACM SIGSOFT Software Engineering Notes, 24: 429-445.

31. Jennings, NR, Sycara, K, and Woolridge, M (1998). A roadmap of agent research and development. Autonomous Agents and Multi-Agent Systems, 1: 7-38.

32. Jones, CB (1972). Formal development of correct algorithms: An example based on Earley's recogniser. In: Proceedings of ACM Conference on Proving Assertions about Programs, ACM, pp.150-169.

33. Katara, M and Katz, S (2003). Architectural views of aspects. In: Proceedings of AOSD 2003, ACM, pp.1-10.

34. Killijian, M-O, Ruiz, J-C, and Fabre, J-C (2002). Portable serialization of CORBA objects: a reflective approach. ACM SIGPLAN Notices, 37: 68-82.

35. Kinzle, DM and Elder, MC (2003). Internet WORMS: past, present, and future: Recent worms: a survey and trends. In: Proceedings of the 2003 ACM workshop on Rapid Malcode, ACM, pp.1-10.

36. Landauer, C and Bellman, KL (2001a). New architectures for constructed complex systems. Applied Mathematics and Computation, 120: 149-163.

37. Landauer C and Bellman, KL (2001b) Self-modelling systems. In: LNCS 2614, pp.238-256.

38. Lee, P.A. and Anderson, T. (1990). Fault Tolerance. Principles and Practice. Wien: Springer-Verlag, 2nd ed.

39. Lee, Y et al. (2003). The nuclear RNase III Drosha initiates microRNA processing. Nature, 425: 415-419.

40. Levine M and Tjian R (2003). Transcription regulation and animal diversity. Nature, 424: 147-151.

41. Luhmann, N (1996). Social Systems. Stanford University Press, Palo Alto, CA.Charlton, BG and Andras, P (2003). The Modernization Imperative, Imprint Academic, Exeter, UK.

42. Maes, P (1987) Concepts and experiments in computational reflection. ACM SIGPLAN Notices, 22: 147-155.

43. Maghrabi, T and Golshani, F (1992). Automatic program generation using sequent calculus. Proceedings of the 1992 ACM Annual Conference on Communications, ACM, pp.73-81.

44. March ,JG and Simon, HA (1993). Organizations. Blackwell, Cambridge, MA.

45. Maturana HR, and Varela, FJ (1980). Autopoiesis and Cognition : the realization of the living. D. Reidel Publishing Company, Boston.

46. Mattick, JS and Gagen, MJ (2001). The evolution of controlled multitasked gene networks: The role of introns and other noncoding RNAs in the development of complex organisms. Molecular Biology and Evolution, 18: 1611-1630.

47. Meister, G and Tuschl, T (2004). Mechanisms of gene silencing by double-stranded RNA. Nature, 431: 343-349.

48. Miller, JG (1978). Living Systems. McGraw-Hill.

49. Newell, A (1990). Unified Theories of Cognition. Harvard University Press, Cambridge, MA.

50. O Cinneide, M and Nixon, P (2001). Patterns and evolution structures: Automated software evolution towards design patterns. In: Proceedings of the 4th International Workshop on Principles of Software Evolution, ACM, pp.162-165.

51. Ortin, F and Cueva, JM (2003). Non-restrictive computational reflection. Computer Standards & Interfaces, 25: 241-251.
52. Ortin, F, Lopez, B, and Perez-Schofield, JBG (2004). Separating adaptable persistence attributes through computational reflection. IEEE Software, 21: 41-49.
53. Pokol, B. (1992) The Theory of Professional Institution Systems. Felsooktatasi Koordinacios Iroda, Budapest.
54. Popovici, A, Alonso, G, and Gross, T (2003). Spontaneous container services. In: LNCS 2743, pp. 29-53.
55. Raghavan, A et al., (2002). Genome-wide analysis of mRNA decay in resting and activated primary human T lymphocytes. Nucleic Acids Research, 30: 5529-5538.
56. Rising, L (1998). The Patterns Handbook. Cambrdige University Press, Cambridge, UK.
57. Rosenblat F (1962) Principles of Neurodynamics : Perceptrons and the Theory of Brain mechanisms. Washington D.C., Spartan.
58. Simon, HA (1976). Administrative Behaviour. The Free Press, New York, NY.
59. Stunkel, CB, Sivaram, R, and Panda, DK (1997). Implementing multidestination worms in switch-based parallel systems: architectural alternatives and their impact. ACM SIGARCH Computer Architecture News, 25: 50-61.
60. Sun, Y-Q, Lu, R-Z, and Bi, H (1985). Program synthesis based on Boyer-Moore theorem proving techniques. Proceedings of the ACM 13th Annual Conference on Computer Science, ACM, pp.348-355.
61. Tanter, E, Noye, J, Caromel, D, and Cointe, P (2003). Partial behavioral reflection: spatial and temporal selection of reification. ACM SIGPLAN Notices, 38: 27-46.
62. Uhrmacher AM, Rohl M, and Kullick B (2002). The role of reflection in simulating and testing agents: An exploration based on the simulation system James. Applied Artificial Intelligence, 16: 795-811.
63. Ungar, D and Smith, RB (1991). SELF: The power of simplicity. LISP and Symbolic Computation, 4: 187-205.
64. Valetto, G and Kaiser, G (2002). A case study in software adaptation. In: Proceedings of WOSS'02, ACM, pp.73-78.
65. Van Moorsel, A and Wolter, K (2004). Analysis and Algorithms for Restart. In: Proceedings of the Quantitative Evaluation of Systems, QEST 2004, pp. 195-204., IEEE Computer Society.

A Case for Design Methodology Research in Self-* Distributed Systems

Indranil Gupta*, Steven Ko, Nathanael Thompson, Mahvesh Nagda,
Chris Devaraj, Ramsés Morales, and Jay A. Patel

Dept. of Computer Science,
University of Illinois at Urbana-Champaign, Urbana IL 61801
{indy, sko, nathomps, nagda, devaraj, rvmorale, jaypatel}@cs.uiuc.edu

Abstract. We argue that "design methodology research" for self-* distributed systems needs to be recognized and enriched. Methodologies encourage systematic design of distributed protocols. They augment the creative activity of innovation, rather than stifle it. They enable easy design of, and automatic code generation for, distributed systems with predictable properties. Through a taxonomy, we show that methodology research is growing slowly but steadily. As a case study, we present and discuss a new methodology that concretely captures the design of a large class of peer-to-peer distributed hash tables (p2p DHTs) and DHT-based applications. We use this to show some advantages of methodology research, such as effective exploration of the design space for protocols. We also summarize some of our ongoing work in the direction of developing methodologies for distributed protocols.

1   Introduction

Today, designing new protocols for self-* distributed systems such as peer-to-peer (p2p) systems, autonomic distributed systems, Grid applications, etc., is an extremely challenging task. Consider a researcher who is asked to design a distributed protocol for a specific p2p application with certain properties. The only resources available to the designer are 1. her basic distributed systems knowledge, 2. prior research literature, and 3. designer's experiences.

This is almost a "seat of pants" approach to protocol design. It has resulted in long research project timelines, as well as long lag times to production and deployment (anecdotes suggest 5 to 15 years). Resultant designs may also be complex, with massive code line counts and inefficiencies when pieces are put together [5, 16].

These shortcomings can be addressed for future systems by populating and enriching a fourth resource for the protocol designer – Protocol Design Methodologies. A protocol design methodology can be loosely characterized as *an organized, documented set of building blocks, rules and/or guidelines for design of a*

---

* This research was partly supported by National Science Foundation Grant ITR-0427089.

O. Babaoglu et al. (Eds.): SELF-STAR 2004, LNCS 3460, pp. 260–272, 2005.

*class of distributed protocols. It is possibly amenable to automated code genera-
tion.*

Given a distributed computing problem then, a collection of methodologies
can be brought to bear, for either innovating novel protocols, or for composing
existing protocols. This would create a range of simple and efficient solutions
to the problem at hand, thus offering several choices for selecting the most appropriate design. In general, the application of methodologies results in a more
systematic approach to design. They augment the creative activity of innovation, rather than stifle it. In the long run, short design times, and compact and
efficient protocol designs, are possible side-effects.

Many disciplines have already used methodologies to systematize and mature
the creative design process. Since the early days of the Internet, TCP/IP layered architectures have helped decentralize design responsibility for infrastructure and applications among different research communities. Hardware design
uses automated synthesis [2], and software engineering uses Design Patterns and
Model-driven architectures [8]. Similar maturity for distributed systems research
requires creation of a critical mass of methodologies, and this can be achieved
through *Design Methodology Research.* As we show in this paper, the discovery
of design methodologies can go hand in hand with protocol design itself.

We make our case for methodology research in distributed systems by first
recognizing that there are already several methodologies for protocol classes. We
present a new taxonomy for classifying methodologies. Then, as a case study, we
present a new *automatable* methodology that retroactively fits a large class of
p2p DHTs and DHT-based applications. We show how this enables exploration
of design space of DHT-based applications, and present experimental results to
justify the benefits.

It will be evident from this paper that the elements of methodology research
are more challenging than, and different from, those of hardcore software engineering. Developing a design methodology requires in-depth understanding of the
protocols being designed, or the desired properties from the protocol, or both. A
design methodology inherently captures the designer's frame of mind and philosophy, a goal that software engineering does not aspire to. The only connection
with software engineering lies in the development of automated toolkits that
enable a designer to generate working code for a new protocol. Although these
toolkits clearly have a very different aim than existing Integrated Development
Environments (IDEs), it is possible that the two might be consolidated in the
future.

Previous Work: We briefly summarize some of the design methodologies that
have emerged for distributed systems, not necessarily restricting discussion to
self-* systems. It should be noted that some of these methodologies have had
considerable impact, while others are less popular, and for many more, it is
too early for the jury to be called out. For example OSI-like architectures are
less popular than the omnipresent TCP/IP design methodology. On the other

hand, the new methodology for DHTs presented in this paper is too young to be judged.

The set of existing design methodologies includes protocol families for survivable storage systems [22], Internet routing protocols [23], peer-to-peer systems [12, 15], extensible router and OS design (e.g., [13]), I/O automata [21], etc.

Strategy design patterns [9] can be used to construct object-oriented code for a large class of deterministically reliable distributed protocols such as consensus. Other tools in this class include ASX and Conduits+. These works have been labeled as *microprotocols*, and include x-kernel based microprotocols and runtime composable systems [20]. Stack-oriented distributed systems such as Horus [19], and composable web services [17] are some other methodologies. However, all of these systems have composition rules that are based on function calls - we have discovered some methodologies that use more complex notions of composition (see Section 3). The above list is by no means comprehensive, and is only a snapshot of the slowly growing body of methodology research.

A new methodology we present captures some popular DHTs and p2p applications. DHTs include Pastry, Chord, Tapestry, Kademlia, Kelips, etc., and applications include CFS, PAST, Bayeux, Squirrel, etc. [1].

Section 2 presents a taxonomy of methodologies. Section 3 presents the p2p methodology, and Section 4 discusses experimental data. Section 5 briefly details our current work. We summarize in Section 6.

2   Taxonomy of Methodologies

In order to motivate an understanding of the features of methodologies, we present a new taxonomy of classification for them.

Formal Versus Informal: We call a methodology that is specified using precise rules or a stringent framework as a *formal* methodology, otherwise we say that it is *informal*. These "rules" could either be mathematical/logical notation, or the grammar of a high level programming language. Respective examples are the probabilistic I/O automata [21], and the methodology of [11] that takes as input a set of differential equations (satisfying certain conditions), and generates code for a distributed protocol that is equivalent. Previous methodologies for DHT design [12, 15] have been informal.

Due to their rigor (either through a formal framework or a compiler), formal methodologies have the capability to create protocols with predictable or provable properties, and also to generate protocol code automatically. For example, the distributed protocols generated from differential equations in [11] are provably equivalent to the original differential equation, and can be generated by a toolkit called DiffGen [11]. On the other hand, informal methodologies are less rigorous and more flexible, but can have multiple possible interpretations. An informal methodology could be converted into a formal one through implementation of a specific interpretation. For example, an informal probabilistic protocol composable methodology can be instantiated through a high level language called Proactive Protocol Composition Language (PPCL) [10, 18], thus making it formal.

Innovative Versus Composable: Design methodologies must be capable of assisting in innovation of new protocols, as well as in the ability to reuse and adapt existing protocols. These are achieved respectively through innovative methodologies and composable methodologies. An innovative methodology describes how completely novel protocols can be created, e.g., [8, 11]. A composable methodology typically describes *building blocks* and *composition rules or guidelines.* Building blocks are either standalone protocols or strategies, and composition rules help combine the blocks to create new protocols with enhanced properties. For example, the informal methodology for DHT design in [12] uses four types of building blocks - overlay, membership, routing, and preprocessing. Strategy design patterns are another example of a composable methodology [9].

Table 1. How Existing Methodologies Fit into the Proposed Taxonomy

METHODOLOGY TYPES	Innovative	Composable
Formal	Protocols from Differential Equations [11]; Bluespec for hardware synthesis [2].	TCP/IP layered architecture; Extensible router and OS designs (e.g., Click [13], SPIN, x-kernel [3, 20]); Routing [23]; Probabilistic I/O automata [21]; Strategy Design Patterns [9]; Stacked architectures (e.g., Horus [19]).
Informal	Design Patterns [8].	DHT design methodologies [12, 15]; Protocol family for survivable storage [22]; Probabilistic protocols [18].

Table 1 summarizes the above discussion.

Discovery of Methodologies: Different approaches are possible for the *discovery* of these methodologies:

1. **Retroactive:** A methodology is discovered for an existing system or class of protocols. Ex: methodologies for routing [23] and probabilistic protocols [10].

2. **Progressive:** A methodology is invented that creates a novel class of protocols. Ex: the design of protocols from differential equations can generate new protocols for dynamic replication and majority voting [11].

3. **Auxiliary:** A methodology is discovered to assist and complement an existing methodology. Ex: protocol families for survivable storage architectures [22] combine several auxiliary methodologies for differing system models.

3   A New Concrete Methodology for P2P Applications

During the past few years, p2p researchers have designed over 25 different DHTs and DHT-based applications. Manku [15] and Iamnitchi et al [12] gave *informal* design methodologies for DHTs. Here, we present the first *formal* composable methodology for a large class of DHTs and DHT-based applications. The DHTs covered include (but are not limited to) Chord, Pastry, Tapestry, Kademlia, Gnutella, CAN, and Kelips[1].

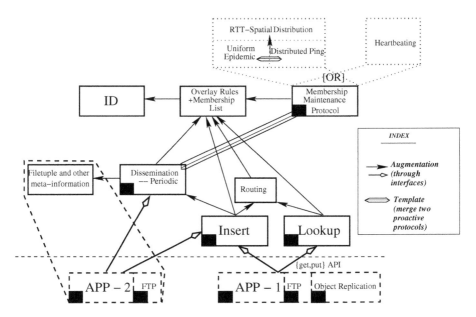

Fig. 1. A New Formal Composable Methodology for the design of a class of DHTs and DHT-based applications. *Covered DHTs include Chord, Pastry, Tapestry, CAN, Kademlia, Kelips. Covered DHT applications include Scribe, PAST, CFS, Squirrel (all App-1) and Kelips-based cooperative web caching (App-2). The methodology consists of standalone building blocks, composed by either (i) (augmentation) simple function calls or (ii) (template) by merging two periodic/proactive blocks together. Composition rules are shown in detail in Figure 2. Building blocks with dark shaded bottom-left corners represent functions that directly talk to their peer functions on other clients.* **This methodology is both retroactive (i.e., fits existing designs) and progressive (i.e., can be used for completely new designs)**

---

[1] The proof discussion of this statement is omitted.

Figure 1 summarizes the methodology. This methodology can be used to create any of the system designs mentioned above. The figure shows several *standalone* building blocks, both at the DHT layer and for two models of DHT-based applications. The building blocks for DHTs include ID (assigns virtual id's to nodes), Overlay Rules and Membership List (encapsulates the overlay structure and maintains neighbors), membership maintenance protocol, dissemination protocol (for updating meta-information such as about files), routing, insert and lookup, and a block that stores meta-information. Two application models (App-1 and App-2) are shown, which we discuss shortly. Blocks with dark corners communicate over the network with corresponding block on peers.

These building blocks are composed by one of two rules - (i) augmentation (i.e., a function call interface), or (ii) template (merges component protocols that have periodically executed main functions). For example, the dissemination protocol and proactive membership maintenance protocol can be merged by the template rule so that one protocol's message is piggybacked on top of the other, saving on communication.

An application of the type App-1 uses the DHT through a {`get(object)`, `put(object)`} API [6]. This is used in a large class of DHT-based p2p applications including CFS, PAST, Squirrel, Ivy, etc. App-2 describes a model where the application is "pushed down into the DHT layer" in the interests of protocol efficiency. This fits the cooperative web caching application built over the Kelips DHT [14]. The App-2 model may recode some blocks from the DHT.

The above two composition rules are borrowed from a different methodology for probabilistic protocols [18]. Like that methodology, Figure 1 is also *automatable*, i.e., the high level language (PPCL) and toolkit described in [18] can be used to generate code for DHTs and applications on the fly. Figure 2 shows salient parts of the PPCL specification for the methodology of Figure 1.

The presented methodology thus encapsulates the philosophy behind a class of DHTs and p2p applications. Besides this retroactive use, it has significant progressive and auxiliary advantages.

In Section 4, we evaluate one progressive use of the methodology. Figure 1 showed an option of two different designs for membership maintenance protocols (heartbeating or random ping-based [7]) - this is an example of auxiliary methodologies brought to bear. Figure 3 shows possible benefits from four other existing methodologies. Other properties such as security may also be introduced through auxiliary composable security protocols.

4   Experimental Results

One benefit of a methodology is the assistance in exploring protocol design space. Consider a designer asked to build a Pastry-based application for an existing (legacy) overlay, where the neighbor relation among nodes may not obey the

```
/* Blocks to be called by App-1. */
component {
    file = dht.c;
    function = char *get(void *);
} lookup;
component {
    file = dht.c;
    function = char *put(void *, char *);
} insert;
/* Blocks with call-in functions. */
component {
    file = overlay.c;
    function = get_neighbor(int dest);
} overlay;
...
/* Compositions -- Augmentation. */
augment {
    target = lookup;
    replace(int forward_search(void *data), overlay);
} lookup-overlay;
        // replace each call to forward_search in lookup
        // with call to main function of overlay
...
/* Periodically Executed Blocks. */
component {
    file = swim.c;
    function = void run();
} membership;
component {
    file = diss.c;
    function = void run();
} dissemination;
/* Composition -- Merging membership and dissemination. */
...
template {
    component = membership;
    component = dissemination;
    match (int send_member_update(),
           int send(),
           int send(),
           piggyback);
    match (int process(char *recv_msg),
           int process(char *recv_msg),
           int process_join(char *piggy_backed, char *recv_msg),
           unpiggyback);
    match (recvmsg, in_buff, recvmsg);
} membership-dissem;
// Merges the main functions of membership.c and dissemination.c. For each
// match statement (a(), b(), c(), d()), a call to a() in membership and b()
// in dissemination are merged, top-down in the code, and replaced with a
// call to c(). d() is an optional user-defined function that merges arguments
// to a() and b() for input into c().
```

Fig. 2. PPCL code (snapshot) for automating the Methodology of Figure 1:
*This specification is derived from existing source code for individual components. The
toolkit in [18] generates code from this and the component source code*

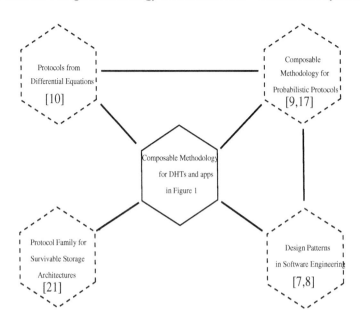

Fig. 3. The Power of Auxiliary Methodologies: *Other methodologies that serve as auxiliary methodologies for (i.e., either benefit, or benefit from) each other as well as for the composable methodology of Figure 1*

Pastry neighbor relation, but is specified by a different application. For instance, this application might be a legacy one that closely relies on a pre-existing membership protocol, but desires to augment itself with Pastry-like search capabilities.

Viewed in the context of Figure 1, the designer's challenge reduces to – the designer can only change the implementation of the App-1, Insert, Lookup and Routing blocks, but not the rest of the design.

Figures 4(a-c) show that if the overlay is just chosen by each node selecting neighbors uniformly at random, the default Pastry routing is inappropriate due to its low query success rate. However, our methodology allows us to explore several alternative designs by modifying the *Routing* block of Figure 1. We consider one such new routing protocol called *multiflow routing*. Here, a node first finds all its neighbors with longer prefix matches to the destination ID than its own. The query is then forwarded to only the top 2 among these neighbors, with such multi-forwarding limited to 3 times per query per route.

The plots show that multiflow routing outperforms prefix routing on query success rate (close to 100%) and latency. The traffic increase is moderate (a factor of about 3) at 10% membership list size. This tradeoff would be acceptable to an overlay running in medium-sized groups, and where the application requires reliable querying.

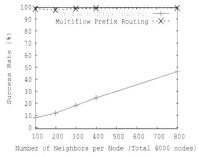

(a) *Query Success Rate.*

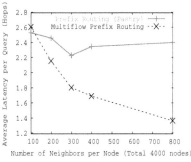

(b) *Query Reply Latency.*

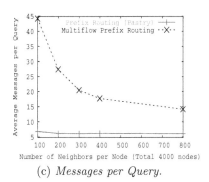

(c) *Messages per Query.*

Fig. 4. Default Pastry Routing versus new Multiflow Routing for random overlays: *Prefix routing is default Pastry routing; multiflow prefix is the new proposed routing protocol within Figure 1. Each point on the plot is averaged from 1000 queries over 10 different random overlays*

5   Our Current Work

We are currently working on both new innovative and composable methodologies. Below, we briefly summarize two methodologies we have developed, along with some of their uses.

5.1   Innovative Methodology – Generating Self-* Protocols from Differential Equations

We have discovered an innovative methodology that translates sets of differential equations into *equivalent* distributed protocols [11]. An equation set generates a state machine, with each variable mapped to a state, and terms mapped to protocol actions. Stable equilibrium points in the original equations map to self-stabilizing behavior (fractions of nodes in respective states), and simplicity of terms maps to scalable communication.

In brief, consider a system of differential equations in the form $\dot{\bar{X}} = \frac{d\bar{X}}{dt} = \bar{f}(\bar{X})$, where $\bar{X}$ is a vector of variables, f is a vector of $|X|$ functions, and the left hand sides denote each of the variables differentiated with respect to time t. An example with $X = \{x, y, z\}$ is:

$$\dot{x} = -\beta xy + \alpha z$$
$$\dot{y} = \beta xy - \gamma y$$
$$\dot{z} = \gamma y - \alpha z \tag{1}$$

Here, α, β, γ are parameters lying in the interval $[0, 1]$. When the methodology of [11] is applied to the above equation, the protocol generated is *equivalent* to the original equation system, viz., *the fractions of processes in different states in the distributed system, at equilibrium, is the same as the values of the variables when the original equations are in equilibrium*. We provide here a summary of the translation techniques and the uses of the derived protocols - for more details, the reader is encouraged to refer to [11].

Summary of Translation Techniques: In order to translate a system of differential equations $\dot{\bar{X}} = \frac{d\bar{X}}{dt} = \bar{f}(\bar{X})$, the right hand sides of these equations are required to each be a sum of polynomial terms $\pm T = \pm c_T \Pi^{y \in X} y^{i_{y, f_x, T}}$ ($0 \le c_T \le 1$, $i_{y, f_x, T}$ non-negative integers), each negative term occurring in $\dot{x}$ should have a power of x that is ≥ 1, and terms should be *pair*-able into matching pairs of positive and negative terms so that each pair sums to zero. The translation methodology then creates a state machine which has one state per original variable in the set $\bar{X}$. It also creates an action for each negative:positive term pair – this action is executed periodically (once every protocol period, protocol period duration fixed) when a process is in the state x, where $\dot{x}$ contains the negative term. Without loss of generality, suppose that the positive part of the pair occurs in $\dot{z}$.

Translating a simple term pair such as $-c.x$:$+c.x$ requires the process in state x to flip a coin with heads probability c, and transition to state z only if this falls heads. Translating other polynomial terms is achieved by not only flipping a local coin but also sampling a random selection of other processes, and deciding whether to transition or not based on their states. For instance a term pair $-T : +T$ with $-T = -x.y^2$ can be translated into an action where a process in state x periodically (once every protocol period) samples two other processes selected uniformly at random from across the group. If both sampled processes happen to be in state y, then p transitions into state z.

Equation systems that do not satisfy the above conditions (e.g., in term matching, or in the form of the basic equation system) may need to be normalized or rewritten. Several equation rewriting techniques are discussed in [11].

Emergent Properties of Derived Protocols and their Uses: The methodology retains the same equilibrium points as in the original differential equation, thus providing the derived protocol with *self-stabilizing behavior* around the stable equilibrium points. The stochastic behavior of the differential equations translates into *fault-tolerance, churn-resistance*, and other interesting properties such as *attacker resilience*, as described below. Finally, the simplicity of the equations is reflected in the simplicity and *constant (hence scalable) communication overhead* of the derived protocol.

Equations (1) above in fact represent the survival of endemic diseases (such as influenza) in a fixed-size human population, with x, y, z respectively the fractions of receptives, infected, and immune individuals. The protocol derived from it is a new *dynamic and migratory replication model*. In this dynamic and migratory replication scheme, once a given file is inserted into a distributed group of computer hosts connected in an overlay, the emergent behavior of the protocol ensures that the file has a small number of replicas moving continuously among the hosts in the distributed system (only "infected" hosts store a replica). Without using too much network bandwidth, this scheme ensures *attacker-resilience* – an attacker only has very short windows (typically tens of seconds) to guess the exact number and location of the current replicas for a given file. This dynamic and migratory replication model is currently being used to design a new distributed file system called "Folklore".

The above methodology can also be used to design a new protocol for majority voting in large-scale distributed systems (derived from a model of biological competition among ecosystem species) [11].

The protocols generated by this methodology are similar to Complex Adaptive Systems, and can be considered as a type of "Emergent Thinker" [4].

This differential equation translation methodology has been incorporated into a design toolkit called *DiffGen*, which enables a designer to input differential equations (in a Mathematica-like format), and outputs compilable and deployable C code for the equivalent protocol.

5.2   Composable Methodology – Probabilistic Protocols for Large-Scale Distributed Systems

In [18], we have developed a toolkit called PPCL that automates a composable methodology for designing probabilistic protocols for large-scale distributed systems. This toolkit extends and implements the methodology of [10]. Multicast, aggregation, leader election, failure detection, membership, are some of the problems solved.

The generated probabilistic protocols are self-adaptive to failures. The protocols have very high reliability, per-process overheads that vary from being either independent of or polylogarithmically dependent on the number of processes in the distributed group, and protocol completion times that are also polylogarithmic.

The methodology consists of seven classes of building blocks, each of which is either a protocol or a strategy: epidemics, distributed ping, tree dissemination, recovery and committee selection are protocols while non-protocol strategies include weak overlays, and topology-aware probability distribution functions. Each building block has well-understood scalability and reliability properties. The composition techniques are either simple *augmentations* or *template compositions*. For example, an epidemic protocol that selects targets uniformly at random can be made topologically aware by augmentation with a network round trip-time-based probability distribution function for target choice. Another example is that a failure detector protocol and a multicast protocol can be composed through a template composition (see Figure 2) to generate a protocol for decentralized membership maintenance.

For such composable design methodologies, one has to ensure that performance properties such as correctness, reliability, scalability are either inherited or preserved to an extent, in spite of the composition. For instance, in the above methodology, template compositions inherit both correctness properties (e.g., eventual delivery of multicasts) as well as performance properties (e.g., overhead, multicast latency, reliability) from components. Augmentation inherits correctness, while preserving performance to a large extent – latency, overhead, etc. degrades by a factor that is typically polylogarithmic in system size.

The reader is refered to [10, 18] for more details.

6 Summary

In this paper, we have presented a new taxonomy for design methodologies, and a new concrete methodology for such self-* distributed systems as DHTs and p2p applications. We have argued that design methodologies for self-* distributed systems can capture the designer's mindframe and the philosophy behind a class of distributed protocols, thus enabling both exploration of the protocol design space and systematic protocol reuse. Many methodologies can be automated to generate ready-to-deploy code.

Methodologies are understood by theoreticians, practitioners, researchers, and vendors alike, e.g., terms familiar to all these communities include "composability" [21, 22]. Cultivation of design methodologies is absolutely essential for systematic protocol design to emerge for self-* distributed systems.

References

1. Proc. 1st-3rd IPTPS, 2002-2004.
2. Arvind. Bluespec: A language for hardware design, simulation, synthesis and verification. In *Proc. MEMOCODE*, page 249, Jun. 2003.
3. B. Bershad and S. Savage et al. Extensibility, safety and performance in the SPIN operating system,. In *Proc. ACM SOSP*, pages 267–284, Dec. 1995.
4. S. Camorlinga and K. Barker. The emergent thinker. In *Proc. SELF-STAR: Intnl. Workshop on Self-* Properties in Complex Information Systems*, May-Jun. 2004.

5. Computing Research Association (CRA). Grand Research Challenges in Distributed Systems. http://www.cra.org/reports/gc.systems.pdf.

6. F. Dabek, B. Zhao, and P. Druschel et al. Towards a common API for structured peer-to-peer overlays. In *Proc. IPTPS*, pages 33–64, 2003.

7. A. Das, I. Gupta, and A. Motivala. SWIM: Scalable Weakly-consistent Infection-style process group Membership protocol. In *Proc. DSN*, pages 303–312, 2002.

8. E. Gamma, R. Helm, R. Johnson, and Vlissides J. *Design Patterns: elements of reusable object-oriented software*. Addison-Wesley, 1st edition, 1995.

9. B. Garbinato and R. Guerraoui. Using the strategy design pattern to compose reliable distributed protocols. In *Proc. USENIX Conf. Obj.-Or. Tech. and Sys.*, pages 221–232, Jun. 1997.

10. I. Gupta. *Building Scalable Solutions to Distributed Computing Problems using Probabilistic Components*. PhD Thesis, Dept. of Computer Science, Cornell University, Jan. 2004.

11. I. Gupta. On the design of distributed protocols from differential equations. In *Proc. ACM PODC*, pages 216–225, 2004.

12. A. Iamnitchi, M. Ripeanu, and I. Foster. Locating data in (small-world?) p2p scientific collaborations. In *Proc. IPTPS*, pages 232–241, 2002.

13. E. Kohler and R. Morris et al. The Click modular router. *ACM Tr. Comp. Sys.*, 18(3), Aug. 2000.

14. P. Linga, I. Gupta, and K. Birman. A churn-resistant peer-to-peer web caching system. In *Proc. ACM Wshop. SSRS*, Oct. 2003.

15. G. S. Manku. Balanced binary trees for id management and load balance in distributed hash tables. In *Proc. ACM PODC*, pages 197–205, 2004.

16. A. Spector. Plenary Talk. ACM SOSP, 2003.

17. B. Srivastava and J. Koehler. Web service composition - current solutions and open problems. In *Wshop. Planning for Web Serv.*, pages 28 – 35, 2003.

18. N. Thompson and I. Gupta. A composable methodology for proactive distributed protocols, Sept. 2004. TR UIUCDCS-R-2004-2490,.

19. R. van Renesse, S. Maffeis, and K. P. Birman. Horus: a flexible group communications system. *CACM*, 39(4):76–83, April 1996.

20. J. Ventura, J. Rodrigues, and L. Rodrigues. Response time analysis of composable micro-protocols. In *Proc. 4th IEEE OORTDC*, pages 335–342, 2001.

21. S.-H. Wu and S. A. Smolka et al. Composition and behaviors of probabilistic I/O automata. *TCS*, 176(1-2):1–38, Apr. 1997.

22. J. Wylie and G.R. Goodson et al. A protocol family approach to survivable storage infrastructures. In *Proc. FUDICO*, 2004.

23. G. Xie and J. Zhan et al. Routing design in operational networks: a look from the inside. In *Proc. ACM SIGCOMM Conf.*, pages 27–40, 2004.

Enabling Autonomic Grid Applications: Requirements, Models and Infrastructure*

M. Parashar, Z. Li, H. Liu, V. Matossian, and C. Schmidt

The Applied Software Systems Laboratory,
Rutgers University, Piscataway NJ 08904, USA

Abstract. The increasing complexity, heterogeneity and dynamism of emerging pervasive Grid environments and applications has necessitated the development of autonomic self-managing solutions, which are based on strategies used by biological systems to deal with similar challenges of complexity, heterogeneity, and uncertainty. This paper introduces Project AutoMate and describes its key components. The overall goal of Project Automate is to investigate conceptual models and implementation architectures that can enable the development and execution of such self-managing Grid applications. Two applications enabled by AutoMate are also described.

1 Introduction

The emergence of pervasive wide-area distributed computing, such as pervasive information systems and computational Grid, has enabled a new generation of applications that are based on seamless aggregation and interactions. For example, it is possible to conceive of a new generation of scientific and engineering simulations of complex physical phenomena that symbiotically and opportunistically combine computations, experiments, observations, and real-time data, and can provide important insights into complex systems such as interacting black holes and neutron stars, formations of galaxies, and subsurface flows in oil reservoirs and aquifers, etc. Other examples include pervasive applications that leverage the pervasive information Grid to continuously manage, adapt, and optimize our living context, crisis management applications that use pervasive conventional and unconventional information for crisis prevention and response, medical applications that use in-vivo and in-vitro sensors and actuators for patient management, and business applications that use anytime-anywhere information access to optimize profits.

However, the underlying Grid computing environment is inherently large, complex, heterogeneous and dynamic, globally aggregating large numbers of independent computing and communication resources, data stores and sensor net-

---

* The research presented in this paper is supported in part by the National Science Foundation via grants numbers ACI 9984357, EIA 0103674, EIA 0120934, ANI 0335244, CNS 0305495, CNS 0426354 and IIS 0430826.

O. Babaoglu et al. (Eds.): SELF-STAR 2004, LNCS 3460, pp. 273–290, 2005.

works. Furthermore, emerging applications are similarly complex and highly dynamic in their behaviors and interactions. Together, these characteristics result in application development, configuration and management complexities that break current paradigms based on passive components and static compositions. Clearly, there is a need for a fundamental change in how these applications are developed and managed. This has led researchers to consider alternative programming paradigms and management techniques that are based on strategies used by biological systems to deal with complexity, dynamism, heterogeneity and uncertainty. The approach, referred to as autonomic computing, aims at realizing computing systems and applications capable of managing themselves with minimal human intervention.

This paper has two objectives. The first is to investigate the challenges and requirements of programming Grid applications and to present self-managing applications as a means for addressing these requirements. The second is to introduce Project AutoMate, which investigates autonomic solutions to deal with the challenges of complexity, dynamism, heterogeneity and uncertainty in Grid environments. The overall goal of Project AutoMate is to develop conceptual models and implementation architectures that can enable the development and execution of such self-managing Grid applications. Specifically, it investigates programming models, frameworks and middleware services that support definition of autonomic elements, the development of autonomic applications as dynamic and opportunistic compositions of these autonomic elements, and the policy, content and context driven execution and management of these applications.

In this paper we introduce AutoMate and its key components, and describe their underlying conceptual models and implementations. Specifically we describe the Accord programming system, the Rudder decentralized coordination framework, and the Meteor content-based middleware providing support for content-based routing, discovery and associative messaging. We also present two autonomic Grid applications enabled by AutoMate. The first application investigates the autonomic optimization of an oil reservoir by enabling a systematic exploration of a broader set of scenarios, to identify optimal locations based on current operating conditions. The second application investigates the autonomic simulations and management of a forest fire propagation based on static and dynamic environment and vegetation conditions.

The rest of this paper is organized as follows. Section 2 outlines the challenges and requirements of Grid computing. Section 3 introduces Project AutoMate, presents its overall architecture and describes its key components, i.e., the Accord programming framework, the Rudder decentralized coordination framework and the Meteor content-based middleware. Section 4 presents the two illustrative Grid applications enabled by AutoMate. Section 5 presents a conclusion.

2   Grid Computing – Challenges and Requirements

The goal of the Grid concept is to enable a new generation of applications combining intellectual and physical resources that span many disciplines and organizations, providing vastly more effective solutions to important scientific, engineering, business and government problems. These new applications must be built on seamless and secure discovery, access to, and interactions among resources, services, and applications owned by many different organizations.

Attaining these goals requires implementation and conceptual models [1]. Implementation models address the virtualization of organizations which leads to Grids, the creation and management of virtual organizations as goal-driven compositions of organizations, and the instantiation of virtual machines as the execution environment for an application. Conceptual models define abstract machines that support programming models and systems to enable application development. Grid software systems typically provide capabilities for: (i) creating a transient "virtual organization" or virtual resource configuration, (ii) creating virtual machines composed from the resource configuration of the virtual organization (iii) creating application programs to execute on the virtual machines, and (iv) executing and managing application execution. Most Grid software systems implicitly or explicitly incorporate a programming model, which in turn assumes an underlying abstract machine with specific execution behaviors including assumptions about reliability, failure modes, etc. As a result, failure to realize these assumptions by the implementations models will result in brittle applications. The stronger the assumptions made, the greater the requirements for the Grid infrastructure to realize these assumptions and consequently its resulting complexity. In this section we first highlight the characteristics and challenges of Grid environments, and outline key requirements for programming Grid applications. We then introduce autonomic self-managing Grid applications that can address these challenges and requirements.

2.1   Characteristics of Grid Execution Environments and Applications

The key characteristics of Grid execution environments and applications are:

Heterogeneity: Grid environments aggregate large numbers of independent and geographically distributed computational and information resources, including supercomputers, workstation-clusters, network elements, data-storages, sensors, services, and Internet networks. Similarly, applications typically combine multiple independent and distributed software elements such as components, services, real-time data, experiments and data sources.

Dynamism: The Grid computation, communication and information environment is continuously changing during the lifetime of an application. This includes the availability and state of resources, services and data. Applications similarly have dynamic runtime behaviors in that the organization and interactions of the components/services can change.

Uncertainty: Uncertainty in Grid environment is caused by multiple factors, including (1) dynamism, which introduces unpredictable and changing behaviors that can only be detected and resolved at runtime, (2) failures, which have an increasing probability of occurrence and frequencies as system/application scales increase; and (3) incomplete knowledge of global system state, which is intrinsic to large decentralized and asynchronous distributed environments.

Security: A key attribute of Grids is flexible and secure hardware/software resource sharing across organization boundaries, which makes security (authentication, authorization and access control) and trust critical challenges in these environments.

2.2   Requirements for Grid Programming Systems

The characteristics listed above impose requirements on the programming systems for Grid applications. Grid programming systems must be able to specify applications which can detect and dynamically respond during execution to changes in both, the state of execution environment and the state and requirements of the application. This requirement suggests that: (1) Grid applications should be composed from discrete, self-managing components which incorporate separate specifications for all of functional, non-functional and interaction-coordination behaviors. (2) The specifications of computational (functional) behaviors, interaction and coordination behaviors and non-functional behaviors (e.g. performance, fault detection and recovery, etc.) should be separated so that their combinations are composable. (3) The interface definitions of these components should be separated from their implementations to enable heterogeneous components to interact and to enable dynamic selection of components.

Given these features of a programming system, a Grid application requiring a given set of computational behaviors may be integrated with different interaction and coordination models or languages (and vice versa) and different specifications for non-functional behaviors such as fault recovery and QoS to address the dynamism and heterogeneity of applications and the environment.

2.3   Grid Computing Research

Grid computing research efforts over the last decade can be broadly divided into efforts addressing the realization of virtual organizations and those addressing the development of Grid applications. The former set of efforts have focused on the definition and implementation of the core services that enable the specification, construction, operation and management of virtual organizations and instantiation of virtual machines that are the execution environments of Grid applications. Services include (1) security services to enable the establishment of secure relationships between a large number of dynamically created subjects and across a range of administrative domains, each with its own local security policy, (2) resource discovery services to enable discovery of hardware, software and information resources across the Grid, (3) resource management services to provide uniform and scalable mechanisms for naming and locating remote resources, support the initial registration/discovery and ongoing monitoring of resources, and incorporate these resources into applications, (4) job management services to enable the creation, scheduling, deletion, suspension, resumption, and synchronization of jobs, (5) data management services to enable accessing, managing, and transferring of data, and providing support for replica management and data filtering. Efforts in this class include Globus [2], Unicore [3], Condor [4] and Legion [5]. Other efforts in this class include the development of common APIs, toolkits and portals that provide high-level uniform and pervasive access to these services. These efforts include the Grid Application Toolkit (GAT) [6], DVC [7] and the Commodity Grid Kits (CoG Kits) [8]. These systems often incorporate programming models or capabilities for utilizing programs written in some distributed programming model. For example, Legion implements an object-oriented programming model, while Globus provides a capability for executing programs utilizing message passing.

The second class of research efforts, which is also the focus of this paper, deals with the formulation, programming and management of Grid applications. These efforts build on the Grid implementation services and focus on programming models, languages, tools and frameworks, and application runtime environments. Research efforts in this class include GrADS [9], GridRPC [10], GridMPI [11], Harness [12], Satin/IBIS [13] [14], XCAT [15] [16], Alua [17], G2 [18], J-Grid [19], Triana [20], and ICENI [21].

These systems have essentially built on, combined and extended existing models for parallel and distributed computing. For example, GridRPC extends the traditional RPC model to address system dynamism. It builds on Grid system services to combines resource discovery, authentication/authorization, resource allocation and task scheduling to remote invocations. Similarly, Harness and GridMPI build on the message passing parallel computing model, Satin supports divide-and-conquer parallelism on top of the IBIS communication system. GrADS builds on the object model and uses reconfigurable object and performance contracts to address Grid dynamics, XCAT and Alua extend the component based model. G2, J-Grid, Triana and ICENI build on various service based models. G2 builds on .Net [22], J-Grid builds on Jini [23] and current implementations of Tirana and ICENI build on JXTA [24]. While this is natural, it also implies that these systems implicitly inherit the assumptions and abstractions that underlie the programming models of the systems upon which they are based and thus in turn inherit their assumptions, capabilities and limitations.

2.4   Self-managing Applications on the Grid

As outlined above, the inherent scale, complexity, heterogeneity, and dynamism of emerging Grid environments result in application programming and runtime management complexities that break current paradigms. This is primarily because the programming models and the abstract machine underlying these models makes strong assumptions about common knowledge, static behaviors and system guarantees that cannot be realized by Grid virtual machines and which are not true for Grid applications. Addressing these challenges requires redefining the programming framework to address the separations outlined above. Specifically, it requires (1) static (defined at the time of instantiation) application requirements and system and application behaviors to be relaxed, (2) the behaviors of elements and applications to be sensitive to the dynamic state of the system and the changing requirements of the application and be able to adapt to these changes at runtime, (3) required common knowledge be expressed semantically (ontology and taxonomy) rather than in terms of names, addresses and identifiers, and (4) the core enabling middleware services (e.g., discovery, messaging) be driven by such a semantic knowledge. In the rest of this paper we describe Project AutoMate, which attempts to address these challenges by enabling autonomic self-managing Grid applications.

3   Project AutoMate: Enabling Self-managing Grid Applications

Project AutoMate [25] investigates autonomic solutions that are based on the strategies used by biological systems to deal with similar challenges of complexity, dynamism, heterogeneity and uncertainty. The goal is to realize systems and applications that are capable of managing (i.e., configuring, adapting, optimizing, protecting, healing) themselves. Project AutoMate aims at developing conceptual models and implementation architectures that can enable the development and execution of such self-managing Grid applications. Specifically, it investigates programming models, frameworks and middleware services that support the definition of autonomic elements, the development of autonomic applications as the dynamic and opportunistic composition of these autonomic elements, and the policy, content and context driven definition, execution and management of these applications.

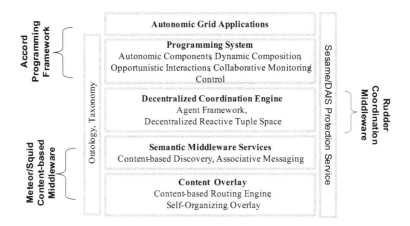

Fig. 1. A schematic overview of AutoMate.

A schematic overview of AutoMate is presented in Figure 1. Components of AutoMate include the Accord [26] programming system, the Rudder [27] decentralized coordination framework, and the Meteor [28] content-based middleware providing support for content-based routing, discovery and associative messaging. Project AutoMate additionally includes the Sesame [29] context-based access control infrastructure, the DAIS [30] cooperative-protection services and the Discover collaboratory [31, 32] services for collaborative monitoring, interaction and control, which are not described here.

3.1 Accord, a Programming Framework for Autonomic Applications

The Accord programming system [26] addresses Grid programming challenges by extending existing programming systems to enable autonomic Grid applications. Accord realizes three fundamental separations: (1) a separation of computations from coordination and interactions; (2) a separation of non-functional aspects (e.g. resource requirements, performance) from functional behaviors, and (3) a separation of policy and mechanism - policies in the form of rules are used to orchestrate a repertoire of mechanisms to achieve context-aware adaptive runtime computational behaviors and coordination and interaction relationships based on functional, performance, and QoS requirements. The components of Accord are described below.

Accord Programming Model: Accord extends existing distributed programming models, i.e., object, component and service based models, to support autonomic self-management capabilities. Specifically it extends the entities and composition rules defined by the underlying programming model to enable computational and composition/interaction behaviors to be defined at runtime using high-level rules. The resulting *autonomic elements* and their *autonomic composition* are described below. Note that other aspects of the programming model, i.e., operations, model of computation and rules for composition are inherited and maintained by Accord.

Autonomic Elements: An autonomic element extends programming elements (i.e., objects, components, services) to define a self-contained modular software unit with specified interfaces and explicit context dependencies. Additionally, an autonomic element encapsulates rules, constraints and mechanisms for self-management, and can dynamically interact with other elements and the system. An autonomic element is illustrated in Figure 2 and is defined by 3 ports:

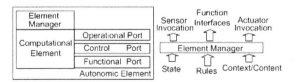

Fig. 2. An autonomic component

The **functional port** (Γ) defines a set of functional behaviors γ provided and used by the element. $\gamma \in \Omega \times \Lambda$, where Ω is the set of inputs and Λ is the set of outputs of the element, and γ defines a valid input-output set.

The **control port** ($\sum$) is the set of tuples (σ, ξ), where σ is a set of sensors and actuators exported by the element, and ξ is the constraint set that controls access to the sensors/actuators. Sensors are interfaces that provide information about the element while actuators are interfaces for modifying the state of the element. Constraints are based on state, context and/or high-level access polices.

The **operational port** (Θ) defines the interfaces to formulate, dynamically inject and manage rules that are used to manage the runtime behavior of the elements and the interactions between elements, between elements and their environments, and the coordination within an application.

Each autonomic element is associated with an element manager (possibly embedded) that is delegated to manage its execution. The element manager monitors the state of the element and its context, and controls the execution of rules. Note that element managers may cooperate with other element managers to fulfill application objectives.

Rules in Accord: Rules incorporate high-level guidance and practical human knowledge in the form of if-then expressions, i.e., IF *condition* THEN *action*, similar to production rule, case-based reasoning and expert systems. *Condition* is a logical combination of element (and environment) sensors, function interfaces and events. *Action* consists of a sequence of invocations of element actuators and/or system actuators, and other interfaces. A rule fires when its condition expression evaluates to be true and causes the corresponding actions to be executed. A priority based mechanism is used to resolve conflicts. Two classes of rules are defined: (1) *behavioral rules* that control the runtime functional behaviors of an autonomic element (e.g., the dynamic selection of algorithms, data representation, input/output format used by the element), and (2)*inter-action rules* that control the interactions between elements, between elements and their environment, and the coordination within an autonomic application (e.g., communication mechanism, composition and coordination of the elements). Note that behaviors and interactions expressed by these rules are defined by the model of computation and the rules for composition of the underlying programming model.

Behavioral rules are executed by an element manager embedded within a single element without affecting other elements. Interaction rules define interactions among elements. For each interaction pattern, a set of interaction rules are defined and dynamically injected into the corresponding elements. The coordinated execution of these rules results in the desired interaction and coordination behaviors between the elements.

Autonomic composition in Accord: Dynamic composition enables relationships between elements to be established and modified at runtime. Operationally, dynamic composition consists of a composition plan or workflow generation and execution. Plans may be created at runtime, possibly based on dynamically defined objectives, policies, and the context and content of applications and systems. Plan execution involves discovering elements, configuring them and defining interaction relationships and mechanisms. This may result in elements being added, replaced or removed or the interaction relationships between elements being changed.

In Accord, composition plans may be generated using the Accord Composition Engine (ACE) [33] or using other approaches, and are expressed in XML. Element discovery uses the Meteor content-based middleware and specifically the Squid discovery service [34]. Plan execution is achieved by a peer-to-peer control network of element managers and agents within Rudder [27]. A composition relationship between two elements is defined by the control structure (e.g., loop, branch) and/or the communication mechanism (e.g., RPC, shared-space) used. A composition agent translates this into a suite of interaction rules, which are then injected into corresponding element managers. Element managers execute the rules to establish control and communication relationships among these elements in a decentralized and parallel manner. Rules can be similarly used for addition or deletion of elements. Note that the interaction rules must be based on the core primitives provided by the system. Accord defines a library of rule sets for common control and communications relationships between elements. The decomposition procedure will guarantee that the local behaviors of individual elements will coordinate to achieve the application's objectives. Runtime negotiation protocols provided by Accord address runtime conflicts and conflicting decisions caused by a dynamic and uncertain environment.

Accord Implementation Issues: The Accord abstract machine assumes the existence of common knowledge in the form of an ontology and taxonomy that defines the semantics for specifying and describing application namespaces, element interfaces, sensors and actuators, and the context and content of systems and applications. This common semantics is used for formulating rules for autonomic management of elements and dynamic composition and interactions between the elements. Further, the abstract machine assumes time-asynchronous system behavior with fail-stop failure modes. Finally, Accord assumes the existence of an execution environment that provides (1) an agent-based control network, (2) support for associative coordination, (3) services for content-based discovery and messaging, (4) support of context-based access control and (4) services for constructing and managing virtual machines for a given virtual organization. These requirements are addressed respectively by Rudder, Meteor, Sesame/DAIS and the underlying Grid middleware on which it builds.

Accord decouples interaction and coordination from computation, and enables both these behaviors to be managed at runtime using rules. This enables autonomic elements to change their behaviors, and to dynamically establish/terminate/change interaction relationships with other elements. Deploying and executing rules does impact performance, however, it increases the robustness of the applications and their ability to manage dynamism. Further, our observations indicate that the runtime changes to interaction relationships are infrequent and their overheads are relatively small. As a result, the time spent to establish and modify interaction relationships is small as compared to typical computation times. A prototype implementation and evaluation of its performance overheads is presented in [35, 36].

3.2   Rudder Coordination Framework

Rudder [27] is a scalable coordination middleware for supporting self-managing applications in decentralized distributed environments. The goal of Rudder is to provide the core capabilities for supporting autonomic compositions, adaptations, and optimizations. Rudder consists of two key components: (1) COMET, a fully decentralized coordination substrate that enables flexible and scalable coordination among agents and autonomic elements, and (2) an agent framework composed of software agents and agent interaction and negotiation protocols. The adaptiveness and sociableness of software agents provides an effective mechanism for managing individual autonomic elements and their relationships in an adaptive manner. This mechanism enables appropriate application behaviors to be dynamically negotiated and enacted by adapting classical machine learning, control, and optimization models and theories. The COMET substrate provides the core messaging and eventing services for connecting agent networks and scalably supporting various agent interactions, such as mutual exclusion, consensus, and negotiation. Rudder effectively supports the Accord programming framework and enables autonomic self-managing applications.

The COMET Substrate: COMET provides a global virtual shared coordination space associatively accessible by all peer agents, and the access is independent of the physical location of the tuples or identifiers of the host. The virtual coordination space builds on an associative messaging substrate and implements a distributed hash table, where the index space is directly generated from the semantic information space (ontology) used by the coordinating entities. COMET also supports dynamically constructed, transient spaces to enable context locality to be explicitly exploited for improved performance.

COMET consists of layered abstractions prompted by a fundamental separation of communication and coordination concerns. It provides an associative communication abstraction and guarantees that content-based query messages, specified using flexible content descriptors, are fully served with bounded costs. This layer essentially maps the virtual information space in a deterministic way to the dynamic set of currently available peer nodes in the system, while maintaining content locality. The COMET coordination abstraction extends the traditional data-driven coordination model with event-based reactivity to changes in system state and data access operations. It defines a reactive tuple abstraction, which consists of additional components: a *condition* that associates *reaction* to events, and a *guard* that specifies how and when the reaction will be executed (e.g., immediately, once). The *condition* is evaluated on an access event. If it evaluates to true, the corresponding reaction is executed. The COMET coordination abstraction provides the basic Linda-like primitives, such as Out, In, and Rd. These basic operations operate on regular as well as reactive tuples and retain their Linda semantics.

The Agent Framework: The Rudder agent framework is composed of a dynamic network of software agents existing at different levels, ranging from individual system/application elements to the overall system/application. Agents monitor the element states, manage element behaviors and dependencies, coordinate element interactions, and cooperate to manage overall system/application behaviors. An agent is a processing unit that perform actions based on rules, which are dynamically defined to satisfy system/application requirements. Further, agents use profiles which are used to identify and describe elements, interact with them and control them. A profile consists of a set of (functional and non-functional) attributes and operators, which are semantically defined using an application-specific ontology. The framework additionally defines a set of protocols for agent coordination and application/system management. Discovery protocols support the registering, unregistering, and discovery of system/application elements. Control protocols allow the agents to query element states, control their behaviors and orchestrate their interactions. These protocols include negotiation, notification, and mutual exclusion. The agent coordination protocol are scalably and robustly implemented in using the abstractions and service provided by COMET. COMET builds on an associative communication middleware, Meteor, which is described below.

3.3   Meteor: A Content-Based Middleware

Meteor [28] is a scalable content-based middleware infrastructure that provides services for content routing, content discovery and associative interactions. The Meteor stack consists of 3 key components: (1) a self-organizing content overlay, (2) a content-based routing engine and discovery service (Squid), and (3) the Associative Rendezvous Messaging Substrate (ARMS). The Meteor overlay is composed of Rendezvous Peer (RP) nodes, which may be any node on the Grid (e.g., gateways, access points, message relay nodes, servers or end-user computers). RP nodes can join or leave the network at any time. The content overlay provides a single operation, *lookup(identifier)*, which requires an exact content identifier (e.g., name). Given an identifier, this operation locates the peer node where the content should be stored or fetched.

Squid [34] is the Meteor content-based routing engine and decentralized information discovery service. It supports flexible content-based routing and complex queries containing partial keywords, wildcards, and ranges. Squid guarantees that all existing data elements that match a query will be found. The key innovation of Squid is the use of a locality preserving and dimension reducing indexing scheme, based on the Hilbert Space Filling Curve (SFC), which effectively maps the multidimensional information space to the peer identifier space. Keywords can be common words or values of globally defined attributes, depending on the nature of the application that uses Squid, and are based on common ontologies and taxonomies.

The ARMS layer [28] implements the Associative Rendezvous (AR) interaction paradigm. AR is a paradigm for content-based decoupled interactions with programmable reactive behaviors. Rendezvous-based interactions provide a mechanism for decoupling senders and receivers, in both space and time. Such decoupled asynchronous interactions are naturally suited for large, distributed, and highly dynamic systems such as pervasive Grid environments. AR extends the conventional name/identifier-based rendezvous in two ways. First, it uses flexible combinations of keywords (i.e, keyword, partial keyword, wildcards and ranges) from a semantic information space, instead of opaque identifiers (names, addresses) that have to be globally known. Interactions are based on content described by these keywords. Second, it enables the reactive behaviors at the rendezvous points to be encapsulated within messages, therefore increasing flexibility and enabling multiple interaction semantics (e.g., broadcast multicast, notification, publisher/subscriber, mobility, etc.).

3.4   Current Status

The core components of AutoMate have been prototyped and are currently being used to enable self-managing applications in science and engineering. The initial prototype of Accord extended an object-oriented framework based on C++ and MPI. The current implementation extends the DoE Common Component Architecture (CCA) [37] and we are working on extending an OGSA-based programming system. Current prototypes of Rudder and Meteor build on the JXTA [24] platform and use existing Grid middleware services. Current applications include autonomic oil reservoir optimizations [31, 38], autonomic forest-fire management [39], autonomic runtime management of adaptive simulations [40], and enabling sensor-based pervasive applications [28]. The first two application are briefly described below. Further information about AutoMate and its components and applications can be obtained from http://automate.rutgers.edu/.

4   Autonomic Grid Applications

4.1   Autonomic Oil-Reservoir Optimization

One of the fundamental problems in oil reservoir production is determining the optimal locations of the oil production and injection wells. However, the selection of appropriate optimization algorithms, the runtime configuration and invocation of these algorithms and the dynamic optimization of the reservoir remains a challenging problem. In this research we use AutoMate to support autonomic aggregations, compositions and interactions and enable an autonomic self-optimizing reservoir application. The application consists of: (1) sophisticated reservoir simulation components that encapsulate complex mathematical models of the physical interaction in the subsurface, and execute on distributed computing systems on the Grid; (2) Grid services that provide secure and coordinated access to the resources required by the simulations; (3) distributed data archives that store historical, experimental and observed data; (4) sensors embedded in the instrumented oilfield providing real-time data about the current state of the oil field; (5) external services that provide data relevant to optimization of oil production or of the economic profit such as current weather information or current prices; and (6) the actions of scientists, engineers and other experts, in the field, the laboratory, and in management offices.

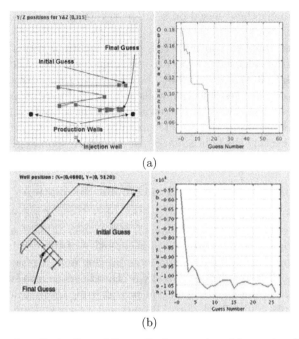

(a)

(b)

Fig. 3. Autonomic optimization of the well placement problem using (a) VFSA algorithm (b) SPSA algorithm

The main components of the autonomic reservoir framework [31, 38] are (i) instances of distributed multi-model, multi-block reservoir simulation components, (ii) optimization services based on the Very Fast Simulated Annealing (VFSA) [31] and Simultaneous Perturbation Stochastic Approximation (SPSA) [38], (iii) economic modeling services, (iv) real-time services providing current economic data (e.g. oil prices) and , (v) archives of data that has already been computed, and (vi) experts (scientists, engineers) connected via pervasive collaborative portals.

The overall oil production process is autonomic in that the peers involved automatically detect sub-optimal oil production behaviors at runtime and orchestrate interactions among themselves to correct this behavior. Further, the detection and optimization process is achieved using policies and constraints that minimize human intervention. Policies are used to discover, select, configure, and invoke appropriate optimization services to determine optimal well locations. For example, the choice of optimization service depends on the size and nature of the reservoir. The SPSA algorithm is suited for larger reservoirs with relatively smooth characteristics. In case of reservoirs with many randomly distributed maxima and minima, the VFSA algorithm can be employed during the initial optimization phase. Once convergence slows down, VFSA can be replaced by SPSA. Similarly, policies can also be used to manage the behavior of the reservoir simulator, or may be defined to enable various optimizers to execute concurrently on dynamically acquired Grid resources, and select the best well location among these based on some metric (e.g., estimated revenue, time or cost of completion).

Figure 3 illustrates the optimization of well locations using the VFSA and SPSA optimization algorithms for two different scenarios. The well positions plots (on the left in 3(a) and (b)) show the oil field and the positions of the wells. Black circles represent fixed injection wells and a gray square at the bottom of the plot is a fixed production well. The plots also show the sequence of guesses for the position of the other production well returned by the optimization service (shown by the lines connecting the light squares), and the corresponding normalized cost value (plots on the right in 3(a) and (b)).

4.2   Autonomic Forest Fire Management Simulation

The autonomic forest fire simulation, composed of *DSM (Data Space Manager)*, *CRM (Computational Resource Manager)*, *Rothermel*, *WindModel*, and *GUI elements*, predicts the speed, direction and intensity of the fire front as the fire propagates using static and dynamic environment and vegetation conditions. *DSM* partitions the forest represented by a 2D data space into sub spaces based on current system resources information provided by *CRM*. Under the circumstance of load imbalance, *DSM* re-partitions the data space. *Rothermel* generates processes to simulate the fire spread on each subspace in parallel based on current wind direction and intensity simulated by the *WindModel*, until no *burning* cells remain. Experts interact with the above elements using the *GUI* element.

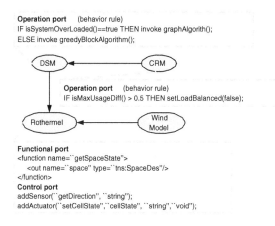

Fig. 4. Examples of the port definition and rules

We use the *Rothermel*, *DSM*, and *CRM* as examples to illustrate the definition of the Accord functional, control and operational ports, as shown in Figure 4. *Rothermel*, for example, provides *getSpaceState* to expose space information as part of its **Functional Port**, and provides the sensor *getDirection* to get the fire spread direction and the actuator *setCellState* to modify the state of a

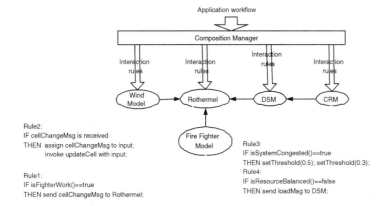

Fig. 5. Add a new component *Fire Fighter Model* and change the interaction relationship between *CRM* and *DSM*

specified cell as part of its **Control Port**. The *DSM* and *CRM* receive rules to manage their runtime behaviors through the **Operation Port**.

Behavior rules can be defined at compile time or at runtime and injected into corresponding element managers to dynamically manage the computational behaviors of elements. As illustrated in Figure 4, *DSM* dynamically selects an appropriate algorithm based on the current system load and *CRM* will detect load imbalance when the maximal difference among resource usage exceeds the threshold according to the behavior rules shown.

The application workflow is decomposed by the *Composition Manager* into interaction rules, which are injected into individual elements. Therefore, addition, deletion and replacement of elements can be achieved using corresponding interaction rules. For example, a new element, *Fire Fighter Model*, modelling the behaviors of the fire fighters, is added to the application as shown in Figure 5, by inserting Rule1 into *Fire Fighter Model* and Rule2 into *Rothermel*. Similarly, changing an interaction relationship can be achieved by replacing the existing interaction rules with new rules. As shown in Figure 5, *CRM* dynamically decreases the frequency of notifications to *DSM* when the communication network is congested based on Rule3 and Rule4.

5   Conclusion

In this paper, we presented Project AutoMate and described its key components. Project AutoMate investigates solutions that are based on the strategies used by biological systems to deal with similar challenges of complexity, dynamism, heterogeneity and uncertainty. This approach, referred to as Autonomic Computing, aims at realizing systems and applications that are capable of managing (i.e., configuring, adapting, optimizing, protecting, healing) themselves. The overall goal of Project AutoMate is to investigate conceptual models and implementation architectures that can enable the development and execution of such self-managing Grid applications. Specifically, it investigates programming models, frameworks and middleware services that support the definition of autonomic elements, the development of autonomic applications as the dynamic and opportunistic composition of these autonomic elements, and the policy, content and context driven definition, execution and management of these applications. Two case-study applications, autonomic oil reservoir optimization and autonomic forest fire management, enabled by AutoMate were also presented.

References

1. Parashar, M., Browne, J.C.: Conceptual and implementation models for the grid. Proceedings of the IEEE, Special Issue on Grid Computing (2005)
2. The globus alliance, http://www.globus.org.
3. Unicore forum, http://www.unicore.org.
4. Thain, D., Tannenbaum, T., Livny, M.: Condor and the Grid. John Wiley & Sons Inc. (2002)
5. Grimshaw, A.S., Wulf, W.A.: The legion vision of a worldwide virtual computer. Communications of the ACM **40** (1997) 39 – 45
6. Allen, G., Davis, K., Dolkas, K.N., Doulamis, N.D., Goodale, T., Kielmann, T., Merzky, A., Nabrzyski, J., Pukacki, J., Radke, T., Russell, M., Seidel, E., Shalf, J., Taylor, I.: Enabling applications on the grid: A Gridlab overview. International Journal of High Performance Computing Applications: Special issue on Grid Computing: Infrastructure and Applications (2003) to appear
7. Taesombut, N., Chien, A.: Distributed virtual computer (dvc): Simplifying the development of high performance grid applications. In: Workshop on Grids and Advanced Networks (GAN '04), IEEE Cluster Computing and the Grid (CCGrid2004) Conference, Chicago, IL USA (2004)
8. Laszewski, G.v., Foster, I., Gawor, J.: Cog kits: A bridge between commodity distributed computing and high-performance grids. In: ACM 2000 Conference on Java Grande, San Francisco, CA USA, ACM Press (2000) 97 – 106
9. Berman, F., Chien, A., Cooper, K., Dongarra, J., Foster, I., Gannon, D., Johnsson, L., Kennedy, K., Kesselman, C., Mellor-Crummey, J., Reed, D., Torczon, L., Wolski, R.: The grads project: Software support for high-level grid application development. International Journal of High Performance Computing Applications **15** (2001) 327–344
10. Nakada, H., Matsuoka, S., Seymour, K., Dongarra, J., Lee, C., Casanova, H.: Gridrpc: A remote procedure call api for grid computing (2003)
11. Ishikawa, Y., Matsuda, M., Kudoh, T., Tezuka, H., Sekiguchi, S.: The design of a latency-aware mpi communication library. In: Proceedings of SWOPP03. (2003)
12. Migliardi, M., Sunderam, V.: The harness metacomputing framework. In: Proceedings of ninth SIAM Conference on Parallel Processing for Scientific Computing, San Antonio, TX, SIAM (1999)
13. Nieuwpoort, R.V.v., Maassen, J., Wrzesinska, G., Kielmann, T., Bal, H.E.: Satin: Simple and efficient java-based grid programming. Journal of Parallel and Distributed Computing Practices (2004)
14. Nieuwpoort, R.V.v., Maassen, J., Wrzesinska, G., Hofman, R., Jacobs, C., Kielmann, T., Bal, H.E.: Ibis: A flexible and efficient java-based grid programming environment. (Concurrency & Computation: Practice & Experience)

15. Govindaraju, M., Krishnan, S., Chiu, K., Slominski, A., Gannon, D., Bramley, R.: Xcat 2.0: A component-based programming model for grid web services. Technical Report Technical Report-TR562, Dept. of C.S., Indiana Univ (2002)
16. Krishnan, S., Gannon, D.: Xcat3: A framework for cca components as ogsa services. In: Proceedings of HIPS 2004, 9th International Workshop on High-Level Parallel Programming Models and Supportive Environments. (2004)
17. Ururahy, C., Rodriguez, N.: Programming and coordinating grid environments and applications. In: Concurrency and Computation: Practice and Experience. Number 5 (2004)
18. Kelly, W., Roe, P., Sumitomo, J.: G2: A grid middleware for cycle donation using .net. In: Proceedings of The 2002 International Conference on Parallel and Distributed Processing Techniques and Applications. (2002)
19. Mathe, J., Kuntner, K., Pota, S., Juhasz, Z.: The use of jini technology in distributed and grid multimedia systems. In: MIPRO 2003, Hypermedia and Grid Systems, Opatija, Croatia (2003) 148–151
20. Taylor, I., Shields, M., Wang, I., Philp, R.: Distributed p2p computing within triana: A galaxy visualization test case. In: International Parallel and Distributed Processing Symposium (IPDPS'03), Nice, France, IEEE Computer Society Press (2003)
21. Furmento, N., Hau, J., Lee, W., Newhouse, S., Darlington, J.: Implementations of a service-oriented architecture on top of jini, jxta and ogsa. In: Proceedings of UK e-Science All Hands Meeting. (2003)
22. Microsoft .net. (http://www.microsoft.com/net/)
23. Jini network technology. (http://wwws.sun.com/software/jini/)
24. Project jxta. http://www.jxta.org (2001)
25. Agarwal, M., Bhat, V., Li, Z., Liu, H., Matossian, V., Putty, V., Schmidt, C., Zhang, G., Parashar, M., Khargharia, B., Hariri, S.: Automate: Enabling autonomic applications on the grid. In: Autonomic Computing Workshop The Fifth Annual International Workshop on Active Middleware Services (AMS 2003), Seattle, WA USA (2003) 365–375
26. Liu, H., Parashar, M., Hariri, S.: A component-based programming framework for autonomic applications. In: 1st IEEE International Conference on Autonomic Computing (ICAC-04), New York, NY, USA, IEEE Computer Society Press (2004) 278 – 279
27. Li, Z., Parashar, M.: Rudder: A rule-based multi-agent infrastructure for supporting autonomic grid applications. In: 1st IEEE International Conference on Autonomic Computing (ICAC-04), New York, NY, USA, IEEE Computer Society Press (2004) 278 – 279
28. Jiang, N., Schmidt, C., Matossian, V., Parashar, M.: Content-based decoupled interactions in pervasive grid environments. In: First Workshop on Broadband Advanced Sensor Networks, BaseNets'04, San Jose, California (2004)
29. Zhang, G., Parashar, M.: Dynamic context-aware access control for grid applications. In: 4th International Workshop on Grid Computing (Grid 2003), Phoenix, AZ, USA, IEEE Computer Society Press (2003) 101 – 108
30. Zhang, G., Parashar, M.: Cooperative mechanism against ddos attacks. In: IEEE International Conference on Information and Computer Science (ICICS 2004), Dhahran, Saudi Arabia (2004)
31. Bhat, V., Matossian, V., Parashar, M., Peszynska, M., Sen, M., Stoffa, P., Wheeler, M.F.: Autonomic oil reservoir optimization on the grid. Concurrency and Computation: Practice and Experience, John Wiley and Sons (2003)

32. Mann, V., Matossian, V., Muralidhar, R., Parashar, M.: DISCOVER: An environment for Web-based interaction and steering of high-performance scientific applications. Concurrency and Computation: Practice and Experience **13** (2001) 737–754

33. Agarwal, M., Parashar, M.: Enabling autonomic compositions in grid environments. In: 4th International Workshop on Grid Computing (Grid 2003), Phoenix, AZ, USA, IEEE Computer Society Press (2003) 34 – 41

34. Schmidt, C., Parashar, M.: Enabling flexible queries with guarantees in p2p systems. IEEE Internet Computing **8** (2004) 19 – 26

35. Liu, H.: A component-based programming framework for autonomic grid applications. Ph.D. Proposal (2004)

36. Liu, H., Parashar, M.: Rule-based monitoring and steering of distributed scientific application. International Journal of High Performance Computing and Networking (IJHPCN) (2005)

37. Allan, B.A., Armstrong, R.C., Wolfe, A.P., Ray, J., Bernholdt, D.E., Kohl, J.A.: The cca core specifications in a distributed memory spmd framework. Concurrency and Computing:Practice and Experience, John Wiley and Sons **14** (2002) 323 – 345

38. Matossian, V., Parashar, M., Bangerth, W., Klie, H., Wheeler, M.: An autonomic reservoir framework for the stochastic optimization of well placement. Cluster Computing: The Journal of Networks, Software Tools, and Applications, Special Issue on Autonomic Computing, Kluwer Academic Press (to appear)

39. Khargharia, B., Hariri, S., Parashar, M.: vgrid: A framework for building autonomic applications. In: 1st International Workshop on Heterogeneous and Adaptive Computing– Challenges of Large Applications in Distributed Environments (CLADE 2003), Seattle, WA, USA, Computer Society Press (2003) 19–26

40. Chandra, S., Parashar, M., Hariri, S.: Gridarm: An autonomic runtime management framework for samr applications in grid environments. In: New Frontiers in High-Performance Computing, Proceedings of the Autonomic Applications Workshop, 10th International Conference on High Performance Computing (HiPC 2003). Elite Publishing, Hyderabad, India (2003) 286 – 295

Pandora: An Efficient Platform for the Construction of Autonomic Applications

Simon Patarin[1] and Mesaac Makpangou[2]

[1] University of Bologna,
Computer Science Department,
Bologna, Italy
patarin@cs.unibo.it
[2] INRIA Rocquencourt,
Regal Group,
Rocquencourt, France
mesaac.makpangou@inria.fr

Abstract. Autonomic computing has been proposed recently as a way to address the difficult management of applications whose complexity is constantly increasing. Autonomic systems will have to diagnose the problems they face themselves, devise solutions and act accordingly. In consequence, they require a very high level of flexibility and the ability to constantly monitor themselves. This work presents a framework, Pandora, which eases the construction of applications that satisfy this double goal. Pandora relies on an original application programming pattern — based on stackable layers and message passing — to obtain a minimalist model and architecture that allows control of the overhead imposed by the full reflexivity of the framework. A prototype of the framework has been implemented in C++, freely available for download on the Internet. A detailed performance study is given, together with examples of use, to assess the usability of the platform in real usage conditions.

1   Introduction

Large-scale distributed applications are being more and more used. Content-delivery networks, computing grids, peer-to-peer file-sharing systems, distributed hash tables, ubiquitous systems: there are many examples and the list keeps growing. The environment in which these applications are deployed, Internet, is characterized by its heterogeneity, the rapid evolution of its various components (hardware, software, but also human) and its lack of reliability. The diversity of the platforms makes it especially difficult to configure these applications. Even if this first step is completed successfully, changes and failures may disturb those choices and annihilate previous efforts. It is then required to ease these operations by automating them as much as possible. Those observations are at the origin of the development of autonomic computing [1]. Its objective is to let the applications diagnose themselves the problems they are facing and solve them without any external intervention. Of course, issues to be addressed are

O. Babaoglu et al. (Eds.): SELF-STAR 2004, LNCS 3460, pp. 291–306, 2005.

numerous before reaching a satisfying solution. Here, we focus on one of them: the necessary system support for the development of such autonomic applications.

It is possible to identify several features that must be provided by a platform enabling the construction of autonomic applications. The first and most important one deals with the flexibility of the applications. It is useless to imagine an application being autonomic if it cannot be modified and reconfigured dynamically. Numerous kinds of reconfiguration may be considered, and all of them will have to be supported: from the simple parameterization, to the addition of non-functional properties likely to drastically change the behavior of the application. Besides, the application itself is often the best candidate to collect the measurements that allow the analyze of its own behavior. The platform must then provide the required mechanisms to disseminate these measurements. It must also ease the interactions among the different components of the system: in particular, the platform should be reflexive [2, 3] to give access to the application current state and observed measurements.

This flexibility that we require should not hinder the performance. This, however, has not been the approach chosen in current systems where only one of those properties is developed, but not both. Thus, in the case of platforms specifically tailored for the development of autonomic applications (e.g. AutoPilot [4] or AutoMate [5]), application flexibility (and hence reconfiguration possibilities) has not been emphasized and is insufficiently developed to address the diversity of application needs that we anticipate. At the opposite, in the domains of aspect programming [6] or component systems [7], a high flexibility is provided to the applications built but overheads are introduced that greatly impact the achieved level of performance.

The approach we propose to address this problem builds on an original compromise. We put forward an alternative programming model instead of imposing the use of interpreted language or sacrificing the provided flexibility. This model consists in the stacking of independent components that communicate by exchanging messages. This approach, which — to the best of our knowledge — has never been applied in this context, is not new and several projects have experimented with it, emphasizing its usefulness and expressiveness. Among the first works in this domain are x-Kernel [8] and Ficus [9] (an operating system and a framework for building file systems, respectively). More recently, two new architecture have been proposed: a modular router, Click [10], and SEDA [11] that allows to build efficient Internet services. While most legacy systems provides flexibility through low-level instrumentation (typically at the level of procedure calls), this programming model allows the definition of a custom intervention degree through the choice of component granularity. The platform presented, Pandora, builds upon these techniques and provides a reflexive interface that allows individual components and external applications to dynamically reconfigure the entire system.

We are now going to present (Section 2) some related work pertaining to this study. We describe next the architecture model proposed by Pandora (Section 3). Deployment, execution and control of the applications built on top of it are presented next (Section 4). Next, the platform implementation and some examples of use of the prototype are described (Section 5). An evaluation of the performance of Pandora (Section 6) and a few concluding remarks (Section 7) finish this paper.

2   Related Work

As mentioned before, there exist some platforms that pursue objectives comparable to ours. We are going to detail their characteristics in a first step. Then, we are going to look at software engineering techniques that relates to the approach we have followed for the design of Pandora. Specifically, we will consider component systems and aspect-oriented programming.

2.1   Autonomic Application Platforms

Platforms explicitly dedicated to the construction of autonomic applications are very few. The originality of AutoPilot [4] comes from its work on the definition of sensors and the means to access them efficiently. Those same sensors are used "back way" (to write a value, instead of reading it) to modify the application parameterization. This is however the only reconfiguration feature provided by the platform. Accord [12] and its predecessor AutoMate [5] target applications deployed on grid computing systems. Both were built on top of DIOS [13] for the construction of objects provided with sensors and actuators that allow them to be parameterized dynamically. The main originality of this platform comes from the specification of a language and of a rule execution engine that allow reconfiguration triggering in response to captured events. Unity [14] also targets grid applications. It promotes the use of "autonomic elements" and provides a platform designed to help these elements interact with each others and their environment. In its current state, however, monitoring facilities are rather limited (polling values from OGSA [15] compatible services) and reconfiguration is not supported by the platform itself (it is left to each element to devise their own strategy).

This rapid panorama of autonomic computing platform shows the limits of the reconfiguration mechanisms provided to applications. Dynamic parameterization consists, at best, in choosing between alternative implementations among a set predefined functionalities. Extensibility and modification of non-functional properties are barely addressed.

2.2   Software Engineering Techniques

This limited flexibility of existing platforms leads us to consider the approaches currently in use to address this issue. Two kinds of techniques are clearly put forward: component systems and aspect-oriented programming.

Component Systems. Legacy component systems — .NET, CCM (Corba Component Model) and EJB (Enterprise Java Beans) — are actually rather poorly adapted to the design of flexible architectures. Coarse component granularity, static component binding, and the limited predefined set of non-functional properties provided by the component containers contribute largely to this fact. This has lead to the development of more lightweight systems, with higher performance. Thus, the OpenCOM [7] platform (that builds on the COM component model) allows for both component and bindings dynamic reconfiguration. This is made possible by a fully reflexive interface that enables the platform to access the entire state of the system (the component graph).

The approach followed by Gravity [16] is more original. Each component publishes a list of interfaces it provides and a list of those it requires. As components get in and out of the system, bindings are dynamically established so that all dependencies are satisfied. For our purposes, the main limitation of this technique is the lack of support for "simple" reconfigurations, like the modification of a single parameter value.

Aspect-Oriented Programming. Aspect-oriented programming [6] promotes separation of concerns. Cross-cutting functionalities that are common to several modules of the same program are isolated (those are the *aspects*) and "weaved" with the rest of the application at compile-time or at run-time. The flexibility of these architectures comes from the relative independence between the various entities involved (modules and aspects). It is then possible to modify any of them without disturbing the other elements of the program.

The JAC [17] (Java Aspect Components) platform is the one that is closer to our objectives. In this case, aspects are encapsulated inside components and weaved at run-time (which allows dynamic reconfiguration). These components are also statically configurable to adapt diverse environments. The main limitation of this platform is the lack of support for the reconfiguration of the modules themselves (those whose functionalities cannot be seen as aspects).

3   Architecture Model for Autonomic Applications

Pandora proposes an original architecture model to build autonomic applications. This model builds upon the notion of component and event-based communication to provide the flexibility and the adaptability required by such applications.

3.1   Fine-Grained Independent Components

Autonomic applications are usually considered to be made of a set of relatively independent modules [18]. Each module is supposed to be able to configure itself, detect problems when they occur, and — ideally — solve them. Naturally, all these decisions depend on the state of the system as a whole and modules cooperate with and monitor each other. In the most recent platforms [12, 14] modules are the smallest entities manipulated by the system.

We believe, however, that there are advantages in considering a finer subdivision of modules. In each module, both "business" logic and "autonomic" logic are present. These two aspects are very different by nature and should be clearly separated from each other. Moreover, a large part of the autonomic logic is generic (threshold triggered alarms, rule processing engine, etc.) and could be reused in different modules. Even business code benefits from being further divided into smaller, cleanly bounded, entities. Having an intermediate granularity (coarser than raw instructions and finer than modules), such entities are much easier to monitor. With adequate support from the platform, the programmer is able to easily indicate what are the meaningful variables to monitor and which are the means to modify the component behavior. Besides, parts of the business code consists in the implementation of non-functional properties (the cross-cutting concerns identified by the aspect-oriented programming community) that are essentially reusable from one module to another.

These considerations have led us to propose an architecture model for autonomic applications based on three layers:

1. *components*: components are the basic and self-contained building blocks in the system. Functional and non-functional business code, as well as autonomic machinery, are encapsulated within these objects.
2. *stacks*: components are assembled to form stacks. A stack defines the nature of components to be used and the order in which they are chained. This corresponds to the notion of modules we have mentioned previously.
3. *tasks*: cooperating stacks form a task, which matches the notion of an application, made of several cooperating modules.

Interactions between these three elements are summarized in Figure 1.

Besides, each component may specify a set of parameters, that we name *options*, identified by their name and whose value can be configured at run-time to adapt the behavior of the component. These options may be of different types (numerical, boolean and character strings). However, we cannot represent every parameter type with such basic types (e.g. file handles, set of values, etc.). This is why the model makes it possible to associate a specific pre-processing step before the parameter is given to the component (e.g. transforming a literal host

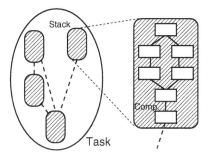

Fig. 1. Interactions between Pandora's elements. Tasks (applications) are made of loosely-coupled stacks (modules). Stacks are made of tightly-coupled components

name into a numerical IP address). Having this step performed outside of the component avoids paying the overhead of these transformations each time a new component instance is created.

The entire independence of the components is an important characteristic of the model, and it is worth considering its implications. A component ignores totally the context in which it is going to be used and interactions with other components are made anonymously. Thus, the reusability of the component is strongly guaranteed. However, the main benefit of this aspect of the model for autonomic applications is simply the very absence of (explicit or hidden) inter-dependencies between components. This helps simplifying the traditionally hard problem of the dynamic reconfiguration of the application. In this case, each component may be safely adapted and modified without having to fear breaking other components that would depend on him. It must be noted that the problem is simplified, not solved, as the component continues to interact with others and radically modifying its behavior might still impact its peers.

The specification of the chaining of components within stacks, together with their initial parameterization, is made through a dedicated language. In order to ease its usage and comprehension by the platform end-users, a compact stack representation has been preferred. However, it would have been possible to use graph description languages (such as `dot` [19]) or markup languages (such as XML) to achieve similar results. It is beyond the scope of this paper to explain it in details, a full description is available in a previous work [20].

3.2   Event-Based Interactions

Components need to interact with each other. In most legacy component models, communication is performed through direct procedure invocations. This establishes a two-way communication channel: the caller chooses the actual method to call and its arguments and, in the other direction, the callee chooses the value to return. However, our component model uses one-way event-passing communication.

Following this approach offers several advantages. The first one is its conceptual simplicity, which contributes largely to the reduction of the component complexity. A component needs only to define a single interface, the one used to receive an event. This also contributes to the flexibility, the extensibility and the modularity of the platform, which is a primary concern when dealing with autonomic applications. Components may be easily inserted within an established event flow, either to modify it, or, at the opposite to provide, non-functional properties to the whole stack. This could not be easily achieved with an interface-based design. In the latter case, such a generic component would need to implement a large set of interfaces to be composed with all other existing components. When components are added or removed, generic ones should be modified.

By favoring the independence of the components, this communication model is complimentary to the component model we have chosen and helps reinforcing its objectives of flexibility and reusability.

Event forwarding between components is one-way, synchronous, and operates in continuous flow. This means that two components, once the communication is established, are durably connected to each other. At the opposite, communications between stacks, seen as a whole, are asynchronous: events are buffered and consumed whenever the receiving stack decides to do so. It must be noted that a stack, in itself, does not "communicate" with another stack. Rather it is a component that chooses to send an event to a stack, rather than to a component. Similarly, an event sent to a stack is actually processed by a specific component in that stack. Having both communication modes available lets the developer freely choose the best compromise for its application. The number of stacks in the system is not limited and it is perfectly legal to encapsulate a single component within a stack. Synchronous communications are much more efficient (in terms of performance) than asynchronous ones. This is easily explained by the fact that asynchronous communications provide thread-safe buffering support, while synchronous ones obviously do not. Another parameter to take into consideration when choosing between these two modes is that inter-component communications are anonymous, while inter-stack ones are named. Being entirely stand-alone, a component cannot choose which components to communicate with. This is entirely determined in the stack configuration. In the general case, a component willing to transmit an event transmits it to its successor, without knowing its identity. At the opposite, stacks are named (different instances of the same stack are identified by a unique handle or an explicit alias), and a component chooses the name of the stack it wants to communicate with.

Each component has a single input port and an arbitrary number of output ports. The usual case for a component is to have one output port. For those with several output ports, two (mutually exclusive) possibilities exist:

1. *switch*: switch ports are identified by a rank number and it is possible to configure the stack so that components of different nature correspond to each port. This matches roughly the *switch* statement found in most imperative

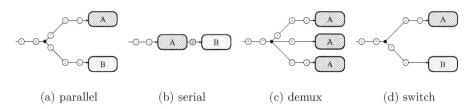

(a) parallel   (b) serial   (c) demux   (d) switch

Fig. 2. Representation of the different component connections modes. Event are represented by a circle and uniquely identified by a rank number (events with the same number are then identical). In parallel mode, each event is sent to all components. In serial mode, components are chained linearly, events sequentially flows from one component to the next one. In demux mode, events are demultiplexed and sent to the component instance that handles the category they belong to. In switch mode, events are sent to one of several alternative components

programming languages. The choice of the branch in which to forward a specific event is determined by the component itself according to its internal logic.

2. *demultiplexing*: demultiplexing ports allow a component to classify events. As soon as a new category is identified, a new port is dynamically created, while events belonging to an existing category are forwarded to the port with which it had been previously associated. All demultiplexing branches are of the same nature (components of the same type are found in the same order) but made of distinct component instances.

This leads to a wide range of possible component connections when constructing a stack which are summarized and illustrated in Figure 2.

In modes that create multiple branches (i.e. all but *serial*), the actual length and definition of the branches is specified in the stack definition. Events flowing out of related branches (that is, those stemming from the same branch point) are naturally merged in the input of the next component in the stack.

3.3   Flexibility and Reconfiguration

Systems manipulated by Pandora exhibit two degrees of flexibility: first, in component parameterization and, second, in the chaining of these components. Parameterization flexibility relates to option usage to modify variables at run-time: this is rather classical. However, its impact may be of great importance as it is possible to use options to specify an alternative demultiplexing algorithm or change an output port in a switch component, modifying the behavior of the whole application.

The second degree of flexibility exposed by Pandora lies in the specification of component chaining (the stack definition). When several components providing different implementations of the same functionality are available, this allows to choose the solution that best fits the current environment (algorithms trading CPU utilization for memory utilization are quite common). Moreover, the model authorizes (and even promotes) using non-functional components. Their insertion in the stack does not modify the general behavior of the system but might alter the way further events are processed or induce side-effects. One can mention the examples of components managing the balance of processing stages across several machines, the persistence of events they receive, application monitoring, failure detection, synchronization, etc. This last issue is very close to the approach followed in aspect-oriented programming: by modifying the application (components in the original definition), it is possible to weave some aspects (by inserting specific components in the definition).

4   Deployment, Execution and Control

Pandora's architecture is organized around a micro-kernel in charge of stack execution. This notion of micro-kernel references works in the operating system domain which gave birth to several generations of minimal kernels, like Chorus [21], L4 [22] or, more recently, Think [23]. In these systems, functionalities (or services) take the form of independent servers, and live outside the kernel itself. Similarly, functionalities provided by the kernel of Pandora are as limited as possible: their implementation within components has always been preferred. This is the case, for example, of event demultiplexing, inter-stack and inter-machine communications, access control, event persistence, etc. In consequence, the main attributions of micro-kernel are to manage the deployment of the applications, supervise the execution of the stacks and implement the reflexive interface of the platform.

4.1   Libraries and Resources Management

Pandora components come within standard dynamic libraries. To deploy an application in Pandora consists in deploying the libraries containing all components in the stack, together with the appropriate configuration files. Pandora uses two kinds of configuration files: stack definitions and library descriptions. The first one contains any number of textual stack specifications expressed in Pandora architecture description language. The second one deals with libraries: it lets Pandora know in which library each component is, and the location of each library. This location may refer either to a file in the local file system or be an URL, which allows its loading from a remote location. Having these different schemes to access library code allows to build and maintain organization-wide component repositories without requiring participating nodes to share a single remotely mounted file system. Library description files also contain information to specify inter-library dependencies, which are automatically taken care of by the platform.

The different configuration files (stack and library descriptions) are named "resources". In order to ease their management (many such files may be required to run a single application), Pandora uses "meta-resource" files (or simply resource files) that contain a list of locations (file or URL) of other resources. Each such resource is accompanied by a priority which tells the order in which they should be visited. These resource files are considered as resources themselves. This makes it possible to organize resources hierarchically by inserting locations of other (sub-)resources in a higher level resource file. Then, one can build an entire resource tree whose leaves would be stack and library descriptions while resource descriptions would be its nodes. In this end, this means that it is possible to boot strap a whole system from one URL.

4.2   Execution

Stacks are the base entities considered by the platform regarding application execution. To guarantee the integrity of the system, the platform performs a verification stage before starting the actual execution of a stack. It checks the correctness of the stack definition, together with the compatibility of component bindings according to the event types they declare supported for input and output (respectively).

The execution phase starts with the creation of a thread in which the stack will be executed. Each stack is run in its own thread and, respectively, each thread contains at most one stack. This one-to-one mapping between stacks and threads has two advantages. The first one is conceptual: the notion of thread is entirely abstracted and the programmer does not have to worry about it. If she wants her application executed in concurrent threads, she just needs to put her components in separate stacks. The second advantage comes from the guaranty that all components within a stack are executed in a single thread. There is no need, then, to synchronize accesses to stack scoped resources: they are made sequentially. As the number of stacks in the system is not limited, and because stacks can be connected in an arbitrary way, it is perfectly legal to split a single logical module into multiple stacks to allow intra-module concurrency and asynchrony.

Tasks are not explicitly defined by the programmer but dynamically created and managed by the platform to be the connected components of the undirected graph whose nodes are stacks and edges are communication channels established between stacks. For example as stack A sends its first event to stack B, the tasks of A and B are merged. This notion of task is used by the platform to allow specific communication modes (see below, in the next section, sensors and monitors) and to collect dead stack cycles (in the garbage collection terminology). It is clear from this operational definition of tasks that, like stacks, their number is not limited in the system.

The kernel is also responsible for the management of each component lifecycle. As events are produced and transmitted, next components are created lazily, only when they first appear as the destination of an event. Pandora maintains access counters for each component so that it can terminate every component that has become inaccessible after the breaking of a connection. This mechanism, which builds on the explicit termination of component bindings, is complemented by a timeout-based mechanism which collects components after a configurable (possibly infinite) period of inactivity.

4.3   Introspection and Dynamic Reconfiguration

We have said how much needed was flexibility for autonomic applications. This is expressed both in the ability to tune such applications as finely as possible, but also in the possibility to reconsider choices as the environment in which the applications are executed evolves.

The entire configuration of the platform and its current state are exposed by the micro-kernel through a reflexive interface. Stack definitions, option values, resource lists: every aspect of the system that is configurable in a configuration file is accessible through this interface. Furthermore, for each element, it is possible to choose whether to modify the stored definition or its active representation (dynamically modifying the platform behavior). Stack management is also exposed, so that it is possible to know the list of running stacks or request to start a new one or stop another one.

Among these operations, the dynamic reconfiguration of a running stack must be given special consideration. Contrary to all the others, this manipulation implies modifying running component instances and bindings between them. As Pandora components are considered stateful, by default, the platform must pay attention to avoid removing components if not strictly necessary. Pandora does so by computing the minimal set of transformations needed to go from the old definition to the new one in terms of component additions and removals. After a removal stage, remaining component are re-linked to each other inserting new component instances as required by the definition.

A meta-object protocol makes these various reconfiguration operations accessible from applications external to the platform. Pandora provides an interface for this protocol in several programming languages, including C, C++, Perl and Guile. Guile [24] is an implementation of the Scheme language and may be used to write scripts with all the standard construction of the original language (procedure definition, flow control, etc.) augmented by primitives accessing the kernel reflexive interface. The ability to write such "control scripts" is original to Pandora and eases the rapid prototyping of (partially) autonomic applications.

However, for autonomic applications to analyze and reconfigure themselves, the utilization of the above protocol is not optimal in terms of performance, as it is designed to allow external applications to interact with the platform. When accesses are made from within the autonomic application (the task in Pandora's terminology), much of the overhead required to locate the targeted option in the system and to serialize the results in the response can be avoided. We have then introduced a specific mechanism that allows a component to "publish" values and make them accessible to all other components within the same task. This operation is made through a dedicated object that we have called a *sensor*. Each sensor is given a name and several component instances may update a single sensor. Accesses are made through another object, called a *monitor*. Monitors are initialized with a set of sensor names they are related to and with a function to apply to the values in order to process them. When this function is actually called depends on the access mode that was chosen for the sensors. There exist two different access modes: a passive mode where monitors pull the values from the sensors when they need it, and an active mode where sensors push the values to the monitors as soon as they are modified. Choosing the best appropriate mode depends on the relative read and write frequencies of monitors and sensors, respectively. Finally, an automatic mode is provided that let the platform do this choice according to access counters it maintains.

5   Implementation

A prototype of this architecture has been developed and has been used in several applications. We present them here briefly.

5.1   Prototype

We have developed a software platform that implements the architecture we have described. It represents more than 50 000 lines of C++ code and, besides the kernel, is made of about 100 components. Approximately a third of those are "base" components: these are components that implement non-functional properties and that may be used in any stack.

Pandora has been ported and tested on a large number of systems, including Linux, FreeBSD, NetBSD, Solaris, Digital Unix (Tru64) and, for the kernel and base components only, Win32. The platform is distributed in its most recent version under an open-source license by INRIA (free for non-commercial use) at the following URL: http://www-sor.inria.fr/projects/relais/pandora/.

5.2   Applications

The Pandora platform has already been used in several projects [20, 25–27]. However, the application that emphasizes most the flexibility of Pandora and the features it offers to build autonomic applications is C/SPAN [28]. C/SPAN is an autonomic Web proxy cache that builds, for the one part, on C/NN [29], a flexible Web cache, and, for the other part, on a HTTP monitoring stack on top of Pandora. In this system, C/NN and Pandora are in a tight interaction loop: C/NN, according to its environment (disk space, request rate, etc.), tunes the behavior of Pandora using its reflexive interface. Respectively, Pandora reconfigures C/NN according to the traffic patters it observes.

6   Performance Evaluation

In this evaluation of the performance of the platform, we have focused on two specific points: the overhead related to the application slicing into components and that related to introspection operations.

All tests have been performed on the same machine which uses a 2.4 GHz Pentium IV processor, running the version 2.6 of the Linux operating system. The measurements that we present are computed from the average of 50 successive runs. The standard error associated with these averages has never gone over 1%. The various procedure execution time have been measured with a loop that executes each one million times. Total execution time expressed in milliseconds gives then the cost a single iteration expressed in nanoseconds.

6.1   Component Traversal

To evaluate the overhead related to the slicing into components, we have measured the time needed for an event to flow through one component, i.e. the time needed to go from one component to its successor. Results presented in Figure 3 show that this time is about 50 ns. Given the other measurements we have performed, we see that this time is superior to the one needed to make simple library calls, but inferior to the one required to make a floating-point division or a system call. This indicates that for non-trivial applications (those that actually do something between each event transmission), the overhead related to the slicing is rather limited, if not negligible.

6.2   Introspection Primitives

To monitor its own behavior, an autonomic application must permanently watch the sensors it is provided with. At the opposite, reconfigurations are supposed to happen only in exceptional circumstances. Then, the most performance critical operation for those applications is the reading of a sensor value, and this is the one we have chosen to evaluate. For the sake of comparison, we have also measured the time needed to read a standard variable when using the reflexive interfaces of two languages commonly used to build flexible applications: Java and C#. In each language, we have reduced the operation to its most simple expression: reading the value of an integer field of an object instance. In both cases, the code used is a one-liner. For Java, we have used different virtual machines, with and without dynamic compilation (Just In Time). We have also statically

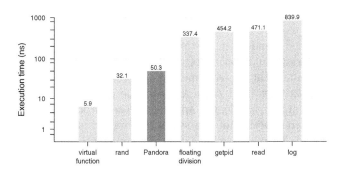

Fig. 3. Average execution time for various library functions, compared to Pandora component traversal time

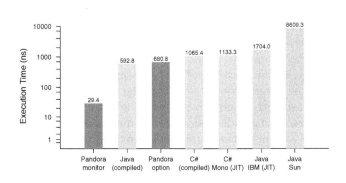

Fig. 4. Average execution time for several language-based introspection functions (Java and C#) compared to those provided by Pandora

compiled the program into native code using the GNU compiler [30]. For C#, we have used the Mono [31] environment whose virtual machine supports both static and dynamic compilation. The results of these experiments are shown Figure 4. Rather than studying the relative performance of compilers and virtual machines compared to each other, what we would like to focus on are orders of magnitude. Pandora sensors (in passive mode) are about 20 times more efficient than natively compiled Java code. The latter, however, corresponds roughly to the time spent when using Pandora options through its external interface. Unsurprisingly, the use of true virtual machine (no static compilation) degrades performance further and the absence of dynamic compilation makes them really catastrophic. This shows how Pandora, for an equivalent CPU load, can support a much higher number (one or two orders of magnitude) of sensors, and thus of applications compared to languages that have been usually used in this domain. It is Pandora specialization in these tasks (the platform has been designed and optimized for this exact purpose), as opposed to the necessary generic approach of a high-level programming language, that explains those differences.

7   Conclusion

We have presented Pandora, a platform for the construction of autonomic applications. Pandora builds on an original programming model, the stacking of components communicating with message exchanges, that provides a compromise between flexibility and performance. The resulting Pandora component model is much simpler than legacy approaches that proceed with standard function calls. The architecture of the system is organized around a micro-kernel that is responsible for managing the system resources (configuration files) whose hierarchical organization eases large-scale deployments. It is also responsible for the chaining of the components according to specified configurations. Its last role is to expose a reflexive interface and propose the necessary abstractions for an application programmer to dynamically configure and reconfigure the entire system. This architecture has been implemented — the prototype is available freely on the Internet — and several applications have already used it. A performance evaluation of the system has shown that its implementation backs up our initial objective to reconcile flexibility and performance.

With Pandora, autonomic application developers needs only to concentrate in implementing the "business logic" of their application. The platform indeed factorizes out most non-functional aspects of the application and provides useful abstractions to deal with monitoring. After some initial effort required to design the application according to Pandora's programming model, easy and powerful deployment and administration support is provided by the system. More importantly, Pandora also makes the application highly flexible and dynamically reconfigurable, basically for free.

References

1. Kephart, J., Chess, D.: The vision of autonomic computing. Computer Magazine, IEEE (2003)
2. Smith, B.C.: Reflection and semantics in lisp. In: Proceedings of the 11th ACM SIGACT-SIGPLAN symposium on Principles of programming languages, ACM Press (1984) 23–35
3. Maes, P.: Concepts and experiments in computational reflection. ACM SIGPLAN Notices **22** (1987) 147–155
4. Ribler, R.L., Vetter, J.S., Simitci, H., Reed, D.A.: Autopilot: Adaptive control of distributed applications. In: Proceedings of the The Seventh IEEE International Symposium on High Performance Distributed Computing, IEEE Computer Society (1998) 172
5. Agarwal, M., Bhat, V., Li, Z., Liu, H., Khargharia, B., Matossian, V., V.Putty, Schmidt, C., Zhang, G., Hariri, S., Parashar, M.: Automate: Enabling autonomic applications on the grid. In: Proceedings of the Autonomic Computing Workshop (AMS 2003), Seattle, WA (2003)
6. Kiczales, G., Lamping, J., Mendhekar, A., Maeda, C., Lopes, C., Loingtier, J.M., Irwin, J.: Aspect-oriented programming. In Aksit, M., Matsuoka, S., eds.: ECOOP'97 — The 11th European Conference on Object-Oriented Programming. Volume 1241 of Lecture Notes in Computer Science., Jyväskylä, Finland, Springer-Verlag (1997) 220–242
7. Clarke, M., Blair, G.S., Coulson, G., Parlavantzas, N.: An efficient component model for the construction of adaptive middleware. Lecture Notes in Computer Science **2218** (2001)
8. Hutchinson, N.C., Peterson, L.L.: The x-Kernel: An architecture for implementing network protocols. IEEE Transactions on Software Engineering **17** (1991) 64–76
9. Heidemann, J.S.: Stackable layers: An architecture for file system development. Technical Report UCLA-CSD 910056, University of California, Los Angeles, CA (USA) (1991)
10. Kohler, E., Morris, R., Chen, B., Jannotti, J., Kaashoek, M.F.: The click modular router. ACM Transactions on Computer Systems **18** (2000) 263–297
11. Welsh, M., Culler, D.E., Brewer, E.A.: SEDA: An architecture for well-conditioned, scalable internet services. In: 18th Symposium on Operating Systems Principles, Lake Louise, Canada (2001) 230–243
12. Liu, H., Parashar, M., Hariri, S.: A component-based programming model for autonomic applications. In: Proceedings of the 1st International Conference on Autonomic Computing (ICAC 2004), New-York, NY, IEEE Computer Society (2004)
13. Muralidhar, R., Parashar, M.: A Distributed Object Infrastructure for Interaction and Steering. In R. Sakellariou, J. Keane, J.G., Freeman, L., eds.: Proceedings of the 7th International Euro-Par Conference (Euro-Par 2001),Lecture Notes in Computer Science. Volume 2150., Manchester, UK, Springer-Verlag (2001) 67–74
14. Chess, D.M., Segal, A., Whalley, I., White, S.R.: Unity: Experiences with a prototype autonomic computing system. In: Proceedings of the 1st International Conference on Autonomic Computing (ICAC 2004), New-York, NY, IEEE Computer Society (2004)
15. Foster, I., Kesselman, C., Nick, J.M., Tuecke, S.: The physiology of the grid: An open grid services architecture for distributed systems integration. Open Grid Service Infrastructure WG, Global Grid Forum (2002) http://www.globus.org/research/papers/ogsa.pdf.

16. Hall, R.S., Cervantes, H.: Gravity: supporting dynamically available services in client-side applications. In: Proceedings of the 9th European software engineering conference held jointly with 10th ACM SIGSOFT international symposium on Foundations of software engineering, ACM Press (2003) 379–382
17. Pawlak, R., Seinturier, L., Duchien, L., Florin, G., Legond-Aubry, F., Martelli, L.: JAC: An aspect-based distributed dynamic framework. Software: Practice and Experience (SPE) (2004)
18. White, S.R., Hanson, J.E., Whalley, I., Chess, D.M., Kephart, J.O.: An architectural approach to autonomic computing. In: Proceedings of the 1st International Conference on Autonomic Computing (ICAC 2004), New-York, NY, IEEE Computer Society (2004)
19. Ellson, J., Gansner, E., Koutsofios, L., North, S.C., Woodhull, G.: Graphviz — open source graph drawing tools. Lecture Notes in Computer Science **2265** (2002)
20. Patarin, S.: Pandora: support pour des services de métrologie à l'échelle d'Internet (english title: Pandora: Support for Internet Scale Monitoring Services). PhD thesis, Université Pierre et Marie Curie – Paris 6 (2003) In French.
21. Rozier, M., Abrossimov, V., Armand, F., Boule, I., Gien, M., Guillemont, M., Herrmann, F., Kaiser, C., Langlois, S., oñard, P.L., Neuhauser, W.: CHORUS distributed operating system. Computing Systems **1** (1988) 305–370
22. Härtig, H., Hohmuth, M., Liedtke, J., Schönberg, S., Wolter, J.: The performance of μ-Kernel-based systems. In: Proceedings of the 16th Symposium on Operating Systems Principles (SOSP-97). Volume 31 of Operating Systems Review., Saint Malo, France, ACM Press (1997) 66–77
23. Fassino, J.P., Stefani, J.B., Lawall, J., Muller, G.: THINK: a software framework for component-based operating system kernels. In: 2002 USENIX Annual Technical Conference, Monterey, CA (2002) 73–86
24. Jaffer, A., Carrette, G., Stachowiak, M., et al.: Guile, project gnu's extension language. software (2002) `http://www.gnu.org/software/guile/`.
25. Patarin, S., Makpangou, M.: On-line Measurement of Web Proxy Cache Efficiency. Research Report RR-4782, INRIA (2003)
26. Fessant, F.L., Patarin, S.: MLdonkey, a Multi-Network Peer-to-Peer File-Sharing Program. Research Report RR-4797, INRIA (2003)
27. Patarin, S., Salamatian, K., Friedman, T.: The Pandora network monitoring platform (2004) Submitted for publication.
28. Ogel, F., Patarin, S., Piumarta, I., Folliot, B.: C/SPAN: a Self-Adapting Web Proxy Cache. In: Proceedings of the Autonomic Computing Workshop (AMS 2003), Seattle, WA (2003)
29. Piumarta, I., Ogel, F., Baillarguet, C., Folliot, B.: Applying the vvm kernel to flexible web caches. In: Proceedings of the IEEE Workshop on Hot Topics in Operating Sy stems, HOTOS-VIII, Schloss Elmau, Germany (2001) 155
30. Bothner, P., Haley, A., Levy, W., et al.: The gnu compiler for the java programming language. software (2004) `http://gcc.gnu.org/java/`.
31. de Icaza, M., Molaro, P., Pratap, R., Porter, D., et al.: The mono project. software (2004) `http://www.go-mono.com/`.

Spatial Computing: The TOTA Approach

Marco Mamei and Franco Zambonelli

DISMI - Università di Modena e Reggio Emilia,
Via Allegri 13, 42100 Reggio Emilia – Italy
{mamei.marco, franco.zambonelli}@unimore.it

Abstract. Spatial abstractions promise to be basic necessary ingredients for a novel "spatial computing" approach to distributed systems development and management, suitable to tackle the complexity of modern distributed computing scenarios and promoting self-organization and self-adaptation. In this paper, we analyze the key concepts underlying spatial computing and show how they can be organized around a sort of "spatial computing stack", in which a variety of apparently very diverse mechanisms and approaches can be properly framed. Following, we present our current research work on the TOTA middleware as a representative example of a general-purpose approach to spatial computing. In particular, we discuss how TOTA can be exploited to support the development and execution of self-organizing and self-adaptive spatial computing applications.

1 Introduction

During the nineties, most researches in distributed computing have focused on the "network of workstations" scenario [7]. However, in the past few years, a number of novel scenarios have emerged including: *(i)* micro-networks, i.e., networks of low-end computing devices typically distributed over a geographically small area (e.g., sensor networks [9], smart dusts [19] and spray computers [26]); *(ii)* ubiquitous networks, i.e., networks of medium-end devices, distributed over a geographically bounded area, and typically interacting with each other via short/medium range wireless connections (pervasive computing systems, smart environments and robot teams [10]); *(iii)* global networks, characterized by high-end computing systems interacting at a world-wide scale (the physical Internet, the Web, P2P networks [23] and multi-agent systems [13]).

Despite clear dissimilarities in structure and goals, one can recognize some key common characteristics distinguishing the above scenarios from more traditional ones:

- **Large Scale:** the number of nodes and, consequently, the number of components involved in a distributed application is typically very high and, due to decentralization, hardly controllable. It is not possible to enforce a strict control over their configuration (consider e.g., the nodes of a P2P network) or to directly control them during execution (consider e.g., the nodes of a sensor network).

- **Network dynamism:** the activities of components will take place in network whose structure derives from an almost random deployment process, likely to

O. Babaoglu et al. (Eds.): SELF-STAR 2004, LNCS 3460, pp. 307–324, 2005.
© Springer-Verlag Berlin Heidelberg 2005

change over time with unpredictable dynamics. This may be due to factors such as environmental contingencies, failures (very likely e.g., in sensor networks and pervasive computing systems), and mobility of nodes (as e.g. in robot teams and in networks of smart appliances). In addition, at the application level, software components can be of an ephemeral or temporary nature (as e.g. the peers of a P2P network).

– **Situatedness:** The activities of components will be strongly related to their location in either a physical or a virtual environment. On the one hand, situatedness can be at the very core of the application goal (as e.g. in sensor networks and pervasive computing systems devoted to improve our interaction with the physical world). On the other hand, situatedness can relate to the fact that components can take advantage of the presence of a structured virtual environment to organize the access to distributed resources (as e.g., in P2P data sharing networks).

The first two characteristics compulsory require systems to exhibit – both at the network and at the application level – properties of self-organization and self-adaptation (or generally, "self-*" properties). In fact, if the dynamics of the network and of the environment compulsory require dynamic adaptation, the impossibility of enforcing a direct control over each component of the system implies that such adaptation must occur without any huma intervention, in an autonomic way. The last characteristic calls for an approach that elects the environment, its spatial distribution, and its dynamics, to primary design dimensions. In any case, the three aspects are strictly inter-related, in that the enforcement of self-* properties cannot abstract from the capability of the system to become "context-aware", i.e., to have components perceive the local properties of the environment in which they are situated and adapt their behavior accordingly.

In the past few years, a variety of solutions exploiting specific self-* properties to solve specific application problems for large-scale systems in dynamic networks are being proposed [8]. The question of whether it is possible to devise a single unifying conceptual approach, applicable with little or no adaptations to a variety of application problems and to scenarios as diverse as P2P networks and networks of embedded sensors, is still open. In this paper, we identify the role that will be played in that process by spatial abstractions, and by their adoption as building blocks for a novel general-purpose "spatial computing" approach for distributed system development. A spatial computing approach – by providing application components with an explicit representation of their operational environment in terms of a space encoding some application-specific features, and by having application level activities expressed in terms of sensing the properties of space and navigating in it – can effectively deal with network dynamics in large scale systems, can facilitate the integration of variety of self-* properties in distributed systems, and also suit systems whose activities are situated in an environment.

The remainder of this paper elaborates on spatial computing and is organized as follows. Section 2 introduces the basic concepts underlying spatial computing and discusses their relations with self-* properties. Section 3 proposes a framework around which to organize the basic abstractions and mechanisms involved in spatial computing. Section 4 presents our current research work on the TOTA middleware, as a representative example of a general-purpose approach to spatial computing. Section 5 concludes by sketching a rough research agenda in the area.

2 Spatial Computing

The key principles underlying spatial computing are that:

- the central role of the network – a discrete system of variously interconnected nodes – evolves into a concept of space. Applications components perceive and act on the basis of some spatial information, distributed across the network and encoding some properties of the components' operational environment that are relevant for a specific application task. Such spatial information decouples components activities from the underlying network structure;
- all application-level activities are abstracted as taking place in such space, and rely on the capability of application components of locally perceiving (and possibly influencing) the local properties of space;

In particular, in spatial computing, any type of networked environment is hidden below some space, mapped as an overlay data structure over the physical network. A space can in fact be represented as an overlay data structure encoding neighborhood and metric relations between nodes. Overlay data structures, realizing the concept of space, are distributed data structures that generalize the idea of overlay networks. Overlay networks are basically routing distributed data structures providing application components with a suitable application-specific view of the network (i.e. they allow components to perceive a specific overlay topology of the network) [22, 24]. An overlay data structure generalizes an overlay network by encoding and providing components with any kind of application-specific spatial representation. In particular, the metric of the represented space defines neighborhood relation and spatial distances accordingly to some specific application need. The nodes of the network are assigned a specific area of the space, and are logically connected to each other accordingly to the spatial neighborhood relations. In this way, components in the network become "space-aware". On the one hand, they perceive their local position in space as well as the local properties of space (e.g., the locally available data and services) and possibly change them. On the other hand, the activities of components in that space are related to some sort of "navigation" in that space, which may include moving themselves to a specific different position of space or moving data and events in space according to "geographical" routing algorithms. The primary way to refer to entities in the network is thus by "position", i.e., any entity is characterized by being situated in a specific position in the physical space.

The above characteristics notably distinguish spatial computing from traditional distributed computing models. In *transparent* distributed computing models [6,7], components are identified by logical names, applications abstract from the presence of a distributed environment, and only a priori known interaction patterns can be effectively supported. This makes them unable to deal with large-scale systems and with network dynamics. In network-aware models [25], components are typically aware of executing in a network and are identified by their location in it (e.g.., the IP). This enables dealing also with applications executing in large-scale networks, but still call for an explicit and complex handling of dynamic changes in the network or in the position of components. With regard to this point it is very important to emphasize that the structure of IP networks, although having a well structured hierarchical topology, cannot be considered a *space*. IPs, in fact, do not relate to each other in such a way that it is possible to effectively exploit their structure for the sake of directing components activities towards a specific application goal. From the application point of view. IPs are just "random labels" attached to application components.

Neither of the two promotes suitable abstractions of environment. Spatial computing overcomes the above limitations in a very effective way:

- **Large Scale:** the size of a network does not influence the models or the mechanisms, which are the same for a small network and for a dramatically large one.
- **Network Dynamics:** the presence of a dynamic network is not directly perceived by components, being hidden behind a stable structure of space that is maintained despite network dynamism. From this perspective, it is effective to set-up interactions and assign tasks on the basis of some space encoding application-related measures. In this way, network changes are automatically taken into account by a changing space representation that shields the application from such low-level events.
- **Situatedness:** the abstraction of space is a conceptually simple abstraction of environment, which also perfectly matches the needs of those systems whose activities are strictly intertwined with a physical or computational environment.

In addition, as discussed in the following sub-section, spatial computing promotes and support self-* computing.

2.1 Self-* Properties in Spatial Computing

Self-* properties, including the capability of a distributed system of self-configuring its activity, self-inspecting and self-tuning its behavior in response to changed conditions, or self-healing it in the presence of faults, are necessary for enabling spatial computing and, at the same time, are also promoted by the adoption of a spatial computing model.

On the one hand, to enable a spatial computing model, it is necessary to envision mechanisms to build the appropriate overlay spatial abstraction and to have such spatial abstraction be coherently preserved despite network dynamics. In other words, this requires the nodes of a network to be able to autonomously connect with each other, set up some sort of common coordinate systems, and self-position themselves in such space. In addition, this requires the nodes of the network to be able to self-reorganize their distribution in the virtual space so as to *(i)* make room for new nodes joining the network (i.e., allocate a portion of the virtual space to these nodes); *(ii)* fill the space left by nodes that for any reason leave the network; *(iii)* re-allocate the spatial distribution of nodes to react to node mobility. It is also worth outlining that, since the defined spatial structure completely shields the application from the network, it is also possible for a system to dynamically tune the structure of the space so as enforce some sorts of self-management of the network, transparently to the higher application levels. As an example, load unbalances in the network can be dynamically dealt, transparently from the application level, by simply re-organizing the spatial structure so as to have overloaded nodes occupy a more limited portion of the space. On the other hand, the so defined spatial structure can be exploited by application level components to organize their activities in space in an autonomous and adaptive way. First of all, it is a rather assessed fact that "context-awareness" and "contextual activity", i.e., the capabilities of a component to perceive the properties of the operational environment and of influencing them, respectively, are basic ingredients to enable any form of adaptive self-organization and to establish the necessary feedback promoting self-adaptation. In spatial computing, this simply translates in the capability of perceiving the local properties of space, which in the end reflect some specific characteristics of either the network or of some application-level characteristics and of changing them. Second, one should also recognize that the vast majority of known phenomena of self-organization and self-adaptation in nature (from ant-foraging to reaction-diffusion systems, just to mention two examples in biology and physics) are actually phenomena of self-organization in space, emerging from the related effect of some "component" reacting to some property of space and, by this reaction, influencing at its turn the properties of space. Clearly, a spatial computing model makes it rather trivial to reproduce in computational terms such types of self-organization phenomena, whenever they may be of some use in a distributed system.

2.2 Examples of Spatial Computing Approaches

The shift towards spatial computing is an emerging trend in diverse scenarios.

As an example, consider a sensor network scenario with a multitude of wireless sensors randomly deployed in a landscape to perform some monitoring of environmental conditions [9]. There, all activities of sensors are intrinsically of a spatial nature. First, each sensor is devoted to local monitoring a specific portion of the physical space (that it can reach with its sensing capabilities). Second, components must coordinate with each other based on their local positions, rather than on their IDs, to perform activities such as detecting the presence and the size of pollution clouds, and the speed of their spreading in the landscape. All of this implies that components must be made aware of their relative positions in the spatial environment by self-constructing a virtual representation of the physical space [18]. Moreover, they can take advantage of "geographical" communication and routing protocols: messages and events flow towards specific position of the physical/virtual space rather than towards specific nodes, thus surviving in an self-adaptive way the possible dismissing of some nodes [21].

Another example in which spatial concepts appear in a less trivial way is worldwide P2P computing. In P2P computing, an overlay network of peers is built over the physical network and, in that networks, peers act cooperatively to search specific data and services. In first generation P2P systems (e.g., Gnutella [23]), the overlay network is totally unstructured, being built by having peers randomly connect to a limited number of other peers. Therefore, in these networks, the only effective way to search for information is message flooding. More recent proposals [22] suggest structuring the network of acquaintances into specific regular "spatial shapes", e.g., a ring or an N-dimensional torus. When a peer connects to the networks, it occupies a portion of that spatial space, and networks with those other peers that are neighbors accordingly to the occupied position of space. Then, data and services are allocated in specific positions in the network (i.e., by those peers occupying that position) depending on their content/description (as can be provided by a function hashing the content into specific coordinates). In this way, by knowing the shape of the network and the content/description of what data/services one is looking for, it is possible to effectively navigate in the network to reach the required data/services. That is, P2P networks define a spatial computing scenario in which all activities of application components are strongly related to self-positioning themselves and navigating in an abstract overlay space. It is also worth outlining that recent researches promote mapping such spatial abstractions over the physical Internet network so as to reflect the geographical distribution of Internet nodes (i.e., by mapping IP addressed into geographical physical coordinates [24]) and, therefore improve efficiency.

In addition to the above examples, other proposals in areas such as pervasive computing [2] and self-assembly [14] explicitly exploit spatial abstractions (and, therefore, a sort of spatial computing model) to organize distributed activities.

3   Framing Spatial Computing

Let us now have a more systematic look at the basic mechanisms that have been exploited so far in distributed computing to promote self-* properties in distributed systems. We will show that most of these mechanisms can be easily interpreted and mapped into very similar spatial concepts, and that they can be framed in a unifying flexible framework.

3.1   A Spatial Computing Stack

In this section, we introduce the "space-oriented" stack of levels (see Figure 1) as a framework for spatial computing mechanisms. In each level of the stack, by introducing a new paradigm rooted on spatial concepts, it is possible to interpret a lot of proposed self-* approaches, in different scenarios, in terms of mechanisms to manage and exploit the space (see Table 1). On this basis, it is likely that a simply unifying model for self-* distributed computing – leading to a single programming model and methodology and – can be actually identified. We want to point out that our stack is not intended to compete with the standard ISO protocol stack, in that it is much more application-oriented.

The "*physical level*" deals on how components start interacting – in a dynamic and spontaneous way – with other components in the systems. This is a very basic expression of self-organizing behavior which is a pre-requisite to support more complex forms of autonomy and of self-organization at higher levels. To this end, one of basic mechanism exploited is broadcast (i.e. communicate with whoever is available). Radio broadcast is used in sensor networks and in pervasive computing systems. P2P systems can relay on different forms of TCP/IP broadcast to find nodes already belonging to the P2P network to initiate a join-protocol. Whatever the case, this physical level can be considered as in charge of enabling a component of a dynamic network application to get into existence and to start interacting with each other.

The "*structure level*" is the level at which a spatial structure is built and maintained by components existing in the physical network. The fact that a system is able to create a stable spatial structure capable of surviving network dynamics and adapting the working conditions of the network is an important expression of self-organizing and self-adapting behavior *per se*. However, such spatial structure is not a goal for the application, and it is instead used as the basic spatial arena to support higher levels activities.

The various mechanisms that are used at the structure level in different scenarios are – again – very similar to each other. Sensor networks as well as self-assembly systems typically structure the space accordingly to their positions in the physical space, by exploiting mechanisms of geographical self-localization. Pervasive computing systems, in addition to mechanisms of geographical localization, often exploit logical spatial structures reflecting some sorts of abstract spatial relationships of the physical world (e.g., rooms in a building) [2]. Global scale systems, as already anticipated, exploits overlay networks built over a physical communication network.

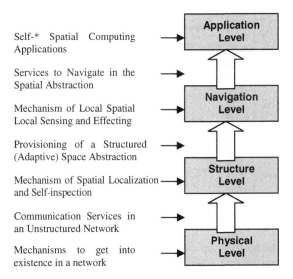

Fig. 1. A Spatial Computing Stack

The "*navigation level*" regards to the basic mechanisms that components exploit to orient their activities in the spatial structure and to sense and affect the local properties of space. If the spatial structure is not associated to some kind of routing information, the only navigation approaches are flooding and gossiping. However, if some sort of routing structure is defined at the structure level (as, e.g., in the geographical spatial structures of sensor networks or in overlay networks) navigation approaches relate in following the routes defined at the structure level. For instance, navigation can imply the capability of components to reach specific points (or of directing messages and data) in the space based on simple geometric considerations as in, e.g., geographical routing [3].

Table 1. Spatial Mechanisms in Modern Distributed Computing Scenarios

	MICRO NETWORKS Nano Networks, Sensor Networks, Smart Dust, Self-Assembly, Modular Robots	UBIQUITOUS NETWORKS Home Networks, MANETs, Pervasive Environments, Mobile Robotics	GLOBAL NETWORKS Internet, Web, P2P networks, multiagent systems
"Application" Level (exploiting the spatial organization to achieve in a *self-organizing and adaptive way* specific app. goals)	Spatial Queries Spatial Self-Organization and Differentiation of Activities Spatial Displacement Motion Coordination & pattern formation DATA: environmental data	Discovery of Services Spatial Displacement Coordination and Distribution of Task and Activities Motion coordination & pattern formation DATA: local resources and environmental data	P2P Queries as Spatial Queries in the Overlay Motion Coordination on the Overlay Pattern formation (e.g., for network monitoring) DATA: files, services, knowledge
"Navigation" Level (dealing with the mechanism exploited by the entities living in the space to *direct activities and movements in that space*)	Flooding Gossiping (random navigation) Geographical Routing (selecting and reaching specific physical coordinates) Directed Diffusion (navigation following sorts of computational fields) Stigmergy (navigation following pheromone gradients)	Computational fields Multi-hop routing based on Spanning Trees Pattern-matching and Localized Tuple-based systems	Flooding Gossiping (random navigation) Metric-based (moving towards specific coordinates in the abstract space) Gossiping (random navigation) Stigmergy (navigation following pheromone gradients distributed in the overlay network)
"Structure" Level (dealing with mechanisms and policies to adaptively *shape a metric space* and let components find their position in that space)	Self-localization (beacon-based triangulation)	Self-localization (Wi-Fi or RFID triangulation) Definition and Maintenance of a Spanning Tree (as a sort of navigable overlay)	Establishment and Maintenance of an Overlay Network (for P2P systems) Referral Networks and e-Institutions (for multiagent systems)
"Physical" Level (dealing with the mechanism to *interact*)	Radio Broadcast Radar-like localization	Radio Broadcast RF-ID identification	TCP broadcast – IP identification Directed TCP/UDP messages Location-dependent Directory services

Starting from the basic navigation capability, is also possible to enrich the structure of the space by propagating additional information to describe "something" which is happening in that space, and to differentiate the properties of the space in different areas. One can say that the structure of space may be characterized by additional types of spatial structures propagating in it, and that components may direct their activities based on navigating these additional structures. In other words, the basic navigation capabilities can be used to build additional spatial structures with different navigation mechanisms.

Typical mechanisms exploited at these additional levels are computational fields and pheromones. Despite the different inspiration of the two approaches (physical versus biological), we emphasize that they can be modeled in a uniform way, e.g., in terms of time-varying properties defined over a space [15]. The basic expression of self-organization that arises here derives from the fact that the structures propagated in the space – and thus the navigation activity of application components – are updated and maintained to continuously reflect the actual structure and situation of the space.

At the "*application level*", navigation mechanisms are exploited by application components to interact and organize their activities. Applications can be conveniently built on the following self-organizing feedback loop: *(i)* having components navigate in the space (i.e., discriminating their activities depending on the locally perceived structure and properties of the space) and *(ii)* having components, at the same time, modifying existing structure due to the evolution of their activities.

Depending on the types of structures propagated in the space, and on the way components react to them, different phenomena of self-organization can be achieved and modeled. For example, processes of morphogenesis (as needed in self-assembly, modular robots and mobile robotics), phenomena mimicking the behavior of ant-colonies and of flocks, phenomena mimicking the behavior of granular media and of weakly correlated particles, as well as a variety of social phenomena, can all be modeled in terms of:

- entities getting to existence in a space explicitly representing some aspects of their operational environment that are relevant for the application task;
- having a position in a structured space and possibly influencing its structure;
- capable of perceiving properties spread in that space;
- capable of directing their actions based on perceived properties of such space and capable of acting in that space by influencing its properties at their turn.

3.2 Multiple Spaces and Nested Spaces

In general, different scenarios and different application problems may require different perceptions of space and different spatial structures. For instance, a world-wide resource-sharing P2P network over the Internet may require – for efficiency reason – a 2-D spatial abstraction capable of reflecting the geographical distribution of Internet nodes over the earth surface. On the other hand, a P2P network for social interactions may require a spatial abstraction capable of aggregating in close regions of the virtual space users with similar interests. Also, one must consider that in the near future, the different network scenarios we have identified will be possibly part of a unique huge network (consider that IPv6 addressing will make it possible to assign an IP address to each and every square millimeter on the earth surface). Therefore, it is hard to imagine that a unique flat spatial abstraction can be effectively built over such a network and satisfy all possible management and application needs.

With this regard, the adoption of the spatial computing paradigm does not prescribe at all to adopt the same set of mechanisms and the same type of spatial structure for all networks and for applications. Instead, being the spatial structure a virtual one, it is possible to conceive both *(i)* the existence, over the same physical network, of multiple complimentary spatial abstraction independently used by different types of applications; and *(ii)* the existence of multiple layers of spatial abstractions, built one over the other in a multi-layered system. With regard to the former point, in addition to the example of the different types of P2P networks calling for different types of spatial abstractions, one could also think at how different problems such as Internet routing, Web caching, virtual meeting points, introduce very different problems and may require the exploitation of very different spatial concepts. With regard to the latter point, one can consider two different possibilities. Firstly, one can think at exploiting a first-level spatial abstractions (and the services it provides) to offer a second-level spatial abstraction enriching it with additional specific characteristics. For examples, one can consider that a spatial abstraction capable of mapping the nodes of the Internet into geographical coordinates can be exploited, within a campus, to build an additional overlay spatial abstraction mapping such coordinates into logical location (e.g., the library, the canteen, the Computer Science department and, within it, the office of Prof. Zambonelli). Such additional spatial abstraction could then be used to build semantically-enriched location dependent services. Secondly, one could think at conceiving a hierarchy of spatial abstractions that provides different levels of information about the space depending on the level at which they are observed, the same as the information we get on a geographical region are very different depending on the scaling of the map on which we study it. As an example, we can consider that the spatial abstraction of a wide-area network can map a sensor network – connected to the large network via a gateway – as a "point" in that space, and that the distributed nature of the sensor networks (with nodes having in turn a specific physical location in space) becomes apparent only when some activity takes place in that point of space (or very close to it).

4   TOTA: A Middleware Approach to Spatial Computing

The ambitious goal of a uniform modeling approach capable of effectively capturing the basic properties of self-organizing computing, and possibly leading to practical and useful general-purpose modeling and programming tools, is far from close. Earlier in this paper we have strongly advocated the generality, flexibility, and modularity of a spatial computing approach. Although we have do not have the ultimate proof that spatial computing can be effectively put to practice and fulfill all its promises, our experience in spatial computing with the TOTA [16] middleware can support in part our claims.

Upon the distributed space identified by the dynamic network of TOTA nodes, each component is capable of locally storing tuples and letting them diffuse through the network. Tuples are injected in the system from a particular node, and spread hop-by-hop accordingly to their propagation rule. In fact, a TOTA tuple is defined in terms of a "content", and a "propagation rule". $T=(C,P)$. The content C is an ordered set of typed fields representing the information carried on by the tuple. The propagation rule P determines how the tuple should be distributed and propagated across the network. This includes determining the "scope" of the tuple (i.e. the distance at which such tuple should be propagated and possibly the spatial direction of propagation) and how such propagation can be affected by the presence or the absence of other tuples in the system. In addition, the propagation rules can determine how the content of a tuple should change while it is propagated. Tuples are not necessarily distributed replicas: by assuming different values in different nodes, tuples can be effectively used to build a distributed data structure expressing contextual and spatial information. So, unlike traditional event based models, propagation of tuples is not driven by a publish-subscribe schema, but it is encoded in tuples' propagation rule and, unlike an event, can change its content during propagation (see figure 2).

Distributed tuples must be maintained coherent despite network dynamism. To this end, the TOTA middleware supports tuples propagation actively and adaptively: by constantly monitoring the network local topology and the income of new tuples, the middleware automatically re-propagates tuples as soon as appropriate conditions occur. For instance, when new nodes get in touch with a network, TOTA automatically checks the propagation rules of the already stored tuples and eventually propa- gates the tuples to the new nodes. Similarly, when the topology changes due to nodes' movements, the distributed tuple structure automatically changes to reflect the new topology.

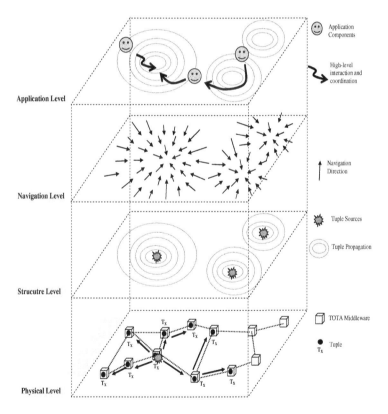

Fig. 2. The General Scenario of TOTA in the spatial computing stack: at the physical level there is the network, communication is broadcast of messages encoding TOTA tuples. At the structure level, the space is represented by means of the TOTA distributed tuples. At the navigation level spatial structures can provide navigation directions. At the Application level coordination tasks can be achieved

The TOTA middleware supports the spatial computing stack introduced in section 4. In fact, from the application components' point of view, executing and interacting basically reduces to create distributed spatial structures in the network (inject tuples), navigate such spatial structures (sense tuples in a neighborhood), and act accordingly to some application-specific policy.

To clarify and ground the discussion we introduce the following exemplary pervasive computing case study application: tourists with wireless PDAs visit a museum provided with an embedded computer network. We suppose that the PDAs and the embedded devices run the TOTA middleware and that they connect with each other forming a multi-hop mobile wireless network. In the following subsections, working on this case study application, we will detail how TOTA deals with all the levels in the spatial computing.

4.1 Physical Level

The physical level deals with how components find and start communicating with each other. At this level, the specific nature of the network scenario has an important role. Since our primary focus is pervasive computing, we mainly consider a wireless network scenario without long-range routing protocols available (like in a "bare" mobile ad-hoc network). In such scenario, it is easy to identify the node's neighborhood with the network local topology (e.g. all the nodes within 10m, for a Bluetooth network). In this case, a TOTA node detects in-range nodes via one-hop message broadcast.

Turning the attention to the case study, each PDA detects neighbor devices, by broadcasting and receiving "here I am" messages. Such discovery operations is executed periodically to take into account the possible movements of users. Upon injecting a tuple, the TOTA middleware broadcasts the tuple to its current neighbors.

To support our experiments, we developed a first prototype of TOTA running on HP IPAQs 36xx equipped with 802.11b wireless card, Familiar LINUX and J2ME-CDC (Personal Profile). IPAQs connect locally in the MANET mode (i.e. without requiring access points) creating the skeleton of the TOTA network. Tuples are being propagated through multicast sockets to all the nodes in the one-hop neighborhood. The use of multicast sockets has been chosen to improve the communication speed by avoiding 802.11b unicast handshake. By considering the way in which tuples are propagated, TOTA is very well suited for this kind of broadcast communication. We think that this is a very important feature, because it will allow in the future implementing TOTA also on really simple devices (e.g. micro mote sensors [19]) that cannot be provided with sophisticate communication mechanisms.

It is important to remark that, despite our focus to wireless networks and pervasive computing, the TOTA mechanisms are general and independent from the underlying physical network. For example, in an Internet scenario (where a long-range routing protocol is available), TOTA identifies the neighborhood of a node with the nodes whose IP address is known (a node can communicate directly with another, only if it knows the other node's address). To realize neighbors discovery, TOTA can either download from a well-known server the list addresses representing its neighbors or it can start an expanding-ring search to detect close nodes [23]). Given that, the multi-hop propagation of a tuple proceeds as previously described.

4.2 Structure Level

TOTA tuples create a "structure of space" in the network. At the basic level, once a tuple is injected from a node and propagates across the network, it creates a source-centered spatial structure identifying some spatial features relative to the source.

For example, a tuple incrementing one of its fields as it gets propagated identifies a spatial structure defining the network distances from the source. This kind of structure of space provides spatial awareness to application agents. In fact, an agent is both able to infer its approximate distance from the source (in terms of hops – i.e. network link range), and the direction of the source by looking at where the gradient of the tuple descends.

Moreover, TOTA allows to combine different tuples to create more complex spatial representations. A particularly significant example of these mechanisms is the creation of shared coordinate systems in the network on the basis of mere connectivity. Localization, in general, can rely on the (geometrically intuitive) fact that the position of a point on a surface can be uniquely determined by measuring its distance from at least three non-aligned reference points ("beacons"), via a process of "triangulation" [18]. Implementing such localization mechanism in TOTA is rather easy. *(i)* A leader election algorithm can elect three beacons nodes. *(ii)* Each beacon "arbitrarily" locates at specific coordinates (without external location information the coordinate system can only be internally coherent [18]). *(iii)* Each beacon injects a TOTA tuple, increasing its content hop-by-hop and marked with the beacon coordinates. As previously pointed out, this tuple allows other nodes to estimate their distance from the beacon. *(iv)* After at least three beacons had propagated their ranging tuples, nodes can apply a triangulation algorithm to infer their coordinates. Moreover, since TOTA tuples self-maintain, the coordinate system remains up to date and coherent despite network dynamism. If upon a node movement the topology of the network changes, the tuples maintenance triggers an update in the coordinate system, making the latter robust.

A shared coordinate system provides a powerful spatial structure in a network and allows to realize complex navigation and coordination tasks (see later).

In addition, although at the primitive level the space is the network space and distances are measured in terms of hops between nodes, TOTA allows to exploit a much more physically-grounded concept of space.

This may be required by several pervasive computing scenarios in which application agents need to interact with and acquire awareness of the physical space. For instance, one can bound the propagation of a tuple to a portion of physical space by having the propagation procedure - as the tuple propagates from node to node - to check the local spatial coordinates, so as to decide whether to further propagate the tuple or not. In order to bound agents' and tuples' behavior to the physical space, nodes must be provided with some kind of localization mechanism [11]. From our perspective, such mechanisms can be roughly divided into two categories:

– A GPS-like localization mechanism provides absolute spatial information (e.g. it provides latitude and longitude of a node in the network). An actual GPS (Global Positioning System) getting spatial coordinates from satellites naturally belongs to this category. Beacon-based signal triangulation (coupled with beacons actual physical location) is anther example of this category (nodes get their coordinates in an absolute coordinate-frame defined by the beacons [18]).

– A RADAR-like localization mechanism provides local information (e.g. relative distances and orientations between nodes). An actual radar or sonar device belongs to this category (radio and sound waves reflected by neighbor devices enable to infer their distance and orientation). A videocamera installed on a node can serve the same purpose (processing the image coming from the camera, a node can infer where other nodes are). Also network roundtrip-time and signal-strength attenuation may serve this purpose.

The kind of localization mechanism being available strongly influences how nodes can express and use spatial information. GPS-like mechanism are more suitable at defining "absolute" regions. For example, they allow to easily create tuples that propagate across a region defined by means of the coordinates of its corners (e.g. propagate in the square area defined by (0,0) and (100,100)). RADAR-like mechanism are more suitable at defining "relative" regions, where for example tuples are constrained to travel north form the source or within a specified distance.

It is fair to report that a similar idea has been developed and exploited in the context of a recently proposed language to program a vast number of devices dispersed in an environment [2]. The idea of this programming language is to identify a number of spatial regions relevant for a given application and to access the devices through the mediation of these regions (e.g. for all the devices on the "hill" do that). In [2], the definition of the regions is performed adopting GPS devices and distributed data structures similar to TOTA tuples.

Other than the network and the physical space, one could think at mapping the peers of a TOTA network in any sort of virtual space. This space must be supported by an appropriate routing mechanism allowing distant peers to be neighbors in the virtual space. Such virtual spaces are particularly useful and enable the definition of advanced application such as content-based routing, as in CAN [22]. TOTA concretely supports the definition of these kinds of applications. Also in this case it is fair to report that similar principles have been used in the Multilayered Multi Agent Situated System (MMASS) model [1]. In MMASS agents' actions take place in a multi-layered environment. Each layer provides agents with some contextual information supporting agents' activities. The MMASS environment is thus a hierarchy of virtual spaces built upon one another, where lower layers provide the routing infrastructure for upper ones.

4.3 Navigation Level

TOTA defines a set of API to allow application components to sense TOTA tuples in their one-hop neighborhood and to locally perceive the space defined by them. Navigation in the space consists in having agents act on the basis of the local shape of specific tuples.

As a first simple example we can consider physical navigation. Turning the attention to our case study, it is clear that a PDA injecting a hop-increasing tuple in the network, becomes immediately reachable by other users. Users, in fact, can move following the gradient of the tuple downhill, to reach the tuple source. Moreover, since the tuple shape is maintained despite network dynamism, users can reach the source of a tuple even if it moves.

Navigation is not related to physical movement only. TOTA allows to relate the propagation of a tuple to other tuples already propagated (e.g. a tuple can propagate following another tuple). This can be at the basis of the routing algorithm detailed in the following [20]. In very general terms, when a node "A" wants to send a message to a node "B", it actually injects the network with a TOTA tuple, that holds: the source identifier i.e. "A", the message, and the number of hops from the source of the message to the current node. Such structure not only trivially hand-off the message to "B", but creates a path leading to "A" that can be exploited for further uses. If node "B" wants to reply, it can just send a message that follows the "A"-field downhill towards node "A". In this case no flooding is involved. The field-like distributed data structures created in this process, can be used further also by other peers to communicate.

Complex spaces enable advanced navigation strategies. A shared coordinate system, like the one described in the previous section, allows, for example, to set-up geographic routing algorithm [3]. A geographic routing algorithm is a mechanism that takes advantage of the established coordinate frame to send messages to the node closer to a specific location. Such algorithm is suitable in a lot of application scenarios because it inherently supports communication decoupling in that senders and receivers are decoupled by the coordinate frame. For example, a sender can send a message to an unknown receiver located at a specific location and the message will be received by whoever is closer to that location.

4.4 Application Level

The spatial abstractions and tools promoted by TOTA enable to easily realize complex coordination tasks in a robust and flexible way.

Our research, up to now, has mainly focused on the problem of enabling a group of agents to coordinate their respective movements (i.e. distributed motion coordination).

Specifically, considering our case study, we focus on how tourists can be supported in planning their movements across a possibly large and unfamiliar museum and in coordinating such movements with other, possible unknown, tourists. Such coordination activities may include scheduling attendance at specific exhibitions occurring at specific times, having a group of students split in the museum according to teacher-specific laws, helping a tourist to avoid crowd or queues, letting a group of tourist to meet together at a suitable location, and even helping to escape accordingly to specific evacuation plans.

An intriguing possibility to realize motion coordination is to take inspiration from the physical world, and in particular from the way masses in our universe move accordingly to the gravitational field. By interpreting (rather roughly) the General Relativity Theory, we can say that the gravitational field actually changes the structure of the space letting particles to globally self-organize their movements. Under this interpretation, particles achieve their "tasks" by simply following the structure of the space.

Realizing this kind of idea with the spatial abstraction promoted by TOTA is rather easy. Under the assumption that users spread hop-counting tuples in the network, it is possible to realize several coordination tasks. A group of tourist following downhill each other tuples will collapse in a single location allowing the tourists to meet somewhere in the building. Analogously, museum's guides could decide to sense each other's tuples (i.e. spaces) so as to maintain a certain distance from each other to improve their reachability by tourists. If a guide has to go away, the same tuples would allows the others to automatically and adaptively re-shape their formation.

Following this approach, agents achieve their goals not because of their capabilities as single individuals, but because they are part of an auto-organized system that leads them to the goal achievement. Such characteristics also imply that the agents' activities are automatically adapted to the environmental dynamism, which is reflected in a changing spatial representation, without forcing agents to re-adapt themselves.

Motion coordination with spatial abstractions is by no means limited to the presented case study. It can be applied to a wide range of scenarios ranging from urban traffic management, mobile software agents on Internet and even self-assembly in modular robots (detailed in the following). A modular or self-reconfigurable robot is a collection of simple autonomous mobile robots with few degrees of freedom. A distributed control algorithm is executed by all the robots that coordinate their respective positions to let the robot assume a global coherent shape or a global coherent motion pattern (i.e. gait).

From a methodological viewpoint, robots can exploit spatial abstraction and TOTA tuples to self-organize their respective positions in space. In particular, starting from any spatial configuration of robots: (i) robots start diffusing specific types TOTA tuples; (ii) robots react to locally perceived tuples by trying to follow them downhill/uphill, or by changing their activity state possibly depending on the perceived values of the tuples (i.e. depending on their position in some abstract space); (iii) changes in the activity state of robots can lead to inhibiting the propagation of some tuples and/or to the diffusion of new types of tuples in the system, leading back to point (i). One can then apply this process several times, with new types of tuples being propagated in different phases, so as to incrementally have robots self-organize into the required shape [14].

In all these application scenario, we verified that the spatial abstractions promoted by TOTA effectively support robust and flexible self-organizing behaviors.

5 Conclusions

By abstracting the execution of distributed applications around spatial concepts, spatial computing promises to be an effective approach towards the identification of general and widely applicable self-* approaches to distributed systems development and management. Our experiences with the TOTA middleware confirm the effectiveness of the approach.

However, besides the claims of this paper and our personal experience, much work is needed to asses the potentials of spatial abstractions in distributed computing, and to verify whether they can actually pave the way to a sound and general-purpose approach to self*- computing. In particular:

- Is the spatial computing stack depicted in Table 1 meaningful and useful, or a better and more practical framing can be proposed?
- If and when such a unifying model will be found, will it be possible to translate it into a limited set of programming abstractions and lead to the identification of a practical methodology for developing self-organizing distributed computing systems?
- Is a middleware-centered approach like that of TOTA the best direction to follow?
- Several self-organization phenomena disregarded by this paper, deals with concepts that can be hardly intuitively mapped into spatial concepts. Would exploring some sorts of spatial mapping be still useful and practical? Would it carry advantages?
- Possibly most important of all questions: is the search for a unifying model fueled by enough applications? Or it is rather the search for specific solutions to specific problems the best direction to follow?

In our hope, further researches and a larger variety of studies about self-* properties in distributed systems will soon provide the correct answers to the above questions.

References

1. S. Bandini, S. Manzoni, G. Vizzari, "Towards a Specification and Execution Environment for Simulations based on MMASS: Managing at-a-distance Interaction", Fourth International Symposium From Agent Theory to Agent Implementation (AT2AI'04), Vienna, Austria, 2004.
2. C. Borcea, "Spatial Programming Using Smart Messages: Design and Implementation", 24th Int.l Conference on Distributed Computing Systems, Tokio (J), May 2004.
3. P. Bose, P. Morin, I. Stojmenovic, J. Urrutia, "Routing with Guaranteed Delivery in Ad Hoc Wireless Networks", Wirleless Networks 7:609-616, Kluwer Academic Publisher, 2001.
4. G. Cabri, L. Leonardi, M. Mamei, F. Zambonelli, Location-dependent Services for Mobile Users, IEEE Transactions on Systems, Man, and Cybernetics-Part A: Systems And Humans, Vol. 33, No. 6, pp. 667-681, November 2003
5. A. Carzaniga, D. Rosenblum, A. Wolf, "Design and Evaluation of a Wide-Area Event Notification Service", ACM Transaction on Computer System, 19(3):332-383.
6. R. S. Chin, S. T. Chanson, "Distributed Object-Based Programming Systems", ACM Computing Surveys, 23(1), March 1991.
7. G. Coulouris, J. Dollimore, T. Kindberg, Distributed Systems. Concepts and Design Addison-Wesley, second edition, 1994.
8. G. Di Marzo, A. Karageorgos, O. Rana, F. Zambonelli (Eds.), Engineering Self-organizing Systems: Nature Inspired Approaches to Software Engineering, LNCS No. 2977, Springer Verlag, May 2004.

9. D. Estrin, D. Culler, K. Pister, G. Sukjatme, "Connecting the Physical World with Pervasive Networks", IEEE Pervasive Computing, 1(1):59-69, 2002.
10. H.W. Gellersen, A. Schmidt, M. Beigl, "Multi-Sensor Context-Awareness in Mobile Devices and Smart Artefacts", Mobile Networks and Applications, 7(5): 341-351, Oct. 2002.
11. Hightower and G. Borriello, "Location Systems for Ubiquitous Computing," Computer, vol. 34, no. 8, Aug. 2001, pp. 57–66.
12. JINI, http://www.jini.org
13. J. Kephart, "Software Agents and the Route to the Information Economy", Proceedings of the National Academy of Science, 99(3):7207-7213, May 2002.
14. M. Mamei, M. Vasirani, F. Zambonelli, "Experiments of Morphogenesis in Swarm of Simple Mobile Robots", Journal of Applied Artificial Intelligence, 18(9-10):903 – 919, Taylor & Francis, Philadelphia (PA), USA, 2004.
15. M. Mamei, L. Leonardi, F. Zambonelli, "Co-Fields: a Unifying Approach to Swarm Intelligence", 3rd Workshop on Engineering Societies in the Agents' Word, LNCS No. 2677, April 2003.
16. M. Mamei, F. Zambonelli, "Programming Pervasive and Mobile Computing Applications with the TOTA Middleware", 2nd IEEE Conference on Pervasive Computing and Communications, Orlando (FL), IEEE CS Press, March 2004.
17. Mamei, M., and F. Zambonelli. 2004b. Co-Fields: a Physically Inspired Approach to Distributed Motion Coordination. IEEE Pervasive Computing, 3(2):52-60.
18. R. Nagpal, H. Shrobe, J. Bachrach, "Organizing a Global Coordinate System from Local Information on an Ad Hoc Sensor Network", 2nd International Workshop on Information Processing in Sensor Networks, Palo Alto (CA), April, 2003.
19. K. Pister, "On the Limits and Applicability of MEMS Technology", Defense Science Study Group Report, Institute for Defense Analysis, Alexandria (VA), 2000.
20. R. Poor, Embedded Networks: Pervasive, Low-Power, Wireless Connectivity, PhD Thesis, Massachusetts Institute of Technology, 2001.
21. A. Rao, C. Papadimitriou, S. Ratnasamy, S. Shenker, I. Stoica. "Geographic Routing Without Location Information". ACM Mobicom Conference. San Diego (CA), USA, 2003.
22. S. Ratsanamy,, P. Francis, M. Handley, R. Karp, "A Scalable Content-Addressable Network", ACM SIGCOMM Conference 2001, Aug. 2001.
23. M. Ripeani, A. Iamnitchi, I. Foster, "Mapping the Gnutella Network", IEEE Internet Computing, 6(1):50-57, Jan.-Feb. 2002.
24. A. Rowstron et al., "PIC: Practical Internet Coordinates", 24th International Conference on Distributed Computing Systems, IEEE CS Press, Tokyo (J), May 2004.
25. J. Waldo et al., "A Note on Distributed Computing", Mobile Object Systems, LNCS No. 1222, Feb. 1997.
26. F. Zambonelli, M.P. Gleizes, M. Mamei, R. Tolksdorf, Spray Computers: Explorations in Self organization", Journal of Pervasive and Mobile Computing 1(1), May 2005.

Towards Self-managing QoS-Enabled Peer-to-Peer Systems

Vana Kalogeraki, Fang Chen, Thomas Repantis,
and Demetris Zeinalipour-Yazti

Department of Computer Science and Engineering,
University of California, Riverside,
CA 92521
{vana, fchen, trep, csyiazti}@cs.ucr.edu

Abstract. Peer-to-peer systems that dynamically interact, collaborate
and share resources are increasingly being deployed in wide-area environments. The inherent ad-hoc nature of these systems makes it difficult
to meet the Quality of Service (QoS) requirements of the distributed applications, thus having a direct impact on their scalability, efficiency and
performance. In this paper we propose adaptive algorithms to meet applications QoS demands and balance the load across multiple peers. These
comprise (a) resource management mechanisms to monitor resource loads
and application latencies and (b) self-organization algorithms to dynamically select peers that maximize the probability of meeting the applications' soft real-time and QoS requirements. Our algorithms use only
local knowledge and therefore scale well with respect to the size of the
network and the number of executing applications.

1 Introduction

In the last few years, the new emerging Peer-to-Peer (P2P) model has become
very attractive for developing large scale file systems [1, 2, 3, 4, 5, 6] and sharing
resources (i.e., CPU cycles, memory, storage space, network bandwidth) [7, 8]
over large scale geographical areas. This is achieved by constructing an overlay
network of many nodes (peers) built on top of heterogeneous operating systems
and networks. P2P systems present the evolution of the client-server model that
was primarily used to manage small-scale distributed environments. The most
distinct characteristic in the P2P overlays is that there is symmetric communication between the peers; each peer has both client and server role.

Many efforts have been made to improve resource usage, minimize network
latencies and reduce the volume of unnecessary traffic incurred in large-scale P2P
overlays. Two main approaches have emerged for constructing overlay networks:
Structured and *Unstructured* overlays. *Structured* overlay networks [4, 3, 5] are
organized in such a way that objects are located at specific nodes in the network and nodes maintain some state information, to enable efficient retrieval of
the objects. These sacrifice atomicity by mapping objects to particular nodes
and assume that all nodes are equal in terms of resources, which can lead to

O. Babaoglu et al. (Eds.): SELF-STAR 2004, LNCS 3460, pp. 325–342, 2005.
© Springer-Verlag Berlin Heidelberg 2005

bottlenecks and hot-spots. In *unstructured* overlay networks, on the other hand, objects can be located at random nodes, and nodes are able to join the system at random times and depart without a priori notification. Recent efforts have shown that a self-organizing unstructured overlay protocol maintains an efficient and connected topology when the underlying network fails, performance changes, or nodes join and leave the network dynamically [9]. More advantages of unstructured overlay networks include their ability for self-organization, for adaptation to different loads, and for resiliency to node failures. Several efforts have demonstrated that P2P systems can be used efficiently in the context of multicast [10], distributed object-location [4, 3] and information retrieval [11].

However, hosting distributed, real-time applications with Quality of Service (QoS) demands, such as predictable jitter and latency on P2P systems imposes many challenges. These types of applications have distinctly different characteristics from content-based or multicast applications traditional being deployed on P2P systems. Examples of such applications include industrial process control systems, avionics mission computing systems and mission-critical video processing systems [12].

For example, consider a surveillance system that transfers public health, laboratory, and clinical data over the Internet. In this example, both continuous and discrete data (such as text, images, audio and video streams and control information) needs to be collected from multiple nodes in the system. Personnel will then analyze the gathered data quickly and accurately to monitor disease trends, identify emerging infectious diseases or track potential bioterrorism attacks. These have end-to-end soft real-time and QoS requirements on data transmission, including fast and reliable transfer, and substantial throughput. In addition, the audio and video streams may need to be transcoded to different formats or presentations (such as lower resolution) to transmit the data over resource constrained links. To support the QoS demands of the distributed applications, the P2P system must be flexible, predictable and adaptable.

Distributed and real-time applications have been successfully developed over middleware technologies, such as OMG's Common Object Request Broker Architecture (CORBA)[13], Microsoft's Distributed Component Object Model (DCOM) [14]), Sun's Java Remote Method Invocation (RMI) [15] and the Simple Object Access Protocol (SOAP) [16]. These typically rely on local management or the use of centralized managers that have a global view of the system [17], [18], [19], [20], [21].

In our view, the inherent advantages of the P2P systems, including scalability, decentralization and ease of use makes it feasible to develop large-scale distributed and real-time applications. However, current P2P systems are limited in capability because of lack of automated and decentralized management mechanisms. There are two main reasons for this limitation: (1) in a large scale system, each node cannot have an accurate global view of the system at all times, since the state of the system changes much faster than it can be communicated to the peers, and (2) the P2P infrastructure can encompass resources with different processing and communication capabilities, therefore, distributed applications that execute over wide-area environments are subject to greater variations due to unpredictable communication latencies and changing resource availability.

QoS properties in the P2P systems can be enabled in two ways: *statically*, where we must ensure that adequate resources are available before the application execution, or *dynamically*, where the resource usage is adjusted based on runtime system monitoring. Examples of static QoS properties include peer geographic location or specific platforms and hardware resources available at the peers. Examples of dynamic QoS properties include runtime resource re-allocation and re-prioritization to handle resource failures or changes in the CPU and network load.

The objective of this work is to build self-managing large-scale P2P systems that are able to meet application QoS requirements. To achieve this, we propose to use self-organization algorithms that revise peer connections dynamically to minimize application latencies and distribute the resource load. These work together with local resource management mechanisms for managing CPU and network bandwidth and prioritizing application requests, and system-wide management mechanisms that run across multiple peers to improve task execution latencies.

Towards this view we present an architecture with two important components:

- A resource management framework to meet the end-to-end soft real-time and QoS requirements of the distributed applications. The framework consists of mechanisms for managing the local resources, prioritizing application requests and propagating resource and timing measurements system-wide. These mechanisms are decentralized, adaptive and use only local information.
- Adaptive self-organization algorithms that improve application latencies and balance the load across multiple peers to meet their end-to-end soft real-time and QoS requirements. The decisions are made in a decentralized manner, thus achieving system scalability.

We implemented the resource management mechanisms and the self organization algorithms in our P2P middleware that uses an unstructured communication protocol to establish connections between the peers. We present empirical results over our P2P system that demonstrate the adaptability, predictability and performance of our resource management mechanisms.

The rest of the paper is organized as follows. Section 2 gives an overview of our P2P architecture and presents the system model and metrics. In Section 3 we describe our self-organization algorithms. In Section 4 we discuss the experimental results. Section 5 presents related work and Section 6 concludes the paper.

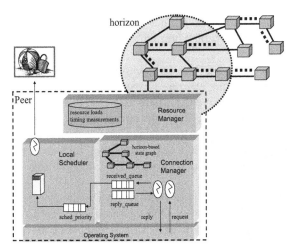

Fig. 1. Our P2P System Architecture

2   Design and Implementation Overview

A P2P system is modeled as an overlay network of nodes (peers[1]) in which each peer comprises a Connection Manager, a Resource Manager and a Local Scheduler, as shown in Figure 1.

The Connection Manager is responsible to manage the peer connections. Each node keeps a small number of connections to other peers; the number of connections is typically limited by the network bandwidth at the peer. Typically, a XP 2000 Athlon PC workstation behind a 100Mbit/s network connection can easily support 20 concurrent peer connections, while the same machine behind a modem 56kbit/s connection can support 1-2 connections. As a result, remote peer invocations may take a long time to complete due to nodes with high latencies or limited network bandwidth, affecting the end-to-end performance of the distributed applications. Peer connections are established as a result of new peers joining the system or are triggered by the self-organization algorithms in which each node tries to connect to better peers. For each peer connection q, the Connection Manager at node p maintains the $Location_q$ that consists of the network address and port number of the peer {IP address, port number} and $Peer\_type_q$: whether the peer is immediate or indirect. The Connection Manager creates and manages a number of connection threads for each peer connection used to handle request and response messages coming from that peer. All the requests coming from the peers, enter the Connection Manager's receiving queue.

---

[1] Two nodes p and q are called **immediate** peers if there is a direct connection between the nodes. Two nodes p and q are called **indirect** peers if there exists a communication path between the nodes. Two peers may not communicate if the graph is disconnected or the shortest path between them is more hops than the maximum allowed TTL.

The Connection Manager constructs and maintains a horizon-based state graph that stores peer resource utilization and application timing measurements and also captures the relationships between the peers. The Connection Manager obtains this information either by propagating updates periodically between the peers, or by recording the parameters carried along with the messages. Note, that, because of the large scale and dynamic nature of the system, the state graph is local at each node and captures only a partial (limited) view of the system. This view is bound by the horizon of the peer. The state graph is constructed and updated dynamically based on the applications executing in the system and the connections established and torn down by the peers.

The Connection Manager works in concert with the Local Resource Manager that controls and monitors the access to the node's local resources (*e.g.,* CPU, memory and network bandwidth) and profiles the behavior of the applications as they execute. For example, if the Resource Manager reports that the processor is overloaded (receiving queue size is full), the Connection Manager does not accept new requests. These requests will be propagated to the node's peers. Our previous measurements [22] indicate that such profiling can be done at run-time with less than 1% overhead, by invoking the /proc interface, but (1) a history of measurements must be maintained and (2) the profiling frequency must be carefully tuned dynamically to adequately capture the load fluctuations in the peer.

The Local Scheduler in the node is responsible for specifying a local ordered list (schedule) for the application object invocations based on the scheduling algorithm implemented in the system. Our scheduling algorithm is based on the Least Laxity Scheduling (LLS) algorithm that allows us to capture timing delays as the applications execute across multiple processors in the system [23, 24].

2.1   Application Tasks

Users request applications from the system that trigger the execution of tasks. An application task is defined as a sequence of invocations of objects distributed across multiple peers in the system. The execution of the task starts at the user invocation and completes when a result is returned back to the user. A task is executed by a single thread executing in sequence on one or more peers. The execution times of the tasks are affected by the load on the peers and the latencies on the communication links. If a node cannot execute the task locally, it propagates the request to one of its peers. This process continues until an appropriate node is found to execute the request. To provide a termination condition so that requests are not propagated indefinitely in the network, we associate a time_to_live (ttl) value with each task that determines the maximum number of hops the task will propagate in the system. To avoid loops in task propagation, we choose not to propagate requests that have previously arrived at the same peer. When the execution finishes, a reply is generated that follows the same path to be reported back to the user. Users may trigger the execution of multiple tasks concurrently and asynchronously.

Each task t is characterized by the $Task\_id_t$ which is a unique identifier that distinguishes each task from the others, generated by the peer initiator of the task. We represent as $Task\_type_t$ the type of task (to be executed), carried along with the message. $Deadline_t$ is the time interval, starting at user invocation within which the task t must complete, specified by the user. $Project\_latency_t$ is the estimated amount of time required for the task to complete. This includes queueing delays and the latencies on communication links. $Laxity_t$ is computed as the difference between the deadline and the projected latency of the task. The laxity value determines the order with which the task will be executed in the system. The task with the smallest laxity value has the highest priority.

3   System Resource Management

In this section, we describe our self-organization algorithm that uses resource and timing measurements monitored locally and collected from remote peers.

3.1   Resource and Timing Measurements

The Resource Managers at the processors monitor the execution of the tasks across multiple peers and record the peer-to-peer messages exchanged. The P2P communication protocol [2] enables interoperability across peers on different nodes in a large scale system and implemented using different languages. The Connection Managers communicate through five message types (**ping, pong, request, reply, update**), of which the ping and pong messages are used to establish connections with remote peers. Ping and pong messages act as the node discovery service. The Connection Manager sends a ping message to discover the IP address and port number of other nodes. Nodes receiving a ping message forward it recursively to all their neighbors. If a node wants to accept new connections it responds with a pong message. The decisions to which peers to connect to or whether to accept an incoming connection, are made by our self-organization algorithm.

For a remote task invocation, the Connection Manager constructs a **request** message that carries the task operation. A request message includes the identifier of the task **task_id**, a **descriptor_id** that uniquely characterizes the peer that propagated the task last, and a **hop_count** that determines the maximum number of times the task will be propagated to the system before it expires. When the task finishes execution, the Connection Manager will generate a **reply** message that carries along the return value of the invocation. It uses the descriptor_id carried along with the messages, to propagate the result, through the same path, back to the user. The Resource Manager attaches a timestamp with each of the messages to measure peer connection times, local computation times and remote task execution times.

The Resource Manager measures the local execution time of the tasks that includes the processing time of the task at a peer and the queueing time at the local Scheduler's task queue. The processing time of the task depends on the type of object to be executed, the parameters carried along with the task and the speed of the processor. The queueing time is affected by the priority (laxity value) of the task and the number of tasks currently being waiting at the Scheduler's queue.

Upon the receipt of a reply message, the Resource Manager measures the end-to-end latency of the task, as the time required for the task to complete, starting at user invocation until the reply message is received back at the user. Thus, the projected latency of the task includes the transmission times to propagate the task from one peer to another and the local execution time of the task. The transmission times are affected by the number of hops the task is propagated and the available bandwidth on the communication links. The Resource Manager measures the percentage of the processing load and the amount of memory used during the task execution. It obtains this information by using system calls to the `/proc` interface.

3.2   Resource and Timing Measurement Propagation

Self-organization is greatly affected by the frequency with which tasks execute in the system and resource and timing measurements are propagated to the peers. The Connection Manager triggers propagation of such measurements in two cases: (1) as a result of the Resource Manager feedback that measures new resource loads and timing measurements at the peer, and (2) when the Connection Manager detects an incoming or withdrawn peer connection. For example, when a connection with a new peer is established, the Connection Manager propagates its current resource and timing measurements to that peer.

Assuming that node p has m immediate peers, the Connection Manager at p constructs an `update` message that carries an array of length l for each of the m immediate peers. The array is constructed based on the measurements stored at p's horizon-based state graph which capture resource and timing information up to l hops away. By bounding l to a small number, we can control the amount of information propagated to the peers. Each entry in the array includes the following information: *(IP address, port num, CPU load, network bandwidth, immediate peers)*. Further, to regulate the rate of update propagation, the Connection Manager can choose to send an update only if the resource measurements have increased above an upper bound `HIGH` or if the peer is underutilized (below `LOW` bound). The advantage is that the amount of network traffic is minimized.

Upon the receipt of an update message from an immediate peer p, node q updates its local horizon-based state graph with p's most recent resource and timing measurements. The Connection Manager detects a new indirect peer, if the array has a new entry and thus updates its state graph. Similarly, if a peer has disconnected, the Connection Manager marks the peer as disconnected and updates the corresponding connection times in the graph.

There are two importance observations in the measurement propagation. First, there is a trade off between the accuracy of the resource utilization information maintained by the Connection Manager peers and the frequency of the update propagation. The higher the propagation frequency, the more accurate the measurements stored. However, a high propagation frequency incurs a high penalty due to the large number of messages that have to be sent. Second, the accuracy of the information decreases as the number of hops between the peers increases. To remedy this, we introduce levels of confidence through weights $(w_0, w_2, ..., w_{l-1})$, $\sum_{i=0,...,l-1} w_i = 1$, where the higher confidence goes to peers one hop away.

3.3   Self-organization

The goal in the peer-based organization algorithm is to improve task execution times by connecting to faster or less loaded peers.

The Connection Manager uses the resource load measurements collected at its horizon-based state graph, to estimate the projected latency of the tasks at the immediate and indirect peers. Let ρ_p be the average load on peer p and τ_{tp} be the mean processing time of task t on peer p. Assuming that ρ_c is the average load on the communication link c and σ_{tc} is the mean transmission time on each communication link c, the Connection Manager (using an M/M/1 queueing model) computes the projected latency of the tasks at peer p as:

$$Projected\_Latency_p = \sum_t \frac{\sigma_{tc}}{1 - \rho_c} + \frac{\tau_{tp}}{1 - \rho_p}$$

Once the projected task latencies have been estimated, the Connection Manager evaluates the relative benefit of its peers. It uses a utility function based on the resource loads and the task computation and communication latencies. Each node computes the utility of both its immediate and indirect peers and tries to connect to indirect peers with the highest utility. These are the peers that have the highest probability of meeting the soft real-time requirements of the tasks.

The Connection Manager at node p estimates the effects on the task latencies by considering the effects of increased or decreased processor loads and communication latencies on the times required to execute the tasks. The Connection Manager estimates the increased latencies of the tasks currently executed at p as a result of the new peer connection. A similar estimate is made for the reduced times of the tasks run in the vicinity.

Thus, the Utility value of both its immediate and indirect peers, as follows:

$$Peer\_Util_p(t) = \alpha * Peer\_Util_p(t - 1) + \beta * e^{-Proj\_Latency_p}$$

where α and β are used to balance between new and previously computed utility values ($\alpha + \beta = 1$). By using exponentially weighted averaging it allows us to track current behavior with a large value yielding rapid response to changing conditions, and a small value yielding more smoothing and less noise. If the types of the executing tasks are stable, our algorithm approximates good peers accurately. If the behavior changes dynamically, the stability of the system is affected by the rate with which each node evaluates its peers and tries to connect to better ones.

The peer-based algorithm determines important indirect peers as peers with high utility values. It identifies immediate peers with low utility values as those where the projected latency of the tasks propagated through those peers increases and the tasks start missing their deadlines. Thus, the Connection Manager at p identifies the peer q with the highest $Peer\_Util_q$ value for node p and peer s with the lowest $Peer\_Util_s$ as a candidate for replacement. Then, it probes peer q for a connection, by generating and sending a `ping` message. If the remote peer q accepts the connection, it replies with a `pong` message including its geographical information {IP address, port number} to allow peer p to connect to. If the maximum number of connections at p has exceeded, the Connection Manager chooses to disconnect from the least important immediate peer.

3.4 Dynamic System Operation

In a large-scale system, the availability of the resources changes as a result of new nodes becoming available, existing nodes failing or disconnecting, and new tasks executing in the system. For example, the execution of a new task increases the load on the processors and requires new projections of the task latencies, triggering self-organization. If the relative utility of an indirect peer increases over time, the node attempts to move closer to that peer and connect to it directly. If the connection is acceptable, it is actually performed. As the maximum number of connections allowed is exceeded or the latency on a peer is too long, then immediate peers with less utility are removed.

One issue in self-organization is how to tear down connections from peers. If a node disconnects from a peer whose tasks are currently being executed to remote peers, the return path of the tasks may be disconnected and the result cannot be propagated back to the source. To avoid this problem, we define a prior_disconnection period, during which two node temporarily remain connected until the results from currently executing tasks are propagated back to the source. During this time, the disconnected peer does not accept new tasks for propagation or execution. Although this will incur some additional overhead, it will allow all the tasks to complete.

The effectiveness of the system is affected by the frequency with which each peer executes the self-organization algorithm to find peers with better utility values. This can affect the stability of our system. To address this issue we choose to restrict the maximum number of times per time interval that a peer can make re-connections. This time interval is determined by considering the characteristics of the tasks in the system.

4 Implementation and Experimental Evaluation

4.1 Experimental Setup

To evaluate the working and performance of our self-organization algorithms we performed empirical experiments. The platform for our implementation consisted of Athlon XP2000 processors and Intel Pentium IV processors with 1GB

memory, running Mandrake Linux 9.0, over a 100Mbit/s network. We built a
P2P system running on these machines. The peers are implemented using the
C++ language and are multi-threaded. To simulate peers of different bandwidth
capabilities we limited the sending and receiving speed of the peers. Figure 2
illustrates the initial topology of the system. The thin lines represent peers with
slow communication links. The bandwidth on those slow peers was restricted
to 200KBytes, the bandwidth on the remaining peers was set to 1MByte. Slow
communication links introduce higher transmission overhead, especially when
the source sends messages at a high transmission speed. In those cases, self-
organization would be beneficial to both peers sending and receiving messages.

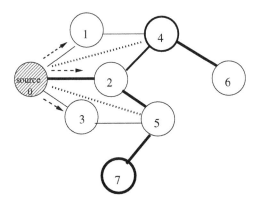

Fig. 2. System topology for the peer-based organization algorithm

4.2   Application Tasks

We used soft real-time distributed multimedia tasks to drive the empirical evaluation of our system. In our scenarios, video streams were generated from the
sources and transmitted over the network from one peer to the other until they
reach the destination, where individual streams received from different sources
are assembled and displayed separately. The multimedia tasks needed to be
transcoded into a different format to reach resource-constrained client machines.
Examples of transcoding operations include changing video compression formats,
reducing video playback bit-rate and adjusting picture resolution.

The multimedia streams consist of a sequence of independent media units,
in the case of MPEG-1 format these are called Group of Pictures (GOPs). For
the experiments, our sources generated video streams of MPEG-1 format with
a resolution of 320x240 and a variable bit rate (VBR) of about 900Kbps, each
Group of Picture (GOP) consists of 12-13 frames which correspond to a 0.5
second playback time. The inter-arrival time between successive GOPs is 0.5
seconds. Transcoding services were implemented using the libavcodec library
[25], which is an open source media library.

In the experiment, our transcoding task was to reduce the bit-rate from
900Kbit/s to 150Kbit/s. The request generator fetches a GOP, encapsulates it

into a request message and forwards it to a peer. When the task finishes execution at a peer, the Connection Manager encapsulates the result in a reply message and sends it back to the request generator, following the same path. The tasks had to travel an average of 2 hops to get transcoded. The figure shows that the average transmission time is 70ms and the average transcoding time is computed to about 53 milliseconds. However, our experiments showed that the transmission times increase rapidly when network connections are slow (*e.g.*, 200Kbit/s) or when the tasks have to propagate more hops in the system. For GOPs of larger data size the transcoding time also increases, although the increase is small.

4.3   Performance Metrics

To evaluate the performance of our self-organization algorithms, we use the following metrics:

- *Miss ratio:* represents the percentage of tasks that miss their deadlines. The miss ratio is primarily affected by the utilization on the nodes and the communication links. As the load on the nodes or the transmission times of the tasks increase, the probability that the tasks miss their deadlines is higher.
- *Task execution time:* defined as the actual execution time of the task in the system. The execution time depends on the computation time of the task that includes transcoding time and queueing time, and the transmission latency experienced at each hop along the path it travels.
- *Estimated Projected Latency:* this is the estimated amount of time for the task to execute, projected by the Connection Manager at the peers. The task's projected latency depends on (1) the accuracy of the measurements recorded by the Resource Managers, (2) the feedback they provide to the Connection Manager and (3) the frequency with which Connection Managers propagate these measurements to their peers. For example, if the update frequency is low, the peers may not have recent resource information about their peers and therefore fail to estimate the task projected latencies accurately.

4.4   Self-organization Algorithm

We conducted three experiments to measure the performance, accuracy and predictability of our self-organization algorithm.

End-to-End Task Execution Times. In the first experiment, we measured the average end-to-end task execution times as a function of the number of transcoding tasks executed in the system. The initial topology is shown in Figure 2, where the dotted lines represent the connections established as a result of the organization algorithm. In this experiment, each peer runs the peer-based organization algorithm. Due to lack of space, we report results only for node 0. Note, that, node 0 is connected to one fast peer 2 and two slow peers 1, 3. Transmission tasks are generated from node 0 with deadlines of 500ms. Resource

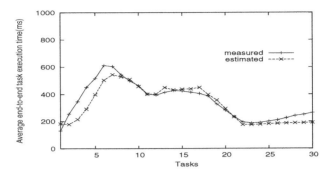

Fig. 3. Measured and estimated end-to-end task execution times as a function of the number of tasks being executed in the system

and timing measurements are propagated at a rate of 200ms and self-organization is triggered every 3-5 seconds.

Figure 3 shows the average end-to-end execution times of the tasks. The solid graph in the figure represents the actual execution times of the tasks, measured by the Resource Managers. The dotted graph in the figure represents the projected latencies of the tasks, estimated by the Connection Managers.

As tasks are generated, the execution times of the tasks increase. The reason is that because node 0 has two slow peers, the tasks are not accepted for execution at those peers, they are propagated to their own peers in the system. As a result, their transmission latencies increase. The Connection Manager at node 0 observes the increase in the task execution times, and triggers the peer-based organization algorithm. This will compute the relative utility values of the peers and will select the peer 4 with the highest utility to connect to (as shown with the dotted line in Figure 2). At this point, the maximum number of connections

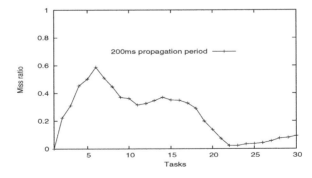

Fig. 4. Task miss ratio as a function of the number of tasks being executed in the system

for the node has being exceeded, and the node chooses to disconnect from peer
1 that has low utility value. This reduces the end-to-end execution times of the
tasks (shown by the decline in Figure 3). At a latter point during the execution,
the Connection Manager discovers another peer 5 with a high utility value and
chooses to connect to that peer directly and disconnect from its immediate peer
3. This will further improve the projected latencies of the tasks.

An important observation in this experiment is that the Connection Managers
accurately estimates the projected latencies of the tasks at all times, even after
organization. The reason is that the Connection Manager propagates the new
resource measurements to their peers, which are stored in their horizon-based
state graphs and are used to compute the new projected latencies for the tasks.

Miss Ratio. Figure 4 shows the corresponding improvement to the miss ratio
of the tasks as a result of running the peer-based self-organization algorithm.
The figure shows that when the execution times of the tasks increase, tasks start
missing their deadlines. This is attributed to two factors: (1) the queueing delays
in the local Schedulers' queues due to the large number of transcoding tasks
concurrently being executed in the system, and (2) the transmission latencies
experienced by the slow communication links and the number of hops that the
tasks are being propagated. For example, when the execution times are 600ms,
60% of the tasks miss their deadlines. After the first organization, the task miss
ratio drops to 35%. The second organization improves the task miss ratio even
further and eventually very few tasks miss their deadlines.

Effect of Propagation Frequency to Task Execution Times. In the last
experiment of the peer-based organization algorithm, we evaluated the effectiveness of the resource and timing measurement propagation frequency to the task
execution times (Figure 5). In these, we varied the frequency with which Connection Managers propagate feedback information to their peers from 200ms to

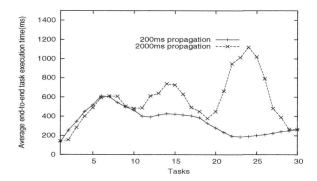

Fig. 5. End-to-end task execution times as a function of different propagation
frequencies

2000ms. Upon the receipt of new resource and timing measurements, the Connection Managers will use the new measurements to decide to which peers to propagate tasks that cannot be executed locally, or whether they need to run the self-organization algorithm to connect to better peers.

When the frequency is high (200ms), the Connection Managers capture load fluctuations at their peers accurately, and therefore the queueing and transmission latencies of the tasks does not increase further. However, if the frequency is low, the Connection Managers do not accurately capture the load fluctuations at their peers. As a result, the end-to-end execution times of the tasks increase, and most of the tasks miss their deadlines. The frequency of propagation depends on the characteristics of the tasks (such as number and distribution of requests, and typical computation times) and resource and communication capabilities of the peers. Our experiments indicate that a frequency of 200ms is adequate to capture load fluctuations and transcode tasks end-to-end without missing their deadlines.

5   Related Work

The task of organizing a large network of peers for efficient data access is a very interesting problem that only recently has been addressed [26], [27], [28], [29], [30], [31]. However, the majority of this work has focused on file sharing applications.

The first wave of the P2P systems [1], [32], [2], [33], [34] perform poorly either because they rely on a centralized manager or they propose simplistic routing mechanisms. For example, Gnutella [2] relies on flooding the network with messages. Limewire [35] organizes the peers on static interest groups based on their preferred music category.

Distributed hash tables (DHTs) have been proposed as an alternative approach for organizing peer-to-peer systems [36], [4], [5], [3], [37], [38], [39] that improve performance by minimizing the number of hops to find the data. These consist of two components: (1) a consistent hashing over a one-dimensional space, and (2) an indexing mechanism to quickly navigate the space. These have the disadvantage that (a) assume that all peers are inherently equal in terms of resources, and (b) impose a a structure in the network by mapping objects to particular nodes and therefore may require a slow connection to be heavily utilized in order to discover a popular item. To the best of our knowledge, ours is the first work, that proposes self-organizing algorithms based on the dynamic properties of the peers to meet the distributed applications end-to-end QoS requirements.

Recent efforts recognize the need to improve the performance of the overlay network by partitioning peers into groups based on the round-trip time (RTT) of the messages. In these, peers in the same group are closes to each other in terms of latency. [40] presents a binning scheme based on landmark nodes to determine the relative latencies for the peer partitioning. In [41], the authors propose to construct an auxiliary network on top of the overlay network using BGP information, and choose neighboring peers based on some random landmark nodes. Eugene *et al* [42] propose an approach that maps overlay peers into individual points in Euclidean space and approximate the distances in IP infrastructures using Euclidean distances. Other work proposes to incrementally improve peer latencies by keeping a list of shortcuts in the routing table. The shortcuts generally point to nodes with smaller latencies. These goals are achieved either through interest-based locality [43], or through random sampling techniques [44]. All of the above work only consider network connectivities and may require extra services, such as node landmarks.

Several efforts have shown [45, 24, 46, 47] that to meet the applications' end-to-end QoS requirements, we need knowledge of real-time task information including the task's deadline, resource requirements and execution times. Most of them have shown that least laxity scheduling is an effective algorithm for distributed scheduling in soft real-time distributed systems.

6   Conclusions

In this paper we have proposed two self-organization algorithms that improve task execution times and system scalability in P2P systems. When a peer is discovered to frequently provide good execution times, the peer-based algorithm attempts to connect directly to that peer. If an underutilized peer discovers slow or overutilized processors, it attempts to move closer to those peers to improve the task execution times and balance the load across multiple processors. The experimental results show that our self-organization algorithms can effectively reduce the task end-to-end execution times, improve task miss ratio, and are able to dynamically adapt to changes in resource availability or peer connections and disconnections.

Acknowledgements. This work is supported by NSF Award 0330481.

References

1. Napster, "Napster home page," http://www.napster.com.
2. Gnutella, "Gnutella home page," http://www.gnutella.com.
3. J. Kubiatowicz, D. Bindel, Y. Chen, S. Czerwinski, P. Eaton, D. Geels, R. Gummadi, S. Rhea, H. Weatherspoon, W. Weimer, C. Wells, and B. Zhao, "OceanStore: An Architecture for Global-Scale Persistent Storage," in *Proceedings of ASPLOS*, Cambridge, MA, 2000.
4. A. Rowstron and P. Druschel, "Storage Management and Caching in PAST, a Large-scale Persistent Peer-To-Peer Storage Utility," in *Proceedings of the 18th SOSP*, Toronto, Canada, 2001.
5. I. Stoica, R. Morris, D. Karger, M.F. Kaashoek, and H. Balakrishnan, "Chord: A Scalable Peer-to-peer Lookup Service for Internet Applications," in *Proceedings of ACM SIGCOMM Conference*, San Diego, CA, August 2001.

6. L. Xiao, X. Zhang, and Z. Xu, "On reliable and scalable peer-to-peer web document sharing," in *Proceedings of the International Parallel and Distributed Computing Symposium*, Fort Lauderdale, Florida, April 2002.

7. SETI Project Home Page, "SETI@home," http://sethiathome.ssl.berkeley.edu.

8. Entropia, "Entropia home page," http://www.entropia.com.

9. S. Jain, R. Mahajan, D. Wetherall, and G. Borriello, "Scalable self-organizing overlays," in *Technical report UW-CSE 02-02-02, University of Washington*, 2002.

10. Y-H Chu, S. G. Rao, and H. Zhang, "A case for end system multicast," in *ACM SIGMETRICS'00*, Santa Clara, CA, 2000.

11. D. Zeinalipour-Yazti, V. Kalogeraki, and D. Gunopulos, "Exploiting locality for scalable information retrieval in peer-to-peer systems," in *Information Systems Journal*, 2004.

12. C. Gill, J. P. Loyall, R. E. Schantz, M. Atighetchi, J. M. Gossett, D. Corman, and D. C. Schmidt, "Integrated Adaptive QoS Management in Middleware: A Case Study," in *Proceedings of the 10th IEEE Real-Time and Embedded Technology and Applications Symposium*, Toronto, Canada, May 2004.

13. Object Management Group, "The Common Object Request Broker: Architecture and Specification," Edition 2.4, formal/00-10-01, October 2000.

14. D. Box, *Essential COM*, Addison-Wesley, January 1998.

15. A. Wollrath, R. Riggs, and J. Waldo, "A distributed object model for the Java system," *Computing Systems*, vol. 9, no. 4, pp. 265–290, Fall 1996.

16. SOAP, "Soap home page," http://www.soap.org.

17. V. Kalogeraki, P. M. Melliar-Smith, and L. E. Moser, "Dynamic scheduling for soft real-time distributed object systems," in *Proceedings of the IEEE Third International Symposium on Object-Oriented Real-Time Distributed Computing*, Newport, CA, March 2000, pp. 114–121.

18. H.-H. Chu and K. Nahrstedt, "A soft real-time scheduling server in unix operating system," 1995, pp. 381–406, Auerbach Publications.

19. Object Management Group, "Real-time CORBA," Edition 1.0, formal/00-10-60, May 1998.

20. Object Management Group, "Dynamic Scheduling," Revised Submission, orbos/00-08-12, August 2000.

21. Todd Tannenbaum, Derek Wright, Karen Miller, and Miron Livny, "Condor – a distributed job scheduler," in *Beowulf Cluster Computing with Linux*, Thomas Sterling, Ed. MIT Press, October 2001.

22. Vana Kalogeraki, *Resource Management for Real-Time Fault-Tolerant Distributed Systems*, Ph.D. thesis, University of California, Santa Barbara, Dec. 2000.

23. V. Kalogeraki, P. M. Melliar-Smith, and L. E. Moser, "Dynamic scheduling of distributed method invocations," in *Proceedings of the 21st IEEE Real-Time Systems Symposium*, Orlando, Florida, November 2000, pp. 57–66.

24. M. L. Dertouzos and A. K.-L. Mok, "Multiprocessor on-line scheduling of hard real-time tasks," *IEEE Transactions on Software Engineering*, vol. 15, no. 12, pp. 1497–1506, December 1989.

25. The FFMPEG Homepage, "http://ffmpeg.sourceforge.net/," .

26. A. Mohan and V. Kalogeraki, "Speculative Routing and Update Propagation: A Kundali Centric Approach," in *International Conference on Communications*, Anchorage, Alaska, May 2003.

27. K. Aberer, M. Punceva, M. Hauswirth, and R. Schmidt, "Improving Data Access in P2P Systems," *IEEE Internet Computing*, vol. 6, no. 1, pp. 58–67, January/February 2002.

28. V. Kalogeraki, A. Delis, and D. Gunopulos, "Peer-to-Peer Architectures for Scalable, Efficient and Reliable Media Services," in *Proceedings of the International Parallel and Distributed Computing Symposium*, Nice, France, April 2003.

29. S. Waterhouse, D.M. Doolin, G. Kan, and Y. Faybishenko, "Distributed Search in P2P Networks," *IEEE Internet Computing*, vol. 6, no. 1, pp. 68–72, January/February 2002.

30. R. Lienhart, M. Holliman, Y-K. Chen, I. Kozintsev, and M. Yeung, "Improving Media Services on P2P Networks," *IEEE Internet Computing*, vol. 6, no. 1, pp. 73–77, January/February 2002.

31. V. Kalogeraki and F. Chen, "Managing distributed objects in peer-to-peer networks," *IEEE Network, special issue on Middleware Technologies for future Communication Netowkrs*, vol. 18, no. 1, pp. 22–29, January 2004.

32. Morpheus, "Morpheus home page," http://www.musiccity.com.

33. Freenet, "Freenet home page," http://freenet.sourceforge.com.

34. Kazaa, "Kazaa home page," http://www.kazaa.com.

35. Limewire, "Limewire home page," http://www.limewire.com.

36. S. Ratnasamy, P. Francis, M. Handley, and R. Karp, "A Scalable Content-Addressable Network," in *Proceedings of the SIGCOMM'01*, San Diego, CA, August 2001.

37. Y. Saito, C. Karamanolis, M. Karlsson, and M. Mahalingam, "Taming Aggressive Replication in the Pangaea Wide-Area File System ," in *Proceedings of OSDI 2002*, Boston, CA, 2002.

38. A. Adya, W. J. Bolosky, M. Castro, G. Cermak, R. Chaiken, J. R. Douceur, J. Howell, J. R. Lorch, M. Theimer, and R. P. Wattenhofer, "FARSITE: Federated, Available, and Reliable Storage for an Incompletely Trusted Environment," in *Proceedings of OSDI 2002*, Boston, CA, 2002.

39. A. Muthitacharoen, R. Morris, T. M. Gil, and B. Chen, "Ivy: A Read/Write Peer-to-Peer File System," in *Proceedings of OSDI 2002*, Boston, CA, 2002.

40. S. Ratnasamy, M. Handley, R. Karp, and S. Shenker, "Topologically-aware overlay construction and server selection," in *Proceedings of IEEE INFOCOM Conference*, June 2002.

41. Z. Xu, M. Mahalingam, and M. Karlsson, "Turning heterogeneity into an advantage in overlay routing," in *Proceedings of IEEE INFOCOM Conference*, April 2003.

42. T.S. Eugene and H. Zhang, "Predicting Internet Network Distance with Coordinates-based Approaches," in *Proceedings of IEEE INFOCOM Conference*, 2002.

43. K. Sripanidkulchai, B. Maggs, and H. Zhang, "Efficient Content Location using Interest-based Locality in Peer-to-Peer Systems," in *Proceedings of IEEE INFOCOM Conference*, April 2003.

44. H. Zhang, A. Goel, and R. Govindan, "Incrementally improving lookup latency in distributed hash table systems," in *Proceedings of ACM SIGMETRICS Conference*, 2003.

45. G. Manimaran and C. R. R. Murthy, "An efficient dynamic scheduling algorithm for multiprocessor real-time systems," *IEEE Transactions on Parallel and Distributed Systems*, vol. 9, no. 3, pp. 312–319, March 1998.

46. F. Sandrini, F. D. Giandomenico, A. Bondavalli, and E. Nett, "Scheduling solutions for supporting dependable real-time applications," in *Proceedings of the IEEE Third International Symposium on Object-Oriented Real-Time Distributed Computing*, 2000.

47. J. Hildebrandt, F. Golatowski, and D. Timmermann, "Scheduling coprocessor for enhanced least-laxity-first scheduling in hard real-time systems," in *Proceedings of 11th Euromicro Conference on Real-Time Systems. Euromicro RTS'99*.

Cooperative Content Distribution: Scalability Through Self-organization

Pascal Felber[1,*] and Ernst W. Biersack[2]

[1] University of Neuchâtel, Switzerland
pascal.felber@unine.ch
[2] Institut EURECOM, France
erbi@eurecom.fr

Abstract. Peer-to-peer networks have often been touted as the ultimate solution to scalability. Although cooperative techniques have been initially used almost exclusively for content lookup and sharing, one of the most promising application of the peer-to-peer paradigm is to capitalize the bandwidth of client peers to quickly distribute large content and withstand flash-crowds (i.e., a sudden increase in popularity of some online content). Cooperative content distribution is based on the premise that the capacity of a network is as high as the sum of the resources of its nodes: the more peers in the network, the higher its aggregate bandwidth, and the better it can scale and serve new peers. Such networks can thus spontaneously adapt to the demand by taking advantage of available resources. In this paper, we evaluate the use of peer-to-peer networks for content distribution under various system assumptions, such as peer arrival rates, bandwidth capacities, cooperation strategies, or peer lifetimes. We argue that the *self-scaling* and *self-organizing* properties of cooperative networks pave the way for cost-effective, yet highly efficient and robust content distribution.

1 Introduction

Peer-to-peer systems, in which peer computers form a cooperative network and share their resources (storage, CPU, bandwidth), have attracted a lot of interest lately. After the apparition of the first truly successful peer-to-peer systems [1, 2], and the significant amount of research conducted in Academia and in the Industry, most researchers now agree that peer-to-peer systems are more than just a fashion phenomenon. They offer great potential for building cooperative networks that are self-organizing, efficient, scalable, and reliable.

Research in peer-to-peer networks has so far mainly focused on content storage and lookup, but fewer efforts have been spent on its actual distribution. By capitalizing the *bandwidth* of peer nodes, cooperative architectures offer great potential for addressing some of the most challenging issue of today's Internet:

---

* This work was performed while the author was at Institut EURECOM.

O. Babaoglu et al. (Eds.): SELF-STAR 2004, LNCS 3460, pp. 343–357, 2005.

the cost-effective distribution of bandwidth-intensive content to thousands of simultaneous users both Internet-wide and in private networks, and the resilience to "flash crowds"—a huge and sudden surge of request traffic that usually leads to the collapse of the affected server, as happened to the Web sites of major media companies during the events of 9/11.

Cooperative content distribution networks are inherently *self-scalable*, in that the bandwidth capacity of the system increases as more peers arrive: each new peer requests service from, but also provides service to, the other peers. The network can thus spontaneously adapt to the demand by taking advantage of the resources provided by every peer.

As an example of the self-scaling properties of cooperative content distribution, consider the situation where a server must replicate a critical file to a large number of clients, e.g., an antivirus update, to all $100,000$ machines of a large company. Given a file size of 4 MB, and a server (client) bandwidth capacity of 100 Mb/s (10 Mb/s) with 90% link utilization, a classical client/server distribution protocol would distribute the file by iteratively serving groups of 10 simultaneous clients in $u = \frac{32 \text{ Mb}}{9 \text{ Mb/s}} = 3.55$ seconds. Updating $100,000$ clients would thus necessitate $\frac{100,000}{10} u$, i.e., almost 10 hours.

In contrast, cooperative distribution leverages the bandwidth of the nodes that have already obtained the file, thus dynamically increasing the service capacity of the system as the file propagates to the clients. As each client that has already received the file can serve another client while the server updates 10 new clients, we can compute the number of clients updated at time t as $n(t) = 2n(t-u)+10 = 2^{\lfloor t/u \rfloor} 10 - 10$. Updating $100,000$ clients would thus necessitate less than 1 minute, as can be observed in Figure 1. The exponential increase of peer-to-peer distribution provides a sharp contrast with the linear progression of traditional client/server distribution, and illustrates the self-scaling property of cooperative networks.

We have studied in [3] the scalability of cooperative distribution architectures, where each peer has equal upload and download rates of b, and there are no failures. We have shown that it takes $1 + \lfloor log_k N \rfloor \cdot \frac{k}{C}$ rounds to serve N peers organized in k spanning trees, where a round is the time needed to download the complete file at rate b and c is the number of chunks the file is split into. This result indicate that the number of peers that complete the download grows exponentially in time and in the number of chunks (large numbers of chunks allow all peers to busy most of the time). Obviously, such static and homogeneous scenarios are rare in real-world systems, where the peers typically have different (often asymmetric) bandwidth, can join and leave anytime, and have only a limited view of the complete system insufficient for global optimizations.

In this paper, we discuss and evaluate the use of peer-to-peer networks for content distribution under various system assumptions, such as peer arrival rates, bandwidth capacities, cooperation strategies, or peer lifetimes. We argue that a key property for the good scalability of content distribution architecture is their ability to *self-organize* by letting each peer select dynamically which other peers to cooperate with over time. This study exhibits the trade offs encountered when deploying a content distribution network and emphasizes that the choice of a specific strategy strongly depends on the considered optimization criteria.

2   Cooperative Content Distribution

In order to maximize the participation of each of the peers in the network, large content is typically split into many blocks (or "chunks") that are directly exchanged between the peers—a technique also known as "swarming." The large number and small size of the chunks are key to quickly create enough diversity in the network for each of the peers to be useful to some other peers.

Cooperative networks are usually build incrementally, with joining peers dynamically connecting to existing peers to eventually create complex mesh topologies. In practice, a peer usually knows only a subset of other peers, and actively trades with an even smaller subset. In addition to the actual structure of the mesh (i.e., which and how many neighbors each peers has), two factors are crucial to the global effectiveness of the content distribution process:

- *Peer selection strategy:* which among our neighboring peers will we actively trade with, i.e., serve or request chunks from?
- *Chunk selection strategy:* which chunks will we preferably serve to, or request from, other peers?

The popular BitTorrent [4] tool, which we have studied extensively in [5], empirically selects the peers that offer the best upload and download rates to trade with ("tit-for-tat" strategy). When a new peers joins the system, it initially requests random chunks in order to quickly receive some data and become useful to the system; thereafter, it requests the rarest chunks among those owned by

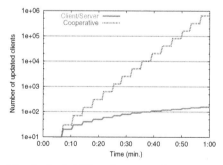

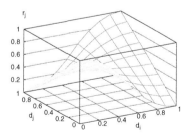

Fig. 1. Scalability of cooperative content distribution: the number of clients that successfully receive a file increases linearly with client/server distribution, and exponentially with cooperative distribution

Fig. 2. *Adaptive-missing* peer selection strategy: Peer i computes the rank r_j of every other peer j as a function of d_i and d_j (here, we have $U(0,1) = 0.5$)

its neighbors, because rare chunks have a higher "trading value" than common chunks.

The main focus of our study is to evaluate several peer and chunk selection strategies, and determine which ones perform best in various deployment scenarios. For the purpose of our evaluation, we only study the extreme case where each peer knows all other peers (fully-connected mesh) and can potentially trade with any of those peers during its lifetime, although we impose a limit on the number of simultaneous active connections. This assumption allows us to observe the asymptotic behavior of the various cooperative strategies.

2.1   Deployment Scenarios

We specifically focus on two deployment scenarios that correspond to real-world applications of cooperative content distribution. In the first scenario, we assume that some critical content need to be quickly replicated on a large number of machines within the private network of a large company. This essentially corresponds to a *push* model where all the peers are known beforehand and distribution stops once the content has been fully replicated on all the machines, which typically have similar connectivity (homogeneous bandwidth).

The second scenario corresponds to the traditional Internet flash-crowd phenomenon, where a large number of clients access almost simultaneously some large popular content. This corresponds to a *pull* model with continuous arrival of the peers. Distribution continues over several peer "generations," with some peers arriving well after the first peers have already left. The clients typically have heterogeneous bandwidth capacities, ranging from dial-up modems to broadband access (asynchronous and synchronous).

2.2   Notation

We denote by $\mathcal{C}$ the set of all chunks in the file being distributed, and by $\mathcal{D}_i$ and $\mathcal{M}_i$ the set of chunks that peer i has already downloaded and is still missing, respectively (with $\mathcal{M}_i \cup \mathcal{D}_i = \mathcal{C}$ and $\mathcal{M}_i \cap \mathcal{D}_i = \emptyset$). Similarly, $d_i \triangleq |\mathcal{D}_i|/|\mathcal{C}|$ and $m_i \triangleq |\mathcal{M}_i|/|\mathcal{C}|$ correspond to the proportions of chunks that peer i has already downloaded and is still missing, respectively. The function $U(a,b)$ returns a random number uniformly distributed in the interval $[a,b]$.

2.3   Peer Selection

The peer selection strategy defines "trading relationships" between peers and is the key factor to the network's *self-organization* property. In our simplified model, we assume that all the peers know one another. When a peer has some chunks available and some free uplink bandwidth capacity, it will use a peer selection strategy to *locally* determine which other peer it will serve next. In this paper, we propose and evaluate the following peer selection strategies:

- *Random:* A peer is selected at random. This strategy is expected to achieve good diversity in peer connectivity.

- *Least missing:* Preference is given to the peers that have many chunks, i.e., we serve in priority peer j with $d_j \geq d_i$, $\forall i$. This strategy is inspired by the SRPT (shortest remaining processing time) scheduling policy that is known to minimize the service time of jobs [6].
- *Most missing:* Preference is given to the peers that have few chunks (newcomers), i.e., we serve in priority peer j with $d_j \leq d_i$, $\forall i$. The rationale behind this strategy is to evenly spread chunks among all peers to allow them to quickly serve other peers.
- *Random least missing:* Similar to *least missing*, but with a random component added in the selection process. We serve in priority peer j with the lowest rank, computed as $U(0, |\mathcal{M}_j|^2)$.
- *Random most missing:* Similar to *most missing*, but with a random component added in the selection process. We serve in priority peer j with the lowest rank, computed as $U(0, |\mathcal{D}_j|^2)$.
- *Adaptive-missing:* Peers that have many chunks serve peers that have few chunks, and vice-versa, with more randomness introduced when download tend to be half complete. A peer i will serve in priority peer j with the lowest rank r_j, computed as:

$$r_j^{Rnd} = U(0, 1)$$
$$r_j^{Det} = \begin{cases} d_j & : \quad d_i \geq 0.5 \\ m_j & : \quad d_i < 0.5 \end{cases}$$
$$f = (1 - |2d_i - 1|)^2$$
$$r_j = f r_j^{Rnd} + (1 - f) r_j^{Det}$$

where r_j^{Rnd} and r_j^{Det} are the random and deterministic ranks of peer j, respectively, and $f \in [0, 1]$ is a weight factor that controls randomness and is maximal when peer i is exactly half-way through the download. A graphical representation of r_j as a function of d_i and d_j is shown in Figure 2. This strategy is expected to give good chances to newcomers without artificially slowing down peers that are almost complete.

Although not shown in this paper because of space constraints, we have also experimented with additional peer selection strategies that take into account the free bandwidth capacities of the peers.

2.4   Chunk Selection

The chunk selection strategy specifies which chunks should preferably be traded between the peers. Chunk selection can be performed by the receiver (which requests specific chunks from its neighbors) or by sender (which decides which chunk it will send next on an active connection). With both interaction models, obviously, the chosen chunk must be held by the sender and not by the receiver. In our simplified model, we assume that every peer knows the list of chunks held by its neighbors (i.e., all peers with a fully-connected mesh topology) and that the chunk selection strategy is applied on the sender's side. In this paper, we evaluate the following chunk selection strategies:

- *Random:* The sending peer i selects a chunk $c \in (\mathcal{D}_i \cap \mathcal{M}_j)$ at random among those that it holds and the receiving peer j needs. This strategy ensures good diversity of the traded chunks.
- *Rarest:* The sending peer i selects the rarest chunk $c \in (\mathcal{D}_i \cap \mathcal{M}_j)$ among those that it holds and the receiving peer j needs. Rarity is computed from the number of instances of each chunk held by the peers known to the sender. This strategy is expected to maximize the number of copies of the rarest chunk in the system.

3   Experimental Setup

For the purpose of evaluating cooperative content distribution, we have developed a simulator that models various types of peer-to-peer networks and allows us to observe step-by-step the distribution of large files among all peers in the systems, according to several metrics. Although we have taken extra care to reproduce realistic operating conditions, we have yet made some assumptions in order to simplify and speed up the simulations. In particular, we do not consider failures (peer or network) nor link congestion in any of the experiments, and we do not favor long-running connections overt short connections as real systems usually do. We also intentionally present here the results of the simulations of extreme scenarios (little heterogeneity, limited server bandwidth) that best exhibit the differences between the various aforementioned strategies; more moderate scenarios have shown the same general trends, albeit with lower intensity.

Our simulator is essentially event-driven, with events being scheduled and mapped to real-time with a millisecond precision. The transmission delay of each chunk is computed dynamically according the link capacities (minimum of the sender uplink and receiver downlink) and the number of simultaneous transfers on the links (bandwidth is equally split between concurrent connections).

Once a peer i holds at least one chunk, it becomes a potential server. It first sorts its neighboring peers according to the specified peer selection strategy. It then iterates through the sorted list until it finds a peer j that (1) needs some chunks from $\mathcal{D}_i$ ($\mathcal{D}_i \cap \mathcal{M}_j \neq \emptyset$), (2) is not already being served by peer i, and (3) is not overloaded. We say that a peer is overloaded if it has reached its maximum number of connections *and* has less than 128 kb/s bandwidth capacity left. Peer i then applies the specified chunk selection strategy to choose the best chunk to send to peer j. Peer i repeats this whole process until it becomes overloaded or finds no other peer to serve.

Our simulator allows us to specify several parameters that define its general behavior and operating conditions. The most important ones relate to the content being transmitted (file size, chunk size), the peer properties (arrival rates, bandwidth capacities, lifetimes, number of simultaneous active connections), and global simulation parameters (number of initial servers or "origin peers," simulation duration, peer selection strategy, chunk selection strategy). Table 1 summarizes the values of the main parameters used in our simulations.

Table 1. Parameters used in the simulations

Parameter	Value
Chunk size	256 kB
File size	200 chunks (i.e., 51.2 MB)
Peer arrival rate	
Simultaneous (push)	5000 peers at t_0
Continuous (flash-crowd)	Poisson with rate $\lambda = \frac{1}{2.5 \text{ s}}$
Peer bandwidth (downlink/uplink)	
Homogeneous, symmetric	100% peers: 128/128 kb/s
Homogeneous, asymmetric	100% peers: 512/128 kb/s
Heterogeneous, asymmetric	50% peers: 512/128 kb/s
	50% peers: 128/64 kb/s
Peer lifetime	
Selfish	Disconnects when complete
Altruistic	Remains 5 minutes online
Active connections per peer	5 inbound and 5 outbound
Number of origin peers	1 (bandwidth: 128/128 kb/s)
Duration of simulation	12 h or more
Peer selection strategy	*Varies*
Chunk selection strategy	*Varies*

We have considered several metrics in our evaluation of cooperative content distribution. We briefly outline below the major properties that we have observed during the simulations:

- *Download times:* The duration of the file download as experienced by individual peers. In general, shorter times are better and variance should be minimized.
- *Download progress:* The progress of the file download over time by each of the peers. In general, regular progress is desirable (i.e., peers should not be stalled for long periods of time).
- *Chunk capacity:* The evolution over time of the number of chunks in the system. Larger numbers of chunks usually correspond to greater "service potential."
- *Chunk distribution:* The evolution over time of the frequency of the chunks in the system. The variance of chunk frequencies should be minimized.
- *Overall efficiency:* The ratio of the effective throughput of the system to its optimal throughput, computed as the sum of the bandwidth capacities of all active peers. Higher values are better.

4   Simulation Results

We now present our simulation results. Due to space constraints, we only discuss here a small selected subset of these results.

4.1   Simultaneous Arrivals

The chunk selection strategy can have a significant impact on the effectiveness of cooperative content distribution, especially when considering selfish peers. As shown in Figure 3, several of the peer selection strategies need a long time to replicate the file on all clients. First consider that the transmission of all 200 chunks of the file over a 128 kb/s connection requires $\frac{200 \cdot 256 \cdot 8 \text{ kb}}{128 \text{ kb/s}} = 3200$ seconds, i.e., slightly less than one hour. If we could construct a linear chain, with each client receiving the file from the previous peer in the chain and serving it *simultaneously* to the next one, we could theoretically approach this asymptotic limit. In practice, because we only consider the transmission of complete chunks and we share bandwidth capacities between several connections, we expect to experience lower efficiency.

We can explain the low performance of the *least missing* peer selection strategy by the fact that the server will initially only serve the same 5 peers that are closest to completion. These peers will in priority exchange chunks with each other and then slowly propagate some chunks to the other peers, which remain mostly idle because they have no rare chunks to trade. As completed peers leave immediately the system, we essentially have one server (the initial peer) that iteratively serves batches of 5 peers at a time, which explains the low efficiency of the *least missing* strategy. One should note, however, that this strategy minimizes the download time of the first complete peer. Figure 4 shows, indeed, that the download times have the highest variance with the *least missing* strategy (each point represents the completion of a peer and 9/10 of the samples have been omitted for clarity; the points for the *most missing* strategy form a horizontal line at the bottom of the graph).

At the other extreme, the *most missing* peer selection strategy tries to make all clients progress simultaneously, thus making them quickly and equally useful to others. This results in a better utilization of the available resources, as can be seen in Figures 5 and 6. By "artificially" delaying the departure of the

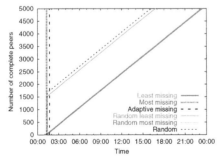

Fig. 3. Completion times for the *random* chunk selection strategy, with simultaneous arrivals, homogeneous and symmetric bandwidth, and selfish peers

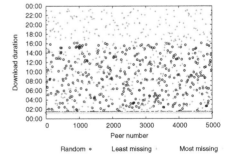

Fig. 4. Download duration for the *random* chunk selection strategy, with simultaneous arrivals, homogeneous and symmetric bandwidth, and selfish peers

peers, we always keep a large service capacity and ensure that all peers complete approximately at the same time. In the case of simultaneous arrivals, we can observe that the *most missing* strategy minimizes the download time of the last complete peer.

The *random* peer selection strategy is expected to let all peers progress at approximately the same rate, and thus to behave roughly like the *most missing* strategy. We observe, however, that only one third of the peers complete simultaneously and the rest essentially follow the same pattern as the *least missing* strategy. This problem can be tracked down to the *random* chunk selection. Indeed, the chunks that were injected first in the system exist in many instances, while the latter chunks are very rare, with the server doing nothing to correct this imbalance. Most of the peers quickly reach near completion, as shown in Figure 7, but many require much time to obtain the few missing chunks—often just one—that are only held by the origin server.

This problem can be observed more clearly in Figure 8, which shows the evolution of the number of copies of each chunk in the system over time (3/4 of the samples have been omitted for clarity and the first, last, and middle chunks have highlighted). We remark that the very first chunk on the right reaches a maximum frequency of approximately 1, 200 copies after 1 hour and falls back to zero after the first batch of peers have left. Thereafter, that extremely rare chunk is served only by the origin peer, because clients behave selfishly and leave as soon as they have downloaded the chunk. In contrast, the *most missing* peer selection strategy ensures regular progress of all the peers and a quick and even dissemination of the chunks after they have been injected in the system, as can be seen in Figures 9 and 10. Indeed, the server gives rare chunks to peers that are expected to remain online for some time and help to their dissemination. In similar settings but with altruistic peers that remain online for some time after

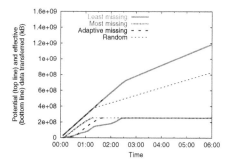

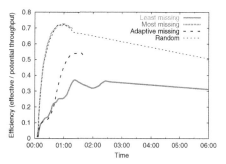

Fig. 5. Potential and effective data transferred for the *random* chunk selection strategy, with simultaneous arrivals, homogeneous and symmetric bandwidth, and selfish peers (the four top lines are all stacked initially)

Fig. 6. Overall efficiency ratio for the *random* chunk selection strategy, with simultaneous arrivals, homogeneous and symmetric bandwidth, and selfish peers

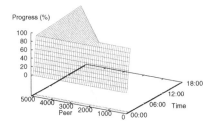

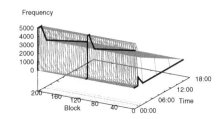

Fig. 7. Download progress for the *random* peer selection strategy, with the *random* chunk selection strategy, simultaneous arrivals, homogeneous and symmetric bandwidth, and selfish peers

Fig. 8. Chunk distribution for the *random* peer selection strategy, with the *random* chunk selection strategy, simultaneous arrivals, homogeneous and symmetric bandwidth, and selfish peers

completion, this pathologic situation does not arise anymore under random peer selection.

As previously mentioned, the download times of the *least missing* strategy have a high variance, with some peers progressing very fast and other very slowly. This can be clearly observed in Figures 11 and 12. The random variants of the *least missing* and *most missing* peer selection strategies exhibit some of the trends of their deterministic counterpart, but with less intensity. We will not discussed them further in this paper. Finally, the *adaptive missing* strategy is interesting because it seems to inherit some of the good properties of each of the extreme *least missing* and *most missing* strategies. It initially quickly and evenly replicates blocks in the system and, at the same time, does not artificially

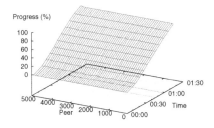

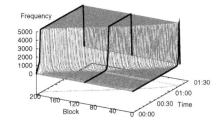

Fig. 9. Download progress for the *most missing* peer selection strategy, with the *random* chunk selection strategy, simultaneous arrivals, homogeneous and symmetric bandwidth, and selfish peers

Fig. 10. Chunk distribution for the *most missing* peer selection strategy, with the *random* chunk selection strategy, simultaneous arrivals, homogeneous and symmetric bandwidth, and selfish peers

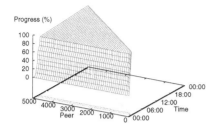

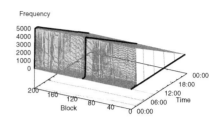

Fig. 11. Download progress for the *least missing* peer selection strategy, with the *random* chunk selection strategy, simultaneous arrivals, homogeneous and symmetric bandwidth, and selfish peers

Fig. 12. Chunk distribution for the *least missing* peer selection strategy, with the *random* chunk selection strategy, simultaneous arrivals, homogeneous and symmetric bandwidth, and selfish peers

prevent near-complete peers to finish their download (this problem is of greater important in the case of continuous arrivals, as we shall see shortly).

When switching to the *rarest* chunk selection strategy, we observe in Figure 13 significant performance improvements, particularly for the *random* peer strategy that becomes as efficient as *most missing*, and the *least missing* strategy that shows a seven-fold improvement. In contrast to the *random* chunk selection strategy, we do not experience the pathological situation where the origin sequentially serves the rare missing chunks to almost-complete peers.

If we consider heterogeneous bandwidths with 128 and 512 kb/s downlink capacities, we can clearly see in Figure 14 the two distinct classes of peers on the basis of their download durations, best visible with the *random* peer selection

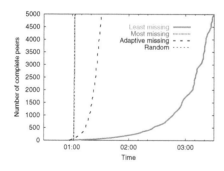

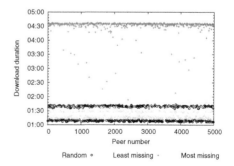

Fig. 13. Completion times for the *rarest* chunk selection strategy, with simultaneous arrivals, homogeneous and symmetric bandwidth, and selfish peers

Fig. 14. Download duration for peers with heterogeneous and asymmetric bandwidth, with the *rarest* chunk selection strategy, simultaneous arrivals, and selfish peers

strategy. The *most missing* strategy tends to diminish this gap by enforcing peers to progress at approximately the same speed. Finally, the *least missing* strategy behaves as for homogeneous bandwidths, with few peers completing very fast and many peer much later.

4.2   Continuous Arrivals

We have studied the case of continuous arrivals and asymmetric bandwidth (512/128 kb/s ADSL) with both selfish and moderately altruistic peers. We observed interesting behaviors that were consistent across both settings but more pronounced in the case of altruistic peers. We can see in Figures 15 and 17 that the *random* and *adaptive missing* peer selection strategies keep up with the arrival rate of the clients, with the latter looking empirically better initially. The *most missing* strategy delays the completion of a first batch of clients, before

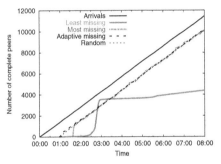

Fig. 15. Completion times for continuous arrivals, with the *rarest* chunk selection strategy, homogeneous and asymmetric bandwidth, and selfish peers

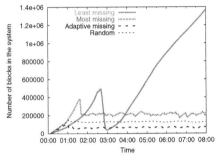

Fig. 16. Chunk capacity of the system, with the *rarest* chunk selection strategy, homogeneous and asymmetric bandwidth, and selfish peers

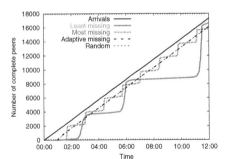

Fig. 17. Completion times for continuous arrivals, with the *rarest* chunk selection strategy, homogeneous and asymmetric bandwidth, and altruistic peers

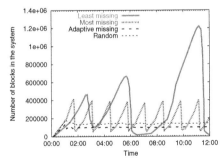

Fig. 18. Chunk capacity of the system, with the *rarest* chunk selection strategy, homogeneous and asymmetric bandwidth, and altruistic peers

following the same slope as the arrivals but with small steps, most notable with altruistic peers. Finally, the *least missing* strategy shows an odd behavior: the number of complete peers is slow to "take off," then makes a big step to overtake all other strategies, then stalls again for a longer period of time before another even higher step, and so on. To better understand this behavior, consider that the origin peer will iteratively serve groups of 5 peers until they complete their download. The peers of a group will exchange chunks with each other in priority, but also slowly propagate some chunks to other less-complete peers, which will quickly disseminate them among all remaining peers (they cannot indeed serve more-complete peers as the *least missing* strategy would require, because they only have blocks that the more-complete peers also hold). Therefore, we have few peers that complete very fast, and a large majority of peers that progresses slowly but steadily and eventually complete all together.

We can better understand the behavior of the peer selection strategies by considering the chunk capacity of the system with respect to time, shown in Figures 16 and 18. The *random* and *adaptive missing* strategies maintain a nearly constant number of chunks in the system. We can note that the latter looks more efficient than the former in this deployment scenario, as it achieves the same completion rate with a lower average chunk capacity. The *most missing* strategy creates a higher chunk capacity by delaying peers until the first batch

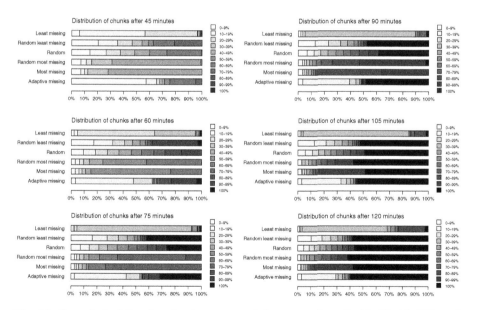

Fig. 19. Snapshot of the download progress of the peers after 45, 60, 75, 90, 105, and 120 minutes, with the *rarest* chunk selection strategy, homogeneous and asymmetric bandwidth, and selfish peers. Each segment of a bar represents the proportion of the peers that have the quantity of chunks specified by the associated color

completes, which corresponds to the sharp drop of chunk capacity. Thereafter, the capacity oscillates with a constant period, driven by the batches of peers that progress and complete together. Finally, the *least missing* strategy exhibits the highest volatility in chunk capacity. The system traverses phases during which it builds an extremely large chunk capacity, and then completely empties it by letting almost all peers terminate simultaneously. Interestingly, the frequency and amplitude of the oscillations increase over time. This corresponds to the steps that we have observed in Figures 15 and 17.

To better understand how each of the peer selection strategies lets the peers progress through their download, one can consider Figure 19 that shows snapshots of the progress of the peers every 15 minutes from 45 to 120 minutes. We see some clear trends: the *random* peer selection strategy lets all peers progress uniformly; with the *most missing* strategy, a large proportion of peers are at the same well advanced stage in their download; the *least missing* strategy pushes a few peers quickly to completion, and maintains the majority of peers early in their download; finally, with the *adaptive missing* strategies, we observe two classes of peers with opposite completion status—early and late—and few peers in between. The random variants of *least* and *most missing* are blends of the *random* peer selection strategy and their deterministic counterpart.

4.3   Discussion

We can draw several conclusions from our simulation results. First, the peer selection strategy, which drives the way the network *self-organizes*, has an huge impact on the efficiency of content distribution. Further, the complexity of the interactions between the peers, as well as the many factors to consider in real-world networks (in particular dealing the dynamics and heterogeneity of the peers) make it hard to develop analytical models. Our simulations raise many open questions, and some of the observed behaviors will require further study for being fully understood.

The peer selection strategies that we have studied have been kept intentionally very simple. In basic scenarios they can be shown to be optimal but, in more complex environments, they need to be extended to take additional factors into account. For instance, in homogeneous settings with simultaneous arrivals, the *most missing* strategy will replicate content in the most efficient manner possible, with the number of copies of each chunk increasing exponentially in time (see [7] for an in-depth analysis). If we now consider two populations of peers of identical sizes but with widely different bandwidth capacities. It can easily be shown that the fast peers should first replicate each chunk among them before transferring it in parallel to the slow peers. This can be achieved by tuning the *most missing* strategy so that it serves in priority, among the peers that have fewest chunks, those with the highest bandwidth capacity. We should additionally take into account dynamic factors such as the number of active connections of each peer, the popularity of the chunks that it holds, or its age. BitTorrent, for instance, uses a peer selection strategy that combines reciprocity ("tit-for-tat") and best experienced transmission rates, coupled with *rarest* chunk selection.

It is therefore necessary to adapt the strategies to the real complexity of the peer-to-peer network in order to optimize content distribution.

5   Conclusion

The *self-scaling* and *self-organizing* properties of peer-to-peer networks offer the technical capabilities to quickly and efficiently distribute large or critical content to huge populations of clients. Cooperative distribution techniques capitalize the bandwidth of every peer to dramatically increase the service capacity of the system. Based on the extensive simulations that we have performed, and the limited set of results shown in this paper, it appears clearly that the deployment scenarios and the cooperative strategies in use have strong influence on the effectiveness of content distribution. In particular, the chunk and peer selection strategies directly impact the delay experienced by the clients and the global throughput of the system. There is no clear "best" strategy, as each of them offers various trade offs and may prove most adequate for specific deployment scenarios. Overall, the *random* and *adaptive missing* peer selection strategies coupled with *rarest* chunk selection consistently deliver good performance and may be safely utilized as general-purpose cooperative strategies for content distribution.

References

1. Napster. (http://www.napster.com)
2. Gnutella. (http://gnutella.wego.com)
3. Biersack, E., Rodriguez, P., Felber, P.: Performance analysis of peer-to-peer networks for file distribution. In: Proceedings of the 5th International Workshop on Quality of future Internet Services (QofIS'04). (2004)
4. Cohen, B.: Incentives to build robustness in BitTorrent. Technical report, http://bitconjurer.org/BitTorrent/bittorrentecon.pdf (2003)
5. Izal, M., Urvoy-Keller, G., Biersack, E., Felber, P., Hamra, A.A., Garces-Erice, L.: Dissecting BitTorrent: Five months in a torrent's lifetime. In: Proceedings of the 5th Passive and Active Measurement Workshop. (2004)
6. Schrage, L.: A proof of the optimality of the shortest remaining service time discipline. Operations Research **16** (1968) 670–690
7. Yang, X., de Veciana, G.: Service capacity of peer-to-peer networks. In: Proceedings of INFOCOM. (2004)

Design and Analysis of a Bio-inspired Search Algorithm for Peer to Peer Networks[*]

Niloy Ganguly, Lutz Brusch, and Andreas Deutsch

Center for High Performance Computing,
Dresden University of Technology, Dresden,
Germany
{niloy, brusch, deutsch}@zhr.tu-dresden.de

Abstract. Decentralized peer to peer ($p2p$) networks like Gnutella are attractive for certain applications because they require no centralized directories and no precise control over network topology or data placement. The greatest advantage is the robustness provided by them. However, flooding-based query algorithms used by the networks produce enormous amounts of traffic and substantially slow down the system. Recently, flooding has been replaced by more efficient k-random walkers and different variants of such algorithms. In this paper, we report immune-inspired algorithms for searching peer to peer networks. The algorithms use the immune-inspired mechanism of affinity-governed proliferation to spread query message packets in the network. Through a series of experiments, we compare the proliferation mechanism with different variants of random walk algorithms. The detailed experimental results show message packets undergoing proliferation spread much faster in the network and consequently proliferation algorithms produce better search output in $p2p$ networks than random walk algorithms. Moreover, theoretical results by calculating the packet spreading speeds are reported which provide an understanding of the improved performance of the proliferation based search algorithm.

1 Introduction

Among different desirable qualities of a search algorithm for peer to peer ($p2p$) networks, robustness is a very important aspect. That is, the performance of a search algorithm should not radically deteriorate in face of the dynamically changing condition of the network. As is known, the big share of Internet users, consequently participants in $p2p$ networks, still use slow and unreliable dial-up modems and also leave the community at very short intervals. Thus in order to give robustness a high priority, precise routing algorithms for forwarding query message packets are generally avoided. Instead random forwarding of the message packets is preferred [8]. The goal of this paper is to study more efficient

[*] This work was partially supported by the Future & Emerging Technologies unit of the European Commission through Project BISON (IST-2001-38923).

O. Babaoglu et al. (Eds.): SELF-STAR 2004, LNCS 3460, pp. 358–372, 2005.

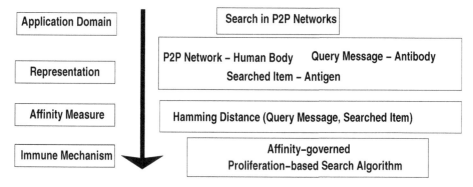

Fig. 1. Immune system concepts used to develop search algorithms

alternatives to the existing k-random walk. In this connection, we draw our inspiration from the immune system.

Our algorithm has been inspired by the simple and well known mechanism of the humoral immune system where B cells upon stimulation by a foreign agent (antigen) undergo proliferation generating antibodies. Proliferation helps in increasing the number of antibodies while mutation implies a variety of generated antibodies. Consequently the antibodies can efficiently track down the antigens (foreign bodies). *Fig. 1* provides an illustration explaining how we have mapped immune system concepts to our search problem. In our problem, the query message packet is conceived as antibody which is generated by the node initiating a search whereas antigens are the searched items hosted by other constituent members (nodes) of the *p2p* network. Like in the natural immune system, the packets undergo proliferation based upon the affinity measure between the message packets and the contents of the node visited which results in an efficient search mechanism. The work presented here is further development of the works reported in [1, 2, 3].

In the next section, we detail the modeling abstractions upon which the algorithms are based. Moreover, we elaborate our algorithms as well as different variants of k-random walk algorithms. Furthermore, the evaluation metrics used to compare the different schemes is introduced. The experimental results are noted next in *Section 3*. *Section 4* provides a theoretical outline explaining the rationale behind the experimental results.

2   Modeling and Evaluation Methodology

It is impossible to model the complete dynamics of a *p2p* system. In this paper, we do not attempt to resolve small quantitative disparities between k-random walk and proliferation algorithms, but instead are trying to reveal fundamental qualitative differences. While our simple models do not capture all aspects of reality, we hope they capture the essential features needed to understand the fundamental qualitative differences between k-random walk and proliferation algorithms.

2.1   Model Definition

P2p networks are networks formed through associations of computers, each providing equivalent services, eg. search facility, to the network. Thus, each peer can be conceived as both client and server of a particular service [8]. To model a search service, we focus on the two most important aspects of a *p2p* system: *p2p* network topology, query and data distribution. For simplicity, we assume the topology and distribution do not change during the simulation of our algorithms. For the purpose of our study, if one assumes that the time to complete a search is short compared to the time of change in network topology and change in query distribution, results obtained from the fixed settings are indicative of performance in real systems.

Network Topology :   By network topology, we mean the graph formed by the *p2p* overlay network; each *p2p* member has a certain number of neighbors and the set of neighbor connections forms the *p2p* overlay network. For our studies, we use random graphs. Random graphs are considered as the best type of topology to represent the majority of the realistic network topologies formed in the Internet [4, 8]. In the experiments reported in this paper, we have considered different random graphs each having 10000 nodes. However, their mean node indegree differs. The random graphs have been generated with the help of the topology generator BRITE[6]. In *Fig. 2*, we show the node degree distribution followed by one of the representative graphs. This particular graph has 10000 nodes and mean node indegree $\mu_{nd} = 4$.

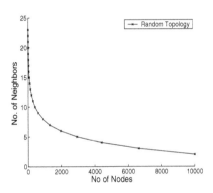

Fig. 2. Cumulative distribution of node degrees in Random graph, 10000 nodes, with $\mu_{nd} = 4$

Data and query distribution : Files are conceived as conglomeration of keywords [5]. Hence the data distribution is represented in terms of keywords. It is assumed that there are 2000 different keywords in the system. Each node hosts some keywords. The number of keywords (not unique) in each node follows a Poisson distribution with mean $\mu_{kw} = 1000$. The data profile (D) of each node can therefore be represented as

$$D = < (\delta_1, n_1), (\delta_2, n_2), \cdots > \& \ n_1 + n_2 + \cdots = N$$

where δ_i are each individual keywords and n_i indicates their weights (number of times they are present in the node), N represents the total number of keywords.

The query comprises of single or multiple keywords and is represented as

$$M = < m_1, m_2, \cdots >$$

where m_i represents each individual keyword. For 95% of the cases, the query length (say n) is ≤ 5 while it is between 6 to 10 in the rest 5% case. In the 95% cases where the query length is ≤ 5, each length 1 to 5 is equiprobable. This is similar for the rest 5% case.

Zipf's distribution[10], is chosen to distribute each of the 2000 unique keywords in the network. In Zipf's distribution the frequency of occurrence of some event (here keywords) t, as a function of the rank r, where the rank is determined by the above frequency of occurrence, follows a power-law $t_i \propto \frac{1}{r^a}$. In the experimental setup, Zipf's exponent (value of a) for both the query and the data is 1. The ranking of keywords in terms of frequency is the same for both data and query distribution.

2.2   Algorithms

In this section, we introduce two proliferation based as well as two random walk based search algorithms. The important aspects of all these algorithms are that although random walk or proliferation is exhibited by the message packets, the algorithms are independently implemented by each node. And coordinated behavior of the nodes produces the required packet dynamics. All the algorithms can be expressed in terms of the following basic premise.

Basic Premise : The search in our $p2p$ network is initiated from the user peer (U). The user peer (U) emanates k ($k \geq 1$) message packets (M) to its neighbors - the packets are thereby forwarded to the surroundings. In the following we present the search initiation process in algorithmic form.

Algorithm 1 InitiateSearch(U)
Input : *Signal to initiate search.*
Form Message Packet (M) = $< m_1, m_2 \cdots >$; m_i represents each individual keyword
Flood k message packets(M) to the neighbors of the user peer.

The message packets travel through the network and when a node (say A) receives a message packet (M), it performs the following two functions.

Function 1 :- It checks whether any $\delta_i \in D$ of A is equal to any $m_i \in M$ (incoming message). The number of successful matches Sm is represented by the following equation.

$$Sm = \sum_{i=1}^{N} \sum_{j=1}^{n} (m_j \oplus \delta_i) \times n_i \qquad (1)$$

where $m_j \oplus \delta_i = 1$, if $m_j = \delta_i$, else 0; N is the total number of keywords present in the node while n represents the length of the search query. The node reports the number of successful matches - Sm.

Function 2 :- It forwards the content of the message packet in some *defined* manner to its neighbor(s).

In algorithmic form, we can represent the functions as *Reaction_p2p*:

Algorithm 2 Reaction_p2p(A)
Input : Message packet(M)
  Calculate Sm from D & M /*Function 1*/
  Algorithm Message_Forward(A) /* Function 2*/

Each of the proliferation and random walk schemes defines *Algorithm Message_Forward(A)* differently. Elaboration of the algorithms corresponding to each of the schemes follows.

Proliferation $\mathcal{P}$: In the proliferation scheme, the packets undergo proliferation at each node they visit. The proliferation is guided by a special function, whereby a message packet visiting a node proliferates to form N_p message packets which are thereby forwarded to the neighbors of the node.

Algorithm 3 $\mathcal{P}$(A)
Input : Message packet(M)
Produce N_p message packets(M)
Spread the N_p packets to N_p randomly selected neighbors of A

The function determining the value of 'N_p' ensures that N_p is $< \eta(A)$, where $\eta(A)$ is the number of neighbors of A and ≥ 1.

Restricted Proliferation ($\mathcal{RP}$) : The restricted proliferation algorithm, similar to $\mathcal{P}$, produces N_p messages. But these N_p messages are forwarded only if the node A has $\geq N_p$ free neighbors. By 'free', we mean that the respective neighbors haven't been previously visited by message M. If A has $\mathcal{Z}$ 'free' neighbors, where $\mathcal{Z} < N_p$, then only $\mathcal{Z}$ messages are forwarded, while the rest are destroyed. However, if $\mathcal{Z} = 0$, then one message is forwarded to a randomly selected neighbor. The rationale behind the restricted movement is to minimize the amount of message wastage. Because, two packets of message M visiting the same peer essentially means wastage of the second packet.

Algorithm 4 $\mathcal{R}P$(A)
Input : Message packet(M)
Produce N_p message packets (M)
$\mathcal{Z}$ = No of 'free' neighbors
if ($\mathcal{Z} \geq N_p$)
    Spread the N_p packets in N_p randomly selected neighbors of A
else
        if ($\mathcal{Z} > 0$)
                Spread $\mathcal{Z}$ packets in $\mathcal{Z}$ free neighbors of A
                Discard the remaining (N_p - $\mathcal{Z}$) packets
        else
                Forward one message packet to a randomly selected neighbor of A
                Discard the remaining (N_p - 1) packets

We now elaborate the function which controls the amount of proliferation.

Proliferation Controlling Function : The proliferation of message packets at any node A is heavily dependent on the similarity between the message packet (M) and the data profile (D) of A. In this connection, we define the measure of similarity between the data profile (D) of the node and the message packet (M).

$$Sim = \frac{Sm}{N}$$

where the value of Sm is calculated through Eq. (1). [Note $Sm \leq$ N, so the value of $Sim \leq 1$.] The number of packets N_p proliferated is defined on the basis of Sm in the following manner

$$N_p = 1 + Sim \times (\eta - 1) \times \rho$$

where η represents the number of neighbors the particular node has; ρ represents the proliferation constant, it is ≤ 1. (ρ is set to 0.5 in all our experiments.) The above formula ensures that $1 < N_p \leq N$.

k-**random walk ($\mathcal{R}W$) :** In k-random walk, when a peer receives a message packet after performing the task of comparison, as mentioned in *Algo. 2*, it forwards the packet to a randomly selected neighbor.

Algorithm 5 $\mathcal{R}W(A)$
Input : Message packet(M)
Send the packet M to a randomly chosen neighbor peer

Restricted Random Walk ($\mathcal{R}RW$): In $\mathcal{R}RW$, instead of passing the message (M) to any random neighbor, we pass on the message to any randomly selected 'free' neighbor. However, if there is no 'free' neighbor, we then pass on the message to any randomly selected neighbor.

Algorithm 6 $\mathcal{R}RW(A)$
Input : Message packet(M)
Send the packet M to a randomly chosen 'free' neighbor peer
    If (no 'free' neighbor)
        Send the packet M to a randomly chosen neighbor peer

2.3   Metrics

In this paper we focus on efficiency aspects of the algorithms solely, and use the following simple metrics in our abstract $p2p$ networks. These metrics, though simple, reflect the fundamental properties of the algorithms.

(a) *Success rate:* The number of similar items found by the query messages within a given time period.
(b) *Coverage rate:* The amount of time required by the messages to cover a percentage of the network.
(c) *Effectivity per message:* The number of search items produced by a single message.

3   Simulation Results

The experimental results compare the efficiency of different algorithms (Algo. 3 - 6), with respect to the metrics defined in *section 2.3*.

As mentioned earlier, each of the above algorithms is distributed in nature and the nodes perform the task independently of the others. However, to assess the speed and efficiency of the algorithm, we have to ensure some sort of synchronous operation among the peers. In this context we introduce the concept of time whereby it is assumed that in one time unit, all the nodes in the network execute the algorithm once. That is, if a peer has some messages in its message queue, it will process one message within that time frame. We believe although approximate, it is a fair abstraction of reality of *p2p* networks where each node is supposed to provide equivalent services. The sequence of operation of the peers during one time step is arbitrary. The length of the message queue is considered to be infinite.

In order to assess the efficiency of different algorithms, we have also to guarantee fairness of 'power' among them which is explained next.

3.1   Fairness in Power

To ensure fair comparison among all the processes, we must ensure that each process ($\mathcal{P}, \mathcal{RP}, \mathcal{RW}, \mathcal{RRW}$) participates in the network with the same 'power'. To provide fairness in 'power' for comparison of a proliferation algorithm (say $\mathcal{P}$) and a random algorithm (say $\mathcal{RW}$), we ensure that the total number of query packets used is roughly the same in all the cases. Query packets determine the cost of the search; too many packets cause network clogging bringing down the efficiency of the system as a whole. It can be seen that the number of packets increase in the proliferation algorithms over the generations, while it remains constant in the case of random walk algorithms. Therefore the number of message packets - k in *Algo. 1* is chosen in a fashion so that the aggregate number of packets used by each individual algorithm is roughly the same.

Besides the cost of the message packets, during comparison between a restricted algorithm (say $\mathcal{RRW}$) and a non-restricted algorithm (say $\mathcal{P}$), we also have to keep in mind that checking 'whether a node was earlier visited or not' involves a cost; this also should be taken into consideration when defining 'fairness'. Therefore, the composite cost[1] for a restricted algorithm can be defined as $C_{comp} = X + \alpha \cdot L$, where X is the average number of message packets, L is the number of neighbor lookup, while α is the ratio of cost of lookup to cost of actually sending the message; α normally ≤ 1. However, in this case, since message length is small, we consider the worst case scenario of $\alpha = 1$ to depict our results.

To ensure fairness in 'power' between two proliferation algorithms (say [$\mathcal{P}$ & $\mathcal{RP}$]), we keep the proliferation constant ρ and the value of k the same for both processes. The value of k for the proliferation algorithm is generally set as $k = \eta(U)$, where $\eta(U)$ is the indegree of the initiator peer U.

---

[1] Henceforth, cost or simple cost indicates the cost of message packets while composite cost always means total cost of messages and neighbor lookup.

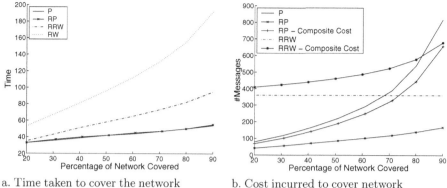

a. Time taken to cover the network   b. Cost incurred to cover network

Fig. 3. Graphs plotting the cost and network coverage time of $\mathcal{P}$, $\mathcal{R}P$, $\mathcal{R}RW$, $\mathcal{R}W$ algorithms in random network. The proliferation constant considered here is $\rho = 0.5$

3.2   Experimental Result – Network Coverage

As mentioned in *Sec 2.1*, we use a random graph, to evaluate the time taken by the message packets to visit all the nodes of the network using different forwarding algorithms. The particular random graph considered here has 10000 nodes and mean node indegree $\mu_{nd} = 4$. Its distribution is shown in *Fig. 2*. The experiment, *network coverage* is detailed in the following two paragraphs.

COVERAGE :   In this experiment, upon initiation of a search (*Algo. 1*), the search operation (*Algo. 2*) is performed till the message packets cover the entire network. The experiment is repeated 1000 times on randomly selected initial nodes.

During the experiment, we collect different statistic at every 10% of coverage of the network that is, we collect statistic at [20%, 30% ⋯ 90%, 100%] of network coverage. Since the message forwarding algorithms (*Algo. 3 -6*) are non-deterministic in nature, message packets find it increasingly difficult to visit the last 10% of the network. This is true for all the different variants of message forwarding algorithms. Consequently, in our results we avoid showing results from the last 10% as it only depicts the aberration arising from the finite size of the network.

Fig. 3(a) shows the network coverage rate of different algorithms $\mathcal{P}$, $\mathcal{R}P$, $\mathcal{R}RW$ and $\mathcal{R}W$. The graph plots the % of network covered in the x-axis, while the time taken to cover the corresponding % of network is plotted on the y-axis. It is seen that $\mathcal{P}$ and $\mathcal{R}P$ take almost identical time to cover up the network. The time taken is, however, much less than that taken by $\mathcal{R}RW$ and $\mathcal{R}W$ respectively. The $\mathcal{R}RW$ is much more efficient than $\mathcal{R}W$. We now assess the cost (both simple and composite) incurred by each algorithm to produce the above mentioned performances.

Fig. 3(b) plots the increase in the average number of message packets present in the network (also referred to as cost) in the y-axis with respect to the percentage of network coverage for $\mathcal{P}$, $\mathcal{R}P$ and $\mathcal{R}RW$. For each $\mathcal{R}RW$ and $\mathcal{R}P$, we show two lines, one for simple and composite cost respectively. Comparing, $\mathcal{R}P$ and $\mathcal{P}$, we see that $\mathcal{R}P$ uses a significantly smaller number of messages (about one-fifth) than

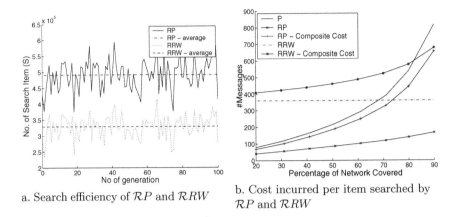

a. Search efficiency of $\mathcal{R}P$ and $\mathcal{R}RW$

b. Cost incurred per item searched by $\mathcal{R}P$ and $\mathcal{R}RW$

Fig. 4. Graphs showing (a). search efficiency, and (b). cost incurred per item searched by $\mathcal{R}P$ and $\mathcal{R}RW$ in random network

$\mathcal{P}$ and achieves the same performance. Even composite cost is significantly lower for $\mathcal{R}P$ (657 for $\mathcal{R}P$ and 818 for $\mathcal{P}$). To ensure the fairness criterion, $\mathcal{R}RW$ initially starts with the number of packets which $\mathcal{R}P$ has used on the average to cover the entire network (361), so it stays constant throughout the experiment; however the composite cost steadily increases. It is the same as for $\mathcal{R}P$ at the 90% coverage ratio. The number of messages $\mathcal{R}W$ uses (not plotted) is 1881. 1881 is the average composite cost incurred by $\mathcal{R}RW$ to cover the entire network.

It is found that $\mathcal{R}RW$ is much more efficient than $\mathcal{R}W$. Similarly, $\mathcal{R}P$ is better than $\mathcal{P}$. So, in our subsequent discussions, we drop $\mathcal{P}$ and $\mathcal{R}W$ and concentrate on a comparison between $\mathcal{R}P$ and $\mathcal{R}RW$.

The next experimental results highlight the search efficiency of $\mathcal{R}P$ and $\mathcal{R}RW$.

3.3   Experimental Results - Search Efficiency

To compare the search efficiency of $\mathcal{R}P$ & $\mathcal{R}RW$, we perform the *time-step* experiment on the random graph for $\mathcal{R}P$ and $\mathcal{R}RW$, each spanning over 100 generations. We use the same random graph as in *Sec 3.2*.

TIME-STEP : In this experiment, upon initiation of a search (*algorithm (1)*), the search operation is performed for $\mathcal{N}$ (= 50) time steps. The number of search items (s) found within 50 time steps from the commencement of the search is calculated. From algorithm (2), we know each visited node returns Sm search items (calculation done through Eq. (1)); s is the summation of Sm over all visited nodes. The experiment is repeated for one generation where one generation is defined as a sequence of 100 searches. The search output (s) is averaged over one generation (100 different searches), whereby we obtain S, where $S = \dfrac{\sum_{i=1}^{100} s}{100}$. The value of S is used to draw the graphs explained next. In this experiment, $\mathcal{R}RW$ always performs the experiment with k packets where k is the average number of packets used by $\mathcal{R}P$ over 100 generations.

The graph of *Fig. 4(a)* shows the average value S against generation number for $\mathcal{R}P$ and $\mathcal{R}RW$. The x-axis of the graph shows the generation number while the y-axis represents the average number of search items (S) found in the last 100 searches. In this figure, we see that the search results for both $\mathcal{R}P$ and $\mathcal{R}RW$ show fluctuations. The fluctuations occur due to the difference in the availability of the searched items selected at each generation. However, we see that on the average, search efficiency of $\mathcal{R}P$ is almost 1.5-times higher than that of $\mathcal{R}RW$. (For $\mathcal{R}P$, the number of hits $\approx 5 \times 10^5$, while it is $\approx 3.25 \times 10^5$ for $\mathcal{R}RW$.)

Fig. 4(b) displays the effectivity per messages (metrics defined in *Sec. 2.3*) of each scheme. As expected, the effectivity of message packets for $\mathcal{R}P$ is much higher than $\mathcal{R}RW$ (keeping in mind the fairness criterion we follow to generate experimental results). However, one more important point to be noted is that the standard deviation is particularly small in the case of $\mathcal{R}P$. Considering σ_E/μ_E (Std. of effectivity/mean effectivity), it is 0.1 for $\mathcal{R}RW$ while it is just 0.08 for $\mathcal{R}P$. This is because in $\mathcal{R}P$, the packets are not generated blindly, but are instead regulated by the availability of the searched item. Therefore, if a particular searched item is sparse in the network, $\mathcal{R}P$ produces a lower number of packets and vice versa.

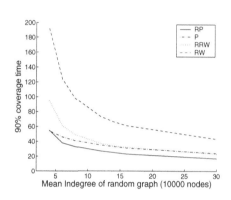

Fig. 5. Graphs illustrating the effect on efficiency with varying indegree

We now describe how efficiency of the different algorithms gets affected when the indegree of the random graph is increased.

3.4   Experimental Results: Changing Indegree

In this experiment, we perform the *coverage* experiment on random graphs each with 10000 nodes, but their mean indegree steadily increases.

Fig. 5 plots the time taken to cover the network (y-axis) by $\mathcal{R}P$, $\mathcal{P}$, $\mathcal{R}RW$ and $\mathcal{R}W$ against different indegree configurations of the random graph (x-axis). The figure shows that as indegree increases each algorithm becomes faster. However, it is to be noted that the speed of random walk algorithms accelerates at a much faster speed. In fact, from around node indegree 12, $\mathcal{R}RW$ and $\mathcal{P}$ take almost identical time. This happens because as indegree of the random graph increases, in effect the dimension (d) of the graph also increases. That is, each node can reach each other node within a shorter time span. Random walk is particularly smart at higher dimensions which consequently provides the result. However, maintaining high indegree in p2p environment typically is a problem [9]. So, at lower indegree level proliferation algorithms are much more effective than random walk algorithms.

We now summarize the results obtained through the above mentioned experiments.

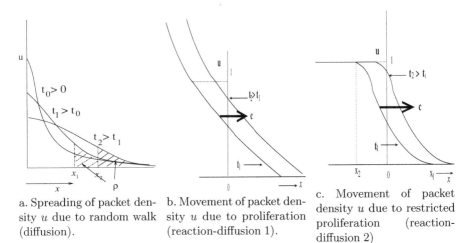

a. Spreading of packet density u due to random walk (diffusion).

b. Movement of packet density u due to proliferation (reaction-diffusion 1).

c. Movement of packet density u due to restricted proliferation (reaction-diffusion 2)

Fig. 6. Packet movement with different algorithms in a continuous system with radial coordinate x

3.5   Summary

The following is the summarization of the results.
(a). $\mathcal{RP}$ is more effective than $\mathcal{P}$.
(b). $\mathcal{RP}$ is more effective than any random walk algorithm.
(c). $\mathcal{RP}$ has an in-built cost regulatory mechanism.
(d). The search efficiency of $\mathcal{RP}$ is roughly one and a half times higher than $\mathcal{RRW}$.
(e). $\mathcal{RRW}$ becomes more effective as the indegree of the graph increases.

4   Theoretical Justification

In this section, we provide insights into the reasons behind the better performance of proliferation compared to random walk algorithms. We provide our explanation in the framework of a continuum model to derive the macroscopic behavior from knowledge about the individual microscopic behavior of the packets. Unlike the model described in the previous sections, for sake of analysis we assume that the system is synchronous in the sense that all nodes operate at the same time. The network is abstracted as a d-dimensional space where the dimension grows with the average node indegree.

We relate the random walk algorithms to a simple diffusive system where the diffusion starts from the origin. The proliferation algorithms can be conceived as reaction-diffusion systems [7], where besides diffusion of packets, new packets are continuously produced by the existing ones. Each of the two processes (diffusion and reaction-diffusion) spreads the message packets through the network. The insights which we will provide are based upon estimates of the *speed of packet spreading* in the radial direction.

Fig. 6 illustrates the basic features of the two processes. *Fig. 6(a)* refers to diffusion, *Fig. 6(b)* to a reaction-diffusion system with unrestricted proliferation,

whereas *Fig. 6(c)* corresponds to a reaction-diffusion system with restricted proliferation. In all three graphs, we plot the density $u(x, t)$ of message packets used to
conduct search versus the radial coordinate x. u can be conceived as a normalized
measure of the number of packets k. u and k is not quantitatively related in this
work, as that is not required to estimate the speed of packet spreading. Each of the
three systems is studied in detail below, here we discuss the figures one by one.

Fig. 6(a) shows three Gaussian curves at three different instances of time (t_0,
t_1, t_2, where $t_0 < t_1 < t_2$). As time increases, a particular density of packets (say ρ)
travels further away from the center. Moreover, since it follows a Gaussian distribution, at time $t \to 0$, at distance $x \to \infty$, there is some concentration of packets u,
where $u \to 0$. However to cover all the nodes at distance x, a finite tangible concentration of packets ρ should reach distance x. As can be seen from the figure, at time
t_1, a concentration ρ covers distance x_1 or more while at time t_2 the same concentration has covered $\geq x_2$ distance. Below we calculate the *speed of diffusive packet
spreading* for this finite density ρ.

On the other hand, in the case of reaction-diffusion systems (proliferation), the
movement of packets follows a traveling front pattern with a uniform front profile.
Figs. 6(b),(c) show such front profiles at time t_1 and t_2. For example, in *Fig. 6(c)*,
we see that at time t_1, till distance x_2, the density $u = 1$, while beyond x_1, it is zero.
The second curve at t_2 is just a uniform shift of the first curve, hence characterized
by a *front speed*. We now elaborate each of the processes one by one.

A. Random Walk (Diffusion): The random walk has traditionally been modeled
as diffusion in continuum systems for which the diffusion equation reads [7]

$$\frac{du}{dt} = D \cdot \frac{d^2u}{dx^2} \tag{2}$$

where D is the diffusion coefficient. We are considering a situation where at time
$t = 0$ all packets are concentrated at the origin from where they diffuse outwards.
Hence, $u(x, t=0) = \delta(x=0)$, where δ has non-zero value at 0 and 0 otherwise. Therefore, solving the differential equation with the given initial condition, we obtain

$$u = \frac{1}{(2 \cdot \sqrt{D \cdot \pi \cdot t})^d} \cdot e^{-\frac{x^2}{4 \cdot D \cdot t}} \tag{3}$$

where d is the dimension of the system.

We transform this equation in order to express the position x_ρ of an arbitrarily
chosen fixed density $\rho \ll 1$ as a function of time.

$$x_\rho(t) = \sqrt{2 \cdot D \cdot d \cdot t \cdot \log \frac{1}{4 \cdot \rho^{2/d} \cdot D \cdot \pi \cdot t}} \tag{4}$$

The speed c of diffusive packet spreading for any fixed density ρ is obtained by dif-
ferentiating $x_\rho(t)$ with respect to time.

$$c = \frac{2 \cdot D \cdot d}{2\sqrt{2 \cdot D \cdot d}} \cdot \frac{\log \frac{1}{4 \cdot \rho^{2/d} \cdot D \cdot \pi \cdot t} - 1}{\sqrt{t \cdot \log \frac{1}{4 \cdot \rho^{2/d} \cdot D \cdot \pi \cdot t}}} \tag{5}$$

For most of the time, the logarithm in the numerator is much larger than 1 and we can neglect the 1, hence obtain simplified

$$c = \sqrt{\frac{D \cdot d}{2}} \cdot \sqrt{\frac{1}{t} \log \frac{1}{4 \cdot \rho^{2/d} \cdot D \cdot \pi \cdot t}} \tag{6}$$

The result shows that packet spreading due to random walk becomes faster in higher dimensions as $c \propto \sqrt{d}$ and is slowing down with time as $c \propto \sqrt{\frac{1}{t} \cdot \log \frac{1}{t}}$.

B. Proliferation (Reaction-Diffusion 1): The proliferation algorithm can be modeled as a system which is undergoing diffusion as well as gaining new packets as copies of existing ones at the rate α at each time step. Therefore, the dynamics can be expressed by the following equation

$$\frac{du}{dt} = D \cdot \frac{d^2 u}{dx^2} + \alpha \cdot u \tag{7}$$

This equation resembles a variation of a well-studied reaction-diffusion equation, the Fisher equation [7]. We therefore utilize the standard result obtained for the *front speed* in a generalized Fisher equation with reaction term $f(u)$ [7].

$$\frac{du}{dt} = \frac{d^2 u}{dx^2} + f(u) \tag{8}$$

has a uniformly moving front as solution and this motion proceeds with the front speed

$$c = 2 \cdot [f'(u_1)]^{\frac{1}{2}}, \tag{9}$$

where $f'(u_1)$ denotes the derivative of $f(u)$ with respect to the packet density u at the position u_1. $u_1 = 0$ is the state of the system that has now yet been visited by the front.

Considering the equation (7), we can rescale it by

$$t^* = \alpha \cdot t; \quad x^* = x \cdot \left(\frac{\alpha}{D}\right)^{\frac{1}{2}}$$

$$dt^* = \alpha \cdot dt; \quad dx^{*2} = dx^2 \cdot \frac{\alpha}{D} \tag{10}$$

Therefore, the equation (7) becomes

$$\alpha \cdot [\frac{du}{dt^*} = \frac{d^2 u}{dx^{*2}} + u] \tag{11}$$

Hence $f'(u) = 1$, which implies $f'(u_1) = 1$. Therefore, the front speed c of the system is given by

$$c = \frac{\Delta x}{\Delta t} = \frac{\Delta x^* \cdot \sqrt{\frac{D}{\alpha}}}{\Delta t^* \cdot \frac{1}{\alpha}} = 2 \cdot \sqrt{\alpha \cdot D} \tag{12}$$

This result shows that the speed of packet spreading due to the proliferation algorithm is constant, *i.e.* independent of time. The speed dependents on the proliferation rate α and diffusion constant D but is independent of the dimension d. Hence, the behavior of the proliferation algorithm drastically differs from that of the random walk.

C. Restricted Proliferation (Reaction-Diffusion 2): In the model of restricted proliferation, the number of packets initially increases at a rate α but the packet production rate is lowered as packets encounter more and more packets, *i.e.* density increases. We can conceive the function as logistic population growth model, where $f(u)$ can be modeled by the following equation

$$f(u) = \alpha \cdot u \cdot (1 - u) \tag{13}$$

Therefore, the corresponding reaction-diffusion equation can be written as

$$\frac{du}{dt} = D \cdot \frac{d^2u}{dx^2} + \alpha \cdot u \cdot (1 - u) \tag{14}$$

By using the same rescaling of space and time as above (10), we obtain

$$\alpha \cdot [\frac{du}{dt^*} = \frac{d^2u}{dx^{*2}} + u(1 - u)] \tag{15}$$

Therefore, $f'(u) = 1 - 2\,u$ and $u_1 = 0$. Hence $f'(u_1) = 1$ and following the same arguments as in case B. we find $c = 2 \cdot \sqrt{\alpha \cdot D}$. This result implies the same speed of packet spreading and dependence on parameters as in the case of unrestricted proliferation.

To sum up, the above theoretical calculations of speeds of packet spreading due to different algorithms can explain the following observations of the coverage experiments (see *Fig. 3(a)*) and their dependence on the average indegree of the network (see *Fig. 5*).

1. Proliferation algorithms propagate packets faster through the network as their speed is independent of time whereas for random walks packet spreading slows down with time $c \propto \sqrt{\frac{1}{t} \cdot \log \frac{1}{t}}$. This explains the differences between the curves $\mathcal{P}, \mathcal{RP}$ and $\mathcal{RW}, \mathcal{RRW}$ in *Fig. 3(a)*.
2. Restricted proliferation is as fast as the simple proliferation algorithm, for both the same speed $c = 2 \cdot \sqrt{\alpha \cdot D}$ was calculated. This result is consistent with our finding in *Fig. 3(a)* that the restricted proliferation scheme works as good as the proliferation scheme and both curves $\mathcal{P}, \mathcal{RP}$ coincide.
3. Random walk becomes faster as the effective dimension d of the network increases, *i.e.* the indegree increases. This explains the strong dependence of performance on the network indegree for both random walk algorithms in *Fig. 5*.

However, the calculations of the package spreading speeds do not account for the differences in cost effectiveness between the different algorithms.

5 Conclusion

In this paper, we have produced detailed experimental results showing that the simple immune-inspired concept of proliferation can be used to cover the network more effectively than random walk. The proliferation algorithm can regulate the number of packets to be produced during a search operation according to the availability of the searched material, thus improving the efficiency of the search. Moreover, we have provided theoretical results by calculating the packet spreading speeds which explain many of the experimental observations and provide an understanding of the improved performance of the immune-inspired search algorithm.

References

1. N Ganguly, G Canright, and A Deutsch. Design of a Robust Search Algorithm for P2P Networks. In 11th *International Conference on High Performance Computing*, December 2004.
2. N Ganguly, G Canright, and A Deutsch. Design Of An Efficient Search Algorithm For P2P Networks Using Concepts From Natural Immune Systems. In 8th *International Conference on Parallel Problem Solving from Nature*, September 2004.
3. N Ganguly and A Deutsch. Developing Efficient Search Algorithms for P2P Networks Using Proliferation and Mutation. In 3rd *International Conference on Artificial Immune Systems*, September 2004.
4. M. A. Jovanovic, F. S. Annexstein, and K. A. Berman. Scalability Issues in Large Peer-to-peer Networks - A Case Study of Gnutella. Technical Report University of Cincinnati, 2001.
5. Dik L. Lee, Huei Chuang, and Kent Seamons. Document ranking and the vector-space model. *IEEE Softw.*, 14(2):67–75, 1997.
6. A Medina, A Lakhina, I Matta, and J Byers. BRITE: An Approach to Universal Topology Generation. In *Proceedings of the International Workshop on Modeling, Analysis and Simulation of Computer and Telecommunications Systems- MASCOTS*, August 2001.
7. J. D. Murray. *Mathematical Biology*. Springer-Verlag, 1990.
8. A. (Ed) Oram. *Peer-to-Peer: Harnessing the Power of Disruptive Technologies*. O Reilly Books, 2001.
9. G. Pandurangan, P. Raghavan, and E. Upfal. Building low-diameter peer-to-peer networks. *IEEE Journal on Selected Areas in Communications (JSAC)*, 21(6), 2003.
10. G. K. Zipf. *Psycho-Biology of Languages*. Houghton-Mifflin, 1935.

Multifaceted Simultaneous Load Balancing in DHT-Based P2P Systems: A New Game with Old Balls and Bins*

Karl Aberer, Anwitaman Datta, and Manfred Hauswirth

Ecole Polytechnique Fédérale de Lausanne (EPFL),
School of Computer and Communication Sciences,
CH-1015 Lausanne, Switzerland
{karl.aberer, anwitaman.datta, manfred.hauswirth}@epfl.ch

Abstract. This paper presents and evaluates uncoordinated on-line algorithms for simultaneous storage and replication load-balancing in DHT-based peer-to-peer systems. We compare our approach with the classical *balls into bins* model, and point out both the similarities as well as the differences which call for new load-balancing mechanisms specifically targeted at P2P systems. Some of the peculiarities of P2P systems, which make our problem challenging are that both the network membership and the data indexed in the network are dynamic, there is neither global coordination nor global information to rely on, and the load-balancing mechanism ideally should not compromise the structural properties and thus the search efficiency of the DHT, while preserving the semantic information of the data (e.g., lexicographic ordering to enable range searches).

1   Introduction

Load balancing problems in P2P systems come along in many facets. In this paper we report on our results on solving simultaneously a combination of two important load balancing problems with conflicting requirements—storage and replication load balancing–in the construction and maintenance of distributed hash tables [1] (DHTs) to provide an efficient, distributed, scalable, and decentralized indexing mechanism in P2P systems. The basic principle of distributed hash tables is the association of peers with data keys and the construction of distributed routing data structures to support efficient search. Existing approaches to DHTs mainly differ in the choice of topology (rings [2], multi-dimensional

---

* The work presented in this paper was supported (in part) by the National Competence Center in Research on Mobile Information and Communication Systems (NCCR-MICS), a center supported by the Swiss National Science Foundation under grant number 5005-67322 and was (partly) carried out in the framework of the EPFL Center for Global Computing and supported by the Swiss National Funding Agency OFES as part of the European project Evergrow No 001935.

O. Babaoglu et al. (Eds.): SELF-STAR 2004, LNCS 3460, pp. 373–391, 2005.

spaces[3], or hypercubes[4]), the specific rules for associating data keys to peer keys (closest, closest in one direction), and the strategies for constructing the routing infrastructure.

To use the available resources of peers best, a *storage load balancing* approach is applied in all DHTs, i.e., associating keys to peers in a way so that the number of data items each peer is associated with, is uniform in terms of storage consumption. Most existing solutions achieve this by first mapping data keys and peer identifiers into the same space using uniform hashing. Using this approach storage load balancing essentially translates into the classical *balls into bins* problem [5], where peers are the bins (the peer identifier determines the data space) and the data items are the balls. Adapting the classical load-balancing mechanisms in the context of P2P systems, such as load-stealing and load-shedding schemes, in which peers share load with random peers, e.g., [6,7], or power of two choices [8], lead to the need of redirections which compromise the search efficiency, because keys become increasingly decoupled from the peers associated with the corresponding key space and other structural properties are violated, since routing needs additional redirections. The problem is further aggravated with the growing recognition of the fact that uniform hashing to generate keys which are uniformly distributed on the key space jeopardizes the possibility to do searches on data using the data key semantics, typically the ordering of keys to enable semantically rich queries like range queries.

The approach which we will follow in this paper is to have peers dynamically change their associated key space ("bin adaptation") decoupled from their (unique and stable) identifier, and the routing between peers is based on the associated key space, rather than on the peer identifiers. Following this approach, the partitioning of the key space dynamically adapts to any data distribution, such that uniform distribution of data items over each partition of the key space is achieved. This leads to uneven sizes of the partitions of the key space, which can be viewed in the one-dimensional case analogously to having an unbalanced search tree. This implies a risk of sacrificing search efficiency. However, we show that due to the distributed and randomized routing process we propose (in P-Grid), this risk can be contained, such that searches can be performed with communication cost of $O(log(|\Pi|))$ with high probability where $|\Pi|$ is the number of partitions of the key space, irrespective of the key space partitioning. This satisfies the condition of efficient searches in the context of P2P systems under the (standard) assumption that in a P2P network, local resources such as computation and storage are cheap, but communication costs (messages or latency) and network maintenance (routing) are expensive.

Beyond search efficiency, another important issue in P2P systems is resilience against failures. The standard response to this problem is to introduce redundancy. In the context of DHTs this corresponds to associating multiple peers with the same partition of the search space, i.e., peers being replicas of each other. A fair use of resources implies uniform replication of all data partitions, which introduces the *replication load* balancing problem. Apart from providing fault-tolerance, replication load balancing also provides query load distribution over several peers. The initial approaches to balance replication used a predefined global constant number of replicas for each data partition [2, 3, 9, 10]. These approaches lack adaptivity to available resources and dynamics in the system.

The challenge is thus to determine adaptively an appropriate replication factor in absence of global knowledge (e.g., total peer population size, total storage space, total data load) in order to distribute the resources in a dynamic environment (change in the peer membership, or the data in the network) in a fair way.

An alternative approach, which we pursue, is to determine the number of replicas for each data space partition dynamically (*resource adaptive replication balancing*) which again induces a load balancing problem, i.e., how to assure that each partition is associated with approximately the same number of replica peers[1]. Here, the key space partitions are the bins, and the peers are the balls. This problem could again be solved by standard distributed load balancing algorithms if the key space partitions were known. However, as mentioned before in the context of storage load balancing, determining key space partitions by itself is a dynamic load balancing problem to solve. This shows that the two problems of storage load balancing and replication load balancing are inherently intertwined.

In this paper we provide decentralized algorithms for both maintaining storage load balance and resource adaptive replication load balance in a self-organizing manner. For storage load balance we use recursive partitioning of the key space performed during bilateral interactions among peers in order to adapt the key space partitioning to the data distribution to ensure storage load balancing. This mechanism also addresses dynamic changes, such that, if over time the data distribution changes, the key space partitioning will change as well. The partitioning process does not ensure replication balancing, and hence we propose a complementary replication maintenance algorithm which decreases imbalance in replication factors. Note that even if the partitioning algorithm were to achieve perfect replication balancing, we would still need the replication maintenance mechanism in order to cope with changes in the peer population, due to node joins and leaves. Since global coordination and knowledge cannot be assumed in a decentralized environment, the replication maintenance algorithm relies on each peer obtaining an approximate local view of the system based on sampling, for example, piggy-backed onto normal query-forwarding, and making an autonomous probabilistic decision to replicate an overloaded key space prioritized according to the load-imbalance between two sub-partitions of the key space.

Though there are some sophisticated data aggregation schemes like Astrolabe [12], the overheads and latency for acquiring a global view at each peer are not amortized. Instead we use partial information gathered by peers in local interactions, such that, both the latency and overheads of partial information

---

[1] Resource adaptive uniform replication of all data items does not provide load-balancing with respect to data item access. For that a complementary *query-adaptive replication* strategy is necessary, which we discuss separately [11].

aggregation are much lower, and still decent load-balancing characteristics are achieved.

Our approach has several advantages: We address multifaceted load-balancing concerns simultaneously in a self-organizing manner without assuming global knowledge, or restricting the replication to a predetermined number. We preserve key ordering which is important for range queries, while retaining the logarithmic search complexity. And we do not compromise structural properties of DHT. Our approach is implemented in our DHT-based P-Grid P2P system which is available at http://www.p-grid.org/.

2   The P-Grid Data Structure

We use our DHT-based P-Grid P2P system [13, 14] to evaluate the approach described in this paper. We assume that the reader is relatively familiar with the standard distributed hash table (DHT) approach [1] and thus only provide P-Grid's distinguishing characteristics.

In P-Grid, peers refer to a common underlying tree structure in order to organize their routing tables (other topologies in the literature include rings [2], multi-dimensional spaces [3], or hypercubes [4]). In the following, for simplicity of presentation, we will assume that the tree is binary. This is not a fundamental limitation as a generalization of P-Grid to k-ary structures has been introduced in [15]. Note that the underlying tree does not have to be balanced but may be of arbitrary shape, thus facilitating to adapt the overlay network to unbalanced data distribution [16].

Each peer $p \in P$ is associated with a leaf of the binary tree. Each leaf corresponds to a binary string $\pi \in \Pi$. Thus each peer p is associated with a path $\pi(p)$. For search, a peer stores for each prefix $\pi(p, l)$ of $\pi(p)$ of length l a set of references $\rho(p, l)$ to peers q with property $\overline{\pi(p, l)} = \pi(q, l)$, where $\overline{\pi}$ is the binary string π with the last bit inverted. This means that at each level of the tree the peer has references to some other peers that do not pertain to the peer's subtree at that level. This enables the implementation of prefix routing for search.

Each peer stores a set of data items $\delta(p)$. Ideally for $d \in \delta(p)$ the key $\kappa(d)$ of d has $\pi(p)$ as prefix. However, we do not exclude that temporarily other data items are also stored at a peer, that is, the set $\delta(p, \pi(p))$ of data items whose key matches $\pi(p)$ can be a proper subset of $\delta(p)$. In addition, peers also maintain references $\sigma(p)$ to peers having the same path, i.e., their replicas.

In a stable state (i.e. where no more maintenance operations are applicable) the set of paths of all peers is prefix-free and complete, i.e., no two peers p and q exist such that $\pi(p) \subset \pi(q)$, i.e., $\pi(p)$ is a proper prefix of $\pi(q)$ and if there exists a peer p with path $\pi(p)$, then there also exists a peer q with $\overline{\pi(p)} = \pi(q)$. This guarantees full coverage of the search space and complete partitioning of the search space among the peers. All data stored at a peer then matches its path.

For search, P-Grid uses a prefix routing strategy. When receiving a search message for key κ from peer p, a peer q checks whether its path is a prefix of κ.

If yes, it checks whether it can return a query result from its data store. If not, it randomly selects a peer r having a common prefix of maximal length with κ from its routing table and forwards the request to peer r.

The algorithm always terminates successfully in the stable state: Due to the definition of $\rho(p, l)$, this prefix routing strategy will always find the location of a peer at which the search can continue (use of completeness) and each time the query if forwarded, the length of the common prefix of $\pi(p)$ and κ increases. It is obvious that this search algorithm is efficient $(O(log(|\Pi|)))$ for a balanced tree, i.e., all paths associated with peers are of equal length. Skewed data distributions may imbalance the tree, so that it may seem that search cost may become non-logarithmic in the number of messages. However, in [16] we show that due to the probabilistic nature of the P-Grid approach this does not pose a problem. The expected search cost measured by the number of messages required to perform the the search remains logarithmic, independently how the P-Grid is structured.

Theorem 1. *The expected search cost for the search of a specific key $\kappa(d)$ using a P-Grid network N that is randomly selected among all possible P-Grids, starting at a randomly selected peer p with $\pi(p) \in \Pi$ is less than $log(|\Pi|)$.*

Although this applies to the special case of prefix-free P-Grids, we have shown by simulation that the result also applies to more general cases. A formal proof of this theorem is given in [16]. Due to space limitations we can only provide the intuition which is underlying the proof. Basically we show that the path resolution in the forwarding process normally is not done bit by bit but for longer bit sequences at the processing peers thus keeping the number of messages required in the forwarding process logarithmic. Additionally, [16] shows that the probability that a search does not succeed after k steps $(1 \leq k \leq max(|\pi|, \pi \in \Pi))$ is smaller than $\frac{log(n|\Pi|)^{k-1}}{(k-1)!}$.

3   P-Grid Construction Algorithm

The construction and maintenance of P-Grid is based exclusively on local inter-actions among peers in order to observe the principle of locality. In this section we give an overview of the *possible* interactions that determine the behavioral options of peers. As peers are autonomous they may use different *strategies* for entering into such local interactions. The choice of concrete strategies will be essential with respect to the global efficiency of the system and discussed later.

Interactions among peers are either performed actively by the peers (similar to the peer discovery in Gnutella using the ping-pong messages) or are performed reactively triggered by earlier interactions or search messages. For maintenance purposes, the following interactions occur among two peers p and q:

- *balancedSplit(p, q)*: The peers check whether their paths are identical. If yes, they extend their paths by complementary bits, i.e., partition (split) the key space they are responsible for. To maintain consistency they exchange their data corresponding to their updated paths and add each other to their routing table. This enables the refinement of the indexing structure into subspaces which are sufficiently populated with data.

– *unbalancedSplit*(*p*, *q*): The peers check whether $\pi(p)$ is a proper prefix of $\pi(q)$. In the case $\pi(p)$ is a proper prefix of $\pi(q)$, *p* extends its path by one bit complementary to the bit of $\pi(q)$ at the same level. The peers exchange their data corresponding to the updated paths and update their routing table. This enables the refinement of the indexing structure into subspaces as in the previous case, but covers the frequently occurring situation that peers have already specialized to different degrees. The case where $\pi(q)$ is a proper prefix of $\pi(p)$ is treated analogously.

– *adoptPath*(*p*, *q*): Peer *p* becomes a copy (replica) of peer *q*. In order to avoid data loss peer *p* attempts to locate peers covering the same subspace and to delegate any non-replicated data items there. If this is not possible it keeps data items not matching the new path to delegate it at a later time.

– *balancedDataExchange*(*p*, *q*): The peers check whether their paths are identical. If yes, they replicate mutually all data pertaining to their common path which increases resilience (availability of the data items).

– *unbalancedDataExchange*(*p*, *q*): The peers check whether $\pi(p)$ is a proper prefix of $\pi(q)$ (or vice versa). If yes, data of *p* pertaining to $\pi(q)$ is moved to *q*.

– *refExchange*(*p*, *q*): The peers exchange entries from their routing tables up to the level corresponding to the length of their common prefix randomly. This interaction randomizes the contents of the routing tables which is essential to maintain routing efficiency, in particular in the unbalanced case [16].

– *forwarding*(*p*, *q*): If the peers' paths are not in a prefix relationship the peer *q* provides the peer *p* with an address of a peer *r* selected from its routing table which shares a prefix of maximal length with $\pi(p)$ (or vice versa). Then peer *p* enters into an interaction with peer *r*.

The conditions under which these rules are applied determine the strategies peers pursue in interactions. From these local interaction strategies a global system behavior emerges. The following sequence of actions performed by peers *p* and *q* entering into an interaction describes a possible strategy to construct a P-Grid structure from an initial state where all peers store some initial data and have empty paths and routing tables.

Algorithm 1
refExchange(*p*, *q*);
if $|\delta(p, \pi(p)) \cup \delta(q, \pi(q))| \leq 2\delta_{max}$**then** *balancedDataExchange*(*p*, *q*)
if $|\delta(p, \pi(p)) \cup \delta(q, \pi(q))| > 2\delta_{max}$;**then** *balancedSplit*(*p*, *q*)
unbalancedSplit(*p*, *q*);
forwarding(*p*, *q*);

In this strategy, peers first exchange routing information if possible. Then depending on the relationship among their paths and the current storage load they select one of the four subsequent actions. (Note that we do not explicitly repeat the necessary conditions on the path relationship for executing these actions). We observe that due to the *forwarding* action any initial interaction will eventually lead to the enabling of one of the balanced or unbalanced split or data exchange operations. For a uniform data distribution and provided that the total number of data items is less than $\delta_{max}n$, where is the total number of peers, this algorithm will end up in a state where each peer carries at most $2\delta_{max}$ data items, the P-Grid structure is (approximately) balanced and all replica peers store the same data.

Theorem 2. *If the total number of data items is less than $\delta_{max}n$ and data keys are uniformly distributed Algorithm 1 results in a steady state in which the P-Grid is prefix-free and complete and each peer p with replicas has a data load smaller than $2\delta_{max}$, all replicas store the same data and in expectation all data items are equally replicated.*

Proof Sketch: First we have to show that the steady state is reached. Prefix-freeness follows from the fact that whenever a peer has a path that is a prefix of another peer's path, it eventually will encounter this peer and perform an unbalanced split. Completeness follows from the fact that new paths can only occur as the result of a balanced split. If a peer has a replica and the data load is larger than $2\delta_{max}$, it will eventually perform a split with its replica. If peers with the same path have different data items then they will eventually perform a balanced data exchange. Second, it is easy to see that once the steady state is reached none of the rules can induce further changes to the paths or data associated with the peers.   □

The problem is that with this strategy peers preferably adapt shorter paths and therefore even though peers try to balance their storage load, the distribution of replicas over the different paths becomes unbalanced in the case of non-uniform distribution of data keys: In a balanced split the same number of peers decide for each side of the data space independent of the actual distribution of data among the two subspaces, and in an unbalanced split peers decide for one side with a probability proportional to the number of peers already specialized for each side of the data space, but independent of the number of data items present in the two subspaces. This has the further effect that fewer peers specialize on paths with higher data load, and sooner end up without replicas. They thus lack the capacity to further refine the path and thus reduce their data load.

To address this problem we consider a different strategy to improve replica balancing already during construction of the P-Grid structure.

Algorithm 2
$refExchange(p, q)$;
if $|\delta(p, \pi(p)) \cup \delta(q, \pi(q))| \leq 2\delta_{max} \wedge \gamma([0, 1]) < \alpha$**then** $balancedDataExchange(p, q)$
if $|\delta(p, \pi(p)) \cup \delta(q, \pi(q))| > 2\delta_{max}$;**then** $balancedSplit(p, q)$
if $\gamma([0, 1]) < \beta$**then** $unbalancedSplit(p, q)$**else** $adoptPath(p, q)$;
$forwarding(p, q)$;

In this strategy two mechanisms work together to improve replica balancing. First, balanced splits are not always performed eagerly, but with reduced probability α, where α may depend on the locally observed load distribution. Thus more unbalanced split situations occur. In those situations peers only either extend their path opposite to the path of the encountered peer or adopt the path. The decision is based on a control parameter β which again may depend on the locally observed load distribution. As a result, if α and β are properly chosen, those subspaces will be populated by more peers that contain more data. Even though, this heuristic approach does not necessarily induce a perfectly uniform replica distribution, it substantially improves the state reached after the P-Grid construction. The remaining balancing is then achieved by the sampling-based replication maintenance algorithm, that we will introduce subsequently. Having a more uniform initial replica distribution substantially reduces the effort required from the maintenance algorithms in order to rectify the distribution.

The construction algorithm can be extended to a maintenance algorithm (path retraction). The path retraction is dual to the path extension, such that if two partitions do not have enough data ($< \delta_{max}/2$), then such partitions would be merged.

4   Replication Maintenance Algorithm

To address the balancing problems discussed in the previous sections, we use a reactive randomized distributed algorithm which tries to achieve globally uniform replication adaptive to globally available resources based on locally available (gathered) information. Before introducing the algorithm we introduce the principles underlying its design.

Consider a P-Grid of leaves as shown in Figure 1(a). Let $N_1 > N_2$ be the actual number of replica peers with paths 0 and 1. To achieve perfect replication balancing $\frac{N_1 - N_2}{2}$ of the peers with path 0 would need to change their path to 1. Since each of the peers has to make an autonomous decision whether to change its path, we propose a randomized decision: Peers decide to change their paths with probability $p_{0 \to 1} = max(\frac{N_1 - N_2}{2N_1}, 0)$ (no $0 \to 1$ transition occurs if $N_2 > N_1$).

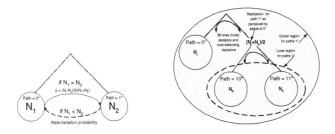

Fig. 1. (a) P-Grid with two leaves, (b) P-Grid with three leaves

Now, if we set $p_0 = \frac{N_1}{N_1 + N_2}$ as the probability that peers have path 0, and similarly $p_1 = \frac{N_2}{N_1 + N_2}$, then the migration probability becomes $p_{0 \to 1} =$

$max(\frac{1}{2}(1 - \frac{p_1}{p_0}), 0)$. It is easy to see that with this transition probability on average an equal replication factor is achieved for each of the two paths after each peer has taken the migration decision. In a practical setting peers do not know N_1 and N_2, but they can easily determinate an approximation of the ratio $\frac{N_1}{N_2}$ by keeping statistics of the peer they encounter in (random) interactions.

Now consider the case of a P-Grid with three leaves, as shown in Figure 1(b), with N_1, N_2 and N_3 replicas for the paths starting with 0, 10 and 11 respectively. This extension of the example captures the essential choices that have to be made by individual peers in a realistic P-Grid. In an unbalanced tree, knowing the count of peers for the two sides at any level is not sufficient because, even if replication is uniform, the count will provide biased information, with a higher value for the side of the tree with more leaves. On the other hand, knowledge of the whole tree (shape and replication) at all peers is not practical but fortunately not necessary either. For example, in the P-Grid with three leaves, peers with path 0 will meet peers with paths 10 and 11. Essentially, they need to know that there are on an average $\frac{N_2+N_3}{2}$ peers at each leaf of the other sub-tree, but do not need to understand the shape of the sub-tree or the distribution of replication factors.

Thus, while collecting the statistical information, any peer p counts the number of peers encountered with common prefix length l for all $0 \le l \le |\pi(p)|$. It normalizes the count by dividing it with $2^{|\pi(q)|-|\pi(p)\cap\pi(q)|}$. Thus peers obtain from local information an approximation of the global distribution of peers *pertaining to their own path*. The latter aspect is important to maintain scalability.

In our example, peers with path 0 will count on an average $\frac{N_2+N_3}{N_1}$ as many occurrences of peers with path 10 or 11 than they will count with path 0, but will normalize their count by a factor of $\frac{1}{2}$. Thus at the top level they will observe replica balance exactly if on average $N_1 = \frac{1}{2}(N_2 + N_3)$. If imbalance exists they will migrate with probability $p_{0\to 1} = max(\frac{1}{2}(1 - \frac{p_1}{p_0}), 0)$, where, now $p_0 = \frac{N_1}{N_1 + \frac{1}{2}(N_2+N_3)}$ and $p_1 = \frac{\frac{1}{2}(N_2+N_3)}{N_1 + \frac{1}{2}(N_2+N_3)}$.

Once balance is achieved at the top level, peers at the second level with paths 10 and 11 will achieve balance as described in the first example. Thus local balancing propagates down the tree hierarchy till global balance is achieved. The peers with longer paths may have multiple migration choices, such that balancing is performed at multiple levels simultaneously. For example, if $N_1 = N_2 < N_3$ peers with path 11 can choose migrations $11 \to 0$ and $11 \to 10$ with equal probability.

Note that N_i changes over time, and thus the statistics have to be refreshed and built from scratch regularly. Thus the algorithm has two phases, (1) gathering statistics and (2) making probabilistic decisions to migrate. It is easy to verify, e.g. by numerical simulation, that this approach is effective in the basic scenario discussed. Now we introduce the algorithms extending the principle idea to the general situation.

Collecting Statistical Information at Peer p: In a decentralized setting, a peer p has to rely on sampling to obtain an estimate of the global load imbalance:

Upon meeting any random peer q, peer p will gather statistical information for all possible levels $l \leq |\pi(p)|$ of its path, and update the number of peers belonging to the same subspace $\Sigma_p(l) = |\{q \text{ s.t. } |\pi(p) \cap \pi(q)| \geq l\}|$ and the complimentary subspace $\overline{\Sigma}_p(l) = |\{q \text{ s.t. } \overline{\pi}(p, l) = \pi(q, l)\}|$ at any level l. When peers p and q interact, statistics gathering is performed as follows

$$l := |\pi(p) \cap \pi(q)|;$$
$$\overline{\Sigma}_{p\|q}(l) := \overline{\Sigma}_{p\|q}(l) + 2^{1+l-|\pi(q\|p)|};$$
$$\forall 0 \leq i < l \; \Sigma_{p\|q}(i) := \Sigma_{p\|q}(i) + 2^{1+i-|\pi(q\|p)|};$$

where the meta-notation $p\|q$ denotes that the operations are performed symmetrically both for p and q.

Choosing Migration Path for Peer p: A path change of a peer only makes sense if it reduces the number of replicas in an underpopulated subspace (data). Therefore, as soon as a minimum number of samples have been obtained, the peer tries to identify possibilities for migration. It determines the largest l_{max} such that $\frac{\Sigma_p(l_{max})}{\overline{\Sigma}_p(l_{max})} > \zeta$ where $\zeta \geq 1$ is a dampening factor which avoids migration if load-imbalance is within a ζ factor. We set $l_{max} := \infty$ if no level satisfies the condition.

If all peers try to migrate to the least replicated subspace, we would induce an oscillatory behavior such that the subspaces with low replication would turn into highly replicated subspaces and vice versa. Consequently, instead of greedily balancing load, peers essentially have to make a probabilistic choice proportional to the relative imbalance between subspaces. Thus $l_{migration}$ is chosen between l_{max} and $|\pi(p)|$ with a probability distribution proportional to the replication load-imbalance $\frac{\Sigma_p(i)}{\overline{\Sigma}_p(i)}, |\pi(p)| \geq i \geq l_{max}$. Thus the migrations are prioritized to the least populated subspace from the peer's current view, yet ensuring that the effect of the migrations is fair, and not all take place to the same subspace. There are subtle differences in our approach to replication balancing in comparison to the classical balls into bins load balancing approach, because in our case there are no physical *bins*, which would share load among themselves, and it is rather the *balls* themselves, which need to make an autonomous decision to migrate. Moreover, the load sharing is not among bins chosen uniformly, but is prioritized based on locally gathered approximate global imbalance knowledge.

To further reduce oscillatory behavior, the probability of migration is reduced by a factor $\xi \leq 1$. As migration is an expensive operation—it leads to increased network maintenance cost due to routing table repairs, apart from the data transfer for replicating a new key space—it should only occur if long-term changes in data and replication distribution are observed and not result from short term variations or inaccurate statistics. The parameters ζ and ξ are design parameters and the impact of their choice on the system behavior will be further explored in Section 5.

Migrating Peer p: The last aspect of replication load balancing is the action of changing the path. For that, peer p needs to find a peer from the complimentary subspace and thus inspects its routing table $\rho(p, l_{migration})$ (s.t. $\pi(p) \cap \pi(q) =$

$l_{migration}$). After identifying a peer q, p clones the contents of q, including data and routing table, i.e., $\delta(p) := \delta(q)$ and $\rho(p, *) = \rho(q, *)$, and the statistical information is reset in order to account for the changes in distribution.

5   Simulation Results

This section highlights some of the many experiments we performed using a simulator implemented in Mathematica to evaluate the construction and maintenance algorithms. The simulations aim at verifying the load balancing characteristics of the algorithms, and do not model aspects related to the physical runtime environment with different network topologies, communication latencies, or heterogeneity of resources of nodes.

Unless mentioned otherwise, simulations were performed with 256 peers. This relatively low number was chosen to keep simulation time manageable. From the design of the algorithms it is clear that the results will scale up to larger populations. To support this, we will give one result for the complete maintenance algorithm with changing peer population at the end. The data was chosen from a Zipf distribution with parameter $\theta = 0.8614$ such that the frequencies of keys were monotonically increasing with decreasing size of the key. We set $\delta_{max} = 50$.

Replication Load Balancing Throughout Construction: In Section 3 we discussed a possibility to maintain better replica load balancing while establishing storage load balance during P-Grid construction, by reducing the probability α of balanced splits of the key space (while choosing $\beta = 1$). In Table 1 we show the results of an experiment in which each peer initially holds 15 data items.

Table 1. Influence of splitting probability α on distribution of replication factor

α	Interactions	R_μ	R_{σ^2}	R_{max}
0.05	40,000	3.32	1.82	10
0.1	35,000	3.20	1.99	9
0.5	20,000	3.55	3.39	21
1.0	20,000	3.28	3.94	23

We see how a reduction of α reduces both the variance R_{σ^2} in the replication factors for the key space partitions and the maximum replication factor R_{max}, where R_μ is the average replication factor with an expected value of 3.33.[2] With lower probabilities more interactions occur to reach a steady state.

Replication Load Balancing Throughout Maintenance: Given a P-Grid that partitions the data space such that the storage load is (approximately) uniform for all partitions, migrations are used to establish simultaneous balancing

---

[2] There are $256 * 15$ data items, on average 50 of them are stored at each peer. They require $\frac{256*15}{50}$ partitions to be replicated among 256 peers, which results in $\frac{50}{15} = 3.33$ replicas on average.

of replication factors for the different partitions without changing the data space partitioning. For the experiments we chose the design parameters $\zeta = 1.1$ (required imbalance for migration), $\xi = 0.25$ (attenuation of migration probability) and a statistical sample size of 10. These parameters had been determined in initial experiments as providing stable (non-oscillatory) behavior.

The performance of the migration mechanism depends on the number of key space partitions and the initial number of peers associated with each partition. Since the expected depth of the tree structure grows logarithmically in the number of partitions, and the maintenance is expected to grow linearly with the depth of the tree (since each peer uses its local view for each level of its current path), we expect the maintenance algorithm to have logarithmic dependency between the number of partitions and the rate of convergence.

Figure 2 shows the reduction of the variance of the distribution of replication factors compared with the initial variance as a function of the number of key space partitions. The simulation was starting from an initially constructed, unbalanced P-Grid network with replication factors chosen uniformly between 10 and 30 for each of the key space partitions. We compared the effect of an increasing number of key space partitions ($p = \{10, 20, 40, 80\}$) on the performance of the replication maintenance algorithm. One observed that the reduction of variance increases logarithmically with the number of partitions. For example, for $p = 80$ the initial variance is reduced by approximately 80%. We conducted 5 simulations for each of the settings. The error bars give the standard deviation of the experimental series.

The right part of Figure 2 shows the rate of the reduction of variance of replication factors as a function of different numbers of peers associated with each key partition. We used a P-Grid with $p = 20$ partitions and assigned to each partition uniformly randomly between k and $3k$ peers, such that the average replication factor was $2k$. The other settings were as in the previous experiment. Actually variance reduction appears to slightly improve for higher replication factors. This results from the possibility of a more fine-grained adaptation with higher replication factors.

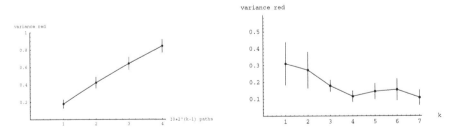

Fig. 2. Maintenance of replication load-balance

Simultaneous Balancing of Storage and Replication Load in a Dynamic Setting: In this experiment we studied the behavior of the system under dynamic changes of the data distribution. Both storage load balancing by restructuring the key partitioning (i.e., extending and retracting paths) and replication balancing by migration were performed simultaneously. We wanted to answer the following two questions: (1) Is the maintenance mechanism adaptive to changing data distributions? (2) Does the combination of restructuring and migration scale for large peer populations?

For the experimental setup we generated synthetic, unbalanced P-Grids with $p = 10, 20, 40, 80$ paths and chose replication factors for each path uniformly between 10 and 30. Thus, for example, for $p = 80$ the expected peer population was 1600. The value δ_{max} was set to 50 and the dataset consisted of approximately 3000 unique Zipf-distributed data keys, distributed over the different peers such that each peer held exactly those keys that pertained to its current path. Since the initial key partition is completely unrelated to the data distribution the data load of the peers varies considerably, and some peers temporarily hold many more data items than their accepted maximal storage $2\delta_{max}$ load would be. Then the restructuring algorithms, i.e., path extension and retraction used for P-Grid construction and path migrations used for replication load balancing, were executed simultaneously.

Table 2 shows the results of our experiments. We executed an average of 382 rounds in which each peer initiated interleaved restructuring and maintenance operations, which was sufficient for the system to reach an almost steady state. R_{σ^2} is the variance of the replication factors for the different paths and D_{σ^2} is the variance of the number of data items stored per peer.

Table 2. Results of simultaneous balancing

Number of peers	Number of paths		R_{σ^2}		D_{σ^2}	
	initial	final	initial	final	initial	final
219	10	43	55.47	3.92	180,338	175
461	20	47	46.30	10.77	64,104	156
831	40	50	40.69	45.42	109,656	488
1568	80	62	35.80	48.14	3,837	364

The experiments show that the restructuring of the network as well as replication balancing was effective and scalable: (1) In all cases the data variance dropped significantly, i.e., the key space partitioning properly reflects the (changed) data distribution. Because of the randomized choices of the initial P-Grid structure and the data set, the initial data variance is high and varies highly. It actually depends on the degree to which the randomly chosen P-Grid and the data distribution already matched. From the case $p = 40$ (number of initial paths), we conclude that this has also a substantial impact on the convergence speed since more restructuring has to take place. Actually, after doubling the number of interactions, the replication variance dropped to 20.93, which is an expected value. (2) With increasing number of replicas per key partition the replication variance increases. This is natural as fewer partitions mean higher replication on average and thus higher variance. (3) With increasing peer population the final data variance increases. This is expected as we used a constant number of interactions per peer and the effort of restructuring grows logarithmically with the number of key partitions.

The algorithms do not require much computation per peer hence have a low overhead. Simulating them, however takes considerable effort: A single experiment with $3 * 10^5$ interactions for the results in this section took up to 1 full day. Thus we had to limit the number and size of the experiments. Nevertheless they indicate the feasibility, effectiveness and scalability of the algorithms.

6 Related Work

For data replication in P2P systems we can distinguish six different methods (partially according to the classification from [17]): *Owner replication* replicates a data object to the peer that has successfully located it through a query (Napster, Gnutella, Kazaa). *Path replication* replicates a data object along the search path that is traversed as part of a search (Freenet, some unstructured P2P networks). *Random replication* replicates data objects as part of a randomized process. [17] shows that for unstructured networks this is superior to owner and path replication. *Controlled replication* replicates a data object a pre-defined number of times upon insertion (Chord [2], CAN [3], and Pastry [9]). This approach does not adapt replication to the changing environment with variable resource availability. The replication balancing mechanism proposed in this paper (and as used in P-Grid) is *adaptive to the available resources* in the system. This mechanism tries to uniformly exploit the storage resources available at peers, and thus achieve uniform distribution of the replicas of data objects. In addition, *query adaptive replication* [11] can be used in various structured overlays, complementing controlled or available resource adaptive replication.

Replication of index information is applied in structured and hierarchical P2P networks. For the super-peer approach it has been shown that having multiple replicated super-peers maintaining the same index information increases system performance [18]. Structured P2P networks maintain multiple routing entries to support alternative routing paths if a referenced node fails. With respect to load balancing in DHT based systems only a few recent works have been reported. The application of uniform hashing and its limited applicability have already been discussed in the introduction.

The load balancing strategy for Chord proposed in [7] uses multiple hash functions instead of only one to select a number of candidate peers. Among those the one with the least load stores the data item and the others store pointers to it. This scheme does not scale in the number of data items due to the effort incurred by redirection pointer maintenance. Moreover, using a predetermined number of hash functions do not give any adaptivity according to the systems requirement. Also Chord's original search no longer works and essentially multiple Chord overlays have to be maintained which are interconnected among themselves in a possibly unpredictable manner.

Another scheme for load balancing for Chord is suggested in [19] based on virtual servers. Nodes are responsible to split the data space to keep the load of each virtual server bounded. The splitting strategy is similar to the splitting used in our storage load balancing strategy, however, this work does not consider the effects on replication nor on search efficiency.

Online load-balancing has been a widely researched area in the distributed systems domain. It has often been modeled as balls into bins [5]. Traditionally randomized mechanisms for load assignment, including load-stealing and load-shedding and power of two choices [8] have been used, some of which can partly be reused in the context of P2P systems as well [7,6]. In fact, from storage load-balancing perspective, [6] compares closest to our approach because it provides storage load-balancing as well as key order preservation to support range queries, but in doing so, they no more provide any guarantee for efficient searches of isolated keys.

As mentioned earlier, load-balancing in DHTs poses several new challenges, which call for new solutions. We need to deal with the dynamic membership (off-online behavior of peers) and dynamic content, and there is neither global coordination nor global information to rely on, and the load-balancing mechanism should ideally not compromise the structural properties and the search efficiency of the DHT, while preserving the semantic information of the data. In [20], storage load-balancing is achieved by reassignment of peer identifiers in order to deal with network churn, but this scheme is designed specifically for uniform load distribution only. The dynamic nature of P2P systems is also different from the online load-balancing of temporary tasks [21] because of the lack of global knowledge and coordination. Moreover, for replication balancing, there are no real bins, and actually the number of bins varies over time because of storage load balancing, but the balls (peers) themselves have to autonomously migrate to replicate overloaded key spaces. Also for storage load balancing, the balls are essentially already present determined by the data distribution, and it is essentially the bins that have to fit the balls by dynamically partitioning the key space, rather than the other way round.

Substantial work on distributed data access structures has also been performed in the area of distributed databases on scalable data access structures, such as [22, 23]. This work is apparently relevant, but the existing approaches apply to a different physical and application environment. Databases are distributed over a moderate number of fairly stable database servers and workstation clusters. Thus reliability is assumed to be high and replication is used only very selectively [24] for dealing with exceptional errors. Central servers for realizing certain coordination functions in the network are considered as acceptable and execution guarantees are mostly deterministic rather than probabilistic. Distributed search trees [25] are constructed by a full partitioning, not using the principle of scalable replication of routing information at the higher tree levels, as originally published in [1] (with exceptions [26]). Nevertheless, we believe that at the current stage the potential of applying principles developed in this area to P2P systems is not yet fully exploited.

7   Conclusions

Existing uncoordinated online load-balancing mechanisms do not address the requirements of DHT-based P2P networks. In this paper we compared the new load-balancing problems of such systems with the standard model of "balls into bins" so that wherever possible we can apply existing solutions. But more importantly, we identified the new and specific requirements of this family of P2P systems, and proposed new algorithms to efficiently achieve simultaneous storage and replication load-balancing relying only on local information. Some of the important novelties of our solution in comparison to other proposed P2P load-balancing mechanisms are: Our mechanism allows the access structure to adapt and restructure dynamically, but preserves its structural properties, unlike other mechanisms which require extrinsic mechanisms like redirection pointers, that make queries inefficient. The effort incurred by our load-balancing approach is low because it requires no extra communication but we gather statistic data from normal interactions and "piggy-back" the load-balancing into the standard information exchanges required by the DHT. We also preserve key ordering, which is vital for semantically rich queries like range queries. Using randomized routing choices, search efficiency is guaranteed with high probability, irrespective of key distribution. Additionally, unlike some other proposals, our solution does not require the peers to change identity which allows us to retain existing knowledge and semantics, that may be exploited by higher level applications. The approach presented in this paper is implemented in our P-Grid system which is available at http://www.p-grid.org/.

References

1. Plaxton, C.G., Rajaraman, R., Richa, A.W.: Accessing Nearby Copies of Replicated Objects in a Distribute d Environment. In: Proceedings of the 9th Annual ACM Symposium on Parallel Algorithms and Architectures (SPAA). (1997)
2. Stoica, I., Morris, R., Karger, D., Kaashoek, F., Balakrishnan, H.: Chord: A Scalable Peer-To-Peer Lookup Service for Internet Applications. In: Proceedings of the ACM SIGCOMM. (2001)
3. Ratnasamy, S., Francis, P., Handley, M., Karp, R., Shenker, S.: A Scalable Content-Addressable Network. In: Proceedings of the ACM SIGCOMM. (2001)
4. Schlosser, M., Sintek, M., Decker, S., Nejdl, W.: Hypercup–hypercubes, ontologies, and efficient search on peer-to-peer networks. LNCS **2530** (2003)
5. Raab, M., Steger, A.: "Balls into Bins" - A Simple and Tight Analysis. In: RANDOM. (1998)
6. Karger, D.R., Ruhl, M.: New Algorithms for Load Balancing in Peer-to-Peer Systems (2003) IRIS Student Workshop (ISW).
7. Byers, J., Considine, J., Mitzenmacher, M.: Simple Load Balancing for Distributed Hash Tables. In: 2nd International Workshop on Peer-to-Peer Systems (IPTPS '03). (2003)
8. Mitzenmacher, M.: The power of two choices in randomized load balancing. IEEE Transactions on Parallel and Distributed Systems **12** (2001) 1094 1104

9. Rowstron, A., Druschel, P.: Pastry: Scalable, decentralized object location, and routing for large-scale peer-to-peer systems. Lecture Notes in Computer Science **2218** (2001)

10. Alima, L.O., El-Ansary, S., Brand, P., Haridi, S.: DKS(N,k,f): A Family of Low Communication, Scalable and Fault-Tolerant Infrastructures for P2P Applications. In: 3rd IEEE/ACM International Symposium on Cluster Computing and the Grid (CCGRID). (2003)

11. Datta, A., Aberer, K., Nejdl, W.: Principles of Query-Adaptive Optimal Replication in DHTs. Technical Report IC/2004/110, Ecole Polytechnique Fdrale de Lausanne (EPFL) (2004)

12. Renesse, R.V., Birman, K.P., Vogels, W.: Astrolabe: A robust and scalable technology for distributed system monitoring, management, and data mining. ACM Trans. Comput. Syst. **21** (2003) 164–206

13. Aberer, K.: P-Grid: A self-organizing access structure for P2P information systems. In: Proceedings of the Sixth International Conference on Cooperative Information Systems (CoopIS). (2001)

14. Aberer, K., Hauswirth, M., Punceva, M., Schmidt, R.: Improving Data Access in P2P Systems. IEEE Internet Computing **6** (2002)

15. Aberer, K., Punceva, M.: Efficient Search in Structured Peer-to-Peer Systems: Binary v.s. k-ary Unbalanced Tree Structures. In: International Workshop On Databases, Information Systems and Peer-to-Peer Computing. Collocated with VLDB 2003. (2003)

16. Aberer, K.: Efficient Search in Unbalanced, Randomized Peer-To-Peer Search Trees. Technical Report IC/2002/79, Swiss Federal Institute of Technology, Lausanne (EPFL) (2002) http://www.p-grid.org/Papers/TR-IC-2002-79.pdf.

17. Lv, Q., Cao, P., Cohen, E., Li, K., Shenker, S.: Search and replication in unstructured peer-to-peer networks. In: International Conference on Supercomputing. (2002)

18. Yang, B., Garcia-Molina, H.: Improving Search in Peer-to-Peer Networks. In: Proceedings of the 22nd International Conference on Distributed Computing Systems (ICDCS'02). (2002)

19. Rao, A., Lakshminarayanan, K., Surana, S., Karp, R., Stoica, I.: Load Balancing in Structured P2P Systems. In: Proceedings of the 2nd International Workshop on Peer-to-Peer Systems (IPTPS '03). LNCS, Springer (2003)

20. Manku, G.S.: Randomized ID Selection for Peer-to-Peer Networks. Technical report, Stanford University (2004) http://dbpubs.stanford.edu:8090/aux/index-en.html.

21. Azar, Y., Kalyanasundaram, B., Plotkin, S., Pruhs, K., Waarts, O.: On-line load balancing of temporary tasks. Journal of Algorithms **22** (1997) 93–110

22. Litwin, W., Neimat, M., Schneider, D.A.: RP*: A Family of Order Preserving Scalable Distributed Data Structures. In: VLDB. (1994) 342–353

23. Litwin, W., Neimat, M., Schneider, D.A.: LH* – A Scalable, Distributed Data Structure. ACM Transactions on Database Systems **21** (1996) 480–525

24. Litwin, W., Schwarz, T.: LH*RS: A High-Availability Scalable Distributed Data Structure using Reed Solomon Codes. In: SIGMOD Conference. (2000) 237–248

25. Kröll, B., Widmayer, P.: Distributing a Search Tree Among a Growing Number of Processors. In: ACM SIGMOD Conference. (1994) 265–276

26. Yokota, H., Kanemasa, Y., Miyazaki, J.: Fat-Btree: An Update-Conscious Parallel Directory Structure. In: International Conference on Data Engineering. (1999) 448–457

A   A Construction Scenario

In the following we provide an elementary example to illustrate constructing and maintaining a P-Grid. We assume 6 peers, each of them being able to store two data items. Let us assume that initially 6 data items are stored by the peers. The states of the peers are represented by triples $[a, \pi(a), \delta(a)]$. Each peer stores some data and initially all paths are empty (ϵ), i.e., no P-Grid has been built yet. For the data items we assume that their corresponding keys have the following 2-bit prefixes: $\kappa(A_i, 2) = 00$, $\kappa(B_i, 2) = 10$, $\kappa(C_i, 2) = 11$ ($i = 1, 2$).

Action	Resulting state.
Initial state.	$[P_1, \epsilon, \{A_1, B_1\}]$ $[P_2, \epsilon, \{B_1, C_1\}]$ $[P_3, \epsilon, \{A_2, B_2\}]$ $[P_4, \epsilon, \{B_2, C_2\}]$ $[P_5, \epsilon, \{A_1, C_1\}]$ $[P_6, \epsilon, \{A_2, C_2\}]$
P_1 initiates a P-Grid network N_1. P_2 joins the network by contacting P_1. We assume that whenever at least 1 data item pertaining to a subspace is available a peer attempts to specialize to that subspace. Thus P_1 and P_2 can split the search space.	$N_1 : [P_1, 0, \{A_1\}], [P_2, 1, \{B_1, C_1\}]$
Independently P_3 starts a P-Grid network N_2 and P_4 joins this network.	$N_2 : [P_3, 0, \{A_2\}], [P_4, 1, \{B_2, C_2\}]$
Next P_5 joins network N_1 by contacting P_2. Since $\pi(P_2) = 1$, P_5 decides to take path 0.	$N_1 : [P_1, 0, \{A_1\}], [P_2, 1, \{B_1, C_1\}],$ $[P_5, 0, \{A_1\}]$
Now P_6 enters network N_1 by contacting P_5. Since $\pi(P_5) = 0$, P_6 decides to adopt 1 as its path and sends $\{d \in \delta(P_6) | \kappa(d) = 0\} = \{A_2\}$ to P_5 which stores it.	$N_1 : [P_1, 0, \{A_1\}], [P_2, 1, \{B_1, C_1\}],$ $[P_5, 0, \{A_1, A_2\}], [P_6, 1, \{C_2\}]$
Next P_3 contacts P_1 and thus the two networks N_1 and N_2 merge into a common P-Grid network N. This shows that P-Grids do not require to start from a single origin, as assumed by standard DHT approaches, but can dynamically merge, similarly to unstructured networks. Since $\pi(P_3) = \pi(P_1) = 0$ and they still have extra storage space, they can replicate their data to increase data availability.	$N : [P_1, 0, \{A_1, A_2\}],$ $[P_2, 1, \{B_1, C_1\}],$ $[P_3, 0, \{A_1, A_2\}],$ $[P_4, 1, \{B_2, C_2\}],$ $[P_5, 0, \{A_1, A_2\}],$ $[P_6, 1, \{C_2\}]$
In order to explore the network P_2 contacts P_4. Network exploration serves the purpose of network maintenance and can be compared to the ping/pong protocol used in Gnutella. $\pi(P_2) = \pi(P_4) = 1$ they can now further refine the search space by specializing their paths and exchange their data according to the new paths.	$N : [P_1, 0, \{A_1, A_2\}],$ $[P_2, 10, \{B_1, B_2\}],$ $[P_3, 0, \{A_1, A_2\}],$ $[P_4, 11, \{C_1, C_2\}],$ $[P_5, 0, \{A_1, A_2\}],$ $[P_6, 1, \{C_2\}]$
Apparently all peers except P_6 have now specialized to the maximum possible degree. So what will happen to P_6? It may eventually contact first P_2 and decide to specialize to $\overline{\pi(P_2)} = 11$ and later encounter P_4 and obtain the missing data item pertaining to path 11. This is the final state.	$N : [P_1, 0, \{A_1, A_2\}],$ $[P_2, 10, \{B_1, B_2\}],$ $[P_3, 0, \{A_1, A_2\}],$ $[P_4, 11, \{C_1, C_2\}],$ $[P_5, 0, \{A_1, A_2\}],$ $[P_6, 11, \{C_1, C_2\}]$

The resulting P-Grid is now not only complete, but also prefix-free. The storage load for all peers is perfectly balanced, as a result of the local decisions made to exchange and replicate data and specialize paths. Globally, however, the replication factors are not balanced. There exist three peers for path 0, two for path 11, and only one for path 10. Consequently data items pertaining to path 0 are replicated more often and thus better available. This imbalance resulted from the specific sequence of interactions performed. Other sequences would have led to other, possibly more balanced replication. However, since no global coordination can be assumed, we cannot exclude such "undesired" sequences of events.

In the paper, we have introduced randomized algorithms requiring no central coordination that reduce global imbalance of replication factors and at the same time maintain local storage balance during construction of P-Grids. Moreover, in case such imbalances occur as a result of the construction or due to changing data distributions, they will re-balance the structure. In our example such re-balancing could be achieved if one of the peers supporting path 0 decided to replicate path 10 instead. The difficulty for the algorithms lies in determining when and how to decide on such changes to the P-Grid structure, and how peers can base their decisions only on locally available information. The heuristics for taking these decisions need to be chosen very carefully so that the overall load-balancing goal is supported and not hampered mistakenly.

Robust Locality-Aware Lookup Networks[*]

Ittai Abraham[1] and Dahlia Malkhi[2]

[1] School of Computer Science and Engineering,
The Hebrew University of Jerusalem, Jerusalem, Israel
ittaia@cs.huji.ac.il
[2] School of Computer Science and Engineering,
The Hebrew University of Jerusalem, Jerusalem, Israel
and Microsoft Research, Silicon Valley
dalia@microsoft.com

1 Introduction

Overlay networks that aim to share information are complex due to numerous factors including scale, decentralization, dynamism, and failures. Deploying, operating and maintaining such overlays can be not only very difficult, but also very costly. In this paper we show how a dynamic overlay can be built and maintained in a cost efficient manner while achieving strong locality properties in a decentralized, dynamic, and faulty environment. In our approach there is no central entity that configures, organizes, and repairs the system. To the contrary, we show that if each peer performs local cost efficient operations then by combining the joint effort of all peers the network manages, configures, and repairs itself.

Building self-maintaining overlay networks for locating information in a manner that exhibits locality-awareness is crucial for the viability of large internets. It means that costs are proportional to the actual distance of interacting parties, and in many cases, that load may be contained locally. At the same time, due to scale and decentralization, these networks must cope with high dynamicity and preserve their qualities in face of churn.

This paper presents the FTLAND approach for robust, locality-aware overlay networks. It starts with a step-by-step decomposition of several locality-aware networks that support distributed content-based location services. As a first contribution of this paper, it explains their common principles and their variations with simple and clear intuition on analysis. As the principles of locality-aware solutions unravel, a significant drawback of all existing designs manifests itself: These networks lose their locality properties in face of high churn. That is, previous overlay lookup schemes achieved either fault tolerance [15, 16, 12, 17, 20] or provably good locality properties [18, 3] but not both. As a second contribution, it presents FTLAND, a novel approach for robustifying locality-aware overlays, that sustains locality qualities for participating nodes in face of high churn. FTLAND deals extremely well with dynamic node departures, arrivals, and temporary inavailabilities.

---

[*] This Research was supported in part by the EC Evergrow project.

O. Babaoglu et al. (Eds.): SELF-STAR 2004, LNCS 3460, pp. 392–402, 2005.
© Springer-Verlag Berlin Heidelberg 2005

Problem Statement. This paper considers the problem of forming a self-organizing, self-maintaining overlay network that locates objects (possibly replicated) placed in arbitrary network locations. Recent studies of scalable content exchange networks, e.g., [11], indicate that up to 80% of Internet searches could be satisfied by local hosts within one's own organization. Therefore, in order for the network to remain viable, it is crucial to consider locality awareness from the outset when designing scalable, decentralized network tools.

More formally, consider that the network constitutes a metric space, with a cost function $c(x, y)$ denoting the "distance" from x to y. Let $s = x_0, x_1, ..., x_k = t$ be the path taken by the search from a source node s to the object residing on a target node t. The main design goal to achieve is constant *stretch*. Namely, that the ratio $\frac{c(x_0, x_1) + ... + c(x_{k-1}, x_k)}{c(s, t)}$ is bounded by a (small) constant. Another important goal is to keep node degree low, so as to prevent costly reconfigurations when nodes join and depart. Thus, trivial solutions that connect all nodes to each other are inherently precluded.

Bounded-Stretch Solutions. The problem of forming overlay routing networks was considered by several recent works in the context of networks that are searchable for content. Many of the prevalent overlay networks were formed for routing search queries in peer-to-peer applications, and exhibit **no** locality awareness.

Bounded stretch network design is a fundamental problem [5], with several important lower bounds [8, 21] and upper bounds [6, 7, 21, 4, 2, 1]. Recently, a practical constant-bounded stretch design was proposed by Plaxton et al. [18] for a limited class of networks. The approach was followed by several improvements and deployments including [19, 22, 14, 3]. All of these solutions borrow heavily from the PRR scheme [18], yet they vary significantly in their assumptions and properties. Some of these solutions are designed for a uniform density space [14]. Others work for a class of metrics space whose growth rate is bounded both from above and from below [18, 19, 22, 9], while others yet cope with an upper bound only on the growth rate [3]. There is also variability in the guarantee provided on the stretch: In [14], there is no bound on stretch (except the network diameter). In [18], the stretch is an expected constant, a rather large one which depends on the growth bound. And in [3], the stretch can be set arbitrarily small $(1 + \varepsilon)$. Diversity is manifested also in the node degree of the schemes.

A Step-by-Step Deconstruction. This paper offers a deconstruction of the principles that underlie these locality-aware schemes step by step, and indicate how and where they differ. It demonstrates the principles of locality awareness in a simplistic, yet reasonable (see [9]) network model, namely, a network with *power law* latencies. In our belief, the simplicity and the intuitive analysis may lead to improved practical deployments of locality-aware schemes.

For clarity, our exposition describes the design of an N-node network. It should be clear however, that this network design is intended to be self-maintaining and incremental. In particular, it readily allows nodes to arrive and depart with no centralized control whatsoever.

Fault Tolerance. The main drawback of PRR-like networks is in their lack of *routing flexibility.* In [10] it is shown that while hypercube and ring geometries have about $(\log n)!$ different routes from a given source to a given target, PRR-like networks have only one. Thus the basic architecture of [18, 22, 13, 19, 3] is fragile and must be augmented with some form of robustness.

In a recent paper, Hildrum and Kubiatowicz [12] make an important contribution for PRR like networks. They show how networks like Tapestry [22] and Pastry [19] can be made robust against random failures. When there are no failures, the construction in [12] can guarantee low stretch. However, when there are random failures, their construction can guarantee reaching the destination, but it cannot bound the stretch to a constant.

In this paper we present the first overlay network that has both a provable low latency for paths and a high fault tolerance. Moreover, we show that these two properties can be combined. Thus our low stretch is achieved even in the presence of constant failure probability of all nodes. The novel technique for achieving the combination of these two properties is general, but we exemplify it by augmenting the basic LAND architecture of Abraham et al. [3]. Our techniques are based on the goal of dramatically increasing the routing flexibility to $(\log n)^{\log n}$ while still maintaining a provably good proximity selection mechanism.

2 Preliminaries

The network consists of N nodes, and an associated metric $c(x, y)$ denoting the "distance" from x to y. The set of nodes within distance r from x is denoted $N(x, r)$. We assume a network model with *power law latencies*, $|N(x, r)| = \Gamma r^2$, for some known constant Γ. For convenience, we define neighborhoods $A_k(x) = N(x, 2^k)$. Thus, we have that $|A_k(x)| = \Gamma 4^k$.

For the purpose of forming a routing structure among nodes, nodes need to have addresses and links. We refer to a *routing entity* of a node as a router, and say that the node *hosts* the router. Thus, each node u hosts an assembly of routers.

Each router $u.r$ has an identifier denoted $u.r.id$, and a level $u.r.level$. Identifiers are chosen uniformly at random. The radix for identifiers is selected for convenience to be 4. This is done so that a neighborhood of radius 2^k shall contain in expectation constant number of routers with a particular length-k identifier. Indeed, the probability of a finding a router with a specific level and a particular prefix of length k is $1/4^k$. According to our density assumption, a neighborhood of diameter 2^k has $\Gamma 4^k$ nodes. Hence, such a neighborhood contains in expectation Γ routers matching a length-k prefix.

Assume a network of N nodes, and let $M = \log_4 N$. Identifier strings are composed of M digits. The level is a number between 1 and M. A level-k router has links allowing it to 'fix' its k'th identifier digit. Routers are interconnected in a butterfly-like network, such that level-k routers are linked only to level-$(k+1)$ and level-$(k-1)$ routers.

Let d be a k-digit identifier. Denote $d[j]$ as the prefix of the j most-significant digits, and denote d_j as the j'th digit of d. A concatenation of two strings d, d' is denoted by $d||d'$.

3   Locality-Aware Solutions

3.1   Step 1: Geometric Routing

The first step builds *geometric routing*, whose characteristic is that the routing steps toward a target increase geometrically in distance. This is achieved by having large flexibility in the choice of links at the beginning of a route, and narrowing it down as the route progresses. More specifically, each router r of level k has four neighbor links, denoted $L(b)$, $b \in \{0..3\}$. Each one of the links $L(b)$ is selected as the closest node within $C_b(r)$, where $C_b(r) = \{u \in V \mid \exists s, u.s.id[k] = v.id[k-1]||b, u.s.level = k+1\}$. The link $L(b)$ 'fixes' the k'th bit to b, namely, it connects to the closest node that has a level-$(k+1)$ router whose identifier matches $v.R_k[k-1]||b$.

Routing from a source to a target is done by fixing the target digits one by one, making up to M hops to completion.

Geometric routing alone yields an expected routing cost which is proportional to the network diameter: The expected distance of fixing one digit is 1. Fixing two digits has expected cost 2. And in general, fixing k digits has expected distance no more than 2^k. The total cost of fixing all M digits of a targets is therefore $O(\Delta)$, where Δ is the network diameter, and so a ball of radius Δ contains all nodes. The designs in [14, 9] make use of this type of geometric routing to bound their routing costs by the network diameter.

3.2   Step 2: Shadow Routers

The next step is unique to the design of LAND in [3]. Its goal is to turn the expectation of geometric routing into a worst-case guarantee. This is done while increasing node degree only by a constant expected factor. The technique to achieve this is for nodes to *emulate* links that are missing in their close vicinity as *shadow nodes*. In this way, the choice of links **enforces** a distance upper bound on each stage of the route, rather than probabilistically maintaining it. If no suitable endpoint is found for a particular link, it is emulated by a shadow node.

The idea of bounding the distance of links is very simple: If a link does not exist within a certain desired distance, it is *emulated* as a shadow router. More precisely, for any level $1 \le k \le M$ let r be a level-k router hosted by node v (this could itself be a shadow router, as described below). For $b \in [0..3]$, if $C_b(v)$ contains no node within distance 2^k, then node v emulates a level-$(k+1)$ *shadow router* s that acts as the $v.r.L(b)$ endpoint. Router s's id is $s.id = v.r.id[k-1]||b$ and its level is $(k+1)$.

Since a shadow router also requires its own neighbor links, it may be that the j'th neighbor link of a shadow router s does not exist in $C_j(s)$ within distance

2^{k+1}. In such a case v also emulates a shadow router that acts as the $s.L(j)$ endpoint.

Emulation continues recursively until all links of all the shadow routers emulated by v are found (or until the limit of M levels is reached).

With shadow routers, we have a deterministic bound of 2^k on the k'th hop of a path, and a bound of $\sum_{i=1..k} 2^i = 2^{k+1}$ on the total distance of a k-hop path.

A different concern we have now is that a node might need to emulate many shadow routers, thus increasing the node degree. Using a standard argument on branching processes, we may obtain that hosting show routers increases a nodes degree only by an expected constant factor.

Shadow emulation of nodes is employed in LAND [3]. In all other algorithms, e.g., [18, 19, 22], a node's out-degree is a priori set so that the stretch bound holds with high probability (but is not guaranteed). Hence, there is a subtle tradeoff between guaranteed out-degree and guaranteed stretch. We believe that it is better to design networks whose outliers are in terms of out-degree than in terms of stretch. Additionally, fixing a deterministic upper bound on link distances results in a simpler analysis than working with links whose *expected* distance is bounded.

3.3   Step 3: Publish Links

The final step in our deconstruction describes how to bring down routing costs from being proportional to the network diameter (which could be rather large) to being related directly to the actual distance of the target. This is done via a technique suggested by Plaxton et al. in [18], that makes use of short-cut links that increase the node degree by a constant factor. With a careful choice of the short-cut links, as suggested by Abraham et al. in [3], this guarantees an optimal stretch.

The technique that guarantees a constant stretch is to 'publish' references to an object in a slightly bigger neighborhood than the regular links distance. The intuition on how to determine the size of the enlarged publishing-neighborhood is as follows. The route that locates obj on t from s starts with the source s, and hops through nodes $x_1 \ldots x_k$ until a *reference* to obj is found on x_k. The length of the route from s to x_k is bounded by 2^{k+1}. The distance from x_k to t is bounded (by the triange inequality) by $2^{k+1} + c(s,t)$. In order to achieve a stretch bound close to 1, we should therefore guarantee that a reference to obj is found on x_k, where 2^k is proportional to $\varepsilon c(s,t)$. This will yield a total route distance proportional to $(1 + \varepsilon)c(s,t)$.

The outgoing publish links for a routing r are as follows: There are 4 sets $r.publish_0, \ldots, r.publish_3$. For each k, $r.publish_k$ contains all of the nodes within distance $2^{k+\delta+1}$ that host a router s such that $s.level = r.level+1$ and $s.id[r.level] = s.id[r.level - 1]||k$. As explained above, the parameter δ is determined so as to capture all relevant level-k routers x_k (the exact formula is provided in [3]).

Therefore, by selecting the range of publish links from to cover x_k, the stretch of any search path is bounded by $1 + \varepsilon$. The total number of outgoing links per node increases only by an expected constant factor.

The increased neighborhood for publishing provides a tradeoff between out-degree and stretch. Setting it large, so as to provide an optimal stretch bound, is unique to the design of LAND [3]. The designs in [18, 19, 22] fix the size of publish neighborhoods indepedently of the network density growth. This yields a stretch bound that depends on the density growth rate of the network.

4   A Robust Low Stretch Lookup Network

Pervious lookup solutions achieved either fault tolerance [12, 17, 20] or provably good locality properties [18, 3] but not both. In this section, we present a resolution of these two important goals. We provide FTLAND, the first lookup network that has, with high probability, low stretch even in the presence of a failure model, where all nodes may have a constant probability of failure. Although our techniques are applicable to general PRR-like networks, FTLAND instantiates them by augmenting the basic LAND architecture of Abraham et al. [3] with novel, locality-aware fault tolerance techniques. The techniques are based on the goal of dramatically increasing the routing flexibility to $(\log n)^{\log n}$ while still maintaining a provably good proximity selection mechanism.

Overview. In order to have fault tolerance, a node must increase the number of outgoing links it may use for routing. Doing so naively, e.g., as in [15, 16, 17, 12], by simply replicating each link to $\log n$ suitable destinations instead of one, compromises locality. More specifically, in PRR-like networks, hops have geometrically increasing distances. If the closest link happens to be down and a replacement link is used, there is no guarantee on the distance, and locality is lost.

The crucial difference in FTLAND from previous approaches is the use of multiple routing entities per host. In FTLAND, every node hosts at each level $O(\log n)$ routers (instead of one). Each router has links to appropriate routers within its vicinity. However, because each host now has $O(\log n)$ routing identities, a router finds in its vicinity w.h.p. $O(\log n)$ outgoing links (instead of an expected constant) for each desired destination.

Herein lies the main idea. Since each node in the network has $\log n$ routers at each level, whose identifiers are independently and uniformly selected, a router finds all $O(\log n)$ replicated destinations at a distance no greater than the distance to the closest router in the LAND scheme. Hence, locality is preserved when using any of these links. The total number of links increases by a poly-log factor (for each of the $O(\log n)$ levels there are $O(\log n)$ routers in place of one, each of which has $O(\log n)$ replicated links w.h.p.).

Another important feature of FTLAND is that routing over the $(\log n)^{\log n}$ possibilities is done deterministically, with no backtracking. At each hop, one live link is followed, and with high probability, it can lead to the target.

Given the redundancy in links and paths, dealing with failures in FTLAND can be done in a very lazy manner, since the network can maintain a successful, locality-aware service in face of a linear fraction of unavailabilities. This property is crucial for coping well with churn, as a sustained quality of service is guaranteed through transitions. It also serves well to cope with transient disconnections and temporary failures, since there is no need for the network to reconfigure itself in response to small changes.

4.1   The FTLAND Scheme

Assume that every node has an independent probability f to fail. Given that we would like our routing protocol to succeed with probability proportional to $1-n^{-\alpha}$, we fix c such that $c = O(\frac{1}{-\log_4 f})$, as determined precisely by Equation 1 in Lemma 5. Each node v has three types of links: closest, publish, and next, as follows:

Closest Links: Let $v.closest$ be the set of the $M^2 4^{\delta+2}$ nodes to v (recall that δ is set in Step 3 of the deconstruction above).

The rest of the links of v depend on the routers it hosts. Each node v hosts a set of $cM(M+1)$ routers. The routers are denoted $v.r(i,j)$ for $1 \leq i \leq M+1$, $1 \leq j \leq cM$. Router $v.r(i,j)$ has level i. The identifiers of routers are all chosen uniformly and independently. For a given router $r = r(i,j)$ and digit $k \in [0, \ldots, 3]$ let $SAME_k(r)$ be the set of all nodes that host a router s such that $s.level = r.level + 1$ and $s.id[r.level] = s.id[r.level - 1] \| k$.

Publish Links: Let $r = r(i,j)$ be a router hosted by node v. The outgoing publish links of r are divided into 4 sets $r.publish_0, \ldots, r.publish_3$. For each k, let $r.publish_k$ be the set of the $\frac{3}{2}cM4^{\delta+2}$ closest nodes from $SAME_k(r)$. In addition denote $r.publish = \bigcup_k r.publish_k$.

Next Links: The outgoing next links are defined as follows: Denote $r.next_k$ as the set of the $\frac{1}{2}cM$ closest nodes in $r.publish_k$ (thus $r.next_k \subseteq r.publish_k$).

Every node hosts $O(\log^2 n)$ routers, and every router has $O(\log n)$ links, therefore:

Lemma 1. *Every node has $O(\log^3 n)$ links.*

Robust Routing Protocol. We now define the basic routing building block. The Robust Routing Protocol (RRP) is given two parameters: An initial node u and a target identifier id. The goal of RRP is to route in a fault tolerant manner from u to a nearby node which hosts a router of level $M + 1$ and identifier id. Routing is done in $M - 2\log(cM)$ hops. Let $x_{(2\log(cM))}, \ldots, x_{M+1}$ denote the sequence of nodes taken, s.t. x_{M+1} hosts a level $M + 1$ router with identifier id. Let $x_i.r$ denote the router in x_i that is involved in the protocol. RRP maintains the invariant that $x_i.r.level = i$ and $x_i.r.id[i - 1] = id[i - 1]$. The first hop is done by using $u.closest$ to reach node $x_{(2\log(cM))}$ that hosts a router r such that $r.id[2\log(cM)] = id[2\log(cM)]$. We will later show that such a node exists w.h.p. Then, at each intermediate node x_i the router $x_i.r$ may use any link from $r.next_j$ such that j is the ith bit of the target identifier id (formally $j = id_i$). The analysis of the Robust Routing Protocol appears in Lemma 5.

Robust Publish Protocol. When a node t wants to store an object obj, it performs the RPP protocol. In the first step, all nodes in $t.closest$ are sent a message to store a pointer of the form $\langle obj; t\rangle$ directly to t. In the second step, the publishing of an object obj residing on a node t uses the basic RRP protocol as a building block. Essentially, node t executes RRP with the target identifier being $H(obj)$. In addition, nodes along the route store references to obj. These references are of the form $\langle obj; U\rangle$ where obj is the name of the object and U is a set of $\frac{1}{2}cM$ different routers that are the next hop towards the location of the object. More specifically, at each step $i > 2\log(cM)$ of RRP, router $x_i.r$ stores a reference on x_i and on all the nodes in $x_i.r.publish$. The reference is of the form $\langle obj; U\rangle$ where U is the $\frac{1}{2}cM$ nodes in $x_{i-1}.r.publish$ that are closest to t.

Lemma 2. *The amount of auxiliary memory for each object is $O(\log^2 n)$ references each with a label of $O(\log^2 n)$ bits.*

Proof. An object is published to $O(\log^2 n)$ closest nodes. In addition there are $O(\log n)$ steps in RRP. At each step, every node in $x_i.r.publish$ stores a reference this adds $O(\log n)$ references for every step. Each reference $\langle obj; U\rangle$ contains $O(\log n)$ node names each requiring $O(\log n)$ bits.

Robust Lookup Protocol. A lookup operation of an object $obj \in \mathcal{A}$ can be initiated by any node in the system, and its purpose is to find the closest node storing obj. The lookup operation from a node x proceeds in three stages:

1. Check if x contains a direct pointer to obj. If it does then use the pointer to reach obj.
2. Otherwise, use RRP to route to $H(obj)$ until a node with a reference to obj is found.
3. Once a reference $\langle obj; U\rangle$ is found, go to a non-failed node in U. Continue this process recursively until the object is found.

4.2   Analysis

The low stretch analysis of FTLAND is based on the analysis provided in [3], and is explained in the simple model of this paper above. In this section, we focus only on the differences.

First, in order to carry the stretch analysis, we need to show that the $\frac{1}{2}cM$ links of a level-i router r all reside w.h.p. within $A_i(r)$. Likewise, we need to prove that the $\frac{3}{2}cM4^{\delta+2}$ publish links of a r cover all suitable nodes within $A_{i+\delta+2}(r)$. Second, we must show fault tolerance in face of independent failure probability f of all nodes. We begin by analyzing the probability that a node contains a relevant router.

Lemma 3. *Given a node u the probability that $u \in SAME_j(r)$ is at least*

$$\frac{cM}{4^{r.level}} - \frac{cM(cM+1)}{2\left(4^{r.level}\right)^2} .$$

Proof. Node u has cM routers of level $r.level$. The probability that all of them do not have a prefix $r.id[r.level - 1]||j$ is $(1 - 4^{-(r.level)})^{cM}$. We can bound this probability using the Taylor polynomial as follows: $Pr[u \in SAME_j(r)] = 1 - \left(1 - \frac{1}{4^{r.level}}\right)^{cM} \geq \frac{cM}{B^{r.level}} - \frac{cM(cM+1)}{2(4^{r.level})^2}$.

For any node v, router $v.r$ of level i, digit j and integer x, Let $Z(v, r, i, j, x)$ be a random variable that equals $|SAME_j(r) \cap A_{r.level+x}(v)|$. In words, $Z(v, r, i, j, x)$ counts the number of nodes suitable as r's links within $A_{r.level+x}(v)$. We now show that Z is centered around its expected value.

Lemma 4. *For $r.level \geq 2\log(cM)$ with high probability,*

$$\frac{1}{2}cM4^x \leq Z(v, r, i, j, x) \leq \frac{3}{2}cM4^x .$$

Proof. We begin by showing that when $r.level \geq 2\log(cM)$ the expected size of Z is roughly $cM4^x$. Note that $A_{r.level+x}(v)$ contains $4^{r.level+x}$ nodes. Using Lemma 3 and the linearity of expectation, for $r.level \geq 2\log(cM)$ we have $E[Z] \geq cM4^x - 1$ and clearly $E[Z] \leq cM4^x$. Applying the Chernoff bounds completes the proof of the Lemma: $Pr\left[|Z - E[Z]| > \frac{1}{2}E[Z]\right] < 2e^{-cM4^x/12}$.

Corollary 1. *W.h.p. any node v, router $v.r$ with $r.level \geq 2\log(cM)$, and digit $j \in [0, \ldots, 3]$:*

(i) $r.next_j \subseteq A_{r.level}(v)$.
(ii) $SAME_j(r) \cap A_{r.level+\delta+2}(v) \subseteq r.publish_j$.

The following lemma shows that RRP is a fault tolerant routing protocol.
Lemma 5. *If each node has an independent probability f to fail, then with high probability, RRP will reach its target.*

Proof. For the first hop, note that there are $M^2 4^{\delta+2}$ nodes in $u.closest$. Thus using the same argument as in Lemma 4 there are at least $\frac{1}{2}cM$ nodes that have a router with the same $2\log(cM)$ digits as the target. The probability that all of them have failed is

$$f^{\frac{1}{2}cM} = n^{\frac{c\log_4 f}{2}} \leq 1/n^{3\alpha} , \tag{1}$$

where the last inequality follows by an appropriate choice of c. For the following levels i, router $x_i.r$ may use $\frac{1}{2}cM$ different nodes. For a given i and $j \in [0, \ldots, 3]$, the probability that all relevant nodes in $x_i.r.next_j$ have failed is again $f^{\frac{1}{2}cM}$. The Lemma is proven by choosing a large enough constant c, and using the union bound for all sources, targets, and routing steps.

The following Lemma is proven in [3]. Using Corollary 1 the same proof shows that the lemma holds in this network w.h.p.

Lemma 6. *[3] Let x_i be the ith step of RRP initiated at node u then $x_i \in A_i(x_{i-1}) \subseteq A_{i+1}(u)$.*

Lemma 7. *If each node has an independent probability f to fail, then with high probability, RLP will reach the desired object.*

Proof. Let t denote the closest node containing the target object obj. Thus t published obj with the RPP. Let x_i denote the ith node in RPP, then from Corollary 1 every node in $A_{i+\delta+2}(x_i)$ that has a router r such that $r.id[i] = H(obj)[i]$ has a reference $\langle obj; U_i \rangle$. From Lemma 6 and the growth bounded assumptions this means that every node in $A_{i+1}(t)$ that has a router r such that $r.id[i] = H(obj)[i]$ has a reference $\langle obj; U_i \rangle$. In addition due to Corollary 1 the set U_i that is written by x_i is a set of nodes that are all inside $A_i(t)$. Thus every node in U_i will have a reference $\langle obj; U_{i-1} \rangle$. Therefore we have shown that once a node containing $\langle obj; U \rangle$ is found then there is a path leading to t. In addition at each step there is a flexibility of $\frac{1}{2}cM$ different nodes at each step thus a next hop exists w.h.p. even in the presence of an independent probability f of failure for every node.

The proof of the stretch factor and exact choice of δ is an adaptation of the proof in [3] thus we only state the main theorem:

Theorem 1. *The routing stretch is w.h.p. $1 + \varepsilon$.*

References

1. I. Abraham, C. Gavoille, and D. Malkhi. Routing with improved communication-space trade-off. In *Eighteenth International Symposium on Distributed Computing (DISC 2004)*, 2004.
2. I. Abraham, C. Gavoille, D. Malkhi, N. Nisan, and M. Thorup. Compact name-independent routing with minimum stretch. In *The Sixteenth ACM Symposium on Parallelism in Algorithms and Architectures (SPAA 04)*, 2004.
3. I. Abraham, D. Malkhi, and O. Dobzinski. LAND: Stretch $(1 + \varepsilon)$ locality aware networks for DHTs. In *Proceedings of the ACM-SIAM Symposium on Discrete Algorithms (SODA04)*, 2004.
4. M. Arias, L. J. Cowen, K. A. Laing, R. Rajaraman, and O. Taka. Compact routing with name independence. In *Proceedings of the fifteenth annual ACM symposium on Parallel algorithms and architectures*, pages 184–192. ACM Press, 2003.
5. B. Awerbuch, A. Bar-Noy, N. Linial, and D. Peleg. Compact distributed data structures for adaptive routing. In *Proceedings of the twenty-first annual ACM symposium on Theory of computing*, pages 479–489. ACM Press, 1989.
6. B. Awerbuch and D. Peleg. Sparse partitions. In *Proceedings of the 31st IEEE Symposium on Foundations of Computer Science (FOCS)*, pages 503–513, 1990.
7. B. Awerbuch and D. Peleg. Routing with polynomial communication-space trade-off. *SIAM J. Discret. Math.*, 5(2):151–162, 1992.
8. C. Gavoille and M. Gengler. Space-efficiency of routing schemes of stretch factor three. *Journal of Parallel and Distributed Computing*, 61:679–687, 2001.

9. A. Goal, H. Zhang, and R. Govindan. Incrementally improving lookup latency in distributed hash table systems. In *ACM Sigmetrics*, 2003.

10. K. Gummadi, R. Gummadi, S. Gribble, S. Ratnasamy, S. Shenker, and I. Stoica. The impact of DHT routing geometry on resilience and proximity. In *Proceedings of the 2003 conference on Applications, technologies, architectures, and protocols for computer communications*, pages 381–394. ACM Press, 2003.

11. K. P. Gummadi, R. J. Dunn, S. Saroiu, S. D. Gribble, H. M. Levy, and J. Zahorjan. Measurement, modeling, and analysis of a peer-to-peer file-sharing workload. In *Proceedings of the nineteenth ACM symposium on Operating systems principles*, pages 314–329. ACM Press, 2003.

12. K. Hildrum and J. Kubiatowicz. Asymptotically efficient approaches to fault-tolerance in peer-to-peer networks. In *Proceedings of the 17th International Symposium on DIStributed Computing (DISC 2003)*, 2003.

13. K. Hildrum, J. D. Kubiatowicz, S. Rao, and B. Y. Zhao. Distributed object location in a dynamic network. In *Proceedings of the Fourteenth ACM Symposium on Parallel Algorithms and Architectures*, pages 41–52, Aug 2002.

14. X. Li and C. G. Plaxton. On name resolution in peer-to-peer networks. In *Proceedings of the 2nd ACM Worskhop on Principles of Mobile Commerce (POMC)*, pages 82–89, October 2002.

15. N. Lynch, D. Malkhi, and D. Ratajczak. Atomic data access in distributed hash tables. In *Proceedings of the International Peer-to-Peer Symposium*, 2002.

16. D. Malkhi, M. Naor, and D. Ratajczak. Viceroy: A scalable and dynamic emulation of the butterfly. In *Proceedings of the 21st ACM Symposium on Principles of Distributed Computing (PODC '02)*, pages 183–192, 2002.

17. M. Naor and U. Wieder. A simple fault tolerant distributed hash table. In *Proceedings of the 2nd International Workshop on Peer-to-Peer Systems (IPTPS '03)*, 2003.

18. C. Plaxton, R. Rajaraman, and A. Richa. Accessing nearby copies of replicated objects in a distributed environment. In *Proceedings of the Ninth Annual ACM Symposium on Parallel Algorithms and Architectures (SPAA 97)*, pages 311–320, 1997.

19. A. Rowstron and P. Druschel. Pastry: Scalable, distributed object location and routing for large-scale peer-to-peer systems. In *IFIP/ACM International Conference on Distributed Systems Platforms (Middleware)*, pages 329–350, 2001.

20. J. Saia, A. Fiat, S. Gribble, A. R. Karlin, and S. Saroiu. Dynamically fault-tolerant content addressable networks. In *Proceedings of the First International Workshop on Peer-to-Peer Systems*, 2002.

21. M. Thorup and U. Zwick. Compact routing schemes. In *Proceedings of the thirteenth annual ACM symposium on Parallel algorithms and architectures*, pages 1–10. ACM Press, 2001.

22. B. Y. Zhao, L. Huang, J. Stribling, S. C. Rhea, A. D. Joseph, and J. Kubiatowicz. Tapestry: A resilient global-scale overlay for service deployment. *IEEE Journal on Selected Areas in Communications*, 2003.

Power-Aware Distributed Protocol for a Connectivity Problem in Wireless Sensor Networks

R. Montemanni and L.M. Gambardella

Istituto Dalle Molle di Studi sull'Intelligenza (IDSIA),
Galleria 2, CH-6928 Manno-Lugano, Switzerland
{roberto, luca}@idsia.ch

Abstract. We consider the problem of assigning transmission powers to the nodes of a wireless network in such a way that all the nodes are connected by bidirectional links and the total power consumption is minimized.

We present a distributed protocol, obtained by extending a connectivity protocol recently appeared in the literature. The new extended protocol is obtained by using in a local, distributed fashion, well-known centralized techniques for power minimization. The result is a self-organization framework where a set of rules, implemented locally at each node, guarantees global properties, i.e. connectivity and power expenditure minimization.

Preliminary computational results are finally presented. They show that the new extended protocol guarantees a substantial saving in the total transmission power.

1 Introduction

Wireless sensor networks have received significant attention in recent years due to their potential applications in battlefield, emergency disasters relief, and other application scenarios (see, for example, Blough et al. [2], Chu and Nikolaidis [3], Kirousis et al. [6], Lloyd et al. [8], Ramanathan and Rosales-Hain [13], Singh et al. [15], Wan et al. [16] and Wieselthier et al. [17]). Unlike wired networks of cellular networks, no wired backbone infrastructure is installed in wireless sensor networks. A communication session is achieved either through single-hop transmission if the recipient is within the transmission range of the source node, or by relaying through intermediate nodes otherwise.

We consider wireless networks where individual nodes are equipped with omnidirectional antennae. Typically these nodes are also equipped with limited capacity batteries and have a restricted communication radius. Topology control is one of the most fundamental and critical issues in multi-hop wireless networks which directly affects the network performance. In wireless networks, topology control essentially involves choosing the right set of transmitter power

O. Babaoglu et al. (Eds.): SELF-STAR 2004, LNCS 3460, pp. 403–416, 2005.

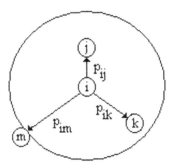

Fig. 1. Communication model

to maintain adequate network connectivity. Incorrectly designed topologies can lead to higher end-to-end delays and reduced throughput in error-prone channels. In energy-constrained networks where replacement or periodic maintenance of node batteries is not feasible, the issue is all the more critical since it directly impacts the network lifetime.

In a seminal paper on topology control using transmission power control in wireless networks, Ramanathan and Rosales-Hain [13] approached the problem from an optimization viewpoint and showed that a network topology which minimizes the maximum transmitter power allocated to any node can be constructed in polynomial time in a centralized fashion, i.e. with the assumption that the network is fully known to the centralized optimizer. This is a critical criterion in battlefield applications since using higher transmitter power increases the probability of detection by enemy radar. In this paper, we attempt to solve the minimum power topology problem in wireless networks. Minimizing the total transmit power has the effect of limiting the total interference in the network.

For a given set of transmitters spatially located in the network's area (nodes), the *minimum power topology (MPT) problem*, sometimes also referred to as the *min-power symmetric connectivity problem*, is to assign transmission powers to the nodes of the network in such a way that all the nodes are connected by bidirectional links and the total power consumption over the network is minimized. Having bidirectional links simplifies one-hop transmission protocols by allowing acknowledgement messages to be sent back for every packet (see Althaus et al. [1]). It is assumed that no power expenditure is involved in reception/processing activities.

Unlike in wired networks, where a transmission from i to m generally reaches only node m, in wireless sensor networks with omnidirectional antennae it is possible to reach several nodes with a single transmission (this is the so-called *wireless multi-cast advantage*, see Wieselthier et al. [17]). In the example of Figure 1 nodes j and k receive the signal originated from node i and directed to node m because j and k are closer to i than m, i.e. they are within the transmission range of a communication from i to m. This property is used to minimize the total transmission power required to connect all the nodes of the network.

Althaus et al. [1], Das et. al [4] and Montemanni and Gambardella [9], [10] proposed exact algorithms for the problem. We refer the interested reader to Montemanni et al. [12] for an overview, comprehensive of theoretical and experimental comparison, of these methods. All of these approaches are based on mixed integer programming models, and all of them are designed to be run in a centralized fashion, on a single computer with full knowledge of the network, i.e. all the information about the network are assumed to be available at a central processor (e.g. power required by each node to reach every other node of the network). Turning into real world, it is very unlikely that all this knowledge is available at the central processor, and even if this is true, there would be the practical problem of transmitting optimal transmission powers to the nodes. For these reasons distributed protocols, i.e. protocols that run at each node of the network, with a partial knowledge of the network - namely the set of neighbors of each node - have to be developed.

Some distributed protocols aiming to guarantee connectivity while minimizing the number of neighbors of each node (an indirect measure of the required transmission power) have been proposed in the literature (see Glauche et al [5] and Krause et al [7]). The aim of this paper is to extend these protocols (that will be briefly described in Section 4.1) in order to preserve connectivity, while directly minimizing the total transmission power over the network.

The MPT problem is formally described in Section 2. Section 3 summarizes an efficient method to solve the problem in a centralized fashion. This method is embedded in the distributed protocol proposed in Section 4. This new protocol can be seen as the power-aware extension of the protocol described in Glauche et al. [5]. Experimental comparison of the original and extended versions of the protocol can be found in Section 5, while Section 6 contains conclusions and future work.

2   Problem Description

To represent the MPT problem in mathematical terms, a model for signal propagation has to be selected. We adopt the model presented in Rappaport [14], and used in most of the papers appeared in the literature (see, for example, Wieselthier et al. [17] and Montemanni et al. [11], [12]). According to this model, signal power falls as $\frac{1}{d^\kappa}$, where d is the distance from the transmitter to the receiver and κ is a environment-dependent coefficient, typically between 2 and 4. Under this model, and adopting the usual convention (see, for example, Althaus et al. [1]) that every node has the same transmission efficiency and the same detection sensitivity threshold, the power requirement for supporting a link from node i to node j, separated by a distance d_{ij}, is then given by

$$p_{ij} = (d_{ij})^\kappa \qquad (1)$$

Technological constraints on minimum and maximum transmission powers of each node are usually present. In particular they state that for each node i, its transmission power must be within the interval $[P_i^{min}, P_i^{max}]$.

The MPT problem can be formally described as follows. Given the set V of the nodes of the network, a *range assignment* is a function $r : V \rightarrow \mathcal{R}^+$. A *bidirectional link* between nodes i and j is said to be established under the range assignment r if $r(i) \geq p_{ij}$ and $r(j) \geq p_{ij}$. Let now $B(r)$ denote the set of all bidirectional links established under the range assignment r. The MPT problem is the problem of finding a range assignment r minimizing $\sum_{i \in V} r(i)$, subject to constraints on minimum and maximum transmission powers and to the constraint that the graph $(V, B(r))$ must be connected.

As suggested in Althaus et al. [1], a graph theoretical description of the MPT problem can be given as follows. Let $G = (V, E, p)$ be an edge-weighted graph, where V is the set of vertices corresponding to the set of nodes of the network and E is the set of edges containing all the possible pairs $\{i, j\}$, with $i, j \in V$, $i \neq j$, that do not violate technological constraints on transmission powers. A cost p_{ij} is associated with each edge $\{i, j\}$. It corresponds to the power requirement defined by equation (1).

For a node i and a spanning tree T of G, let $\{i, i_T\}$ be the maximum cost edge incident to i in T, i.e. $\{i, i_T\} \in T$ and $p_{ii_T} \geq p_{ij} \ \forall \{i, j\} \in T$. The *power cost* of a spanning tree T is then $c(T) = \sum_{i \in V} p_{ii_T}$. Since a spanning tree is contained in any connected graph, the MPT problem can be described as the problem of finding the spanning tree T with minimum power cost $c(T)$.

3   Centralized Approach

The approach discussed in this section aims to solve the MPT problem in a centralized fashion, i.e. the full network is supposed to be known. When the problem has been solved, the results (and the respective transmission powers for all the nodes) would have to be communicated all around the network. This is clearly impractical.

Notwithstanding the assumption about the full network knowledge, that can appear very strong, and somehow unrealistic, the method remains of our interest since it will be embedded within the distributed protocol described in Section 4.1.

3.1   An Integer Programming Formulation

A weighted, directed graph $G' = (V, A, p)$ is derived from G by defining $A = \{(i, j), (j, i) | \{i, j\} \in E\} \cup \{(i, i) | i \in V\}$, i.e. for each edge in E there are the respective two (oriented) arcs in A, and a dummy arc (i, i) with $p_{ii} = 0$ is inserted for each $i \in V$. Power p_{ij} is defined by equation (1) when $i \neq j$. In order to describe the new integer programming formulation for MPC, we also need the following definition.

Given $(i, j) \in A$, we define the *ancestor* of (i, j) as

$$a_j^i = \begin{cases} i & \text{if } p_{ij} = \min_{\{i,k\} \in E} \{p_{ik}\} \\ arg \max_{k \in V} \{p_{ik} | p_{ik} < p_{ij}\} & \text{otherwise} \end{cases} \qquad (2)$$

According to this definition, (i, a_j^i) is the arc originated in node i with the highest cost such that $p_{ia_j^i} < p_{ij}$. In case an *ancestor* does not exist for arc (i, j), vertex i is returned, i.e. the dummy arc (i, i) is addressed.

In formulation IP a spanning tree (eventually augmented) is defined by z variables: $z_{ij} = 1$ if edge $\{i, j\}$ is on the spanning tree, $z_{ij} = 0$ otherwise. Variable y_{ij} is 1 when node i has a transmission power which allows it to reach node j, $y_{ij} = 0$ otherwise.

$$(IP) \quad \text{Min} \sum_{(i,j) \in A} c_{ij} y_{ij} \tag{3}$$

$$\text{s.t. } y_{ij} \leq y_{ia_j^i} \qquad \forall (i, j) \in A, a_j^i \neq i \tag{4}$$

$$z_{ij} \leq y_{ij} \qquad \forall \{i, j\} \in E \tag{5}$$

$$z_{ij} \leq y_{ji} \qquad \forall \{i, j\} \in E \tag{6}$$

$$\sum_{i \in S, j \in V \setminus S, \{i,j\} \in E} z_{ij} \geq 1 \qquad \forall S \subset V \tag{7}$$

$$y_{ij} = 1 \qquad \forall (i, j) \in A \text{ s.t. } p_{ij} \leq P_{min} \tag{8}$$

$$y_{ij} = 0 \qquad \forall (i, j) \in A \text{ s.t. } p_{ij} \geq P_{max} \tag{9}$$

$$z_{ij} \in \{0, 1\} \qquad \forall \{i, j\} \in E \tag{10}$$

$$y_{ij} \in \{0, 1\} \qquad \forall (i, j) \in A \tag{11}$$

In formulation IP an incremental mechanism is established over y variables (i.e. transmission powers). The costs associated with y variables in the objective function (3) are given by the following formula:

$$c_{ij} = p_{ij} - p_{ia_j^i} \quad \forall (i, j) \in A \tag{12}$$

c_{ij} is equal to the power required to establish a transmission from node i to node j (p_{ij}) minus the power required by node i to reach node a_j^i ($p_{ia_j^i}$). In Figure 2 a pictorial representation of the costs arising from the example of Figure 1 is given.

Constraints (4) realize the incremental mechanism by forcing the variable associated with arc (i, a_j^i) to assume value 1 when the variable associated with arc (i, j) has value 1, i.e. the arcs originated in the same node are activated in increasing order of p. Inequalities (5) and (6) connect the spanning tree variables z to transmission power variables y. Basically, given edge $\{i, j\} \in E$, z_{ij} can assume value 1 if and only if both y_{ij} and y_{ji} have value 1. Equations (7) state that all the vertices have to be mutually connected in the subgraph induced by z variables, i.e. the (eventually augmented) spanning tree. Constraints (8) and (9) model minimum and maximum possible transmission powers. Constraints (10) and (11) define variable domains.

In Montemanni and Gambardella [10] a set of facet defining valid inequalities is presented. These inequalities, that are strongly based on the incremental mechanism described by equations (2), (3) and constraints (4), are able to better

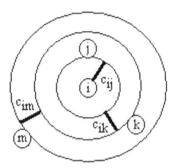

Fig. 2. Costs for the mathematical formulation IP

define the polytope associated with the linear relaxation of IP, which is obtained by substituting constraints (10) and (11) with the following ones:

$$0 \leq z_{ij} \leq 1 \quad \forall \{i,j\} \in E \tag{13}$$

$$0 \leq y_{ij} \leq 1 \quad \forall (i,j) \in A \tag{14}$$

Since methods to solve integer programs are based on the iterative refinement of the solution of the linear relaxation, a tighter relaxation usually produces a speed up. In Montemanni and Gambardella [10] it is shown that for the MPT problem the speed up factor can reach 1200. For this reason it is convenient to incorporate these extra inequalities into formulation (IP).

3.2   The Exact Algorithm IEX

In this section we describe an algorithm which efficiently solves to optimality the integer program IP (i.e. the minimum power symmetric connectivity problem).

It is very difficult to deal with constraints (7) of formulation IP, because they are in a huge number. For this reason some techniques which leave some of them out have to be considered. We present an *iterative exact algorithm* (IEX) which in the beginning does not consider constraints (7) at all, and then adds them step by step only in case they are violated.

In order to speed up the approach, the following inequality should also be added to the initial integer problem IP:

$$\sum_{\{i,j\} \in E} z_{ij} \geq |V| - 1 \tag{15}$$

Inequality (15) forces the number of active z variables to be at least $|V| - 1$ - this condition is necessary in order to have a spanning tree - already at the very first iterations of the algorithm.

The integer program defined as IP without constraints (7) but with inequality (15), is solved and the values of the z variables in the solution are examined. If the edges corresponding to z variables with value 1 form a spanning tree then the problem has been solved to optimality, otherwise constraints (16), described below, are added to the integer program and the process is repeated.

At the end of each iteration, the last available solution is examined and, if edges corresponding to z variables with value 1 generate a set $\mathcal{CC}$ of connected components with $|\mathcal{CC}| > 1$, then the following inequalities are added to the formulation:

$$\sum_{i \in C, j \in V \setminus C, \ \{i,j\} \in E} z_{ij} \geq 1 \ \ \forall C \in \mathcal{CC} \tag{16}$$

Inequalities (16) force z variables with value 1 to connect the (elsewhere disjoint) connected components in $\mathcal{CC}$ to each other.

The IEX algorithm is summarized by the pseudo-code presented in Figure 3:

```
IEX()
Build integer program IP;
sol := optimal solution of IP;
CC := connected components defined by
      variables z of sol;
While (|CC| > 1)
    Add inequalities (16) to IP;
    sol := optimal solution of IP;
    CC := connected components defined by
          variables z of sol;
EndWhile
return sol.
```

Fig. 3. Pseudo-code for the centralized exact algorithm IEX

It is important to observe that the exact method discussed in this section is able to solve to optimality, in reasonable time, problems with up to 50 nodes. When the method is used in a distributed fashion - e.g. when it is used within the protocol we will describe in Section 4.2 - the practical problems of interests are sensibly smaller.

4   Distributed Protocols

Glauche et al. [5] conducted a detailed study showing that there is a very close correlation between the (minimum) number of neighbors of the nodes of a network and the probability of the network to be fully connected. In particular they observed that this indicator (number of neighbors) is more interesting than transmission power when connectivity issues are studied. Following this observation they propose a simple protocol able to provide full connectivity (with high probability) with a much smaller total transmission power expenditure than methods working directly on power.

This protocol will be extended in order to locally optimize transmission powers while maintaining the good theoretical properties of the original protocol. The original protocol is sketched in Section 4.1, while the new extended version is presented in Section 4.2.

4.1   Protocol LMLD (Glauche et al. [5])

The LMLD (*Local Minimum Link Degree*) protocol has been originally proposed in Glauche et al. [5]. It has been inspired by the following observation, motivated by reasonings based on percolation theory. By exchanging so-called *hello* and *hello-reply* messages each ad hoc node is able to access direct information only from its immediate neighbors, defined by its links. The simplest local observable for a node is the number of its links, which is equal to the number of its one-hop neighbors. Based on this observable alone, a simple strategy for a node would be to decrease/increase its transmission power once it has enough neighbors. Consequently the target node degree should be defined by a parameter, that we will refer to as ngb. A value of the latter has to be chosen such that all nodes are part of one connected network and reflects the only external input to this otherwise fully local link rule.

The simple protocol just lined out has two main drawbacks. The first one is that the value of ngb must be very conservative in order to guarantee full connectivity in case of clustered networks (with an undesired high density of links in density populated areas as a side effect). The second drawback is that the protocol does not take into account that links have to be bidirectional.

The idea introduced in Glauche et al. [5] elaborates on the protocol described above, aiming to eliminate these drawbacks. In particular, upon setting up the communication links to the other nodes, a node attaches to its hello message information about its current link neighborhood list and its current transmission power. Starting with P_{min}, the node increases its transmission power by a small amount once it has not reached a minimum link degree ngb_{min}. Whenever another node, which so far does not belong to the neighborhood list, hears the hello message of the original node for the first time, it realizes that the latter has too few neighbors, either sets its power equal to the transmission power of the hello-sending node or leaves it as before, whichever is larger, and answers the hello message. Now the original and new node are able to communicate back and forth and have established a new link. The original node adds one new node to its neighborhood list. Only once the required minimum link degree is reached, the original node stops increasing its power for its hello transmissions. At the end each node has at least ngb_{min} neighbors. Some have more because they have been forced to answer nodes too low in ngb; their transmission power is larger than necessary to obtain only ngb_{min} neighbors for themselves.

In Glauche et al. [5] it is shown that small values of parameter ngb_{min} (e.g. 10) already guarantee, from a theoretical and practical point of view, full connectivity with probability almost 1 for very large networks (e.g. 1600 nodes).

4.2   Protocol LMPT

Our aim here is to enrich the LMLD protocol described in the previous section by introducing explicit transmission power minimization. In order to do this, we need a little bit more of local information about neighbors, and a slightly more articulated protocol. We will refer to this new protocol as the LMPT protocol, which stands for *Local Mimimum Power Topology* protocol.

Similarly to the LMLD protocol sketched in Section 4.1, where each node is, in turn, in charge of establishing links with ngb_{min} neighbors, here each node is, in turn, in charge of local optimization. We will refer to this node as the (temporarily) head node. It needs to know the list of neighbors (at the time of the local optimization) for each of its ngb_{min} potential neighbors. Moreover, each node has to send to the head node the power required to reach each one of its neighbors (it collected these information while it incrementally increased its power in order to reach a minimum number of neighbors or when it receives a connection request by another node).

Once the head node has collected these information for the ngb_{min} nodes (same parameter of LMLD protocol) closest to it, it solves the local optimization problem involving itself and these nodes (details about the constructions of the local problem are given below). In the meantime the nodes in its neighborhood wait for the optimization to be concluded. At these point, according to the solution of the optimization, the head node distributes the new neighbors lists and the new transmission powers for its (current) neighbors. Once they receive this information they update their state and lists.

The overhead introduced for information exchange (and for solving the local optimization problem) is justified by the efficiency gained in terms of transmission power expenditure.

It is very important to stress that when the new protocol LMPT is applied, all the theoretical results of Glauche et al, that guarantee connectivity "almost for sure" for proper values of ngb_{min}, are still completely valid, since after the local optimization has been concluded, each node is able to reach at least ngb_{min} nodes, although now a multi-hop transmission could be necessary. The power saving we guarantee is consequently directly related to the acceptance of multi-hop transmission instead of direct one-hop transmissions only.

Figure 4 illustrates the algorithmic implementation of the distributed rule in more detail. Initially, all nodes come with a minimum transmission power $P_i = P_{min}$ and an empty neighborhood list $\mathcal{N}_i = \emptyset$ (with the respective list of required transmission powers $\mathcal{I}_i$ empty as well). All of them start in the receive mode. Then, at random, one of the nodes switches into the discovery mode. By subsequently sending Ask4Info messages and receiving replies, the picked node increases its power until it has discovered enough neighbors to guarantee connectivity with high probability. At this point it uses the collected information to set up the optimization problem IP (see below) and solves it.

Once IP has been solved, the optimal solution of IP is distributed to the set of neighbors that sent their information in order to set up problem IP. The

```
LMPT()
P_i := P_i^min;
N_i := ∅;
ReceiveMode();
DiscoveryMode();
ReceiveMode();


DiscoveryMode()
P_i^disc := P_i^min;
N_i^disc := ∅;
I_i := ∅;
While ( P_i^disc ≤ P_i^max and |N_i^disc| < ngb_min )
      P_i^disc := P_i^disc(1 + Δ );
      Ask4Info(i, P_i^disc, N_i^disc);
      (j_1, info_{j_1}, i),... := ReceiveInfo();
      N_i^disc := N_i^disc ∪ {j_1,...} ;
      Update I_i according to info_{j_1}, ...;
EndWhile
Create IP according to I_i;
Sol := Optimal solution of IP;
SendSol(i, N_i^disc, sol);
Set P_i, N_i and I_i according to sol;


ReceiveMode()
(j, P_j, N_j) := ReceiveReq4Info();
If ( i ∉ N_j )
      P_i := max(P_i, P_j);
      info_i := combination of N_i and I_i;
      SendInfo(i, info_i, j);
      sol := ReceiveSol();
      Set P_i, N_i and I_i according to sol;
EndIf
```

Fig. 4. Pseudo-code for the Local Minimum Power Topology (LMPT) protocol

head node can now set up its new transmission power P_i, its set of neighbors N_i with the respective required transmission powers I_i.

The other nodes will use the information received to set up their power and their new neighbor lists. The node returns then into the receive mode.

For simplicity we assume that only one node at a time is in the discovery mode; furthermore, we assume the maximum transmission power P_{max} to be sufficiently large, so that each node is able to discover at least ngb_{min} neighbors.

In the receive mode a node listens to incoming Req4Info messages. Upon receipt of such a message, the node first checks whether it already belongs to the incoming neighborhood list. If yes, the requesting node has already asked before with a smaller discovery power and there is no need for the receiving node to react. Otherwise, it updates its transmission power to $\max(P_i, P_j)$. Then it sends back information about its neighbors and the respective transmission powers required to reach them. The node then waits for the head node j to solve IP and collects the results. These results are used to update transmission power P_i, the set of neighbors $\mathcal{N}_i$ and the respective transmission powers $\mathcal{I}_i$.

Construction of the local mixed integer program IP. The set of nodes V of the local IP for head node i is given by the elements of $\mathcal{N}_i^{disc}$, while power requirements between nodes are set according to the following rule: if $j \in V \cap \mathcal{N}_i$ then p_{ij} is given by the respective power requirement (contained in $\mathcal{I}_i$), otherwise $p_{ij} := +\infty$. This last assignment is equivalent to state that node i will never reach node j in the optimal solution of IP (since they are not aware of each other and do not know the required power to reach each other). Another issue has to be taken into account while setting up problem IP. In case there exists a node $j \in \mathcal{N}_k \backslash V, k \in \mathcal{N}_i^{disc}$ (j is not a neighbor of i, but j is a neighbor of k, that in turn is a neighbor of i), we have to force k to keep transmitting to j in order to ensure global connectivity. This can happen when k has already been replying to Ask4Info messages before the current round. In the situation depicted we have to force node k to reach (at least) node j. We then add the following constraints to IP.

$$y_{kl} = 1 \quad \forall (k, l) \in A \text{ s.t. } p_{kl} \leq p_{kj} \tag{17}$$

Constraints (17) are enough to keep the valid global properties that guarantee connectivity with high probability for appropriate values of parameter ngb_{min}. It is interesting to observe that they also reduce the complexity of IP (new facets are added), making it easier to solve.

5   Preliminary Experimental Results

In this section we aim to compare the results obtained by the distributed protocol described in Glauche et al. [5] with those of the power-aware $LMPT$ protocol, discussed in Section 4.1.

The following three indicators are taken into account for the comparison:

- **Total transmission power:** the sum of the transmission power of all the nodes of the network;
- **Average number of neighbors:** the average number of connections each node has to maintain in the solution generated by the protocols. This indicator is important because having too many neighbors leads to problematic communications due to the resulting high noise over the network;
- **Maximum number of neighbors:** the maximum number of connections a node within the network has to maintain.

Is is important to stress that in the comparison we do not take into account the overhead generated by the extra operations carried out by the new $LMPT$ protocol. This overhead is however marginal, and can be reduced to the extra transmission power dissipated when information about (old and new) neighbors

Table 1. Homogeneous networks. Averages over 50 networks

	LMLD ([5])	LMPT	Gain (%)
Total transmission power	2.547	1.403	44.92
Average number of neighbors	7.085	2.879	59.36
Maximum number of neighbors	12.317	7.683	37.62

Table 2. Multifractal networks. Averages over 50 networks

	LMLD ([5])	LMPT	Gain (%)
Total transmission power	4.311	2.047	52.44
Average number of neighbors	8.320	3.393	59.22
Maximum number of neighbors	14.146	9.334	34.02

Table 3. Manhattan networks. Averages over 50 networks

	LMLD ([5])	LMPT	Gain (%)
Total transmission power	3.417	0.618	81.91
Average number of neighbors	11.890	3.514	70.45
Maximum number of neighbors	24.789	12.684	48.83

are exchanged within the local neighborhood of each node. However this overhead is very marginal, since the extra operations are carried out only once when the network is established.

The network topologies considered are those already adopted in Glauche et al. [5]. Namely, we consider *homogeneous, multifractal* and *Manhattan* topologies. We refer the interested reader to Glauche et al. [5] for details about these topologies and how to generate the networks. All the networks considered here have 1600 nodes, path loss exponent $\kappa = 2$ and are generated according to [5]. Parameter ngb_{min}, that defines the minimum number of neighbors of each node, has been set to 6 for homogeneous networks, to 7 for multifractal networks and to 10 for Manhattan networks. These value are those suggested in [5] and guarantee full connectivity with probability almost 1.

Average results of the indicators over 50 networks are summarized in Tables 1, 2 and 3 for the three families of networks considered. Percentage gains achieved by the extended protocol LMPT also appear in the tables.

For all the experiments reported in Tables 1, 2 and 3 the use of the extended protocol $LMPT$ brings a substantial gain over protocol $LMLD$, in terms of both the total transmission power and the number of neighbors (average and maximum).

In particular the most impressive results have been obtained on Manhattan networks (Table 3), where the gains for the three indicators are in the order of

81.91 %, 70.45 % and 48.83 % respectively. These results are due to the intrinsic characteristics of these networks, that in fact are critical cases for the original protocol presented in [5].

We can conclude that the results are indeed very encouraging and they completely justify the marginal overhead generated by the extra operations carried out by the extended protocol $LMPT$.

6   Conclusions and Future Work

In this paper we have considered the problem of assigning transmission powers to the nodes of a wireless network in such a way that all the nodes are connected by bidirectional links with probability almost 1 and the total power consumption is minimized.

We have presented a distributed protocol, which can be seen as the power-aware extension of a protocol recently appeared in the literature. The extended protocol uses a well-known centralized technique for power minimization in a local, distributed fashion. An important characteristic of the new protocol is that all the nice theoretical and experimental properties about connectivity of the original protocol, can be directly transferred to it.

Preliminary computational results are very encouraging, and our future work will be in the direction of assessing more in detail the potentialities of the new approach, both from a theoretical and experimental point of view. In particular it will be very interesting to compare the quality, in terms of power consumption, of the solution computed by the power-aware distributed protocol we propose, with the theoretical optimal solution, obtained by assuming full knowledge of the network at a centralized location.

Acknowledgements

The work was partially supported by the Future & Emerging Technologies unit of the European Commission through Project "BISON: Biology-Inspired techniques for Self Organization in dynamic Networks" (IST-2001-38923).

References

1. E. Althaus, G. Călinescu, I.I. Măndoiu, S. Prasad, N. Tchervenski, and A. Zelikovsky. Power efficient range assignment in ad-hoc wireless networks. In *Proceedings of the IEEE Wireless Communications and Networking Conference (WCNC 2003)*, pages 1889–1894, 2003.
2. D. Blough, M. Leoncini, G. Resta, and P. Santi. On the symmetric range assignment problem in wireless ad hoc networks. In *Proceedings of the 2nd IFIP International Conference on Theoretical Computer Science (TCS 2002)*, pages 71–82, 2002.
3. T. Chu and I. Nikolaidis. Energy efficient broadcast in modile ad hoc networks. In *Proceedings of AD-HOC NetwOrks and Wireless Conference (AD-HOC NOW 2002)*, 2002.

4. A.K. Das, R.J. Marks, M. El-Sharkawi, P. Arabshani, and A. Gray. Optimization methods for minimum power bidirectional topology construction in wireless networks with sectored antennas. Submitted for publication.

5. I. Glauche, W. Krause, R. Sollacher, and M. Greiner. Continuum percolation of wireless ad hoc communication networks. *Physica A*, 325:577–600, 2003.

6. L. Kirousis, E. Kranakis, D. Krizanc, and A. Pelc. Power consumption in packet radio networks. *Theoretical Computer Science*, 243:289–305, 2000.

7. W. Krause, R. Sollacher, and M. Greiner. Self-⋆ topology control in wireless multihop ad hoc communication networks. Submitted for publication.

8. E. Lloyd, R. Liu, M. Marathe, R. Ramanathan, and S. Ravi. Algorithmic aspects of topology control problems for ad hoc networks. In *Proceedings of the Third ACS International Symposium on Mobile Ad Hoc Networking and Computing (MobiHoc 2002)*, pages 123–134, 2002.

9. R. Montemanni and L.M. Gambardella. Minimum power symmetric connectivity problem in wireless networks: a new approach. In *Mobile and wireless communications networks* (E.M. Belding-Royer et al. eds.), pages 496–508. Springer, 2004.

10. R. Montemanni and L.M. Gambardella. Exact algorithms for the minimum power symmetric connectivity problem in wireless networks. *Computers and Operations Research*, 32(11):2891–2904, 2005.

11. R. Montemanni, L.M. Gambardella, and A.K. Das. The minimum power broadcast problem in wireless networks: a simulated annealing approach. In *Proceedings of the IEEE Wireless Communication & Networking Conference (WCNC 2005)*, 2005, to appear.

12. R. Montemanni, L.M. Gambardella, and A.K. Das. Mathematical models and exact algorithms for the min-power symmetric connectivity problem: an overview. In *Handbook on Theoretical and Algorithmic Aspects of Sensor, Ad Hoc Wireless, and Peer-to-Peer Networks* (J. Wu ed.). CRC Press, to appear.

13. R. Ramanathan and R. Rosales-Hain. Topology control of multihop wireless networks using transmit power adjustment. In *Proceedings of the IEEE Infocom 2000 Conference*, pages 404–413, 2000.

14. T. Rappaport. *Wireless Communications: Principles and Practices*. Prentice Hall, 1996.

15. S. Singh, C. Raghavendra, and J. Stepanek. Power-aware broadcasting in mobile ad hoc networks. In *Proceedings of the IEEE International Symposium on Personal, Indoor and Mobile Radio Communications (PIMRC 1999)*, 1999.

16. P.-J. Wan, G. Călinescu, X.-Y. Li, and O. Frieder. Minimum energy broadcast routing in static ad hoc wireless networks. In *Proceedings of the IEEE Infocom 2001 Conference*, pages 1162–1171, 2001.

17. J. Wieselthier, G. Nguyen, and A. Ephremides. On the construction of energy-efficient broadcast and multicast trees in wireless networks. In *Proceedings of the IEEE Infocom 2000 Conference*, pages 585–594, 2000.

Self-management of Virtual Paths in Dynamic Networks

Poul E. Heegaard[1], Otto Wittner[2], and Bjarne E. Helvik[2]

[1] Telenor R&D* and Department of Telematics,
Norwegian University of Science and Technology, Norway
poulh@item.ntnu.no

[2] Centre for Quantifiable Quality of Service in Communication Systems**
Norwegian University of Science and Technology, Trondheim, Norway
{bjarne, wittner}@q2s.ntnu.no

Abstract. Virtual path management in dynamic networks poses a number of challenges related to combinatorial optimisation, fault and traffic handling. Ideally such management should react immediately on changes in the operational conditions, and be autonomous, inherently robust and distributed to ensure operational simplicity and network resilience. Swarm intelligence based self management is a candidate potentially able to fulfil these requirements. Swarm intelligence achieved by cross entropy (CE) ants is introduced, and two CE ants based path management approaches are presented. A case study of a nation wide communication infrastructure is performed to demonstrate their abilities to handle change in network traffic as well as failures and restoration of links.

Keywords: Cross-entropy, Swarm intelligence, Ant-based optimisation, elite CE ants, Network management, Resilience.

1   Introduction

Paths between all source destination pairs in a communication network should be chosen such that an overall good utilisation of network resources is ensured, and hence high throughput, low loss and low latency achieved. At the same time the set of paths chosen must enable utilisation of the available spare capacity in the network in such a manner that a failure results in a minimum disturbance of the directly affected traffic flows as well as other traffic flows in the network. The combinatorial optimisation aspects of this task are typically NP-hard, see for instance [1]. Nevertheless, considerable knowledge has been acquired for planning paths in networks [2]. Establishment of virtual path layouts and deployment of backup paths are issues discussed in this paper. Insight and practical methods

* This work was partially supported by the Future& Emerging Technologies unit of the European Commission through ProjectBISON (IST-2001-38923).
** Centre for Quantifiable Quality of Service in CommunicationSystems, Centre of Excellence appointed by The Research Council of Norway,funded by the Research Council, NTNU and UNINETT. http://www.ntnu.no/Q2S/

O. Babaoglu et al. (Eds.): SELF-STAR 2004, LNCS 3460, pp. 417–432, 2005.
© Springer-Verlag Berlin Heidelberg 2005

for obtaining such paths by mathematical programming are available. For an overview, see the recently published book by Piro and Medhi [2] and references therein. Several stochastic optimisation techniques which may be used to address these kinds of problems, have been proposed [3, 4, 5, 6]. However, common to these are that they deal with path finding as an optimisation problem where the "solution engine" has a global overview of the problem and that the problem is unchanged until a solution is found. This differs from the requirement that path management should be truly distributed and adaptive. On the other hand, one should be aware that applying truly distributed decision-making typically yields solution which are less fine tuned with respect to optimal resource utilisation.

In addition to finding good paths, proper path management requires that: a) the set of operational paths should be continuously updated as the traffic load changes, b) new paths should become almost immediately available between communication nodes when established paths are affected by failures, and c) new or repaired network elements should be put into operation without unnecessary delays. Near immediate and robust fault handling advocates distributed local decision-making on how to deal with failures. This is reflected by the commonly applied protection switching schemes in today's telecommunication networks, e.g. in SDH and ATM [7, 8]. Typically two (or more) disjoint paths are established, one serving as a backup for the other. Protection switching requires preplanning, is rather inflexible and is not very efficient in utilising network resources. Shortest path, distance vector and policy based routing as applied in the Internet, is distributed, have local decision-making and applies to some degree planning inherent in the network, see for instance [9]. However, routes (paths) are restored after a failure, which may incur a substantial delay before traffic flows along a route are fully reestablished. Furthermore, it is not unusual that Internet operators use static link weights. This requires preplanning and lessens the adaptivity. In general, making plans that are able to cope efficiently with every combination of traffic load and network state is difficult, if at all possible.

Schoonderwoerd & al. introduced the concept of using multiple agents with a behaviour inspired by ants to solve problems in telecommunication networks [10]. The concept is known as *swarm intelligence* [11] and has been pursued further by others, see for instance [12, 13, 14] and references therein. Self-management by swarm intelligence is a candidate to meet the aforementioned requirements and to overcome some of the drawbacks of the current path and fault management strategies. This is elaborated further in Section 2. For dealing with path management in communication networks we have developed the CE ants (cross-entropy ants) which are based on Rubinstein's method for stochastic optimisation [6]. CE ants and their application in two path management approaches are presented in Section 3. The first approach, adaptive paths, presented for the first time in this paper, applies a stochastic routing scheme and is promising with respect to robust and adaptive forwarding. In Section 4, a case study demonstrates the adaptive abilities of the two CE ants based path management approaches. The approaches are confronted with a changing traffic load as well as failures and restorations of links in the network. This demonstration is one of the original contributions of the paper. Some concluding remarks are given in Section 5.

2   Position on Path Management

Being able to transfer addressed information between sources and destinations is the prime function of a communication network, and hence, how to find a way for the information through the network is one of the most salient issues in network architecture and operation. How this has been done throughout history is a trade-off between requirements and available technology. We raise the question: is self-management by emergent behaviour a viable approach to path finding in future networks, meeting the requirement of an integrated multi-service transport network? Paths are in this context both explicit paths as virtual connections realized for instance by multiprotocol label switching (MPLS), [15], and implicit paths given by for instance open shortest path first (OSPF) routing tables, [9].

To substantiate our position on this question we first introduce the main objectives of routing/path management in networks, discuss basic architectural issues and outline two alternative algorithms and their rationale with respect to management. Details and the performance of these algorithms are presented later in the paper.

By path management we address medium length temporal characteristics of network, i.e., how to use the available network resources to establish paths that best meet the requirements of the offered traffic on a time scale in the range from 100 ms to some hours. Long term planning, involving installation and rearrangement of physical equipment, is outside the scope of path management together with the short term management issues dealing with the real time characteristics of the individual flows. The objective of path management may be summarised by the following obviously interrelated items.

Path Finding Ability. This is the obvious objective; if a path exists between a source and a destination in a network, it should be found. There may be additional objectives to find multiple node and/or link disjoint paths for better resource utilisation and resilience.

Resource Utilisation. The network resources should be used efficiently. The exact interpretation of efficiency will depend on the QoS objectives of the network, e.g., be close to some optimal value with respect to traffic carried (or operator income) when constrained by QoS requirements. The efficiency should be maintained under changes in the loading of the network, in the topology and in the capacities of the network elements, i.e., *adaptivity* is mandatory for efficient resource utilisation.

Resilience. If feasible, the dependability requirements of the service provided should be met in terms of availability, reliability and down time. In some services, the temporal aspects, e.g. continuity of service or negligible down times, are of great importance. A prerequisite for resilient services is the *resilience of the management system itself,* i.e., it should be robust to failures of network elements as well as loss of management information due to failures and overload.

Priorities and Fairness. Common to most networks is that they should provide a fair service, i.e., all users (or traffic flows) having the same "status", should statistically receive the same QoS. Future networks will carry a variety of services with highly differing dependability requirements and importance (end-users' willingness to pay). In these networks, the management system has to implement priorities to deal with an offered load exceeding the capacity and with failures, while maintaining a generally high resource utilisation.

There are two major design axis for management systems, a spatial axis, i.e., degree of centralisation or distribution, and a temporal axis, i.e., the degree of preplanning. It would be too lengthy to go into detail on various solutions, so the discussion is limited to establishing the main pros and cons of the various options.

Centralisation has the advantage that decisions may be based on a global view, and hence, in theory, better decisions with respect to resource utilisation and priorities may be made. Its drawback is that it is vulnerable since centralisation yields a single point of failure, and since these systems have to rely on a potentially partially overloaded or failed network for extraction of measurements and status information, as well as for dissemination of control information. Centralised decision-making may also be slow due to a long decision cycle. *Distribution* tends to yield poorer resource utilisation, but has a potentially better resilience. preplanning is needed to be able to rapidly respond to network element failures, e.g. by protection switching, and may be used to deal with anticipated changes in the load, e.g. daily variations. For *long term preplanning*, it is impossible to plan for all eventualities making it necessary to plan for ranges of eventualities which may result in more costly solutions. On the other end of the scale, we have the *reactive* systems. Their drawback is the restoration time, i.e. the inability to provide continuity of service shortly after a failure. To avoid the extremes we advocate *short term planning*, dynamically making contingency plans for the current network state and load, or a *pro-active* preparation for a fast restoration, cf. Section 3.1.

In the public telecom networks, primarily designed for telephony, preplanned protection switching schemes (with a distributed implementation) is typically used to achieve fast fault management. This scheme is rather inflexible and costly in terms of spare equipment. It is combined with otherwise centralised management to obtain high resource utilisation and control of delays and loss. The Internet, which has its architecture governed by the requirement to survive a nuclear attack, has an inherent robustness in part achieved by distributed path finding. Resilience is the prime objective, while QoS is less focused. The major drawback of the Internet approach is the relative long time needed for restoration after failures, which results in missing ability to provide continuity of service when failures occur. Another issue is that fixed link costs are typically used in the routing algorithms, and hence, the ability to adapt the flows in the network to changes in the load is restricted. MPLS and the generalised multiprotocol label switching (GMPLS) for management of underlaying circuit switched networks, have been introduced as means that may be used to overcome these drawbacks. However, the tendency is toward using (G)MPLS based on "off-line" centralised preplanning and thereby missing some of Internet's inherent robustness and adaptivity.

It is our research hypothesis that self-management of path finding by emergent behaviour has the potential to provide the advantages of both these approaches, inherent robustness and adaptivity, a good resource utilisation as well as continuity of service by protection-like schemes or pro-active path routing schemes. A drawback is that in order to achieve this, determinism is sacrificed. To support this hypothesis we have developed an emergent path finding algorithm based on the CE ants approach to stochastic optimisation [6], and performed extensive experiments on two variants of self-management algorithms with decreasing "designedness" in order to meet the continuity of service objective. The **primary backup** scheme has as its prime objective to establish disjoint primary and backup (MPLS) paths for (all) source destination pairs. The primary and backup paths are to be established such that backup-paths reuse network resources without preventing (due to overload) the scheme to provide continuity of service when a network element fails. Its main pro is the explicit knowledge of the immediately restorable traffic. Its scalability for increasing network sizes and complex priority schemes is not yet investigated. The other approach is the **adaptive path** scheme, which has stochastic paths for all source destination pairs in all nodes of the network. This approach will pro-actively provide alternative paths in case of failure. Its main pros are simplicity and fast adaption to major chances in the network. It lacks, however, the ability to give explicit indication of the fraction of traffic that will experience continuity of service. Differentiation or priority is also difficult to provide. In order to substantiate our position, the remainder of the paper will present, compare and discuss these two schemes in the context of the objectives listed at the beginning of this section.

3   Cross Entropy Ants (CE Ants)

The CE ant system which forms the foundation for the work presented in this paper, is a swarm intelligent system originally inspired by the foraging behaviour of ants, as outlined in the introduction. The overall idea is to have a number of simple ant-like mobile agents iteratively search for paths in a network. An ant, having found a path, backtracks and leaves markings, denoted *pheromones,* resembling the chemicals left by real ants during ant trail development. The strength of the change in markings depends on the quality of the path found. Hence, nodes hold distributions of pheromones pointing toward their neighbour nodes. A new ant in its searching phase visiting a node selects the next node to visit stochastically based on the pheromone distribution seen in the visited node. Using such trail marking ants, together with evaporation of pheromone, the overall process converges quickly toward having the majority of the ants follow a single trail that tends to be a near optimal path. The behaviour of the cross entropy ants, to be presented in Sections 3.2 to 3.4, is in addition to mimicking ants in nature, founded in Rubinstein's method for stochastic optimisation [6].

Due to space limitation, the rest of this section presents only an outline of the CE ant system. For details readers are referred to [14].

The path management strategy implemented by the ants is governed by how the "quality of a path found" is determined. We denote this quality (or the lack of quality) *cost*. Traffic streams between pairs of nodes in the network is indexed by m. A path for this stream found by the t'th ant is denoted π_t^m. A link connecting two adjacent nodes i, j has a link cost L_{ij}. The link cost is chosen to a measure appropriate for the problem at hand. It may for instance be in terms of incurred delay by using the path, "fee" paid to the operator of the link, a penalty for using a scare resource like free capacity, etc., or a combination of such measures. The link cost may depend on the traffic stream to be carried and when the cost is observed. If this is the case the cost observed by the t'th ant is denoted $L_{t,ij}^m$. The cost function, L, of a path is the sum of the link costs, i.e.

$$L(\pi_t^m) = \sum_{ij \in \pi_t^m} L_{t,ij}^m \tag{1}$$

3.1   Management Strategies

The management strategy should be reflected in the cost function determining the cost for the individual ants. Below two such strategies and their corresponding cost functions are presented.

Primary Backup. This strategy is designed to provide soft guarantees for retaining service under single link failures. This is done by finding pairs of mutually disjoint primary and back-up paths. Hence, the ants seeking primary paths and backup paths should detest each other. The capacity of the primary paths will be used in fault free operation, and ants finding primary paths should detest each other if using a common link would cause overload. The capacity on the back-up paths will be allocated and shared with other backup paths. Backup paths having primary paths with common links should also avoid using common links in the backup path that may be overloaded if the common primary link fails. The cost function should give high penalty to the primary backup paths where the accumulated traffic demand exceeds the capacity of at least one link. Hence, a penalty related to the approximate expected potential link overload, including the above mention detestation, is chosen as the link cost. The primary backup link cost expression relating to stream m_r, where r indicates rank of path ($r = 0 \Rightarrow$ primary and $r = 1 \Rightarrow$ backup), has the following structure:

$$L_{t,ij}^{m_r} = S \left[a_m + \sum_{\forall n_s:\, ij \in \pi_t^{n_s}} P_{t,ij}^{n_s} V_{t,i}^{n_s} Q_{t,m_r}^{n_s} a_n - c_{ij} \right] \tag{2}$$

where a_m, and a_n represent the load put by streams m and n, and c_{ij} capacity available on link ij. $P_{t,ij}^{n_s}$ is the probability that an ant n_s of rank s ($s = 0 \Rightarrow$ primary and $s = 1 \Rightarrow$ backup) for stream n will follow link ij when it visits node i, and $V_{t,i}^{n_s}$ is the probability that ant n_s visits node i. The factor $P_{t,ij}^{n_s} V_{t,i}^{n_s}$

indicates the likelihood, at the current state of the emerging process, that the actual link will be chosen as a path for stream n. These quantities are derived directly from pheromone levels in node i. $Q_{t,m_r}^{n_s}$ is a weight function controlling the intensity of the detestation. $S[...]$ is a smoothening function ensuring $L_{t,ij}^{m_r} > 0$. For details see [13].

Adaptive Path. This strategy is designed for fast restoration and adaptivity to both link failures and change in traffic loads. Hence, the cost function should be sensitive to the carried traffic, which makes a delay based link cost measure a natural choice. The link cost measure includes both the queueing and processing delay in a node, and the transmission delay of a link. The link cost measure for a link in a path for stream m is therefore $L_{t,ij}^m = d_{t,ij}^m$, where $d_{t,ij}^m$ is average delay induced by the link ij measured in the short time period between ant t and the succeeding ant traversing link ij.

3.2   The Cross Entropy Method

In [6] Rubinstein presents an algorithm for iteratively finding optimal solutions to hard combinatorial problems. It stems from the recognition of that finding the optimal solution by random selection is an extremely rare event. For instance, the probability of finding the shortest Hamiltonian cycle in a 26 node network is $\frac{1}{25!} \approx 10^{-26}$. Hence, a successive importance-sampling-like technique is used to increase the probabilities of finding good solutions. In our context, his approach may be regarded as a centralised search for a single best path in a network. For the sake of presentation, the cross entropy (CE) method is summarised with the above "ant terminology" with the modification that t is now interpreted as a batch of N ants rather than a single ant, cf. step 2 below. Hence Rubinstein's algorithm is batch oriented.

The total allocation of pheromones in a network is represented by a probability matrix P_t where an element $P_{t,ij}$ reflects the normalised intensity of pheromones pointing from node i toward node j. An ant's stochastic search for a sample path resembles a Markov Chain selection process based on P_t. By importance sampling in multiple iterations Rubinstein alters the transition matrix $(P_t \rightarrow P_{t+1})$ and increases, as mentioned, certain probabilities such that ants eventually find near optimal paths with high probabilities. Cross entropy is applied to ensure efficient alteration of the matrix. To speed up the process further, a performance function weights the path qualities such that high quality paths have greater influence on the alteration of the matrix, cf. step 2 below. Rubinstein's CE algorithm has 4 steps. The indexes m and r are omitted since a single path and single kind of ant is considered:

1. At the first iteration $t = 0$, select a start transition matrix $P_{t=0}$ (e.g. uniformly distributed).
2. Generate N paths from P_t. Calculate the minimum parameter γ_t, denoted *temperature*, to fulfil average path performance constraints, i.e.

$$\min \gamma_t \text{ s.t. } h(P_t, \gamma_t) = \frac{1}{N} \sum_{k=1}^{N} H(\pi_k, \gamma_t) > \rho \tag{3}$$

where $H(\pi_k, \gamma_t) = \exp(-L(\pi_k)/\gamma_t)$ is the performance function returning the quality of path π_k. $L(\pi_k)$ is the cost of using path π_k as in Section 3.1, and $10^{-6} \leq \rho \leq 10^{-2}$ is a search focus parameter. The minimum solution for γ_t implies a certain reinforcement (dependent on ρ) of high quality paths and produces a minimum average $h(P_t, \gamma_t) > \rho$ over all path qualities in the current batch of N paths.

3. Using γ_t from step 2 and $H(\pi_k, \gamma_t)$ for $k = 1, 2..., N$, generate a new transition matrix P_{t+1} which maximises the "closeness" (i.e. minimises distance) to the optimal matrix, by solving

$$\max_{P_{t+1}} \frac{1}{N} \sum_{k=1}^{N} H(\pi_k, \gamma_t) \sum_{ij \in \pi_k} \ln P_{t+1,ij} \tag{4}$$

where $P_{t+1,ij}$ is the transition probability from node i to j at iteration $t+1$. The solution of (4) is shown in [6] to be

$$P_{t+1,ij} = \frac{\sum_{k=1}^{N} I(\{i, j\} \in \pi_k) H(\pi_k, \gamma_t)}{\sum_{l=1}^{N} I(\{i\} \in \pi_l) H(\pi_l, \gamma_t)} \tag{5}$$

where $I(X) = 1$ if $X = true$, 0 otherwise. (5) results in a minimised cross entropy between P_t and P_{t+1}, and ensures an optimal shift in probabilities with respect to γ_t and the performance function.

4. Repeat steps 2-3 until $H(\hat{\pi}, \gamma_t) \approx H(\hat{\pi}, \gamma_{t+1})$ where $\hat{\pi}$ is the best path found.

3.3   Distributed Cross Entropy Method

In [16] a distributed and asynchronous version of Rubinstein's CE algorithm is developed, today known as *CE ants*. By a few approximations, (5) and (3) may be replaced by autoregressive counterparts based on

$$P_{t+1,ij} = \frac{\sum_{k=1}^{t} I(\{i, j\} \in \pi_k) \beta^{t-k} H(\pi_k, \gamma_t)}{\sum_{l=1}^{t} I(\{i\} \in \pi_l) \beta^{t-l} H(\pi_l, \gamma_t)} \tag{6}$$

and

$$\min \gamma_t \text{ s.t. } h_t'(\gamma_t) > \rho \tag{7}$$

where

$$h_t'(\gamma_t) = h_{t-1}'(\gamma_t)\beta + (1 - \beta)H(\pi_t, \gamma_t) = \frac{1 - \beta}{1 - \beta^t} \sum_{k=1}^{t} \beta^{t-k} H(\pi_k, \gamma_t)$$

and where $\beta \in \langle 0, 1 \rangle$ (typically close to 1) controls the history of paths remembered by the system (i.e. replaces N in step 2). See [16] for details on the auto-regression. Step 2 and 3 in the algorithm can now be performed immediately after a single new path π_t is found (i.e. t again represents the t'the ant), and a new probability matrix P_{t+1} can be generated. Hence CE ants may be viewed as an algorithm where search ants evaluate a path found (and calculate γ_t by (7)) right after they reach their destination node, and then immediately return to their source node backtracking along the path. During backtracking, pheromones are placed by updating the relevant probabilities in the transition matrix, i.e applying $H(\pi_t, \gamma_t)$ through (6).

Due to the compact autoregressive schemas applied in a CE ant system, the system becomes both computationally efficient, requires limited amounts of memory and is simple to implement.

3.4   Elite CE Ants

In [17] elitism is introduced in the CE ants system. The new system, denoted *elite CE ants,* performs significantly better in terms of the number on path traversals required to converge toward a near optimal path. The kind of contribution an ant makes depends on the cost of the path it has traversed relative to the cost of paths found by other ants. All ants contribute in updating the temperature γ_t as in (7). However, a limited set of ants, denoted the *elite set*, updates a different temperature γ_t^*. Only ants belonging to the elite set backtrack their paths and update pheromones applying $H(\pi_k, \gamma_t^*)$ in (6), and hence, reducing the total number of backtracking traversals and pheromone updates.

The criterion for determining if an ant is in the elite set is based on the fact that the best solutions in the CE ants method relates to ρ through $e^{-L(\pi_t)/\gamma_t} > \rho$, cf. step 2 in Section 3.2. The elite criterium of (8) is a rearrangement of this relationship. An ant is considered an elite ant if the cost of the path found by the ant satisfies

$$L(\pi_t) < -\gamma_t \ln \rho \tag{8}$$

Note that the temperate γ_t updated by *all* ants is applied in (8). Hence, when removing parts of the search space which enables elite ants to find their paths, e.g. by a link breakdown in the best path found, the temperature γ_t will increase and allow ants with higher path costs to perform pheromone updates. Hence dynamic network conditions are handled. Note also that the elite criterium does not introduce any additional parameters. It is self-tuning.

4   Case Studies of a National-Wide Internet Topology

In order to demonstrate the effect of the swarm-based path management approaches, case studies are carried out based on a topology extracted from a national-wide Norwegian Internet provider. In this section the simulation cases are described, and results are given from the studies of adaptivity and robustness of the primary-backup and adaptive path strategies. A few comments on the efficiency, i.e. the management overhead relative to its reactiveness, are also included. As previously mentioned, relative to more traditional centralised path finding schemes under static conditions, we expect to loose some "performance", but not necessary too much [16].

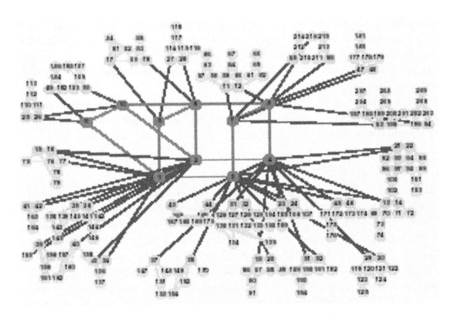

Fig. 1. The network topology in case studies

4.1   The Simulation Case Description

The network in Figure 1 consists of a core network with 10 core nodes in a sparsely meshed topology, ring based edge networks with a total of 46 edge nodes, and dual homing access network with 160 access nodes. The relative transmission capacities are 1, 1/4 and 1/16 for core, edge and access links, respectively. In the processing delay in the nodes only includes the variable queueing delay as a function of the load level.

The path management of 10 separate paths is studied in details. The paths are exposed to network link failures, drops of management information, and changes in offered traffic loads. The terminal nodes, i.e. the ingress and egress nodes, of the 10 paths are all access nodes. Each path is routed through an edge and the core network. The average load, ρ, is the link utilisation of every link of the paths through the network. The traffic is routed according to the (multi) paths provided by the management algorithm. This traffic represents the background traffic and is added to study how the algorithm reacts to load variations. In order to stress the algorithm and create instabilities, the load changes are in significant steps, see Table 1. All results in the following are from 10 simulation replications.

The objective is to study the transient behaviour, i.e. the adaptivity and robustness, of this distributed management approach. Hence, the dynamism simulated are specific, and abrupt, changes in the network environments. The main observations from these experiments are given in the following.

4.2   Adaptivity

In order to test the adaptivity of the path management approach, a scenario with changes in traffic pattern and load level, and changes in structure (link failures and restorations) is defined. The details of the 9 phases of the scenario are given in Table 1.

Adaptive Path Strategy. The results presented in Figure 2 are the average cost values from 10 simulation replications over the 9 phases. The results are from 3 of the 10 paths, selected from the paths that are affected by at least one of the changes in network conditions given in Table 1. There are three main observations from the series of simulation experiments.

1. The adaptive path strategy will switch to an alternative path almost immediately. This will in some cases cause a transient decrease in the quality (e.g. delay) but not necessary an interruption of the transport service. As an example, follow the path VC1. When a core link fails (phase 5 to 6), a sudden increase in the cost value of VC1 is observed because the preferred path is no longer available. An alternative path is immediately available. The elite CE ants continue to search for better paths. In this experiment the alternative eventually found in phase 6 has the same cost value as the best in phase 5. If a prescribed upper bound on the delay of the transport service relying on the VC, the service will not be conform with the requirements and hence unavailable. E.g. if this delay bound is 200 ms (see horizontal grid line in Figure 2), the VC2 will at start of phase 3 and 5 experience a short interruption of the transport service. Measuring the unavailability, U, as the relative time with delay above 200, this gives $U_{VC1} = 0.036$, $U_{VC2} = 0.022$, and $U_{VC3} = 0.0$ for this simulation experiment. This unavailability can be reduced by increasing the number of updating messages per time unit, but this will increase the overhead of the management function.
2. If the increase in traffic load causes an overload on a link, the load sharing property of the adaptive path strategy will resolve this rather quickly. E.g.

Table 1. Dynamic scenario for testing of adaptivity

Phase	Average load, ρ	Link events	Comments
-	0	-	Exploration phase
1	0	-	Initial topology
2	0.3	-	Increased load
3	0.6	-	Increased load
4	0.3	-	Decreased load
5	0.9	-	Sign. increase in load
6	0.9	Down [4,8], [6,8], [1,2]	Core links failed
7	0.9	Down [3,20], [1,42], [7,55], [3,22]	Edge links failed
8	0.9	Down [19,86]	Access link failed
9	0.9	Restored [19,86]	Access link restored

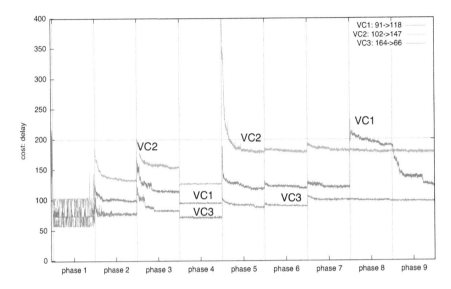

Fig. 2. Adaptive path strategy: adaptivity in dynamic environment

the sudden increase in traffic load of VC2 from 30 to 90% (phase 4 to 5) will cause a sudden peak in the cost value because one of the access links is overloaded. But, after a while (during phase 5), a new and good solution is found.

Primary Backup Strategy. Figure 3 shows the results from the most illustrative simulation out of 10 replications applying the primary backup strategy for the scenario describe above. The cost of the operational paths for three selected VCs during the phases 5-9 are plotted. An operational path is either a primary or a backup path. The cost value function for the primary backup strategy is not sensitive to the carried load and hence the phases 1-5 from Table 1 are indistinguishable and represented by phase 5 in Figure 3. The cost value indicated at the y-axis is the loss penalty, as specified in Section 3.1. Note that the loss penalty is greater than 0 even if no traffic is lost. This is due to smoothening function in (2). Two lessons learned from the experiments are emphasised.

1. A switch-over from a disconnected operational path to an alternative path, either by protection switching (primary to backup) or by restoration (primary to a new primary), will cause an *interruption of service*. E.g. observe the behaviour of VC2. After the core link failure at the beginning of phase 6, the primary path of VC2 is disconnected and VC2 is broken (regarded as *down time*). After a short period, the backup path takes over and is made operational. The backup path, which has a higher cost value, is operational until a new good primary path is found (primary is restored) at the end of phase 6. For VC1, the failed primary path at the beginning of phase 6 is quickly restored to a new primary path of equal cost (hence no shift in

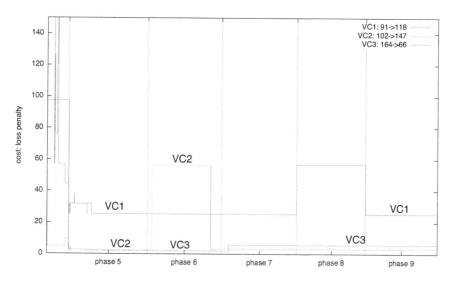

Fig. 3. Primary backup strategy: adaptivity in dynamic environment

the curve in Figure 3), i.e. the restoration mechanism reacts faster than the protection switching mechanism. Again, from phase 7 to 8, the operational primary path becomes unavailable, but is very quickly restored to a new primary path (space between the vertical start-line of phase 8 and the cost curve for VC1 is almost not observable). Again restoration is faster than protection switching. The reason is that the nodes contains (in pheromone values) alternative primary paths that are almost immediately available, at least quicker than switching to the protection, or backup, path. The cost value is increased because the new best path needs extra hops to establish a path from the ingress to the egress node. Also for VC3 restoration works faster than protection switching, however as observed in the beginning of phase 7 a more significant (and visible) delay is experienced, i.e. a down time, before a new primary path is found.

2. *Explicit link failure notification* will improve the path availability by making the protection switching mechanism more reactive. In the current implementation, no explicit notification of link failure is given to the ingress node of the path. The switch-over from primary to backup is triggered by a significant increase in the elite selection criterion from E.g.. (8) in Section 3.4. This type of "ant driven" failure reporting is robust, but may be inefficient because more than one ant is required to trigger and update. Even so, down times for VC1, 2 and 3 are short. The unavailabilities are $U_{VC1} = 0.0003$, $U_{VC2} = 0.012$, and $U_{VC3} = 0.018$.

4.3   Robustness

To test the robustness of the strategies two critical kinds of events are studied. First, *loss of information packages* (i.e. ants), and secondly, *loss of information* (i.e. pheromone values) in a node N_c along a specific primary path. As in previous experiments, we have studied the performance of the 10 paths using both the adaptive and primary backup path strategies.

In the first series of experiments, the management information was lost in all phases of the experiments, also in the exploration and transient phases. The strategies performed as if the number of ants where reduced and therefore the convergence rate was reduced, which is a desired and very robust behaviour indeed. The second series of experiments introduced failures after a path is established. These results for both loss of information packages and loss of information in a node are reported in this section.

Loss of Information Packages. The ants are dropped on a specific interface that is a part of the preferred path for ingress node 194 and egress node 84. One of the interfaces of this path drops packets with a probability p_d. When $p_d = 1$ this is similar to a link failure and the method reacts as described in previous section. When $p_d < 1$ at least some of the searching (forward) and updating (backward) ants will get through and the pheromone values are updated. For the adaptive path strategy, if a single best path exists, it will remain the best even with $p_d > 0$. The reason is that the cost function does not reflect this performance degradation. However, when there are several paths with the same best value, the paths with packet loss will be updated less frequent than the paths without failure, and hence their pheromones will evaporate relative to the paths with less, or no, loss of ants.

Loss of Information. The second simulated failure mode is deleting all the pheromone values, i.e. removing all routing information in a specific node. This means that all interfaces of this node are affected. The specific node studied is a core node with 9 edges (interfaces). This node holds routing information about the preferred paths for 2 out of 10 VCs. When the routing information is removed, it means that an ant (and the data traffic) will be routed randomly according to a uniform distribution over the 9 available interfaces. The probability of deleting pheromones is $p_f = 0.05$, which corresponds to that on average every 20th ants will meet an empty routing tables in this node. The main observation is that the best paths are retained and that loosing all routing information in one single node only causes minor problems. After very few ants (less than the average 20 in between node failures) the routing table is restored. This is because the neighbour nodes contain sufficient information to avoid an extensive exploration to re-establish the routing tables again. The adaptive strategy is more robust than the primary backup strategy because no explicit resource reservation and establishment of path is necessary. The primary backup strategy will suffer from the same problems as standard MPLS LSP management with respect to loss of soft state establishment (LSP) messages.

Based on the experiments in this section, it seems that both methods are robust to random loss of information packages (ants) and to loss of routing information (pheromones). In both cases, the paths are retained or restored quickly, without loss of consistency. As a general comment, the adaptive strategy seems robust to the random loss of any management information. This strategy is less sensitive to loss of specific control packets like the routing updates messaged, or LSP establishment messages you find in primary backup path strategy and in MPLS. The adaptive path strategy relies on small but redundant pieces of information. However, this redundancy comes with a price, and good and adaptive rules for managing the overhead must carefully be looked into.

5   Concluding Remarks

In this paper, we look at virtual path management in dynamic networks that poses a number of challenges related to combinatorial optimisation, fault and traffic handling. We claim that swarm intelligence based self-management is a promising candidate which reacts immediately to changes in the operational conditions, is autonomous, inherently robust and distributed, all necessary conditions to achieve operational simplicity and network resilience. Swarm intelligence achieved by elite CE ants is introduced and two path management strategies based on these are presented, denoted *adaptive path* and *primary backup*. A case study of a nation-wide communication infrastructure is presented to demonstrate the ability to handle change in network traffic as well as failures and restoration of links. The adaptive path strategy is designed to react quickly to loss and overload of resources. This reaction is demonstrated through the case study, in addition to a slower observable reaction when resources become available or underloaded. The latter is dependent on the number of ants used, i.e. the overhead. Note, however, that it is acceptable to operate on a sub-optimal solution for a short period as long as the prescribed QoS requirements are fulfilled. The primary backup is designed to guarantee, by establishing link disjoint primary and backup paths, that sufficient bandwidth is available if an arbitrary link fails. The case study demonstrates that fast switch-over to backup paths as well as fast restoration of primary paths is possible. The case study also demonstrated that both methods are robust to loss of management state and updating information.

Further work includes continued work on the principles of applying emergent behaviour for managing QoS in networks, as well as dealing with engineering issues for introduction of these principles in operational networks.

References

1. M. O. Ball, *Handbooks in Operation Research and Management Science, Network Models*, vol. 7. North Holland, 1995.
2. M. Pióro and D. Medhi, *Routing, Flow and Capacity Design in Communication and Computer Networks.* ISBN 0125571895, Morgan Kaufmann Publishers, March 2004.
3. S. Kirkpatrick, C. D. Gelatt, and M. P. Vecchi, "Optimization by Simulated Annealing," *Science 220*, pp. 671–680, 1983.
4. F. Glover, *Tabu Search.* Kluwer, 1996.
5. D. Goldberg, *Genetic Algorithms in Search, Optimization and MachineLearn ing.* Addison Wesley, 1998.

6. R. Y. Rubinstein, "The Cross-Entropy Method for Combinatorial and Continuous Optimization," *Methodology and Computing in Applied Probability*, pp. 127–190, 1999.
7. ITU-T G.841 (10/98), "Types and characteristics of SDH network protection architectures," 1998.
8. ITU-T I.630 (02/99), "ATM protection switching," 1999.
9. C. Huitema, *Routing in the Internet*. Prentice Hall PTR, 2 ed., November 1999.
10. R. Schoonderwoerd, O. Holland, J. Bruten, and L. Rothkrantz, "Ant-based Load Balancing in Telecommunications Networks," *Adaptive Behavior*, vol. 5, no. 2, pp. 169–207, 1997.
11. E. Bonabeau, M. Dorigo, and G. Theraulaz, *Swarm Intelligence: From Natural to Artifical Systems*. Oxford University Press, 1999.
12. G. D. Caro and M. Dorigo, "AntNet: Distributed Stigmergetic Control for Communications Networks," *Journal of Artificial Intelligence Research*, vol. 9, pp. 317–365, Dec 1998.
13. O. Wittner and B. E. Helvik, "Distributed soft policy enforcement by swarm intelligence; application to loadsharing and protection," *Annals of Telecommunications*, vol. 59, pp. 10–24, Jan/Feb 2004.
14. O. Wittner, *Emergent Behavior Based Implements for Distributed Network Management*. PhD thesis, Norwegian University of Science and Technology, NTNU, Department of Telematics, November 2003.
15. E. Rosen, A. Viswanathan, and R. Callon, "RFC3031: Multiprotocol Label Switching Architecture." IEFT, January 2001.
16. B. E. Helvik and O. Wittner, "Using the Cross Entropy Method to Guide/Govern Mobile Agent's Path Finding in Networks," in *Proceedings of 3rd International Workshop on Mobile Agents for Telecommunication Applications*, Springer Verlag, August 14-16 2001.
17. P. E. Heegaard, O. Wittner, V. F. Nicola, and B. E. Helvik, "Distributed asynchronous algorithm for cross-entropy-based combinatorial optimization," in *Rare Event Simulation & Combinatorial Optimization [RESIM2004]*, (Budapest, Hungary), September 7-8 2004.

Sociologically Inspired Approaches for Self-*: Examples and Prospects

David Hales

The University of Bologna, Italy
dave@davidhales.com
http://davidhales.com

Abstract. One way of approaching the engineering of systems with self-* properties is to examine naturally occurring systems that appear to have such properties. One line of work examines biological theories and phenomena. Ideas from the social sciences are less well explored as a possible source of self-* techniques. We briefly overview some recent work that follows this latter approach and consider some specific prospects for future work.

1   Why Social Science?

Human social systems appear to be scalable, self-repairing and self-regulating and often robust. They spontaneously form, and emerge apparently functional structures, institutions and organisations.

Much social scientific research has been produced concerning why and how social phenomena occur and social science itself has numerous sub-discplines, sub-schools, methodologies and approaches.

We believe that many of the deep engineering problems inherent in the self-* approach can be thought of as sociological questions.

Recently, new computational approaches have been applied to explore the complex processes of emergence that often characterise social phenomena. This approach forces a new kind of rigour on social theory construction and offers the prospective self-* engineer a possible source of ideas to plunder.

2   Computational Social Science

It is only very recently, with the arrival of cheap, fast, desktop computers and social science researchers who know how to program them, that a new area of 'computational social science' has begun to emerge.

There has been an explosion of published work concerning sociologically motivated computational models [5, 6, 7, 14]. In contrast to early equation-based 'high-level' models, in which there was no space of individual behaviours, much of these models are described as 'agent-based'.

O. Babaoglu et al. (Eds.): SELF-STAR 2004, LNCS 3460, pp. 433–445, 2005.

Agent-based modelling in these contexts means a discreet, individual and event-based approach. Individual behaviours of agents (representing people, groups or institutions) are programmed explicitly as a computer program. A population of such agents (or programs) inhabiting a shared environment are then allowed to interact over time and the emergent results and outcomes are observed. It is therefore a prerequisite of such work that agent behaviours must be specified algorithmically.

The emphasis of much computational social science is on the emergent properties of these 'artificial societies'. By experimentation and observation researchers attempt to gain general insights into mechanisms of social emergence and then to relate these to real human societies.

It should be noted that the relationship between real social systems and computer models is, and probably always will be, highly controversial — human social systems are so complex, fluid and political (by definition) that debates about what constitutes adequate validation and verification of models rarely converge to agreement. However, these kinds of debates do not need to trouble an engineer looking for new techniques to construct self-* systems.

3   A Brief Note on Game Theory

Some branches of economics, particularly classical game theoretical approaches, formalised their subject matter, analytically, some time ago. This was due, in part, to the advances made by von Neumann and Morgenstern's seminal work [23] and early pioneers such as Nash [18].

However, due to the focus and strong assumptions of classical game theory — quite proper for the original focus and application of the work — a lot of results are hard to apply to typical self-* scenarios (e.g. noisy, dynamic and with little information concerning the possible behaviour of other units in the system). The classical approach gives analytical proofs of the 'best' way to act in a given situation under the assumption that each actor or agent has complete information and infinite computational resources.

Despite these qualifications, classical game theoretical analysis has many possible areas of application [3] — but we will not concentrate on these here. Also the abstracted scenarios (games) constructed by game theorists to capture certain kinds of social interactions are useful as a basis for evaluating other kinds of modelling techniques (as we shall see later with the Prisoner's Dilemma game).

Interestingly, within economics there are now many researchers using agent-based modelling to concentrate on issues, such as emergence, using agents employing simple heuristics or evolutionary learning algorithms — this area is often termed 'Agent-based Computational Economics' (ACE) [16].

We contrast the 'sociologically inspired' approach we overview in this paper with a classical game theoretic approach — specifically we are more interested in dynamics than equilibrium and in the development of algorithms that can function in noisy environments with incomplete information.

4   Example: BitTorrent and World War I

A general issue explored by much computational sociological work is that of maximising the collective performance of a group while allowing individual agents reasonable levels of autonomy. In many situations there arises a contradiction between these two aspects. This kind of thing happens in human societies all the time, for example, when someone decides to not to pay on a short train ride (free-ride) or evade tax by not declaring income.

One way to stop these anti-social behaviours is to impose draconian measures via centralised government control — ensuring all individuals behave for the common good stopping free-riders. However, this is costly and hard to police and raises other issues such as: who polices the police? In the parlance of distributed systems engineering — the method does not scale well, is sensitive to noise and has a high computational overhead.

In the context of actually deployed massively distributed software systems, Peer-2-Peer (P2P) file sharing applications (such as the KaZaA and eDonkey systems) have similar problems — most users only download files rather than sharing them [1]. This limits the effectiveness of such systems. Even when the P2P client software is coded to force some level of sharing, users may modify and redistribute a hacked client. It has been noted that P2P file sharing is one of the applications in which only a small number of altruists are needed to support a large number of free riders [1]. Consequently it can be argued that this might be why popular P2P applications tend to be limited to only file sharing rather than, say, processor or distributed storage for example.

These sort of cases can be seen as examples of a more fundamental issue: how can one maintain cooperative (socially beneficial) interactions within an open system under the assumption of high individual (person, agent or peer) autonomy. An archetype of this kind of social dilemma has been developed in the form of a minimal game called the Prisoner's Dilemma (PD) game.

In the PD game two players each selected a move from two alternatives and then the game ends and each player receives a score (or pay-off). Figure 1 shows a so-called 'pay-off matrix' for the game. If both choose the 'cooperate' move then both get a 'reward' — the score R. If both select the 'defect' move they are 'punished' — they get the score P. If one player defects and the other co-operates then the defector gets T (the 'temptation' score), the other getting S (the 'sucker' score). When these pay-offs, which are numbers representing some kind of desirable utility (for example, money), obey the following constraints: $T > R > P > S$ and $2R > T + S$ then we say the game represents a Prisoner's Dilemma (PD). When both players cooperate this represents maximising of the collective good but when one player defects and another cooperates this represents a form of free-riding. The defector gains a higher score (the temptation) at the expense of the co-operator (who then becomes the 'sucker').

A game theoretic analysis drawing on the Nash equilibrium solution concept (as defined by the now famous John Nash [18]) captures the intuition that a utility maximising player would always defect in such games because whatever the other player does a higher score is never attained by choosing to cooperate. The

	Cooperate	Defect
Cooperate	R, R	S, T
Defect	T, S	P, P

Fig. 1. A payoff matrix for the two-player single round Prisoner's Dilemma (PD) game. Given $T > R > P > S \wedge 2R > T + S$ the Nash equilibrium is for both players to select Defect but both selecting Cooperate would produce higher social and individual returns. However, if either player selects Cooperate they are exposed to Defection by their opponent — hence the dilemma

Nash Equilibrium (NE) might be a partial explanation for why there is so much free-riding on existing P2P file-sharing systems users are simply behaving to maximise their utility. However, do we have any way to solve this problem without going back to centralised control or closed systems? The NE analysis gives us a good explanation for selfish behaviour but not for altruistic behaviour. As stated earlier, even in P2P file sharing systems there are some altruists (keeping the show on the road).

It has been argued by many researchers from the social and life sciences that human societies produce much more cooperation than a Nash analysis would predict. Consequently, various cooperation promoting mechanisms (often using the PD as their test case) have been proposed by social scientists.

BitTorrent, designed by Bram Cohen [4], employs a strategy popularised in the 1980's by computer simulation tournaments applied to the PD. Researchers were asked to submit programs (agents if you like) that repeatedly played the PD against each other [2]. The result of all these tournaments was that a simple strategy called 'Tit-For-Tat' did remarkably well against the majority of other submitted programs.

Tit-for-tat (TFT) operates in environments where the PD is played repeatedly with the same partners for a number of rounds. The basic strategy is simple: an agent starts by cooperating then in subsequent rounds copies the move made in the previous round by its opponent. This means defectors are punished in the future: the strategy relies on future reciprocity. To put it another way, the "shadow" of future interactions motivates cooperative behaviour in the present. In many populations and scenarios this simple strategy can outperform pure defection in the repeated PD.

In the context of BitTorrent, while a file is being downloaded between peers, each peer maintains a rolling average of the download rate from each of the peers it is connected to. It then tries to match it's uploading rate accordingly. If a peer determines that another is not downloading fast enough then it may 'choke' (stop uploading) to that other. Additionally, peers periodically try new peers randomly by uploading to them testing for better rates [4].

Axelrod used the TFT result to justify sociological hypotheses such as understanding how fraternisation broke out between enemies across the trenches of World War I. Cohen has applied a modified form of TFT to produce a decentralised file sharing system resistant to free-riding, robust against a number of possible exploitative strategies and scalable.

However, TFT has certain limitations and it is not guaranteed to always be the best way of avoiding free-riding strategies, but its simple to implement and performs 'well enough' (currently at least) — BitTorrent traffic currently constitutes a major portion of bandwidth usage on the Internet.

The Tit-For-Tat (TFT) strategy employed by BitTorrent works well when agents exchange many file parts over a period of time (repeat the game interaction many times) but is next to useless if interactions follow a single interaction (such as a single game of the Prisoner's Dilemma). This tends to limit it's use to the sharing of very large files where mutual co-operation can be established.

But how might "strangers" who interact only once come to co-operate? We discuss a recent technique developed from socially motivated computer models in the next section.

5   Example: File Sharing and the 'Old School Tie'

Recent work, drawing on agent-based simulations of cooperative group formation based on 'tags' (surface features representing social labels or cues [13]) suggests a novel co-operation mechanism which does not require reciprocal arrangements [8, 19]. It is based on the idea of a kind of 'cultural group selection' and the well known social psychological phenomena that people tend to favour those believed to be similar to themselves even when this is based on seemingly arbitrary criteria (e.g. wearing the same coloured tie). Like TFT, the mechanism is refreshingly simple. Individuals interact in cliques (subsets of the population sharing the same tags). Periodically, if they find another individual who is getting higher utility than themselves they copy them — changing to their clique and adopting their strategy. Also, periodically, individuals form new cliques and / or randomly change their strategies.

Defectors can do well initially, suckering the co-operators in their clique — but ultimately all the co-operators leave the clique for pastures new — leaving the defectors alone with nobody to free-ride on. Those copying a defector (who does well initially) will also copy their strategy, further reducing the free-riding potential in the clique. So a clique containing any free-riders quickly dissolves but those containing only co-operators grow.

Given an open system of autonomous agents all cliques will eventually be invaded by a free-rider who will exploit and dissolve the clique. However, so long as other new cooperative cliques are being created then co-operation will persists in the population as a whole.

In the sociologically oriented models, cliques are defined as those individuals sharing the same labels and their interpretation is as some kind of socially observable marking attached to individuals. There is no population structure other than the cliques themselves and the population changes over time by employing a population level evolutionary algorithm employing replication and mutation [8, 19].

In the context of application to P2P systems the clique to which a node belongs is defined by it's immediate neighbourhood. Movement between cliques

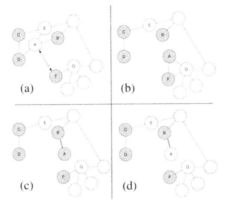

Fig. 2. An illustration of 'replication' and 'mutation' as applied in the Evolutionary Rewiring Algorithm (ERA) from [12]. Shading of nodes represents strategy. In (a) the arrowed link represents a comparison of utility between A and F. Assuming F has higher utility then (b) shows the state of the network after A copies Fs links and strategy and links to F. A possible result of applying mutation to As links is shown in (c) and the strategy is mutated in (d)

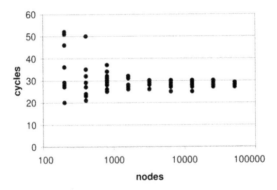

Fig. 3. The chart shows the number of cycles required before high file-sharing behaviour is attained. Ten independent runs for each network size are shown. Note that increasing the network size does not increase the time to high performance — from [12]

and copying of strategies follows a process of network 're-wiring' which brings a form of evolutionary process into the network — an Evolutionary Rewiring Algorithm (ERA). Figure 2 gives an example of this simple re-wiring process followed by each node over time.

The adapted tag mechanisms have been shown to be effective in a simulated P2P file-sharing scenario [12] based on that given by Sun et al [22]. The mechanism demonstrates high scalability with zero scaling cost i.e. it does not take longer to establish cooperation in bigger populations (see figure 3). Although there are outstanding issues to be addressed before the technique can be deployed it offers applications beyond file sharing (such as load sharing or co-operative routing). The ERA algorithm bears some comparison with the SLIC algorithm [22] which makes use of incentives. The ERA appears to achieve similar results by producing an emergent incentive structure.

The tag-based process has been likened to 'old school tie' in-group effects [20, 9] that appear to permeate many human societies. It offers a possible explanation for why individuals may behave more altruistically towards perceived in-group members, even if they have never met before — a puzzle for self-interest based social theory. Here we have given an overview of how the same mechanism was adapted and applied within a simulated file-sharing P2P scenario to control free-riding when nodes act selfishly [12].

6   Prospect: Specialisation with 'Foraging Tribes'

Specialisation between individuals is the basis of human society. Agents come to specialise in particular tasks and then use methods of exchange or communal ownership to meet the needs of the collective. But how can agents with only local knowledge and simple learning rules come to specialise in this way — particularly if they behave selfishly?

Some models have demonstrated how group processes similar to those discussed previously (i.e. tag-based) can produce internally specialised co-operative groups [10, 11, 21]. Instead of agents evolving behaviours relating to just co-operation or non-co-operation they evolve discreet skill-types in addition to altruistic giving behaviour.

In [10, 11] a resource foraging and harvesting scenario is modelled. Agents forage for resources and then harvest them to gain energy. Different resources require different skills but agents can only posses one skill at a time and are therefore only able to harvest those resources that match their specific skill. An agent may pass a resource it can not harvest to a fellow agent at a cost to itself (an altruistic act) or it may simply ignore such resources (act selfishly). When an agent harvests a resource it attains energy (utility) which can be considered as a form of 'fitness'. Figure 4 gives a schematic of the scenario.

If agents follow a tag-based evolutionary algorithm (similar to that previously described) then they form groups (which can be thought of as cliques or 'tribes') that contain a diversity of skills within them and sharing becomes high.

Figure 5 gives some results from [10]. The main result worth noting is that donation rates are high even when the cost of giving is high to the donating agent. The cost values given are as a proportion of the the harvest value of a resource (one unit of energy).

As can be seen, even when donation costs half as much as a harvested resource, donation rates are still high if the environment is sufficiently 'resource rich' and a 'smart' method of locating recipients is used (the smart method simply means that agents are able to locate others within their group directly rather than search randomly in the population for them — we do not concern ourselves hear with this issue).

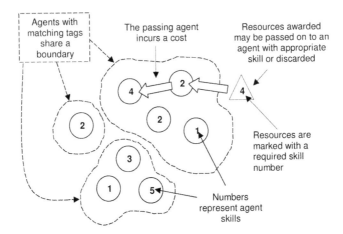

Fig. 4. A schematic representation of how resources are passed to an in-group with the required skill at a cost to the passing agent and hence making use of in-group altruism (from [11])

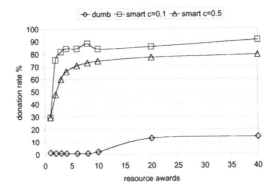

Fig. 5. The chart shows averaged results from a number of runs where there are five skills associated with five unique resource types. The x-axis indicates how 'resource rich' the environment is. The y-axis indicates the amount of altruistic donation within groups. The comparison of dumb and smart agents refers to the method of locating a recipient for the donation and the cost indicates the cost to the donating agent (from [10])

We can envisage prospects for application of this technique to the formation of internally specialised cliques within P2P networks. The skills would become different kinds of services that nodes could offer (e.g. processing, query answering, storage) and resources could represent job requests submitted at nodes. Figure 6 shows a schematic of this.

The process of translation from the abstract sociologically oriented models previously produced [10, 11] to a P2P type application is a non-trivial exercise —

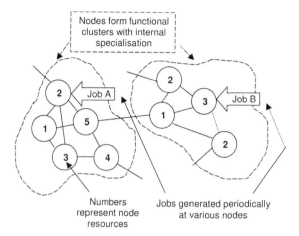

Fig. 6. The specialisation mechanism could be applied within a peer-to-peer network. The above schematic shows an example network fragment. Jobs are submitted at nodes and may require services (or resources) from other nodes. Using a similar mechanism to the ERA algorithm described previously, the network could be made to self-organise into functional clusters to satisfy job requests

for example, the previous exercise of applying 'tag' models of co-operation to P2P file-sharing involved a four stage process in which an abstract model was adapted towards an application domain [12]. At each stage a simulation model needed to be extensively explored to ensure that the desirable emergent properties had not been lost.

However, we are given confidence that specialisation can be generated within working systems since recent work, applied to simulated robotics, applying similar techniques based on tags (combined with genetic programming) produced specialised and altruistic behaviour within in-groups (or 'tribes') [21].

7   Prospect: Power, Leadership and Hierarchy

A major area of interest to social scientists is the concept of power — what kinds of process can lead to some individuals and groups becoming more powerful than others? Most explanations are tightly related to theories of inequality and economic relationships, hence this is a vast and complex area.

Here we give just a brief very speculative sketch of recent computational work, motivated by sociological questions, that could have significant import into understanding and engineering certain kinds of properties (e.g. in peer-to-peer systems), in which differential power relationships emerge and may, perhaps, be utilised in a functional way.

Interactions in human society are increasing seen as being situated within formal and informal networks [16]. These interactions are often modelled us-

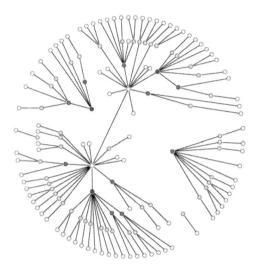

Fig. 7. Forms of 'hiearchy', 'leadership' and unequal wealth distribution have been observed to emerge in simulated interaction networks (from [24]). Nodes play PD-like games with neighbours and break connections based on a simple satisfaction rule. Hierarchies are produced in which some nodes are more connected and hence can effect the network dramatically by their individual actions — a form of 'topological power'

ing the abstraction of a game capturing interaction possibilities between linked agents [24]. When agents have the ability to change their networks based on past experience and some goals or predisposition, then, over time, networks evolve and change.

Interstingly, even if agents start with more-or-less equal endowments and freedom to act, and follow the same rules, vastly unequal outcomes can be produced. This can lead to a situation in which some nodes become objectively more powerful that other nodes through topological location (within the evolved network) and exploitative game interactions over time.

Zimmerman et al found this in their simulations of agents playing a version of the Prisoner's Dilemma on an evolving network [24]. Their motivation and interpretation is socio-economic: agents accumulate 'wealth' from the payoffs of playing games with neighbours and make or break connections to neighbours based on a simple satisfaction heuristic (based on a rule discussed in [15]).

Figure 7 (from [24]) shows a an example of an emergent stable hierarchical network structure. Interestingly, it was found that, over time, some nodes accumulate large amounts of 'wealth' (through exploitative game behaviour) and other nodes become 'leaders' by being at the top of a hierarchy. These unequal topological and wealth distributions emerge from simple self-interested behaviour within the network. Essentially, leaders, through their own actions, can re-arrange significantly the topology of the network — those on the bottom of the hierarchy have little 'topological power'.

The idea of explicitly recognising the possibility of differential power between sub-units in self-* systems and harnessing this is an idea rarely discussed in engineering contexts but could offer new ways to solve difficult co-ordination problems.

Considering P2P applications, one can envisage certain kinds of task in which differential power would be required for efficient operation — e.g. consider two nodes negotiating an exchange on behalf of their 'group' or 'follower' nodes. This might be more efficient than individual nodes having to negotiate with each other every time they wished to interact. Or consider a node reducing intra-group conflict by imposing a central plan of action.

We mention the notion of engineering emergent power structures, briefly and speculatively here, because we consider power to be an under-explored phenomena within evolving information systems. Agents, units or nodes are often assumed to have equal power. It is rare for human societies to possess such egalitarian properties and perhaps many self-* like properties are facilitated by the application of unequal power relationships. We consider this a fascinating area for future work.

8   Conclusion and Summary

Here we have provided some examples and prospects of sociologically inspired approaches to engineering self-* systems. Rather than attempt an extensive overview we have focused on a few encouraging specific results and possible P2P-type applications.

We believe that the computational social science literature can be a potential source of new techniques and ideas for prospective self-* engineer because social phenomena are generally self-organising, robust and scalable — all desirable properties for self-organising information systems.

Computational social science tries to reverse engineer general properties at a fairly abstract level whereas self-* engineers need to apply techniques to specific concrete problem domains. As we have hoped to show, however, it is possible to import useful techniques (see [12] for a case study in applying a technique to realistic domain) from the one approach to the other.

The idea of using social metaphors and approaches for the construction of smart information systems is far from new [17]. What is new is that distributed systems engineers are increasing asking sociological questions (even if they are unaware of it!) and social scientists are increasingly turning to algorithmic specification and computer simulation to explore their theories. We hope that advances from both areas can be brought together and used to reinforce each other. Experience so far indicates this not to be an unreasonable hope.

Acknowledgements

This work partially supported by the EU within the 6th Framework Program under contract 001907 (DELIS).

References

1. Adar, E. and Huberman, B.: Free Riding on Gnutella. *First Monday* Volume 5, No. 10. (2000).
2. Axelrod, R.: *The evolution of cooperation.* N.Y.: Basic Books, (1984).
3. Binmore, K.: *Game Theory and the Social Contract. Volume 2: Just Playing.* Cambridge, MA: The MIT Press, (1998).
4. Cohen, B.: Incentives Build Robustness in BitTorrent. Presented at the *1st Workshop on the Economics of Peer-2-Peer Systems*, June 5-6, 2003, Berkley, CA. Available at: http://www.sims.berkeley.edu/research/conferences/p2pecon/
5. Epstein, J.M. and Axtell, R.: *Growing Artificial Societies: Social Science From The Bottom Up.* London: MIT Press, (1996).
6. Gilbert, N. and Doran J., (eds.): *Simulating Societies: the Computer Simulation of Social Phenomena.* London: UCL Press, (1994).
7. Gilbert, N. and Conte, R. (eds.): *Artificial Societies: the Computer Simulation of Social Life.* London: UCL Press, (1995).
8. Hales, D.: Cooperation without Space or Memory: Tags, Groups and the Prisoner's Dilemma. In Moss, S., Davidsson, P. (eds.) *Multi-Agent-Based Simulation. Lecture Notes in Artificial Intelligence 1979.* Berlin: Springer-Verlag, (2000).
9. Hales, D.: Tag Based Cooperation in Artificial Societies. Ph.D. Thesis, Department of Computer Science, University of Essex, UK, (2001).
10. Hales, D.: Evolving Specialisation, Altruism and Group-Level Optimisation Using Tags. In Sichman, J. S., Bousquet, F. Davidsson, P. (eds.) *Multi-Agent-Based Simulation II. Lecture Notes in Artificial Intelligence 2581.* Berlin: Springer-Verlag, (2002).
11. Hales, D.: Searching for a Soulmate — Searching for Tag-Similar Partners Evolves and Supports Specialization in Groups. In Lindemann, G., Moldt, D. and Paolucci, M., (eds.) *Regulated Agent-Based Social Systems — 1st Intnerational Workshop, Lecture Notes in Artificial Intelligence 2934.* Berlin: Springer-Verlag, (2004).
12. Hales, D. (2004) From selfish nodes to cooperative networks — emergent link based incentives in peer-to-peer networks. In *Proc. of the 4th IEEE International Conference on Peer-to-Peer Computing (P2P2004).* IEEE Computer Soc. Press, (2004).
13. Holland, J.: The Effect of Labels (Tags) on Social Interactions. Santa Fe Institute Working Paper 93-10-064. Santa Fe, NM, (1993).
14. The Journal of Artificial Societies and Social Simulation (JASSS). Available at: http://jasss.soc.surrey.ac.uk
15. Kirman, A.: Ants, Rationality and Recruitment. *Quarterly Journal of Economics*, 108, 137156, (1993).
16. Kirman, A.P., and Vriend, N.J.: Evolving Market Structure: An ACE Model of Price Dispersion and Loyalty. *Journal of Economic Dynamics and Control*, 25, Nos. 3/4, 459-502, (2001).
17. Minsky, M.: *Society of Mind.* Simon & Schuster, (1988).
18. Nash, J. F.: Equilibrium Points in N-Person Games, *Proc. Natl. Acad. Sci.* USA 36, 48-49, (1950).
19. Riolo, R., Cohen, M. D. & Axelrod, R.: Cooperation without Reciprocity. *Nature* 414, 441-443, (2001).
20. Sigmund & Nowak: Tides of tolerance. *Nature* 414, 403-405, (2001).

21. Spector, L., J. Klein, C. Perry, and M. Feinstein.: Emergence of Collective Behavior in Evolving Populations of Flying Agents. In E. Cantu-Paz, et al (Eds.), *Proceedings of the Genetic and Evolutionary Computation Conference (GECCO-2003)*, pp. 6173. Berlin: Springer-Verlag, (2003).
22. Sun Q. & Garcia-Molina, H.: SLIC: A Selfish Link-based Incentive Mechanism for Unstructured Peer-to-Peer Networks. In *Proceedings of the 24th IEEE international Conference on Distributed Systems*. IEEE computer Society, (2004).
23. von Neumann, J. and Morgenstern, O.: Theory of Games and Economic Behavior. Princeton, (1944).
24. Zimmermann, M.G., Egufluz, V.M. and San Miguel.: Cooperation, adaptation and the emergence of leadership. In A. Kirman and J.B. Zimmermann (eds.) *Economics with Heterogeneous Interacting Agents*, pp. 73-86. Berlin: Springer, (2001).

Author Index

Lecture Notes in Computer Science

For information about Vols. 1–3392

please contact your bookseller or Springer